F. Hoffmann, E. Hüllermeier (Hrsg.)

Proceedings 20. Workshop Computational Intelligence

Dortmund, 1. - 3. Dezember 2010

Schriftenreihe des

Instituts für Angewandte Informatik / Automatisierungstechnik

am Karlsruher Institut für Technologie

Band 33

Eine Übersicht über alle bisher in dieser Schriftenreihe erschienenen Bände finden Sie am Ende des Buchs.

Proceedings
20. Workshop Computational Intelligence

Dortmund, 1. - 3. Dezember 2010

F. Hoffmann
E. Hüllermeier
(Hrsg.)

Impressum

Karlsruher Institut für Technologie (KIT)
KIT Scientific Publishing
Straße am Forum 2
D-76131 Karlsruhe
www.ksp.kit.edu

KIT – Universität des Landes Baden-Württemberg und nationales
Forschungszentrum in der Helmholtz-Gemeinschaft

KIT Scientific Publishing 2010
Print on Demand

ISSN: 1614-5267
ISBN: 978-3-86644-580-2

Inhaltsverzeichnis

20 Jahre CI in Bommerholz – Zufälle und Notwendigkeiten

Harro Kiendl

Technische Universität Dortmund

Die Geschichte und Vorgeschichte des GMA-Ausschusses Computational Intelligence wird anhand von wegweisenden Meilensteinen nachgezeichnet. Dies geschieht aus der Sicht eines Zeitzeugen, der einen der legendären weltweit ersten Computer von Zuse noch mit eigenen Händen angefasst hat. Durch eine mikroskopische Brille betrachtet, erscheinen diese Geschichte und ihre Vorgeschichte als evolutionäre Prozesse, die durch viele Zufälle und oft im Widerspruch zueinander stehende Impulse einzelner Akteure geprägt worden sind. Bei Betrachtung durch eine makroskopische Brille verschwindet dagegen der Eindruck von Zufällen. Vielmehr meint man dann, notwendige – emergente? – Entwicklungen zu erkennen.

In diesem Beitrag werden zunächst die erwähnten Meilensteine dargelegt. Damit verbindet sich die Hoffnung, dass eine genauere Kenntnis der Vergangenheit eine bessere Prognose der zukünftigen Entwicklung ermöglicht. Dieser Beitrag möchte aber auch das ungeklärte Spannungsverhältnis, das sich aus dem Vergleich einer mikroskopischen und einer makroskopischen Betrachtung komplexer Systeme ergibt, ins Bewusstsein rücken. Diese Intention soll durch folgende Fabel unterstrichen werden:

Die Biene Maja staunte über die Perfektion der sechseckigen Bienenwaben und fragte ihre kluge Schwester Melissa, wie ihre Form entstanden sei. Sie erfuhr, dass die Bienen zunächst einzeln lebten und isoliert stehende, runde Waben bauten. Erst im Rahmen der später erfolgenden Staatenbildung wurden die Waben in Gruppen aneinander gebaut. Schließlich erfand die Biene Summ die sechseckige Wabenform, die seither überall verwendet wird. „Wie sähen die Bienenwaben heute aus – vielleicht dreieckig oder viereckig – wenn Summ nicht zufällig auf die Idee der Sechseckform gekommen wäre?" fragte Maja dann ihre Schwester. Diese antwortete: „Der Zufall hat keine entscheidende Rolle gespielt, auch ohne Majas Einfall wären die Bienenwaben heute sechseckig. Schon ca. 300 v.Chr. stellte der griechische Geometer und Philosoph Pappus von Alexandria die „Bienenwaben-Vermutung" auf: Danach kommt man mit einem Minimum von Baumaterial für die Zwischenwände aus, wenn man sechseckige Waben baut. Diese Vermutung wurde 1998 vom Mathematiker Thomas C. Hales auch bewiesen. Da eine ökonomische Bauweise für Bienen äußerst wichtig ist, wäre also früher oder später auch irgendeine andere Biene auf die Idee gekommen, den Waben eine sechseckige Form zu geben. Bevor es überhaupt Bienen gab, stand also schon fest, dass ihre Waben letztendlich sechseckig sein würden." Maja hätte ihre Schwester gerne noch gefragt, ob auch die Sechseckform der Facettenaugen und andere seit Jahrmillionen etablierte Strukturen der Bienenanatomie und die Bienenarchitektur aus mathematisch-ökonomischen Gründen vorherbestimmt waren. Aber da war Melissa schon zur Suche nach einer neuen Futterstelle fortgeflogen.

On Robust Feature Extraction and Classification of Inhomogeneous Datasets

Markus Reischl, Rüdiger Alshut, Ralf Mikut

Karlsruhe Institute of Technology (KIT), Institute for Applied Computer Science,
D-76021 Karlsruhe, P.O. Box 3640, Germany
Phone: (07247) 82-5749, Fax: (07247) 82-5786,
Email: markus.reischl@kit.edu

1 Introduction

Natural scientists carry out experiments to find significant differences between experimental setups. Significance is usually proven by statistically testing features extracted out of an experimental dataset (time series, images etc.) which measures the outcome of the experiment. However, the measurement often suffers from being inhomogeneous due to varying side effects. I.e. data may be collected on different time points, with different platforms or by different experimenters. Therefore, also feature quality suffers as features do not only reflect the properties of the experiment but also the properties of the side effects on the measurement. Accordingly, an accurate and/or consistent conclusion regarding the outcome of two experiments can not be made.

The high-throughput screening of zebrafish larvae is a typical example. In different experimental setups potential influences on the development of a larva (i.e. the presence of a chemical substance) are examined. Microscope images of a larva are taken and features like grayscale values, histograms, morphological properties etc. are used to provide evidence that developmental differences exist [1, 2, 3]. However, the amount of images often enforces experiments on multiple days using multiple microscopes with varying fish lines, incubation times etc. As all these side effects influence the images and therefore the features, data-mining approaches will most likely find highly significant features proving developmental differences. However the significance is not necessarily caused by the experimental setup but by the influence of the side effects.

Similar problems are well-known in different applications. Classification of handwritings is long known to be unrobust without a normalization filter approach [4].

To automate feature extraction and image preprocessing, there are classification filter approaches in image processing using classifiers for segmentation [5], wrapper approaches for segmentation [6] or for optimization of extracted features [7]. However, there are no wrapper approaches to optimize robustness with respect to the influence of side effects. In this paper we present a framework to process microscope images and extract reliable and robust features such that the influence of the side effects is minimized. The framework transforms images into features based on a set of normalizations. A data mining routine is set up to quantify the influence of the known side effects on the features. Sequentially, the parameters are then optimized such that the influence becomes minimal. As a result, we obtain a calculation routine for robust and significant features. The results are discussed using a dataset from an Olympus ScanR microscope containing 136 images of zebrafish larvae.

This paper is organized as follows. Section 2 explains the proposed methodology, Section 3 the adaptation strategy and Section 4 the used benchmark datasets. In Section 5, the methodology is applied to the benchmark datasets and the results are discussed.

2 Methods

A set of n images is described by matrices containing gray values $\mathbf{A}_i = ((a_{\nu\mu}))_i \in \mathbb{N}_0^{\nu_{max} \times \mu_{max}}, i = 1...n$, and each image by its intended properties $\mathbf{y}_i = (y_1, ..., y_k)_i \in \mathbb{N}^k$ and its unintended properties $\mathbf{z}_i = (z_1, ..., z_l)_i \in \mathbb{N}^l$ where $\mathbb{N}$ refers to the set of all natural numbers. Intended properties are asked for in the assay design (i.e. y_1: coagulation status as indicator for dead larvae, y_2: heartbeat status etc.) and need to be estimated by a classifier, unintended properties are based on side effects (i.e. z_1: microscope type, z_2: experimenter, z_3: day of experiment etc.) and are usually given. Each intended property y_j is specified by n_j classes $y_j \in \{1, ..., n_j\}$, each unintended property z_j by m_j classes $z_j \in \{1, ..., m_j\}$ (i.e y_1 may have $n_1 = 3$ classes: dead, alive, unknown). Ideally, an automated system is able to classify each image according to its intended properties and is not able to classify it according to its unintended properties (Fig. 1).

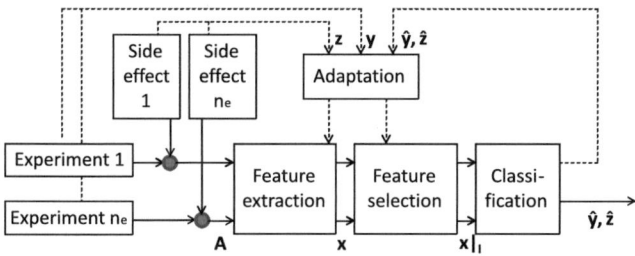

Figure 1: Intended and unintended properties in an image processing pipeline

To set up such an automated system, an image needs to be reduced to a set of significant features which is then classified. In our case, s features like grayscale values etc. are generated out of a set of n images $\mathbf{A}_i, i = 1, ..., n$ by the *feature extraction* $S_1(\mathbf{p})$

$$S_1(\mathbf{p}) : \mathbf{A}_i \mapsto \mathbf{x}_i = (x_1, ..., x_s)_i^T. \tag{1}$$

$\mathbf{p}$ denotes a set of parameters used for feature extraction (i.e. threshold values in image processing). This step can split up into two substeps for an image transformation (with operations like normalization and standardization)

$$S_{1A}(\mathbf{p}_A) : \mathbf{A}_i \mapsto \mathbf{A}_i^* \tag{2}$$

resulting in transformed images with $\mathbf{A}_i^* = ((a_{\nu\mu}^*))_i \in \mathbb{N}_0^{\nu_{max} \times \mu_{max}}, i = 1...n$; followed by a feature extraction from the transformed image

$$S_{1B}(\mathbf{p}_B) : \mathbf{A}_i^* \mapsto \mathbf{x}_i = (x_1, ..., x_s)_i^T. \tag{3}$$

$\mathbf{p}_A$ and $\mathbf{p}_B$ denote the set of parameters for the substeps with $\mathbf{p} = (\mathbf{p}_A; \mathbf{p}_B)$.

A *feature selection* S_2 uses the multivariate analysis of variances (MANOVA, [8]) to find the most important s_m features for a classification problem

$$S_2 : \mathbf{x}_i = (x_1, ..., x_s)_i^T \mapsto \mathbf{x}_i|_{\mathcal{I}} = (x_{i_1}, ..., x_{i_{s_m}})_i^T, s > s_m. \tag{4}$$

$\mathcal{I}$ contains the indices of the chosen s_m features.

The classification S_3 estimates for each feature set intended and unintended properties [9]

$$S_3 : \mathbf{x}_i|_{\mathcal{I}} \mapsto \hat{\mathbf{y}}_i, \hat{\mathbf{z}}_i. \tag{5}$$

If the estimation of a property $\hat{y}_{j,i}, \hat{z}_{j,i}$ equals the real property $y_{j,i}, z_{j,i}$, this is called a match. The sum of matches related to the number of properties defines the match rates $\xi_{y,i}, \xi_{z,i}$ per image i

$$\xi_{y,i} = \frac{1}{k} \sum_{j=1}^{k} \xi_{y,j,i} \quad \text{with} \quad \xi_{y,j,i} = \begin{cases} 1 & \hat{y}_{j,i} = y_{j,i} \\ 0 & \text{else} \end{cases}, \tag{6}$$

$$\xi_{z,i} = \frac{1}{l} \sum_{j=1}^{l} \xi_{z,j,i} \quad \text{with} \quad \xi_{z,j,i} = \begin{cases} 1 & \hat{z}_{j,i} = z_{j,i} \\ 0 & \text{else} \end{cases}. \tag{7}$$

The mean classification accuracies $\overline{\xi_y}, \overline{\xi_z}$ are given by

$$\overline{\xi_y} = \frac{1}{n} \sum_{i=1}^{n} \xi_{y,i}, \quad \overline{\xi_z} = \frac{1}{n} \sum_{i=1}^{n} \xi_{z,i}. \tag{8}$$

In case of a perfect classifier, the estimated intended properties $\hat{\mathbf{y}}$ perfectly match the real intended properties $\mathbf{y}$, whereas the estimated unintended properties $\hat{\mathbf{z}}$ match the real unintended properties $\mathbf{z}$ by chance

$$\overline{\xi_{y,\text{goal}}} = 1, \quad \overline{\xi_{z,\text{goal}}} \approx \frac{1}{l} \sum_{j=1}^{l} \frac{1}{m_j}. \tag{9}$$

The latter indicates the independence of features from the side effects.

However, independence is not given in real world systems. Feature extraction S_1 or feature selection S_2 and thus, $\mathbf{p}$ or $\mathcal{I}$ have to be adapted to decrease the influence of side effects. According to classification theory [10, 11], the adaptation step can be realized by filter or wrapper approaches. Filter approaches determine values for $\mathbf{p}$ or $\mathcal{I}$ independent of the classifier output:

$$\mathbf{p}^* = f(\mathbf{A}_i), \quad \mathcal{I}^* = f(\mathbf{x}_i). \tag{10}$$

Wrapper approaches use the classifier output for adaptation:

$$\mathbf{p}^{**} = f(\mathbf{A}_i, \mathbf{y}_i, \mathbf{z}_i, \hat{\mathbf{y}}_i, \hat{\mathbf{z}}_i), \quad \mathcal{I}^{**} = f(\mathbf{x}_i, \mathbf{y}_i, \mathbf{z}_i, \hat{\mathbf{y}}_i, \hat{\mathbf{z}}_i). \tag{11}$$

In general, wrapper approaches deliver better results, however they are more computation intensive.

3 Adaptation

Exemplary the adaptation process is achieved using three different standardization/normalization procedures for S_{1A} which are typical adaptation approaches for feature extraction out of images independent from $\mathbf{y}_i$, $\mathbf{z}_i$. For 2D-instances of 3D-objects the scale-invariant feature transform (SIFT) [12, 13] can be used. Subsequently, for 2D images, brightness transforms may be applied. Here, each pixel value is centered by a value c and divided by a variation s

$$a^*_{\nu\mu} = \frac{a_{\nu\mu} - c}{s}. \tag{12}$$

For example, normalization can be based on statistical parameters like mean value and standard deviation

$$c = \frac{1}{\nu_{\max}\mu_{\max}} \sum_{\nu,\mu} a_{\nu\mu}, \quad s = \sqrt{\frac{1}{\nu_{\max}\mu_{\max} - 1} \sum_{\nu,\mu} (a_{\nu\mu} - c)^2} \tag{13}$$

or on quantiles or extreme values

$$c = \min_{\nu\mu} a, \quad s = \max_{\nu\mu} a_{\nu\mu} - \min_{\nu\mu} a_{\nu\mu}. \tag{14}$$

Eq. (14) can be further optimized by introducing a percentage of saturated pixels using the 2% percentile a_{low} and the 98% percentile a_{high}:

$$a^*_{\nu\mu} = \begin{cases} 0 & \text{for } a_{\nu\mu} \leq a_{\text{low}} \\ \frac{a_{\nu\mu} - a_{\text{low}}}{a_{\text{high}} - a_{\text{low}}} & \text{for } a_{\text{low}} < a_{\nu\mu} < a_{\text{high}} \\ 1 & \text{for } a_{\nu\mu} \geq a_{\text{high}} \end{cases}. \tag{15}$$

Further normalization can be done by introducing centering value $c(\mathbf{z}_i)$ and variation value $s(\mathbf{z}_i)$ dependent on unintended properties.

The wrapper approach aims for a feature extraction S_1 and a feature selection S_2 minimizing $\overline{\xi_y} - \overline{\xi_{y,\text{goal}}}$ and minimizing $\overline{\xi_z} - \overline{\xi_{z,\text{goal}}}$

$$\min_{\mathbf{p},\mathcal{I}} \left| \overline{\xi_y} - \overline{\xi_{y,\text{goal}}} \right|, \quad \min_{\mathbf{p},\mathcal{I}} \left| \overline{\xi_z} - \overline{\xi_{z,\text{goal}}} \right|. \tag{16}$$

A possible criterion for a wrapper approach is[1]

$$\min_{\mathbf{p},\mathcal{I}}(Z) \quad \text{with} \quad Z = \alpha \left| \overline{\xi_y} - \overline{\xi_{y,\text{goal}}} \right| + (1 - \alpha) \left| \overline{\xi_z} - \overline{\xi_{z,\text{goal}}} \right|, \quad \alpha \in [0.5, 1]. \tag{17}$$

The parameter α weights the classification results from intended to unintended properties and needs to be set to values bigger than 0.5 in order to have a significant influence of the intended properties. If $\alpha = 1$ a common wrapper approach is used for feature extraction and selection [14].

A combination of filter and wrapper approaches is possible, i.e. by applying a wrapper criterion on normalized features.

Conventional machine learning algorithms perform well in crossvalidation and even on test data, if all data points of training and test data belong to the same unintended property

---

[1] We use absolute differences instead of a quadratic criterion - the latter would rather compensate values for ξ_y with values of ξ_z than finding extreme values.

class [15, 16]. They will fail dramatically if test data belongs to another unintended class. However, performance in crossvalidation is not decreased in this case. Thus, crossvalidation is no means to check validity of classification. All criterions perform best if the training dataset contains all instances of the output classes $\mathbf{y}_i, \mathbf{z}_i$.

For all analysis steps, the open source MATLAB toolbox Gait-CAD [17][2] was used.

4 Benchmark dataset

Features extracted out of each embryonic image S_1 are according to [18, 19]

- Center of gravity of pixel values,

- Variation of horizontal image center line,

- Mean of horizontal image center line,

- Number of pixels exceeding threshold,

- Number of edges according to log-algorithm and

- Number of edges according to Canny-algorithm.

To restrict complexity, we focus on one intended property $\mathbf{y}_i = y_i = \{1, 2\}$ and one unintended property $\mathbf{z}_i = z_i = \{1, 2\}$, thus $\overline{\xi_{z,\text{goal}}} = 0.5$ and $\overline{\xi_{y,\text{goal}}} = 1$. The intended property is called 'coagulation status' and describes the developmental status of a zebrafish larva (see rows of images in Fig. 2a), the unintended property is the microscope setting of two identical microscopes (see columns of images in Fig. 2a). Although the images look quite similar, a feature derived out of an image processing routine shows clear differences for a set of images (see. Fig. 2b).

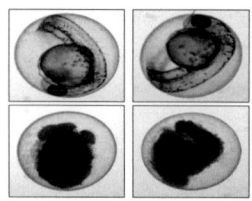 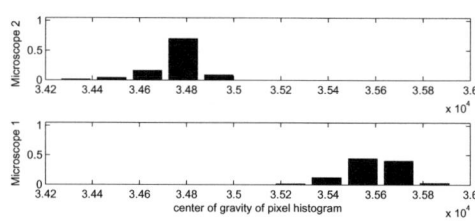

Figure 2: a (left): Images with differing intended properties (alive in row 1, dead in row 2) and unintended properties (microscope 1 in column 1, microscope 2 in column 2). b (right): Histogram of center of gravity of all images of two microscopes

We introduced the following datasets to discuss the classifiers' adaptation:

- Dataset 1 (D1) contains all data points from microscope 1 ($n = 67$) and is validated by a test dataset from microscope 2 ($n = 69$).

---

[2]http://sourceforge.net/projects/gait-cad/

- Dataset 2 (D2) contains all data points from microscope 2 ($n = 69$) and is validated by a test dataset from microscope 1 ($n = 67$).

- Dataset 3 (D3) contains every second data point from microscope 1 and microscope 2 ($n = 68$) and is validated by a test dataset containing all left over data points[3] ($n = 68$).

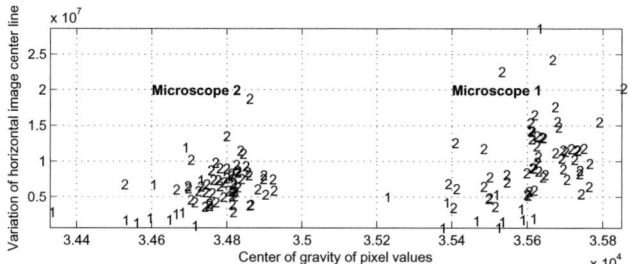

Figure 3: Feature space for two classes, dataset D1

Fig. 3 shows the heterogeneity of datasets 1 and 2. There are two clusters representing the two microscopes. Each of the clusters contains the two classes 'alive'(1) and 'coagulated'(2). Both datasets build clusters with different centers.

5 Results

5.1 Classifier settings

The machine learning process consists of a feature selection with MANOVA ($s_m = 2$) and classification using a Bayes classifier. We apply the machine learning routine to classifiers without adaptation, classifiers adapted with the filter approach and to classifiers adapted with the wrapper approach.

5.2 Filter approach

To validate the filter approach, we compared the performance of the classification without adaptation to the performance of the three filter approaches (13), (14) and (15). Table 1 shows the results.

Without adaptation MANOVA chooses the feature 'Mean of horizontal image center line' delivering a good classification on the training dataset. However, the feature is strongly related to the brightness settings of the microscope. Thus, the found discriminant function is not valid for the test dataset and tends to deliver high misclassification rates ($1-\xi_y = 0.38$) - a lot of data points of class two are assigned to class one. By contrast, the normalization

---
[3]To obtain comparable results, also a crossvalidation or bootstrap could be used. However, as data with different unintended properties do not fit a crossvalidation or bootstrap approach, we decided to split the data in training and test dataset. Furthermore, crossvalidation and bootstrap are computational intensive.

	D1	D2	D3	Ø
w/o adaptation	0.38	0.03	0.01	0.14
filter approach (eq. (13))	0.07	0.01	0.01	0.03
filter approach (eq. (14))	0.33	0.13	0.26	0.24
filter approach (eq. (15))	0.03	0.01	0.01	**0.02**

Table 1: Classification error $1 - \overline{\xi_y}$ without adaptation and with filter approaches

by (15) decreases the influence of the brightness settings in all images and the classifier stays valid for the test dataset ($1 - \overline{\xi_y} = 0.03$). The feature space of D1 of the test dataset and the discriminant functions of the training dataset are given in Figs. 4 and 5.

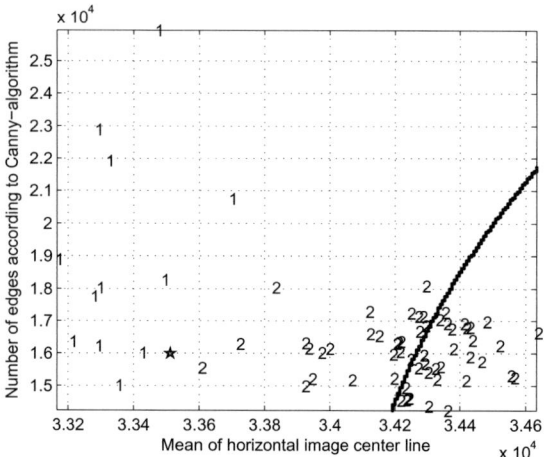

Figure 4: Feature space and discriminant function on test dataset for D1 without adaptation

The filter approach normalized to maximum and minimum (14) delivers also a high misclassification rate ($1 - \overline{\xi_y} = 0.33$). This is due to the sensitivity of the normalization procedure to outliers which affect maximum and minimum dramatically. The filter approach based on mean value and standard deviation (13) delivers better results ($1 - \overline{\xi_y} = 0.07$) because the influence of outliers is decreased. The results are not as good as with normalization by equation (15), because here, outliers are not taken into account at all.

Datasets D2 and D3 show the same tendency. In both datasets, a the training dataset is more valid for a classifier to deliver good results on the test dataset. Thus, also the classifier without adaptation delivers good results ($1 - \overline{\xi_y} = 0.03$ for D2, $1 - \overline{\xi_y} = 0.01$ for D3). The filter approach normalized to maximum and minimum (14) delivers bad results on both datasets ($1 - \overline{\xi_y} = 0.13$ for D2, $1 - \overline{\xi_y} = 0.26$ for D3).

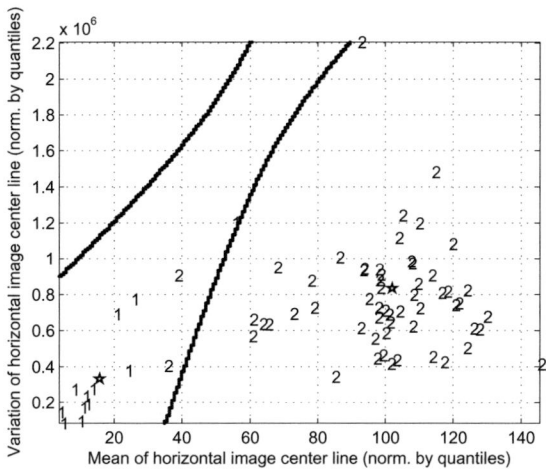

Figure 5: Feature space and discriminant function on test dataset for D1 with filter approach (eq. (15))

5.3 Wrapper approach

The wrapper approach is used to select an appropriate set of features. Due to the need of data points of both microscopes we only used dataset D3 to validate the approach. We applied equation (17) and set $\alpha = 0.8$. The results for the optimization criterion with respect to the selected features and classification rates are given in Table 2.

$s_{m,1}$	$s_{m,2}$	$1-\overline{\xi_y}$	$1-\overline{\xi_z}$	Z	$s_{m,1}$	$s_{m,2}$	$1-\overline{\xi_y}$	$1-\overline{\xi_z}$	Z
1	2	0.18	0	0.24	2	6	0.13	0.34	0.14
1	3	**0.01**	0	0.11	3	4	0.03	0.12	0.10
1	4	0.24	0	0.29	3	5	**0.01**	0.18	**0.08**
1	5	0.25	0	0.30	3	6	**0.01**	0.13	0.09
1	6	0.16	0	0.23	4	5	0.15	0.44	0.13
2	3	0.06	0.15	0.12	4	6	0.10	0.49	0.09
2	4	0.16	0.32	0.16	5	6	0.18	0.35	0.17
2	5	0.21	0.32	0.20					

Table 2: Validation results for wrapper without adaptation. Chosen features $s_{m,1}$, $s_{m,2}$, classification errors $1-\overline{\xi_y}$, $1-\overline{\xi_z}$ and wrapper criterion Z, $\alpha = 0.8$.

Both methods - classification without adaptation and wrapper approach - deliver a misclassification rate of $(1 - \overline{\xi_y} = 0.01)$. The classifier without adaptation already delivers a very good result, which can hardly be improved. However, a glimpse in the feature space (Fig. 6 and Fig. 7) shows that the wrapper approach chooses robust features whereas the classifier without adaptation chooses features generating clusters for each microscope in the feature space being less robust. However, this assumption needs to be validated on a bigger dataset. Decreasing the parameter α would lead to the choice of features 4 and 6 and thus to higher misclassification rates ($1 - \overline{\xi}_y = 0.10$) - however, classification of the unintended properties would then become impossible ($1 - \overline{\xi}_z = 0.51$).

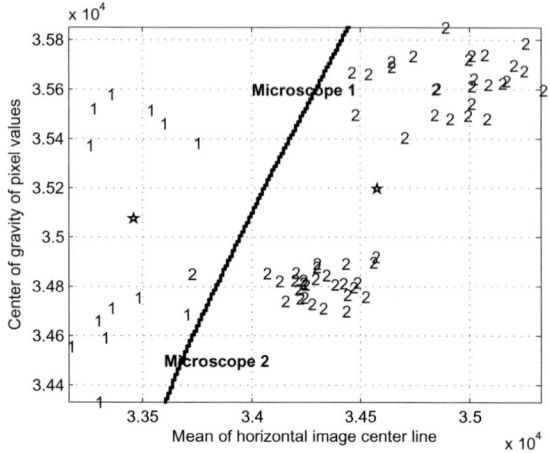

Figure 6: Feature space and discriminant function on test dataset for D3 without adaptation

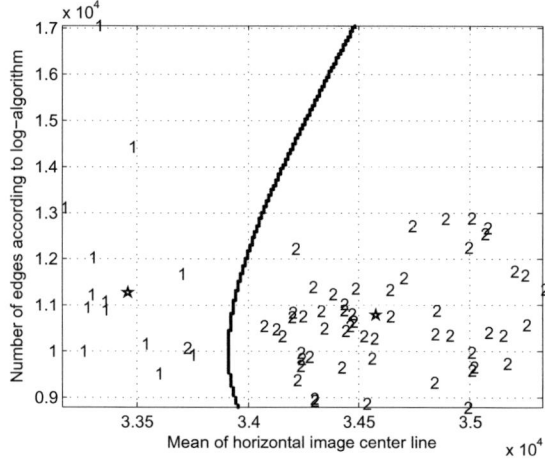

Figure 7: Feature space and discriminant function on test dataset for D3 with wrapper approach

6 Conclusions and outlook

We addressed the problem of classifying heterogeneous datasets. It was shown, that if the heterogeneity consists of differences between training and test dataset, a filter approach for image normalization improves the classification results. The normalization needs to be done such that the influence of outliers is minimized. If the heterogeneity is given in the training dataset, also a wrapper approach may be applied for feature selection. It was shown, that the wrapper produces a coherent feature space which will improve robustness.

All results need to be validated in larger scale. Therefore, experiments are running validating the effect of toxic substances on the organism of fish larvae. Thousands of data points are gathered being described by the intended properties chemical, concentration of chemical and effect on different organs and unintended properties like microscopes, experiment day and experimenter. With the new data, a validation of the preliminary results of this article will become possible.

References

[1] Gehrig, J.; Reischl, M.; Kalmar, E.; Ferg, M.; Hadzhiev, Y.; Zaucker, A.; Song, C.; Schindler, S.; Liebel, U.; Müller, F.: Automated High Throughput Mapping of Promoter-Enhancer Interactions in Zebrafish Embryos. *Nature Methods* 6 (2009) 12, pp. 911–916.

[2] Alsmadi, M.; Omar, K.; Noah, S.; Almarashdeh, I.: Fish Recognition Based on Robust Feature Extraction from Size and Shape Measurements using Neural Networks. *Journal of Computer Science* 6 (10) (2010), pp. 1059–1065.

[3] de Weerd, E.: *Hochdurchsatz-Evaluierung von konfokalen Mikroskopiebildern biologischer Modellorganismen*. Master's thesis, Karlsruher Institut für Technologie (KIT). 2010.

[4] Guedesen, A.: Quantitative Analysis of Preprocessing Techniques for the Recognition of Handprinted Characters. *Pattern Recognition* 8 (1976), pp. 219–227.

[5] Andres, B.; Köthe, U.; Helmstaedter, M.; Denk, W.; Hamprecht, F.: Segmentation of SBFSEM Volume Data of Neural Tissue by Hierarchical Classification. *Pattern Recognition, Proc. 30th DAGM Symposium* 5096 (2008), pp. 142–152.

[6] Farmer, M.; Jain, A.: A Wrapper-based Approach in Image Segmentation and Classification. *IEEE Transactions on Image Processing* 14 (12) (2005), pp. 2060–2072.

[7] Beller, M.; Stotzka, R.; Müller, T.: Application of an Interactive Feature-Driven Segmentation. *Biomedizinische Technik* 49 (E2) (2004), pp. 210–211.

[8] Tatsuoka, M. M.: *Multivariate Analysis*. New York: Macmillan. 1988.

[9] Mitchell, T.: *Machine Learning*. McGraw-Hill. 1997.

[10] Kohavi, R.; John, G. H.: Wrappers for Feature Subset Selection. *Artificial Intelligence* 97 (1-2) (1997), pp. 273–324.

[11] Hall, M.: *Correlation-based Feature Selection for Machine Learning*. Ph.D. thesis, University of Waikato, Hamilton, New Zealand. 1999.

[12] Lindeberg, T.: Scale-Space Theory: A Basic Tool for Analysing Structures at Different Scales. *Journal of Applied Statistics* 21 (1994), pp. 224–270.

[13] Lowe, D. G.: Distinctive Image Features from Scale-Invariant Keypoints. *International Journal of Computer Vision* 60 (2004) 2, pp. 91–110.

[14] Reischl, M.; Gröll, L.; Mikut, R.: Optimierte Klassifikation für Mehrklassenprobleme am Beispiel der Bewegungssteuerung von Handprothesen. In: *Proc., 13. Workshop Fuzzy Systeme*, pp. 124–143. Forschungszentrum Karlsruhe. 2003.

[15] Efron, B.; Tibshirani, R.: Cross-Validation and the Bootstrap: Estimating the Error Rate of a Prediction Rule. Tech. Rep. TR-477, Dept. of Statistics, Stanford University. 1995.

[16] Kohavi, R.: A Study of Cross-Validation and Bootstrap for Accuracy Estimation and Model Selection. In: *Proc., International Joint Conference on Artificial Intelligence*. 1995.

[17] Mikut, R.; Burmeister, O.; Braun, S.; Reischl, M.: The Open Source Matlab Toolbox Gait-CAD and its Application to Bioelectric Signal Processing. In: *Proc., DGBMT-Workshop Biosignalverarbeitung, Potsdam*, pp. 109–111. 2008.

[18] Alshut, R.; Legradi, J.; Mikut, R.; Strähle, U.; Reischl, M.: Robust Identification of Coagulated Zebrafish Eggs using Image Processing and Classification Techniques. In: *Proc., 19. Workshop Computational Intelligence*, pp. 9–21. 2009.

[19] Alshut, R.; Legradi, J.; Liebel, U.; Yang, L.; van Wezel, J.; Strähle, U.; Mikut, R.; Reischl, M.: Methods for Automated High-Throughput Toxicity Testing using Zebrafish Embryos. *Lecture Notes in Artificial Intelligence* 6359 (2010), pp. 219–226.

On the Evaluation of Direct Search Methods

Steffen Finck, Hans-Georg Beyer

Fachhochschule Vorarlberg Forschungszentrum PPE
Hochschulstrasse 1, A-6850 Dornbirn, Österreich
Tel.: (0043) 5572 792 7122
Fax: (0043) 5572 792 9510
E-Mail: {steffen.finck,hans-georg.beyer}@fhv.at

Abstract

Direct search methods are the means of choice when dealing with optimization problems where the objective (or goal) functions are hidden in a black box. Under such conditions the optimization strategy can only send queries to the black box and receives quality signals (objective function values) the reliability of which might be disturbed by noise. There is a plethora of such methods and the question arises which of these are the best for a specific problem. This question can be tackled from different perspectives and with different methods. On the one hand side, there are theoretical investigations dealing with the performance on simplest test functions. Such an analysis based on the dynamical systems approach is presented for the Simultaneous Perturbation Stochastic Approximation (SPSA) strategy using the sphere model. The results are compared with three variants of Evolution Strategies (ESs). On the other hand, there are empirical evaluations based on well crafted testbeds. The second part is devoted to the Black Box Optimization Benchmarking framework. After a short introduction, exemplary results are provided for several strategies considering noise-free and noisy test functions. Furthermore, the performance on the sphere model is discussed.

1 Introduction

Given the increase in computational power during the last decade, one is able to model and simulate large and complex problems like traffic scheduling problems, the behavior of an aircraft under different flow conditions, and bio-chemical processes amongst others. As a consequence, the optimization of such models is the logical next step. However, the optimization problems arising from these models are often characterized by non-availability of derivatives of the control (or design) variables. Making things even more complex, the models and the values of the objective functions might be corrupted by noise. Gradient-based optimization strategies will usually fail in such situations. Therefore, one rather needs strategies which send ("intelligent") queries to the model and adapt the decision parameters according to the information contained in the received quality signal (objective function value). This form of optimization is referred to as *black box optimization* and frequently occurs in engineering sciences in terms of simulation optimization and robust design optimization.

Optimization strategies which fit above description are also referred to as *direct search strategies*. While all these strategies use objective function values only (in contrast to gradient-based methods), they yet rely on different concepts which can be subdivided into evolutionary, derivative approximating, and response surface modeling approaches. For a more comprehensive introduction one is referred to [1].

The problem practitioners face is to select the best method for their application from the plethora of available methods. In most cases the application of interest exhibits only a restricted set of function properties like multi-modality, noise, or separability amongst others. Thus, if one knows these properties one can select the appropriate optimization strategy from a set of possible strategies. This assumes one has information about the performance of these strategies w.r.t. the function properties. This is the main motivation for comparing (direct search) strategies.

Such a comparison can be done on a theoretical level and on an experimental level. In the latter one defines a set of different test functions which feature function properties of interest. Such a setup is usually called a benchmark set. There exist different benchmarks each concerned with a specific area of interest, e.g. for multi-objective optimization algorithms [2], dynamic and uncertain environments [3], large scale optimization [4], constrained optimization [5], and real-parameter optimization [6, 7]. Note, these benchmarks are not fully equivalent to black box optimization since the test functions are known a priori. This cannot be easily avoided since this information is needed to run the benchmark on the contestants' machines. Furthermore, using this knowledge allows the algorithm designers to draw their own conclusions regarding the performance of the optimization strategy evaluated. The drawback of such an approach is, however, that in principle one can adapt the parameters of the optimization strategy to the test functions. This is, of course, not desirable. Therefore, using the identity of the test function for tuning the optimization strategy parameters (e.g., population sizes, mutation rates, shrinking factors, etc.) is highly discouraged by the benchmark designers. In Section 3 the setup of the Black Box Optimization Benchmark (BBOB) [7] will be described in more detail. This benchmark was used during the Genetic and Evolutionary Computation Conferences in 2009 and 2010.

In general, using a (well-defined) benchmark allows one to compare different optimization strategies over a broad range of test functions w.r.t. the experimental setup used. This should provide an indication on the performance for real-world problems. While experimental results can be used to obtain guidelines for the strategy specific parameters, the more profound way is the theoretical analysis of the dynamic behavior. A method for such an analysis will be presented in Section 2. Further, if theoretical results for several strategies exist, one can compare the dynamic behaviors. This might help to identify promising concepts for algorithm design. However, the obtained results are usually only valid for a certain function class and can not be transferred easily to other function classes. This is one reason why progress in this line of research proceeds gradually.

In the remainder of this work an approach for theoretical analysis of strategies will be presented in Section 2. Recently obtained results for the Simultaneous Perturbation Stochastic Approximation (SPSA) algorithm will be presented and compared with respective results for different Evolution Strategies from literature. In Section 3 the BBOB setup will be described in more detail and some exemplary results for the strategies considered in Section 2 will be shown.

2   Theoretical Analysis

In this work we are interested in the dynamical behavior of the algorithms to infer conclusions w.r.t. the approximate optimal setting of the strategy parameters. A prerequisite for such an analysis is that the function class of interest can be specified by simple analytical expressions (e.g., linear functions, quadratic forms). On the other hand, if one is interested in general convergence behavior only, other approaches do exist. These methods yield upper and/or lower performance bounds in terms of order notations. However, order notations do hide constants. As a consequence, it is rather difficult or even impossible to draw guidelines w.r.t. *optimal* choice of strategy parameters from this kind of analysis.

The approach considered in this work is to first analyze the optimization strategy of interest and later on to perform a comparison with other results available. This is different to the work presented in [8]. There Random Search, SPSA, Evolution Strategies, Genetic Algorithms, and Simulated Annealing were compared based on existing theoretical results for the respective convergence rate. The work showed the challenges involved of attaining comparable results from different analysis approaches.

2.1 Analysis Concept: Dynamical Systems Approach

The dynamical system approach considers the optimization strategy as a physical process and the test function as the physical environment. As in physics, one has to identify the forces driving the system and the governing equations of motion. In the case of Evolution Strategies (ESs) one has to consider the mapping

$$\{\mathcal{P}^{(g)}, \mathbf{s}^{(g)}, f\left(\mathbf{x}^{(g)}\right)\} \mapsto \{\mathcal{P}^{(g+1)}, \mathbf{s}^{(g+1)}, f\left(\mathbf{x}^{(g+1)}\right)\},$$

where $\mathcal{P}$ contains the population of object parameters (to be optimized), s contains the strategy parameters, $f(\mathbf{x})$ is the test (objective) function value (*fitness*), and g is the iteration counter. From mathematical point of view, this mapping is a memoryless stochastic process (inhomogeneous Markovian process). One way to analyze such a mapping is to model the Markovian process by determining the necessary probability and transition densities and to solve the corresponding Chapman-Kolmogorov equations. Apart from the problem of analytical tractability of the integral equations, the resulting densities are hard to interpret and yield therefore no insight w.r.t. the strategy parameter settings.

Another way is to look at the change of certain measures related to the algorithm's optimization performance which can be derived from the Chapman-Kolmogorov equation. Such performance measures can concern the change in the fitness space (*fitness gain*), the change in the search space (*progress rate*), or the change of certain strategy parameters, e.g. the mutation strength in the case of simple ESs. These measures will be called *local* measures to emphasize that they describe the change in one iteration. Further, the measures represent *expected* changes. The resulting dynamics are described by difference equations. For example,

$$q^{(g)} := \mathrm{E}\left[f\left(\mathbf{x}^{(g)}\right) - f\left(\mathbf{x}^{(g+1)}\right)\right]$$

is the fitness gain for a minimization problem ($q > 0$ indicate progress towards the optimizer). The calculation of the local measures is still a demanding task. Therefore, one is aiming at asymptotically exact local measures depending on the strategy and test function parameters. That is, these measures are considered for infinite search space dimensionality $N \to \infty$. Technically, this is done by neglecting terms with higher order of N in the denominator. A pleasant side effect is that often the variance of the local measure tends to vanish and one can replace the stochastic system by a deterministic one. However, due to the $N \to \infty$ assumption, the derived expressions are not exact for finite N and must be regarded as approximations. To check the approximation quality for medium and small search space dimensionalities, simulation experiments must be performed. In most cases, the approximation quality is rather good (i.e., only marginal differences between predicted and observed behavior) for $N \geq 30$. For smaller search space dimensionalities, the approximation still predicts the correct qualitative behavior, but the difference in the quantitative behavior is not negligible anymore.

Once $q^{(g)} = h\left(\mathcal{P}^{(g)}, \mathbf{s}^{(g)}, f\left(\mathbf{x}^{(g)}\right)\right)$ is determined one can extract the dynamic properties. For example in the case of the fitness gain q, one can determine convergence criteria by requiring $q > 0$, or in the case of noisy optimization one can determine the noise strength σ_ϵ until which progress can be achieved. From these results one will be able to derive guidelines for the choice of the strategy parameters.

As known from similitude concept and dimensional analysis in engineering sciences, introducing normalizations can simplify and unify results. Therefore, the progress measures are usually presented in normalized form, indicated by a superscripted star "*". It turns out that these progress quantities often approach a steady state after a certain transient time: In the case of the fitness gain, this can be written as $q^{*,(g)} = q^{*,(g+1)} = q^*$ for $g > g_0$ where $g \leq g_0$ is called transition phase. Such a steady state allows one easily to determine the long term dynamic behavior. One can simply iterate the steady state local measure or one can transform the difference equation into a differential equation. With the latter method an analytical solution for the long term dynamic behavior can be determined, however, in some cases a closed form solution of the integrals involved exists only in special cases.

Concerning noisy optimization, the analyzed noise models can be written as

$$\tilde{f}\left(\mathbf{x}\right) = f\left(\mathbf{x}\right) + \sigma_\epsilon\left(\mathbf{x}\right)\mathcal{N}(0,1),$$

where $\tilde{f}\left(\mathbf{x}\right)$ is the observed noisy fitness, $f\left(\mathbf{x}\right)$ is the true (undisturbed) fitness, $\sigma_\epsilon\left(\mathbf{x}\right)$ is the noise strength, and $\mathcal{N}(0,1)$ is a standard normally distributed random variate. The two most common noise models are:

- The additive noise model $\sigma_\epsilon = \text{const.}$, where the noise strength is independent of the current search point.

- The multiplicative noise model $\sigma_\epsilon^* = \text{const.}$, where the normalized noise strength is constant and the noise strength depends on the current search point. In most cases the noise strength vanishes at the optimizer.

Both noise models can be analyzed with the described analysis approach without much effort. In most cases, the noise-free case is obtained as special case of the more general noisy case. In contrast, the analysis of SPSA in [9] was only valid for noisy functions and the noise-free case could not be derived from the noisy results. An additional analysis [10] was necessary to determine the noise-free convergence behavior. Note, in the mentioned analyses the aim was to determine the convergence for the general case, i.e., the test function(s) considered must satisfy certain conditions and the results obtained are stated in order notation.

An analysis approach based on the dynamic systems theory applied to ES was first published in [11]. Since then the approach was successfully applied to the sphere model [12], ridge functions [13], general quadratic functions [14], and ill-conditioned functions [15].

Amongst others one was able to determine the dynamics of the mutation strength for self-adaptation strategies [16] and investigate the effects of different noise distributions [17]. There exist also analyses which derive N-dependent formulas for the local measures [16].

2.2 Results for SPSA

Recently, above procedure was applied to Simultaneous Perturbation Stochastic Approximation (SPSA) [18] in connection with the sphere model. The aim was to find out whether this strategy – which is not an ES – can be analyzed with such an approach and how the results obtained compare with available results of other methods.

Before stating the results obtained and comparing them with ESs, the basic concept of SPSA will be introduced. SPSA was developed in [9] and belongs to the class of stochastic gradient approximation strategies. The gradient itself is approximated by evaluating trial points and using the difference in the respective fitness. The early variants of such methods used $N + 1$ or $2N$ function evaluations per iteration to approximate the gradient. The novelty of SPSA is that only 2 function evaluations per iteration are necessary independent of the search space dimensionality. This was achieved by using random directions Δ for the creation of the trial points. In Alg. 1 the pseudo code for the basic variant is shown. The strategy parameters of SPSA are: Initial update step size a_0, α as rate for the decrease

---

Algorithm 1 Simultaneous Perturbation Stochastic Approximation

1: initialize $\mathbf{x}_1$
2: initialize a_0 and c_0
3: choose α, γ, and A
4: **for** $g := 1$ to $g_{\max}$ **do**
5: $\qquad c_g = c_0 g^{-\gamma}$
6: $\qquad$ choose random perturbation vector Δ
7: $\qquad f_g^+ = f(\mathbf{x}_g + c_g\Delta)$ $\qquad\qquad\qquad\qquad$ ▷ evaluate trial points
8: $\qquad f_g^- = f(\mathbf{x}_g - c_g\Delta)$
9: $\qquad \mathbf{g}_g = \dfrac{f_g^+ - f_g^-}{2c_g}\Delta^{-1}$ $\qquad\qquad\qquad$ ▷ gradient approximation
10: $\qquad a_g = a_0(g + A)^{-\alpha}$
11: $\qquad \mathbf{x}_{g+1} = \mathbf{x}_g - a_g\mathbf{g}_g$ $\qquad\qquad\qquad$ ▷ update of the current solution
12: $\qquad$ check termination criteria
13: **end for**

---

of the update step size a_g, constant A to allow for larger update step sizes, initial test step size c_0, and the decrease rate γ for the test step size c_g. Guidelines for the settings of these parameters can be found in [19]. The perturbation vector Δ is usually drawn from the symmetric ± 1 Bernoulli distribution. This distribution satisfies the conditions of zero mean, finite variance, symmetry, and finite inverse moments required by the analysis in [9]. See [20] for discussions on other possible distributions. Note, for the Bernoulli distribution $\Delta = \Delta^{-1}$, where

$$\Delta^{-1} := \left(\Delta_1^{-1}, \Delta_2^{-1}, \ldots, \Delta_N^{-1}\right)^{\mathrm{T}}.$$

Additionally, given that g represents a (noisy) gradient approximation, one can resample the steps 6–9 W-times per iteration and use the respective g-average as gradient approximation for the update of the solution. Note, each gradient approximation sample uses different perturbation vectors $\mathbf{\Delta}$ (which are i.i.d.), but the same test step size c_g. More information on SPSA can be found in [21] and on the web site http://www.jhuapl.edu/spsa/.

Applying the steps of the analysis approach (for the technical details refer to [18]) yields

$$q \stackrel{N \to \infty}{=} 4a_g R^2 \left(1 - \frac{a_g}{W}(N + W - 1)\right) - \frac{a_g^2 N \tilde{\sigma}_\epsilon^2}{4W c_g^2}, \tag{1}$$

where R is the distance to the optimizer and $\tilde{\sigma}_\epsilon$ is the overall variance of the noisy influences. For the noise models considered one obtains $\tilde{\sigma}_\epsilon = \sqrt{2}\sigma_\epsilon$. Note, in the case of the noise model with $\sigma_\epsilon^* = \sigma_\epsilon \frac{N}{2R^2} = \text{const.}$ the noise strength itself depends only on the current search point $\mathbf{x}_g$ and not on the evaluated points $\mathbf{x}_g \pm c_g \mathbf{\Delta}_g$. This assumption is exact for $N \to \infty$ and simplifies the math involved.

To not duplicate the work in [18], only some of the results will be presented here. The first question of interest is how the derived results compare with the results from other theoretical analyses. The first step is to obtain the long term dynamic behavior from (1). Assuming this behavior is described by

$$\frac{df}{dg} \approx -q$$

a solution to this ordinary differential equation is searched for. With the initial condition $f(\mathbf{x}_1) = f_{\text{start}}$ the asymptotic behavior $g \to \infty$ yields

$$\log(f(\mathbf{x}_g)) \sim -g^{1-\alpha}, \quad \text{for } \alpha < 1, \tag{2}$$
$$f(\mathbf{x}_g) \sim g^{-4a_0}, \quad \text{for } \alpha = 1 \tag{3}$$

for the noise-free sphere model. In [10] the respective result for the noise-free sphere model is stated as

$$\lim_{g \to \infty} \frac{1}{g} \log |f(\mathbf{x}_g))| = \beta \tag{4}$$

where $\beta < 0$ is a small constant depending on a_g. See [10] for the necessary proof conditions. Comparing (2) and (3) with (4) one can draw the conclusion that for $\alpha = 0$ both statements agree[1]. The advantage of the dynamical systems approach is that also the dynamic behavior for $\alpha > 0$ was obtained. Overall, for the noise-free sphere using $\alpha = 0$ yields the best convergence behavior. The convergence rates in (2) and (3) hold also for the sphere model with constant normalized noise, however, with additional restrictions. Only the special cases $\alpha = 1, A = 0$ (Eq. 3) and $\alpha = 0, \gamma = 0$ (Eq. 2) could be derived since for other cases no closed form solution of the integrals involved exist. For the sphere model with constant noise the results differ. With $\alpha = 0, \gamma = 0$ SPSA will stagnate within a certain distance to the optimizer (*residual location error*). On the other hand, for SPSA with $\alpha = 1$ the asymptotic results ($k \to \infty$) reads

$$f(\mathbf{x}_g) \sim g^{2\gamma - 1}, \quad \text{for } \gamma < 1/2. \tag{5}$$

From literature the general convergence rate of SPSA for noisy optimization reads

$$g^{\frac{\alpha - 2\gamma}{2}}(\mathbf{x}_g - \mathbf{x}_{\text{opt}}) \xrightarrow{dist.} \mathcal{N}(\mu, \Sigma) \quad \text{as } g \to \infty, \tag{6}$$

---

[1]Note, in [10] the results was stated in terms of convergence in the search space.

under the conditions given in [21]. As one can see, for $\alpha = 1$ both, (5) and (6), will yield the same convergence rate. Note, (6) must be squared to obtain the convergence in the fitness space.

Another important aspect is the approximate optimal choice for a_g. This can be derived by trying to find the a_g which maximizes q, Eq. (1). The following step size sequences were obtained

$$a_g = \frac{W}{2(N + W - 1)}, \quad \text{for } \sigma_\epsilon = 0, \tag{7}$$

$$a_g = \frac{4WR^2}{8R^2(N + W - 1) + N\left(\frac{\sigma_\epsilon}{c_g}\right)^2}, \quad \text{for } \sigma_\epsilon = \text{const.}, \tag{8}$$

$$a_g = \frac{W}{2(N + W - 1) + \frac{R^2}{N}\left(\frac{\sigma_\epsilon^*}{c_g}\right)^2}, \quad \text{for } \sigma_\epsilon^* = \text{const.} \tag{9}$$

From (7) one confirms that the optimal steps size is constant and only depends on the search space dimensionality N and the number W of gradient approximations per iteration step. For the noisy cases, both sequences (8) and (9) need information which are not accessible by optimization strategies (basically the distance R to the optimizer). Nevertheless, the following conclusions can be drawn: For the case with constant standard deviation noise $\sigma_\epsilon = \text{const.}$ the steps size should decrease with R, whereas the opposite is the case for the fitness proportional noise model $\sigma_\epsilon^* = \text{const.}$

2.3 Comparison with Evolution Strategies

In this part we are interested in comparing the results from the previous section with respective results of different ESs. First, the ESs variants will be presented: the $(\mu/\mu_I, \lambda)$-ES [12], the $(\lambda)_{\text{opt}}$-ES [22] and the Evolutionary Gradient Search (EGS) [23].

The $(\mu/\mu_I, \lambda)$-ES is an ES where λ offspring will be created in each step and the best μ ($\mu < \lambda$) offspring will be selected for recombination. The creation (also called mutation step) will be achieved by adding $\sigma \mathcal{N}(0, \mathbf{I})$ to the current search point $\mathbf{x}$. The parameter σ is called mutation strength and $\mathcal{N}(0, \mathbf{I})$ is a multi-variate standard normally distributed vector. Selection will be done w.r.t. the fitness values, To express the ordering the order notation

$$f_{1;\lambda} \leq f_{2;\lambda} \leq \ldots \leq f_{\lambda;\lambda}$$

is frequently used. Note, all problems considered are minimization problems. In the recombination step the centroid of the μ selected offspring will be determined. See Alg. 2 for the pseudo code.

The weighted recombination strategy $(\lambda)_{\text{opt}}$-ES is quite similar except all offspring will be considered for recombination. Each offspring will be weighted w.r.t. the fitness rank. In [22], the optimal weights for the sphere were determined as

$$w_l = \frac{e_{l-1,\lambda}^{0,1}}{\kappa} \quad \text{for } l = 1, \ldots, \lambda,$$

where $e_{l-1,\lambda}^{0,1}$ is a special case of the general progress coefficient, an integral constant defined in [12], and κ is a rescaling factor. The latter is set to $\kappa = 1$ for noise-free optimization

Algorithm 2 Basic steps for $(\mu/\mu_I, \lambda)$-ES and $(\lambda)_{\text{opt}}$-ES. In the case of $(\mu/\mu_I, \lambda)$-ES $w_{1\ldots\mu} = 1/\mu$ and $w_{\mu+1\ldots\lambda} = 0$ applies. For the $(\lambda)_{\text{opt}}$-ES $w_l = \frac{e^{0,1}_{l-1,\lambda}}{\kappa}, l = 1, \ldots, \lambda$ applies.

1: Initialize σ, $\mathbf{x}^{(0)}$, and $w_{1\ldots\lambda}$
2: Set $g = 0$
3: **repeat**
4:     **for** $l := 1$ to λ **do**
5:         $\mathbf{z}_l := \mathcal{N}(\mathbf{0}, \mathbf{I})$
6:         $f_l := f\left(\mathbf{x}^{(g)} + \sigma\mathbf{z}_l\right)$
7:     **end for**
8:     sort f_l
9:     $\langle\mathbf{z}\rangle := \mathbf{0}$
10:     **for** $l := 1$ to λ **do**
11:         $\langle\mathbf{z}\rangle = \langle\mathbf{z}\rangle + w_l\mathbf{z}_{l;\lambda}$
12:     **end for**
13:     $\mathbf{x}^{(g+1)} := \mathbf{x}^{(g)} + \sigma\langle\mathbf{z}\rangle$
14:     adapt mutation strength σ
15:     $g := g + 1$
16: **until** termination criteria are fulfilled

and $\kappa > 1$ for noisy optimization. The same weights were found to be optimal also for a subset of positive definite quadratic forms [24], the parabolic ridge [13], and the cigar function [25]. See Alg. 2 for the basic steps performed by the strategy.

The EGS is an exception since it is not an ES-type strategy. It is much closer to SPSA. As in SPSA, an even number 2λ of symmetric trial points will be evaluated and the difference in the fitnesses will be used to approximate the gradient. However, the creation of the trial points and the scheme for approximating the gradient differ from SPSA. Similar to the ES algorithms, EGS uses the mutation strength σ and the creation of the trial points is similar to the scheme used in $(\mu/\mu_I, \lambda)$-ES and $(\lambda)_{\text{opt}}$-ES. Note, in EGS the strategy needs 2λ function evaluations per step. The $(\mu/\mu_I, \lambda)$-ES and $(\lambda)_{\text{opt}}$-ES use λ evaluations per step.

Algorithm 3 Basic steps for Evolutionary Gradient Search.

1: Initialize σ and $\mathbf{x}^{(0)}$
2: Set $g = 0$ and κ
3: **repeat**
4:     **for** $l := 1$ to λ **do**
5:         $\mathbf{z}_l := \mathcal{N}(\mathbf{0}, \mathbf{I})$
6:         $\tilde{f}_l^{\pm} := f\left(\mathbf{x}^{(g)} \pm \sigma\mathbf{z}_l\right)$
7:     **end for**
8:     $\mathbf{z}^{(avg)} := \sum_{l=1}^{\lambda}\left(f_l^{-} - f_l^{+}\right)\mathbf{z}_l$
9:     $\mathbf{z}^{(prog)} := \frac{\sqrt{N}}{\kappa}\frac{\mathbf{z}^{(avg)}}{\|\mathbf{z}^{(avg)}\|}$
10:     $\mathbf{x}^{(g+1)} := \mathbf{x}^{(g)} + \sigma\mathbf{z}^{(prog)}$
11:     adapt mutation strength σ
12:     $g := g + 1$
13: **until** termination criteria are fulfilled

Algorithm	Fitness Gain q^*	opt. step size ($\sigma_\epsilon = 0$)
$(\mu/\mu, \lambda)$-ES	$c_{\mu/\mu_I,\lambda}\dfrac{\sigma^{*2}}{\sqrt{\sigma^{*2}+\sigma_\epsilon^{*2}}} - \dfrac{\sigma^{*2}}{2\mu}$	$\mu c_{\mu/\mu_I,\lambda}$
EGS	$\dfrac{1}{\kappa}\left[\sigma^{*2}\sqrt{\dfrac{\lambda}{\sigma^{*2}+\sigma_\epsilon^{*2}/2}} - \dfrac{\sigma^{*2}}{2\kappa}\right]$	$\kappa\sqrt{\lambda}$
$(\lambda)_{\mathrm{opt}}$-ES	$\dfrac{W_\lambda}{\kappa}\left(\dfrac{\sigma^{*2}}{\sqrt{\sigma^{*2}+\sigma_\epsilon^{*2}}} - \dfrac{\sigma^{*2}}{2\kappa}\right)$	κ
SPSA	$2Na_g - \dfrac{a_g^2}{W}\left(2N(N+W-1) + \dfrac{R^2\sigma_\epsilon^{*2}}{c_g^2}\right)$	$\dfrac{1}{2N}\,(W=1)$

Table 1: Overview of the normalized fitness gain $q^* = q\frac{N}{2R^2}$ for the sphere model. The optimal step size (σ^* and a_g, respectively) column applies for the noise-free case. Note, the term W_λ for the $(\lambda)_{\mathrm{opt}}$-ES is defined as $W_\lambda = \sum_{l=1}^{\lambda} w_l^2$.

For all three strategies the adaptation of the mutation strength is vital to the performance. There exist different methods, however, for the theoretical comparison an *ideal* adaptation scheme will be assumed. This scheme is characterized by $\sigma^* = \sigma\frac{N}{R}$ being constant throughout the optimization process. Therefore, the comparison will be based on optimal results and no effects of the applied mutation strength adaptation will be considered.

2.4 Efficiency Comparison

In a first attempt one can compare the respective fitness gains with each other. This is done in Table 1 where additionally the optimal step sizes for the noise-free case are given. Further, for the ES variants and EGS the progress rate $\varphi = \mathrm{E}\left[R^{(g+1)} - R^{(g)}\right]$ has been used instead of the fitness gain. However, the normalized progress rate and the normalized fitness gain are identical for the sphere as $N \to \infty$.

The fitness gain does not account for how many function evaluation are used per iteration step. To this end, the fitness *efficiency* has been introduced which is defined as

$$\nu = \frac{q^*}{\#FEs}, \tag{10}$$

where $\#FEs$ denotes the number of function evaluations per step. In Fig. 1 the efficiency curves for the noise-free sphere model are displayed. In the case of SPSA, $W = 1$ was used since it yields the highest efficiency. Increasing W reduces the efficiency ν. In comparison, the efficiency of EGS does not depend on the number of trial points λ used. As one can observe, the best efficiency is achieved by the $(\lambda)_{\mathrm{opt}}$-ES which reaches $\nu = 1/2$ for $\lambda \to \infty$. Thus, the $(\lambda)_{\mathrm{opt}}$-ES can achieve twice the efficiency than the next best strategies (EGS, SPSA) considered. For the $(\mu/\mu, \lambda)$-ES the efficiency depends on the truncation ratio $\vartheta = \mu/\lambda$ which was determined to be optimal at $\vartheta \approx 0.27$. The respective optimal efficiency is $\nu \approx 0.202$.

In the case of the sphere with constant normalized noise $\sigma_\epsilon^* = \mathrm{const.}$, the comparison is more involved. First, from Table 1 one can infer that the effect of the noise appears in a different term for SPSA. For the three other considered algorithms, the noise affects the *gain term* of the fitness gain. This term contributes positively to the overall fitness

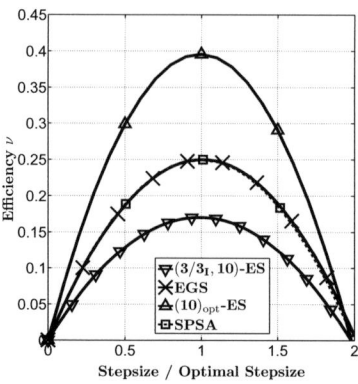

Figure 1: Efficiency curves for the noise free sphere model.

gain and it is reduced due to the noise. Further, using the normalization yields fitness gain expressions which only dependent on the noise strength σ_ϵ^* and the strategy parameters (e.g., population sizes μ and λ or the rescaling factor κ). For SPSA the noise affects the *loss term* (the one having the a_g^2 factor) which reduces the overall fitness gain and it is increased by $\sigma_\epsilon > 0$. Moreover, the resulting normalized fitness gain still depends on the search space dimensionality N and more importantly on the current distance to the optimizer R. Hence, the efficiency is not constant during the optimization process. This is illustrated in the left plot of Fig. 2 where the efficiency as a function of the noise strength is shown. All strategies use their respective optimal step size for the given noise strength and it is assumed that the strategy parameters are constant. In the case of SPSA, the efficiency curve can only be shown w.r.t. search space dimensionality N and current distance to the optimizer R. If one compares both SPSA curves (black curves with square markers), one observes that the efficiency is reduced if the strategy is farther away form the optimizer. One can adjust the behavior by the choice of c_g, however, this shows that SPSA is rather sensitive w.r.t. the strategy parameter choice and that information about the fitness landscape or the noise model are needed to make an appropriate choice. Similar curves will be obtained for different sets of the parameters. For the other strategies, the efficiency can be increased by either increasing the rescaling factor κ (EGS, $(\lambda)_{\text{opt}}$-ES) or increasing the population size λ with simultaneously holding the selection ratio ϑ constant $((\mu/\mu, \lambda)$-ES). Note, the shown results were obtained for the sphere with $N \to \infty$ and there seems to be no bound on the value of κ or the population size. Note, however, investigations which consider N-dependent fitness gain expressions showed that these bound do exist [26, 27]. Overall, the most robust choice seems to be the $(\mu/\mu, \lambda)$-ES, especially for large noise strengths (which is usually not known a priori).

In the case of the sphere with constant noise $\sigma_\epsilon = \text{const.}$ the efficiency ν can not be used as a measure for comparison. The three ESs (including EGS) will always achieve a residual location error, where the strategy stagnates and no more progress is possible. In the case of SPSA, using the optimal step size (8) for this noise model one can always reach the optimizer under the assumption $g \to \infty$. However, a similar problem as for the constant normalized noise model appears, namely the change in the efficiency during the

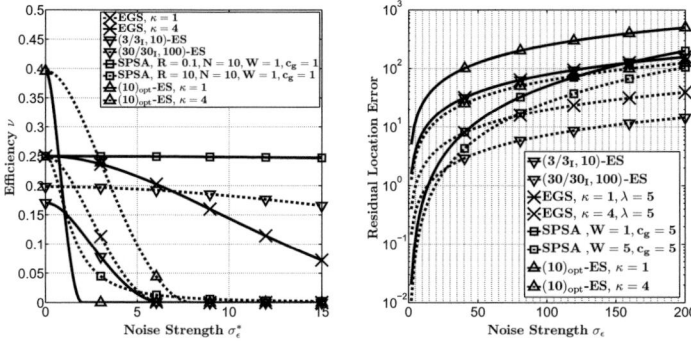

Figure 2: Efficiency curves for the noisy sphere model (left plot) and Residual Location Error for the sphere model with constant noise and search space dimensionality $N = 10$ (right plot). In the right plot, the curve for the $(3/3_I, 10)$-ES is almost identical to the one for the EGS with $\kappa = 1$.

optimization run. In this case a high-efficient strategy far away from the optimizer (noise almost negligible) will turn into a low-efficient strategy close to the optimizer (strong noisy influence). For comparison purposes one can use SPSA with constant step size a_g (7). In that case one also exhibits a residual location error. Such a scenario can happen in practice if the noise strength is small compared to the fitness at the initial point. Using several function evaluations one might not be able to detect the noise.

For all strategies the attained residual location error depends on the strategy parameters and the noise strength σ_ϵ. In the case of SPSA it additionally depends on the search space dimensionality N. In the right plot of Fig. 2 the different curves are shown. One can observe that the increase for SPSA is the strongest which is due to the residual location error being a function of the square of the noise strength. For all other strategies the noise strength influences the residual location error linearly. From the right plot in Fig. 2 it appears that the $(\mu/\mu, \lambda)$-ES is the most robust one w.r.t. the noise strength. As before, the result were derived for a sphere with $N \to \infty$, which neglects effects of the rescaling factor κ and the population sizes. In the case of the ESs-type strategies also $\sigma^* \leq 1$ was assumed. As a summary, the residual location errors and the maximal normalized noise strengths are listed in Table 2 for all strategies.

3 Experimental Analysis

In the previous section profound knowledge about the dynamic behavior has been presented. However, the results are restricted to the sphere model and can not be extrapolated easily to other function classes. Still, one is interested how SPSA (or any other optimization strategy of interest) compares with other strategies on more complex test functions. Empirical comparisons are the means of choice. Such a comparison will be based on a set of test functions and the respective performance (evaluation) criteria. Recently, such a benchmark suite was designed for the evaluation of strategies in a black box setting. In the following the setup and the performance criteria for the Black Box Optimization Benchmark (BBOB) will be reviewed.

Algorithm	Residual Location Error $f_{\min}$	max. σ_ϵ^*
$(\mu/\mu, \lambda)$-ES	$\dfrac{N\sigma_\epsilon}{4\mu c_{\mu/\mu_I,\lambda}}$	$2\mu c_{\mu/\mu_I,\lambda}$
EGS	$\dfrac{N\sigma_\epsilon}{4\kappa\sqrt{2\lambda}}$	$2\kappa\sqrt{2\lambda}$
$(\lambda)_{\text{opt}}$-ES	$\dfrac{N\sigma_\epsilon}{4\kappa}$	2κ
SPSA	$\dfrac{a_g N\sigma_\epsilon^2}{8c_g^2\left(W - a_g(N + W - 1)\right)}$	$\dfrac{c_g}{R}\sqrt{\dfrac{2N}{a_g}\left[W - a_g\left(N + W - 1\right)\right]}$

Table 2: Residual location error (measured as the expected fitness difference to the optimum) and maximal normalized noise strength σ_ϵ^* until which progress can be achieved for the strategies considered.

3.1 The BBOB Setup and Evaluation Criteria

Since this will be a summary, only some aspects of the BBOB setup will be considered. For the complete documentation one is referred to http://coco.gforge.inria.fr/doku.php?id=bbob-2010 where the up-to-date documents can be obtained. Additionally, one is referred to [28]. Note, the BBOB is an ongoing effort and therefore changes in the setup can occur over time.

The aim of the proposed setup is to analyze and to increase the knowledge of the optimization strategies benchmarked. The results obtained should further help to improve the strategies. The intent behind the selection of the test functions is to reflect a rather difficult portion of the problems encountered in practice to a certain extent. The BBOB itself comprises two testbeds, a noise-free one with 24 test functions and a noisy setup with 10 test functions and 3 noise models (30 functions altogether). In the noise-free benchmark the test functions are divided into five categories: separable (5 functions), low or moderate conditioning (4), high conditioning and unimodal (5), multi-modal with adequate global structure (5), and multi-modal with weak global structure (5). In the noisy benchmark three categories exist: moderate noise (2), severe noise (5), and highly multi-modal with severe noise (3). All test functions are scalable with the search space dimensionality N.

In the "Gaussian Noise" model, the noise is multiplicative and drawn from a log-normal distribution. The "Uniform Noise" model is also multiplicative and the noise is drawn from a uniform distribution. In comparison with "Gaussian Noise" it is more severe and the noise strength increases with decreasing function value. The last model is "Cauchy Noise" which is an additive noise model where the noise is drawn from a Cauchy distribution which is modeled as ratio of two independent standard normal distributions. Moreover, the noise acts only with a certain frequency (i.e., not all function evaluations will be noisy). Note, these models differ from the ones used in the theoretical analysis. For all test functions in the noisy testbed the function value observed by the algorithm is created in the following way: First the true function value f will be determined where $f \geq 0$ for all test functions by definition. Afterwards the respective noise model will be applied yielding the noisy function value $\tilde{f}$. All noise models were designed to yield $\tilde{f} \geq 0^2$. Further, if $f < 10^{-8}$ the true function value will be returned, i.e., $\tilde{f} = f$. The last step will be the addition of a penalty value (if necessary) and a shift of the function

---

[2]In case f_{target} is not reached an additional value of $1.01 * 10^{-8}$ is added to $\tilde{f}$.

value w.r.t. the current optimal function value f_{opt}. The conditions $\tilde{f} + f_{\text{opt}} \geq f_{\text{opt}}$ and $\tilde{f} < 10^{-8} \Rightarrow \tilde{f} = f$ were necessary to allow for testing whether the strategy reached the target function value $f_{\text{target}} = f_{\text{opt}} + 10^{-8}$. Normally, in noisy optimization the observed function value can not be used as termination criterion since it will be a random value. Instead a utility function must be defined (e.g., the expected value) and used as quality criterion. However, optimization strategies do not always optimize for a utility value and different strategies might have different utility targets. Therefore, using a "utility-free" setup allows to compare strategies independently of their implicitly build-in or explicitly defined utility function. Above conditions allow for such a utility-free setup and – most importantly – enables one to use the same evaluation methods as in the noise-free testbed.

For both testbeds, the search domain is $[-5, 5]^N$ while all functions can be evaluated within $\mathbb{R}^N$. The search space dimensionalities of interest are $N = (2, 3, 5, 10, 20, 40)$. The location of the optimizer is for most functions drawn uniformly from the $[-4, 4]^N$ box. The function value of the optimizer is sampled from a truncated Cauchy distribution within $[-1000, 1000]$ bounds. The input to the test function is transformed for some test functions. The transformations include linear transformations (e.g. rotation) which generate non-separable test functions and nonlinear transformations which break symmetries and introduce irregularities. A boundary penalty is applied if the current search point is outside the search domain for some test functions to possibly guide the strategy back towards the search domain.

An important aspect of any benchmark suite is the choice of the performance criteria. There seems to be two different viewpoints for this choice. One can base the performance on a fixed function evaluation budget or on a given target function value. While the former is (probably) closer to real-world situations, the latter allows for a quantitative comparison of algorithms: Instead of stating "A is better than B" one can state "A is x-times better than B" measured in the number of function evaluations needed to reach a given target function value[3]. Note, independent from the performance measure each strategy will always have termination criteria based on the function value and the function evaluation budget. In the BBOB design a prominent performance criterion is the expected running time (ERT). It estimates the expected number of function evaluations to reach a given target function value (assuming infinite time horizon) and is defined as

$$\text{ERT} = \frac{1 - p_{\text{s}}}{p_{\text{s}}} RT_{\text{us}} + RT_{\text{s}}, \qquad (11)$$

where RT_{s} is the average number of function evaluations in a successful run, RT_{us} is the average number of function evaluations in a unsuccessful run (i.e., the function budget), and p_{s} is the success probability. A successful run is defined as a run where f_{target} is reached. ERT is a well-interpretable measure which yields quantitatively comparable measurements. See [29, 7] for a derivation of ERT[4] and a theoretical comparison with a similar performance measure.

To have sufficient data for the computation of ERT, 15 trials are performed for each test function and each search space dimensionality. In each trial the location of the optimizer and the shift in the fitness space are drawn anew. The same holds for the linear search

---

[3] If two algorithms attain different target levels for a given function evaluation budget, no interpretation can be given w.r.t. the observed difference.

[4] It is denoted as SP2 in the reference.

space transformation. In order to take into account user performed strategy parameter tuning, the crafting effort [7]

$$\text{CrE} = -\sum_{k=1}^{K} \frac{n_k}{n} \log\left(\frac{n_k}{n}\right)$$

was used as a measure. If for all $n = \sum_{k=1}^{K} n_k$ test functions the same strategy parameter setting was used $\text{CrE} = 0$. If $K > 1$ different strategy parameter settings were used, with n_k being the number of test functions to which parameter setting $k = 1, \ldots, K$ was applied. In such cases one obtains $\text{CrE} > 0$. The calculated ERT value of the strategy will be multiplied by $\exp(\text{CrE})$ to account for the parameter tuning. The standard BBOB plot for the ERT-values (similar to Fig. 5) shows the scaling w.r.t. the search space dimensionality for a single algorithm and a single test function.

Using the experimental data as basis for a *simulated* run, one is able to estimate a dispersion measure for ERT. With bootstrapping [30], i.e., sampling with replacement repeatedly from the experimental data until a run is drawn which achieves the desired target function value, one can estimate the empirical cumulative distribution function (ECDF) of ERT. The ECDF can also be seen as the empirical cumulated probability of success for an event. In the here considered framework, such an event occurs when a horizontal line (fixed target value) in the convergence plot (function value vs. number of function evaluations) intersects the convergence curve. Thus, one can condense the empirical data into a single curve by considering several convergence curves, e.g. for different trials, different test functions, or search space dimensionalities. Moreover, considering more than one target value yields ultimately curves which depict the performance of the strategy on the complete testbed over a range of target values. The standard BBOB plots display the ECDF curves for several test functions w.r.t. a target value and also w.r.t. a given function budget[5] for a single search space dimensionality. Note, the ECDF is closely related to the proposed data and performance profiles in [31].

For the second BBOB workshop the arsenal of available plots was extended to include plots for direct comparison between two or many strategies. However, the performance criteria remained the same. One is referred to above mentioned web site for more information.

3.2 Examples

In the following, some example figures from the BBOB framework will be presented. The strategies of interest will be those from Section 2. They have been implemented with their respective standard parameter settings, however, in each strategy the number of function evaluations per iteration step is increased if a restart is performed. For all strategies $\text{CrE} = 0$ holds. For the ES-type strategies (including EGS) the cumulative step length adaptation method (CSA) [32] was used for the adaptation of the mutation strength. The same mutation strength adaptation procedure is used in the state-of-the-art covariance matrix adaptation (CMA-ES) [33]. A function evaluation budget of $10^4 \times N$ was used by all strategies. Note, each strategy has also a second order version where either

---

[5]The same procedure is easily extend by using a vertical line (fixed number of function evaluations) in the convergence plot.

a covariance matrix (ES) or the Hessian matrix (SPSA) will be estimated. See [33, 34] for more information.

In Fig. 3 the ECDF of the bootstrapped ERT for $N = 10$ is shown for the test function subgroups of the noise-free testbed. In each plot the y-axis shows the percentage of the reached target values for the considered test functions. For example, in the top left plot a value of 1 on the y-axis means that all target values (50 for *each* test function) for all test functions (24) were reached by the algorithm. The 'x'-markers in the plots indicate the maximal number of function evaluations used in the experiments. The data right of the marker is obtained by the bootstrapping. Additionally to the results of the four strategies considered, the best obtained result for each target value from BBOB 2009 is displayed. Note, the curves show compressed information, meaning one can not determine which target value on which test functions was reached from these plots. The conclusion one can draw are that CSA-EGS has the best overall performance (of the considered strategies), however, if one is interested in a certain subgroup this changes. For example, for the test functions with moderate condition number the $(\lambda)_{\mathrm{opt}}$-CSA-ES is the best. One can also draw a conclusion w.r.t. the used parameter setup. In case of SPSA, the used strategy parameters perform well on separable functions and multi-modal functions with a weak global structure, but for functions with moderate conditioning and multi-modal functions with adequate global structure the chosen setup seems not to be a good choice. Similar conclusions can be drawn for the other strategies. In Fig. 4 the ECDF is shown for the noisy testbed. There the performance of the ES-type strategies (including EGS) is quite similar in all plots. The performance of SPSA is always worse compared with the other strategies. In Fig. 5 the ERT on the sphere model (with and without noise) is displayed for all search space dimensionalities and a target function value of $f_{\mathrm{target}} = 10^{-8}$. The ordinate values represent $\log_{10} \left(\frac{\mathrm{ERT}}{N} \right)$. These type of plots allow to obtain information about a specific target function value on a specific test function. For the noise-free sphere (top left) the performance of the strategies are quite similar and for the strategies with CSA one can observe that the performance is better for higher search space dimensionalities. In case of SPSA, the performance is best for $N = 5$. The theoretical analysis ($N \to \infty$) predicted that the $(\lambda)_{\mathrm{opt}}$-ES is the best strategy which is confirmed by the experimental analysis for $N \geq 20$. However, the experimental results are influenced by the use of the non-optimal step sizes. For the noisy sphere models, SPSA reaches $f_{\mathrm{target}} = 10^{-8}$ only for $N \in \{2, 3\}$ in two of three noise models. The curves with the gray-scaled markers indicate the maximal number of function evaluation used in the experiments. All other strategies reach the target value for all search space dimensionalities and all noise models, and exhibit a similar performance.

4   Conclusions and Outlook

The analyses presented showed what kind of information can be gained by theoretical and empirical investigations, respectively. For the former, one obtains information as to the choice of the strategy parameters and the convergence properties in an idealized setting for simple test function classes. However, the results can not be easily transferred to other test functions of interest. From empirical investigations one obtains the performance for a set of (arbitrary) test functions. One can further draw conclusions on the chosen parameter setting, (e.g., satisfactory or not), however, no information on how to choose (better) parameters is obtained. This shows that both type of analysis can be seen as

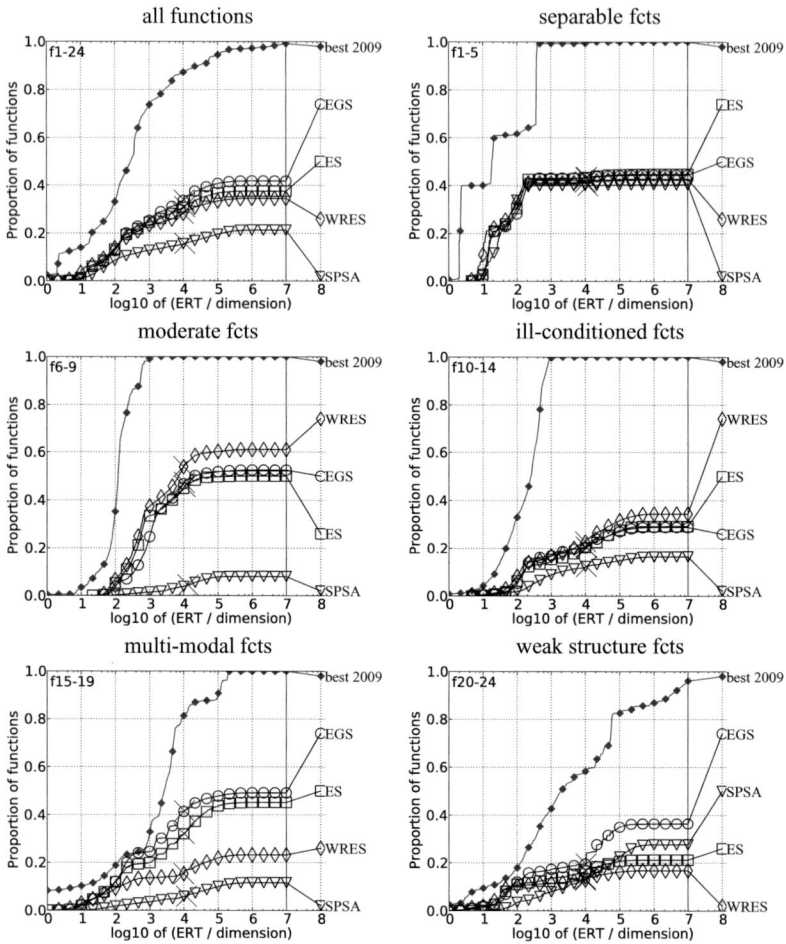

Figure 3: Empirical cumulative distribution of the bootstrapped distribution of ERT over dimension for 50 targets in $10^{[-8..2]}$ for all noise-free functions and subgroups for $N = 10$. The best ever line corresponds to the algorithms from BBOB 2009 with the best ERT for each of the targets considered.

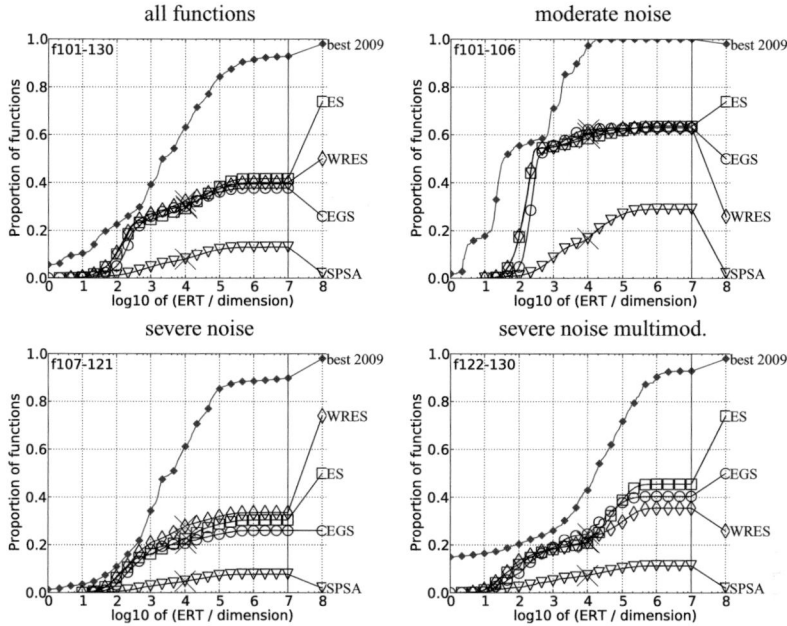

Figure 4: Empirical cumulative distribution of the bootstrapped distribution of ERT for all noisy functions and subgroups for $N = 10$. See also caption of Fig. 3.

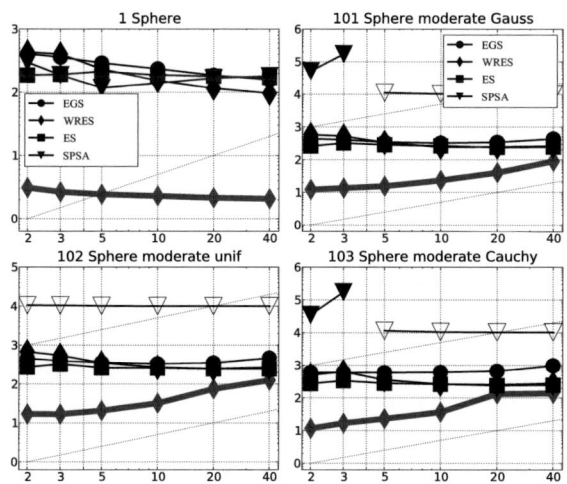

Figure 5: Scaling graphs giving the decimal logarithm of ERT divided by dimension versus dimension for the target function value 10^{-8}. The thick line corresponds to the best algorithm from BBOB 2009 for this target value and function.

complementary to each other.

The theoretical analysis proceeds rather gradually due to the math involved. Yet, this analysis has not only its merits in providing functional dependencies between performance and strategy parameters, it also provides a deeper insight into the working mechanisms of the optimization algorithms investigated. This opens the possiblity of feedback to the algorithms design based on first principles. While the set of test functions analyzed steadily increases, the effort for the respective performance analysis is rather high. This makes the decision as to what kind of test functions should be analyzed next a crucial step. The same holds for the choice of the optimization strategies to be investigated. Of course, one would like to analyze more complex strategies (e.g. CMA-ES) and other types of direct search methods (e.g. response surface techniques). It is still unclear whether these strategies can be treated by the presented approach.

For empirical analyses, the challenge is to improve the benchmark framework. While one is clearly interested in an accepted standard benchmark, one must avoid overfitting. Thus, if an algorithm performs well on the benchmark it should perform well on similar problems not included in the benchmark. This also raises the principal question whether the functions in the testbed do qualitatively represent the optimization behavior of typical real-world optimization problems. Do the test scenarios and noise models currently implemented in the BBOB really reflect the needs and performance criteria practitioners are interested in? And does it make sense to look at a 10^{-8} precision at all?

References

[1] Kolda, T. G.; Lewis, M. R.; Torczon, V.: Optimization by Direct Search: New Perspectives on Some Classical and Modern Methods. *SIAM Review* 45 (2003) 3, S. 385–482.

[2] Huang, V. L.; Qin, A. K.; Deb, K.; Zitzler, E.; Suganthan, P. N.; Liang, J. J.; Preuß, M.; Huband, S.: Problem Definitions for Performance Assessment of Multi-Objective Optimization Algorithms, Special Session on Constrained Real-Parameter Optimization. Technical Report, Nanyang Technological University, Singapore. URL http://www3.ntu.edu.sg/home/epnsugan/index_files/CEC-07/CEC07.htm. 2007.

[3] Li, C.; Yang, S.; Nguyen, T. T.; Yu, E. L.; Yao, X.; Jin, Y.; Beyer, H.-G.; Suganthan, P. N.: Benchmark Generator for CEC'2009 Competition on Dynamic Optimization. Technical Report, University of Leicester, UK. URL http://www.cs.le.ac.uk/people/syang/ECiDUE/ECiDUE-Competition09. 2009.

[4] Tang, K.; Yao, X.; Suganthan, P. N.; MacNish, C.; Chen, Y. P.; Chen, C. M.; Yang, Z.: Benchmark Functions for the CEC'2008 Special Session and Competition on Large Scale Global Optimization. Technical Report, Nature Inspired Computation and Applications Laboratory, USTC, China. URL http://nical.ustc.edu.cn/cec08ss.php. 2007.

[5] Mallipeddi, R.; Suganthan, P. N.: Problem Definitions and Evaluation Criteria for the CEC 2010 Competition on Constrained Real-Parameter Optimization. Technical Report, Nanyang Technological University, Singapo-

re. URL http://www3.ntu.edu.sg/home/EPNSugan/index_files/ CEC10-Const/CEC10-Const.htm. 2010.

[6] Suganthan, P. N.; Hansen, N.; Liang, J. J.; Deb, K.; Chen, Y. P.; Auger, A.; Tiwari, S.: Problem definitions and evaluation criteria for the CEC 2005 Special Session on Real Parameter Optimization. Technical Report, Nanyang Technological University. URL http://www3.ntu.edu.sg/home/EPNSugan/index_files/ CEC-05/CEC05.htm. 2005.

[7] Hansen, N.; Auger, A.; Finck, S.; Ros, R.: Real-Parameter Black-Box Optimization Benchmarking 2010: Experimental Setup. Technical Report RR-7215, INRIA. URL http://coco.gforge.inria.fr/bbob2010-downloads. 2010.

[8] Spall, J. C.; Hill, S. D.; Stark, D. R.: Theoretical Comparison of Evolutionary Computation and Other Optimization Approaches. In: *Proceedings of the CEC'99 Conference* (Angeline, P., Hg.), S. 1398–1405. Piscataway, NJ: IEEE. 1999.

[9] Spall, J. C.: Multivariate Stochastic Approximation Using a Simultaneous Perturbation Gradient Approximation. *IEEE Transactions on Automatic Control* 37 (1992) 3, S. 332–341.

[10] Gerencsér, L.; Vágó, Z.: SPSA in Noise Free optimization. In: *Proceedings of the American Control Conference*, Bd. 5, S. 3284–3288. 2000.

[11] Beyer, H.-G.: Toward a Theory of Evolution Strategies: Some Asymptotical Results from the $(1, + \lambda)$-Theory. *Evolutionary Computation* 1 (1993) 2, S. 165–188.

[12] Beyer, H.-G.: *The Theory of Evolution Strategies*. Natural Computing Series. Heidelberg: Springer. 2001.

[13] Arnold, D.; MacLeod, A.: Step Length Adaptation on Ridge Functions. *Evolutionary Computation* 16 (2008) 2, S. 151–184.

[14] Beyer, H.-G.: Actuator Noise in Recombinant Evolution Strategies on General Quadratic Fitness Models. In: *GECCO-2004: Proceedings of the Genetic and Evolutionary Computation Conference* (Deb et al., K., Hg.), Bd. LNCS Volume 3102, S. 654–665. Heidelberg: Springer-Verlag. 2004.

[15] Beyer, H.-G.; Finck, S.: Performance of the $(\mu/\mu_I, \lambda)$-σSA-ES on a Class of PDQFs. *IEEE Transactions on Evolutionary Computation* 14 (2010) 3, S. 400–418.

[16] Meyer-Nieberg, S.: *Self-Adaptation in Evolution Strategies*. Dissertation, University of Dortmund, CS Department, Dortmund, Germany. 2007.

[17] Arnold, D. V.; Beyer, H.-G.: A General Noise Model and Its Effects on Evolution Strategy Performance. *IEEE Transactions on Evolutionary Computation* 10 (2006) 4, S. 380–391.

[18] Finck, S.; Beyer, H.-G.: Convergence Analysis of SPSA on the Noisy Sphere. *Theoretical Computer Science* (2010). Submitted.

[19] Spall, J. C.: Implementation of the Simultaneous Perturbation Algorithm for Stochastic Optimization. *IEEE Transactions on Aerospace and Electronic Systems* 34 (1998) 3, S. 817–823.

[20] Hutchinson, D. W.: On an Efficient Distribution of Perturbation for Simulation Optimization using Simultaneous Perturbation Stochastic Approximation. In: *Proceedings of the IASTED AMS 2002* (Hamza, M. H., Hg.), S. 440–444. ACTA Press. ISBN 0-88986-331-8. 2002.

[21] Spall, J. C.: *Introduction to Stochastic Search and Optimization.* Hoboken, NJ: John Wiley & Sons. 2003.

[22] Arnold, D. V.: Optimal Weighted Recombination. In: *Foundations of Genetic Algorithms 8* (Wright et al., A. H., Hg.), S. 215–237. Springer Verlag. 2005.

[23] Arnold, D. V.; Salomon, R.: Evolutionary Gradient Search Revisited. *IEEE Trans. Evolutionary Computation* 11 (2007) 4, S. 480–495.

[24] Finck, S.; Beyer, H.-G.: Weighted Recombination Evolution Strategy on a Class of PDQF's. In: *FOGA '09: Proceedings of the tenth ACM SIGEVO workshop on Foundations of genetic algorithms*, S. 1–12. New York, NY, USA: ACM. ISBN 978-1-60558-414-0. 2009.

[25] Arnold, D. V.; Beyer, H.-G.; Melkozerov, A.: On the Behaviour of Weighted Multi-Recombination Evolution Strategies Optimising Noisy Cigar Functions. In: *GECCO-2009: Proceedings of the Genetic and Evolutionary Computation Conference* (Raidl et al., G., Hg.), S. 483–490. New York: ACM. 2009.

[26] Beyer, H.-G.: Evolutionary Algorithms in Noisy Environments: Theoretical Issues and Guidelines for Practice. *Computer Methods in Applied Mechanics and Engineering* 186 (2000) 2–4, S. 239–267.

[27] Arnold, D. V.: *Local Performance of Evolution Strategies in the Presence of Noise.* Ph.D. Thesis, University of Dortmund, Dortmund. 2001.

[28] Ros, R.: *Real-Parameter Black-Box Optimisation:Benchmarking and Designing Algorithms.* Dissertation, University Paris-South. 2009.

[29] Auger, A.; Hansen, N.: Performance Evaluation of an Advanced Local Search Evolutionary Algorithm. In: *Proceedings of the CEC'05 Conference*, S. 1777–1784. IEEE. 2005.

[30] Efron, B.; Tibshirani, R.: *An introduction to the bootstrap.* Chapman & Hall/CRC. 1993.

[31] More, J. J.; Wild, S. M.: Benchmarking Derivative-Free Optimization Algorithms. *SIAM J. Optimization* 20 (2009) 1, S. 172–191.

[32] Hansen, N.; Ostermeier, A.; Gawelczyk, A.: Step-size adaption based on non-local use of selection information. In: *Parallel Problem Solving from Nature - PPSN III* (et al., Y. D., Hg.), S. 189–198. Springer Verlag. 1994.

[33] Hansen, N.; Ostermeier, A.: Completely Derandomized Self-Adaptation in Evolution Strategies. *Evolutionary Computation* 9 (2001) 2, S. 159–195.

[34] Spall, J. C.: Feedback and Weighting Mechanisms for Improving Jacobian Estimates in the Adaptive Simultaneous Perturbation Algorithm. *IEEE Transactions on Automatic Control* 54 (2009), S. 1216–1229.

Clustering Based Niching for Genetic Programming in the R Environment

Oliver Flasch, Thomas Bartz-Beielstein, Patrick Koch, and Wolfgang Konen

Fakultät für Informatik und Ingenieurwissenschaften, Fachhochschule Köln
E-Mail: {oliver.flasch | thomas.bartz-beielstein |
patrick.koch | wolfgang.konen}@fh-koeln.de

Abstract

In this paper, we give a short introduction into RGP, a new genetic programming
(GP) system based on the statistical package R. The system implements classical untyped tree-based genetic programming as well as more advanced variants including,
for example, strongly typed genetic programming and Pareto genetic programming.
The main part of this paper is concerned with the problem of premature convergence
of GP populations, accompanied by a loss of genetic diversity, resulting in poor effectiveness of the search. We propose a clustering based niching approach to mitigate
this problem. The results of preliminary experiments confirm that clustering based
niching is effective in preserving genetic diversity in GP populations.

1 Introduction

The goal of this paper is twofold: first, it provides a short introduction into RGP, a new
open source genetic programming system implemented as an extension package for the
statistical language and software package R [1]. Second, it reports on our ongoing research in diversity preservation methods for tree-based genetic programming (GP).

GP is a class of evolutionary algorithms for the automatic generation of computer programs from high-level problem definitions [2, 3, 4]. In our work, we apply a strongly-
typed tree-based multi-objective GP variant for symbolic regression to solve real-world
time series regression problems from water resource management and from finance [5, 6].
We recently developed RGP, a modular GP system based on the R statistical package. By
building on R, our system can leverage extensive tools for statistics, data handling, and visualization. Because GP individuals are represented as R functions, arbitrary R functions
may be used as GP building blocks. Furthermore, GP individuals can be used and analyzed by all available R-based tools. By distributing our system as open source software,
we enable others to verify the results of our experiments and to apply our algorithms and
techniques to their problems and datasets.

In our application of GP, we experienced the common problem of premature convergence
into local optima, accompanied by a loss of genetic diversity, resulting in poor effectiveness of the search. This problem is perhaps more severe in GP for symbolic regression
than in other evolutionary algorithms or GP applications because of the highly difficult
structure of the symbolic regression GP search space: depending on the set of GP building
blocks (the function set), the fitness landscape is highly multi modal and rough, making
it especially difficult to escape from local optima.

A typical means to circumvent the impact of premature convergence is to use multiple independent runs in parallel, combining their results only after a certain number of fitness evaluations m have passed [7]. The hyperparameter m can be fixed at the start of a run or controlled dynamically. This algorithm is a form of static niching, where genetic diversity is preserved by isolating possibly structurally, i.e., genotypically, different solutions from direct competition [8, 9]. Multi-objective GP methods, such as Pareto GP, also result in an implicit form of niching by maintaining a set of Pareto-optimal solutions that may be structurally different. Furthermore, explicit static niching schemes based on trivial geographies, demes or islands, or on individual age have shown promising potential in several GP applications [10, 3, 11, 12].

The remainder of this paper is organized as follows: Section 2 gives a high-level introduction into the design and features of the RGP system. Section 3 motivates and describes clustering based niching in the abstract and, building on this description, presents our algorithm. Section 4 explains preliminary experiments and gives first results. Section 5 concludes this paper with a short summary and an outlook to further research.

2 Genetic Programming in the R Environment

The recent availability of fast multi-core systems has enabled the practical application of GP in many real-world application domains. This has lead to the development of software frameworks for GP, including DataModeler, Discipulus, ECJ, Eurequa, and GPTIPS[1].

All of these systems are complex aggregates of algorithms for solving not only GP specific tasks, such as solution creation, variation, and evaluation, but also more general Evolutionary Computation (EC) tasks, like single- and multi-objective selection, and even largely general tasks like the design of experiments, data pre-processing, result analysis and visualization. Packages like Matlab, Mathematica, and R already provide solutions for the more general tasks, greatly simplifying the development of GP systems based on these environments [1].

RGP[2] is based on the R environment for several reasons. First, there seems to be a trend towards employing statistical methods in the analysis and design of evolutionary algorithms, including modern GP variants [13, 14]. Second, R's open development model has led to the free availability of R packages for most methods from statistics and many methods from EC. Also, the free availability of R itself makes RGP accessible to a wide audience. Third, the R language supports "computing on the language", which greatly simplifies symbolic computation inherent in most GP operations. In addition, parallel execution of long-running GP experiments is easily supported by R packages such as Snow [15].

---

[1]DataModeler is a commercial Mathematica-based GP system focused on symbolic regression in industrial applications (evolved-analytics.com). Discipulus is a commercial linear GP system (www.rmltech.com). ECJ is an open source framework for evolutionary computation (cs.gmu.edu/~eclab/projects/ecj). Eurequa is a graph GP system optimized for symbolic regression (ccsl.mae.cornell.edu/eureqa). GPTIPS is an open source Matlab toolbox for symbolic regression by GP (sites.google.com/site/gptips4matlab).

[2]The RGP package and documentation is freely available at rsymbolic.org.

2.1 RGP Features

RGP was mainly developed as a research tool for exploring time series regression and prediction problems with GP. Nevertheless, the system is modular enough to be easily adapted and extended to new application domains.

Individual Representation   RGP represents GP individuals as R expressions that can be directly evaluated by the R interpreter. This allows the whole spectrum of functions available in R to be used as building blocks for GP. Because R expressions are internally represented as trees, RGP may be seen as a tree-based GP system. However, the individual representation can be easily replaced together with associated variation and evaluation operators, if an alternative representation is found to be more effective for a given application [16].

Besides classical untyped GP, strongly typed GP is supported by a type system based on simply typed lambda calculus [17]. A distinctive feature of RGP's typed tree representation is the support for *function defining subtrees*, i.e. anonymous functions or lambda abstractions. In combination with a type system supporting function types, this allows the integration of common higher order functions like folds, mappings, and convolutions, into the set of GP building blocks.

RGP also includes a rule based translator for transforming R expressions. This mechanism can be used to simplify GP individuals during the evolution process as a means the reduce bloat, or just to simplify solution expressions for presentation. The default rule base implements simplification of arithmetic expressions. It can be easily extended to simplify expressions containing user-defined operators and functions.

GP Operators   RGP provides default implementations for several initialization, variation, and selection operators. The system also provides tools for the analysis and visualization of populations and GP individuals.

Initialization   Individual initialization can be performed by the conventional *grow* and *full* strategies of tree building. When using strongly-typed GP, the provided individual initialization strategies respect type constraints and will create only well-defined expressions. Initialization strategies may be freely combined, e.g. to implement the well known *ramped-half-and-half* strategy [3].

Variation   RGP includes classical and type-safe subtree crossover operators. Also, several classical and type-safe mutation operators are provided. The variation step can be freely configured by combining several mutation and recombination operators to be applied in parallel or consecutively, with freely configurable probabilities.

Selection   The system provides an implementation of single-objective tournament selection with configurable tournament size. Other selection strategies can be easily added and will be provided in later versions. Additionally, multi-objective selection is supported via the EMOA package by implementing the Pareto GP algorithm [7]. This algorithm optimizes solution quality while, at the same time, controlling solution complexity. For this purpose, RGP implements multiple complexity measures for GP individuals.

3 Clustering Based Niching

Preserving genetic diversity in the population of an evolutionary algorithm (EA) is important for reaching two related goals: first, high diversity is a resource for exploratory crossover, helping in the discovery of multiple optima in multi-modal search spaces. Second, high diversity decreases the probability of the whole population converging to a local optimum.

Most diversity-preserving EA are based on altering the selection operator to prevent premature convergence to a local optimum, examples include Fitness Sharing, Crowding, and Tagging [18, 19, 20]. A different approach is to use multiple independent populations or niching, like in Multinational GA and Forking GA [21, 22].

The underlying idea of niching in evolutionary algorithms is to apply the biological concept of isolated non-interbreeding species living in separate ecological niches to preserve genetic diversity in EA populations. Individuals of different species do not interbreed and individuals living in different niches do not compete for the same resources. Each niche is implemented as an independent EA run, convergence of the species in a single niche has no influence on the genetic diversity of other species in other niches. Inside each niche, individuals breed and compete like in a traditional EA, converging to a local optimum. This has the benefit that all possible EA extensions and specialized EA operators can still be applied at the niche level.

Given a technique for dynamically creating and merging niches, speciation can occur. By merging species, the higher genetic diversity of the resulting species can be exploited as a resource for exploratory crossover. By splitting a species into separate niches, the now isolated sub-species can evolve independently, creating new genetic diversity. In clustering based niching, clustering algorithms are used to divide an initial global population into species which are then distributed to niches. Clustering algorithms group individuals into species so that the individuals within the same species are relatively similar, while individuals in different species are relatively distinct. The similarity of individuals can be measured in several different ways, leading to different clusterings and different algorithm behaviour.

Clustering based niching methods have shown to be effective in preserving genetic diversity in Evolution Strategy (ES) populations [23]. In this work, we apply clustering based niching to GP for the first time. This leads to our main hypotheses:

H1 Niching is effective in preserving genetic diversity in GP populations.

H2 Clustering based niching yields significantly better results than static niching when applied to GP for symbolic regression.

If these hypotheses can be accepted is not clear, mainly because of the difficult nature the GP search space for symbolic regression. Table 1 shows the results of an experiment designed to highlight this difficulty. The phenotypic distance (see Section 3.1) between a GP individual and its mutated variant after a single mutation step of three different standard GP mutation operators is given. The phenotypic effect of a single mutation is highly random. Mutating constants in an GP individual can change its behaviour and therefore its fitness significantly, the effect of mutating function nodes or replacing subtrees is even stronger. These observations tell us that GP individuals might be unrelated phenotypically, even if they have very similar genotypes. We study empirically if clustering based niching is effective under these conditions.

Table 1: Effect of standard genetic programming mutation operators: in each experiment, a random full tree T_A of depth 6 is generated and the phenotypic distance to another tree T_B is measured. In mutation type (Mut. Type) *Random*, T_B is another random full tree of depth 6. In *Const. Mut.*, T_B is created by mutating constants in T_A. In *Func. Mut.*, T_B is created by mutating function labels in T_A. In *Subtree Mut.*, T_B is created by replacing random subtrees of T_A. The results shown are summaries of 500 experiments for each mutation type.

Mut. Type	Min.	1st Qu.	Median	Mean	3rd Qu.	Max.
				Phenotypic Distance (RMSE)		
Random	0	30.4959	197.2396	1.9161×10^6	1.3951×10^3	5.8326×10^8
Const. Mut.	0	0.0030	1.1040	5.5765×10^3	17.2065	7.8703×10^5
Func. Mut.	0	0.4273	19.9414	3.6973×10^7	408.7947	1.6742×10^{10}
Subtree Mut.	0	6.8196	78.2556	2.7572×10^5	1.1684×10^3	4.5585×10^7

What is the expected advantage of clustering based niching in contrast to a conventional static niching approach? In contrast to fixed niching, in clustering based niching individuals inside a single niche can be expected to be more similar than individuals of two different niches. This could be beneficial because successful crossover is much more likely between similar individuals, i.e. individuals which share homologous subtrees.

The general scheme of clustering based niching GP consists of four steps:

1. Cluster the GP population P_i into N_i niches.

2. Perform parallel GP passes in each of the N_i niches until the pass stop criterion is met at each niche.

3. Join the N_i populations into the GP population P_{i+1}, adding the best performing individuals into an elite set E.

4. Unless the run stop criterion is met, set $i := i + 1$ and return to step 1, otherwise return the resulting population P_{i+1} and the elite set E.

3.1 Distance Measures for Clustering GP Populations

In order to perform a clustering of a GP population into niches, a distance measure for GP individuals is needed. This distance measure is then used to calculate a distance matrix which can be used as an input for several hierarchical or partitioning clustering algorithms. There are basically three classes of distance measures that are suitable for this purpose: *Fitness distance*, *phenotypic distance*, and *genotypic distance*. Each of these measures has distinct requirements, advantages, and drawbacks.

Fitness Distance   Given two GP individuals T_A and T_B, a (possibly multi-objective) fitness function f and a distance measure d, the Fitness Distance d_{fitness} between T_A and T_B is given by the formula $d_{\text{fitness}} := d(f(T_A), f(T_B))$. Trivially, d_{fitness} is a metric iff d is a metric. Typically, the Euclidean metric is used for d, but other choices are possible. For example, the Euclidean Squared metric is sometimes used for efficiency reasons.

The main benefit of d_{fitness} is that it is comparatively efficient to calculate if the values of the fitness function f are already known for most individuals in a population, as it is the case in later stages of a GP run. At the start of a GP run, fitness values must be expected to be mostly random, with a high (when fitness values are minimized) mean, making d_{fitness} unsuitable for meaningful clustering in this stage of a run.

Phenotypic Distance   The phenotypic distance $d_{\text{phenotype}}$ measures the behavioral difference between two GP individuals T_A and T_B. Its definition is highly dependent on the interpretation of GP individuals, i.e. the GP application. In symbolic regression, given an error measure ϵ and a set of fitness cases $F \subseteq D$, we define $d_{\text{phenotype}} := \epsilon(\llbracket T_A \rrbracket(F), \llbracket T_B \rrbracket(F))$. The operator $\llbracket \cdot \rrbracket$ interprets a GP individual tree as a function defined on a domain D. In practice, typically the mean square error (MSE) or the root mean square error (RMSE) are used as an error measure ϵ.

Phenotypic distance can give meaningful clusterings in every stage of a GP run. Its main drawback is its possibly high computational effort, depending on the mean computational cost of calculating $\llbracket \cdot \rrbracket(F)$.

Genotypic Distance   As a GP population is a set of expression trees, there is no "natural" genotypic distance measure. To give meaningful and stable clusterings, a genotypic distance measure d_{genotype} should reflect the impact of the GP variation operators in the (informal) sense that $d_{\text{genotype}}(T_A, T_B) \leq d_{\text{genotype}}(T_A, T_C)$ iff $P(\text{variate}(T_A) = T_B) \geq P(\text{variate}(T_A) = T_C)$: an individual T_A is closer to an individual T_B than it is to an individual T_C iff the probability of arriving at T_B by a fixed number of stochastic variation steps from T_A is higher than the probability of arriving at T_C. Finding an appropriate d_{genotype} that is also efficiently computable is a difficult problem, particularly in the presence of a crossover operator.

We employ *norm-induced tree distance metrics* as genotypic distance measures because of their flexibility. A norm-induced tree distance metric $\delta_{(p,d)}$ uses a norm p defined on expression trees and a metric d on tree node labels to induce a metric on expression trees T_A and T_B: if both T_A and T_B are empty trees, $\delta_{(p,d)}(T_A, T_B) := 0$. If exactly one of T_A and T_B is empty, assume without loss of generality T_A is empty, then $\delta_{(p,d)}(T_A, T_B) := p(T_B)$. If neither T_A or T_B is empty, the difference of their root node labels $d(\text{root}(T_A), \text{root}(T_B))$ is added to the sum of the differences of the children as measured by $\delta_{(p,d)}$. The children lists are padded with empty trees to equalize their lengths.

In the remainder of this paper, we use $\delta_{(p_{\text{vl}}, d_{\text{discrete}})}$ as our implementation of d_{genotype}, where d_{discrete} is the discrete metric and p_{vl} is the expression visitation length norm [24, 25]. The expression visitation length is a fine-grained expression complexity measure which is calculated for each (sub-)expression as part of the Pareto GP algorithm. When using Pareto GP, we are therefore able to calculate $\delta_{(p_{\text{vl}}, d_{\text{discrete}})}$ more efficiently by reusing individual complexity information we already calculated.

3.2 Dynamic Restart of GP Passes

As in each niche, we perform a standard GP run (a GP pass), the pass might fail in the sense that the niche population converges into a local optimum of unsatisfactory fitness. We implement a dynamic restart strategy to mitigate this problem [26]. Many different criteria for detecting convergence are conceivable, such as monitoring the standard deviation of the best, median, or mean fitness in a fixed time window during the run and triggering restarts once the standard deviation drops below a certain fixed limit given as an algorithm parameter.

We take a different approach to detect convergence by taking advantage of the distance measures we defined for clustering GP populations (see Section 3.1). This enables us to reuse a niche's sub-matrix of the distance matrix calculated for population clustering to derive a convergence criterion for that niche. We consider a niche to be converged if its median genotypic distance has dropped below a certain fixed limit given as an algorithm parameter. When triggering a restart, the fittest individual in a niche is saved into an elite set, then the niche is reinitialized with newly generated random individuals.

3.3 Clustering Based Niching with Dynamic Restart

After all components of our clustering based niching GP algorithm have been described in the abstract, this section shows how these components are integrated into our concrete RGP implementation. The description follows the general scheme given in Section 3.

Figure 1 shows an outline of the algorithm. After creating an initial population of GP individuals using the standard ramped half-and-half initialization strategy, the population is clustered into N_i niches using the R implementation of Ward's agglomerative hierarchical clustering algorithm "hclust" [3, 27]. [3] The clustering can be based on any distance measure described in Section 3.1. Due to time constraints, we only use the genotypic distance measure $\delta_{(p_{vl}, d_{discrete})}$ in this paper.

In the next step, the N_i niches are distributed to a compute cluster where each compute node performs an isolated GP run (a GP pass) on its niche population. Figure 2 shows a flow diagram of a single GP pass in a niche $k \in [1, N_i]$. Starting at the initial niche population, a standard GP step consisting of tournament selection, mutation, and crossover is performed. Based on either fitness distance, phenotypic distance, or genotypic distance, a diversity measure for the niche is calculated. In this paper, we use the niche's median of the genotypic distance $\delta_{(p_{vl}, d_{discrete})}$ as a diversity measure. If this measure drops below a fixed limit given as an algorithm parameter, the niche population is reinitialized with new individuals created by the same strategy as the initial population. Before, the fittest existing individual in the niche is saved to a fixed size niche local elite set E_k, replacing surplus individuals based on their relative fitness. This process is repeated until a pass stop criterion holds. When the pass ends, the best individuals of the current niche population are joined into the niche population's local elite set E_k.

After all parallel passes have met their stop conditions, the pass results, i.e. the niche populations and elite sets, are joined. All niche populations are again combined into a

---

[3] For practical reasons, N_i is fixed in the current implementation to simplify distribution to a compute cluster. Yet in principle a dynamic number of clusters could be used, which would lead to a different N_i for each clustering pass i.

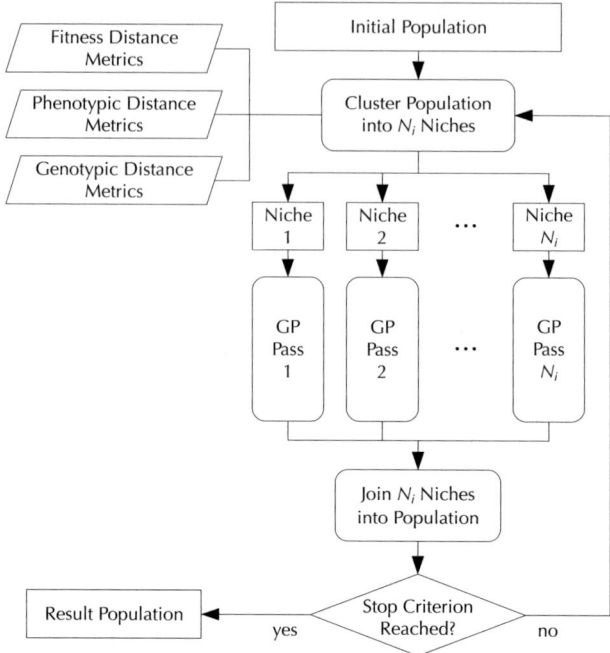

Figure 1: Outline of the distributed clustering based niching with restarts algorithm: an initial population is clustered into N_i niches, based on fitness distance, phenotypic distance, or genotypic distance. The niches are distributed to a compute cluster where each node performs an isolated GP run (a GP pass) on its niche population. The pass results are collected from the cluster nodes and joined into a single population. This process is repeated until a run stop criterion holds.

single population. All niche elite sets are joined into a fixed size global elite set E stored as a separate part of the population, where surplus individuals are replaced based on their relative fitness. If a global stop criterion holds, the current combined population and the global elite set E is returned as the algorithm's result. Otherwise, the process is repeated, starting at the clustering step.

4 Preliminary Experiments

In a set of preliminary experiments, we compared the performance of our algorithm as described in Section 3.3 (referred to as CBNGP in the remainder of this paper) with standard GP (SGP) and with a static fixed niche strategy (FNGP). SGP uses a single global population without any niching. In contrast to CBNGP, FNGP randomly divides the initial population into N_i fixed niches of equal size at the start of the run. That division is never changed until the end of the run. In this respect, FNGP resembles basic multi-deme or island strategies often employed in GP [3, 11]. All algorithms are granted a

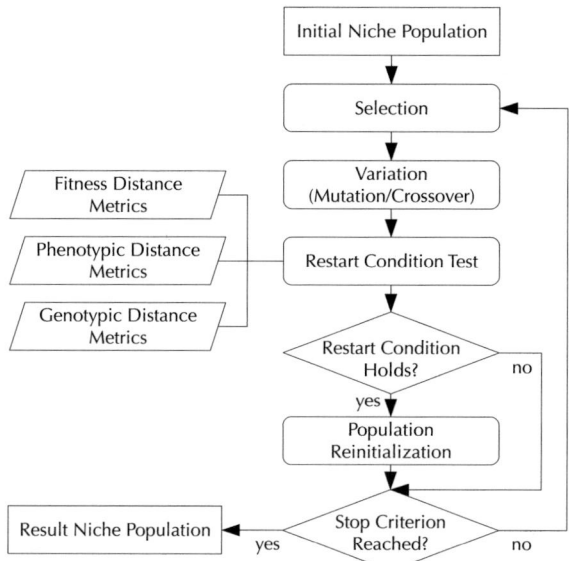

Figure 2: Outline of a single pass of the clustering based niching with restarts algorithm: Starting from an initial niche population, a standard GP step consisting of tournament selection and variation (mutation and crossover) is performed. Based on fitness distance, phenotypic distance, or genotypic distance, a diversity measure for the niche population is calculated and used to test a restart condition. If this condition holds, the niche population is reinitialized with new individuals, while the fittest existing individual is saved into a niche local elite set, otherwise the niche population is not changed. This process is repeated until a pass stop criterion holds. After the pass ends, the best individuals of the current niche population are joined into the niche population's elite set.

budget of 300,000 fitness evaluations, all algorithms use the same parameter settings as far as applicable, all algorithms use the same set of random seeds, and all algorithms use the same restart condition. Note that in our experiments FNGP and CBNGP can run 10 GP passes in parallel while SGP relies on a single sequential run, resulting in an about tenfold lower total runtime of FNGP and CBNGP in relation to SGP.

The parameter settings used in our experiment runs are shown in Table 2. Parameters that only apply to FNGP and CBNGP are marked by the phrase "FNGP and CBNGP only".

We used the following three univariate test functions, which are plotted in Figure 3, in our preliminary experiments. Descriptions of the fitness cases (equally spaced samples) for each test function are given in parenthesis:

Damped Oscillator 1D $\frac{3}{2} e^{-\frac{x}{2}} \sin(\pi x + \pi)$ (512 fitness cases from $[1, 4\pi]$)

Salustowicz 1D $e^{-x} x^3 \sin x \cos x (\sin^2 x \cos x - 1)$ (512 fitness cases from $[0, 12]$)

Unwrapped Ball 1D $\frac{10}{(x-3)^2+5}$ (512 fitness cases from $[-2, 8]$)

Table 2: GP parameters of the experiment runs: note that some parameters do not apply to all experiments, these are marked by the phrase "FNGP and CBNGP only".

Objective:	symbolic regression of a test function f with fitness cases F
Fitness:	$\text{RMSE}(f(F), [\![\cdot]\!](F))$ (RMSE between real and predicted function values)
Terminal set:	$\{x\} \cup [0.0, 1.0]$ (function parameter x and uniform distributed random constants)
Function set:	$\{+, \times, -, \div, \sin, \cos, \tan, \sqrt{\cdot}, \exp, \ln\}$
Selection:	tournament selection with tournament size 10
Population size:	200 expression trees
Initialization:	ramped half-and-half with maximum tree depth of 6
Variation:	constant node mutation (prob. 0.1), function node mutation (prob. 0.1), replacement of node by new subtree (prob. 0.1), single-point crossover (prob. 1.0)
Restart:	restart when median of genotypic distance $\delta_{(p_{\text{vl}}, d_{\text{discrete}})}$ is less than 4
Clustering:	FNGP: fixed, same at every pass; CBNGP: dynamic, based on $\delta_{(p_{\text{vl}}, d_{\text{discrete}})}$ (FNGP and CBNGP only)
Niches:	10 (FNGP and CBNGP only)
Pass termination:	terminate after $6,000$ fitness evaluations (FNGP and CBNGP only)
Run termination:	terminate after $300,000$ fitness evaluations

By using these very simple test functions, we are able to obtain usable results in comparatively short run time. A single experiment run takes about 10 minutes on a Intel Xeon 5550 system equipped with two 2.66 GHz quad core CPUs.

4.1 Results

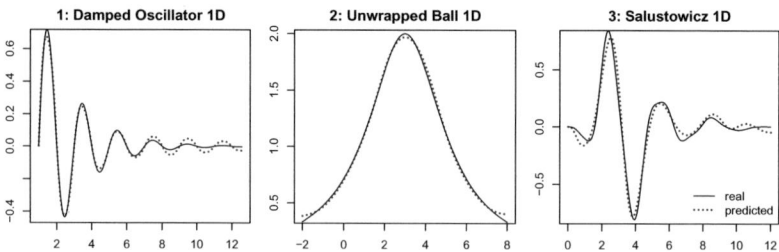

Figure 3: Plots of the univariate test functions for symbolic regression used in our experiments and best results: the test functions are plotted in solid black, the overall best symbolic regression models are plotted in dotted gray.

Table 3 shows a summary of the results of 10 runs for each algorithm (SGP, FNGP, and CBNGP) and each test function (Damped Oscillator 1D, Salustowicz 1D, and Unwrapped Ball 1D). The 10 runs for each algorithm are based on the same set of 10 random seeds. The lowest, i.e. best, RMSE values are highlighted by gray rectangles. Figure 3 shows dotted gray line plots of the overall best individuals from Table 3 overlayed over the solid black line plots of the test functions. Figure 4 shows the data of Table 3 in the form of box plots.

It is readily apparent from Table 3 that SGP results in the best minimum RMSE of 10

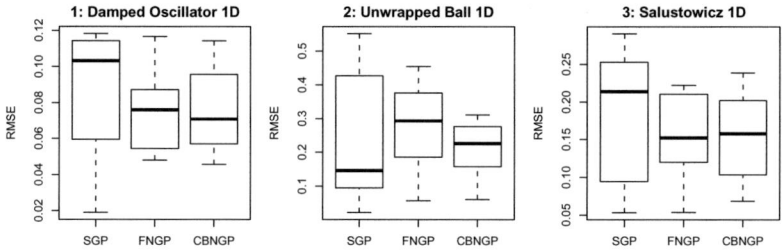

Figure 4: Box plots of our preliminary results: the plots are based 10 runs for each test function and each algorithm.

Table 3: Overview on our preliminary results: this table shows a summary of 10 runs for each algorithm and each test function. The best, i.e. lowest, RMSE values are highlighted by gray rectangles.

		RMSE					
Algorithm	*Test Fun.*	*Min.*	*1st Qu.*	*Median*	*Mean*	*3rd Qu.*	*Max.*
	Damp. Osc. 1D	0.01909	0.06051	0.10320	0.08644	0.11410	0.11830
SGP	Salust. 1D	0.05322	0.09828	0.21390	0.17760	0.24520	0.29030
	Unwr. Ball 1D	0.02185	0.09492	0.14560	0.23240	0.39940	0.55140
	Damp. Osc. 1D	0.04810	0.05699	0.07612	0.07630	0.08613	0.11660
FNGP	Salust. 1D	0.05356	0.12440	0.15210	0.15630	0.20640	0.22240
	Unwr. Ball 1D	0.05653	0.19530	0.29290	0.27530	0.36890	0.45460
	Damp. Osc. 1D	0.04564	0.05730	0.07084	0.07498	0.09282	0.11430
CBNGP	Salust. 1D	0.06842	0.11040	0.15770	0.15840	0.20200	0.23870
	Unwr. Ball 1D	0.06063	0.16260	0.22560	0.20690	0.27280	0.31130

runs in all three test functions, in case of Damped Oscillator 1D and Unwrapped Ball 1D it does so by a large margin. At the same time, SGP's 10 run maximum RMSE is the worst in all three test functions. The question of which algorithm is best in the 10 run median case yields no conclusive answer. In the 10 run mean and in the 10 run maximum case, FNGP yields the best RMSE on the Salustowicz 1D test function, while CBNGP yields the best RMSE on the other two test function. Overall the differences between FNGP's and CBNGP's results are less pronounced than the differences between each of these niching GP algorithms and standard GP.

4.2 Discussion and First Conclusions

A possible explanation for the preliminary results shown is the high sensitivity of a GP run to its initial population. This explains the high standard deviation in the best fitness reached over 10 SGP runs: when starting with a favorable initial population, spending a high budget of fitness evaluations on a single run leads to good results. Naturally, the converse is also true, when starting a GP run with an unfavorable initial population, even a high budget of fitness evaluations leads to a poor result.

Both niching strategies, FNGP as well as CBNGP, result in significantly better mean results. This indicates that niching is effective in preserving genetic diversity in GP populations, leading us to accept hypothesis **H1**. Regarding hypothesis **H2**, i.e. whether clustering based niching is superior to static fixed niching in the domain of symbolic regression, our results are still inconclusive. Further experiments with more realistic test functions and real-world test cases should illuminate this question further.

5   Summary and Outlook

In this paper we introduced RGP, a new GP system for the R environment, and described our ongoing research in diversity preservation for GP populations through clustering based niching. We applied clustering based niching to symbolic regression with GP for the first time and conducted first experiments. Three classes of distance measures to be used for GP population clustering and convergence detection where introduced, while only genotypic distance was used in preliminary experiments.

In future work, we plan to study the relative benefits and drawbacks of fitness distance, phenotypic distance and genotypic distance measures for population clustering and convergence detection in a series of experiment runs. These runs will be based on a much broader set of test functions, including multivariate functions. We will also include difficult real-world regression problems from the financial and water resource management domains into our test function set [6, 5].

Regarding the further development of RGP, we are currently implementing optimized versions of the most important GP operators, which should enable RGP to solve more difficult problems in less compute time. We will also extend RGP's type system to allow the finer description of the relevant solution space. This will reduce the time spent searching infeasible regions of the solution space and will contribute to a more efficient and effective GP search.

6   Acknowledgements

This work has been supported by the Bundesministerium für Bildung und Forschung (BMBF) under the grants FIWA and SOMA (AiF FKZ 17N2309 and 17N1009, "Ingenieurnachwuchs") and by the Cologne University of Applied Sciences under the research focus grant COSA. We are grateful to Dr. Wolfgang Kantschik (DIP GmbH) for helpful discussions on niching strategies for GP.

References

[1] R Development Core Team: *R: A Language and Environment for Statistical Computing*. R Foundation for Statistical Computing, Vienna, Austria. URL http://www.R-project.org. 2008.

[2] Banzhaf, W.; Francone, F. D.; Keller, R. E.; Nordin, P.: *Genetic programming: an introduction: on the automatic evolution of computer programs and its applications*. San Francisco, CA, USA: Morgan Kaufmann Publishers Inc. ISBN 1-55860-510-X. 1998.

[3] Koza, J.: *Genetic Programming: On the Programming of Computers by Means of Natural Selection*. Cambridge MA: MIT Press. 1992.

[4] Poli, R.; Langdon, W. B.; McPhee, N. F.: *A field guide to genetic programming*. Published via `http://lulu.com` and freely available at `http://www.gp-field-guide.org.uk`. (With contributions by J. R. Koza). 2008.

[5] Flasch, O.; Bartz-Beielstein, T.; Koch, P.; Konen, W.: Genetic Programming Applied to Predictive Control in Environmental Engineering. In: *Proceedings 19. Workshop Computational Intelligence* (Hoffmann, F.; Hüllermeier, E., eds.), p. 101–113. Karlsruhe: KIT Scientific Publishing. 2009.

[6] Flasch, O.; Bartz-Beielstein, T.; Davtyan, A.; Koch, P.; Konen, W.; Oyetoyan, T. D.; Tamutan, M.: Comparing CI Methods for Prediction Models in Environmental Engineering. In: *Proc. 2010 Congress on Evolutionary Computation (CEC'10) within IEEE World Congress on Computational Intelligence (WCCI'10), Barcelona, Spain* (Fogel, G.; and others, eds.). Piscataway NJ: IEEE Press. 2010.

[7] Smits, G.; Vladislavleva, E.: Ordinal Pareto Genetic Programming. In: *Proceedings of the 2006 IEEE Congress on Evolutionary Computation* (Yen, G. G.; and others, eds.), p. 3114–3120. Vancouver, BC, Canada: IEEE Press. URL `http://ieeexplore.ieee.org/servlet/opac?punumber=11108`. 2006.

[8] Mahfoud, S. W.: *Niching methods for genetic algorithms*. Phd Thesis, University of Illinois at Urbana-Champaign, Champaign, IL, USA. 1995.

[9] Shir, O. M.: *Niching in derandomized evolution strategies and its applications in quantum control*. Phd Thesis, Natural Computing Group, LIACS, Faculty of Science, Leiden University. 2008.

[10] Spector, L.; Klein, J.: Trivial Geography in Genetic Programming. In: *Genetic Programming in Theory and Practice III*. Springer. 2005.

[11] Carbajal, S. G.; Levine, J.; Martinez, F. G.: Multi Niche Parallel GP with a Junk-Code Migration Model. In: *EuroGP*, p. 327–334. 2003.

[12] Hornby, G. S.: ALPS: the age-layered population structure for reducing the problem of premature convergence. In: *GECCO 2006: Proceedings of the 8th annual conference on Genetic and evolutionary computation* (Keijzer, M.; and others, eds.), vol. 1, p. 815–822. Seattle, Washington, USA: ACM Press. ISBN 1-59593-186-4. 2006.

[13] Sun, Y.; Wierstra, D.; Schaul, T.; Schmidhuber, J.: Efficient natural evolution strategies. In: *GECCO '09: Proceedings of the 11th Annual conference on Genetic and evolutionary computation*, p. 539–546. New York, NY, USA: ACM. ISBN 978-1-60558-325-9. 2009.

[14] Bartz-Beielstein, T.; Chiarandini, M.; Paquete, L.; Preuss, M. (eds.): *Experimental Methods for the Analysis of Optimization Algorithms*. Berlin, Heidelberg, New York: Springer. Im Druck. 2010.

[15] Tierney, L.; Rossini, A. J.; Li, N.; Sevcikova, H.: *snow: Simple Network of Workstations*. R package version 0.3-3. 2009.

[16] Schmidt, M.; Lipson, H.: Comparison of tree and graph encodings as function of problem complexity. In: *GECCO '07: Proceedings of the 9th annual conference on Genetic and evolutionary computation* (Thierens, D.; Beyer, H.-G.; Bongard, J.; Branke, J.; Clark, J. A.;

Cliff, D.; Congdon, C. B.; Deb, K.; Doerr, B.; Kovacs, T.; Kumar, S.; Miller, J. F.; Moore, J.; Neumann, F.; Pelikan, M.; Poli, R.; Sastry, K.; Stanley, K. O.; Stutzle, T.; Watson, R. A.; Wegener, I., eds.), vol. 2, p. 1674–1679. London: ACM Press. 2007.

[17] Barendregt, H.; Abramsky, S.; Gabbay, D. M.; Maibaum, T. S. E.; Barendregt, H. P.: Lambda Calculi with Types. In: *Handbook of Logic in Computer Science*, p. 117–309. Oxford University Press. 1992.

[18] Goldberg, D. E.; Richardson, J.: Genetic algorithms with sharing for multimodal function optimization. In: *Proceedings of the Second International Conference on Genetic Algorithms on Genetic algorithms and their application*, p. 41–49. Hillsdale, NJ, USA: L. Erlbaum Associates Inc. ISBN 0-8058-0158-8. 1987.

[19] De Jong, K.: *An analysis of the behaviour of a class of genetic adaptive systems*. Phd Thesis, University of Michigan. 1975.

[20] Bäck, T.; Fogel, D.; Michalewicz, Z.: *Handbook of Evolutionary Computation*. New York NY: IOP Publishing and Oxford University Press. 1997.

[21] Ursem, R. K.: Multinational GAs: Multimodal optimization techniques in dynamic environments. In: *Proceedings of the Genetic and Evolutionary Computation Conference* (Whitley, D.; Goldberg, D. E.; Cantu-Paz, E.; Spector, L.; Parmee, I.; Beyer, H.-G., eds.), p. 19–26. Las Vegas, Nevada, USA: Morgan Kaufmann. 2000.

[22] Tsutsui, S.; Fujimoto, Y.: Forking genetic algorithm with blocking and shrinking modes (FGA). In: *Proceedings of the 5th International Conference on Genetic Algorithms* (Forrest, S., ed.), p. 206–215. San Mateo, CA: Morgan Kaufman. 1993.

[23] Streichert, F.; Stein, G.; Ulmer, H.; Zell, A.: A Clustering Based Niching Method for Evolutionary Algorithms. In: *Genetic and Evolutionary Computation GECCO 2003* (Cantu-Paz, E.; and others, eds.), Lecture Notes in Computer Science. Springer. 2003.

[24] Barile, M.: Discrete Metric. MathWorld – A Wolfram Web Resource, created by Eric W. Weisstein. URL http://mathworld.wolfram.com/DiscreteMetric.html. 2010.

[25] Keijzer, M.; Foster, J.: Crossover Bias in Genetic Programming. In: *Genetic Programming* (Ebner, M.; O'Neill, M.; Ekart, A.; Vanneschi, L.; Esparcia-Alcazar, A., eds.), vol. 4445 of *Lecture Notes in Computer Science*, p. 33–44. Springer. 2007.

[26] Jansen, T.: On the Analysis of Dynamic Restart Strategies for Evolutionary Algorithms. In: *PPSN VII: Proceedings of the 7th International Conference on Parallel Problem Solving from Nature*, p. 33–43. London, UK: Springer-Verlag. ISBN 3-540-44139-5. 2002.

[27] Ward, J. H.: Hierarchical Grouping to Optimize an Objective Function. *Journal of the American Statistical Association* 58 (1963), p. 236–244.

Entscheidungskriterien zur methodischen Realisierung multikriterieller Optimierungsalgorithmen in industriellen Anwendungen am Beispiel der Feuerführung eines Großdampferzeugers

Matthias Freund, Wolfgang Kästner, Rainer Hampel, Tom Förster,
Michael Wagenknecht

Hochschule Zittau/Görlitz, IPM
Theodor-Körner-Allee 16
02763 Zittau
Tel.:+49 3583 611383
Fax: +49 3583 611288
E-Mail: {mfreund,w.kaestner,r.hampel,tfoerster,m.wagenknecht}@hs-zigr.de

Dietmar Haake, Heiko Kanisch

Vattenfall Europe Generation AG
Vom-Stein-Straße 39
03050 Cottbus, Germany
Tel.: +49 355 2887 3704
Fax: +49 355 2887 3703
E-Mail: {dietmar.haake, heiko.kanisch}@vattenfall.de

Ulrich-Steffen Altmann

CombTec GmbH
Theodor-Körner-Allee 16
02763 Zittau, Germany
Tel.: +49 3583 518398
Fax: +49 3583 518832
E-Mail: altmann@combtec.de

1   Einleitung

Hintergrund des Projektes ist die Reduzierung der rauchgasseitigen Hochtemperaturkorrosion an Verdampferheizflächen. Das wesentliche Merkmal zur Beeinflussung dieses Schadensbefundes ist die Feuerlage. Derzeit obliegt es dem Anlagenfahrer, durch Vertrimmung der Mühlenzuteiler eine möglichst symmetrische Position des Flammenkörpers zu gewährleisten [3], da hohe Partikelkonzentrationen in Wandnähe, verbunden mit überhöhter Rauchgastemperatur, ein erhebliches Gefährdungspotential bezüglich der Hochtemperaturkorrosion bedeuten [2]. Als Projektziel wurde die Entwicklung eines onlinefähigen Assistenzsystems (Demonstrator) formuliert, um das Betriebspersonal angesichts der sich stetig verändernden Betriebsbedingungen zu entlasten und eine Objektivierung der Entscheidungsfindung zu erreichen.

Der verwendete Referenzdampferzeuger des Kraftwerkes Jänschwalde zeichnet sich durch eine Zweipunkt-Feuerung aus (Abb. 1 links). Von den sechs Mühlen, die den Braunkohlestaub über zugeordnete Haupt- und Brüdenbrenner in die Brennkammer einblasen, sind aufgrund von Instandhaltungsarbeiten im Normalfall fünf in Betrieb [3]. Somit ergibt sich bei einer gleichmäßigen Aufteilung der Gesamtbrennstoffmenge auf die Mühlen eine asymmetrische Feuerlage in der Brennkammer, welche als eine maßgebliche Ursache für die Hochtemperaturkorrosion (Abb. 1 rechts) ausgemacht werden kann. Eine Verlagerung des Feuerkörpers zur Brennkammermitte hin ist durch eine geeignete Aufteilung des Brennstoffes und somit der zugehörigen Luftmengen auf die in Betrieb befindlichen Mühlen möglich.

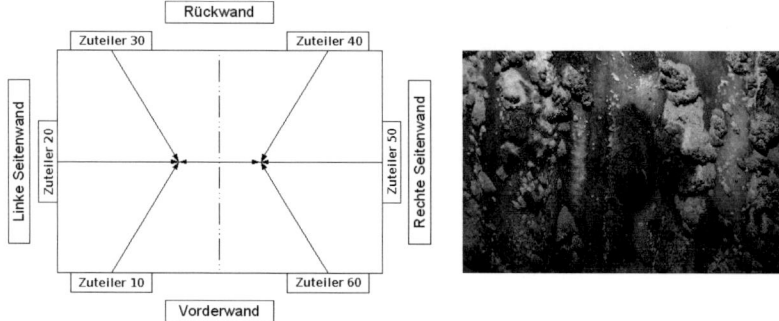

Abb. 1. Schematische Darstellung der Zweipunkt-Feuerung (links) und Verdampferheizfläche mit Korrosionsangriff (rechts)

Um die momentane Feuerlage korrekt beurteilen zu können, wurden die Messwerte des installierten CombPyr-2D$^+$-Diagnosesystems der Firma CombTec genutzt [1]. Hierbei wird mit Hilfe von zwölf Flammenpyrometern auf einer Ebene oberhalb des Brennergürtels eine Temperaturverteilung über dem Feuerraumquerschnitt ermittelt. Eine abstrahierte Darstellung der Temperaturverteilung ergibt sich mit der 4-Zonen-Trapez-Anzeige (Abb. 2). Die vier zu betrachtenden Randzonen weisen die Abweichung der mittleren Zonentemperatur vom Mittelwert des gesamten Querschnittes aus. Die zu optimierende Feuerschieflage kann mit diesen vier Werten ($TABW_{1...4}$) qualitativ und quantitativ beschrieben werden.

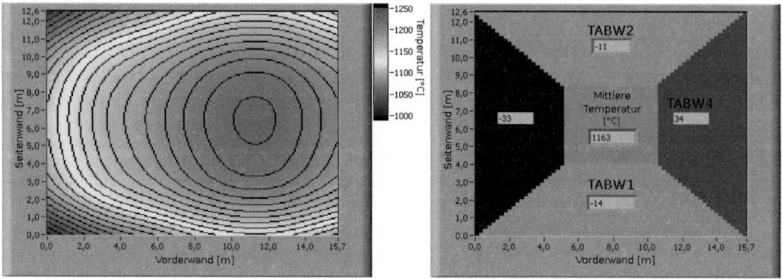

Abb. 2. Isothermendarstellung der Temperaturverteilung (links) und abstrahierte 4-Zonen-Trapez-Anzeige (rechts)

2   Realisierungskonzept

Zur Realisierung eines onlinefähigen Assistenzsystems wurde ein modulares Projektkonzept entwickelt (siehe Abb. 3). Ausgehend vom realen Prozess der Braunkohlestaubfeuerung wurde nach einer Signalvalidierung eine Daten- und Wissensbasis erstellt, in die sowohl Aufzeichnungen der Prozessdaten als auch Expertenwissen einging. Darauf aufbauend wurde das Prozessmodell mittels Künstlicher Neuronaler Netze (KNN) erstellt, welches die Grundlage für die Optimierung mittels Evolutionärer Algorithmen (EA) bildet. Die Optimierungsausgabe wird anschließend an die Prozessführung in Form eines ausgewählten Vorschlages übergeben.

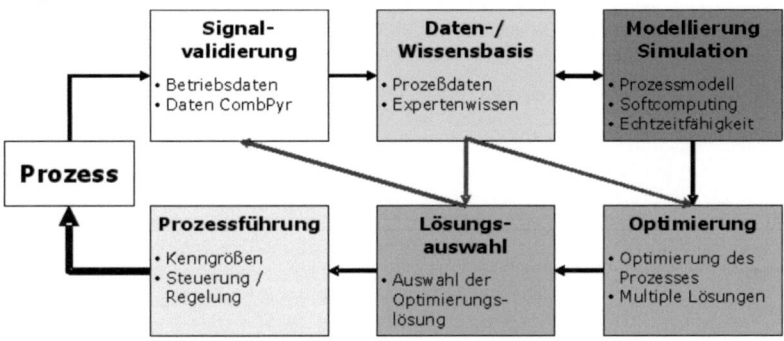

Abb. 3. Schema des Realisierungskonzept

2.1   Datenaufbereitung

Als Grundlage stand eine umfangreiche Datenbasis, bestehend aus einer Auswahl von Betriebsmessdaten des Kraftwerksbetreibers Vattenfall Europe Generation und dem Mess- und Berechnungswersten des CombPyr-2D$^+$-Diagnosesystems, über einen Zeitraum von ca. 10 Monaten zur Verfügung. Die Daten entstammen dem normalen Betrieb. Dies hat Vorteil, dass davon ausgegangen werden kann, dass jeder, für einen Normalbetrieb (5-Mühlen-Betrieb) relevante Arbeitspunkt auch ohne aufwendigen Versuchsbetrieb mindestens einmal angefahren wurde. Des Weiteren enthalten die Daten wichtige Aussagen über das generelle Verhalten der Referenzanlage und des Bedienpersonals. Es lassen sich somit Feststellungen treffen, wie die Anlage betrieben wird und wie sie auf Eingriffe reagiert [4]. Allerdings beinhalten die Daten somit auch jegliche Störeinflüsse. Mit der eingehenden Überprüfung des Datenmaterials sollten mehrere Ziele erreicht werden. Allgemein ist die Datenreinheit (Eliminierung von Fehlstellen und vom Normalbetrieb abweichenden Arbeitspunkten) als Notwendigkeit für eine gewünschte Modellgüte anzusehen. Zudem galt es, die Kompatibilität der Zeitstempel der beiden Mess- bzw. Aufzeichnungssysteme herzustellen. Für die Beschreibung des Brennkammerzustandes mittels KNN war es notwendig, dass der verwendete Datensatz nur Arbeitspunkte ohne zeitliche Verzögerungen von Signalen enthält. So müssen Ursache und Wirkung eines verfahrenstechnischen Effektes in einer Matrixzeile stehen, auch wenn die technisch-physikalische Wirkung nicht zeitgleich mit der Ursache einzuordnen ist.

2.2   Prozessmodellierung

Die chemisch-physikalischen Prozesse bei der Kohleverbrennung sind hoch komplex und vielfältigen, teils unbekannten Einflüssen ausgesetzt. Mit aktuell genutzten Methoden zur Berechnung von Flammen und Feuerräumen (Strömungs-/ Turbulenz-, Strahlungs- und Reaktionsmodelle), wie sie zur dreidimensionalen Berechnung von Brennkammern mit numerischen Feuerraummodellen (Finite-Volumen-Methoden für reagierende Strömungen) verwendet werden, ist die für dieses Vorhaben benötigte Rechengeschwindigkeiten nicht zu realisieren [8]. Es wurde daher entschieden, ein Verhaltensmodell auf der Basis Künstlicher Neuronaler Netze der speziellen Ausprägung Multilayer Perzeptron (MLP) zu entwerfen. Die vornehmliche Eignung dieses Teilgebietes der Künstlichen Intelligenz ergibt sich aus der Tatsache, dass der abzubildende funktionale Zusammenhang nicht analytisch bekannt sein muss, sondern anhand von charakteristischen Prozessmustern approximiert wird [5].

Aus den als signifikant für die Bestimmung der Feuerlage erkannten Mess- und Berechnungsgrößen (u. a. Massen- und Volumenströme, Kohlequalitätsmerkmale, Mühlentemperaturen nach Sichter, Sauerstoffregime), werden die vier vom CombPyr-System ermittelten Zonenabweichungen modelliert [8]. Es entsteht eine abstrakte und generalisierungsfähige Form des Modellgegenstands durch Verknüpfung der Eingangs-mit den Ausgangsdaten über verdeckte Schichten künstlicher Neuronen und den trainierten Gewichtsmatrizen zwischen ihnen (Netzstrukturbeispiel in Abb. 4). Die Form, in der die zu lernenden Daten dem Netz präsentiert werden, hat entscheidenden Einfluss auf die Lerngeschwindigkeit und die Reproduktionsgüte. Je präziser das Problem durch die Datenaufbereitung definiert wird, desto erfolgreicher kann ein KNN dieses verarbeiten [5]. Um den erfahrungsgemäß wenig übertragbaren Eigenschaften der einzelnen Mühlenkombinationen zu begegnen, wurden für jede mögliche Fünfer-Kombination von im Betrieb befindlichen Mühlen separate Modelle erstellt.

Abb. 4. Beispiel einer KNN-Netzstruktur

2.3 Prozessoptimierung

Um den Erfolg komplexer Optimierungsprobleme in industriellen Anwendungen zu beherrschen, ist eine systematische Analyse des Optimierungsproblems notwendig, welche in vier Teile untergliedert werden kann [7].

1. Definition der Optimierungsziele
2. Definition der Eingangsvariablen und eventueller Abhängigkeiten zwischen den Eingangsgrößen
3. Beschreibung weiteren Problemswissens (Anzahl der erwarteten Minima, Stetigkeit und Differenzierbarkeit der verwendeten Modelle)
4. Analyse des Anwendungsbereiches (Häufigkeit der Anwendung, Qualitätserwartungen, Anzahl alternativer Lösungsvorschläge)

Diese Analyse dient zudem als Grundlage zur Definition von Anforderungen an den Optimierungsalgorithmus und dessen Operatoren.

Die KNN geben die vier Temperaturabweichungen $TABW_{1...4}$ der 4-Zonen-Trapez-Anzeige zurück. Eine zentrale Feuerlage liegt dann vor, wenn die jeweils gegenüberliegenden Zonen eine gleichmäßige Temperaturabweichung aufweisen. Die Optimierung erfolgt somit auf Grundlage der Minimierung der Differenzen der Temperaturabweichungen zwischen den Zonen 1 und 2 (ΔT_1) bzw. den Zonen 3 und 4 (ΔT_2) des Trapez-Modells. Es kann das zweikriterielle Optimierungsproblem entsprechend Gl. 1 formuliert werden.

$$\Delta T_1 = |TABW_1 - TABW_2| \rightarrow \min$$
$$\Delta T_2 = |TABW_3 - TABW_4| \rightarrow \min \qquad (1)$$

Insgesamt haben die KNN 34 Eingangsgrößen. Als zu optimierende Stellgrößen des Prozesses eignen sich die Drehzahlen der einzelnen Mühlenzuteiler $DRZ_{10...60}$. Ihr Wert ist proportional zur jeweils eingebrachten Kohlemenge und folglich der Brennerleistung.

Aus den technologischen und anlagenspezifischen Rahmenbedingungen im zu betrachtenden Arbeitspunkt ergeben sich Restriktionen für die Optimierungsrechnung [8]. Diese einschränkenden Faktoren sind beispielsweise die wechselnde Kohlequalität, der Verschleißzustand der Kohlemühlen oder die momentane Schadstoffemission. Hieraus ergeben sich aus Messgrößen abgeleitete oder vom Anlagenfahrer manuell vorzugebende obere und untere Grenzwerte für die zu optimierenden Drehzahlen der Mühlenzuteiler. Diese Realisierungsbandbreite ist vom Optimierungsalgorithmus zwingend einzuhalten (Gl. 2).

$$DRZ_{i,\min} \leq DRZ_{i,\text{opt}} \leq DRZ_{i,\max} \qquad (2)$$

Ebenso ist die globale Leistungsvorgabe des Dampferzeugers von den jeweiligen Lösungskandidaten beizubehalten (Gl. 3).

$$\sum_{i=10...60} DRZ_i = const \qquad (3)$$

Neben der Quantität des eingebrachten Kohlestaubs wird die Leistung des Dampferzeugers auch durch die Verbrennungsluftmenge, bestehend aus Primärluft $PRIMLU_{10...60}$ und Sekundärluft $SEKLU_{10...60}$, beeinflusst. Die Summe aus Primärluft und Sekundärluft muss demnach konstant gehalten werden (Gl. 4).

$$\sum_{i=10..60} PRIMLU_i + SEKLU_i = const \ . \tag{4}$$

Die Primärluft- und die Sekundärluftmengen sind über Regelungskennlinien an die Zuteilerdrehzahlen gekoppelt. Dabei erfolgt eine Anpassung der Primärluft $\Delta PRIMLU_{10...60}$ an die Änderung der Zuteilerdrehzahlen $\Delta DRZ_{10...60}$ entsprechend Gl. 5.

$$\Delta PRIMLU_{10..60} = \begin{cases} 0 & falls \quad DRZ_{10..60} \leq 670\,\dfrac{1}{min} \\ K_1 \cdot \Delta DRZ_{10..60} & falls \quad 670\,\dfrac{1}{min} < DRZ_{10..60} \leq 780\,\dfrac{1}{min} \\ 0 & falls \quad 780\,\dfrac{1}{min} < DRZ_{10..60} \end{cases} \tag{5}$$

$$K_1 = const.$$

Die Änderung der Sekundärluft $\Delta SEKLU_{10..60}$ ist entsprechend Gl. 6 an die Änderung der Zuteilerdrehzahlen gekoppelt. Zur Bewahrung eines konstanten Gesamtluftregimes entsprechend Gl. 4 wird die Änderung der Primärluft von der Sekundärluft abgezogen.

$$\Delta SEKLU_{10..60} = K_2 \cdot \Delta DRZ_{10..60} - \Delta PRIMLU_{10..60}$$
$$K_2 = const. \tag{6}$$

Durch die Einbindung der Regelungskennlinien wird die Nebenbedingung entsprechend Gl. 4 implizit eingehalten. Für die weiteren Eingangswerte wird angenommen, dass sie aufgrund hoher Zeitkonstanten der Regelstrecken über einen Vertrimmungseingriff hinweg konstant bleiben. Sie dienen somit zur Charakterisierung des momentanen Arbeitspunktes des Dampferzeugers.

Weitere Charakteristika des Optimierungsproblems können aufgrund der Verwendung KNN für die Modellierung gefunden werden. So zeichnen sich KNN durch einen nichtlinearen und multimodalen Suchraum aus. Der Optimierungsalgorithmus muss erkennen, welche Mühle inaktiv ist und das entsprechend gültige Modell zur Berechnung der Zielfunktionswerte auswählen. Die Anwendung des Optimierungsalgorithmus als Teil eines onlinefähigen Assistenzsystems zur Unterstützung des Betriebspersonals bedingt die Echtzeitfähigkeit des Optimierungsalgorithmus. Um dies zu gewährleisten ist eine maximale Rechenzeit von 20 Sekunden gegeben. Um auf unterschiedliche Betriebssituationen reagieren zu können, wird eine Menge von Lösungsalternativen benötigt.

Es liegt somit ein nichtlineares, multimodales und bikriterielles Optimierungsproblem zugrunde. Als Optimierungsalgorithmus bieten sich somit EA an. Für eine Einschätzung der Anwendbarkeit eines EA diente eine Abschätzung der benötigten Zeit zur Berechnung der Funktionswerte eines Lösungskandidaten. Hierbei ergab sich eine durchschnittliche Rechenzeit von 1,6 Millisekunden. Für eine Online-Anwendung steht somit eine ausreichende Anzahl an Berechnungen zur Verfügung. Der Entwurf des Funktionsprinzips der Operatoren ist ein kreativer Prozess. Hierzu mussten Operatoren zur Generierung, Bewertung und Selektion der Lösungskandidaten entworfen werden. Als Grundlage dienten sowohl schon bekannte Strukturen und Algorithmen, als auch selbst entworfene bzw. angepasste Operatoren. Alle Operatoren und Algorithmen mussten hinsichtlich ihrer effektiven Wirkungsweise für die Anwendung zur Optimierung der Feuerlage getestet werden.

Die Operatoren zur Generierung neuer Lösungskandidaten (Rekombination und Mutation) müssen wiederum gültige Lösungskandidaten erzeugen. Werden die Nebenbedingungen verletzt, ist zusätzlich eine Reparaturfunktion notwendig. Als

Mutationsoperator wird die uniforme Mutation verwendet, wobei für jede Zuteilerdrehzahl separat entschieden wird, ob diese verändert wird. Die Verwendung dieses Mutationsoperators kann nicht gewährleisten, dass die Nebenbedingungen entsprechend Gl. (2) und (3) erfüllt werden, sodass eine Reparaturfunktion notwendig ist. Zusätzlich müssen die Luftmengen entsprechend Gl. (5) und (6) angepasst werden. Ein Rekombinationsoperator findet keine Anwendung, da er für die vorliegende konkrete Aufgabenstellung keine Optimierungsverbesserung mit sich bringt.

Als Grundlage zur Bewertung der Lösungskandidaten dient das Optimierungsziel entsprechend Gl. 1. Da als Optimierungsausgabe eine Menge von Lösungsalternativen erwartet wird, ist ein Algorithmus notwendig, der die Pareto-Front des Optimierungsproblems annähert. Aufgrund der Komplexität des Zielfunktionsraumes kann nicht garantiert werden, dass die Pareto-Front stets konvex ist, sondern vielmehr eine nicht konvexe Form ausprägt. Zur Berechnung der Fitness wird somit das Pareto-Ranking angewendet. Da keine Rekombination stattfindet, kann die Population eine nicht ausreichende Divergenz aufweisen. Aufgrund des multimodalen Zielfunktionsraumes besteht zusätzlich die Gefahr der Konvergenz in einem Suboptimum. Demnach muss eine Nischentechnik verwendet werden, die sowohl die Konzentration der Population in wenigen Nischen verhindert, als auch die Erforschung des Suchraumes gewährleistet. Hierfür wurde das Fitness-Sharing als geeigneter Operator gefunden. Die so berechnete und modifizierte Fitness ist die Grundlage für die Selektion und Ersetzung. Alle Lösungskandidaten der Population werden als Eltern selektiert. Als Ersetzungsstrategie wird die Selektion der Lösungskandidaten mit der höchsten Güte aus der Menge der Lösungskandidaten der vorherigen Population und den Kindern verwendet.

Als Grundlage für die Parametrierung des EA dienten statistische Experimente mit unterschiedlichen Parametereinstellungen. Hierbei wurde auf die Konvergenz und Diversität der Population, sowie auf eine minimale Ausführungsdauer des Algorithmus geachtet.

2.4 Lösungsauswahl

Der Algorithmus gibt 80 Lösungskandidaten zurück, welche sich der theoretischen Pareto-Front annähern. Aus dieser Menge muss die für den aktuellen Betriebsfall geeignetste Lösung ausgewählt werden. Hierzu werden die Lösungskandidaten hinsichtlich ausgewählter Kriterien untersucht und bewertet. Die so erhaltenen Bewertungskennziffern können je nach eingestellter Betriebspriorität variierend gewichtet werden. Nach Aufsummierung der gewichteten Kennziffern beschreibt die numerisch kleinste Gesamtbewertung die einzustellende Vorzugslösung. Die Kriterien beurteilen dabei neben der Qualität des Kandidaten bezüglich der Fitness vor allem die komplexen feuerungs- und betriebstechnischen Konsequenzen. So gilt es unter anderem die zu erwartende Emissionsentwicklung, die notwendigen Mühlenbelastungen oder die sich ergebende Dynamik des Flammenkörpers zu berücksichtigen. Aufgrund der in Vorversuchen nachgewiesenen Tatsache, dass unterschiedliche Lösungsvarianten des Evolutionären Algorithmus eine äquivalente Feuerlage erzielen können, ist es möglich, die für die momentane Betriebssituation optimale Lösung zu ermitteln bzw. mit einer Neuberechnung oder Neubewertung auf sich verändernde Bedingungen zu reagieren. Insbesondere die Berücksichtigung der stetig variierenden Betriebsparameter führt zu einer immensen Entlastung des Betriebspersonals und zu einer Objektivierung der Entscheidungsfindung.

3   Funktionsnachweis

Der Optimierungsalgorithmus einschließlich der KNN-Modelle und das Modul zur Lösungsauswahl wurden in eine Softwareumgebung implementiert, welche zudem die Messwertverarbeitung, die Zustandsdiagnose der Anlage sowie die Kommunikation mit dem Anlagenfahrer realisiert. In vom Entwicklerteam betreuten Testläufen an der Referenzanlage konnte die Funktionsweise des entwickelten Konzeptes und die Leistungsstärke des Evolutionären Algorithmus bezüglich der Feuerlageverbesserung nachgewiesen werden [8]. Abbildung 5 zeigt die Temperaturverteilung vor (oben) und nach dem Optimierungseingriff (unten).

Vor der Optimierung

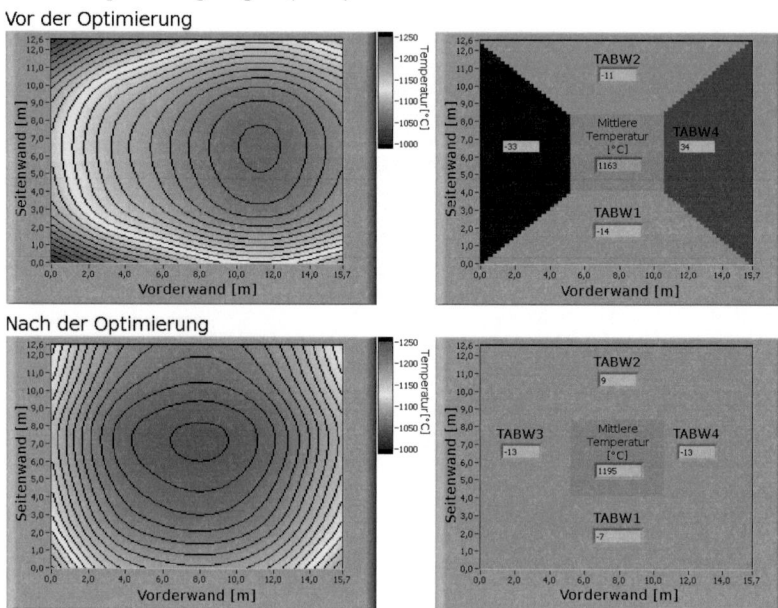

Abb. 5. Anwendungsbeispiel für einen umgesetzten Lösungsvorschlag

Danksagung

Das diesem Bericht zugrunde liegende Vorhaben wurde mit Mitteln des Bundesministeriums für Wirtschaft und Technologie (BMWi) unter dem Förderkennzeichen 1718X07 gefördert. Die Verantwortung für den Inhalt dieser Veröffentlichung liegt bei den Autoren.

Literatur

[1]   Altmann, U.-S.; Förster, T.: *Entwicklung eines Feuerungsdiagnosesystems für Kraftwerks-Dampferzeuger unter Anwendung von Soft-Computing-Verfahren. Abschlußbericht aFuE-Projekt (Förderkennzeichen 1744X04) mit Förderung der BMBF.* IPM, Zittau; 2007

[2]   Altmann, U.-S.; Grusla, S.; Müller, F.; Marschner, C; Bischoff, H; Sturm, A: *Verfahren zur Beurteilung des Ansatzbildungspotentials von Kraftwerkskohlen*

und Gewährleistung einer anlagenschonenden Feuerführung. In: Tagungsband 40. Kraftwerkstechnisches Kolloquium 2008 Band 2, pp. 103-114. TU Dresden, Dresden; 2008

[3]   Vattenfall Europe: *Bedienvorschrift - Kraftwerk Jänschwalde (BV 500) Ausgabe 04 / 2004.* Vattenfall Europe; 2004

[4]   Müller, F.: *Diagnose des Betriebszustandes eines Dampferzeugers. Diplomarbeit.* CombTec GmbH / IPM, Zittau; 2008

[5]   Förster, T.: *Untersuchungen zu hierarchischen Netzstrukturen mit Multilayer Perzeptren.* IPM, Zittau; 2005

[6]   Weicker, K.: *Evolutionäre Algorithmen.* B. G. Teubner Verlag / GWV Fachverlage GmbH, Wiesbaden; 2007

[7]   Freund, M.: *Entwicklung Genetischer Algorithmen zur mehrkriteriellen Optimierung einer Braunkohlestaubfeuerung. Diplomarbeit.* IPM, Zittau; 2008

[8]   Hampel, R; Förster, T; Freund, M; Kästner, W: *Modell- und Regelbasierte Prozessführung der Feuerlage und Verbrennungsgüte in Großdampferzeugern. Abschlußbericht aFuE-Projekt (Förderkennzeichen 1718X07) mit Förderung des BMWi.* IPM, Zittau; 2009

Entwicklung von Künstlichen Neuronalen Netzen und deren evolutionäre Strukturoptimierung mit einem Computer Cluster

S. C. Schäfer, U. Lehmann, J. Krone, M. Schneider, H. Brenig

Institut für Computer Science, Vision and Computational Intelligence,
Fachhochschule Südwestfalen, Frauenstuhlweg 31, 58644 Iserlohn
Tel. (02371) 566-465, Fax -209
E-Mail: {Schaefer.s, Lehmann, Krone, MSchneider, Brenig}@fh-swf.de

1   Einleitung

Bevor ein Künstliches Neuronales Netz eingesetzt werden kann, muss es zuerst dimensioniert und trainiert werden. Die Generalisierungsleistung eines Künstlichen Neuronalen Netzes hängt dabei stark von seiner Struktur und den beim Training verwendeten Daten ab. Um die optimale Struktur des Künstlichen Neuronalen Netzes [1] für die gegebenen Daten zu ermitteln ist daher ein langwieriger manueller trial and error Prozess vonnöten.

Um diesen Prozess zu automatisieren wurde eine Software konzeptioniert und entwickelt, welche mit Techniken der Evolutionären Optimierung die optimale Struktur ermittelt. Dazu wird ein modifizierter Genetischer Algorithmus [2] eingesetzt, der automatisch die Anzahl der Hidden-Layer, der künstlichen Neuronen und die Aktivierungsfunktion der Hidden-Layer für einen gegebenen Trainingsdatensatz optimiert. Durch die Benutzung dieser Software kann der Anwender wertvolle Zeit, welche ansonsten für das manuelle trial and error oder für Brute-Force-Methoden nötig wäre, sparen.

Im Rahmen der Evolutionären Strukturoptimierung muss eine große Menge Künstlicher Neuronaler Netze trainiert werden. Die Software wurde daher für den Einsatz auf einem Computer Cluster mit dem MATLAB Distributed Computing Server [3] entwickelt um optimal mit der aufkommenden Rechenlast zu verfahren. Dabei werden die Trainings- und Auswertungsaufträge automatisiert auf dem Computer Cluster verteilt, verarbeitet und ausgewertet.

2 Ausgangssituation

Die Struktur eines Künstlichen Neuronalen Netzes, unter anderem die Anzahl der Hidden-Layer, der Neuronen pro Hidden-Layer und der auf den Hidden-Layern eingesetzten Aktivierungsfunktion hat sehr großen Einfluss auf das Training und damit die letztendlich erreichte Generalisierungsleistung des Netzes [4]. Jedoch ist es bisher nicht möglich die optimale Struktur für ein KNN ohne großen manuellen Aufwand zu ermitteln. Daher ist es beim Dimensionieren eines KNN für eine bestimmte Problemstellung bisher üblich eine große Testreihe mit verschiedenen Strukturen, welche anhand von Expertenwissen erstellt wurden, durchzuführen. Diese Testreihen sind langwierig und keinesfalls Garant dafür, dass an ihrem Ende eine optimale KNN-Struktur gefunden wird. Besonders in der industriellen Anwendung spielt der Zeitfaktor eine sehr bedeutende Rolle, weshalb für manuelle Testreihen nicht viel Zeit zur Verfügung steht und daher sehr stark auf das Expertenwissen vertraut werden muss. Dadurch tritt oft der Fall ein, dass eine Netzstruktur Verwendung findet, welche möglicherweise keine optimalen Eigenschaften aufweist. Daher wäre eine automatisierte Lösung zur Ermittlung der optimalen Struktur für ein Künstliches Neuronales Netz bei einer gegebenen Problemstellung wünschenswert.

Der primitivste Ansatz für eine derartige automatisierte Strukturermittlung, welcher auch mit hoher Wahrscheinlichkeit zielführend wäre, würde die Prüfung und Bewertung aller möglichen Strukturkombinationen in einem gegebenen Bereich umfassen. Diese Brute-Force Methode wäre jedoch ineffizient und zeitaufwändig, selbst bei Einsatz eines Computer Clusters.

3 Lösungskonzept

Um die optimale Struktur eines Künstlichen Neuronalen Netzes für eine gegebene Problemstellung automatisiert zu ermitteln, wird bei der im Rahmen dieses Projekts entwickelten Softwarelösung auf einen Genetischen Algorithmus zurückgegriffen. Genetische Algorithmen haben sich in der Wissenschaft vielfach zur Lösung von Optimierungsproblemen verschiedenster Art bewährt. Sie werden eingesetzt, um aus einem großen Raum potentieller Lösungen für ein gegebenes Problem in einem vertretbaren Zeitrahmen eine möglichst optimale Lösung zu finden.

Der Anwendung des Genetischen Algorithmus auf das diesem Projekt zugrunde liegenden Problem ging eine Analyse der für die Ermittlung der KNN-Struktur wichtigsten Parameter voraus. Dabei sollten jene Parameter ermittelt werden, welche die Struktur und damit die letztendlich erreichte Generalisierungsleistung entscheidend beeinflussen. Für diese ermittelten Parameter wurde anschließend ein Genetischer Algorithmus zur Ermittlung der optimalen Struktur konzipiert. Dieser Genetische Algorithmus optimiert die Struktur der Künstlichen Neuronalen Netze über eine festgelegte Anzahl an Iterationen, auch Generationen genannt. Da im Laufe des Optimierungsprozesses eine große Menge an Künstlichen Neuronalen Netzen trainiert wird, besteht eines der Hauptziele der Implementierung in der automatisierten Verteilung der Trainingspakete auf einem Computer Cluster.

4 Ermittelte Strukturparameter

Als Strukturparameter mit dem größten Einfluss auf die Qualität des Künstlichen Neuronalen Netzes wurden die folgenden Parameter ermittelt:

- Anzahl der Hidden-Layer
- Anzahl der Neuronen auf den Hidden-Layern
- Aktivierungsfunktion der Hidden-Layer

Da die Hidden-Layer und insbesondere die künstlichen Neuronen auf den Hidden-Layern, das Vorbild des biologischen Gehirns von Säugetieren abbilden, sind die künstlichen Neuronen für den Informationsverarbeitungsprozess des Künstlichen Neuronalen Netzes enorm wichtig. Die gewichteten Verbindungen zwischen den künstlichen Neuronen beinhalten dabei das durch das Training erlernte Wissen. Die Verteilung der künstlichen Neuronen auf die Hidden-Layer und deren Anzahl pro Hidden-Layer sind daher von großer Bedeutung für die nach dem Trainingsvorgang erreichte Güte und damit der Generalisierungsleistung des Künstlichen Neuronalen Netzes.

Ebenfalls besondere Bedeutung kann der Aktivierungsfunktion der künstlichen Neuronen beigemessen werden. Mit ihrer Hilfe wird der Aktivierungsgrad eines jeden künstlichen Neurons bestimmt. Dieser Aktivierungsgrad hat wiederum entscheidenden Einfluss auf die nachfolgenden künstlichen Neuronen und ist daher während des Trainingsvorgangs des KNN von großer Bedeutung. Da den verschiedenen Aktivierungsfunktionen unterschiedliche mathematische Formeln zugrunde liegen, können sie das Trainingsergebnis, je nach verwendeten Trainingsdaten, stark beeinflussen.

5 Genetischer Algorithmus

Um die im vorherigen Kapitel vorgestellten Strukturparameter zu optimieren wird ein speziell auf diesen Anwendungsfall zugeschnittener Genetischer Algorithmus verwendet. Dieser weicht in einigen Bereichen vom Standard-GA ab, um den Eigenheiten des Trainings Künstlicher Neuronaler Netze Rechnung zu tragen. Bei dem hier eingesetzten Genetischen Algorithmus repräsentiert jedes Individuum der Population ein Künstliches Neuronales Netz. Die im vorigen Kapitel ermittelten Strukturparameter werden dabei als die zu optimierenden Gene jedes Individuums repräsentiert.

Zunächst soll der Ablauf des Genetischen Algorithmus zur Strukturoptimierung eines Künstlichen Neuronalen Netzes anhand des folgenden Aktivitätsdiagramms näher veranschaulicht werden:

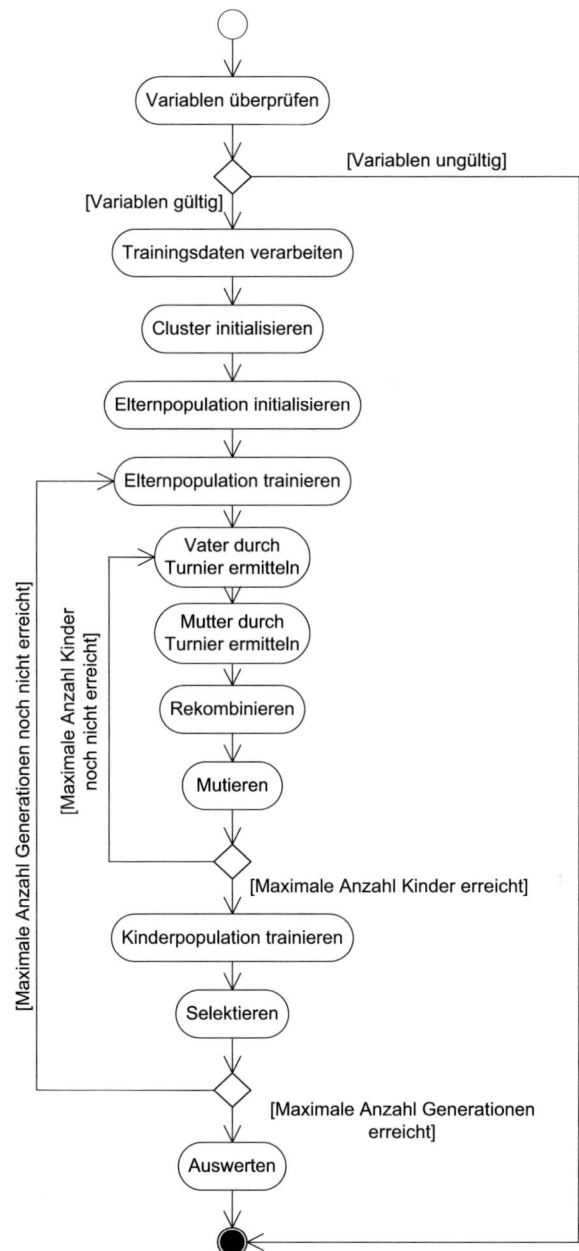

Abbildung 1: Beschreibung des Ablaufs einer Strukturoptimierung mithilfe eines Aktivitätsdiagramms

Wie das Diagramm veranschaulicht, werden nach dem Programmstart alle nötigen Funktionen initialisiert. Dazu werden im ersten Schritt die Variablen und Parameter überprüft. Bei Feststellung eines Fehlers wird das Training mit einer Fehlermeldung mit weiterführenden Informationen abgebrochen. Nach der Überprüfung folgt die Verarbeitung der Trainingsdaten für das Training der Künstlichen Neuronalen Netze. Im Anschluss wird die Initialisierung des Computer Clusters durchgeführt. Nachdem diese Schritte erfolgreich abgearbeitet wurden, findet im letzten Schritt der Initialisierung die Erstellung der Individuen der Grundpopulation des Genetischen Algorithmus statt.

Nun startet die eigentliche Evolutionäre Optimierung. Dazu werden alle Individuen der Population, die Eltern, auf dem Computer Cluster trainiert und nach Abschluss des Trainings in ihrer Fitness bewertet. Nachdem alle Individuen der Elternpopulation trainiert wurden, beginnt die Erstellung der Kind-Individuen. Dazu werden zuerst über eine Turnierfunktion ein Mutter- und ein Vater-Individuum aus der Elternpopulation ausgewählt. Aus diesen wird anschließend ein Kind-Individuum über eine Rekombinationsfunktion erstellt. Nach dessen Erstellung wird es zusätzlich über eine Mutationsfunktion modifiziert. Dieser Prozess wird solange wiederholt bis alle Kind-Individuen erstellt wurden.

Nach der Erstellung der Kinder werden diese, ebenso wie die Eltern, auf dem Computer Cluster trainiert und in ihrer Fitness bewertet. Da nun alle Individuen, die Eltern und Kinder, trainiert und bewertet wurden, folgt im vorletzten Schritt die Selektionsfunktion. Diese stellt die neue Elternpopulation aus einem Teil der besten aktuellen Eltern, der Elite, und den besten Kindern zusammen.

Die Schritte, startend beim Training der Eltern bis zur Selektion der neuen Elternpopulation, werden solange durchgeführt bis die maximale Anzahl an Generationen erreicht ist.

Nach Erreichen der maximalen Anzahl an Generationen wird im letzten Schritt die Auswertung durchgeführt. Dabei werden die Netze nach ihrer Leistung klassifiziert und die besten Netze an den Benutzer zurückgeliefert.

Bei diesem Prozess ist eine Besonderheit zu beachten, welche diesen Genetischen Algorithmus stark vom Standard-GA unterscheidet [5]: Am Anfang jeder Generation wird die aktuelle Elternpopulation, welche zuletzt am Ende der letzten Generation erzeugt wurde, noch einmal trainiert und in ihrer Fitness bewertet. Beim Standard-GA findet diese Bewertung der Elternpopulation nur einmalig in der 0. Generation, direkt nach ihrer Initialisierung, statt.

Dass die Population in diesem Programm am Start jeder Generation noch einmal trainiert wird liegt in der Eigenheit des Trainings Künstlicher Neuronaler Netze begründet. Beim Trainingsprozess eines Künstlichen Neuronalen Netzes wird dieses für eine bestimmte Anzahl an Epochen trainiert. Die Anzahl der durchzuführenden Epochen ist jedoch statisch vom Benutzer festgelegt. Daher kommt es oft vor, dass aufgrund der verschiedenen Anfangsinitialisierungen der KNN manche Netze nach dieser Anzahl an Epochen bereits optimal trainiert sind. Andere hingegen sind noch nicht an ihrem endgültigen Optimum angelangt und würden noch weitere Trainingsepochen benötigen, um dieses zu erreichen. Um dem entgegenzuwirken und allen Netzen zu ermöglichen möglichst ihr Optimum zu erreichen, werden die bereits trainierten Netze, welche die jeweils neue Population bilden, nochmals mit derselben Anzahl Epochen trainiert.

6 Optimierungsversuch & Auswertung

Im Folgenden wurde ein Optimierungsversuch mit dem zuvor beschriebenen Genetischen Algorithmus durchgeführt.

Im weiteren Verlauf soll das aus diesem Optimierungsversuch resultierende KNN mit dem bisher für die vorliegenden Daten verwendeten KNN verglichen werden. Dieses bisher verwendete KNN entstand im Rahmen eines Vorgänger-Projekts und wurde in einem Zeitraum von ca. 2-3 Monaten entwickelt. Im Vergleich dazu benötigte der in diesem Projekt entwickelte Genetische Algorithmus lediglich ca. 2-3 Tage um das KNN mit der im folgenden Diagramm dargestellten Fehlerkurve (durchgezogene Linie) zu ermitteln:

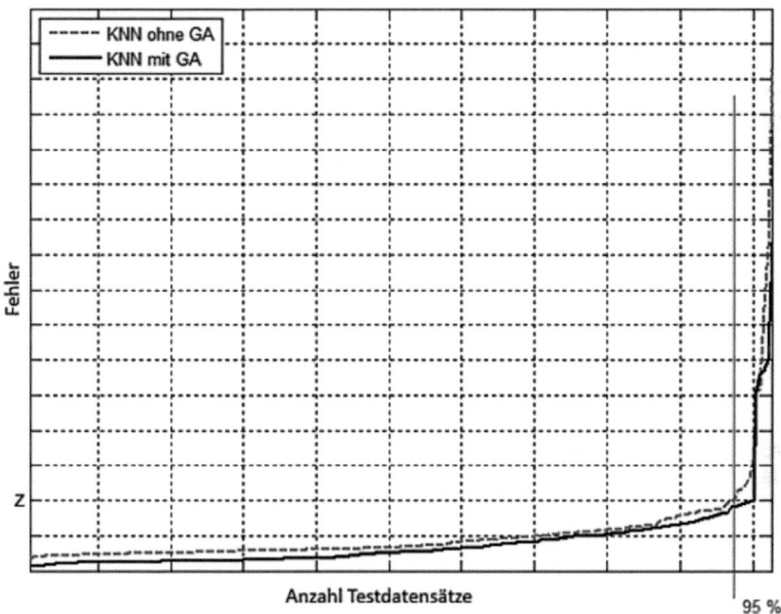

Abbildung 2: Diagramm zum Vergleich der Vorhersagefehler

Wie anhand des Diagramms gut zu erkennen ist, konnte die Generalisierungsleistung des mit dem Genetischen Algorithmus trainierten KNN im Vergleich zum vorher eingesetzten KNN verbessert werden. Bei dem durch den Genetischen Algorithmus ermittelten KNN liegen 97.5% der Testdatensätze bei kleiner gleich z, wohingegen das vorher eingesetzte KNN nur dazu in der Lage war 95% der Datensätze mit einem

Vorhersagefehler kleiner gleich z zu berechnen. Weiterhin konnte der maximale Fehler um 35% von ca. $7 * z$ auf ca. $4,5 * z$ reduziert werden.

7 Zusammenfassung

Im Rahmen dieses Projekts wurde eine Softwarelösung zur Evolutionären Strukturoptimierung auf einem Computer Cluster mithilfe eines Genetischen Algorithmus konzipiert und implementiert.

In der Konzeptionierungsphase der Evolutionären Strukturoptimierung wurden im ersten Schritt die Strukturparameter Künstlicher Neuronaler Netze analysiert. Dabei wurde ermittelt, welche dieser Parameter den größten Einfluss auf die Güte und damit die Generalisierungsleistung eines Künstlichen Neuronalen Netzes haben. Die folgenden Parameter wurden dabei für die Optimierung ausgewählt:

- Anzahl der Hidden-Layer
- Anzahl der Neuronen pro Hidden-Layer
- Aktivierungsfunktion der Hidden-Layer

Anschließend wurde ein Genetischer Algorithmus konzipiert, der in der Lage ist die zuvor ermittelten Strukturparameter innerhalb zuvor vom Benutzer festgelegter Grenzen zu optimieren. Dieser Genetische Algorithmus wurde anschließend so umgesetzt, dass alle anfallenden Berechnungen auf einen Computer Cluster verteilt werden. Dadurch wurde es ermöglicht die große Menge an Künstlichen Neuronalen Netzen, die im Rahmen der Evolutionären Strukturoptimierung ausgewertet werden müssen, in einem annehmbaren Zeitrahmen zu trainieren.

Bei dem abschließend durchgeführten Optimierungsversuch kam ein Referenzdatensatz des Instituts zum Einsatz. Für diesen Datensatz sollte die optimale Struktur eines Künstlichen Neuronalen Netzes ermittelt werden.

Der notwendige Aufwand für die Ermittlung der optimalen Struktur eines Künstlichen Neuronalen Netzes konnte mithilfe des implementierten Verfahrens der Evolutionären Strukturoptimierung signifikant reduziert werden. Die Ermittlung der Architektur des aktuell im Institut eingesetzten Künstlichen Neuronalen Netzes geschah in monatelanger manueller Optimierung. Mithilfe der Evolutionären Strukturoptimierung war es durch den Einsatz eines Computer Clusters möglich, innerhalb eines Bruchteils dieser Zeit mehrere Netzarchitekturen zu ermitteln, die in der Lage sind den maximal zulässigen Vorhersagefehler deutlich genauer einzuhalten.

8 Ausblick

Mit der Evolutionären Strukturoptimierung werden in der aktuellen Version des Programms die Anzahl der Hidden-Layer, die Anzahl der Neuronen pro Hidden-Layer und die Aktivierungsfunktion der Hidden-Layer optimiert. In der Zukunft sollen Tests durchgeführt werden, in denen auch die Werte der gewichteten Verbindungen in die Optimierung mit einbezogen werden. Es soll dadurch ermittelt werden, ob sich durch deren Einbeziehung das Optimierungsergebnis verbessern lässt.

Aktuell handelt es sich bei dem hier entwickelten Programm um ein rein textbasiertes MATLAB-Skript, weshalb es für die Benutzung erforderlich ist, sich zuerst in die textbasierte Konfiguration einzuarbeiten. Um die Benutzung des Programms in Zukunft einfacher zu gestalten, ist es vorgesehen eine Grafische Benutzeroberfläche zu konzipieren und zu implementieren.

9 Danksagung

Diese Arbeit entstand am Institut CV&CI der Fachhochschule Südwestfalen im Rahmen des vom Bundesministerium für Bildung und Forschung geförderten Projekts „Neuroadaptiver Bauplatz im Flugzeugbau".

10 Literatur

[1]   Zell, Andreas. *Simulation neuronaler Netze.* 4. unveränderte Auflage. München: Oldenbourg Wissenschaftsverlag GmbH 2003.

[2]   Bäck, Thomas. *Evolutionary Algorithms in Theory and Practice - Evolution Strategies - Evolutionary Programming - Genetic Algorithms.* New York: Oxford University Press, Inc., 1996

[3]   The MathWorks, Inc. [Hrsg.]: *MATLAB Distributed Computing Server - MATLAB Distributed Computing Server Introduction & Key Features.* [Online] http://www.mathworks.com/products/distriben/description1.html. [Zitat vom: 30. September 2010.]

[4]   Rojas, Raúl. *Neural Networks - A Systematic Introduction.* Springer-Verlag, Berlin, 1996

[5]   Schöneburg, Eberhard, Heinzmann, Frank und Feddersen, Sven. *Genetische Algorithmen und Evolutionsstrategien - Eine Einführung in Theorie und Praxis der simulierten Evolution.* Bonn/Paris : Addison-Wesley (Deutschland) GmbH, 1994.

Zur Modellierung unstetiger sowie heterogener nichtlinearer Systeme mittels Takagi-Sugeno-Fuzzy-Systemen

Andreas Kroll

Fachgebiet Mess- und Regelungstechnik,
Fachbereich Maschinenbau, Universität Kassel
Mönchebergstrasse 7, 34125 Kassel
Tel.: (0561) 804 3248, Fax: (0561) 804 2847
E-Mail: andreas.kroll@mrt.uni-kassel.de

1   Einführung

Modellbasierte Analyse- und Synthesemethoden für technische Systeme versprechen deutlich verbesserte System-Performanz. Der Aufwand und die erforderliche domainen-spezifische Kompetenz bei physikalischer Modellbildung verhindern allerdings eine breite Durchdringung in der Praxis. So beziffern die industrielle Praxis betreffende Schätzungen den Modellierungsaufwand bei gehobenen Regelungsprojekten auf 50-80% [1], 75% [2], 75% für Aufgaben in Chemie/Petrochemie [3], 80-90% [4] und 90% [5]. Dies motiviert die Entwicklung von Verfahren zur automatisierten Modellbildung. Hierzu bietet sich die Systemidentifikation an. Dabei ist es von Interesse, mit einem überschaubaren Methodenportfolio viele Systemklassen modellieren zu können.

Für die datengetriebene Modellierung nichtlinearer Systeme werden gerne Takagi-Sugeno-(TS-)Fuzzy-Modelle [6] mit überlappenden oder stückweise affine (piece-wise affin, PWA) Modelle mit disjunkten Partitionen verwendet, z. B. [7]. Für beide Beschreibungsformen sind Analyse- und Synthesemethoden der Regelungstheorie (Stabilitätsanalyse, Reglersynthese usw.) verfügbar, z. B. [7,8]. TS-Modelle werden üblicherweise für Systeme mit glatten Nichtlinearitäten und ausgeprägten lokal affinen Bereichen eingesetzt. PWA-Modelle finden insbesondere Einsatz für hybride (z. B. schaltende) Systeme. Bisherige Arbeiten zu TS- und PWA-Modellen nehmen eine homogene Modellstruktur an, d. h. einen einheitlichen lokalen Modellansatz und gleich-artige Übergänge zwischen den lokalen Modellen.

Der vorliegende Beitrag untersucht die Modellierbarkeit unstetiger sowie heterogener nichtlinearer Systeme mittels TS-Modellen. Unter heterogenen Systemen sollen hier Systeme verstanden werden, die lokal signifikant variierendes nichtlineares Verhalten aufweisen. Dies erschwert eine Modellierung mit TS- oder PWA-Modellen, da sie eine gewisse Homogenität der Verhaltensmuster annehmen. Abbildung 1 zeigt als Beispiel eine Turboladerkennlinie: Sie weist einen „wasserfallartigen Verlauf" mit entlang des oberen „Plateaurandes" deutlich variierender Krümmung auf. Zudem zeigt sie einen scharfen Knick beim Übergang des steilen Bereichs in den niedrigen Plateaubereich auf. Dabei beschreibt die „Knicklinie einen Bogen. Das ebenfalls dargestellte PWA-Modell [9] kann trotz Verwendung von 17 Teilmodellen das Übertragungsverhalten nur mäßig approximieren. Der Beitrag zeigt, welche Ergebnisse sich mit TS-Modellen bei der-artigen Modellierungsproblemen erreichen lassen. Dazu finden affine TS-Modelle mit mehrdimensionalen Zugehörigkeitsfunktionen Verwendung, die mittels Clusterung ermittelt werden. Die Fallstudien zeigen exemplarisch den Unterschied zum LOLI-

MOT-Algorithmus. Für die Modellierung heterogener Systeme wird eine Erweiterung von TS-Modellen auf lokal einstellbare und somit heterogene Unschärfe vorgestellt.

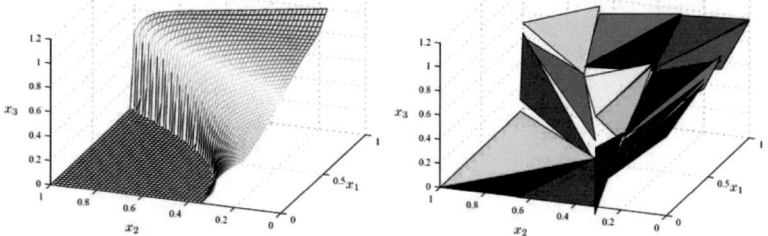

Abbildung 1: Kennfeld eines Turboladers: Normierte Messdaten (links) und identifiziertes PWA-Modell (rechts) [9].

Der folgende Abschnitt beinhaltet eine Beschreibung von TS- und PWA-Modellen. Der 3. Abschnitt behandelt deren Identifikation. Der 4. Abschnitt fasst die Ergebnisse zusammen und gibt einen Ausblick auf zukünftig geplante Arbeiten.

2 Beschreibung von Takagi-Sugeno- und PWA-Modellen

TS-Modelle können als ein Satz von c semi-linguistischen Regeln der Form (i-te Regel)

WENN $\mathbf{Z}$ IST $\mathbf{A}_i$ DANN $\mathbf{y}_i = \mathbf{f}_i(\mathbf{x})$, $i = 1;...;c$

zuzüglich der Überlagerungsvorschrift dargestellt werden. Dabei definiert $\mathbf{f}_i(\mathbf{x})$ ein Teilmodell mit den (scharfen) Ausgangsgrößen $\mathbf{y}_i \in \mathfrak{R}^q$ und den (scharfen) Eingangsgrößen $\mathbf{x} \in \mathfrak{R}^p$. Der unscharfe Gültigkeitsbereich der Regel wird durch die Fuzzy-Referenzmenge $\mathbf{A}_i$ festgelegt. $\mathbf{Z} = \mathcal{F}(\mathbf{z})$ mit $\mathbf{z} \in \mathfrak{R}^r$ beschreibt die fuzzifizierte Prämissenvariable; Prämisse und Konklusion können also andere Größen bewerten.

Alternativ kann eine mathematische Beschreibung gewählt werden, die eine bessere Gegenüberstellung mit PWA- oder schaltenden ARX- (Switched AutoRegressiv with eXternal input, SARX-)Modellen gestattet. Die folgenden Ausführungen beschränken sich auf Modelle mit einer Ausgangsgröße, da i.d.R. nichtlineare Modelle mit $q > 1$ Ausgangsgrößen in q Modelle mit einer Ausgangsgröße zerlegt werden. So kann für jede Ausgangsgröße gezielt auf das nichtlineare Übertragungsverhalten eingegangen werden (z. B. durch eine andere Partitionierung). Der Ansatz für die Teilmodelle ist bei beiden Ansätzen

$$\hat{y}_i(k) = \mathbf{\Theta}_i^T [\varphi^T(k);1]^T \tag{1}$$

mit dem Parametervektor $\mathbf{\Theta}_i$ und dem Regressionsvektor φ^T. Im Fall statischer Modelle gilt

$$\hat{y}_i(k) = [a_{1,i};...;a_{p,i};c_i][\varphi^T(k);1]^T \text{ mit } \varphi^T(k) = [\varphi_1(k);...;\varphi_p(k)]. \tag{2}$$

und dem Datenindex k. Für dynamische Teilmodelle vom ARX-Typ gilt

$$\varphi(k) = [-y(k-1);...;-y(k-n_y);u(k-1-T_\tau);..;u(k-n_u-T_\tau)]^T$$
$$\mathbf{\Theta}_i = [a_{1,i};....;a_{ny,i};b_{1,i};...;b_{nu,i};c_i]^T \tag{3}$$

mit der diskreten Zeit k und der Totzeit T_τ. Für Teilmodelle vom OE- (Output Error, Ausgangsfehler-)Typ ändert sich der Regressor zu

$$\varphi = [-\hat{y}(k-1);...;-\hat{y}(k-n_y);u(k-1-T_\tau);...;u(k-n_u-T_\tau)]^T, \tag{4}$$

wobei $\hat{y}$ die vom Modell prädizierte Ausgangsgröße bezeichnet. OE-Modelle berücksichtigen somit die Fehlerfortpflanzung bei Mehrschrittprädiktion/Simulation bei der Identifikation. Im Fall $c_i = 0$ handelt es sich um lineare, im Fall $c_i \neq 0$ um affine Teilmodelle. Das Übertragungsverhalten des gesamten TS- bzw. PWA-Modells folgt zu

$$\hat{y} = \sum_{i=1}^{c} \phi_i \cdot \hat{y}_i. \tag{5}$$

Bei PWA-Modellen wird der Beschreibungsraum R mittels der Funktionen

$$\phi_i = \begin{cases} 1 \forall \ \varphi \in R_i \\ 0 \ \text{sonst} \end{cases} \tag{6}$$

lückenlos in konvexe Polyeder $R_i \in \mathfrak{R}^r, \bigcup_{i=1}^{c} R_i = R$, zerlegt, wobei in jedem Polyeder genau ein Teilmodell gilt. Die Polyeder/Partitionen überlappen sich nicht $(R_i \cap R_j = 0 \forall i \neq j)$ und es gibt keine leeren Partition $(R_i \neq 0 \forall i)$.

Bei TS-Modellen wird der Beschreibungsraum R i.d.R. lückenlos in unscharf voneinander abgegrenzte Partitionen zerlegt. Partitionierend wirken die Fuzzy-Basisfunktionen

$$\phi_i := \frac{\mu_i}{\sum_{i=1}^{c} \mu_i}; \ i \in \{1;...;c\}. \tag{7}$$

Nicht-orthogonale μ_i und korrespondierende ϕ_i können deutlich und zudem nicht-intuitiv voneinander abweichen. Probabilistische Clusteralgorithmen wie Fuzzy-c-Means- und Gustafson-Kessel-Algorithmus liefern orthogonale μ_i, für die $\mu_i \equiv \phi_i$ gilt.

Als Zugehörigkeitsfunktionen (ZF) können skalare Funktionen wie Trapeze oder Gaußglocken verwendet werden. Diese lassen sich zu multivariaten, achsparallel orientierten Zugehörigkeitsfunktionen z. B. mittels des Produktoperators überlagern:

$$\mu_i(\mathbf{z}) = \prod_{j=1}^{r} \mu_{i,j}(z_j). \tag{8}$$

Im Fall gaußglockenförmiger ZF folgt somit

$$\mu_i(\mathbf{z}) = \exp\left(-\frac{1}{2}\left(\frac{(z_1 - v_{1,i})^2}{\sigma_{1,i}^2} + \cdots + \frac{(z_r - v_{r,i})^2}{\sigma_{r,i}^2}\right)\right). \tag{9}$$

Dabei geben die $v_{1,i};...;v_{r,i}$ die Zentrumsposition der jeweiligen univariaten Gaußglocke und $\sigma_{1,i};...;\sigma_{r,i}$ deren jeweilige „Ausdehnung/Breite" an. „Echt-" multivariate ZF

$$\mu_i(\mathbf{z}) = \left[\sum_{j=1}^{c}\left(\frac{\|\mathbf{z}-\mathbf{v}_i\|_{Ai}^2}{\|\mathbf{z}-\mathbf{v}_j\|_{Aj}^2}\right)^{\frac{1}{m-1}}\right]^{-1} \tag{10}$$

wie sie aus einer Fuzzy-Clusterung hervorgehen, stellen eine Alternative dar. Dabei bezeichnen die $\mathbf{v}_i, \mathbf{v}_j$ die Lage der Prototypen bzw. Zentren des i-/j-ten Clusters und $m \in \Re^{>1}$ stellt den sogenannten Unschärfeparameter dar. $\|\cdot\|$ ist eine Vektornorm, wie z. B. eine innere Produktnorm oder eine Lp-Norm:

$$\|\mathbf{z} - \mathbf{v}_j\|_{Aj} = \sqrt{(\mathbf{z} - \mathbf{v}_j)^T \cdot \mathbf{A}_j \cdot (\mathbf{z} - \mathbf{v}_j)} \quad \text{bzw.} \quad \|\mathbf{z} - \mathbf{v}_j\|_p = \sqrt[p]{\sum_{l=1}^{r} |z_l - v_{l,j}|^p} \quad (11)$$

mit positiv definiter Matrix $\mathbf{A}_j \in \Re^{r \times r}$ und $p \in \Re^{\geq 1}$.

In Bezug auf die Beschreibung unstetiger und heterogener Systeme bleibt anzumerken: PWA-Modelle können einen stetigen Übergang zwischen den Teilmodellen aufweisen, wenn die Partitionsgrenzen aus den Schnittlinien der überlagerten Teilmodelle folgen. Wird eine Partitionierung anders festgelegt, so folgen i.d.R. unstetige Übergänge zwischen den Teilmodellen. Die Partitionierung besteht aus polyedrischen Teilgebieten, die sich bei PWA-Modellen lückenlos zum Beschreibungsraum zusammenfügen. TS-Modelle interpolieren (für $m > 1$ bzw. $\sigma > 0$) zwischen ihren Teilmodellen, was zu einem weichen Übergang führt. Die Schärfe des Übergangs lässt sich durch die Form der Zugehörigkeitsfunktionen einstellen. Bei der Verwendung von Zugehörigkeitsfunktionen aus einer Clusterung folgt diese aus der Wahl des (global einheitlichen) Unschärfeparameters m sowie aus Anzahl und Anordnung der Partitionszentren. Für $m \to 1$ folgt an den Partitionsgrenzen ein abrupter Übergang zwischen den Teilmodellen. Die Partitionsgrenzen können achsübergreifend liegen. Im Fall gaußförmiger Zugehörigkeitsfunktionen beeinflusst die Wahl der $\sigma_{1,i}; ...; \sigma_{r,i}$ deren Ausdehnung und so die die Schärfe des Übergangs. Die Partitionsgrenzen können achsübergreifend gelegt werden; gewöhnlich werden aber achsparallele univariate Gaußglocken überlagert, die zu achsparallelen Partitionsgrenzen führen.

3 Identifikation von Takagi-Sugeno- und PWA-Modellen

Im Folgenden werden die Festlegung der Partitionierung sowie die Parameterschätzung für die lokalen Modelle besprochen. Zum gesamten Identifikationsprozess gehören weitere Aufgaben wie Testsignalentwurf, Wahl der Regressoren, Skalierung/Filterung von Messdaten und Modellvalidierung. Hierfür sei z. B. auf [10], [11] verwiesen.

3.1 Übersicht

Die Lage der Gültigkeitsgrenzen der Teilmodelle (Partitionierung) legt das nichtlineare Übertragungsverhalten der betrachteten Modelle fest, da die Teilmodelle linear/affin sind. Deshalb ist sie von zentraler Bedeutung. Hierzu gibt es mehrere Ansätze (siehe Abbildung 2), insbesondere:

1. Regelmäßiges Gitter („Schachbrettmuster"),

2. Rechteckstruktur,

3. Ermittlung ebener Partitionierungsgrenzen (Hyperebenen) mittels numerischer Optimierung oder Klassifikationsalgorithmen oder

4. Clusteranalyse im Eingangs-, Ein-/Ausgangs- (Produkt-)größenraum und/oder im Modellparameterraum.

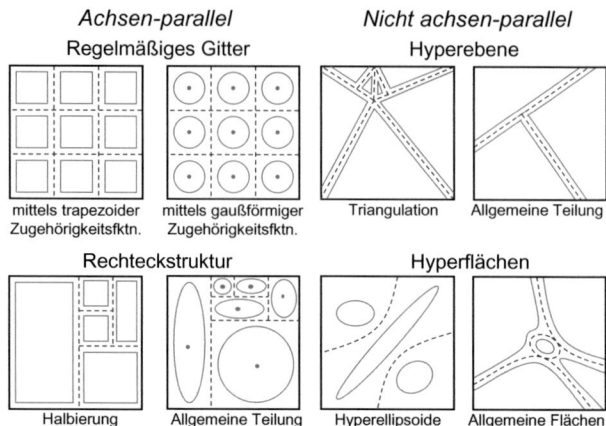

Abbildung 2: Beispiele verschiedener Partitionierungsarten; gestrichelte Linien deuten den Verlauf der Partitionierungsgrenzen, durchgezogene den Verlauf der Zugehörigkeitsfunktionen an.

Die Vorgehensweise 1 kann bei höherdimensionalen Problemen zu explodierender Parameteranzahl führen („curse of dimensionality").

Ein prominenter, zu Vergleichszwecken in diesem Beitrag mit untersuchter Vertreter der 2. Methodik ist der LOLIMOT-Algorithmus [12]. Dabei wird eine Gitterpartitionierung (startend von einer einzigen Partition) sukzessive dort durch Halbierung verfeinert, wo die größte Steigerung der Modellgüte bzgl. eines quadratischen Fehlerkriteriums folgt. Diese Vorgehensweise wird wiederholt, bis ein Abbruchkriterium erfüllt ist. Diese Wachstumsstrategie gehört zu den „Greedy"-Suchstrategien, die nicht zu global optimalen Ergebnissen führen.

Vorgehensweise 3 ist eher bei PWA-als TS-Modellen üblich. Insbesondere wird die simultane Festlegung von Partitionierung und lokalen Modellparametern untersucht. Dieses Optimierungsproblem ist wegen seiner Größe und Multimodalität mit verfügbaren Werkzeugen nur für kleine Aufgaben lösbar.

Beachtung hat der Einsatz clusterungsbasierter Identifikationsmethoden gefunden, z. B. [13, 14, 15]. Die aus der Clusterung resultierenden echt-mehrdimensionalen Zugehörigkeitsfunktionen können für das TS-Modell übernommen werden. Sie erlauben eine vorteilhafte spärliche Parametrierung der Modelle, führen aber zu schwieriger zu interpretierenden multivariaten Zugehörigkeitsfunktionen. Eine Überführung in einfacher zu interpretierende achsparallele Zugehörigkeitsfunktionen kann z. B. durch Projektion erfolgen, was allerdings i.d.R. die Modellgüte reduziert.

Die folgenden Ausführungen fokussieren auf TS-Modelle; für Details der Identifikation von PWA-Modellen sei z. B. auf [7] verwiesen.

3.2 Fuzzy-Clusterung

Der Fuzzy-c-means-(FCM-)Algorithmus gruppiert Objekte zu unscharfen Teilmengen, so dass ähnliche Objekte (definiert über ihren Abstand im Merkmalsraum) zu Gruppen zusammengefasst werden. Gegeben sei eine Menge X von N jeweils durch r Merkmale beschriebenen Objekten $\mathbf{z}_k \in \mathfrak{R}^r, k = 1; ...; N$. Der FCM-Algorithmus [16, 17] ermittelt dann c Clusterzentren $\mathbf{v}_i \in \mathfrak{R}^r, i = 1; \ldots; c$ und die $c \times N$ Zugehörigkeiten $\mu_{i,k} \in [0;1]$ aller Daten zu allen Clustern, so dass die Zielfunktion

$$J_{\text{FCM}} = \sum_{k=1}^{N} \sum_{i=1}^{c} (\mu_{i,k})^m \|\mathbf{z}_k - \mathbf{v}_i\|_{A_i}^2 \tag{12}$$

unter Beachtung von

$$\sum_{i=1}^{c} \mu_{i,k} = 1 \forall k \in \{1; \ldots; N\} \text{ und } \sum_{k=1}^{N} \mu_{i,k} > 0 \forall i \in \{1; \ldots; c\} \tag{13}$$

minimiert wird. Das Optimierungsproblem wird iterativ durch Lösung zweier reduzierter Probleme gelöst. Dies führt auf die Vorschrift, für festgehaltene Zugehörigkeiten $\mu_{i,k}$ der Objekte die Clusterzentren zu berechnen über

$$\mathbf{v}_i = \frac{\sum_{k=1}^{N} (\mu_{i,k})^m \cdot \mathbf{z}_k}{\sum_{k=1}^{N} (\mu_{i,k})^m} \quad \forall i \in \{1; \ldots; c\} \tag{14}$$

und für anschließend festgehaltene Clusterzentren die Zugehörigkeiten zu aktualisieren

$$\mu_{i,k} = \left[\sum_{j=1}^{c} \left(\frac{\|\mathbf{z}_k - \mathbf{v}_i\|_{A_i}^2}{\|\mathbf{z}_k - \mathbf{v}_j\|_{A_j}^2} \right)^{\frac{1}{m-1}} \right]^{-1} \quad \forall i \in \{1; \ldots; c\}, k \in \{1; \ldots; N\}. \tag{15}$$

Diese Prozedur wird wiederholt, bis ein Terminierungskriterium erreicht wird, z. B. dass die Partitionierung sich kaum noch ändert ($\|[\mu_{i,k}]\| < \varepsilon$ oder $\|[\mathbf{v}_1; \ldots; \mathbf{v}_c]\| < \tilde{\varepsilon}$). Beim Gustafson-Kessel- (GK-)Algorithmus werden zusätzlich noch die lokalen Fuzzy-Streumatrizen berechnet und zur Adaption der lokalen inneren Produktnormen verwendet [14, 16, 18].

Für die TS-Identifikation ist i.d.R. eine Clusterung im Produktdatenraum sinnvoll, da sonst die Nichtlinearität des Zusammenhangs zwischen Ein- und Ausgangsgrößen nicht in die Partitionierung einfließt, wie das Beispiel in Abbildung 3 zeigt. Dargestellt ist die Anwendung des FCM ($c=2$, $m=1,6$, $\|.\|_2$) auf $N=20$ Daten, die mittels sign-Funktion für zufällig in [-1; 1] verteilte Argumente erzeugt wurden. Bei Clusterung im Eingangsdatenraum werden die Partitionen schlecht getrennt und entsprechend schlecht ist das Ergebnis der anschließenden Modellbildung. Für die Modellauswertung sind die Zugehörigkeitsfunktionen auf den Eingangsgrößenraum zu reduzieren, da die Ausgangsinformation nicht vorliegt. Dies lässt sich dadurch erreichen, dass die Prototypen auf den Eingangsgrößenraum projiziert werden und die Abstandsnorm angepasst wird. (Beim GK-Algorithmus wird dazu die Fuzzy-Kovarianzmatrix auf den Eingangsgrößenraum reduziert und daraus eine neue Formenmatrix berechnet [14].)

3.3 Schätzung der lokalen Modellparameter

Liegt die Partitionierung vor, so werden die Parameter der lokalen Modelle i.d.R. aus der Minimierung einer quadratischen Kostenfunktion ermittelt. Dabei kann eine (lokale) Schätzung der Parameter separat für alle c Teilmodelle erfolgen

$$\hat{\boldsymbol{\Theta}}_i : \arg\min_{\boldsymbol{\Theta}i} \sum_{k=1}^{N} w_i(k) \cdot \left(y(k) - \hat{y}_i(k, \boldsymbol{\Theta}_i) \right)^2, i \in \{1; \ldots; c\} \tag{16}$$

oder die Parameter aller Teilmodelle können simultan (global) geschätzt werden:

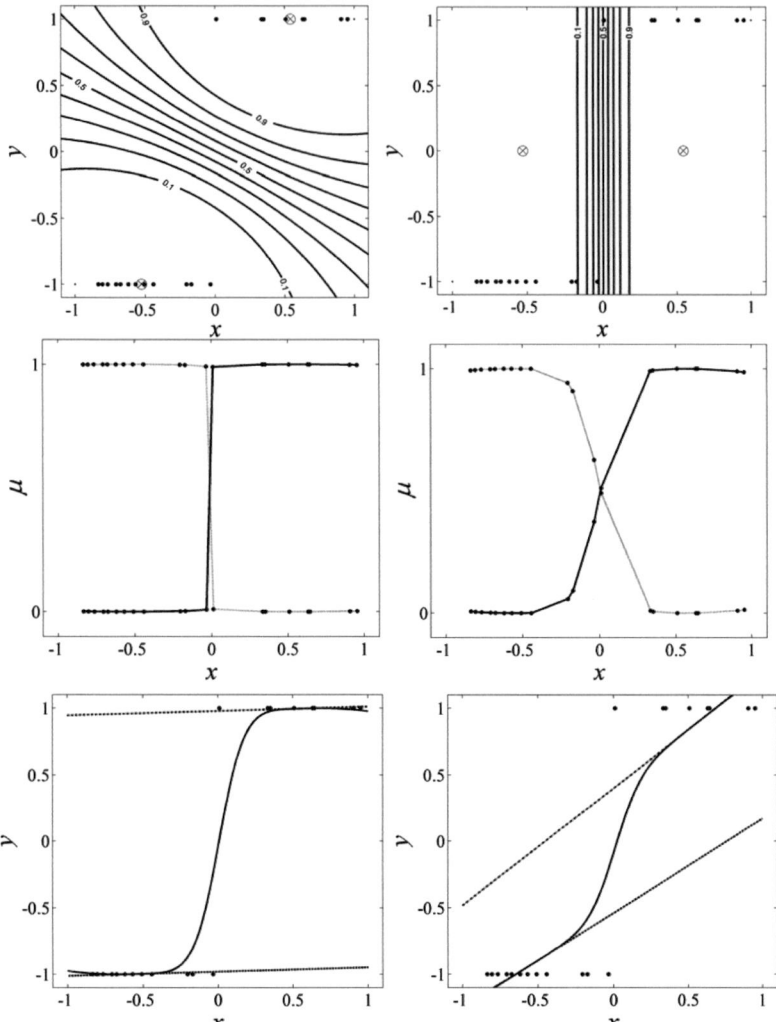

Abbildung 3: TS-Approximation einer sign-Funktion: Clusterungsergebnis im Ein- (o.r.) oder Produktgrößenraum (o.l.; Clusterzentren: ○) für gleiche Entwurfsparameter, Zugehörigkeitsfunktionen (Mitte), lokal geschätzte Teilmodelle und Gesamtübertragungsverhalten (unten).

$$\hat{\boldsymbol{\Theta}} : \arg\min_{\boldsymbol{\Theta}} \sum_{k=1}^{N} (y(k) - \sum_{i=1}^{c} \phi_i(k)\hat{y}_i(k,\boldsymbol{\Theta}_i))^2; \quad \hat{\boldsymbol{\Theta}} := [\hat{\boldsymbol{\Theta}}_1;...;\hat{\boldsymbol{\Theta}}_c]. \tag{17}$$

Bei statischen oder NARX-Modellen führt dies auf ein Schätzproblem, das linear in den Parametern ist und einfach mittels des Verfahrens der kleinsten Fehlerquadrate gelöst werden kann: Bei einer lokalen Schätzung (LS) folgt:

$$\hat{\boldsymbol{\Theta}}_i = [\boldsymbol{\Phi}^T \mathbf{W}_i \boldsymbol{\Phi}]^{-1} \boldsymbol{\Phi}^T \mathbf{W}_i \mathbf{Y} \text{ mit } \boldsymbol{\Phi} = [\varphi_k^T \ 1], \mathbf{W}_i = \text{diag}[\ w_{i,k}\ ], \ \mathbf{Y} = [y_k] \text{und} k = 1;...;N. \tag{18}$$

Die Lösung bei globaler Schätzung (GS) folgt analog. Die Identifikation von NOE-Modellen stellt ein nichtlineares Schätzproblem dar, das mit nichtlinearen Optimierungsverfahren gelöst werden kann. Mit abnehmender Größe von m verringert sich der Unterschied zwischen lokaler und globaler Schätzung; im Grenzfall $m \to 1$ ist das Ergebnis identisch. Abbildung 4 illustriert die unterschiedliche Wirkung von LS und GS am Beispiel einer einfachen Sprungfunktion. Die LS führt hier zu besseren lokalen Modellen und qualitativ besserem Gesamtübertragungsverhalten. Allerdings ist der (radizierte) mittlere quadratische Fehler im Fall der GS etwa 10% geringer. Dies wird darauf zurückgeführt, dass bei einer LS im Gegensatz zur GS der Verlauf des Übergangsbereichs nicht in die Kostenfunktion eingeht. Dies kann gerade im Fall sprungförmiger Wechsel zwischen den Teilmodellen zu großen Abweichungen im Übergangsbereich führen, die die Summe der quadratischen Fehler dominieren können. In Abbildung 4 werden äquidistante unverrauschte Daten verwendet, analoge Ergebnisse treten bei verrauschten Daten auf.

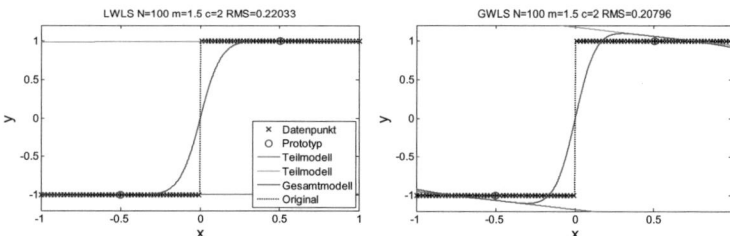

Abbildung 4: Funktionsapproximation einer Sprungfunktion mittels FCM-Clusterung ($c=2$, $m=1,5$, $\|.\|_2$) und lokaler (links) bzw. globaler Parameterschätzung (rechts).

Bei der Parameteridentifikation können sowohl im Produkt- als auch im Eingangsgrößenraum definierte Zugehörigkeitsfunktionen verwendet werden. Bei der LS erscheint ersteres sinnvoll, da während der Identifikation mehr Informationen über das Verhalten ausgenutzt werden und die Rahmenbedingungen bei Identifikation und Modellauswertung ansatzbedingt voneinander abweichen. Bei der GS führt eine Beschränkung auf im Eingangsgrößenraum definierte Zugehörigkeitsfunktionen zu konsistenten Bedingungen während Identifikation und Auswertung. Wegen des auf numerische Anpassung des gesamten Übertragungsverhaltens ausgelegten Ansatzes liegt deshalb eine konsistente Betrachtung im Eingangsdatenraum nahe. Gute Ergebnisse lassen sich aber auch beim Vorgehen analog zur LS erzielen.

3.4   Wahl des Unschärfeparameters m

Bei der Auswertung des Modells entscheidet die Wahl von m über den Ausprägungsgrad des gewünschten interpolierenden Verhaltens sowie unerwünschter Interpolations- und Reaktivierungseffekte. Bei Problemen mit unstetigen/abrupten Übergängen ist eine Wahl von m nahe 1 günstig. Dies illustriert die Approximation einer Sprungfunktion in Abbildung 5. Dazu wurden für $N=81$ im Intervall [-1; 1] äquidistante verteilte Argumente Daten generiert. Für ein TS-Modell ($c=2$) werden die mittels FCM ($\|.\|_2$) bestimmten Prototypen dargestellt sowie Teil- und Gesamtmodelle bei LS für verschiedene Kombinationen von m bei Identifikation und Auswertung. Analoge Ergebnisse folgen bei GS oder verrauschten Daten.

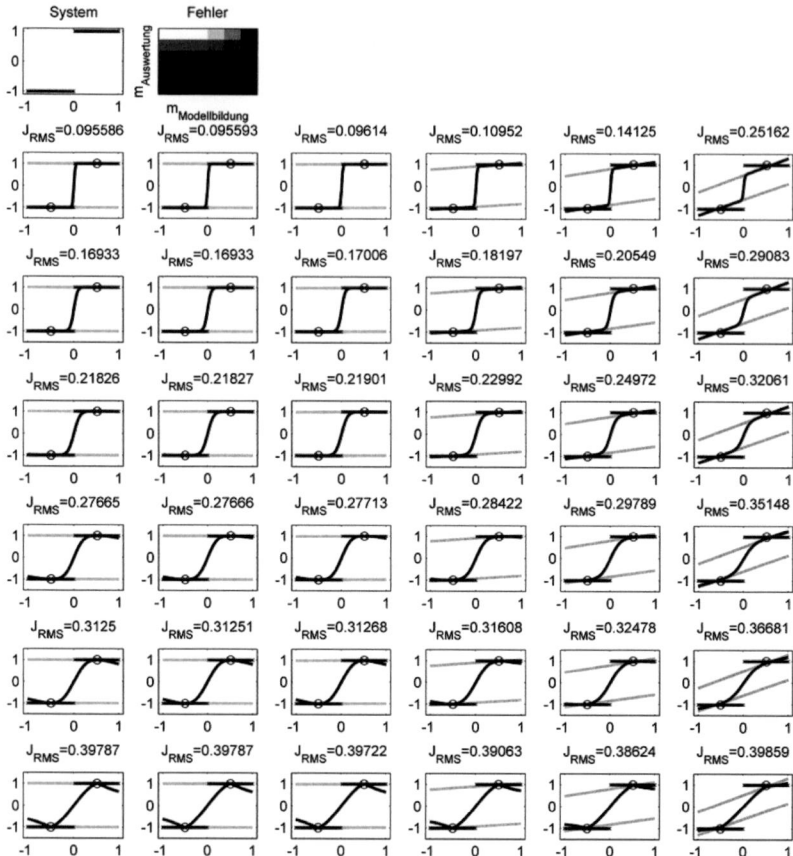

Abbildung 5: Einfluss der Wahl von *m* auf die TS-Approximation einer Sprungfunktion (o.l.). Bei den Einzelbildern nimmt *m*(Clusterung und Parameterschätzung) von oben nach unten zu, *m*(Auswertung) von links nach rechts. Die betrachteten Werte sind: 1,1; 1,3; 1,5; 1,8; 2,0; 2,5. Über den Bildern ist die Wurzel des mittl. quadr. Fehlers (rms) notiert. Das Grauwertbild o.r. gibt eine qualitative Übersicht über den quadratischen Fehler: hell $\hat{=}$ klein bis dunkel $\hat{=}$ groß.

Bei glatten Nichtlinearitäten ist eine kleine Wahl von *m* ebenfalls günstig, da dann unerwünschte Reaktivierungs- und Interpolationseffekte geringer ausfallen. Dies illustriert die Approximation der sigmoiden Funktion

$$f(x) = 2\left(\frac{1}{\exp(-15x) + 1} - 0,5 \right). \tag{19}$$

Abbildung 6 zeigt die Ergebnisse der Parameterstudien analog zu Abbildung 5. Es zeigt sich ein klares Optimum für *m*=1,5. Bei heterogenen Nichtlinearitäten mit unstetigen Übergängen und glatten Nichtlinearitäten kann also ein Zielkonflikt für die Einstellung des globalen Parameters *m* bestehen. Dies motiviert die Erweiterung/Verallgemeinerung clusterungsbasierter TS-Systeme um eine lokal anpassbare Unschärfe.

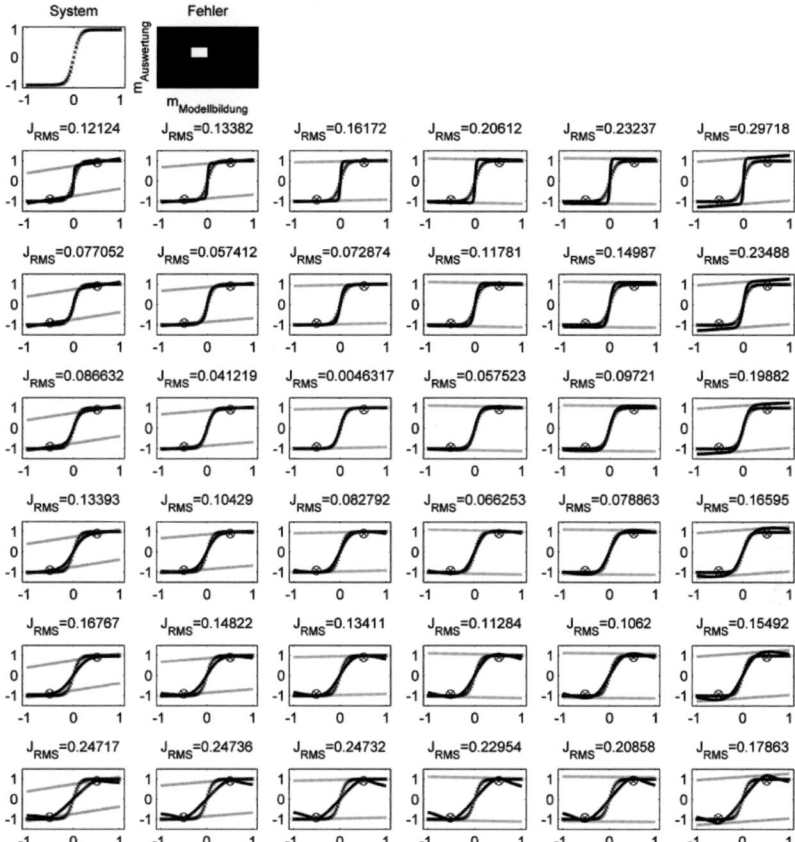

Abbildung 6: Einfluss der Wahl von _m_ auf die TS-Approximation einer sigmoiden Funktion (o.l.). Bei den Einzelbildern nimmt _m_(Clusterung und Parameterschätzung) von oben nach unten zu, _m_(Auswertung) von links nach rechts. Die betrachteten Werte sind: 1,1; 1,3; 1,5; 1,8; 2,0; 2,5. Über den Bildern ist die Wurzel des mittl. quadr. Fehlers (rms) notiert. Das Grauwertbild o.r. gibt eine qualitative Übersicht über den quadratischen Fehler: hell ≙ klein bis dunkel ≙ groß.

Bei der Nutzung von Clustermethoden und Verwendung clusterungsbasierter Zugehörigkeitsfunktionen im TS-Modell tritt der Parameter _m_ an drei Stellen auf:

- Im Clusteralgorithmus für die Clusteranalyse,

- in den resultierenden Zugehörigkeitsfunktionen zwecks Gewichtung bei der Parameterschätzung für die lokalen Modelle und

- im ausgewerteten resultierenden Modell.

Dabei können sich günstige Wertebereiche für _m_ unterscheiden:

Bei der Clusteranalyse führt eine Wahl von _m_ nahe 1 häufiger zu ungünstiger lokaler Konvergenz, insbesondere bei verrauschten Daten. Begegnet wird dem i.d.R. mit mehrfacher Clusterung mit verschiedenen Startwerten. (Moderate) Verbesserungen lassen sich mittels 2-stufiger Clusterung erreichen: Zuerst wird mit hoher Unschärfe geclustert (z. B. $m=3$) und mit dem Ergebnis eine Clusterung mit kleinerem m entsprechend der Anforderung aus der Modellbildung initialisiert. Theoretische Betrachtungen [19] zeigen, dass – lässt man die Problematik lokaler Konvergenz außer acht – die optimale Lage der Clusterzentren nur geringfügig von m abhängt. Vereinfacht können so direkt die Prototypen einer unscharfen Clusterung übernommen und nur das m in der Definition der Zugehörigkeitsfunktionen im gewünschten Maß verkleinert werden.

Bei der Identifikation der lokalen Modelle sind die Daten zu gewichten. Üblich ist eine scharfe Gewichtung z. B. mit den Elementen einer α-Schnittmenge der Zugehörigkeitsfunktionen oder eine weiche Gewichtung mit den Zugehörigkeiten $\mu_i(\mathbf{z}_k)$ der Daten. Ist das Systemverhalten nahezu lokal affin und dergestalt, dass die Partitionsgrenzen gut identifiziert werden können, so ist es sinnvoll die zur Identifikation benutzten Daten relativ scharf abzugrenzen. Ist das nicht der Fall, so ist eine moderat unscharfe Gewichtung ($m \approx 1,2....1,5$) sinnvoll. (Dieser Aspekt ist nicht mit der gegenseitigen Beeinflussung bei der GS zu verwechseln.) Verallgemeinert kann eine Gewichtung $f(\mu_i(\mathbf{z}_k))$ zugelassen werden, um z. B. Daten mit hoher Zugehörigkeit überproportional zu gewichten. So leitet [14] die Teilmodelle direkt aus einer GK-Clusterung im Produktdatenraum ab, was nicht einer Gewichtung mit $\mu(\mathbf{z}_k)$ entspricht. In eigenen Untersuchungen wurde $f(\mu) = \mu^a, a \in [0;1]$, exemplarisch untersucht. In den Tests ließ sich in einigen Teilbereichen die Modellgüte verbessern, in anderen verschlechterte sie sich allerdings. Deshalb wurde dieser Ansatz nicht weiter verfolgt.

Der Einfluss von m bei der Auswertung des Modells wurde bereits zu Beginn dieses Teilabschnitts diskutiert.

3.5 Achsparallele vs. mehrdimensionale Partitionierungsstrategien

Achsparallele Partitionierungsstrategien wie der LOLIMOT führen zu einer hohen Anzahl an Partitionen, wenn die nichtlinearen Effekte nicht achsparallel liegen, während sich clusterungsbasierte Partitionen achsübergreifend ausrichten können. Abbildung 7 illustriert die Unterschiede am Beispiel der Approximation einer achsdiagonalen Sprungfunktion. Ein auf einer GK-Clusterung aufbauendes TS-Modell kann die Funktion mit 2 Partitionen sehr gut approximieren und benötigt ein vergleichsweise geringe Anzahl an Identifikationsdaten. Ein LOLIMOT-Modell mit 49 Partitionen liefert nur eine moderate Approximationsqualität, da die diagonal liegende Nichtlinearität mittels achsparallel orientierter Partitionen nachzubilden ist. Deshalb wurden verbesserte LOLIMOT-Varianten entwickelt, siehe z. B. [20].

Ein Vergleich von Abbildung 7 o.m. und o.r. illustriert die Wirkung des Entwurfsparameters σ: Eine kleinere Wahl bedeutet eine geringer ausgeprägte Überlappung der Partitionen. Dies führt einerseits zu erhöhtem „Überschwingen" bei den Übergängen zwischen dem Bereich großer Steigung und den Plateaus, weil die Modelle mit großer Steigung bei der Interpolation in ihrem Einfluss weniger gedämpft werden. Vice versa werden die Plateaus besser (ebener) approximiert. Abbildung 7 u.l. zeigt die Folgen einer ungünstigen Verteilung der Identifikationsdaten. Für Abbildung 7 wurden unverrauschte Daten verwendet; verrauschte Daten führen zu qualitativ vergleichbaren Ergebnissen. In [21] findet sich ein ausführlicherer Vergleich.

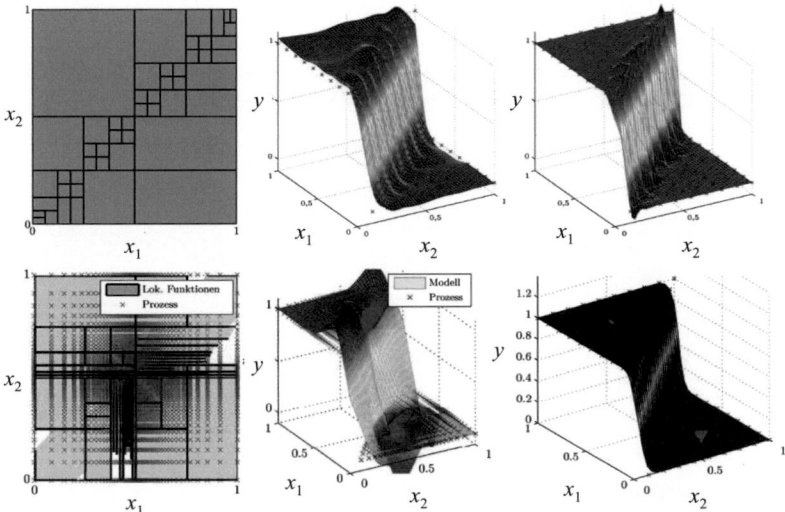

Abbildung 7: Approximation einer achsdiagonalen Sprungfunktion: LOLIMOT-Partitionierung (o.l. für σ=1/16) und resultierendes Übertragungsverhalten für σ=1/16 (o.m.) und σ=1/64 (o.r.) bei N=50×50 äquidistant verteilten Eingangsdaten; Ergebnisse bei ungleichförmiger Datenverteilung: Daten (x) und Partitionierung (u.l.) sowie Übertragungsverhalten (u.m.); Clusterung mittels GK-Algorithmus für N=10×10 mit c=2 und m=1,1 (u.r.).

3.6 TS-Systeme mit heterogener Unschärfe

Die Annahme bei affinen TS-Modellen mit clusterungsbasierten Zugehörigkeits-funktionen ist, dass das zu modellierende System lokal gut affin approximierbar und ein global einheitlicher Interpolationsansatz ausreichend ist. Wenn diese Annahmen verletzt sind, entsteht der Zielkonflikt, auf welche Effekte der global einzustellende Unschärfe-parameter m angepasst werden soll. Abbildung 8 illustriert dies mit einem einfachen Beispiel: Zu approximieren ist eine Funktion, die aus zwei Gaußglocken hart zusammengesetzt wurde und dadurch eine achsdiagonale Unstetigkeit aufweist (Abbildung 8 o.r.). FCM- oder GK-clusterungsbasierte TS-Modelle können die Funktion moderat gut approximieren. Im Beispiel wurde ein relativ kleiner Wert von $m=1,1$ gewählt, um die Unstetigkeit gut abbilden zu können. Dadurch werden die Krümmungen der beiden Gaußglocken flach abgebildet. In den Plots sind Originaldaten als Kreuze und Modellprädiktionen flächig dargestellt.

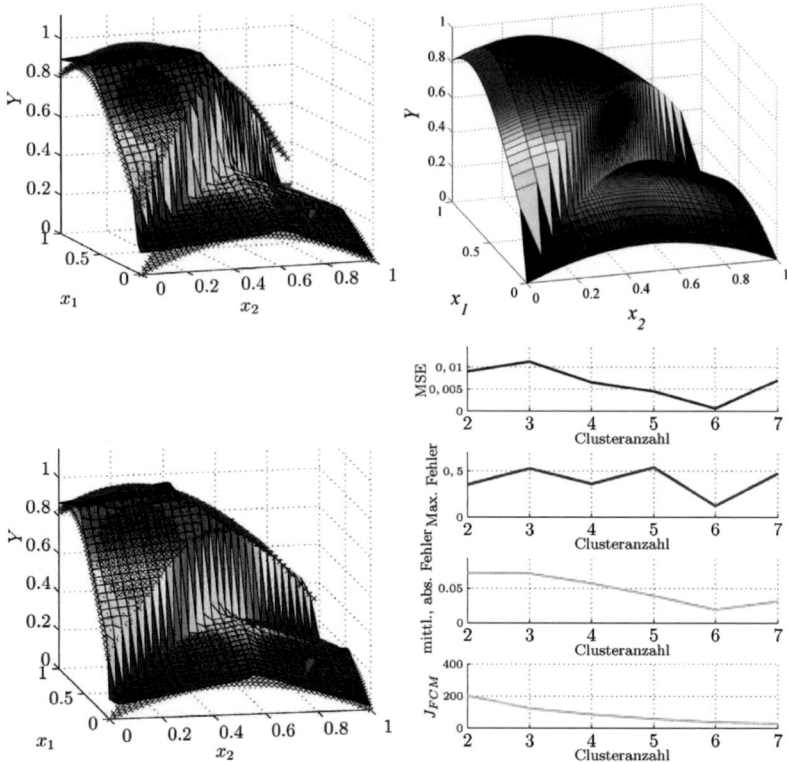

Abbildung 8: Approximation einer heterogenen Nichtlinearität (o.r.) mittels FCM- (o.l.; $\|.\|_2$) sowie GK-Algorithmus (u.l.) mit jeweils $c=6$, $m=1,1$, $N=50\times50$; verschiedene Fehlermaße[1] weisen $c=6$ als günstig bei GK-Clusterung mit $m=1,1$ aus (u.r.).

Ein schwierigeres Beispiel stellen Kennflächen von Strömungsmaschinen wie Turboladern eines Common-Rail Vierzylinder-Turbodieselmotors dar (Abbildung 1). (u.r.) zeigt die dem Verlauf von Abbildung 1 sehr ähnliche Kennfläche des einstufigen Axialkompressors Nasa CR-72694 (basierend auf Daten von [22]), die exemplarisch als Modellierungsaufgabe betrachtet werde. Ein auf eine FCM-Clusterung ($c=6$, $m=1,2$, $\|.\|_2$, 20 Zufallsinitialisierungen) aufbauendes TS-Modell (LS mit Gewichtung über die Zugehörigkeiten) führt nur zu einem mäßigen Modell (Abbildung 9m.l.).

Dies liegt insbesondere daran, dass die Partitionierung den Verlauf der Unstetigkeit nicht richtig wiedergibt. Die Ursache ist die der Clusterung zu Grunde liegende Ziel-funktion, die die Datengruppierung aber nicht den Prädiktionsfehler bewertet. Eine deutliche Verbesserung lässt sich durch numerische Optimierung von Partitionszentren und m bzgl. des mittleren quadratischen Modellfehler erreichen (Abbildung 9 o.r., m.r.): Die Partitionierung spiegelt nun die Kontur der Unstetigkeit wieder.

---

[1] Mittl. Quadr. Fehler, max. Fehlerbetrag, mittl. absoluter Fehler, Werte der Clusterungs-Zielfunktion

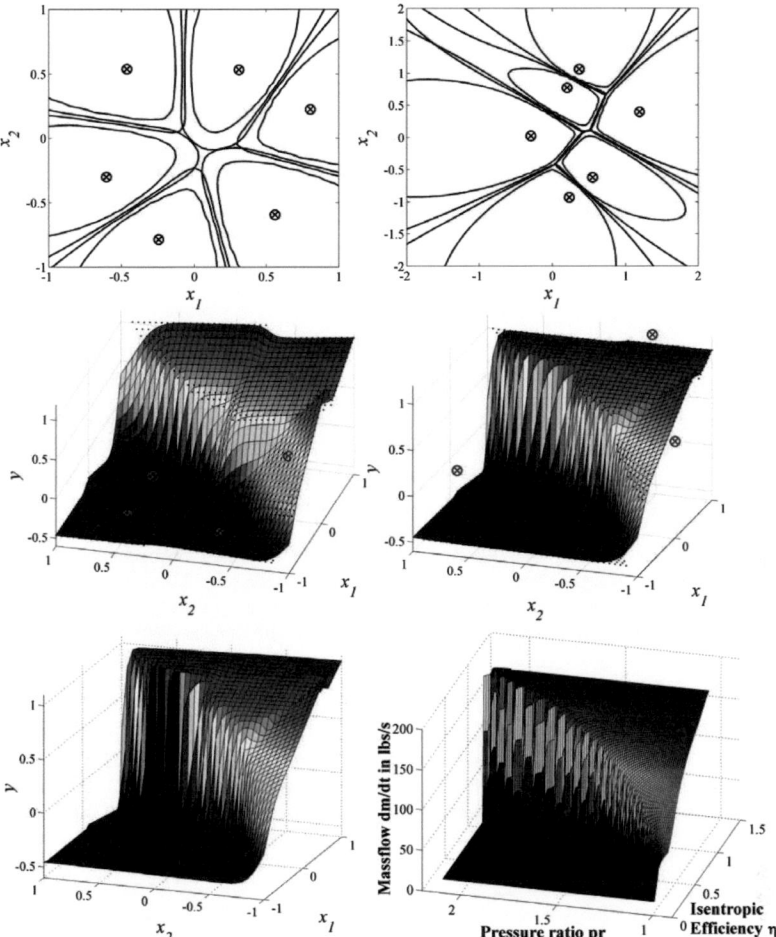

Abbildung 9: Beispiel Axialkompressor: FCM-Partitionierung (o.l., Zentren: ○) und TS-Modell (m.l.), optimierte Partitionierung (o.r.) und resultierendes TS-Modell (m.r.), TS-Modell mit heterogener Unschärfe (u.l.) sowie unnormierte Originaldaten (u.r.).

Für eine bessere lokale Anpassung können TS-Modelle mit lokal anpassbarer Unschärfe verwendet werden. Das Konzept wird in [23] im Detail beschrieben, weshalb im Folgenden nur Eckpunkte skizziert werden. Die Zugehörigkeitsfunktionen werden dazu modifiziert zu

$$\mu_i(\mathbf{z}) = \left[\sum_{j=1}^{c} \left(\frac{\|\mathbf{z} - \mathbf{v}_i\|_{Ai}^2}{\|\mathbf{z} - \mathbf{v}_j\|_{Aj}^2} \right)^{\frac{1}{m(\mathbf{z})-1}} \right]^{-1} \quad ; i \in \{1;...;c\}.$$ (21)

Dabei wird die lokale Unschärfe $m(\mathbf{z}) \in \mathfrak{R}^{>1}$ berechnet mittels

$$m(\mathbf{z}) = \sum_{i,j \neq j} \mu_{i,j}(\mathbf{z}) \cdot m_{i,j} \quad \text{mit } \mu_{i,j}(\mathbf{z}) = \left[\sum_{r,s} \left(\frac{\|\mathbf{z} - \mathbf{v}_{i,j}\|_{Ai}^2}{\|\mathbf{z} - \mathbf{v}_{r,s}\|_{Aj}^2} \right)^{\frac{1}{\tilde{m}-1}} \right]^{-1}.$$ (22)

Mit den $m_{i,j}$ und $\tilde{m}$ als neuen Parametern. Die Zentren $\mathbf{v}_{i,j}$ werden mittig zwischen jeweils zwei Prototypen aus der Clusterung platziert: $\mathbf{v}_{i,j} = (\mathbf{v}_i + \mathbf{v}_j)/2; i \neq j$. Davon werden nur die Zentren $\mathbf{v}_{i,j}$ übernommen, die ein „Nächstes-Nachbar"-Kriterium erfüllen. Zur Ermittlung wird eine Delaunay-Triangulation durchgeführt. In Anbetracht des gewünschten Unschärfeprofils erwies sich $\tilde{m} = 1,3$ als günstiger Wert. Die $m_{i,j}$ können z. B. mit dem m-Wert einer vorausgehenden Modellbildung mit einheitlicher Unschärfe initialisiert und anschließend mittels numerischer Optimierung eingestellt werden. Im vorliegenden Beispiel des Axialkompressors ließ sich durch das so erweiterte TS-Modell der mittlere quadratische Fehler auf den Identifikationsdaten um 20% reduzieren. Vergleicht man das resultierende TS-Modell (Abbildung 9 u.l.) mit dem PWA-Modell aus Abbildung 1 für eine sehr ähnliche Approximationsaufgabe, so zeigen sich deutlich die Vorzüge des vorgestellten Modellierungskonzeptes.

4 Zusammenfassung und Ausblick

Im vorliegenden Beitrag wurde auf der Basis von Fallstudien gezeigt, dass sich TS-Modelle auch für unstetige und heterogene Modellierungsprobleme eignen. Dazu wurde systematisch untersucht, welchen Einfluss die Entwurfsentscheidungen auf die Modell-charakteristik haben und Handlungsvorschläge wurden abgeleitet. Um Zielkonflikte bei der Einstellung des globalen Unschärfeparameters zu umgehen, wurde eine Erweiterung des Modellansatzes um eine lokal anpassbare Unschärfe vorgestellt. Im nächsten Schritt sollen unstetige und heterogene dynamische nichtlineare Systeme untersucht werden, bei denen weitere Effekte wie das mögliche Auftreten von im System nicht vorhandenen Ruhelagen durch Modellierungsfehler auftreten können.

5 Danksagungen

Gedankt sei Herrn Dipl.-Ing. Samuel Soldan und Herrn Dipl.-Ing. Alexander Schrodt, die in ihren Diplomarbeiten wichtige Beiträge zum vorliegenden Artikel geliefert haben.

6 Literatur

[1]   A. Kroll, D. Abel, "Modellbasierte Prädiktive Regelung," *at-Automatisierungs-technik*, vol. 54, no. 12, pp. 587-589, 2006.

[2]   M. Gevers, "Identification for Control: from the early achievements to the revival of experiment design," *European Journal of Control*, vol. 11, pp. 1-18, 2005.

[3]   M.A. Hussain, "Review of the applications of neural networks in chemical process control - simulation and online implementation," *Artificial Intelligence in Engineering*, vol. 13, pp. 55-68, 1999.

[4]   K.H. Jorgensen, J.H. Lee, "Recent advances and challenges in process control," *Chemical process Control*, vol. 6, pp. 55-74, 2002.

[5]   M. Vašak, N. Perc, "Combining identification and constrained optimal control of piecewise affine systems," *AUTOMATIKA*, vol. 48, pp. 145-160, 2007.

[6]   T. Takagi, M. Sugeno, "Fuzzy identification of systems and its application to modelling and control," *IEEE Trans. Systems, Man, and Cybernetics*, vol. 15, no. 1, pp. 116-132, 1985.

[7]   J. Lunze, F. Lamnabhi-Lagarrigue (Hrsg): *Handbook of hybrid systems control: Theory, tools, applications.* Cambridge Univ. Press, 2010.

[8]   K. Tanaka, H.O. Wang, *Fuzzy Control Systems design and analysis: A linear matrix inequality approach*, New-York: Wiley, 2001.

[9]   E. Münz, *Identifikation und Diagnose hybrider dynamischer Systeme.* Universitätsverlag Karlsruhe, 2006.

[10]   O. Nelles, *Nonlinear System Identification.* Heidelberg: Springer, 2001.

[11]   M. Jelali, A. Kroll, *Hydraulic Servo-Systems.* London: Springer, 2003.

[12]   O. Nelles, "LOLIMOT - Lokale, lineare Modelle zur Identifikation nichtlinearer, dynamischer Systeme," *at-Automatisierungstechnik*, vol. 45, no. 4, pp. 163-174, April 1997.

[13]   J. Abonyi, B. Feil, *Cluster analysis for data mining and system identification.* Basel: Birkhäuser, 2007.

[14]   R. Babuska, *Fuzzy Modeling for Control.* Boston: Kluwer, 1998.

[15]   A. Kroll, "Identification of functional fuzzy models using multidimensional reference fuzzy sets," *Fuzzy Sets and Systems*, vol. 80, pp. 149-158, 1996.

[16]   J.C. Dunn, "A fuzzy relative of the isodata process and its use in detecting compact, well-separated clusters," *J. Cybernet.*, vol. 3, pp. 22-57, 1974.

[17]   J.C. Bezdek, *Pattern recognition with fuzzy objective function algorithms.* New York: Plenum, 1981.

[18]   F. Höppner, F. Kruse, F. Klawonn, T. Runkler, *Fuzzy Cluster Analysis.* Chichester: Wiley, 1999.

[19]   A. Kroll, "On choosing the fuzziness parameter in clustering-based systems modeling: theoretical constraints and recommendations" (submitted).

[20]   B. Hartmann, O. Nelles, "Automatic Adjustment of the Transition between Local Models in a Hierarchical Structure Identification Algorithm," in *Proc. European Control Conf.*, Budapest, 2009, pp. 1599-1604.

[21]   O. Nelles, A. Fink, R. Babuska, M. Setnes, "Comparison of two construction algorithms for Takagi-Sugeno Fuzzy models," *Int. J. Appl. Math. Comput. Sci.*, vol. 10, no. 4, pp. 835-855, 2000.

[22]   J.T. Flynn, M.J. Keenan, D.H. Sulam, "Single-stage evaluation of highly-loaded high Mach-number compressor stages," NASA Technical Report, 1970.

[23]   A. Kroll, S. Soldan, "On Data-driven Takagi-Sugeno Modelling of Heterogeneous Systems with Multidimensional Membership Functions" (submitted).

Topology optimization of artificial neural networks using $\mathcal{L}_1$-penalization

L. Görlitz, R. Loosen, Th. Mrziglod

Systems Biology and Computational Solutions, Bayer Technology Services
51368 Leverkusen
E-Mail: thomas.mrziglod@bayertechnology.com

Abstract

Learning with artificial neural networks (ANN) is usually performed as a two-step procedure: Identification of the optimal network topology (i.e. number of nodes in the hidden layer(s) and which inputs to use) and identification of the optimal network weights. The identification of the correct topology is often performed using cross-validation or bootstrapping approaches. In the case of limited training data or if combinatorial issues arise (e.g. in the context of structured hybrid models) these approaches are infeasible. In these situation weight decay with squared $\mathcal{L}_2$-norm penalty can be applied. But it is structurally incapable of selecting a topology as it drives parameters only close to zero.

We propose to replace the squared $\mathcal{L}_2$-norm of the weights of the ANN by the $\mathcal{L}_1$-norm. The resulting optimization problem is non-differentiable and it will be solved using a generalization of the Levenberg-Marquardt algorithm. We show that this leads to sparsely connected neural networks. Applying it to production data from solar cells demonstrates that this approach can be used to identify the correct number of hidden layer nodes. In the example, it reduces the number of required parameters by 75% compared to a model optimized using an explicit test set. The predictive accuracy of the sparse model is only slightly smaller compared to the fully connected model. In future research we want to combine this method with ideas from automatic relevance determination to automatically identify the correct value of the trade-off parameter and with formulations using structured norms to identify the relevant input parameters.

1 Introduction

Learning with artificial neural networks (ANN) consists of two tasks: identification of the optimal network topology (i.e. number of nodes in the hidden layer(s) and which inputs to use) and identification of the optimal network weights. The latter is usually performed using back-propagation although superior approaches exist [3]. The optimal network topology should be the one allowing a model with low generalization error, i.e. a model which well predicts unseen data. Many methods exist for this with many having significant drawbacks in case of few training data. Obviously, all methods have to take special care not to memorize the data.

The approaches to topology identification can roughly be divided into two general strategies: continuous and discrete approaches. While discrete approaches pick a number of nodes in the hidden layer, evaluate the optimal model (i.e. try to estimate its predictive accuracy) and then change the number of nodes, continuous approaches start with a sufficiently complex topology and identify the correct topology by penalizing complex models more severely than simple ones (motivated by Occam's razor).

If sufficient training data is available the topology can be inferred using any of the well established methodologies like cross-validation [7] (k-fold or leave-one-out) or bootstrapping [4, 2, 5] (especially the ".632+" estimator). If only few independent data points are available for training (a situation often encountered in process data modeling due to the large autocorrelations) splitting the data into training and test set seems suboptimal and methods allowing the use of the complete data set should be preferred. This is possible if criteria like the Akaike Information Criterion (AIC) [1] or Schwarz-Bayes Criterion (BIC) [15], consisting of an explicit trade-off between goodness-of-fit and model complexity, to score different models are used. These two criteria only differ in the amount of penalization they add for an extra complexity parameter with the BIC usually selecting the simpler model. Their applicability to neural networks is restricted as the efficient degrees of freedoms for neural networks are hard to calculate.

The major drawback of these approaches is the amount of models to be checked in order to identify the optimal one. Especially in the case of nested parameters (resulting in nested cross-validation or bootstrapping approaches) or hybrid models [10] containing more than one black box model the computational burden grows exponentially. Therefore, greedy heuristics are mostly applied to restrict the number of evaluated models.

Continuous selection methods start with a sufficiently complex model (in our case, a network with many nodes in the hidden layer) and include an extra term in the optimization function which prefers smaller values of the weights. For artificial neural networks with weight vector $p = (p_1, \ldots, p_n)$ the squared $\mathcal{L}_2$-norm of the parameter vector as weight decay term $\sum p_i^2$ has found widespread use [14] although several other formulation have been proposed (e.g. weight elimination [16]). In the context of linear models this approach is well known as "ridge-regression" [7]. The disadvantage of using a squared norm is that this formulation tends to shrink all parameters but sets none of them exactly to zero. Therefore, after optimizing the weight decay extended error function a threshold is chosen and all weights below the threshold are set to zero. Again in the context of linear models this problem is dealt with by replacing the squared $\mathcal{L}_2$-norm by the $\mathcal{L}_1$-norm of the parameter vector, an approach known as Least Absolute Shrinkage and Selection Operator (LASSO). Using the $\mathcal{L}_1$-norm leads to estimated parameters being exactly zero. Therefore, this approach can be used to perform model-selection in the linear model case.

In this paper we transfer this formulation to ANN's (chapter 2) and discuss why this will lead to sparsely connected nets. In chapter 3 an optimization algorithm is presented which explicitly handles the non-differentiability of the optimization problem. In chapter 4 we demonstrate that this approach leads to sparsely connected ANNs with good generalization abilities by applying it to real process data. Conclusions and directions for future research are discussed in chapter 5.

2 Methods

Due to the often limited amount of independent data sets in process data modeling it is advisable to apply methods for model selection which use all available data. Approaches like cross-validation or bootstrapping which iteratively subsample the data often select models being either too complex (if correlated data points are assumed to be independent the resulting model will overfit the data) or too simplistic (as the few data points only allow to identify simple models with sufficient stability). Continuous model selection and weight inference methods which combine the ability of a model to explain data (often measured via residual sum of squares terms) with a term leading to simple models into one optimization task have been applied to neural networks. The most prominent formulation in the context of ANN is weight decay with squared $\mathcal{L}_2$-norm of the parameter vector resulting in the following optimization functional:

$$\arg\min_p \sum_i \left(y_i - f(x_i, p)\right)^2 + \lambda |p|_{\mathcal{L}_2}^2 \tag{1}$$

This approach has twofold impact on the structure of the optimization problem. It leads to less effective parameters which have to be estimated (i.e. requires fewer training data) and shrinks the weights of the identified neural network toward zero. But a pitfall of this approach is the fact that no weight will exactly be zero. This can easily be understood by looking at the (negative) gradient field associated with this penalty function (cf. left image in fig. 1). The gradients always point towards zero and thus no single weight will reach zero as no axis will be crossed. Changing the parameter according to this direction will shrink all weights proportionally towards zero but will never result in zero entries of the parameter vector. Post-hoc thresholding of the weights has to be applied to set them to zero without knowing the correct threshold value.

In the context of linear models this behavior was analyzed in detail and different improvements have been proposed. The behavior of different penalty terms in the case of linear models is extensively investigated in [6]. One formulation which has shown to lead to sparse models is given by exchanging the squared $\mathcal{L}_2$-norm by an $\mathcal{L}_1$ penalty. This behavior can again be well understood by investigating the directions of the gradient of the $\mathcal{L}_1$-norm penalty in fig. 1. All entries of the gradient vector are either 1 or -1 and point accross the axis of the smallest entry. Changing the parameters according to this direction shrinks all parameters by the same amount. Changing the parameter vector iteratively according to the gradient vector will thus lead to zero parameter values and sparse parameter vectors.

Therefore, we propose to use the following formulation for model selection and weight inference for neural networks with trade-off parameter λ which governs the sparseness of the identified network (larger values will lead to sparser models):

$$\arg\min_p \sum_i \left(y_i - f(x_i, p)\right)^2 + \lambda |p|_{\mathcal{L}_1} \tag{2}$$

It will be of utmost interest if this formulation will be able to drive all weights into one node of the hidden layer jointly driven towards zero. If this is possible the method will be directly applicable to model selection tasks.

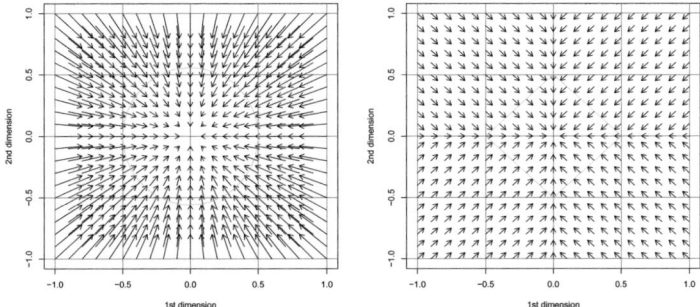

Figure 1: Gradient fields for squared $\mathcal{L}_2$ norm (left) and $\mathcal{L}_1$ norm (right) in the two-dimensional case. The gradient in the left case always points towards zero. Therefore, in each step all weights are shrunk but none is set to zero. The gradient in the right image does not always point towards zero. Changing parameters according to this direction shrinks all entries by the same amount. The direction itself points across the axis and can thus lead to zero parameter values. The gradient field is, of course, not smooth in this situation.

3 Optimization method

The main disadvantage of the $\mathcal{L}_1$-penalty compared to the $\mathcal{L}_2$-penalty is that it is much more difficult to solve the underlying minimization problem. In the case of linear models and $\mathcal{L}_2$-penalization the optimization problem can be reduced to the solution of a linear system, whereas for the $\mathcal{L}_1$-penalization a nonlinear system has to be solved. For ANN (and all other models) using $\mathcal{L}_1$-penalization leads to an optimization function which is only piecewise differentiable with a discontinuity at value 0 for any parameter p_j (cf. right image in Fig. 1). Hence usual optimization algorithms run into difficulties as some parameter values approach zero. Therefore, we modify the well-known Levenberg-Marquardt method [9] to deal with the non-differentiability of the optimization function in a fashion similar to the approach introduced in [12] for the case of linear models. A detailed discussion for related problems with discontinuities in the derivative can be found in [13].

The main idea of our approach is that a parameter p_j can be omitted if its contribution to the penalty term exceeds its contribution to the error term (locally near the optimum parameter value p and $p_j = 0$). In terms of the minimizing function this is equivalent to the absolute value of the partial derivative of the error term with respect to p_j at $p_j = 0$ being less than the partial derivative of the penalty term with respect to p_j near $p_j = 0$ which is equal to λ. Hence we have the sufficient and necessary condition

$$2\left|\sum_i (y_i - f(x_i, p)) \frac{\partial f}{\partial p_j}(x_i, p)\right| < \lambda \tag{3}$$

at the optimum parameter value p and $p_j = 0$ for a parameter p_j to be omitted. Due to the nonlinear nature of the optimization system this condition is valid only locally in a neighborhood of a minimizing point.

The aim of the continuous selection method is to solve the optimization and parameter selection problem simultaneously. Due to the discontinuity of the derivative of the optimizing function many optimization methods will run into difficulties in the neighborhood of vanishing parameters. For example this parameter values may oscillate around zero and the method may not terminate properly. On the other hand such an oscillation behavior indicates that inequality (3) is satisfied. This is due to the discontinuity of the derivative of the penalty term with respect to p_j since this leads to changing sign of that part of the gradient vector. Oscillating behavior then means that the corresponding component in the gradient vector changes sign hence inequality (3) is satisfied. Therefore we modified the (generalized) Levenberg-Marquardt method such that this oscillating behavior is recognized and the corresponding parameter p_j is fixed at $p_j = 0$. The optimization method is then carried on without consideration of p_j. Essentially we modify the optimization method locally according to (3). As a consequence several parameters were fixed at the value 0 sequentially during the optimization procedure.

4 Example

Polymer solar cells have high potential for future applications due to the theoretically low energy and material costs during production and their flexible handling in applications. The aim of the BMBF project NanoPolySol is the development and optimization of polymer solar cells and the overall production process. We used data from this project to optimize the topology of a standard feed forward neural network with one inner layer. The neural network model is used to describe the relationship between input parameters as the used polymer type, geometry parameters of the nanoparticles, the formulation and some parameter of the production process and the resulting efficiency of the solar cell. The data consist of overall 100 data points and 6 input parameter were considered for the model. For testing purposes we added an additional input parameter containing only noise.

We used the modified Levenberg-Marquardt method described in section 3 to identify simultaneously network topology (number of nodes in the inner layer) and the parameter values. Different values for the parameter λ were tested and the results were compared with the resulting neural network trained with the standard learning set - test set procedure. Thereby 80 data points were used for the learning set and the remaining 20 data points for the test set. For the parameter identification the classical Levenberg-Marquardt method was used resulting in a network with 10 nodes in the inner layer. Starting point for the continuous selection method using the modified Levenberg-Marquardt algorithm was the resulting complex model topology with 10 nodes in the inner layer. For the case $\lambda \simeq 0.005$ the resulting model topology is visualized in fig. 2. The number of parameters is reduced from 80 for the classical case to only 20 for the continuous selection method. Thereby the prediction error increases only slightly (correlation coefficient 96.74% vs. 95.55%). The resulting scatter plots for both cases are shown in fig. 3. This increase in prediction error might well be due to weights being inferred in a biased manner (weights are shrunken towards zero). Bias free retraining of the identified topology would again

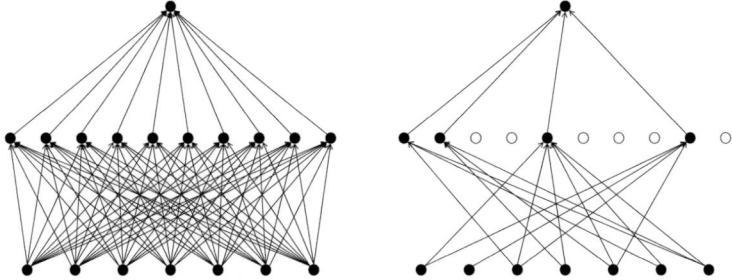

Figure 2: Resulting topology for the model trained using a fixed test set (left) and the continuous selection method (right). In the latter case, only 4 nodes in the hidden layer are leftover. Remarkably, all weights belonging to a hidden node with zero hidden-to-output weight are automatically set to zero. In the resulting topology further weights are automatically set to zero leading to a highly sparse network structure. The additional input parameter which contains only noise is not completely eliminated but connected to 3 of the 4 inner nodes with parameters of small absolute value.

reduce the prediction error.

The weights belonging to the noise input are not completely set to zero but two connec-

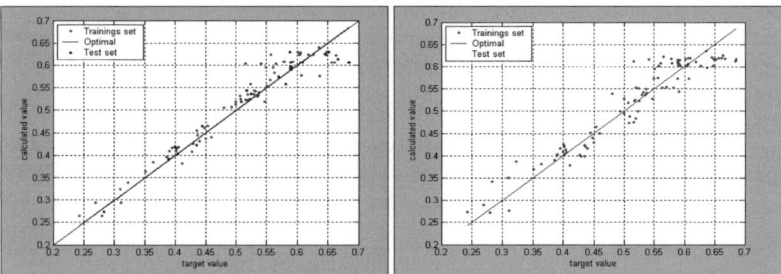

Figure 3: Scatter plot for prediction quality of the model trained in classical way (left) and with help of the continuous selection method (right). For the case $\lambda \simeq 0.005$ the prediction quality decreases only slightly.

tions remain although the absolute value of these weights is low compared to all other weights in the network.

5 Conclusion & Future Research

Model or complexity selection is the main problem in building predictive models with ANNs or structured hybrid models. Many well established discrete procedures exist to deal with this problem in case of sufficient (independent) training data (for ANN) and few structural assumptions (hybrid models). Continuous approaches like weight decay might be capable of dealing with low sample size situations if they are capable of selecting sparse models. But $\mathcal{L}_2$ penalties (often used in weight decay) fail to do so. Thus we have proposed to use a $\mathcal{L}_1$ penalty which in the case of linear models is known to select only few parameters. The resulting non-differentiable optimization problem is solved using an adapted Levenberg-Marquardt optimization strategy.

The method is successfully applied to production data of solar cells. It selects a model containing only 25% of the parameters with only slightly reduced accuracy compared to a neural network with structure optimized using an explicit test set. This reduced accuracy could be overcome by retraining the optimized structure without using any penalty term (and thus trained without any bias). The example demonstrates that using $\mathcal{L}_1$ penalties can select the correct number of nodes in the hidden layer but seems incapable of deselecting irrelevant inputs. This might be overcome by further subgrouping of weights in the penalty term.

The main problem is the identification of the value of the trade-off parameter λ. One way is to use cross-validation to identify the optimal value. But this approach would again result in subsampling of the data. A heuristic approach widely used in the case of linear models is to calculate the residual sum-of-squares (RSS) for different values of λ and pick the one where the kink in the RSS vs. λ curve occurs. In future research we want to use ideas from Bayesian inference of hyperparamters to automatically identify the correct value. For example, we want to add automatic relevance determination priors [8, 11] to automatically identify the trade-off parameter λ. A second direction of future research will be the use of structured $\mathcal{L}_1$-norms for identification of the correct topology and the correct number of inputs within one optimization framework.

References

[1] H. Akaike. Information theory and an extension of the maximum likelihood principle. In *Proceedings of the Second International Symposium on Information Theory*, 1973.

[2] J. Anil, R. Dubes, and C. Chen. Bootstrap techniques for error estimation. *IEEE Transactions on Pattern Analysis and Machine Intelligence*, 9(5):628–633, 1987.

[3] F. Bärmann and F. Biegler-König. On a class of efficient leraning algorithms for neural networks. *Neural Networks*, 5(1):139–144, 1992.

[4] B. Efron. Bootstrap methods: Another look at the jackknife. *Annals of Statistics*, 7(1):1–26, 1979.

[5] B. Efron and R. Tibshirani. Improvements on cross-validation: The .632+ bootstrap method. *Journal of the American Statistical Association*, 92:548–560, 1997.

[6] J. Fan and R. Li. Variable selection via nonconcave penalized likelihood and its oracle properties. *Journal of the American Statistical Association*, 96(456):1348–1360, 2001.

[7] T. Hastie, R. Tibshirani, and J. Friedman. *The Elements of Statistical Learning*. Springer, 2001.

[8] D. MacKay. Bayesian methods for backpropagation networks. In E. Domany, J. van Hemmen, and K. Schulten, editors, *Models of Neural Networks III*, chapter 6, pages 211–254. Springer, 1994.

[9] D. Marquardt. An algorithm for least-squares estimation of nonlinear parameters. *SIAM Journal of Applied Mathematics*, 11:431–441, 1963.

[10] G. Mogk, T. Mrziglod, and A. Schuppert. Application of hybrid models in chemical industry. In *Computer Aided Chemical Engineering*, volume 10, pages 931–936, 2002.

[11] R. Neal. *Bayesian Leraning for Neural Networks*. Springer, 1996.

[12] M. R. Osborne, B. Presnell, and B. A. Turlach. On the LASSO and its dual. *Journal of Computational and Graphical Statistics*, 9:319–337, 1999.

[13] M. Owerton. Algorithms for nonlinear l_1 and l_∞ fitting. In M. Powell, editor, *Nonlinear Optimization*, 1981.

[14] B. Ripley. *Pattern Recognition and Neural Networks*. Cambridge University Press, 1996.

[15] G. Schwarz. Estimating the dimension of a model. *Annals of Statistics*, 2(6):461–464, 1978.

[16] A. Weigend, D. Rumelhart, and B. Huberman. Generalization by weight-elimination with application to forecasting. In R. Lippmann, J. Moody, and D. Touretzky, editors, *Advances in Neural Information Processing Systems*, 1991.

Evolving Fuzzy Pattern Trees for Binary Classification on Data Streams

Ammar Shaker, Robin Senge, and Eyke Hüllermeier

Department of Mathematics and Computer Science
University of Marburg, Germany
Tel.: (06421) 2821567
Fax: (06421) 2821573
{shaker, senge, eyke}@mathematik.uni-marburg.de

Abstract

Fuzzy pattern trees have recently been introduced as a novel model class for machine learning. In this paper, we consider the problem of learning fuzzy pattern trees for binary classification in the setting of data streams. Apart from its practical relevance, this problem is also interesting from a methodological point of view. First, the aspect of efficiency plays an important role in the context of data streams, since learning has to be accomplished under hard time (and memory) constraints. Moreover, a learning algorithm should be adaptive in the sense that an up-to-date model is offered at any time, taking new data items into consideration as soon as they arrive and perhaps forgetting old ones that have become obsolete due to a change of the underlying data generating process. In this paper, we develop methods for pattern tree learning that meet these requirements. In a first experimental study, we compare our method to Hoeffding trees, a state-of-the-art classifier on data streams.

1 Introduction

Fuzzy pattern tree induction was recently introduced as a novel machine learning method for classification by Huang, Gedeon and Nikravesh [1]. Independently, the same type of model was proposed in [2] under the name "fuzzy operator tree". Roughly speaking, a fuzzy pattern tree is a hierarchical, tree-like structure, whose inner nodes are marked with generalized (fuzzy) logical and arithmetic operators, and whose leaf nodes are associated with fuzzy predicates on input attributes. A pattern tree propagates information from the leafs to the root node: A node takes the values of its descendants as input, combines them using the respective operator, and submits the output to its predecessor. Thus, a pattern tree implements a recursive mapping producing outputs in the unit interval.

The model class of fuzzy pattern trees is interesting for several reasons, especially from an interpretation point of view. Generally, each tree can be considered as a kind of logical description of a class.[1] In this regard, pattern trees can be considered as a viable alternative to classical fuzzy rule models. However, compared to rule-based models, the hierarchical structure of pattern trees further allows for a more compact representation and for trading off accuracy against model simplicity in a seamless manner.

In this paper, we consider the problem of learning fuzzy pattern trees for binary classification in the setting of evolving data streams. More specifically, building on the algorithm

---

[1] Actually, the description is not purely logical, since arithmetic (averaging) operators are also allowed.

for pattern tree induction as proposed in [3], we develop an online version capable of learning from a stream of data in an incremental manner.

The rest of the paper is organized as follows. In Section 2, we start with a brief description of the data stream scenario and recall the special requirements it involves for learning. Fuzzy pattern trees are explained in Section 3, in which we also introduce an algorithm for learning such trees in batch mode. An extension of this algorithm for learning from data streams in then proposed in Section 4. Finally, an empirical evaluation of this method is presented in Section 5, where evolving fuzzy pattern trees are compared with so-called Hoeffding trees [4] on different types of data streams, both in terms of performance and readability.

2 Learning on Data Streams

In recent years, so-called data streams have attracted considerable attention in different fields of computer science, including database systems, data mining, and distributed systems. As the notion suggests, a data stream can roughly be thought of as an ordered sequence of data items, where the input arrives more or less continuously as time progresses [5, 6, 7]. There are various applications in which streams of this type are produced, such as network monitoring, telecommunication systems, customer click streams, stock markets, or any type of multi-sensor system.

A data stream system may constantly produce huge amounts of data. Regarding aspects of data storage, management, processing, and analysis, the continuous arrival of data items in multiple, rapid, time-varying, and potentially unbounded streams raises new challenges and research problems. Indeed, it is usually not feasible to simply store the arriving data in a traditional database management system in order to perform operations on that data later on. Rather, stream data must generally be processed in an online, incremental manner so as to guarantee that results are up-to-date and that queries can be answered with small time delay.

Domingos and Hulten [8] list a number of properties that an ideal stream mining system should possess, and suggest corresponding design decisions: the system uses only a limited amount of memory; the time to process a single record is short and ideally constant; the data is volatile and a single data record accessed only once; the model produced in an incremental way is equivalent to the model that would have been obtained through common batch learning (on all data records so far); the learning algorithm should react to concept drift in a proper way and maintain a model that always reflects the current concept.

Apart from processing and querying tools, methods for mining and learning on data streams have attracted a lot of attention in recent years [9, 7]. Corresponding algorithms must not only work in an incremental manner, but should also be *adaptive* in the sense of being able to adapt to an evolving environment in which the data (stream) generating process may change over time. Thus, the handling of changing concepts is of utmost importance in mining data streams [10].

A few frameworks and software systems for mining data streams have been released in recent years, including VFML [11] and MOA [12]. VFML is a toolkit for mining high-speed data streams and very large data sets. MOA is a framework for dealing with massive

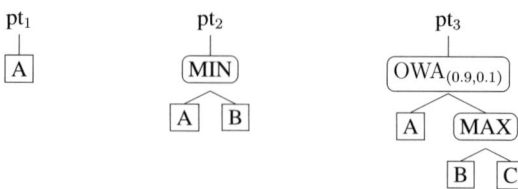

Figure 1: Examples of fuzzy pattern trees. MIN and MAX denote, respectively, the minim t-norm and maximum t-conorm. OWA stands for the ordered weighted average operator (parameterized by a weight vector).

amounts of evolving data streams. It includes data stream generators and several classifiers, and also offers different methods for classifier evaluation. MOA is also able to interact with the popular WEKA environment [13].

3 Fuzzy Pattern Trees

A fuzzy pattern tree (FPT) is a hierarchical, tree-like structure, whose inner nodes are marked with generalized (fuzzy) logical and arithmetic operators, and whose leaf nodes are associated with fuzzy predicates on input attributes. A pattern tree propagates information from the leaf to the root node: A node takes the values of its descendants as input, combines them using the respective operator, and submits the output to its predecessor. Thus, a pattern tree implements a recursive mapping producing outputs in the unit interval.

3.1 Tree Structure and Model Components

We proceed from the common setting of supervised learning and assume an attribute-value representation of instances, which means that an instance is a vector

$$x \in \mathbb{X} = \mathbb{X}_1 \times \mathbb{X}_2 \times \ldots \times \mathbb{X}_m \ ,$$

where $\mathbb{X}_i$ is the domain of the i-th attribute A_i. Each domain $\mathbb{X}_i$ is discretized by means of a fuzzy partition, that is, a set of fuzzy subsets

$$F_{i,j} : \mathbb{X}_i \to [0,1] \qquad (j = 1, \ldots, n_i)$$

such that $\sum_{j=1}^{n_j} F_{i,j}(x) > 0$ for all $x \in \mathbb{X}_i$. The $F_{i,j}$ are often associated with linguistic labels such as "small" or "large", in which case they are also referred to as *fuzzy terms*. In the case of binary classification, each instance is associated with a class label $y \in \mathbb{Y} = \{y_0, y_1\}$, where y_1 denotes the positive and y_0 the negative class, respectively. A training example is a tuple $(x, y) \in \mathbb{X} \times \mathbb{Y}$.

Unlike decision trees [14], which assume an input at the root node and output a class prediction at each leaf, pattern trees process information in the reverse direction. The input of a pattern tree is entered at the leaf nodes. More specifically, a leaf node is labeled by an attribute A_i and a fuzzy subset $F_{i,j}$ of the corresponding domain $\mathbb{X}_i$. Given an instance $x = (x_1, \ldots, x_m) \in \mathbb{X}$ as an input, the node produces $F_{i,j}(x_i)$ as an output, that is, the degree of membership of x_i in $F_{i,j}$. This degree of membership is then propagated to the parent node.

Internal nodes are labeled by generalized logical or arithmetic operators, including t-norms and t-conorms [15] as well as weighted and ordered weighted average [16, 17]. These operators provide a continuous spectrum ranging from very strict, conjunctive over averaging to compensatory, disjunctive aggregation; for technical details, we refer to [3].

The results of the evaluations of internal nodes are propagated to the parents of these nodes in a recursive way. The output eventually produced by a pattern tree is given by the output of its root node; like for all other nodes, it is a number in the unit interval. In the case of binary classification, a discrete prediction can be produced via thresholding: The positive class is predicted if the output exceeds a threshold t (typically $1/2$), otherwise the negative class. Fig. 1 shows some exemplary pattern trees.

3.2 Learning Fuzzy Pattern Trees in Batch Mode

The basic algorithm for learning a pattern tree for binary classification in batch mode is presented in pseudo-code in Fig. 2. It implements a beam search and maintains the B best models (trees) so far ($B = 5$ is used as a default value). The algorithm starts by initializing the set of all primitive pattern trees $\mathbf{P}$. A primitive tree is a tree that consists of only one node, labeled by a fuzzy term. Additionally, the first candidate set, $\mathbf{C}^0$, is initialized by the B best primitive pattern trees, i.e., the trees being maximally similar to the target (see Section 3.3).

After initialization, the algorithm iterates over all candidate trees. Starting from line 11, it seeks to improve the currently selected candidate C_i^{t-1} in terms of performance. To this end, new candidates are created by tentatively replacing exactly one leaf node L (labeled by a fuzzy term) of C_i^{t-1} by a new subtree. This new subtree is a three-node pattern tree that again contains L as one of its leaf nodes (see Fig. 3 for an illustration). The new candidate tree thus obtained is then evaluated by computing its performance. Having tried all possible replacements of all leaf nodes of the trees in $\mathbf{C}^i$, the B best candidates are selected and passed to the next iteration, unless the termination criterion is fulfilled. More specifically, our algorithm stops if

$$\text{perf}_{max}^t < (1 + \epsilon)\text{perf}_{max}^{t-1} , \tag{1}$$

i.e., if the relative improvement is smaller than ϵ, where $\epsilon \in (0, 1)$ is a user-defined parameter.

3.3 Performance Evaluation

To evaluate the performance of a pattern tree, we compare the output of our pattern tree for each training example to its respective target output. More precisely, a tree will make predictions in the unit interval, which can be considered as membership degrees of a fuzzy subset B of the training data: $B(x^{(i)}) = \text{PT}(x^{(i)})$ for all training instances $x^{(i)}$. This fuzzy subset can then be compared to the true subset of positive (and hence implicitly

Top-down Algorithm

1: {Initialization}
2: $\mathbf{P} = \{A_{ij}\}, i = 1, ..., n; j = 1, ..., m$
3: $\mathbf{C}^0 = argmaxB_{P \in \mathbf{P}}[Sim(P, X_0)]$
4: $\epsilon = 0.0025$
5: $t = 0$
6: {Induction}
7: {Loop on iterations}
8: **while** true **do**
9:    $t = t + 1$
10:    $\mathbf{C}^t = \mathbf{C}^{t-1}$
11:    {Loop on each candidate}
12:    **for all** $C_i^{t-1} \in \mathbf{C}^{k-1}$ **do**
13:       {Loop on each leaf of the chosen candidate}
14:       **for all** $l \in leafs(C_i^{t-1})$ **do**
15:          {Loop on each available operator ψ}
16:          **for all** $\psi \in \Psi$ **do**
17:             {Loop on nearly each primitive pattern tree}
18:             **for all** $P \in \mathbf{P} \backslash l$ **do**
19:                $\mathbf{C}^t = \mathbf{C}^t \cup ReplaceLeaf(C_i^{t-1}, l, \psi, P)$
20:             **end for**
21:          **end for**
22:       **end for**
23:    **end for**
24:    $\mathbf{C}^t = argmaxB_{C_i^t \in \mathbf{C}^t}[Perf(C_i^t, X_0)]$
25:    $perf_{max}^t = max_{C_i^t \in \mathbf{C}^t}(Perf(C_i^t, X_0))$
26:    $perf_{max}^{t-1} = max_{C_i^{t-1} \in \mathbf{C}^{t-1}}(Perf(C_i^{t-1}, X_0))$
27:    **if** $perf_{max}^t < (1 + \epsilon)perf_{max}^{t-1}$ **then**
28:       **break**
29:    **end if**
30: **end while**
31: **return** $argmax_{C_i^t \in \mathbf{C}^t}[Perf(C_i^t, X_0)]$

Figure 2: Top-down algorithm for learning fuzzy pattern trees.

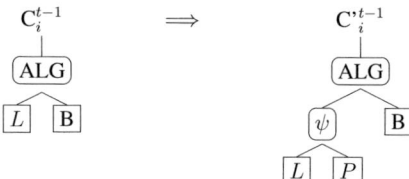

Figure 3: Top-down induction: A leaf node is expanded through replacement with a three-node tree.

to the true subset of negative) examples, namely the set A defined by $A(\boldsymbol{x}^{(i)}) = 1$ if $\boldsymbol{x}^{(i)}$ is a positive example and $A(\boldsymbol{x}^{(i)}) = 0$ if it is a negative example.

The measure is distance-based and inversely related to the root mean squared error (RMSE) between the respective fuzzy sets:

$$Perf(A, B) = 1 - \sqrt{\frac{\sum_{i=1}^{n} (A(\boldsymbol{x}^{(i)}) - B(\boldsymbol{x}^{(i)}))^2}{|\mathcal{T}|}} . \tag{2}$$

3.4 Fuzzy Partitions

To make pattern tree learning amenable to numeric attributes, these attributes have to be "fuzzified" and discretized beforehand. Fuzzification is needed because fuzzy logical operators at the inner nodes of the tree expect values between 0 and 1 as input, while discretization is needed to limit the number of candidate trees in each iteration of the learning algorithm. Besides, fuzzification may also support the interpretability of the model.

Fuzzy partitions can of course be defined in various ways. In our implementation, we discretize a domain $\mathbb{X}_i$ using three fuzzy sets $F_{i,1}, F_{i,2}, F_{i,3}$ associated, respectively, with the terms "low", "medium" and "high". The first and the third fuzzy set are defined as

$$F_{i,1}(x) = \begin{cases} 1 & x < min \\ 0 & x > max \\ \frac{max - x}{max - min} & otherwise \end{cases}, \tag{3}$$

$$F_{i,3}(x) = \begin{cases} 1 & x > max \\ 0 & x < min \\ \frac{x - min}{max - min} & otherwise \end{cases}, \tag{4}$$

with min and max being the minimum and the maximum value of the attribute in the training data. Noting that all operators appearing at inner nodes of a pattern tree are monotone increasing in their arguments, it is clear that these fuzzy sets can capture two types of influence of an attribute on the class membership, namely a positive and a negative one: If the value of a numeric attribute increases, the membership of the "high"-term of that attribute also increases (positive influence), whereas the membership of the "low"-term decreases (negative influence).

Apart from monotone dependencies, it is of course possible that a non-extreme attribute value is "preferred" by a class. The fuzzy set $F_{i,2}$ is meant to capture dependencies of this type. It is defined as a triangular fuzzy set with center c:

$$F_{i,2}(x) = \begin{cases} 0 & x \leq min \\ \frac{x - min}{c - min} & min < x \leq c \\ 1 - \frac{x - c}{max - c} & c < x < max \\ 0 & x \geq max \end{cases} \tag{5}$$

The parameter c is determined so as to maximize the absolute (Pearson) correlation between the membership degrees of the attribute values in $F_{i,2}$ and the corresponding class information (encoded by 1 for instances belonging to the class and 0 for instances of other classes) on the training data. In case of a negative correlation, $F_{i,2}$ is replaced by its negation $1 - F_{i,2}$.

Finally, nominal attributes are modeled as degenerated fuzzy sets: For each value v of the attribute, a fuzzy set with the following membership function is introduced:

$$Term_v(x) = \begin{cases} 1 & x = v \\ 0 & otherwise \end{cases}$$

4 Evolving Fuzzy Pattern Trees

The basic idea of the evolving version of fuzzy pattern tree learning (eFPT) is to maintain an ensemble of pattern trees, consisting of a current (active) model and a set of neighbor models. The current model is used to make predictions, while the neighbor models are kept ready to replace this model in case of a drop in performance, caused, for example, by a drift of the concept to be learned. More generally, the current model is replaced whenever its performance appears to be significantly worse than the performance of one of the neighbor models; in this case, the set of neighbors it revised, too.

More specifically, this set is always defined by the set of trees that are "close" to the current model—hence the term "neighbor"—in the sense of being derivable from this model by means of a single expansion or pruning step. Like in batch learning, an expansion replaces a leaf L of the current tree by a three-node pattern tree that again contains L as one of its leaf nodes. A pruning step is essentially undoing an expansion. More precisely, each inner node except the root can be replaced by one of its sibling nodes (which means that the subtree rooted by this node is lifted by one level, while the subtree rooted by the other sibling is pruned).

Looking at the neighbor trees as the local neighborhood of the current model in the space of pattern trees, the algorithm is performing a kind of adaptive local search in this space and, therefore, is somewhat comparable to a discrete variant of a swarm-based search procedure (the collective movement of the active model and its "surrounding" neighbor models in the search space is similar, for example, to the flocking of a group of birds).

4.1 Performance Monitoring and Hypothesis Testing

The error rate of the current model PT and, likewise, of all neighbors is calculated on a sliding window consisting of the last n training examples:

$$\tau = \frac{1}{n} \sum_{i=1}^{n} (y_i - \hat{y}_i)^2 \; , \tag{6}$$

where y_i is the class observed in the i-th time step and $\hat{y}_i$ its prediction. The length of the sliding window, n, is a parameter of the method (our default value is $n = 100$).

Storing the predictions and observed class labels, τ can easily be updated in a incremental way:

$$\tau \leftarrow \tau - \frac{1}{n} \left((y_{n+1} - \hat{y}_{n+1})^2 - (y_1 - \hat{y}_1)^2 \right) \; , \tag{7}$$

where y_{n+1} is a new observation and y_1 the oldest example in the current window.

In order to decide whether or not one of the neighbor trees is superior to the current model, each update of the error rates is followed by a statistical hypothesis test. Let τ_0 and τ_1 denote, respectively, the error rate of the current model and a neighbor tree. We are then testing the null hypothesis $H_0 : \tau_0 \leq \tau_1$ against the alternative hypothesis $H_1 : \tau_0 > \tau_1$. A suitable test statistic for doing so is

$$\frac{\sqrt{n}\,(\tau_0 - \tau_1)}{\sqrt{2\hat{\tau}(1-\hat{\tau})}} \ ,$$

where $\hat{\tau} = \frac{\tau_0 + \tau_1}{2}$ and n is the sample size (window length). This test statistic approximately follows a normal distribution, and the null hypothesis is rejected if it exceeds a critical threshold Z_α; here, α denotes the required significance level. Note that this level controls the proneness of the algorithm toward changes of the model: The smaller α, the less often the model will be changed (our default value is $\alpha = 0.01$).

The above test is conducted for each alternative tree, and if H_0 is rejected in at least one of these tests, the current model is replaced by the alternative for which the test statistic was the highest. In this case, the fuzzy partitions of the numerical attributes are recomputed, too, using the data in the current window.

4.2 Summary of the Algorithm

The algorithm for learning evolving fuzzy pattern trees on data streams is summarized in Fig. 5. The main steps of this algorithm are as follows:

1. In the initialization phase, a first pattern tree is learned in batch mode on a small set of training examples. The current model is initialized with this tree.

2. The set of neighbor trees is generated for the current model (line 3).

3. Upon the arrival of a new example, the sliding window is shifted, the error rates for the current model and all neighbors are updated, and the error rates of the neighbors are compared to the one of the current model.

4. If a neighbor is significantly better than the current model, the latter is replaced by the former; in this case,

   (a) the primitive pattern trees are reinitialized,
   (b) the operators used in the pattern trees are optimized (e.g., by recomputing optimal weight parameters for averaging operators),
   (c) the set of neighbor trees is recomputed (see Fig. 4).

5. Loop at step 3

Procedure GenerateNeighborTrees(*C*)

1: {Initialization}
2: $\mathbf{P} = \{A_{ij}\}, i = 1, ..., n; j = 1, ..., m$
3: $\mathbf{N} = Null$
4: {Creating the neighbor extension trees}
5: {Loop on each leaf of the current tree}
6: **for all** $l_{chosen} \in leafs(C)$ **do**
7:     {Loop on each available operator ψ}
8:     **for all** $\psi \in \Psi$ **do**
9:         {Loop on nearly each primitive pattern tree}
10:         **for all** $P \in \mathbf{P} \backslash l_{chosen}$ **do**
11:            $\mathbf{N} = \mathbf{N} \cup ReplaceLeaf(C, l_{chosen}, \psi, P)$
12:         **end for**
13:     **end for**
14: **end for**
15: {Creating the neighbor pruning trees}
16: {Loop on each internal node of the current tree}
17: **for all** $n_{chosen} \in Internalnodes(C)$ **do**
18:     {Replacing the chosen node by its children nodes}
19:     $\mathbf{N} = \mathbf{N} \cup ReplaceNode(C, n_{chosen}, child1)$
20:     $\mathbf{N} = \mathbf{N} \cup ReplaceNode(C, n_{chosen}, child2)$
21: **end for**
22: **return** N

Figure 4: Algorithm for generating neighbor trees.

5 Empirical Evaluation

In this section, we compare our evolving fuzzy pattern trees (eFPT) with Hoeffding trees [4], a state-of-the-art approach for classification on data streams, in terms of performance and stability. In particular, we are interested in how these two algorithms react to concept drift.

The experiments are performed using the MOA framework, which offers the Concept-DriftStream procedure for simulating concept drift. The idea underlying this procedure is to mix two pure distributions in a probabilistic way, smoothly varying the corresponding probability degrees. In the beginning, examples are taken from the first pure stream with probability 1, and this probability is decreased in favor of the second stream in the course of time. More specifically, the probability is controlled by means of the sigmoid function

$$f(t) = \left(1 + e^{-s(t-t_0)}\right)^{-1} .$$

This function has two parameters: t_0 is the mid point of the change process, while s controls the length of this process.

A non-trivial issue in learning from data streams concerns the evaluation of an evolving classifier system. In fact, compared to standard batch learning, simple one-dimensional

Evolving Fuzzy Pattern Tree

1: {Initialization}
2: $C = BatchPatternTree$
3: $\mathbf{N} = GenerateNeighbourTrees(C)$
4: {New instance form the stream is present}
5: **while** incoming instance t **do**
6:     {Update the error rate for the current tree}
7:     $\tau_{current}^{t} = \tau_{current}^{t-1} - \frac{1}{n}L(y_1, \hat{y}_1) + \frac{1}{n}L_{(y_{n+1}, \hat{y}_{n+1})}$
8:     {Loop on each neighbor tree}
9:     **for all** $N_k \in \mathbf{N}$ **do**
10:         {Update the error rate for each neighbor tree}
11:         $\tau_k^{t} = \tau_k^{t-1} - \frac{1}{n}L(y_{1,k}, \hat{y}_1) + \frac{1}{n}L_{(y_{n+1,k}, \hat{y}_{n+1})}$
12:     **end for**
13:     {Testing the null hypothesis that the current error rate is lower than that of all neighbor trees}
14:     **if** $\exists N_k \in \mathbf{N}$: Reject $H_0(\tau_{current}^{t} < \tau_k^{t})$ **then**
15:         {A neighbor tree with a lower error rate is found}
16:         $C = N_k$
17:         {Recompute all primitive pattern trees}
18:         $\mathbf{P} = \{A_{ij}\}, i = 1, ..., n; j = 1, ..., m$
19:         $OptimizeUsedOperator(C)$
20:         $\mathbf{N} = GenerateNeighborTrees(C)$
21:     **end if**
22: **end while**

Figure 5: Evolving Fuzzy Pattern Trees.

performance measures such as classification accuracy are not immediately applicable, or at least not able to capture the time-varying behavior of a classifier in a proper way. Besides, additional criteria become relevant, too, such as the handling of concept drift, many of which are rather vague and hard to quantify. In our experiments, we employ a holdout procedure for measuring predictive accuracy, which is offered by the MOA framework. Here, the idea is to interleave the training and the testing phase of a classifier as follows: the classifier is trained incrementally on a block of m instances and then evaluated (but no longer adapted) on the next n instances, then again trained on the next m and tested on the subsequent n instances, and so forth; as parameters, we use $m = 5000$ and $n = 1000$.

5.1 First Experiment: Hyperplane Data

The first experiment uses data taken from a hyperplane generator. Here, the instance space is given by the d-dimensional Euclidean space, and the decision boundary is defined in terms of a hyperplance in this space. The ConceptDriftStream procedure mixing streams produced by two different hyperplanes simulates a rotating hyperplane. Using this procedure, we generated one million examples connecting two hyperplanes in 4-dimensional space, with $t_0 = 500,000$ and $w = 100,000$.

As can be seen in Fig. 6, eFPT fits the pattern trees quite well to the data, without a significant drop in accuracy during the concept drift. The Hoeffding tree, on the other hand, needs quite a long time to learn the concept and, moreover, is strongly affected by the drift; it recovers only lately, but then reaches almost the same level of accuracy as eFPT.

5.2 Second Experiment: Decision Tree Data

In the above experiment, the Hoeffding tree was arguably put as a disadvantage, since fitting a hyperplane with a decision tree is a quite difficult problem. In a second experiment, we therefore use a random tree generator to produce examples. This generator constructs a decision tree by making random splits on attribute values and then assigns random class labels to the leaf nodes. Obviously, this generator is favorable for the Hoeffding tree.

Again, the same ConceptDriftStream is used, but this time mixing two random tree generators. As can be seen in Fig. 7, the Hoeffding tree is now able to outperform eFPT in the first phase of the learning process; in fact, it reaches an accuracy of close to 100%, which is not unexpected given that the Hoeffding tree is ideally tailored for this kind of data. Once again, however, the Hoeffding tree is much more affected by the concept drift than the pattern tree learner, which is remarkably stable.

The same figure shows results for different parameterizations of eFPT. As can be seen, for example, using a significance level of $\alpha = 0.015$ yields slightly better results than $\alpha = 0.01$. We also tried a version in which the primitive pattern trees are not recomputed after a replacement of the current model. As expected, this variant performs worse than the original one, showing that a recomputation is indeed useful.

5.3 Model Size

Apart from comparing the performance of the methods, we also looked at the size of the models they produce. In this regard, eFPT is clearly superior. In fact, the size of the fuzzy pattern trees is rather stable over time and remains on a low level—the maximum size observed in the two experiments is 19 nodes. As opposed to this, the Hoeffding tree seems to grow linearly with the length of the stream and becomes as large as 747 nodes in the hyperplane and 851 nodes in the random trees setting (see Fig. 8). Needless to say, a model of that size is no longer understandable.

6 Summary and Conclusions

We have proposed an evolving version of the fuzzy pattern tree classifier that meets the increased requirements of incremental learning on data streams. The key idea of eFPT is to maintain, in addition to the current model, a set of neighbor trees that can replace the current model if the performance of the latter is no longer optimal. Thus, a modification of the current model is realized implicitly in the form of a replacement by an alternative

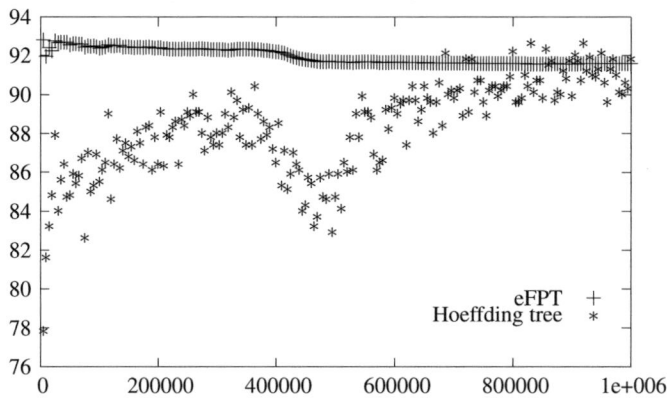

Figure 6: Comparison of the performance in case of the hyperplane generator.

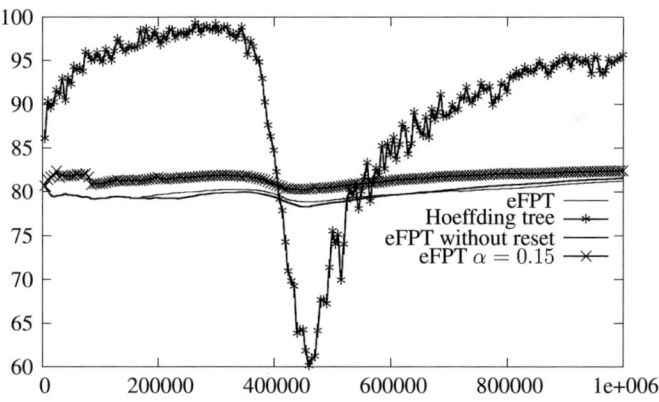

Figure 7: Comparison of the performance in case of a random tree generator.

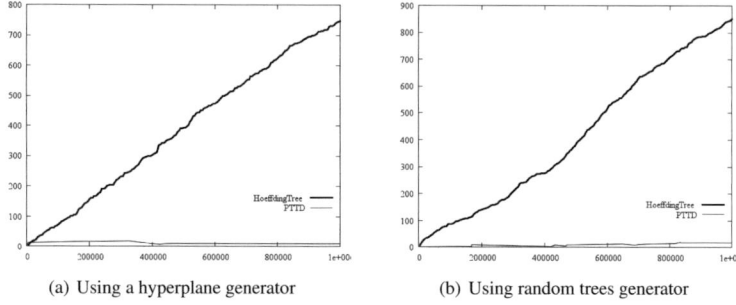

(a) Using a hyperplane generator (b) Using random trees generator

Figure 8: Comparision of the model size between eFPT and Hoeffding trees.

tree. A replacement decision is made on the basis of the performance of all models, which is monitored continuously on a sliding window of fixed length.

In a first experimental study, we compared eFPT with Hoeffding trees, a state-of-the-art classifier for data streams. The results we obtained are quite promising. Put in a nutshell, they suggest that eFPT is competitive in terms of accuracy, while being less affected by concept drift and producing models that are much smaller.

Needless to say, however, our experiments are not comprehensive enough to draw general conclusions and, therefore, should be expanded in future work. Apart from using more data sets, we are especially interested in comparing our approach with other evolving fuzzy systems that have been proposed in the literature [18, 19]. Another important aspect of future work concerns the computational efficiency of eFPT, which still offers scope for improvement. In particular, we are currently working on strategies for limiting the number of neighbor models, since this number may become large and significantly hamper the performance of the method.

References

[1] Huang, Z.; Gedeon, T. D.; Nikravesh, M.: Pattern Trees Induction: A New Machine Learning Method. *IEEE T. Fuzzy Systems* 16 (2008) 4, S. 958–970.

[2] Yi, Y.; Fober, T.; Hüllermeier, E.: Fuzzy Operator Trees for Modeling Rating Functions. *International Journal of Computational Intelligence and Applications* 8 (2009) 4, S. 413–428.

[3] Senge, R.; Hüllermeier, E.: Top-Down Induction of Fuzzy Pattern Trees. *IEEE Transactions on Fuzzy Systems* (2010). To appear.

[4] Hulten, G.; Spencer, L.; Domingos, P.: Mining time-changing data streams. In: *Proceedings of the seventh ACM SIGKDD international conference on Knowledge discovery and data mining, August 26-29, 2001, San Francisco, CA, USA. ACM, 2001*, S. 97–106.

[5] Golab, L.; Özsu, M. T.: Issues in data stream management. *SIGMOD Record* 32 (2003) 2, S. 5–14.

[6] Garofalakis, M. N.; Gehrke, J.: Querying and Mining Data Streams: You Only Get One Look. In: *Proceedings of 28th International Conference on Very Large Data Bases, August 20-23, 2002, Hong Kong, China.*

[7] Gama, J.; Gaber, M. M.: *Learning from Data Streams.* Springer-Verlag, Berlin, New York. 2007.

[8] Domingos, P.; Hulten, G.: Catching up with the Data: Research Issues in Mining Data Streams. In: *ACM SIGMOD Workshop on Research Issues in Data Mining and Knowledge Discovery, Santa Barbara, CA, USA, May 20, 2001.*

[9] Gaber, M. M.; Zaslavsky, A. B.; Krishnaswamy, S.: Mining data streams: a review. *SIGMOD Record* 34 (2005) 2, S. 18–26.

[10] Kifer, D.; Ben-David, S.; Gehrke, J.: Detecting Change in Data Streams. In: *Proceedings of the Thirtieth International Conference on Very Large Data Bases, Toronto, Canada, August 31 - September 3 2004*, S. 180–191.

[11] Hulten, G.; Domingos, P.: VFML a toolkit for mining high-speed time-changing data streams. URL http://www.cs.washington.edu/dm/vfml/. 2003.

[12] Bifet, A.; Kirkby, R.: *Massive Online Analysis Manual.* 2009.

[13] Witten, I. H.; Frank, E.: *Data Mining: Practical machine learning tools and techniques.* Morgan Kaufmann, 2 Aufl. 2005.

[14] Quinlan, J. R.: *C4.5: Programs for Machine Learning.* Morgan Kaufmann. ISBN 1-55860-238-0. 1993.

[15] Klement, E. P.; Mesiar, R.; Pap, E.: *Triangular Norms.* Kluwer Academic Publishers. 2002.

[16] Schweizer, B.; Sklar, A.: *Probabilistic Metric Spaces.* New York. 1983.

[17] Yager, R.: On ordered weighted averaging aggregation operators in multi criteria decision making. *IEEE Transactions on Systems, Man and Cybernetics* 18(1) (1988), S. 183–190.

[18] Angelov, P. P.; Lughofer, E.; Zhou, X.: Evolving fuzzy classifiers using different model architectures. *Fuzzy Sets and Systems* 159 (2008) 23, S. 3160–3182.

[19] Lughofer, E.: FLEXFIS: A Robust Incremental Learning Approach for Evolving Takagi-Sugeno Fuzzy Models. *IEEE T. Fuzzy Systems* 16 (2008) 6, S. 1393–1410.

Automatische Segmentierung von Zellkernen und den dazugehörigen Zellen in Zellclustern für die Biokompatibilitätsprüfung

S. Buhl, E. Eisenbarth, B. Neumann, M. Schneider, U. Lehmann

Institut für Computer Science, Vision und Computational Intelligence,
Fachhochschule Südwestfalen, Frauenstuhlweg 31, 58644 Iserlohn
Tel. (02371) 566-214 Fax (02371) 566-420
E-Mail: {Buhl, Eisenbarth, Neumann.B, MSchneider, Lehmann}@fh-swf.de

1 Zusammenfassung

Im vorliegenden Paper wird ein Verfahren vorgestellt, mit dem zuerst zytologisch gefärbte Zellen in mikroskopischen Bildaufnahmen mit Hilfe des Histogram Backprojection (HB) Algorithmus [1] segmentiert und in Einzelzellen und Zellclustern klassifiziert werden. Mit dem HB Algorithmus werden dann die Zellkernregionen der Zellen segmentiert und durch geeignete CV-Methoden aufbereitet. Die so ermittelten Zellkernbereiche unterstützen das Segmentieren der Zellen in den Zellverbänden. In den Zellclustern werden nun die sogenannten „Dominant Contour Points" [2] gesucht, die bevorzugt innerhalb von Zellverengungen liegen. An diesen Stellen macht eine Zelltrennung aus biologischer Sicht am meisten Sinn. Zum Festlegen der Trennlinien werden pro Trennung jeweils zwei sich gegenüberliegende Konturpunkte benötigt. Zum Auffinden korrespondierender Konturpunkte wird durch den Zellcluster von einem Zellkern zum nächsten Zellkern der kürzeste Pfad mit dem A*-Algorithmus[3] berechnet und unter Berücksichtigung bestimmter Regeln die idealen Konturpunkte zwischen zwei Zellkernen für die Zellseparation ermittelt.

2 Einführung

Bei der Biokompatibilitätsprüfung von Implantatwerkstoffen weisen die zu untersuchenden Zellen komplexe Zellgeometrien auf, ebenso variiert das Material auf dem die Zellen aufgebracht werden, z.B. Titan oder Stahl. Da, wie in Abb. 1 zu erkennen, die Zellmorphologie stark variiert, wird die Segmentierung von Zellen in Zellclustern sehr erschwert.

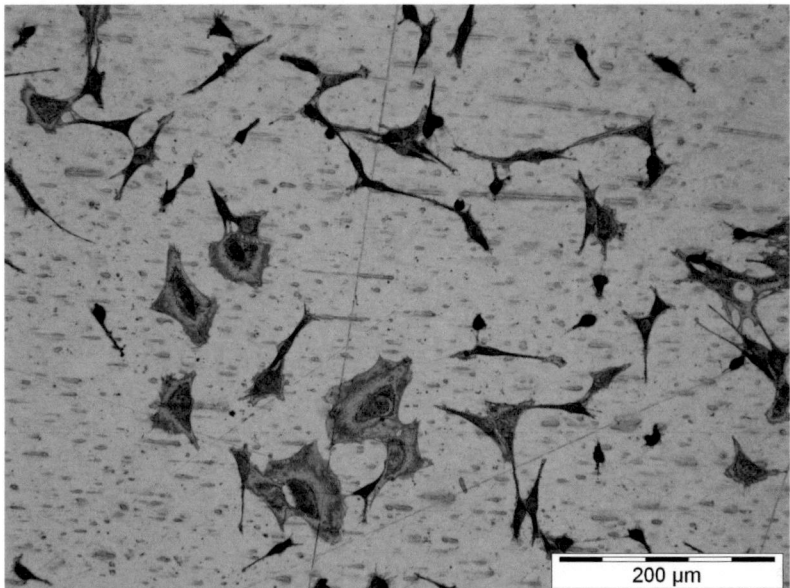

200 µm

Abbildung 1: Zytologisch gefärbte Zellen auf dem Substrat Titan

3 Segmentierung der Zellen und Detektion der Zellkernbereiche

3.1 Zellsegmentierung

Die Zellsegmentierung erfolgt mit Hilfe des Histogram Backprojection (HB) Algorithmus. Er dient zur Lokalisierung von Objekten in einem Bild auf Basis ihrer Farbwerte, wobei im Vorfeld ein geeignetes Farbtemplate des zu suchenden Objektes erstellt werden muss.

Da sich das Zellmaterial farblich gut vom Substrat unterscheidet, bietet sich eine Segmentierung mit dem HB Algorithmus an. Im Vergleich zu anderen Segmentierungsverfahren wie zum Beispiel die Wasserscheidentransformation (siehe Abb. 2 und Abb. 3) oder verschiedene Kantenfilter werden deutlich bessere Segmentierungsergebnisse erzielt. Dies liegt u.a. daran, dass sich im Bild Kratzer vom Poliervorgang wiederfinden und gerade Kantenfilter sensibel darauf reagieren und so das Segmentierungsergebnis verfälschen können. Da die Kratzer in der Regel dunkel erscheinen, stellen sie für den HB Algorithmus meistens kein Problem dar. Das Farbtemplate des zu suchenden Objektes, in unserem Fall die Zellen, wurde mit Hilfe eines entwickelten Software Tools erstellt. In diesem Tool hat man die Möglichkeit in das Bild hineinzuzoomen und Bildbereiche einfach herauszukopieren. Diesen Vorgang kann man beliebig wiederholen und am Ende wird aus den vielen verschiedenen Bildbereichen ein Farbtemplate erstellt.

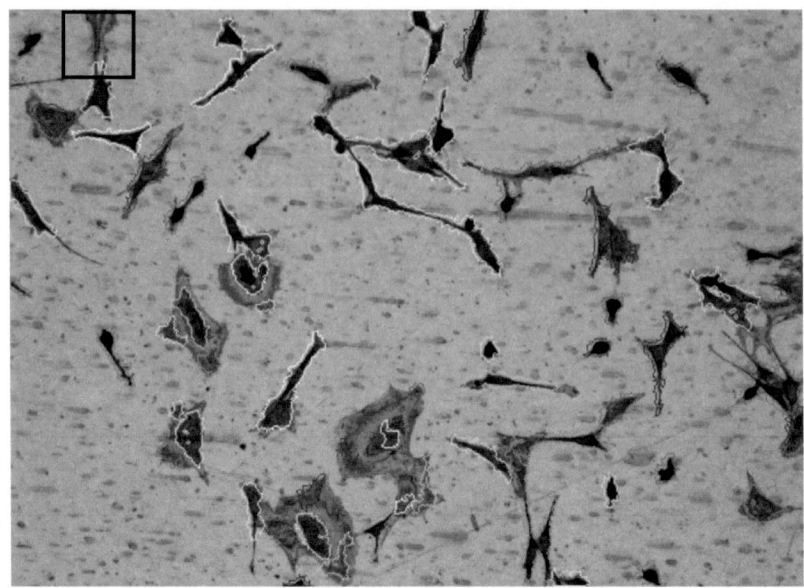

Abbildung 2: Zellsegmentierung mit der Wasserscheidentranformation

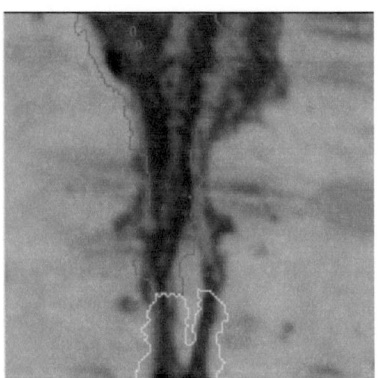

Abbildung 3: Vergrößerung des eingerahmten Bildausschnittes in Abb. 2

In Abb.2 ist das Ergebnis einer Wasserscheidentransformation zur Zellsegmentierung zu sehen. In dem vergrößerten Bildausschnitt in Abb. 3 wird deutlich, dass die Wasserscheidentransformation schlecht zur Zellsegmentierung geeignet ist. Zwar kann der Anfälligkeit gegenüber Bildrauschen z.B. durch eine Glättung des Bildes entgegengewirkt werden, dennoch sind die Segmentierungsergebnisse einer Wasserscheidentransformation bezogen auf unser Bildmaterial nicht zufriedenstellend. Zum einen wurden die Zellkonturen nicht immer korrekt erfasst und zum anderen enthalten die Zellkonturen oft Unterbrechungen, so dass dieselbe Zelle zunächst aus mehreren Konturen besteht und Korrekturarbeiten notwendig macht.

Im Vergleich zur Wasserscheidentransformation liefert der HB Algorithmus bessere Segmentierungsergebnisse (Abb. 4), wobei auch dieses Segmentierungsergebnis noch optimierbar ist, da teilweise Kratzer an den Zellen als Zellbereiche segmentiert werden.

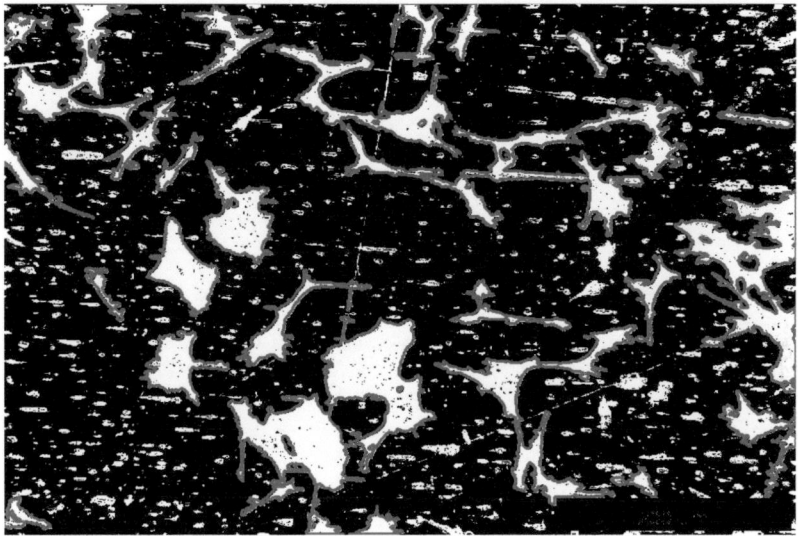

Abbildung 4: Ergebnis einer Zellsegmentierung mit dem HB Algorithmus

3.2   Detektion der Zellkerne

Die Segmentierung der Zellkerne innerhalb der Zellflächen erfolgt auch mit dem HB Algorithmus. Dazu werden im Vorfeld geeignete Farbtemplates erstellt, die möglichst gut die Farben des Zellkernbereiches wiederspiegeln. Da bei diesem Zellmaterial die Kerne in größeren Zellen andere Farbeigenschaften besitzen als in kleineren Zellen, werden zwei verschiedene Farbtemplates benötigt. Bei dem Ergebnisbild des HB Algorithmus handelt es sich um eine Punktewolke mit 2 verschiedenen Farben, wobei eine Farbe jeweils eine bestimmte Klassifizierung wiederspiegelt.

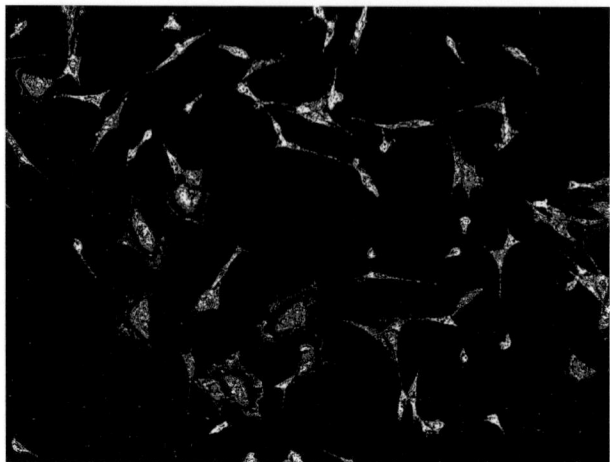

Abbildung 5: Ergebnisbild des Histogram Backprojection Algorithmus zur Zellkernerkennung

Helle Pixel in Abb. 5 stehen für den klassifizierten Zellkernbereich auf Basis der Farben in Template 1 und dunkle Pixel für solche auf Basis der Farben in Template 2. Weiterhin wird das Ergebnis mit CV-Methoden bearbeitet um die Zellkernbereiche festzulegen. Hierzu werden nach einer Bereichsegmentierung erst kleinere Bereiche eliminiert und mit einem Closing benachbarte Farbpunkte zu einer zusammenhängenden Fläche vereinigt.

4   Klassifikation der Zellflächen

Da eine Segmentierung von Zellen auch in Zellclustern erfolgen soll, müssen zunächst die Zellcluster im Bild klassifiziert werden. Die hier verwendeten Zellen sind allerdings sehr variantenreich und so kann kaum durch geometrische Merkmale wie z.B. Zellfläche oder Kompaktheit sicher zwischen Einzelzelle und Zellcluster unterschieden werden. Eine einfache aber sehr effektive Methode ist die iterative Ausführung der Erosion auf eine Zellfläche. Dabei wird die Erosion mit einem kreisförmigen Strukturelement mit Radius 1 Pixel auf die Zellfläche angewandt und anschließend geprüft, ob eine Teilung der Zellfläche erfolgte. Ist dies nicht der Fall, wird die Erosion erneut auf die neu entstandene kleinere Zellfläche angewandt (Abb. 6 und 7).

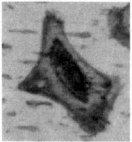   

Abbildung 6: Erosion einer segmentierten Einzelzelle nach 10 bzw. 20 Iterationen

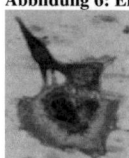  

Abbildung 7: Erosion eines segmentierten Zellclusters nach 5 Iterationen

Ist bis zu einer Grenze I_{max} eine Teilung der Zellfläche erfolgt, so wird ein Zellcluster mit mindestens 2 Zellkernen angenommen. Ist nach I_{max} Iterationen keine Flächentrennung erfolgt oder wurde die vorhandene Zellfläche eliminiert, so wird auf eine Einzelzelle geschlossen.

5   Berechnung der dominanten Konturpunkte

Die zu Zellclustern verbundenen Zellen weisen sehr oft die Gemeinsamkeit auf, dass sich an den zusammengewachsenen Zellbereichen verengte Übergänge befinden, die durch Pfeile in Abb. 8 markiert sind.

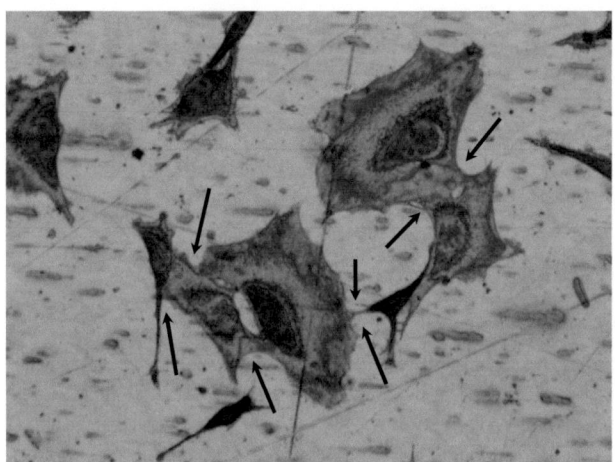

Abbildung 8: Zellverengungen im Cluster, als Ansatzpunkte für eine sinnvolle Zelltrennung

Für eine ordentliche Zellsegmentierung innerhalb eines Clusters ist es nun hilfreich, diese markanten Punkte (DCP) an den Verengungen zu ermitteln. Die Detektion der DCP basiert weitestgehend auf dem Verfahren nach [2], musste allerdings für unsere Aufgabenstellung modifiziert werden. Dazu wird im ersten Schritt der Abstand von jedem Konturpunkt der Zelle in eine vorgegebene Richtung bis zur umschließenden bounding box berechnet.

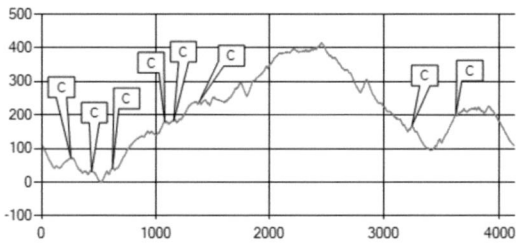

Abbildung 9: Abstandsfunktion zur rechten Seite der bounding box des Zellclusters

In Abb. 9 ist nun die Distanzfunktion beispielhaft für eine Richtung aufgetragen. Die mit einem „C" markierten Funktionswerte stellen ein lokales Maximum da. Diese Punkte müssen für unsere Zwecke noch eine weitere Eigenschaft besitzen. Es wird geprüft, ob der nächste Konturpixel in aktueller Richtung Teil der Zelle ist. Ist dies der Fall, liefert die Funktion true zurück, andernfalls false. Der Punkt wird also nur ein DCP, wenn es sich um ein lokales Maximum handelt und der nächste Punkt in aktueller Richtung Teil der Zelle ist. Diese Berechnung wird dann insgesamt für vier Richtungen wiederholt (oben, unten, links und rechts).

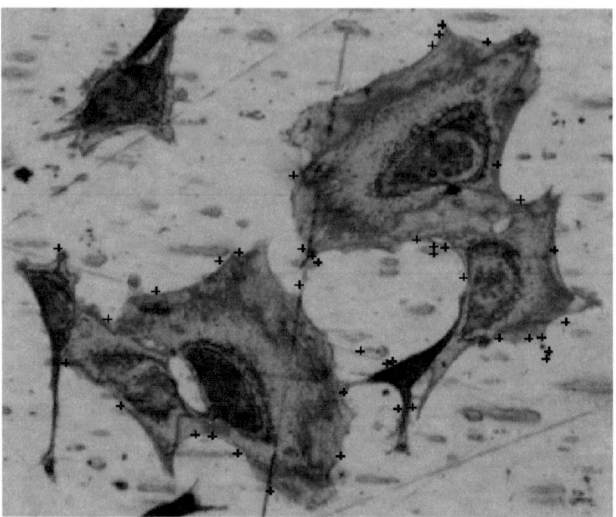

Abbildung 10: Die ermittelten DCPs im Zellcluster

In Abb.10 sind schwarz die gefundenen DCPs für alle Richtungen eingezeichnet. Im Vergleich zu [2] erfolgt die Bestimmung der Maxima in unserem Fall auf eine andere Weise. Es werden nur die Konturpixel als lokale Maxima definiert, bei denen sich der Abstand der vorherigen Pixel zur Bounding Box fünfmal monoton vergrößert hat und die nachfolgenden Pixel analog fünfmal den Abstand zur Bounding Box monoton verringern. Der Grund dafür ist, dass die Zellkontur meist stufig aufgebaut ist, und so eine Bestimmung der lokalen Maxima durch digitale Ableitung unmöglich macht. Die Anzahl der notwendigen Stufen, bei denen sich monoton der Abstand zur bounding box vergrößern muss, ist parametrisiert. So kann die Sensibilität des Algorithmus eingestellt und je nach Bedarf eher mehr oder weniger DCPs erzeugt werden. Wie in Abb. 10 zu sehen, werden auch einige DCPs an ungeeigneten Konturabschnitten erzeugt. Also wird nun eine Methode benötigt, mit der die korrekten DCPs verbunden werden.

6   Pfadberechnung zwischen den Zellkernbereichen

Die Herausforderung liegt nun darin, die DCPs an den aus biologischer Sicht optimalen Stellen miteinander zu verbinden, so dass eine sinnvolle Zelltrennung entsteht. Dazu werden im ersten Schritt von den gefundenen Zellkernen im Cluster die Schwerpunkte berechnet. Ausgehend von dem am meisten links liegenden Schwerpunkt wird der kürzeste Weg zum nächstgelegenen Zellkernschwerpunkt bestimmt und dann wieder zum nächstgelegenen usw. Dafür wird der A*-Algorithmus [3] eingesetzt, der häufig auch in der Spielebranche zum Einsatz kommt.

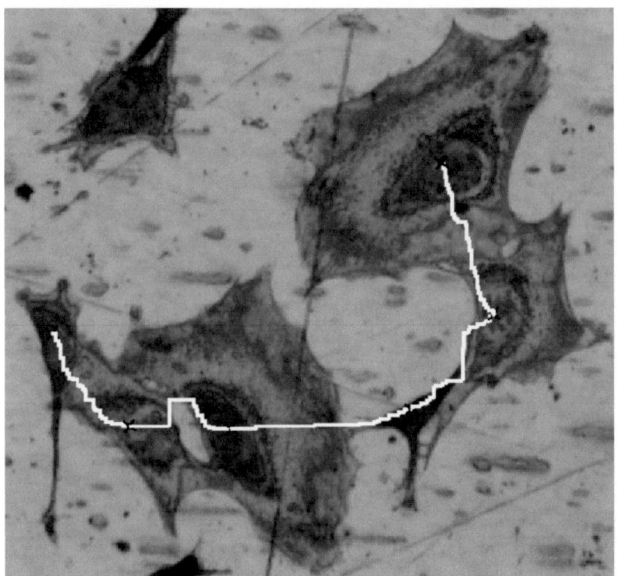

Abbildung 11: Mit dem A*-Algorithmus berechneter kürzester Pfad durch die Zellkernschwer-punkte im Cluster

Dabei müssen mögliche Hindernisse wie z.b. innenliegende Löcher in der Zelle berücksichtigt werden, denn der kürzeste Pfad soll Hindernisse nicht durchkreuzen. Der Algorithmus stellt ausgehend vom Startpunkt für alle Nachbarpixel eine Kostenfunktion auf.

$$f(x,y) = g(x,y) + h(x,y)$$

$g(x,y)$ beschreibt die Kosten vom Startpunkt ausgehend zum aktuellen Punkt und $h(x,y)$ die geschätzten Kosten vom aktuellen Punkt zum Zielpunkt. Wichtig dabei ist, dass die verwendete Heuristik die Kosten nie überschätzt, deshalb ist es sinnvoll die „Luftlinie" vom aktuellen Punkt zum Zielpunkt zu berechnen. Die Kosten für $g(x,y)$ werden in unserem Fall über den Manhatten-Block Abstand berechnet, da die Rechenzeit erheblich kürzer ist im Vergleich zum euklidischen Abstand. Nachdem die Kosten für jeden Nachbarpunkt berechnet wurden wird der Nachbar mit den geringsten Gesamtkosten ausgewählt und die Prozedur wiederholt. Wichtig dabei ist, dass jeder untersuchte Punkt einen Zeiger auf seinen Vorgängerpunkt erhält. So kann der Weg vom Zielpunkt zum Startpunkt zurückverfolgt werden.

Nun werden von den berechneten Pfadpunkten nur die übernommen, die sich außerhalb der Zellkernbereiche befinden, da eine Zelltrennung durch einen vorhandenen Zellkern keinen Sinn macht.

7   Zelltrennung innerhalb der Cluster

Zuerst werden für die Pfadpunkte zwischen zwei Zellkernen die Abstände zu allen DCPs berechnet und der erste DCP übernommen, der die kürzeste Trennlinie zu einem Pfadpunkt außerhalb der Kernregion aufweist. Die Trennlinie muss allerdings die Bedingung erfüllen, dass kein Zellkernbereich geschnitten wird. Schneidet die Linie den Kernbereich wird sie wieder verworfen und das Punktepaar mit dem nächsten niedrigsten Abstand gesucht. Dieser Vorgang wird so oft wiederholt, bis eine gültige Trennlinie erzeugt wurde.

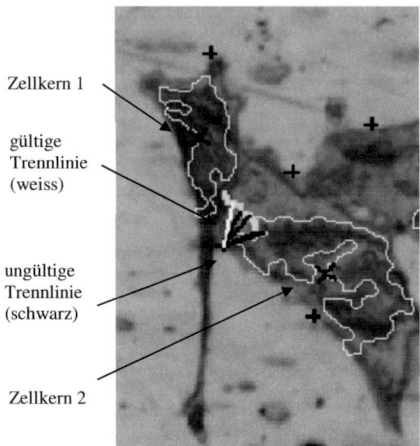

Zellkern 1

gültige
Trennlinie
(weiss)

ungültige
Trennlinie
(schwarz)

Zellkern 2

Abbildung 12: Berechnung einer gültigen Trennlinie zur Zellseparation

Wurde eine gültige Trennlinie hergestellt muss nun der nächstgelegene DCP auf der anderen Seite des Pfades gefunden werden, der mit demselben Pfadpunkt verbunden wird und die Zelltrennung vervollständigt. Um zu prüfen ob ein DCP auf der anderen Seite des Pfades liegt wird das Skalarprodukt der beiden potentiellen Trennungsvektoren gebildet, mit der Bedingung, dass das Ergebnis < 0 sein muss. Nicht in jedem Fall muss es einen passenden zweiten DCP geben, es kann der Fall eintreten, dass alle Trennlinien durch einen Zellkern führen und somit nicht verwendet werden können. Alternativ wird dann der Pfadpunkt auf der Hälfte des Weges zwischen den beiden Kernen selektiert und von dort aus der nächste Konturpunkt auf der einen Seite des Pfades sowie derjenige auf der anderen Seite des Pfades bestimmt. Wenn die Verbindungslinien keinen Zellkernbereich schneiden, handelt es sich um den neuen Grenzbereich der Zellen, ansonsten wird die Verbindungslinie zum danach nächstgelegenen Konturpunkt geprüft, solange bis gültige Trennlinien erzeugt wurden.

8   Ergebnisse und Ausblick

Zellen werden mit Hilfe des iterativen Erosionsklassifikators zu 90% richtig als Zellcluster identifiziert. Probleme bekommt der Klassifikator, wenn z.B. zwei Zellen relativ kompakt aneinander gewachsen sind, so dass eine mehrfache Erosion zu keiner Teilung führt. Hier wird an weiteren Klassifikatoren gearbeitet, die z.B. mittels AdaBoost [4] zu einem stärkeren Gesamtklassifikator trainiert werden könnten. Die Zellteilung mit dem vorgestellten Verfahren funktioniert gut für die meisten Zellcluster. In einigen Fällen, wo der Anteil an Zellkernfarben im Cluster relativ hoch ist, schlägt die Zelltrennung fehl, wie in Abb. 13 die nicht farbigen Clusterkonturen rechts im Bild. Hier wird an einer neuen Methode zur Zelltrennung innerhalb dieser Art von Cluster gearbeitet. Derzeit werden ca. 70% der zu Clustern verbundenen Zellen korrekt isoliert.

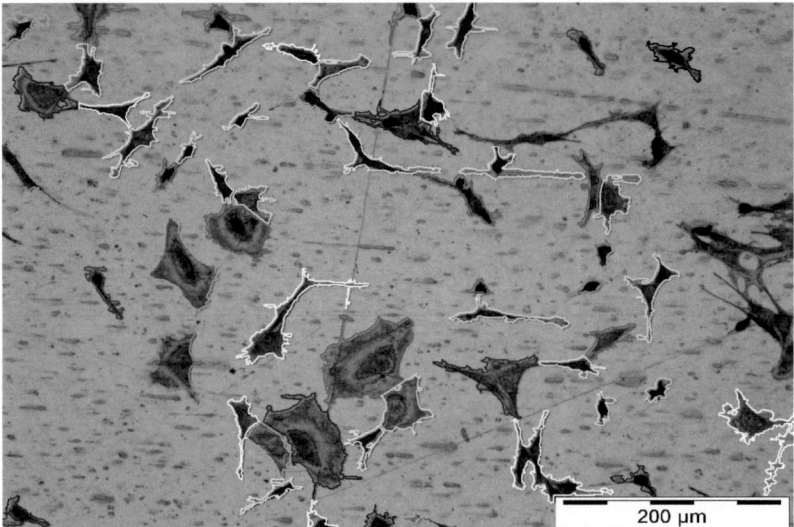

Abbildung 13: Separierte Zellen in den Clustern und segmentierte Einzelzellen

Des Weiteren ist die Rechenzeit der Klassifizierung und Zelltrennung sehr groß. Das Verfahren benötigt bei einem Zellbild mit einer Auflösung von 3 MP bei einem Single Core PC bis zu 3 Minuten für die Analyse. Eine Parallelisierung des Algorithmus auf 4 CPU Kernen reduziert die Verarbeitungszeit zwar auf 10-60s, abhängig von der Komplexität der enthaltenen Cluster, jedoch ist eine weitere Optimierung erstrebenswert. Ziel ist nun, an geeigneten Stellen die Berechnungen auf der Grafikkarte durchzuführen zu lassen, um die Rechenzeit deutlich zu reduzieren.

9   Literatur

[1]   M. Swain, J. Ballard, D., H.: *Indexing via Color Histograms*, Proc. ICCV, pp. 390-393, 1990

[2]   U. Pal, K. Rodenacker and B.B. Chaudhuri: *Automatic cell segmentation in cyto- and histometry using dominant contour feature points*, Analytical cellular pathology, European Society for Analytical Cellular Pathology, pp.243-250, Amsterdam, 1998

[3]   P. E. Hart, N. J. Nilsson and B. Raphael: *Correction to A Formal Basis for the Heuristic Determination of Minimum Cost Paths*, SIGART Newsletter, 37, pp. 28–29, 1972

[4]   Y.Freund, R.E. Schapire : *A Short Introduction to Boosting*, Journal of Japanese Society for Artificial Intelligence, 14(5), pp. 771-780, September, 1999

Bessere Generalisierungsleistung durch Verwendung mehrerer künstlicher Neuronaler Netze

M. Schneider, F. Calcagno, M. Stieglitz, U. Lehmann, J. Krone

Institut für Computer Science, Vision und Computational Intelligence,
Fachhochschule Südwestfalen, Frauenstuhlweg 31, 58644 Iserlohn
Tel. (02371) 566-303 Fax (02371) 566-209
E-Mail: {MSchneider, Lehmann, Krone}@fh-swf.de
{Fabrizio.Calcagno, Marcel.Stieglitz}@stud.fh-swf.de

Zusammenfassung

In dieser Veröffentlichung wird eine Möglichkeit vorgestellt, um die Generalisierungsleistung von künstlichen Neuronalen Netzen (KNN) zu verbessern. Hierbei wird die Datenbasis pro Inputneuron sortiert und in Teildatenmengen aufgeteilt. Pro Inputneuron wird eine individuelle Sortierung benötigt, da es nur anhand dieser individuellen Sortierung möglich ist, einen unbekannten Datensatz zu simulieren. Für jede dieser sortierten Teildatenmengen wird ein eigenes KNN trainiert. Bei mehreren Ausgabeneuronen kann es zur Reduzierung des Modellfehlers hilfreich sein, auch für jedes einzelne Ausgabeneuron ein KNN zu trainieren. Bei der Simulation wird für jede Sortierung der passende Teilbereich für den neuen Datensatz ermittelt. Demnach wird eine Berechnung mit den KNN der jeweiligen Teilbereiche durchgeführt. Pro Ausgabeneuron ergeben sich somit so viele Ergebnisse wie Inputneuron vorhanden sind. Diese werden mit Ausnahme der Extremwerte zusammengeführt, indem der arithmetische Mittelwert über die verbleibenden Teillösungen berechnet wird.

Mit dieser Methode lassen sich sehr große Datenbasen ohne Datenreduktion trainieren, die ansonsten aufgrund mangelnder (Standard-)Hardwareressourcen nicht so einfach trainiert werden könnten.

1 Motivation und Zielsetzung

Beim Training Künstlicher Neuronaler Netze (KNN) unter der Verwendung großer Datenbasen von komplexen Prozessen besteht häufig das Problem, dass das trainierte künstliche Neuronale Netz nur für Teilbereiche der Daten eine gute Generalisierungsleistung aufweist. Des Weiteren erhöht sich bei großen Datenmengen je nach Trainingsverfahren der Zeitaufwand für das Training von künstlichen Neuronale Netzen enorm. Eine geringere Datenmenge pro künstliches Neuronales Netz reduziert die Trainingsdauer und erhöht gleichzeitig die Modellgenauigkeit. Dies kann durch eine Reduzierung der Datenbasis erreicht werden, wobei Datenreduktion auch immer mit Datenverlust verbunden ist. Dies kann jedoch verhindert werden, wenn die vorhandene Datenbasis auf mehrere Teilmodelle aufgeteilt wird, welche zusammen ein Gesamtmodell bilden [1].

2 Modellbildung

Die Datenbasis muss vor dem Training eines künstlichen Neuronalen Netzes entsprechend aufbereitet werden. Hierfür wird davon ausgegangen, dass die Input-Datenbasis aus M Zeilen und N Spalten besteht.

N Spalten

1	5	7	2	6
3	3	4	7	1
2	4	6	9	0

M Zeilen

Abbildung 2.1: Datenbasis aus N Spalten und M Zeilen

N = Anzahl der Datensätze

M = Anzahl der Inputneuronen

Für jede der M Zeilen wird eine Kopie der Input-Datenbasis angefertigt. Diese wird jeweils nach einer der M Zeilen aufsteigend oder absteigend sortiert. Auf diese Weise werden M sortierte Input-Datenbasen generiert.

Eine solche sortierte Datenbasis ist in Abbildung 2.2 beispielhaft dargestellt. Jede dieser sortierten Input-Datenbasen wird nun in D Teilbereiche zerlegt. Die minimalen und maximalen Werte lassen sich somit einfach in je einen Teilbereich zusammenfassen.

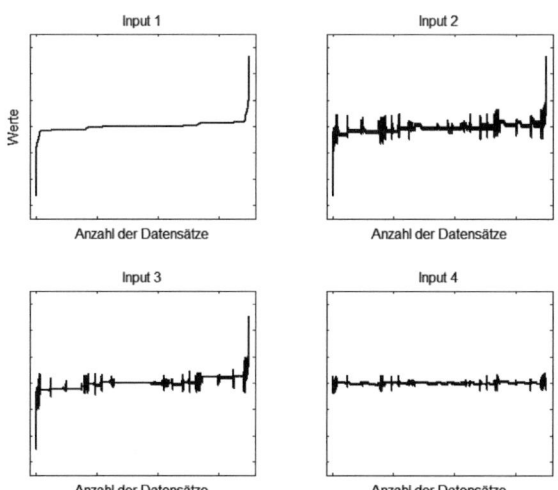

Abbildung 2.2: Sortierung der Datenbasis nach Input 1

Die restlichen Daten können auf die Bereiche D = 1 bis D = n-2 gleichmäßig aufgeteilt werden. In Abbildung 2.3 ist eine solche Aufteilung exemplarisch zu sehen. D ist je nach Größe der Datenbasis und der verwendeten Hardware zu wählen. Die Größe von D beeinflusst auch die Trainingsdauer jedes einzelnen künstlichen Neuronalen Netzes, da bei einem kleineren D mehr Datensätze und bei einem größeren D weniger Datensätze pro Teilbereich verwendet werden.

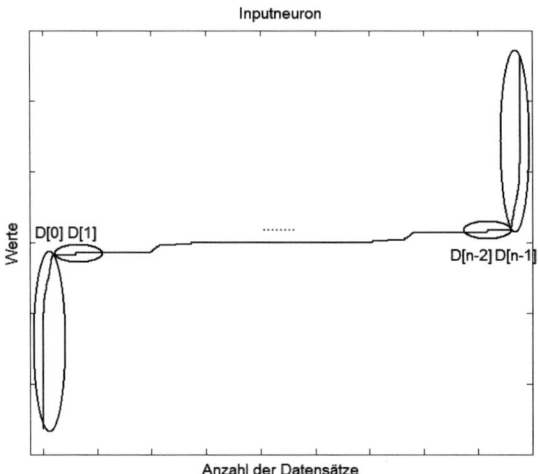

Abbildung 2.3: Aufteilung der Datenbasis

Zusätzlich zur Aufteilung und Sortierung der Datenbasis, können zudem noch für jede Zeile einer Outputdatenbasis eigene künstliche Neuronale Netze trainiert werden. Auf diese Weise wird jedes künstliche Neuronale Netz auf eine bestimmte Zeile der Datenbasis spezialisiert.

Die Anzahl der so zu trainierenden künstlichen Neuronalen Netze lässt sich mit folgender Formel berechnen:

$$Anzahl\ der\ KNN = D \ \times\ I \ \times\ O \qquad (1)$$

D   = Anzahl von Datenaufteilungen

I   = Anzahl der Inputneuronen

O   = Anzahl der Outputneuronen

Beispiel:

Die Input-Datenbasis besteht aus einer 20x200000 Matrix und die Output-Datenbasis besteht aus einer 10x200000 Matrix. Ein einzelnes großes künstliches Neuronales Netz hätte demnach 20 Eingabe- und 10 Ausgabeneuronen. Teilt man die Datenbasis nun wie in diesem Kapitel beschrieben auf, entstehen 20 Datenbasen, wenn D = 10 gewählt wird. Das bedeutet, dass jede Datenbasis in 10 Teilbereiche aufgeteilt wird. Zusätzlich hat die Ausgabematrix 10 Zeilen. Jede dieser Spalten kann einzeln betrachtet werden. Somit werden nach Formel 1 insgesamt 2000 einzelne künstliche Neuronale Netze trainiert.

In Abbildung 2.4 ist der Aufbau eines Teilmodells mit einem Ausgabeneuron dargestellt.

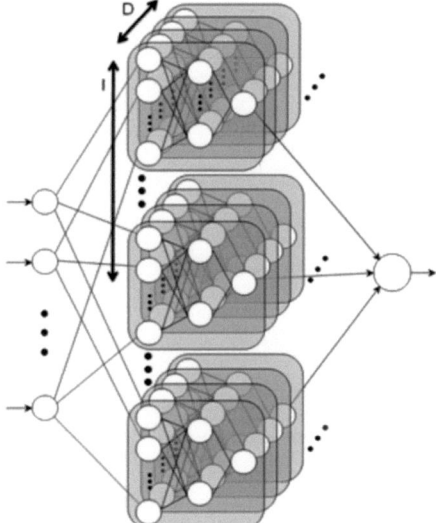

Abbildung 2.4: Aufbau eines Teilmodells

Der Datensatz der durch die künstlichen Neuronalen Netze simuliert werden soll, muss zunächst eingeordnet werden. Für jede Sortierung muss zunächst ermittelt werden, in welchen Teilbereich der Datensatz fällt. Auf diese Weise wird pro Sortierung ein künstliches Neuronales Netz ausgewählt. Pro Sortierung findet für jedes Outputneuron eine Simulation statt. Somit entspricht die Anzahl der Ergebnisse jedes Outputneurons der Anzahl der Inputneuronen bzw. der Sortierungen. Die berechneten Ausgaben werden in einer Matrix abgespeichert. Für die Berechnung einer einzigen Ausgabe aus dem Gesamtmodell werden die beiden maximalen und minimalen Ausgabewerte gestrichen und über die verbleibenden Ausgabewerte das arithmetische Mittel gebildet.

3   Ergebnis

In diesem Kapitel wird das Ergebnis zwischen dem in dieser Veröffentlichung vorgestellten Verfahren und einem Verfahren bei dem nur ein künstliches Neuronales Netz für die gesamte Datenbasis trainiert wurde, verglichen

In Abbildung 3.1 ist der mittlere absolute Fehler (MAE) über die Ausgabeneuronen für die Testdaten dargstellt . Um den MAE besser darzustellen, wurde dieser aufsteigend sortiert. Dabei ist ersichtlich, dass viele kleine künstliche Neuronale Netze ein besseres Ergebnis liefern als ein einziges großes KNN. Die Fehlerkurve der vielen kleinen künstlichen Neuronalen Netze liegt deutlich unter der Fehlerkurve eines einzelnen großen künstlichen Neuronalen Netzes.

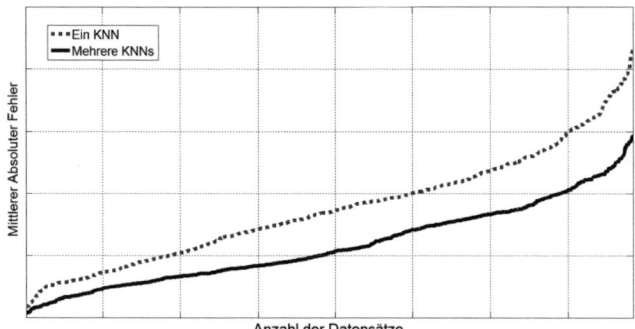

Abbildung 3.1: Vergleich zwischen einem KNN und multiplen KNNs

Mit folgender Formel wurde der mittlere absolute Fehler berechnet:

$$MAE = \frac{1}{N} \sum_{n=1}^{N} |E_n| \qquad (2)$$

N   = Anzahl der Ausgaben pro Datensatz

E   = Fehler an jedem Ausgabeneuron pro Datensatz

MAE   = Mittlerer absoluter Fehler

In Abbildung 3.2 ist der mittlere absolute Fehler jedes einzelnen Outputs zu sehen. Dabei wird ersichtlich, dass für die meisten Outputs signifikante Verbesserungen erzielt werden konnten. Hervorzuheben ist, dass der maximale Fehler pro Ausgabeneuron wesentlich verbessert werden konnte.

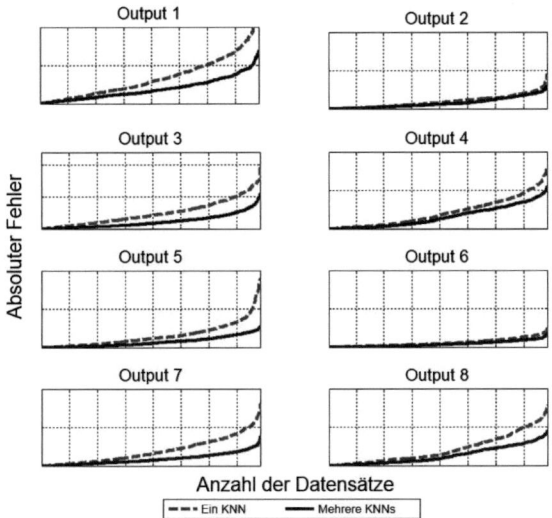

Abbildung 3.2: Vergleich zwischen einem KNN und multiplen KNNs pro Ausgabeneuron

In folgender Tabelle ist die Verbesserung prozentual angegeben. Zur Berechnung der Werte wurde das arithmethische Mittel über alle Fehlerwerte beider Verfahren herangezogen.

Tabelle 3.1: Verbesserung der Generalisierungsleistung pro Ausgabeneuron

Output 1	39,53 %	Output 2	25,56 %
Output 3	56,15 %	Output 4	34,14 %
Output 5	52,97 %	Output 6	38,37 %
Output 7	52,89 %	Output 8	37,67 %

Folgende Formel wurde zur Berechnung der Verbesserung der Generalisierungsleistung verwendet:

$$AI = 1 - \frac{MAE(E_{mANN})}{MAE(E_{ANN})} \qquad (3)$$

E_{mKNN} = Fehler von allen Datensätzen pro Ausgabeneuron mit mehreren KNN

E_{KNN} = Fehler von allen Datensätzen pro Ausgabeneuron mit nur einem KNN

MAE = Mittlerer absoluter Fehler

AI   = Durchschnittliche Verbesserung

Durch diese Art der Verteilung des Prozesswissens auf mehrere kleine künstliche Neuronale Netze konnte die Generalisierungsleistung des Gesamtmodells wesentlich erhöht werden. Darüber hinaus konnte die gesamte Trainingsdauer um 42% stark verkürzt werden.

4   Ausblick

Das bisher vorgestellte Verfahren teilt die Datenbasis nur statisch nach fest vorgegebenen Grenzen auf. Dies könnte durch eine dynamische Aufteilung verbessert werden. So kann zum Beispiel die Steigung der Sortierung zwischen den verschiedenen Datensätzen berechnet werden. Alle Datensätze die in einem bestimmten Intervall von Steigungen liegen, könnten so in eine eigene Teildatenbasis zusammengeführt werden. Bei einem großen Intervall entstehen wenige Datenbasen, während bei einem kleinen Intervall viele Datenbasen generiert werden.

Wenn in der Datenbasis eine größere Lücke zwischen den Werten der Datensätze ist und die Datenbasis genau so aufgeteilt ist, so dass diese Grenze nicht betrachtet wird, dann müssen die künstlichen Neuronalen Netze bei dieser Lücke extrapolieren. Damit wäre es denkbar, die generierten Teildatenbasen überlappen zu lassen. Das bedeutet, dass die einzelnen Teildatenbasen zusätzlich noch Datensätze aus den benachbarten Datenbasen erhalten, mit Ausnahme der Teildatenbasen am Rand. Auf diese Weise wird der Datenbereich komplett abgedeckt und das Extrapolieren der künstlichen Neuronalen Netze verhindert.

5   Danksagung

Diese Arbeit entstand am Institut für Computer Science, Vision und Computational Intelligence der Fachhochschule Südwestfalen (http://cvci.fh-swf.de) im Rahmen des vom Bundesministerium für Bildung und Forschung (BMBF) geförderten Forschungsprojektes „Neuroadaptiver Bauplatz im Flugzeugbau".

Literatur/Veröffentlichungen

[1]   H. Braun: Neuronale Netze. Optimierung durch Lernen und Evolution, Springer Berlin, 1997
[2]   R. Rojas: Theorie der neuronalen Netze, Springer-Verlag Berlin/Heidelberg, 1993
[3]   A. Zell: Simulation neuronaler Netze. Oldenburg Verlag, 1994
[4]   W. Schweizer: Matlab kompakt, Oldenbourg, Auflage 4, 2009

Preference Learning using the Choquet Integral: The Case of Multipartite Ranking

Ali Fallah Tehrani, Weiwei Cheng and Eyke Hüllermeier

Dept. of Mathematics and Computer Science
University of Marburg, Germany
{fallah, cheng, eyke}@mathematik.uni-marburg.de

Abstract

In this paper, we propose a novel method for two types of ranking problems that have recently been introduced in the context of preference learning, an emerging subfield of machine learning. In the literature, these problems are referred to, respectively, as *object ranking* and *multipartite ranking*. In both cases, the task is to learn a ranking model that accepts as input a subset of alternatives, with each alternative typically represented in terms of a feature vector, and produces a ranking of these alternatives as output. Our approach is based on the idea of using the (discrete) Choquet integral as an underlying model for representing rankings. Being an established aggregation function in multiple criteria decision making and information fusion, the Choquet integral offers a number of interesting properties that render it attractive from a machine learning perspective, too. The learning problem itself, which comes down to properly specifying the fuzzy measure on which the Choquet integral is defined, is formalized as a margin maximization problem. For testing the performance of our method, we apply it to a real problem, namely the ranking of scientific journals.

1 Introduction

Preference learning is an emerging subfield of machine learning that has received increasing attention in recent years [1]. Roughly speaking, the goal in preference learning is to induce preference models from observed data revealing information about the preferences of an individual or a group of individuals in a direct or indirect way; these models are then used to predict the preferences in a new situation. In this regard, predictions in the form of *rankings*, i.e., total orders of a set of alternatives, constitute an important special case [2–6]. A ranking can be seen as a specific type of *structured output* [7], and compared to conventional classification and regression functions, models producing such outputs require a more complex internal representation.

In this paper, we propose novel methods for two types of ranking problems, using the (discrete) Choquet integral [8] as an underlying model for representing rankings. The Choquet integral is an established aggregation function that has been used in various fields of application, including multiple criteria decision making and information fusion. It can be seen as a generalization of the weighted arithmetic mean that is not only able to capture the importance of individual features but also information about the redundancy, complementarity and interaction between different features. Moreover, it obeys certain monotonicity properties in a rather natural way. Due to these properties, the Choquet integral appears to be very appealing for preference learning, especially for aggregating the evaluation of individual features in the form of interacting criteria. The learning problem itself comes down to specifying the fuzzy measure underlying the definition of the Choquet integral in the most suitable way. In this regard, we explore connections to kernel-based machine learning methods [9].

We develop learning algorithms for two types of problems that have been referred to, respectively, as *object ranking* and *multipartite ranking* in the literature [2, 6]. In both cases, the task is to learn a ranking model that accepts as input an arbitrary set of alternatives, with each alternative typically represented in terms of a feature vector, and produces a ranking of these alternatives as output. The main difference concerns the training information, which is given in the form of *absolute* judgments in multipartite ranking and *relative* judgments in object ranking. More specifically, it consists of a set of evaluated alternatives in the former case, rated in terms of preference degrees on an ordinal scale (such as bad, good, very good), and of a set of pairwise comparisons between alternatives in the second case (suggesting that one alternative is preferred to another one).

For testing the performance of our methods, we apply them to a real problem, namely the ranking of scientific journals based on various properties and indicators, such as impact factor. A corresponding data set will not only be used to compare our methods with existing approaches in terms of predictive performance but also to highlight the advantages of the Choquet integral from a modeling and knowledge representation point of view.

The rest of this paper is organized as follows. In the next section, we give a brief overview of related work. In Section 3, we recall the basic definition of the Choquet integral and related notions. The ranking problems we are dealing with are explained in Section 4, and our approach for tackling them is introduced in Section 5. Finally, some first experimental results are presented in Section 6.

2 Related Work

Although the Choquet integral has been widely applied as an aggregation operator in multiple criteria decision making [10–12], it has been used much less in the field of machine learning so far. There are, however, a few notable exceptions.

First, the problem of extracting a Choquet integral (or, more precisely, the non-additive measure on which it is defined) in a data-driven way has been addressed in the literature. Essentially, this is a parameter identification problem, which is commonly formalized as a constraint optimization problem, for example using the sum of squared errors as an objective function [13, 14]. To this end, a heuristic, gadient-based method called HLMS (Heuristic Least Mean Squares) was introduced in [15], while [16] proposed an alternative approach based on the use of quadratic forms. Besides, genetic algorithms have been used as a tool for parameter optimization [17]. Some mathematical results regarding this optimization problem can be found in [18, 19].

Second, the Choquet integral has been used in a few works for learning classification models. Recently, for example, it has been used for ordinal classification [20, 21]. In [22], the problem of learning an optimal classification function is cast in the setting of margin-maximization. Although the learning problem is different, this approach is especially relevant for us, since we shall employ quite similar techniques (cf. Section 5).

3 The Discrete Choquet Integral

In this section, we recall the basic definition of the Choquet integral and related notions. The first definition of the Choquet integral for additive measures is due to Vitali [23]. For the general case of a capacity (i.e., a non-additive measure or fuzzy measure), it was later on introduced by Choquet [24]. Yager proposed a generalized version in [25].

Definition 1 (Fuzzy measure) *Let $X = \{x_1, x_2, \ldots, x_n\}$ be a finite set. A discrete fuzzy measure (also called capacity) is a set function $\mu : 2^X \rightarrow [0, 1]$ which is monotonic ($\mu(A) \leq \mu(B)$ for $A \subseteq B \subseteq X$) and normalized ($\mu(\emptyset) = 0$ and $\mu(X) = 1$). A fuzzy measure μ is called additive if $\mu(A \cup B) = \mu(A) + \mu(B)$ for all $A, B \subseteq X$ such that $A \cap B = \emptyset$. Obviously, in the case of an additive measure, $\mu(A)$ is simply obtained as follows:*

$$\mu(A) = \sum_{i \in A} \mu(\{i\}) \tag{1}$$

Definition 2 (Choquet integral) *Let μ be a fuzzy measure on $X = \{x_1, x_2, \ldots, x_n\}$. The discrete Choquet integral of a function $f : X \rightarrow \mathbb{R}_+$ with respect to μ is defined as follows:*

$$C_\mu(f) = \sum_{i=1}^{n} \big(f(x_{(i)}) - f(x_{(i-1)}) \big) \cdot \mu(A_{(i)}) \ ,$$

where $(\cdot)$ is a permutation of $\{1, \ldots, n\}$ such that $0 \leq f(x_{(1)}) \leq f(x_{(2)}) \leq \ldots \leq f(x_{(n)})$. Moreover, $A_{(i)}$ is given by the set $\{x_{(i)}, \ldots, x_{(n)}\}$. Finally, $f(x_{(0)}) = 0$ by definition.

Definition 3 (Möbious transform) *The Möbius transform $\mathbf{m}_\mu$ of a fuzzy measure μ is defined as follows:*

$$\mathbf{m}_\mu(A) = \sum_{B \subseteq A} (-1)^{|A|-|B|} \mu(B)$$

for all $A \subseteq X$.

As a useful property of the Möbius transform, that we shall exploit later on for learning Choquet integrals, we mention that is allows for reconstructing the underlying fuzzy measure:

$$\mu(B) = \sum_{A \subseteq B} \mathbf{m}(A)$$

for all $B \subseteq X$. More specifically, we shall make use of the following representation of the Choquet integral:

$$\begin{aligned}
C_\mu(f) &= \sum_{i=1}^{n} \big(f(x_{(i)}) - f(x_{(i-1)}) \big) \cdot \mu(A_{(i)}) \\
&= \sum_{i=1}^{n} f(x_{(i)})(\mu(A_{(i)}) - \mu(A_{(i+1)})) \\
&= \sum_{i=1}^{n} f(x_{(i)}) \sum_{R \subseteq T_{(i)}} \mathbf{m}(R) \\
&= \sum_{T \subseteq X} \mathbf{m}(T) \times \min_{(i) \in T} f(x_{(i)})
\end{aligned} \tag{2}$$

where $T_{(i)} = \{S \cup \{(i)\} \mid S \subseteq \{(i+1), \ldots, (n)\}\}$.

Definition 4 (k-Additivity) *A fuzzy measure μ is said to be k-order additive or simply k-additive if k is the smallest integer such that $\mathbf{m}(A) = 0$ for all $A \subseteq X$ with $|A| > k$.*

Thus, while a Choquet integral is determined by 2^n coefficients in general, the k-additivity of the underlying measure reduces the number of required coefficients to at most

$$\sum_{i=1}^{k} \binom{n}{i} \; .$$

The (discrete) Choquet integral is often used as an aggregation operator, namely to aggregate the assessments $f(x_i)$ of an object on different criteria x_i into a single evaluation. If the underlying measure μ is additive (i.e., k-additive with $k = 1$), the Choquet integral reduces to a linear aggregation

$$C_\mu(f) = \sum_{i=1}^{n} w_i \cdot f(x_i) \; ,$$

with $w_i = \mu(\{x_i\})$ the weight or, say, the importance of the criterion x_i. Besides, in this case, there is obviously no interaction between the criteria x_i, i.e., the influence of evaluation $f(x_i)$ on the overall assessment is independent of the other values $f(x_j), j \neq i$.

Measuring the importance of a criterion x_i becomes obviously more involved if μ is nonadditive. Besides, one may then also be interested in a measure of interaction between the criteria, either pairwise or even of a higher order. In the literature, measures of that kind have been proposed, both for the importance of single as well as the interaction between several criteria.

Given a fuzzy measure μ on X, the *Shaply value* (or importance index) of x_i is defined as follows:

$$\varphi(x_i) = \sum_{A \subseteq X \setminus \{x_i\}} \frac{1}{n \binom{n-1}{|A|}} (\mu(A \cup \{x_i\}) - \mu(A))$$

The Shaply value of μ is the vector $\varphi(\mu) = (\varphi(1), \ldots, \varphi(n))$. One can show that $0 \leq \varphi(x_i) \leq 1$ and $\sum_{i=1}^{n} \varphi(x_i) = 1$. Thus, $\varphi(x_i)$ is a measure of the *relative* importance of x_i. Obviously, $\varphi(x_i) = \mu(\{x_i\})$ if μ is additive.

The *interaction index* between criteria x_i and x_j, as proposed by Murofushi and Soneda [26], is defined as follows:

$$I(x_i, x_j) = \sum_{A \subseteq X \setminus \{x_i, x_j\}} \frac{\mu(A \cup (\{x_i, x_j\})) - \mu(A \cup (\{x_i\})) - \mu(A \cup (\{x_j\})) + \mu(A)}{(n-1)\binom{n-2}{|A|}}$$

This index ranges between -1 and 1 and indicates a positive (negative) interaction between criteria x_i and x_j if $I(x_i, x_j) > 0$ ($I(x_i, x_j) < 0$).

Interestingly, the Shaply value can also be expressed in terms of the interaction index:

$$\varphi(x_i) = \mathbf{m}(\{x_i\}) + \frac{1}{2} \sum_{x_j \in X \setminus \{x_i\}} I(x_i, x_j)$$

4 Multipartite and Object Ranking

As mentioned earlier, different types of ranking problems have recently been studied in the machine learning literature. Here, we are specifically interested in so-called *object ranking* and *multipartitle ranking*. In both problems, the goal is to learn a *ranking function* that accepts a subset $\mathcal{O} \subset \mathbf{O}$ of objects as input, and produces as output a ranking (total order) $\succeq$ of these objects. Typically, a ranking function of that kind is implemented by means of a scoring function $U : \mathbf{O} \to \mathbb{R}$, so that

$$o \succeq o' \quad \Leftrightarrow \quad U(o) \geq U(o')$$

for all $o, o' \in \mathbf{O}$. Obviously, $U(o)$ can be considered as a kind of utility degree assigned to the object $o \in \mathbf{O}$. Seen from this point of view, the goal in object and multipartite ranking is to learn a latent utility function on a reference set $\mathbf{O}$. In the following, we shall also refer to $U(\cdot)$ itself as a ranking function. Moreover, we assume that this function produces a strict order relation $\succ$, i.e., that ties $U(o) = U(o')$ do either not occur or are broken at random.

The difference between the two problems is the type of training data available for learning such a function, and the way in which a prediction is evaluated. In object ranking, the ground truth is supposed to be a total order $\succ^*$ on $\mathbf{O}$, and training data consists of pairwise preferences of the form $o_i \succ o_j$. Given a new set of objects $\mathcal{O}$ to be ranked, the predicted order $\succ$ is then compared with the true order $\succ^*$ (restricted to $\mathcal{O}$). This can be done, for example, by means of a rank correlation measure such as Kendall's tau [27].

In multipartite ranking, the ground truth is supposed to be an ordinal categorization of the objects. That is, each object $o \in \mathbf{O}$ belongs to one of the classes in $\mathcal{L} = \{\lambda_1, \lambda_2, \ldots, \lambda_k\}$. Correspondingly, training data consists of labeled objects $(o_i, \ell_i) \in \mathbf{O} \times \mathcal{L}$. Assuming that the classes are sorted such that $\lambda_1 < \lambda_2 < \ldots < \lambda_k$, the goal is to learn a ranking function $U(\cdot)$ that agrees well with this sorting in the sense that objects from higher classes are ranked higher than objects from lower classes. In [6], it was proposed to use the so-called C-index as a suitable performance measure:

$$C(U, \mathcal{O}) = \frac{1}{\sum_{i<j} |\mathcal{O}_i| \cdot |\mathcal{O}_j|} \sum_{1 \leq i < j \leq k} \sum_{(o,o') \in \mathcal{O}_i \times \mathcal{O}_j} S(U(o), U(o'))$$

where $\mathcal{O}_i$ is the subset of objects $o \in \mathcal{O}$ whose true class is λ_i and

$$S(u, v) = \begin{cases} 1 & u < v \\ 0 & u > v \end{cases} \tag{3}$$

indicates whether or not a pair of objects has been ranked correctly.

5 Learning to Rank using the Choquet Integral

The idea of our approach is to represent the latent utility function $U(\cdot)$ in terms of a Choquet integral. Assuming that objects $o \in \mathbf{O}$ are represented as feature vectors

$$f_o = (f_o(x_1), \ldots, f_o(x_n)) \ ,$$

where $f_o(x_i)$ can be thought of as the evaluation of object o on the criterion x_i, this means that

$$U(o) = C_\mu(f_o) \ . \tag{4}$$

This approach appears to be interesting for a number of reasons, notably the following:

- The representation (4) covers the commonly used linear utility functions as a special case.

- Generalizing beyond the linear case, however, it is also able to capture more complex, non-linear dependencies and interactions between criteria.

- The Choquet integral offers various means for explaining and understanding a utility function, including the importance value and the interaction index.

- As opposed to many other models used in machine learning, the Choquet integral guarantees monotonicity in all criteria. This is a reasonable property of a utility function which is often required in practice.

We assume training data to be available in the form of a set of objects $\{o_1, \ldots, o_N\} \subset O$, together with their feature representations f_{o_i} $(i = 1, \ldots, N)$ and a subset D of pairwise preferences between these objects; each pairwise preference is represented by a tuple $(o_i, o_j) \in D$, suggesting that $o_i \succ o_j$. While these preferences are given directly in the case of object ranking, they can be derived from the class information in the case of multipartite ranking: $(o_i, o_j) \in D$ if the original training data contains (o_i, ℓ_i) and (o_j, ℓ_j), and $\ell_i > \ell_j$.

Following the idea of empirical risk minimization [9], we seek to induce a Choquet integral that minimizes the number of ranking errors (3) on the training data D. Since the Choquet integral is uniquely identified by the underlying measure μ on the set of criteria $X = \{x_1, \ldots, x_n\}$, this comes down to defining this measure in a most suitable way. In this regard, we make use of the representation (2) of μ in terms of its Möbius transform.

Inspired by the maximum margin principle in kernel-based machine learning [9], we formulate the problem of learning μ as an optimization problem:

$$\max_{M, \xi_1, \ldots, \xi_N} \left\{ M - \frac{\gamma}{|D|} \sum_{(o_s, o_t) \in D} \xi^s + \xi^t \right\}$$

s.t.

$$C_\mu(f_{o_s}) - C_\mu(f_{o_t}) > M - \xi^s - \xi^t \qquad \forall (o_s, o_t) \in D$$

$$\xi^s \geq 0 \qquad \forall s \in \{1, \ldots, N\}$$

$$\sum_{T \subseteq X} \mathbf{m}(T) = 1$$

$$\sum_{B \subseteq A} \mathbf{m}(B) \geq 0 \qquad \forall A \subseteq X$$

$$\sum_{L \subseteq A} \mathbf{m}(L) \leq \sum_{K \subseteq B} \mathbf{m}(K) \qquad \forall A \subset B \subseteq X$$

In this problem, M denotes the margin to be maximized, that is, the smallest difference between the utility degrees of two training objects o_s and o_t with $o_s \succ o_t$. More specifically, M is a *soft margin*: Accounting for the fact that it will generally be impossible to satisfy all inequalities simultaneously, each object o_s is associated with a slack variable ξ^s. The slack variables are non-negative, and a positive slack is penalized in proportion to its size. Finally, γ is a trade-off parameter that controls the flexibility of the model; the higher γ, the stronger the slacks are punished.

The last three constraints formalize, respectively, the normalization, non-negativity and monotonicity of the Möbius transform. Obviously, the non-negativity and monotonicity conditions are quite costly and produce as many as $3^n - 2^n$ constraints, since each subset of X is compared with all its subsets:

$$\sum_{i=1}^{n} \binom{n}{i} (2^i - 1) = \sum_{i=1}^{n} \binom{n}{i} 2^i - \sum_{i=1}^{n} \binom{n}{i} = 3^n - 2^n$$

Fortunately, the last two constraints can be represented in a more compact way, exploiting a transitivity property:

$$\sum_{B \subseteq A \setminus \{x_i\}} \mathbf{m}(B \cup \{x_i\}) \geq 0 \qquad \forall A \subseteq X, x_i \in X$$

This representation reduces the number of constraints to $n2^n$, which, despite still being large, is a significant reduction in comparison to the original formulation.

Another way of reducing complexity is to restrict the class of fuzzy measures to k-additive measures, that is, setting $\mathbf{m}(A) = 0$ for all $A \subseteq X$ with $|A| > k$. In fact, choosing a $k \ll n$ is not only interesting from an optimization but also from a learning point of view: Since the degree of additivity of μ offers a way to control the *capacity* of the underlying model class, selecting a proper k is crucial in order to guarantee the generalization performance of the learning algorithm. More specifically, the larger k is chosen, the more flexibly the Choquet integral can be fitted to the data. Thus, choosing k too large comes along with a danger of overfitting the data.

6 Experimental Results

We conucted experiments using a data set that classifies 172 scientific journals in the field of pure mathematics into categories A^*, A, B and C [21]. Each journal is moreover scored in terms of 5 criteria, namely

- cites: the total number of citations per year;

- IF: the well-known impact factor (average number of citations per article within two years after publication);

- II: the immediacy index measures how topical the articles published in a journal are (cites to articles in current calendar year divided by the number of articles published in that year);

- articles: the total number of articles published;

- half-line: cited half-life (median age of articles cited).

6.1 Comparison with Linear and Polynomial Kernel Methods

In a first study, we compared our approach with kernel-based methods for ranking, using the RankSVM approach with a linear and a polynomial kernel [28]. A comparison with this class of methods is interesting for several reasons. First, kernel-based methods belong to the state-of-the-art in the field of learning to rank. Second, they make use of the same type of learning algorithm (large margin maximization). Third, the use of a polynomial kernel leads to a model that bears some resemblence with a Choquet integral. In fact, using a polynomial kernel of degree k on the original feature representation of objects, i.e., a kernel of the form

$$K(\boldsymbol{o}, \boldsymbol{o'}) = (\langle f_{\boldsymbol{o}}, f_{\boldsymbol{o'}} \rangle + \lambda)^k \ , \tag{5}$$

essentially comes down to fitting a linear model in an expanded feature space, in which the original features $f(x_1), \ldots, f(x_n)$ are complemented by all monomials of order $\leq k$. Thus, a polynomial kernel of degree k captures the same interactions between criteria as a Choquet integral on a k-additive fuzzy measure.

We use an experimental setup that randomly splits the data into two parts, one half for training and one half for testing. From the training data, a total number of T object pairs is sampled, and the corresponding preferences are used for training. The model induced from this training data is then evaluated on the test data, using the C-index as a performance measure. This procedure is repeated 100 times, and the results are averaged.

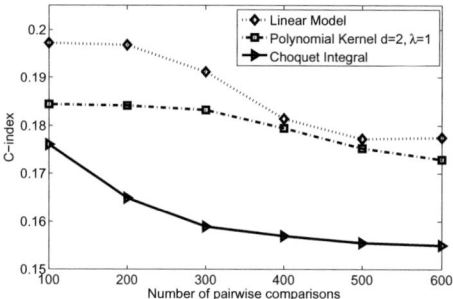

Figure 1: Average test accuracy for Choquet intregral, the linear model and the polynomial kernel of order 2.

Fig. 1 shows the average accuracy of the Choquet integral[1], the linear model and the polynomial kernel (5) with parameters $k = 2$ and $\lambda = 1$ as a function of the size T of the training set. As can be seen, the linear model performs the worst, suggesting the presence of important interactions between criteria. The kernel method is slightly better, but the best results are obtained by the Choquet integral.

6.2 Choquet Integral on k-Additive Fuzzy Measures

In a second experiment, we applied the Choquet integral with k-additive fuzzy measures, varying the value of k from 1 to 5. As can be seen in Fig. 2, there is a significant increase

---

[1]The trade-off parameter γ was set to 1.

cites	IF	II	articles	half-life
0.0989	0.1643	0.5379	0.0984	0.1006

Table 1: Importance of criteria in terms of the Shaply value.

in performance when going from $k = 1$ (the linear model) to $k = 2$. Increasing k beyond the value 2, however, does not seem to be beneficial.

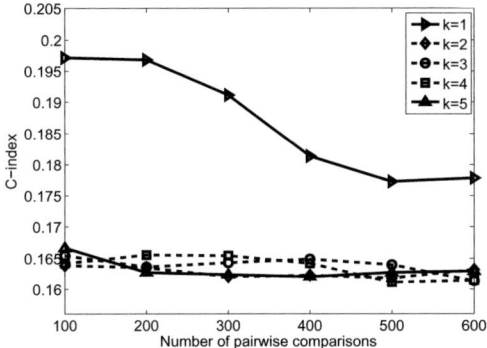

Figure 2: Performance of the Choquet integral on a k-additive fuzzy measure.

6.3 Importance of Criteria and Interaction

As mentioned before, the Choquet integral does also offer interesting information about the importance of individual criteria and the interaction between them. In fact, in many practical applications, this type of information is at least as important as the predictive accuracy of the model.

Table 1 shows the importance of the five criteria in terms of the Shaply value. As can be seen, the immediacy index and the impact factor seem to have the strongest impact on the assessment of a journal, which is hardly surprising. However, the weight of the former is even much higher than the weight of the latter, which is arguably less expected.

Table 2 shows the measures of pairwise interaction between the criteria. Interestingly, the interaction is positive throughout, i.e., there seems to be a kind of synergy between each pair of criteria. Moreover, while the degree of interaction is in general quite comparable accross all pairs of criteria, it is again maximal for the impact factor and immediacy index.

7 Summary and Conclusions

In this paper, we have advocated the use of the discrete Choquet integral in the context of preference learning. More specifically, we have used the Choquet integral for representing a latent utility function in two types of ranking problems, namely object ranking and

	IF	II	articles	half-line
cites	0.24	0.26	0.34	0.29
IF		0.40	0.32	0.24
II			0.26	0.26
articles				0.29

Table 2: Pairwise interaction between criteria.

multipartite ranking. This idea is motivated by several appealing properties offered by the Choquet integral, including its ability to capture dependencies between criteria and to obey natural monotonicity conditions, as well as its interpretability.

Algorithmically, our approach is inspired by large margin methods that have been developed in the field of kernel-based machine learning. First experimental studies, in which we applied this approach to a journal ranking data set and compared it to a kernel-based ranking method, are quite promising.

Needless to say, this study is only a first step and should be complemented by more extensive experiments including diverse types of data sets. Another problem to be addressed in future work concerns the (soft) margin maximization problem. In fact, due to the large number of constraints that have to be satisfied, this problem may become computationally complex. Dedicated techniques for solving it in a more efficient way are therefore desirable.

References

[1] Fürnkranz, J.; Hüllermeier, E. (Hg.): *Preference Learning*. Springer-Verlag. 2010.

[2] Cohen, W.; Schapire, R.; Singer, Y.: Learning to Order Things. *Journal of Artificial Intelligence Research* 10 (1999), S. 243–270.

[3] Har-Peled, S.; Roth, D.; Zimak, D.: Constraint classification for multiclass classification and ranking. In: *Advances in Neural Information Processing Systems 15 (NIPS-02)* (Becker, S.; Thrun, S.; Obermayer, K., Hg.), S. 785–792. 2003.

[4] Fürnkranz, J.; Hüllermeier, E.: Pairwise Preference Learning and Ranking. In: *Proc. ECML–03, 13th European Conference on Machine Learning*. Cavtat-Dubrovnik, Croatia. 2003.

[5] Dekel, O.; Manning, C.; Singer, Y.: Log-linear models for label ranking. In: *Advances in Neural Information Processing Systems*. 2003.

[6] Fürnkranz, J.; Hüllermeier, E.; Vanderlooy, S.: Binary Decomposition Methods for Multipartite Ranking. In: *Proceedings ECML/PKDD–2009, European Conference on Machine Learning and Knowledge Discovery in Databases*. Bled, Slovenia. 2009.

[7] Bakir, G.; Hofmann, T.; Schölkopf, B.; Smola, A.; Taskar, B.; Vishwanathan, S. (Hg.): *Predicting structured data*. MIT Press. 2007.

[8] Choquet, G.: Theory of Capacities. *Annales de l'Institut Fourier* 5 (1954), S. 131–295.

[9] Schölkopf, B.; Smola, A.: *Learning with Kernels: Support Vector Machines, Regularization, Optimization, and Beyond*. MIT Press. 2001.

[10] Grabisch, M.; Roubens, M.: *Fuzzy measures and integrals*. Physica. 2000.

[11] Grabisch, M.: Fuzzy integral in multicriteria decision making. *Fuzzy set and system* 69 (1995), S. 279–298.

[12] Torra, V.: Learning aggregation operators for preference modeling. In: *Preference Learning* (Fürnkranz, J.; Hüllermeier, E., Hg.). 2010.

[13] Torra, V.; Narukawa, Y.: *Modeling decisions: Information fusion and aggregation operators*. Spinger. 2007.

[14] Grabisch, M.: Modelling data by the Choquet integral. In: *Information Fusion in Data Mining* (Torra, V., Hg.), S. 135–148. Physica. 2003.

[15] Grabisch, M.: A new algorithm for identifying fuzzy measures and its application to pattern recognition. In: *Int. Joint Conf. of the 4th IEEE Int. Conf. on Fuzzy Systems and the 2nd Int. Fuzzy Engineering Symposium*, S. 145–150. 1995.

[16] Murofushi, T.; Mori, T.: An Analysis of Evaluation Model Using Fuzzy Measure and the Choquet Integral. In: *The 5th Fuzzy System Symposium*, S. 207–212. Kobe, Japan. 1989.

[17] Ishii, Y.; Murofushi, T.: Identification of fuzzy measures using real valued GA and considering outliers. In: *The 6th Workshop on Evaluation of Heart and Mind*. Japan. 2001.

[18] Imai, H.; Miyamori, M.; Miyakosi, M.; Sato, Y.: An algorithm based on alternative projections for a fuzzy measures identification problem. In: *International Conference on Soft Computing*. Iizuka, Japan. 2000.

[19] Imai, H.; Asano, D.; Sato, Y.: An algorithm based on alternative projections for a fuzzy measures identification problem. In: *Information Fusion in Data Mining* (Torra, V., Hg.), S. 149–159. Springer. 2003.

[20] Angilella, S.; Greco, S.; Matarazzo, B.: Non-additive robust ordinal regression with Choquet integral, bipolar and level dependent Choquet integrals. In: *IFSA-EUSFLAT*. Lisbon, Portugal. 2009.

[21] Beliakov, G.; James, S.: Citation-based journal ranks: the use of fuzzy measures. *Fuzzy Sets and Systems* (2010).

[22] Angilella, S.; Greco, S.; Matarazzo, B.: The most representative fuzzy measure for non-additive robust ordinal regression. In: *IPMU*. Dortmund, Germany. 2010.

[23] Vitali, G.: Sulla definizione di integrale delle funzioni di una variabile. *Annali di Matematica Serie IV Tomo* 2 (1925), S. 111–121.

[24] Choquet, G.: Theory of capacities. *Annales de l'Institut Fourier* 5 (1954), S. 131–295.

[25] Yager, R. R.: Generalized OWA aggregation operators. *Fuzzy Optimization and Decision Making* 3 (2004), S. 93–107.

[26] Murofushi, T.; Soneda, S.: Techniques for reading fuzzy measures (III): Interaction index. In: *The 9th Fuzzy Systems Symposium*, S. 693–696. Sapporo, Japan. 1993.

[27] Kendall, M.: *Rank correlation methods*. London: Charles Griffin. 1955.

[28] Herbrich, R.; Graepel, T.; Obermayer, K.: Large Margin Rank Boundaries for Ordinal Regression. In: *Advances in Large Margin Classifiers*, S. 115–132. 2000.

Parameter-Tuned Data Mining: A General Framework

Wolfgang Konen, Patrick Koch,
Oliver Flasch and Thomas Bartz-Beielstein

Fakultät für Informatik und Ingenieurwissenschaften, Fachhochschule Köln
E-Mail: {wolfgang.konen | patrick.koch |
oliver.flasch | thomas.bartz-beielstein}@fh-koeln.de

Abstract

Real-world data mining applications often confront us with complex and noisy data, which makes it necessary to optimize the data mining models thoroughly to achieve high-quality results. We describe in this contribution an approach to tune the parameters of the model and the feature selection conjointly. The aim is to use *one* framework to solve a variety of data mining tasks. We show that tuning is of large importance for high-quality results in benchmark tasks like the Data Mining Cup: tuned models achieve rank 2 or 4 in the ranking tables, where the untuned model had rank 21 out of 67. We discuss several issues of special relevance for the tuning of data mining models, namely resampling strategies and oversearching.

1 Introduction

How can we find good data mining models with a small amount of manual intervention? – The practitioner in data mining is confronted with a wealth of machine learning methods containing an even larger set of method parameters to be adjusted to the task at hand. In addition, careful feature selection and feature generation (constructive induction) is often necessary to achieve good quality. This increases even more the number of possible models to consider. It is the aim of the BMBF-funded research project SOMA (**S**ystematic **O**ptimization of **M**odels for **A**utomation and IT) to provide a general framework for constructing data mining models in a systematic, semi-automated or automated fashion: Tuned data mining (TDM) for applications in industry and science. In this paper we describe the first steps undertaken along this alley.

Features of TDM The goal of TDM as a subproject of SOMA for classification and regression tasks can be formulated as follows: Find a recipe / template for a generic data mining process which works well on many data mining tasks. That is more specifically:

- Besides from reading the data and task-specific data cleansing, the template is the same for each task. This makes it easily reusable for new tasks.
- Well-known machine learning methods, e.g., Random Forest (RF) [1, 2] or Support Vector Machines (SVM) [3, 4] available in R are reused within the R-based template implementation, and the template is open to the integration of new user-specific learning methods.

- Feature selection and/or feature generation methods are included in a systematic way within the optimization / tuning loop.
- Parameters are either set by general, non-task-specific rules or they are tuned by an automatic tuning procedure. We propose here to use SPOT (**S**equential **P**arameter **O**ptimization **T**oolbox) [5] in its recent R-implementation [6]. To our knowledge this is the first time that SPOT is used for systematic parameter tuning in data mining. The hyperparameters of SPOT are again either constant or set by general, non-task-specific rules.
- Special care should be taken not to overfit / oversearch: The quality of results, especially after parameter tuning, is checked on independent test sets and with independent test runs.

The interesting points from a learning perspective are: Is it possible to derive a data mining template together with an automated tuning procedure which achieves high-quality results on a variety of tasks? Which are the general rules that work well for many data mining (DM) tasks?

Related work There are several other data mining frameworks with a similar scope in the literature, e.g. ClearVu Analytics [7], Gait-CAD [8], MLR [9], RapidMiner [10]. We plan to compare our findings with results from these framework at a later point in time. Bischl et al. [11] have recently given an interesting overview of well-known resampling strategies. Their findings that careful model validation is essential to avoid overfitting and oversearching in tuning is compatible with our results in Sec. 3.2.

2   Methods

2.1   Tuned Data Mining (TDM) Template

The application of advanced machine learning models to different tasks is often difficult, because the selection of relevant features and the precise setting of model parameters is often a tedious trial-and-error task. Therefore our goal is to develop a general framework (you may call it a script or a program) which can be applied in the same manner to different tasks. Of course there is inevitably a task-specific part concerned with data reading and task-specific data cleansing and data preprocessing; we assume for the moment that this has been done and a prepared data set is at hand.

We consider here classification tasks, but the approach can be – and is in our framework – easily generalized to regression tasks as well. If we have a prepared data set, the following steps of the data mining process can be formulated in a generic way:

DATA MINING TEMPLATE:

- Sampling, i.e. the division of the data in training and test set (random, k-fold CV, ...)
- Generic feature selection: currently variable ranking based on RF, but also EA, see Sec. 2.2

- Modeling: currently SVM, RF, Metacost.RF (see Sec. 2.3), but other models, especially all those available in R can easily be integrated
- Model application: predict class and (optional, depending on model) class probabilities
- User-defined postprocessing (optional)
- Evaluation of model: confusion matrix, gain matrix, score, ...

All these steps are controlled by general or model-specific parameters. Some of these parameters may be fixed by default settings or by generic rules, other parameters usually need task-specific optimization, a process which is generally referred to as "tuning". With a general-purpose tuning algorithm like SPOT (Sequential Paramater Optimization Toolbox, cf. Sec. 2.4) it is now possible to embed the above data mining template in a tuning optimization loop:

TUNED DATA MINING TEMPLATE:
    while (budget not exhausted) **do**
        Choose specific parameter values for all the parameters to be tuned.
        Run the DATA MINING TEMPLATE with these values and report result.
    end while

Our goal is: Construct *one* template (program) for the whole generic process, which can be equally well applied to a variety of tasks and reach high-quality results.

Although we have with SPOT a general-purpose tuning algorithm, some points concerning the tuning part deserve further attention: the passus 'for all the parameters to be tuned' in the above pseudo-code requires that - given a model - the set of parameters to be tuned as well as their range (ROI = region of interest) has to be prescribed beforehand. It is a question which can be only answered by experiments whether *one* such triple {model, parameter set, ROI} fits for a large variety of tasks. If it turns out to be difficult to find one triple for all tasks, the condition can be somewhat relaxed if we allow for n tripels {model, parameter set, ROI}, run the generic TDM process for each triple and select the best-out-of-n result. This allows for the possibility that for task A a tuned triple 1 reaches the best result, while task B has a tuned triple 2 as its best choice. In order to select the right triple it is then of course important that the best performance measure on the tuning data is also a reliable predictor of the best performance on unseen test data. It means that we have to be careful to avoid overfitting and oversearching, an issue which is covered in Sec. 3.2.

2.2 Generic feature selection

Selecting the right features is often of large importance for high-quality results in data mining.[1] Standard approaches like sequential forward selection or sequential backward elimination [12] allow quite accurate selection of the right features for a certain model, but they have the disadvantage of high computational costs proportional to N^2, N being the number of input variables, which makes them difficult to use for large N.

---

[1]In this paper the term *feature* is equivalent to *input variable*, but future work might include the possibility to form out of the given inputs new derived features.

Table 1: Gain matrices for the tasks DMC-2007 and DMC-2010. A gain-sensitive matrix is a matrix where not all off-diagonal matrix elements are the same or where not all diagonal elements are the same.

DMC 2007		predict (p)		
		A	B	N
true (t)	A	3	-1	0
	B	-1	6	0
	N	-1	-1	0

DMC 2010		predict	
		0	1
true (t)	0	1	0
	1	-5	0

Another option is variable ranking where a certain pre-model (e.g. a Random Forest with reduced number of trees) allows to rank the input variables according to their importance. Given this importance (where it is a tacit assumption that the importance of the pre-model is also representative for the full model), it is possible to transform the combinatoric feature selection problem into a simpler numeric optimization problem which has moderate computational costs for arbitrary numbers of input variables:

> *Importance selection rule:* Sort the input variables by decreasing importance $I_n, n = 1, \ldots, N$ and select the first K variables such that

$$\sum_{n=1}^{K} I_n \geq X_{perc} \sum_{n=1}^{N} I_n \tag{1}$$

This means that we select those K variables which capture at least the fraction $X_{perc} \in [0, 1]$ of the overall importance. A nice feature of this approach is that a range $0.8 \leq X_{perc} \leq 1.0$ is usually a reasonable choice for tuning, irrespective of the number of features in the task and also irrespective of the number of unimportant features among them.

We use the importance delivered by R's `randomForest` package [2] in our current implementation, but other importance measures could be used equally well. A general remark to keep in mind: The validity of variable ranking rests on the validity of the pre-model and its predictions. If the pre-model is not appropriate for the task, it is also likely that the selections based on variable ranking will not result in optimal classification models.

Another option for feature selection are Genetic Algorithms (GA), which were studied by us in application to a regression task using SVM [13]. GA-based feature selection is more time-consuming but valuable if a variable ranking based on RF as pre-model does not produce good predictions.

2.3 Cost-sensitive modeling

Many classification problems require cost-sensitive or equivalently gain-sensitive modeling. This is the case if the cost (or negative gain) for different misclassifications differs or if the gain for correct classifications differs, see for example

Tab. 1. Advanced classification algorithms can be made gain-sensitive by adjusting different parameters. For example in Random Forest the following options are available (N_c is the number of classes):

CLASSWT: a class weight vector with length N_c indicating the importance of class i.

CUTOFF: a vector c_i with length N_c and sum 1 specifying that the predicted class i is that one which maximizes v_i/c_i where v_i is the fraction of trees voting for class i. The default is $c_i = 1/N_c$ $\forall i$.

Sample size: a vector of length N_c specifying the number of training records drawn from each class.

These are many parameters and it is often difficult to find the right settings by manual adjustment, because the precise value of the above parameters depends in a complex manner on the gain matrix, the a-priori probability of each class in the training data, and the interaction between these three parameter options. Therefore careful tuning of those parameters is often of utmost importance to reach high-quality results.

MetaCost An alternative to task-specific parameter tuning are wrapper models which can turn any (cost-insensitive) base model into a cost-sensitive meta model. We consider as an example the MetaCost algorithm by Domingos [14]. This algorithm maximizes the structural gain by relabeling the training data: It assigns to each training record x such a class label $c(x)$ that the structural gain is maximized:

$$c(x) = \arg\max_p \sum_t P(t|x)G(t,p) \qquad (2)$$

Here $G(t,p)$ is the gain associated with true class t when predicting it as class p. $P(t|x)$ is the (usually unknown) a-posteriori probability that t is the true class, given the observed input x. $P(t|x)$ can be either estimated by training $k = 1, \ldots, K$ different base models M_k, feeding each input x into every M_k and assigning to $P(t|x)$ the fraction of models M_k voting for class t. Or the base model itself offers already an estimate for $P(t|x)$ which is simply used by MetaCost. – Once the training records are relabeled, MetaCost trains a final model M on the relabeled target. This model M will maximize the gain when used for further predictions.

MetaCost for RF We implemented an RF-based MetaCost algorithm which we will abbreviate with MC.RF in the following. In the case of Random Forest (RF) the fraction of OOB-votes [2] for class t and input x is already a reliable estimate for $P(t|x)$ and therefore used in our MC.RF-implementation. This allows to shorten the time-consuming training of K models M_k: We need only one RF for relabeling and a second RF for model M. – With a first look on the above description of MetaCost it might appear that MetaCost already finds by construction the best settings for all cost-sensitive parameters. However, we will examine below the question whether MC.RF can be further optimized by tuning the RF-specific parameters CLASSWT and CUTOFF and we will find evidence that there is indeed room for considerable improvement.

Table 2: Tunable parameters and their ROI for the classification models RF and MC.RF. Index $i \in 1, \ldots, N_c - 1$, where N_c is the number of classes. As an example the best tuning results from Sec. 3.1 for DMC-2010 are shown.

	RF		MC.RF	
	ROI	best DMC-2010	ROI	best DMC-2010
CUTOFF[i]	[0.1,0.8]	0.734	[0.1,0.8]	0.448
CLASSWT[i]	[2.0,18]	5.422	[2.0,18]	4.6365
XPERC	[0.9,1.0]	0.999	[0.9,1.0]	0.9505

2.4 Generic tuning with SPOT

The Sequential Parameter Optimization Toolbox (SPOT) [5, 6] allows to tune of many parameters simultaneously. It is well-suited for optimization problems with noisy output functions (as they occur frequently in data mining) and it can reach good results with few model-building experiments since it builds during its sequence of runs a surrogate model which is constantly refined as the tuning progresses. SPOT has been recently made available as R-package [6].

We use SPOT here to answer the following question: Is it – given a certain data mining model – possible to specify *one* set of tunable parameters together with their ROI (region of interest) such that for several challenging data mining tasks a high-quality result is reached after tuning? – If the answer to this question is 'Yes', we can combine machine learning and its parameter tuning in a black-box fashion which will facilitate its wide-spread use in industry and economy.

After some initial experiments the set of parameters and ROIs as specified in Tab. 2 was used for all the results reported below. We have $3, 5, 7, \ldots$ parameters for a $(N_c = 2, 3, 4, \ldots)$-class problem, since one of the parameters in each vector CUTOFF and CLASSWT is fixed by a constraint: CUTOFF$[N_c]$ = $1 - \sum_{i=1}^{N_c-1}$ CUTOFF[i] and CLASSWT[1]=10. If SPOT should suggest a constraint-violating parameter choice, e.g.

$$CUTOFF[1] + CUTOFF[2] = 0.7 + 0.8 > 1,$$

this is transformed by appropriate scaling to a constraint-compliant choice.

All SPOT-tuning experiments were performed with the following settings (see [6] for further details): 50 sequence steps, 3 new design points in each step, up to 5 repeats per design point (to dampen statistical fluctuations), and 10 initial design points. This leads to 747 data mining models to be built for each SPOT tuning experiment. Random Forest was used as a fast surrogate model building tool, but other techniques as Kriging could have been used as well.

Table 3: Task overview

Task	number of records (training / test)	number of inputs	number of classes	cost-sensitive?
Sonar (UCI)	208	60	2	no
DMC-2007	50000 / 50000	20	3	yes
DMC-2010	32428 / 32427	38	2	yes

3   Results

3.1   Benchmark tasks

The benchmark tasks studied in this paper are briefly summarized in Tab. 3. The Sonar dataset as one simple benchmark from the UCI Machine Lerning Repository [15] gave the expected result that the default RF or SVM model already achieved 84.8% accuracy which is close to the best result obtained in the original work by Gorman and Sejnowski [16] and which can not be significantly improved by tuning.

We concentrate in the following on the two different DMC (Data Mining Cup) competitions [17] as benchmarks. These tasks with their realistic size (60000-100000 records, 25-50 input variables) provide interesting benchmarks as they go beyond the level of toy problems. Many comparative results from other teams participating in the Data Mining Cup allow to gauge the quality of our results achieved with the general template.

Note that in all results described below no task-specific model adjustment or task-specific postprocessing has taken place. Only the general TDM framework with its general models (with either default settings or tuned settings) has been used.

3.1.1   DMC-2007

DMC-2007 is a three-class, cost-sensitive classification task with the gain matrix shown in Tab. 1, left. The data consists of 50000 training records with 20 inputs and 50000 test records with the same inputs. Class N has with 76% a much higher frequency than the other classes A and B, but only a correctly classified A or B will contribute positively to the gain. The DMC-2007 contest had 230 participants whose resulting score distribution are shown in Fig. 1 as boxplots (we removed 13 entries with score < 0 in order to concentrate on the important participants). Our results from different models are overlayed as horizontal lines and arrows to this diagram. We can learn from this:

- Using the default parameters in RF or MC.RF gives only bad results, well below the mean of the DMC participants' distribution. This is no surprise for the base RF[2], because it minimizes the misclassification error and is thus

---

[2]with CLASSWT=CUTOFF=NULL

not well-suited for a cost-sensitive problem. But it is a surprise for MC.RF which is supposed to behave optimally in the presence of cost-sensitive effects. We will discuss this topic further at the end of Sec. 3.1.

- The tuned results delivered by SPOT are much better: Model RF.tuned reaches the highest quartile and the results of model MC.RF.tuned are close to this quartile. It is thus crucial to tune CLASSWT and CUTOFF for cost-sensitive problems.
- The CV estimate of the total gain (red dashed line) is in good agreement with the final gain (blue arrows).

We note in passing, that hand-tuning CLASSWT and CUTOFF usually leads to gains in the range 6000-7000, and it is in general a very time-consuming task since no good rules-of-thumb exist for these parameters .

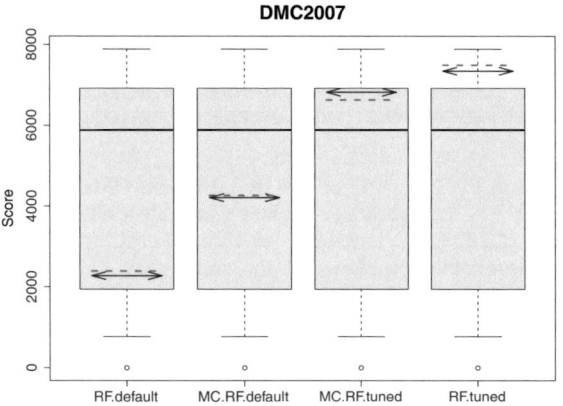

Figure 1: Results for the DMC-2007 benchmark: The boxplot shows the spread of score (gain) among the competition participants, the red dashed lines show the score of our models on the training data (10-fold cross validation), the blue arrows show the score of these trained models on the real test data.

3.1.2   DMC-2010

DMC-2010 is a two-class, cost-sensitive classification task with the gain matrix shown in Tab. 1, right. The data consists of 32428 training records with 37 inputs and 32427 test records with the same inputs. Class 0 is with 81.34% of all trainings records much more frequent than the other class 1. Given this a-priori probability and the above gain matrix, there is a very naïve model "always predict class 0" which gives a gain of $32428 \cdot (1.5 * 81.34\% - 5 * 18.66\%) = 9310$ on the training data. Any realistic model should do better than this.

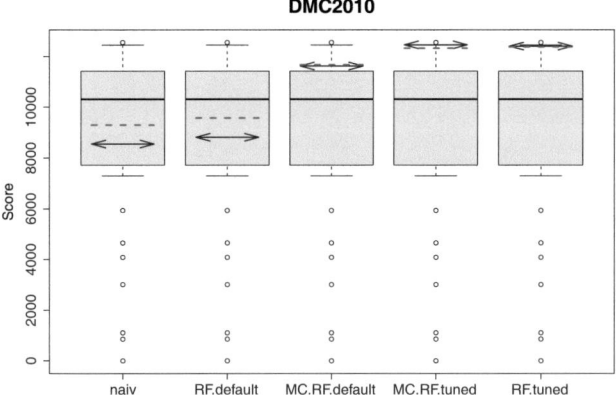

Figure 2: Results for the DMC-2010 benchmark.

The data of DMC-2010 require some preprocessing, because they contain a small fraction of missing values, some obviously wrong inputs and some factor variables with too many levels which need to be grouped. This task-specific data preparation was done beforehand.

The DMC-2010 contest had 67 participating teams whose resulting score distribution is shown in Fig. 2 as boxplot (we removed 17 entries with score < 0 or NA in order to concentrate on the important teams). Our results from different models are overlayed as horizontal lines and arrows in this diagram. We can learn from this:

- For the naïve model the blue arrow is lower than the red line because the class-0-percentage is with 80.9% lower in the test set than in the training set (81.34%).
- The model RF.default is hardly better than the naïve model. Indeed it behaves nearly identical to the naïve model in an attempt to minimize the misclassification error.
- Except for the naïve model, the CV estimates of the total gain (red dashed lines) are again in good agreement with the final gain (blue arrows).
- MC.RF.default is now already quite good (at the lower rim of the highest quartile), but both tuned models achieve again considerably better results: They are at the upper rim of the highest quartile; within the rank table of the real DMC-2010 contest this corresponds to rank 2 and rank 4 for MC.RF.tuned and RF.tuned, resp.

3.1.3 Parameter Sensitivity

It is an advantage of parameter tuning with SPOT that the user can investigate the sensitivity of the model with respect to the tuned parameters. This is done with

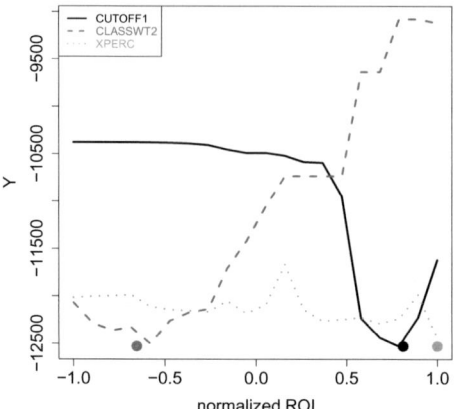

Figure 3: Sensitivity plot for the best parameter set found by SPOT when tuning the DMC-2010 task. Each circle indicates the location of the best value for a parameter within its ROI. The lines are the responses from SPOT's surrogate model when varying a certain parameter within its ROI.

SPOT's addin `spotReportSens` which delivers a diagram as shown in Fig. 3. The curves show certain slices from the surrogate model constructed by SPOT: If we set all parameters to the best point found by SPOT and vary one of the parameter within its ROI, we get a sensitivity curve of the model on that parameter. The x-axis has each parameter range (ROI, seeTab. 2) normalized to the interval [-1,1]. This demonstrates for example that CUTOFF1 is an important parameter in the DMC-2010 task (narrow, deep valley), while the model is relatively insensitive to the precise setting of XPERC (broad, shallow valley).

3.1.4 Limitations of MetaCost

Why is MC.RF so bad in the DMC-2007 task, especially with its default values? – We believe that this is due to the fact that input data in the DMC-2007 task allow only weak predictability: even the best participant of the contest reached just 17.2% of the maximal gain. (This is very different to the DMC-2010 task where the relative gain of the winner was 31.4%.) It makes the relabeling process more difficult and might result in many records not optimally relabeled. In this case a direct tuning of CLASSWT, which directly influences on which part of the given input information the trees put more emphasis, seems to yield better results than MetaCost.

Table 4: Different total gains compared for the tuned models and the benchmark tasks considered. See main text for explanation of the columns BST-OOB, OOB, CV, TST. Each cell contains mean ± std.dev. from 5 repeated runs with different random seeds. The column "Rank DMC" is the rank of gain TST within the result table of the corresponding DMC contest. The maximum gain within each contest was 7890 and 12455 for DMC-2007 and DMC-2010, resp.

task	model	total gain				Rank
		BST-OOB	OOB	CV	TST	DMC
DMC2007	RF.tuned	7584 ± 52	7493 ± 66	7491 ± 24	7343 ± 38	37/230
	MC.RF.tuned	7574 ± 99	7590 ± 96	6632 ± 33	6822 ± 131	61/230
DMC2010	RF.tuned	12549 ± 44	12475 ± 49	12368 ± 83	12400 ± 23	4/67
	MC.RF.tuned	14250 ± 121	14110 ± 99	12322 ± 94	12451 ± 103	2/67

3.2 Overfitting and Oversearching

3.2.1 Resampling Strategies

It is of utmost importance for building high-quality data mining models to obtain – given only the training data – a good, unbiased estimate of the expected gain (or error) on unseen test data . Several resampling options exist and are compared in Tab. 4, but all have their specific pros and cons:

CV: k-fold cross validation, commonly used with $k = 10$, is a reliable estimate for the gain to expect on unseen data. However, it is also 10 times more costly and thus often prohibitively slow for tuning processes. Tab. 4 shows the CV for the final tuned models.

OOB: Random Forest allows with its OOB-prediction[3] [2] to compute an unbiased gain much faster, because only one RF is needed. The column OOB in Tab. 4 is the average of 5 independent runs (model building with different random initializations plus OOB-prediction), all based on the final tuned parameter set.

BST-OOB: The OOB-gain is used as maximization criterion during SPOT-tuning. The best result BST-OOB returned from the tuning process is the highest average of 5 repeated OOB-gains obtained with a certain parameter set during tuning.

TST: While the three options CV, OOB and BST-OOB all operate on the training data alone, this last measure TST operates on unseen test data and is used to check the validity of the above measures. It is the average gain obtained with the final tuned parameter set when building 5 independent models on the training data and evaluating the gain on unseen test data.

---

[3]OOB = out-of-bag prediction: use for a certain training record's prediction only those trees which had this record *not* in their training 'bag'. This gives an unbiased estimate of the test set gain.

For other models than RF the OOB-prediction might not be available. In this case it can be replaced by

RSUB: random subsampling, i.e. partitioning the data randomly in training and test set,

BLOC: blocking, i.e. $1, \ldots, k$ set pairs {training,test} are randomly formed but hold constant throughout the whole (tuning) process.

Both options are available in the TDM framework, but they were not used in this paper. The random selection in RSUB will often introduce some difficulties when used for tuning: An otherwise better parameter set might be rejected simply because it is evaluated on a more difficult test set. The strategy BLOC keeps the test set(s) fixed which is better for tuning, however, at the price that either only a part of the data is tested or that the computation cost becomes close to that of CV.

3.2.2   Comparison of Resampling Methods

We study on our DMC benchmarks how different resampling strategies perform. Tab. 4 compares the different gain estimates and some interesting observations can be made:

Oversearching   One could have expected that OOB and BST-OOB were the same since they measure the same thing on the same parameters. But it turns out that BST-OOB is slightly (1%) but significantly[4] higher than OOB. This is an issue of **oversearching** which we expect to observe always when tuning a stochastic optimization function: the model building process of RF (or many other data mining models) has an inherent stochastic element due to the random assignment of training data to each tree. If there are several parameter settings which give comparable results, then the tuning process will return that pair {parameter setting, gain} which happens to have the highest average gain out of 5 repeats (column BST-OOB). When the same parameter set is evaluated *after* the tuning process in 5 independent runs (column OOB), the gain will be on average a bit lower.

We note in passing, that even larger oversearching effects in the range of 16% to 60% have been observed recently in SPOT tuning experiments for regression [13]. These large effects are observed if training is done on one quarter of the data, tuning on a second quarter and evaluation is either done on this second quarter (oversearching) or it is done on the remaining two quarters (no oversearching).

Overfitting   In the case of the MetaCost-implementation MC.RF we see that both columns BST-OOB and OOB severely overestimate the gain by 11-14%.[5] This is an issue of **overfitting** which can be attributed to the two-staged nature of Meta-Cost: The OOB-data at each tree are no longer independent, since the relabeling

---

[4]The p-values for Student's t-test on the two RF.tuned models are p=0.041 and p=0.036, resp., meaning that the means of BST-OOB and OOB are significantly different at the 5%-level.

[5]Note that the winner of the DMC-2010 contest had a gain 12545, well below the claimed OOB-gain.

process made use of all training data. Nevertheless, we expect the OOB-gain to have roughly the same bias for all parameter settings, so that it may be a valuable measure for steering the tuning process, although its absolute value is not reliable.

Cross Validation The gain in column CV is in all cases quite a good estimate of the gain on the unseen test data (the observable difference might be attributed to differences in the two data sets).

Therefore we suggest to use the different gain estimates in the following manner: use OOB (or RSUB or BLOC) resampling for steering the tuning process, but do not take the final gain reported from this tuning process as granted. Instead, perform with the best parameter set found by tuning a new and independent model building process with 10-fold CV (which might be repeated m times). The average of these m CV-gains is a good and fairly unbiased estimate of the real gain on unseen test data.

4 Conclusion

This paper has shown first steps towards a general data mining framework which combines feature selection, model building and parameter tuning within one integrated optimization environment. We have studied with TDM two challenging classification tasks with cost-sensitivity where standard models using default parameters do not achieve high-quality results. This puts the necessity of parameter tuning for data mining into focus: We have shown

1. that parameter tuning with SPOT gives large improvements, yielding results in the upper quartil, sometimes even rank 2 to 4, of the DMC-contest table;
2. that one generic template can be used for quite different classification tasks;
3. that MetaCost is not always the best model for cost-sensitive classification tasks and
4. that MetaCost can be improved by parameter tuning with SPOT.

In future work we want (a) to compare our TDM framework with other DM frameworks with a similar scope [7, 8, 9, 10], (b) to test TDM on more of tasks, including regression applications and (c) to provide a broader range of models with prescribed tunable parameter sets and corresponding ROIs.

5 Acknowledgements

This work has been supported by the Bundesministerium für Bildung und Forschung (BMBF) under the grant SOMA (AiF FKZ 17N1009, "Ingenieurnachwuchs") and by the Cologne University of Applied Sciences under the research focus grant COSA.

References

[1] Breiman, L.: Random Forests. *Machine Learning* 45 (2001) 1, S. 5 –32.

[2] Liaw, A.; Wiener, M.: Classification and Regression by randomForest. *R News* 2 (2002), S. 18–22. http://CRAN.R-project.org/doc/Rnews/.

[3] Vapnik, V. N.: *Statistical Learning Theory.* Wiley-Interscience. ISBN 0471030031. 1998.

[4] Schölkopf, B.; Smola, A. J.: *Learning with Kernels: Support Vector Machines, Regularization, Optimization, and Beyond.* Cambridge, MA, USA: MIT Press. 2002.

[5] Bartz-Beielstein, T.: *Experimental Research in Evolutionary Computation—The New Experimentalism.* Natural Computing Series. Berlin, Heidelberg, New York: Springer. 2006.

[6] Bartz-Beielstein, T.: SPOT: An R Package For Automatic and Interactive Tuning of Optimization Algorithms by Sequential Parameter Optimization. arXiv.org e-Print archive, http://arxiv.org/abs/1006.4645. 2010.

[7] Bäck, T.; Krause, P.: ClearVu Analytics. http://divis-gmbh.de/ClearVu. accessed 21.09.2010.

[8] Mikut, R.; Burmeister, O.; Reischl, M.; Loose, T.: Die MATLAB-Toolbox Gait-CAD. In: *Proceedings 16. Workshop Computational Intelligence* (Mikut, R.; Reischl, M., Hg.), S. 114–124. Karlsruhe: Universitätsverlag, Karlsruhe. 2006.

[9] Bischl, B.: The mlr package: Machine Learning in R. http://mlr.r-forge.r-project.org. accessed 25.09.2010.

[10] Mierswa, I.: Rapid Miner. http://rapid-i.com. accessed 21.09.2010.

[11] Bischl, B.; Mersmann, O.; Trautmann, H.: Resampling Methods in Model Validation. In: *Workshop WEMACS joint to PPSN2010* (Bartz-Beielstein, T.; et al., Hg.), Nr. TR10-2-007 in Technical Reports. TU Dortmund. 2010.

[12] Liu, H.; Yu, L.: Toward integrating feature selection algorithms for classification and clustering. *IEEE TRANSACTIONS ON KNOWLEDGE AND DATA ENGINEERING* 17 (2005), S. 491–502.

[13] Koch, P.; Konen, W.; Flasch, O.; Bartz-Beielstein, T.: Optimizing of Support Vector Regression Models for Stormwater Prediction. In: *Proceedings 20. Workshop Computational Intelligence* (Mikut, R.; Reischl, M., Hg.). Karlsruhe: Universitätsverlag, Karlsruhe. 2010.

[14] Domingos, P.: MetaCost: A General Method for Making Classifiers Cost-Sensitive. In: *Proceedings of the Fifth International Conference on Knowledge Discovery and Data Mining (KDD-99)*, S. 195–215. 1999.

[15] Frank, A.; Asuncion, A.: UCI Machine Learning Repository. URL http://archive.ics.uci.edu/ml. 2010.

[16] Gorman, R. P.; Sejnowski, T. J.: Analysis of Hidden Units in a Layered Network Trained to Classify Sonar Targets. *Neural Networks* 1 (1988), S. 75–89.

[17] Kögel, S.: Data Mining Cup DMC. `http://www.data-mining-cup.de`. accessed 21.09.2010.

Optimization of Support Vector Regression Models for Stormwater Prediction

Patrick Koch, Wolfgang Konen,
Oliver Flasch, and Thomas Bartz-Beielstein

Cologne University of Applied Sciences
E-Mail: {patrick.koch | oliver.flasch |
wolfgang.konen | thomas.bartz-beielstein}@fh-koeln.de

Abstract

In this paper we propose a solution to a real-world time series regression problem: the prediction of fill levels of stormwater tanks. Our regression model is based on *Support Vector Regression* (SVR), but can easily be replaced with other data mining methods. The main intention of the work is to overcome frequently occuring problems in data mining by automatically tuning both preprocessing and hyperparameters. We highly believe that many models can be improved by a systematic preprocessing and hyperparameter tuning. The optimization of our model is presented in a step-by-step manner which can easily be adapted to other time series problems. We point out possible issues of parameter tuning, e.g., we analyze our tuned models with respect to overfitting and oversearching (which are effects that might lead to a reduced model generalizability) and present methods to circumvent such issues.

1 Introduction

In environmental engineering stormwater tanks are installed to stabilize the load on the sewage system by preventing rainwater from flooding the system and by supplying a base load in dry periods. Heavy rainfalls are the most common reason for overflows of stormwater tanks, causing environmental pollution from wastewater contaminating the environment. To avoid such situations, the effluent of the stormwater tanks must be controlled effectively and possible future state changes in the inflow should be recognized as early as possible. This problem can be defined as a classical time series regression problem of predicting a stormwater tank fill level at time t from a fixed window of past rainfall data from time t back to time $t - W$ (for a fixed window size W) and will be referred to as the *stormwater problem* in the remainder of this paper.

A model that predicts fill levels by means of rainfall data can be an important aid for the controlling system. Special sensors (Fig. 1) record time series data which can be used to train such a model.

Although many methods exist for time series analysis [1], ranging from classical statistical regression to computational statistics, such methods often require time-consuming investigations on the hyperparameter selection and preprocessing of the data. Besides that, the results are often worse than special-purpose models which are designed from scratch for each new problem. This situation is of course very unsatisfying for the practitioner in environmental engineering, because new models have to be created and parameters have to be tuned manually for each problem.

Figure 1: Left: rain gauge (pluviometer). Right: stormwater tank.

For this reason, it would be an advantage to have some standard repertoire of methods which can be easily adapted to new problems. In this paper we use Support Vector Machines (SVM) [2] for Support Vector Regression as a state-of-the-art method from machine learning and apply them to the stormwater problem. SVMs are known to be a strong method for classification and regression. However, it has to be noted that because of the time series structure of the data consecutive records are not independent from each other, as it is the case in normal regression. Therefore we investigate a generic preprocessing operator to embed time series data and to generate new input features for the SVM model. In addition, we apply the sequential parameter optimization toolbox (SPOT) [3] and a genetic algorithm (GA) to the preprocessed data, to find good hyperparameter settings for both preprocessing and SVM parameters. We analyze the robustness of our method against overfitting and oversearching of hyperparameters.

Previous work in stormwater prediction has been done by Hilmer [4], Konen et al. [5], Bartz-Beielstein et al. [6] and Flasch et al. [7]. A conclusion of these previous publications is that good results can be obtained with specialized models (which are 'hand-crafted' and carefully adapted to the stormwater problem). A first step towards a more generic model based on Support Vector Regression has recently been presented by Koch et al. [8]. It has been shown, that superior results can be achieved, if hyperparameters are tuned and time series preprocessing is taken into account. Therefore, we point out the main hypotheses of this paper:

H1 It is possible to move away from domain-specific models for time series prediction without loss in accuracy by applying modern machine learning algorithms and modern parameter tuning methods on data augmented through generic time series preprocessing operators.

H2 Parameter tuning for stormwater prediction leads to oversearching, yielding too optimistic results on the dataset during tuning.

Hypothesis **H2** puts emphasis on the fact that a distinction between validation set (used during tuning) and test set (used for evaluation) is essential to correctly quantify the benefits from parameter tuning in data mining. The oversearching issue is prevalent in data mining since the output function to tune shows often a high variance when the data used for training or tuning are changed. This effect is also shown for other benchmark problems in a work of Konen et al. [9] in the same book.

2 Methods

2.1 Stormwater Tank Data

Time series data for this case study are collected from a real stormwater tank in Germany and consists of 30,000 data records, ranging from April to August 2006. Rainfall data are measured in three-minute intervals by a pluviometer as shown in Fig. 1. All models described in this paper were trained on a 5,000 record time window (Set 2, Fig. 2) in order to predict another 5,000 record time window for testing (Set 4, Tab. 1).

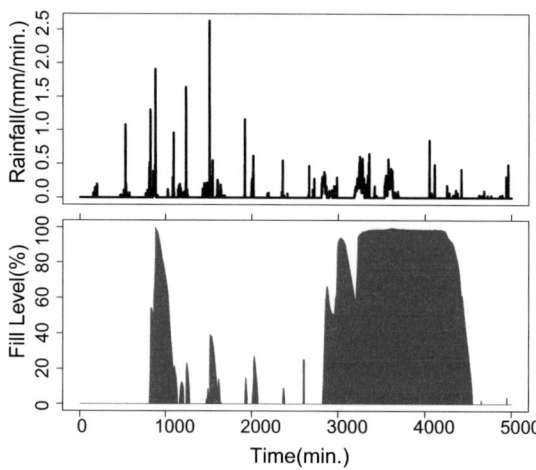

Figure 2: Training set showing rainfall and fill level time series data of the stormwater tank.
Table 1: Real-world time series data from a stormwater tank in Germany.

Set	Start Date	End Date
Set 1	2006-04-28 01:05:59	2006-05-15 09:40:59
Set 2	2006-05-15 09:40:59	2006-06-01 18:20:59
Set 3	2006-06-19 03:01:00	2006-07-06 11:41:00
Set 4	2006-07-23 20:21:00	2006-08-10 05:01:00

2.2 Evaluation of Models

The prediction error on the datasets is taken as objective function for SPOT and for the GA. For comparing models, we calculate the root mean squared error (RMSE) as a quality measure:

$$RMSE = \sqrt{(mean((Y_{predicted} - Y_{true})^2))} \tag{1}$$

We also incorporate the Theil's U index of inequality [10], where the RMSE of the trained model is compared to the RMSE of a naïve predictor. Here we are using the mean of the training data target as a naïve predictor:

$$U = \frac{RMSE(model)}{RMSE(naive)} \tag{2}$$

U values greater than 1 indicate models that perform worse than the naïve predictor, while values smaller than 1 indicate models that perform better than the naïve predictor.

2.3 Sequential Parameter Optimization Toolbox

The main purpose of SPOT is to determine improved parameter settings for search and optimization algorithms and to analyze and understand their performance.

During the first stage of experimentation, SPOT treats an algorithm A as a black box. A set of input variables $\vec{x}$, is passed to A. Each run of the algorithm produces some output $\vec{y}$. SPOT tries to determine a functional relationship F between $\vec{x}$ and $\vec{y}$ for a given problem formulated by an objective function $f : \vec{u} \to \vec{v}$. Since experiments are run on computers, pseudorandom numbers are taken into consideration if:

- the underlying objective function f is stochastically disturbed, e.g., measurement errors or noise occur, and/or

- the algorithm A uses some stochastic elements, e.g., mutation in evolution strategies.

SPOT employs a sequentially improved model to estimate the relationship between algorithm input variables and its output. This serves two primary goals. One is to enable determining good parameter settings, thus SPOT may be used as a tuner. Secondly, variable interactions can be revealed for helping in understanding how the tested algorithm works when confronted with a specific problem or how changes in the problem influence the algorithm's performance. Concerning the model, SPOT allows for insertion of virtually any available model. However, regression and Kriging models or a combination thereof are most frequently used. The Kriging predictor applied in this study uses a regression constant λ which is added to the diagonal of the correlation matrix. Maximum likelihood estimation was used to determine the regression constant λ [11, 12].

2.4 The INT2 Model for Predictive Control of Stormwater Tanks

In previous work [6, 5], the stormwater tank problem was investigated with different modeling approaches, among them FIR, NARX, ESN, a dynamical system based on ordinary differential equations (ODE) and a dynamical system based on integral equations (INT2). All models in these former works were systematically optimized using SPO [3]. Among these models the INT2 approach turned out to be the best one [6]. The INT2 model is an analytical regression model based on integral equations. Disadvantages of the INT2 model are that it is a special-purpose model only designed for stormwater prediction and that it is practically expensive to obtain an optimal parameter configuration: the parameterization example presented in [6] contains 9 tunable parameters which must be set. In this paper we compare hand-tuned INT2 parameters with the best parameter configuration found by SPOT in former study [6].

2.5 Support Vector Regression

Support Vector Machines have been successfully applied to regression problems by Drucker
et al. [2], Müller *et al.* [13], Mattera and Haykin [14], and Chan and Lin [15]. In these
studies the method has been shown to be superior to many other methods especially when
the dimensionality of the feature space is very large.

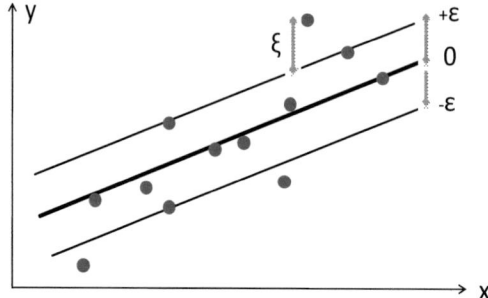

Figure 3: Example for Support Vector Regression. A tube with radius ϵ is learned to represent the
real target function. Possible outliers are being regularized considering a positive slack
variable ξ.

The idea of Support Vector Regression (SVR) is to transform the input space of the training
data usually to a higher-order space using a non-linear mapping, e.g. a radial basis function.
In this higher-order space a linear function is learned, which has at most ϵ deviation
from the real values in general and at most ξ deviation for certain outliers. An example
for Support Vector Regression and its parameters ϵ and ξ is depicted in Fig. 3. The
transformation to a higher-order space by a non-linear kernel function with parameter γ is
not shown here. For a more detailed description of SVR we refer to Smola and Schölkopf
[16].

3   Preprocessing for Stormwater Prediction Models

Time series prediction models can benefit from preprocessing operators which generate
new features based on the input data. There are two possibilities to integrate such operators
into the SVM modeling process:

- Integration into the SVR kernel function, i.e. replacing standard kernel functions by
  kernel functions that incorporate preprocessing operators

- Direct preprocessing of the data, i.e. by augmenting the input feature set with results
  of preprocessing

In this work we choose the second approach, because the effect of this integration into a
model is easier to analyze. In a first step, we compare the effects of applying different types
of time series preprocessing operators on SVM model accuracy. Details on preprocessing

operators as the *embedding* operator and *leaky rain* as an integral operator suited for time series analysis are given in Sec. 3.2 and Sec. 3.3 respectively. All preliminary models built on the following varieties of input features were used in the following experimental setups to make them comparable:

E1 Predicting fill levels based only on current rainfall

E2 Predicting fill levels with embedding of rainfall

E3 Predicting fill levels with embedding of leaky rain and rainfall

E4 Predicting fill levels with embedding of leaky rain only

E5 Predicting fill levels with embedding of multiple leaky rain kernel functions

In our experiments we used the radial basis SVM kernel from the *e1071* SVM-implementation in R, since we achieved best results with this kernel choice. Other SVR hyperparameters were obtained by SPO, namely parameters γ, ϵ and ξ, to make our results comparable to each other. All models created for optimization of the preprocessing were trained on set 2 and evaluated on set 4 (see Tab. 1). As objective function for SPOT tuning we used the prediction error on the test set, which is topic of criticism and will be treated in the discussion section of this work. In the following subsections, we describe the setup of the preprocessing operators used for these different model variants in more detail.

3.1 E1: Predicting Fill Levels without Preprocessing

The most simple approach is to predict fill levels solely based on the current rainfall, taken as only input feature for the SVM. Regardless of which SVR hyperparameter configuration was used, the obtained RMSE for this model on the test set couldn't get about 45.8% better than a naïve prediction.[1] Although the SVM prediction is more accurate than the naïve one, it can be seen in Fig. 4 that the length of high fill level periods are frequently underestimated throughout the whole test period. For this reason, this very simple model is not competitive to models like the INT2 by Konen *et al.* [5].

3.2 E2: Embedding of Rainfall

One major difference of time series problems in comparison to standard regression problems is that timeseries usually have certain dependencies of successive records. This has not been taken into consideration in our last model, which might be a main reason for its poor accuracy. Therefore usually an embedding of the input data [17] is conducted. Here, the fill level of stormwater overflow tanks $l(t)$ can be represented by a function F on past input features, more precisely by the rainfall $r(t)$ up to $r(t - W)$, where t indicates time and $W \in \mathbb{N}^+$ is the embedding dimension:

$$l(t) := F(r(t), r(t-1), r(t-2), ..., r(t-W)) \tag{3}$$

---

[1]Naïve prediction means predicting the mean value of the training set.

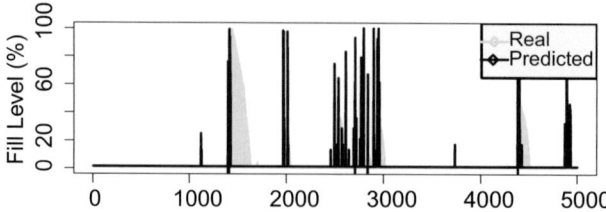

Figure 4: Plot of predicted fill levels using only rain data without any preprocessing.

Table 2: Best SPOT parameter configuration for rainfall embedding. The region of interest (ROI) bounds have been refined after preliminary runs with SPO.

Parameter	Best Value found	ROI
Embedding W_{rain}	43	$[2, 60]$
SVM γ	0.0116667	$[0.005, 0.3]$
SVM χ	1.25	$[0, 10]$
SVM ϵ	0.0116667	$[0.005, 0.3]$

The influence of past data points on the current data point is generally unknown, but might be detected by the SVM model, if we augment each record $r(t)$ with its predecessors $r(t-1), ..., r(t - W_{rain})$. Since the embedding parameter might have a crucial meaning for our model quality, we add this parameter to the SPOT tuning. This setup led us to a tuning of either the embedding dimension W_{rain} and of the SVM parameters γ, χ and ϵ. SPOT tuned parameter values which are presented in Tab. 2.

With an RMSE of 14.98 (cf. Tab. 4), the SVM model has gained accuracy by using an embedding of past rainfall in comparison to just using the current rainfall data point.

3.3 E3: Leaky Rain and Rainfall Embedding

In the design of the previous model, the rainfall at time $t - 40$ has been considered to be of the same importance as the rainfall at time $t - 5$. This is of course not true, because loosely speaking, the rainfall from two days in the past should not have the same impact on the fill level as the rainfall from the last 20 minutes. Or more precisely, the rain is a measurable quantity which drains into the soil and then – depending on the consistence of the soil – flows into the stormwater tanks with a certain delay. Therefore the rainfall could be summed up and this integrated quantity could than be used as a new feature of the input data. How can it be expressed that, given $w_2 > w_1$, rainfall from time $t - w_2$ has less influence than $t - w_1$ on $l(t)$? We define the preprocessing operator *leaky rain*

$$\sum_{i=0}^{T} \left(\lambda^i \cdot r(t - i) \right) \tag{4}$$

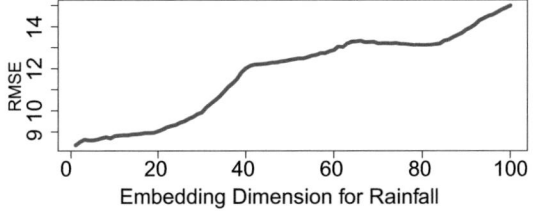

Figure 5: Progressively increasing the rainfall embedding dimension W_{rain}, while keeping leaky rain embedding dimension W constant at 43.

where $\lambda \in [0, 1]$, T is the length of the integration and t is the current time. The formula can be efficiently computed by Fast Fourier Transformation (FFT) even for large datasets.

The summarized results in Tab. 4 show that there is a vast reduction of prediction error by using this more sophisticated input feature: the RMSE with leaky rain embedding decreases from 14.98 to 10.14.

3.4 E4: Embedding of Leaky Rain Only

Surprisingly the rainfall embedding is no longer advantageous when leaky-rain embedding is taken into account. This fact can be clearly deduced from Fig. 5, where the RMSE is nearly monotonously increasing with higher rainfall embedding dimensions, given a constant leaky rain embedding dimension of $W = 43$. Besides that, the modeling process is slower when higher embedding dimensions are used, because the SVM has to cope with more input dimensions and much more data.

Learning from this observation, we omit the rainfall embedding W_{rain} and concentrate on optimizing the embedding dimension for the leaky rain embedding. Therefore, we performed a similar embedding dimension experiment for leaky rain. Results are shown in Fig. 6. The plot shows clearly that there is an almost monotonous decrease of prediction error when using embeddings up to 40 dimensions. The prediction error increases again for more than 40 dimensions. This effect could be explained by two processes. First, the infomation gain decreases with increasing embedding dimension, because the influence of rainfall on the target decreases with increasing time lag. This may lead to a model with worse generalization capabilities. Secondly, the model is fitted to a higher number of input dimensions, including disturbing factors as noise, measurement errors, etc. Summarized, these factors may lead to more complex models which are prone to overfitting.

When tuning the parameters, SPOT delivered an embedding dimension of 43 which is not the global optimum, but is very close to it. Possible improvements to this result can be achieved by increasing the function evaluations in the SPOT settings or incorporating a local search strategy on the SPOT parameters for fine-tuning.

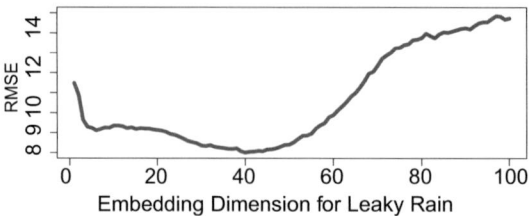

Figure 6: Progressively increasing the leaky rain embedding dimension W. The optimal embedding dimension is at $W = 40$ which was almost found by SPO. No rainfall embedding was used here.

3.5 E5: Two Leaky Rain Functions

Leaky rain has shown to be an adequate preprocessing function to simplify learning of the target function. However, the true function might be more complex due to factors not incorporated in our simple leaky rain function. Therefore, we employed a more complex preprocessing by using two leaky rain functions at the same time (Fig. 7). We tuned the parameters λ, T, and W independently for each of the two functions by SPOT leading to a new parameter configuration as shown in Tab. 3.

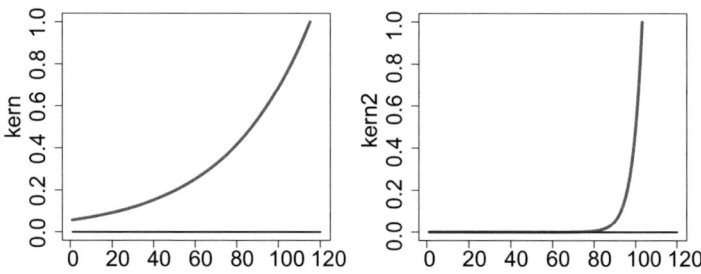

Figure 7: Left and right curve: the two leaky rain kernel functions obtained by SPO. Bottom lines: zero level.

After integrating the two kernel functions in our model, the RMSE slightly improves from 8.09 to 7.80 compared with a single leaky rain function, outperforming the INT2 model again. Note that one leaky kernel function uses a larger λ value and a shorter embedding dimension (less than half size of the first embedding dimension), so that both functions seem to support each other (Fig. 7).

Table 3: Best SPOT parameter configuration for all tuned parameters evaluated on set 4. The region of interest (ROI) bounds are the final values after preliminary runs.

Type	Parameter	Best found	ROI	Remark
Embedding	W_1	39	$[2, 60]$	embed. dimension 1
	W_2	16	$[2, 60]$	embed. dimension 2
	T_1	114	$[50, 120]$	leaky window size 1
	T_2	102	$[50, 120]$	leaky window size 2
	λ_1	0.0250092	$[0.00001, 0.3]$	leaky decay 1
	λ_2	0.225002	$[0.00001, 0.3]$	leaky decay 2
SVM	γ	0.0116667	$[0.005, 0.3]$	RBF kernel width
	ϵ	0.0116667	$[0.005, 0.3]$	ϵ-insensitive loss fct.
	χ	1.25	$[0, 10]$	penalty term

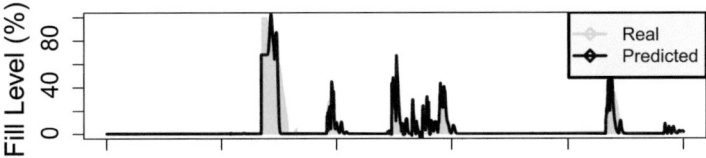

Figure 8: Prediction gathered by SVM with two leaky rain embeddings optimized separately by SPOT.

3.6 Summary of Preprocessing

A comparison of the results of all models obtained so far can be found in Tab. 4. It can be concluded that the model with the most complex preprocessing (two different leaky rain embeddings) leads to the best prediction accuracy. The worst results are obtained when no prepocessing is employed, indicating that no satisfying model for the stormwater problem can be found without using a special preprocessing. It seems that rainfall itself does not contain enough accessible information to do accurate predictions of the fill level. As soon as leaky rain is added as a feature for the SVM model, prediction accuracy increases considerably.

Table 4: Precision comparison of all models on set 4

Model type	RMSE	Theil's U
Naïve prediction	33.34	1.00
E1: Only Rainfall	18.07	0.54
E2: Rainfall Emb. w/o Leaky	14.98	0.45
E3: Rainfall and Leaky Rain	10.14	0.30
INT2	9.00	0.27
E4: Leaky Rain Embedding	8.09	0.24
E5: Two Leaky Embeddings	7.80	0.23

Table 5: Results of SPOT tuning on the stormwater problem. In each row 1-3 of the table, SPOT tunes the RMSE on validation set 1,3,4 leading to different SPOT-tuned parameter configurations. These configurations were applied to the test sets (columns) to make the results comparable. Each experiment was repeated five times with different seeds and we show the mean RMSE; bold-faced numbers are best values on the test set and the numbers in brackets indicate standard deviations.

		Test		
		Set 1	Set 3	Set 4
	Set 1	**9.11** (0.56)	16.40 (6.42)	12.88 (5.50)
Validation	Set 3	10.82 (1.55)	**12.78**(0.34)	12.36 (3.46)
	Set 4	10.45 (0.28)	12.93 (0.35)	**7.69** (0.48)
	S_t	10.64	14.67	12.62
	V_t	16.7%	14.7%	64.1%

4 Discussion

4.1 T1: Parameter Tuning by SPOT

In our last models we used the prediction error gathered on the test dataset as the objective function value for the hyperparameter tuning with SPOT. In the real world this value is unknown and when available during optimization it gives the tuned model an unfair advantage. In order to perform a fair comparison and to show the benefits of parameter tuning in a more realistic setting, we should use a different objective function. Otherwise the test set error might be too optimistic since the model has been tuned and tested on the same set. In Tab. 5, we present the mean results of five SPOT runs for the SVR model to determine optimal parameter settings which are then alternately evaluated on the sets 1,3,4. Again, dataset 2 has been used for training. The best configuration found by SPOT is then applied in turn to the other sets (columns) resulting in 3 RMSE values for each parameter configuration. We used the Matlab implementation of SPO[2] allowing a total budget of 200 SVM models to be built and a maximum number of 500 samples in the metamodel.

A strong indication of oversearching is when best values are often present in the diagonal of the table. It can be seen that this is the case for all validation sets of Tab. 5. Besides this, standard deviations of the offdiagonal values are also larger than the values on the diagonal.

We quantify the oversearching effect by evaluating the following formula: let R_{vt} denote the RMSE for row v and column t of Tab. 5. We define

$$V_t = \frac{S_t - R_{tt}}{R_{tt}} \quad \text{with} \quad S_t = \frac{1}{3}\left(\sum_{v=1}^{4} R_{vt} - R_{tt}\right) \tag{5}$$

With S_t we evaluate the mean off-diagonal RMSE for the columns $t = \{1, 2, 3\}$ which is an indicator of the true strength of the tuned model on independent test data. The diagonal elements R_{tt} are considerably lower in each column of Tab. 5. In case of no oversearching,

---

[2] The Sequential Parameter Optimization Toolbox for Matlab can be downloaded at http://www.gm.fh-koeln.de/~bartz/experimentalresearch/

a value of V_t close to zero would be expected, whereas values larger than zero indicate oversearching.

In summary, a systematic tuning is beneficial but the tuned RMSE is often subject to oversearching effects. E.g. in our case the RMSE on a certain test set was on average 32% higher[3] when the tuned model had not seen the test data before (the realistic case) as compared to the lower value when the test data were used during tuning (T=V).

4.2 T2: Feature Selection by Genetic Algorithms

A Genetic Algorithm (GA) is used to determine good feature subsets for the SVM regressor. We rely here on the GA approach because it has some advantages compared to other feature selection methods: iterative search algorithms can be used to determine feature subsets, where more features are added or eliminated to build the final feature set (Feature Forward Selection and Feature Backward Elimination). Unfortunately these methods often get stuck in locally optimal feature subsets where they finally converge. GAs offer the possibility to escape from such local optima and find the global optimum given enough iterations.

Experimental Setup In our experimental analysis we started five GA runs, each with a population size of 100, elitist selection strategy (e.g. the best 20% of total population were definitely survivors) and termination after 100 generations. GA parameters where chosen by means of preliminary runs. Each GA individual has N genes, each of which representing whether a certain feature should be included in the model or not. The basis input feature set consisted of all features drawn from a sample SPOT-tuned configuration set as described in Sec. 4.1. Here, the gene length N equals the sum of the embedding dimensions for the two leaky rain functions, ranging from 55 to 92. The candidate solution is mapped to a feature vector which is passed to the feature selection preprocessing script before the SVM model is built. This process has an overall runtime of about 17 hours on a 2.4 GHz Intel Xeon CPU.

Results In each objective function, the RMSE was calculated on the validation sets as defined in Sec. 2.1. This resulted in different feature vectors, which were evaluated again on each validation set. The number of selected features ranges from a minimal feature set of 5 (mean value of GA runs when set 1 was used for evaluation) up to a maximum feature set of 50 (mean value of 5 GA runs). The number of features only varies slightly for runs of the same configuration, but usually differs for different configurations.

The evaluation is presented in Tab. 6. Again it has to be noted that all configurations seem to suffer from oversearching, when the validation set V (the set on which the GA was performed) is equal to the test set T: the diagonal in Tab. 6 shows always the seemingly best values. Compared with the results gathered by the SPOT tuning (Tab. 5), GA feature selection leads to a slightly better predictive performance if we look at S_t, the mean off-diagonal RMSE.

Even when feature selection does not produce much better results than SPOT tuning alone, it has an obvious positive effect on the RMSE ranges: the standard deviations of the

---

[3]average of all V_t in Tab. 5

Table 6: Mean results of five runs using feature selection by genetic algorithms. SVM and preprocessing parameters were obtained using the SPOT configurations 1,3,4 (see Sec. 4.1). The table shows the RMSE values for feature subsets on the validation sets leading to different feature configurations (rows). These configurations were evaluated on the test sets (columns); bold-faced numbers are best values on the test set and the numbers in brackets indicate standard deviations over five runs.

		Test		
		Set 1	Set 3	Set 4
	Set 1	**9.36 (0.11)**	15.48 (0.90)	11.44 (0.91)
Validation	Set 3	10.80 (0.19)	**12.11(0.59)**	7.78 (0.30)
	Set 4	10.99 (0.07)	13.04 (0.04)	**7.36 (0.03)**
S_t		10.90	14.26	9.61
V_t		16.40%	17.75%	30.57%

configurations are considerably smaller with feature selection than without, leading to better generalizing models. Also the variance between the three off-diagonal RMSEs is lower than the high off-diagonal variance observed in experiment **T1**. A reason for this might be the complexity decrease of the models due to the lower number of input features. In addition to this, the runtime for model-building is also reduced, although the GA runtime has should be considered of course.

5 Conclusion and Outlook

In this work we analyzed different predictive models based on Support Vector Machines for a practical application named stormwater prediction. Summarizing the results obtained on real world test data our models are in most cases better than the best-known special-purpose model INT2 under the assumption that i.) preprocessing of the data and ii.) tuning of SVM and preprocessing parameters is conducted. This can be seen as a confirmation of our hypothesis **H1**. This might have a great impact for applications which need a lot of similar models to be built since with our approach most of the time-consuming work of defining and tuning domain-specific models can be replaced by automatic processes.

Our results have also shown that one has to be careful when optimizing data mining models by means of parameter tuning, e.g., SPOT and GA: parameter tuning will often lead to oversearching and to too optimistic error estimates on the datasets used for tuning (as measured by V_t in Tab. 5 and Tab. 6), which was the statement of our hypothesis **H2**. Therefore the distinction between validation datasets (used for tuning) and independent test sets is essential to obtain a realistic estimate on the improvement reached by tuning. Nevertheless, our results have shown that tuning leads to better models as measured by independent test set RMSE. Also feature selection led to more stable results in our case study, which indicates better generalizing models. In a nutshell, feature selection and SPOT tuning can help to improve results, but must always be validated on different test sets to detect possible overfitting and oversearching effects.

In future work we plan to extend and validate our study on other datasets, first by applying our methodology to different stormwater tanks and more comprehensive data (time periods stretching over several years). Besides that, we want to compare our models with special time series regression frameworks, e.g., Gait-CAD [18], or with software as ClearVu Analytics [19] and MLR [20].

Acknowledgements

This work has been supported by the Bundesministerium für Bildung und Forschung (BMBF) under the grants FIWA (AiF FKZ 17N2309, "Ingenieurnachwuchs") and SOMA (AiF FKZ 17N1009, "Ingenieurnachwuchs") and by the Cologne University of Applied Sciences under the research focus grant COSA. We are grateful to Prof. Dr. Michael Bongards and his research group for discussions and for the stormwater tank data.

References

[1] Brockwell, P.; Davis, R.: *Time series: theory and methods.* Springer Verlag. 2009.

[2] Drucker, H.; Burges, C.; Kaufman, L.; Smola, A.; Vapnik, V.: Support vector regression machines. *Advances in neural information processing systems* (1997), S. 155–161.

[3] Bartz-Beielstein, T.: *Experimental Research in Evolutionary Computation—The New Experimentalism.* Natural Computing Series. Berlin, Heidelberg, New York: Springer. 2006.

[4] Hilmer, T.: *Water in Society – Integrated Optimisation of Sewerage Systems and Wastewater Treatment Plants with Computational Intelligence Tools.* Dissertation, Open Universiteit Nederland, Heerlen. 2008.

[5] Konen, W.; Zimmer, T.; Bartz-Beielstein, T.: Optimierte Modellierung von Füllständen in Regenüberlaufbecken mittels CI-basierter Parameterselektion. *at – Automatisierungstechnik* 57 (2009) 3, S. 155–166.

[6] Bartz-Beielstein, T.; Zimmer, T.; Konen, W.: Parameterselektion für komplexe Modellierungsaufgaben der Wasserwirtschaft – Moderne CI-Verfahren zur Zeitreihenanalyse. In: *Proc. 18th Workshop Computational Intelligence* (Mikut, R.; Reischl, M., Hg.), S. 136–150. Universitätsverlag, Karlsruhe. 2008.

[7] Flasch, O.; Bartz-Beielstein, T.; Koch, P.; Konen, W.: Genetic Programming Applied to Predictive Control in Environmental Engineering. In: *Proceedings 19. Workshop Computational Intelligence* (Hoffmann, F.; Hüllermeier, E., Hg.), S. 101–113. Karlsruhe: KIT Scientific Publishing. 2009.

[8] Koch, P.; Konen, W.; Flasch, O.; Bartz-Beielstein, T.: Optimizing Support Vector Machines for Stormwater Prediction. In: *Proceedings of Workshop on Experimental Methods for the Assessment of Computational Systems joint to PPSN2010* (Bartz-Beielstein, T.; Chiarandini, M.; Paquete, L.; Preuss, M., Hg.), Nr. TR10-2-007. TU Dortmund. 2010.

[9] Konen, W.; Koch, P.; Flasch, O.; Bartz-Beielstein, T.: Parameter-Tuned Data Mining: A General Framework. In: *Proceedings 20. Workshop Computational Intelligence* (Hoffmann, F.; Hüllermeier, E., Hg.). Karlsruhe: KIT Scientific Publishing. 2010.

[10] Theil, H.: Economic Forecasts and Policy. *Bayesian Analysis, Journal of the American Statistical Associa-Amsterdam: North-Holland* (1961), S. 776–800.

[11] Forrester, A.; Sobester, A.; Keane, A.: *Engineering Design via Surrogate Modelling.* Wiley. 2008.

[12] Bartz-Beielstein, T.: SPOT: An R Package For Automatic and Interactive Tuning of Optimization Algorithms by Sequential Parameter Optimization. Techn. Ber. arXiv:1006.4645. CIOP TECHNICAL REPORT 05-10. COLOGNE UNIVERSITY OF APPLIED SCIENCES. Comments: Article can be downloaded from: http://arxiv.org/abs/1006.4645. Related software can be downloaded from http://cran.r-project.org/web/packages/SPOT/index.html. 2010.

[13] Müller, K.; Smola, A.; Rätsch, G.; Schölkopf, B.; Kohlmorgen, J.; Vapnik, V.: Predicting time series with support vector machines. *Artificial Neural Networks–ICANN'97* (1997), S. 999–1004.

[14] Mattera, D.; Haykin, S.: Support vector machines for dynamic reconstruction of a chaotic system. In: *Advances in kernel methods*, S. 211–241. MIT Press. 1999.

[15] Chang, C.; Lin, C.: IJCNN 2001 challenge: Generalization ability and text decoding. In: *Neural Networks, 2001. Proceedings. IJCNN'01. International Joint Conference on Neural Networks*, Bd. 2. 2001.

[16] Smola, A.; Schölkopf, B.: A tutorial on support vector regression. *Statistics and Computing* 14 (2004) 3, S. 199–222.

[17] Kantz, H.; Schreiber, T.: *Nonlinear time series analysis.* Cambridge Univ. Press. 2004.

[18] Mikut, R.; Burmeister, O.; Reischl, M.; Loose, T.: Die MATLAB-Toolbox Gait-CAD. In: *Proceedings 16. Workshop Computational Intelligence* (Mikut, R.; Reischl, M., Hg.), S. 114–124. Karlsruhe: Universitätsverlag, Karlsruhe. 2006.

[19] Bäck, T.; Krause, P.: ClearVu Analytics. http://divis-gmbh.de/ClearVu. accessed 21.09.2010.

[20] Bischl, B.: The mlr package: Machine Learning in R. http://mlr.r-forge.r-project.org. accessed 25.09.2010.

Zur regelungsspezifischen Ableitung dynamischer Takagi-Sugeno-Modelle aus rigorosen Modellen

Andreas Kroll, Axel Dürrbaum

Fachgebiet Mess- und Regelungstechnik
Fachbereich Maschinenbau, Universität Kassel
Mönchebergstraße 7, 34277 Kassel
Tel.: (0561) 480 3268, Fax: (0561) 804 7768
E-Mail: {andreas.kroll, axel.duerrbaum}@mrt.uni-kassel.de

1 Einleitung

In der Praxis stellt ein Modell immer eine Approximation der Wirklichkeit dar, die bezüglich seines Einsatzzwecks hinreichend genau sein muss. Bei Parameterschätzung und Bewertung von Modellen werden üblicherweise Prädiktionsfehlermaße verwendet und die verfügbaren Freiheitsgrade so ausgenutzt, dass diese minimiert werden. Üblich sind globale Fehlermaße wie der kumulierte quadratische Fehler, sowie lokale wie der maximale Fehler. Prädiktionsfehlermaße stellen approximations- bzw. prognoseorientierte Bewertungskriterien dar. Sie zielen darauf ab, gut für Prognose- und Simulationsaufgaben geeignete Modelle zu erhalten. Eine gute Modelleignung für die Regelungssynthese entscheidet sich dagegen an Hand anderer Kriterien. Für die Synthese linearer Regelungssysteme ist z.B. die Güte des zum Modell zugehörigen Frequenzgangs im mittleren Frequenzbereich wegen dessen Bedeutung für die Stabilität besonders wichtig [1]. Andere Frequenzbereiche dürfen weniger gut erfasst werden. Die Freiheitsgrade bei der Modellbildung sollten eigentlich im Sinne anwendungsspezifischer Kriterien optimal ausgenutzt werden.

Im vorliegenden Beitrag wird dazu die Problemstellung behandelt, aus einem rigorosen bzw. physikalischen Modell in Form eines nichtlinearen Differentialgleichungssystems (DGLS) ein für die Reglersynthese günstiges Takagi-Sugeno-(TS)-Modell abzuleiten. Die üblichen Ansätze [2] linearisieren dazu das DGLS mittels Taylorreihenentwicklung in mehreren Punkten. Diese werden als gleichförmiges Gitter im Zustands- oder Hilfsvariablenraum angeordnet und ggf. per Optimierung so verschoben, dass der Prädiktionsfehler minimiert wird. Wünschenswert wäre dagegen, dass die Linearisierungspunkte so gelegt werden, dass lokale Modelle resultieren, die „günstig" für den Regelungsentwurf sind.

Die Regelungstheorie bietet Kriterien, die binäre Aussagen zur Stabilität sowie Steuer- und Beobachtbarkeit von dynamischen Systemen liefern. Dabei sind einfach anwendbare Methoden für lineare Systeme verfügbar [1, 3, 4]. Die Verallgemeinerung und Übertragung auf nichtlineare dynamische Systeme wird z.B. behandelt in [5, 6]. Im Rahmen dieses Beitrags interessieren dagegen quantitative „Günstigkeitsmaße", mit denen nichtlineare TS-Systeme strukturell bewertet werden sollen. Dazu wird erstens ein Kriterium eingeführt, das mittels des Grades der Hermitizität der lokalen Systemmatrizen die Stabilitätseigenschaften bewertet, zweitens wird der Grad der Regularität der lokalen Steuerbarkeitsmatrizen bewertet wird. Diese Kriterien treten neben die Bewertung der Approximationsgüte des Modells.

Im folgenden Abschnitt werden Takagi-Sugeno-Systeme kompakt beschrieben. Im dritten Abschnitt werden die Bewertungskriterien für regelungsspezifische Modelle eingeführt. Im vierten Abschnitt demonstriert eine Fallstudie „Inverses Pendel", welche Auswirkung die Nutzung regelungsspezifischer im Vergleich zu rein prädiktionsfehlerorientierten Modellen auf die erreichbare Regelgüte hat. Der Beitrag schließt mit einer Zusammenfassung und einem Ausblick im letzten Abschnitt.

2 Tagaki-Sugeno-Systeme

Für die Beschreibung der zentralen Idee dieses Beitrags reicht eine Betrachtung von Eingrößensystemen aus, auf die sich wegen der vereinfachten Notation die folgenden Ausführungen beschränken werden. Die vorgestellten Konzepte sind direkt auf Mehrgrößensysteme übertragbar. Betrachtet werde ein nichtlineares dynamisches System

$$
\begin{aligned}
\dot{\mathbf{x}}(t) &= \mathbf{f}(\mathbf{x}(t), u(t), \quad \mathbf{x}(0) = \mathbf{x}_0 \\
y(t) &= g(\mathbf{x}(t), u(t))
\end{aligned}
\tag{1}
$$

aus einem Satz von n Differentialgleichungen 1. Ordnung und einer Ausgabegleichung. Dabei sei $\mathbf{x} \in \mathbb{R}^n, u, y \in \mathbb{R}$. Dieses System soll durch ein TS-Modell aus c Regeln mit affinen Zustandsmodellen

WENN z ist Z_i
DANN $\dot{\mathbf{x}}_i(t) = \mathbf{A}_i \cdot \mathbf{x}(t) + \mathbf{b}_i \cdot u(t) + \mathbf{f}_{0i}$ $\qquad$ (2)
$\qquad y_i(t) = \mathbf{c}_i^{\mathsf{T}} \cdot \mathbf{x}(t) + d_i \cdot u(t) + g_{0i}$

approximiert werden:

$$
\dot{\mathbf{x}}(t) = \sum_{i=1}^{c} \phi_i(\mathbf{x}, u) \cdot x_i(t), \qquad y(t) = \sum_{i=1}^{c} \phi_i(\mathbf{x}, u) \cdot y_i(t)
\tag{3}
$$

Dabei sei z die unscharfe Prämissenvariable und Z_i eine mehrdimensionale Fuzzy-Referenzmenge. Zudem ist ϕ_i die i-te Fuzzy-Basisfunktion

$$
\phi_i = \frac{\mu_i}{\sum_{i=1}^{c} \mu_i}, \quad i \in \{1; \ldots; c\}
\tag{4}
$$

wobei die ϕ_i orthogonal sind, d.h. es gilt $\sum_{i=1}^{c} \phi_i = 1$. Die lokalen Zustandsmodelle können jeweils im Betrachtungspunkt EP mittels Taylorreihenentwicklung und Abbruch nach dem ersten Glied ermittelt werden

$$
\begin{aligned}
\mathbf{A}_i &= \left. \frac{\partial \mathbf{f}}{\partial \mathbf{x}} \right|_{\mathrm{EP}_i}, \qquad \mathbf{b}_i = \left. \frac{\partial \mathbf{f}}{\partial u} \right|_{\mathrm{EP}_i}, \qquad \mathbf{c}_i = \left. \frac{\partial g}{\partial \mathbf{x}} \right|_{\mathrm{EP}_i}, \qquad d_i = \left. \frac{\partial g}{\partial u} \right|_{\mathrm{EP}_i}, \\
\mathbf{f}_{0i} &= f(\mathbf{x}_{\mathrm{EP}_i}, u_{\mathrm{EP}_i}), \quad g_{0i} = g(\mathbf{x}_{\mathrm{EP}_i}, u_{\mathrm{EP}_i}),
\end{aligned}
\tag{5}
$$

Bei EPs, die in eine Ruhelage fallen, verschwindet der affine Term in der Zustandsgleichung und es folgt jeweils ein lineares Modell. Im Folgenden wird als Prämissenvariable der Zustandsvektor verwendet. Es sollen mehrdimensionale gaußförmige Zugehörigkeitsfunktionen

$$
\mu_i(\mathbf{x}) = \exp \left(-\frac{\|\mathbf{v}_i - \mathbf{x}\|_2^2}{2 \cdot \sigma_i^2} \right)
\tag{6}
$$

verwendet werden. Dabei geben die $\mathbf{v}_i$ die Zentrumspositionen der radialsymmetrischen Gaußglocke und σ_i ihre „Ausdehnung/Breite" an. In diesem Beitrag wird $\sigma_i = 1/64 \; \forall i$ verwendet.

Zur Regelung wird das „Parallel Distributed Compensator (PDC)" Konzept [7] mit c lokalen Zustandsreglern

$$u_i(t) = w(t) - \mathbf{k}_i^\mathsf{T} \cdot \mathbf{x}(t) \tag{7}$$

eingesetzt. Dabei ist w die Führungsgröße und $\mathbf{k}_i$ der Vektor der Reglerparameter. Vernachlässigt man die $\mathbf{f}_{0i}$, so folgt

$$\dot{\mathbf{x}}_i(t) = \left(\mathbf{A}_i - \mathbf{b}_i \cdot \mathbf{k}_i^\mathsf{T}\right) \cdot \mathbf{x}(t) + \mathbf{b}_i \cdot w(t) \tag{8}$$

Die Reglerparameter $\mathbf{k}_i$ können mittels Polvorgabe festgelegt werden. In der Regel werden für alle c Teilsysteme die gleichen Pole vorgegeben. Angenommen sei, dass das System eine Ruhelage in 0 habe, in der es der Regler halten soll. Dann wird einer der c EP fix in den Ursprung gelegt, um eine bleibende Regelabweichung zu vermeiden.

3 Bewertungkriterien

3.1 Modellgütebewertung

Üblicherweise werden die EP als gleichförmiges Gitter im Zustands- oder Hilfsvariablenraum angeordnet. Die Auflösung des Gitters wird entsprechend den Approximationsanforderungen gewählt. Die einzelnen EPs können zudem einzeln verschoben werden, um die Güte der Approximation zu verbessern. Im Folgenden werden nun Bewertungsmaße zur zusätzlichen Berücksichtigung vorgestellt, die insgesamt zu einem für den Regelungsentwurf günstigen Modell führen, das dennoch das Systemverhalten gut repräsentiert. Von besonderem Interesse sind Strukturmaße, da sie test-/bewertungssignalunabhänig sind.

3.1.1 Approximationsorientiertes Kriterium

Bei der Systemidentifikation erfolgt üblicherweise eine Modellgütebewertung anhand des Prädiktionsfehlers auf einer endlichen Menge von N Testdaten. Typische Fehlermaße sind die mittlere quadratische Abweichung zwischen Prädiktion und Referenz

$$e_{SS} = \frac{1}{N} \cdot \sum_{k=1}^{N} \left(y(k) - \hat{y}(k)\right)^2 \tag{9}$$

oder die betragsmäßig maximal auftretende Abweichung

$$e_{\max} = \max_k |y(k) - \hat{y}(k)| \,. \tag{10}$$

Diese Kriterien liefern keine strukturellen, sondern eine testsignalbezogenen Aussage. In der Fallstudie wird ein instabiles System betrachtet, so dass brauchbare Daten in der offenen Wirkungskette kaum zu gewinnen sind. Stattdessen soll ein Kriterium eingesetzt werden, welches die ausreichende Abdeckung des Beschreibungsraumes bewertet.

Eine einfache Möglichkeit ist die Bewertung der Abweichung der EP von einem regelmäßigen Gitter

$$J_{\text{Approx},i} = ||\mathbf{v}_i - \mathbf{v}_{i0}||^2 \overset{!}{=} \min .$$ (11)

Dieses Kriterium bewertet nicht, ob die EP günstig bzgl. der Ausprägung der Nichtlinearität von $\mathbf{f}$ liegen. Vielmehr verhindert es, das die Bewertungsmaße bzgl. der Regelbarkeit nicht alle EP in denselben Punkt verschieben, wodurch eine Systembeschreibung nicht mehr repräsentativ wäre. Im Folgenden wird bei J_{Approx} das Quadrat der Euklidische Norm verwendet.

3.1.2 Steuerbarkeitsorientiertes Kriterium:

Mittels eines Steuereingriff wird ein System beeinflusst, um ein gewünschtes Regelungsziel zu erreichen. Bei technischen Systemen ist einerseits die Amplitude des Steuersignals beschränkt, da Stellglieder endliche Stellwege haben. Andererseits korrespondiert in vielen Anwendungen die Stellamplitude direkt mit den Energie-/Ressourcenverbrauch. Deshalb interessiert technisch der *Grad der Steuerbarkeit* eines Systems, und nicht nur eine Ja/Nein-Aussage.

Als Bewertungkriterium soll dazu der Grad der Regularität der Steuerbarkeitsmatrix

$$\mathbf{C} = [\mathbf{b}|\mathbf{A} \cdot \mathbf{b}] =: [c_{jl}]$$ (12)

der Teilsysteme verwendet werden. Dazu kann z.b. die Konditionszahl oder der kleinste Singulärwert von $\mathbf{C}_j$ bewertet werden. Die Konditionszahl sollte nahe bei 1 liegen, der kleinste Singulärwert möglichst groß sein. Für Systeme 2. Ordnung lässt sich der kleinste Singulärwert einfach ermitteln als [8]:

$$\underline{\sigma}(\mathbf{C}) = \sqrt{\frac{\tilde{b} - \sqrt{\tilde{b}^2 - 4 \cdot \tilde{c}}}{2}}$$ (13)

mit $\tilde{b} = \sum_{j,l=1}^{2} |c_{jl}|^2$ und $\tilde{c} = (\det \mathbf{C})^2$.

Als Steuerbarkeitskriterium wird der Betrag des kleinsten Singulärwertes verwendet:

$$J_{\text{Steuer}} = \underline{\sigma}(\mathbf{C}).$$ (14)

Bezüglich steuerbarkeitsspezifischer Modellbildung sollte der Bereich schlechter Steuerbarkeit gut approximiert werden, da dort hohe Reglerverstärkungen folgen.

Zur weiteren in der Literatur vorgeschlagenen Kriterien gehören insbesondere die modalen Bewertungsmaße, die allerdings eine Ähnlichkeitstransformation erfordern. Auch ist für stabile Matrizen $\mathbf{A}$ eine Bewertung mittels der Regularität der Gramschen Steuerbarkeitsmatrix $\mathbf{W}_S$ möglich. Für $\mathbf{W}_S$ gilt:

$$\mathbf{A} \cdot \mathbf{W}_S + \mathbf{W}_S \cdot \mathbf{A}^\mathsf{T} = -\mathbf{B} \cdot \mathbf{B}^\mathsf{T}$$ (15)

Die Größe des kleinsten Eigenwertes von $\mathbf{W}_S$ ist dann ein Maß für die „Beeinflussbarkeit des Systems".

3.1.3 Stabilitätsorientiertes Kriterium

Betrachtet werde ein autonomes lineares System

$$\dot{\mathbf{x}}(t) = \mathbf{A} \cdot \mathbf{x}(t), \quad \mathbf{x} \in \mathbb{R}^n, \quad \mathbf{x}(0) = \mathbf{x}_0. \tag{16}$$

Dies hat die Lösung

$$\mathbf{x}(t) = e^{\lambda_1 \cdot t} \cdot k_1 \cdot \tilde{\mathbf{v}}_1 + \cdots + e^{\lambda_n \cdot t} \cdot k_n \cdot \tilde{\mathbf{v}}_n \tag{17}$$

mit den Eigenvektoren $\tilde{\mathbf{v}}_i$ zu den Eigenwerten λ_i. Ist (16) stabil und $\mathbf{A}$ hermitesch, so laufen die Trajektorien monoton auf die Ruhelage in $\mathbf{0}$ zu. Bei nicht-hermitescher Matrix $\mathbf{A}$ kann sich dagegen eine Trajektorie deutlich von der Ruhelage entfernen, bevor sie gegen diese konvergiert, siehe Bild 1.

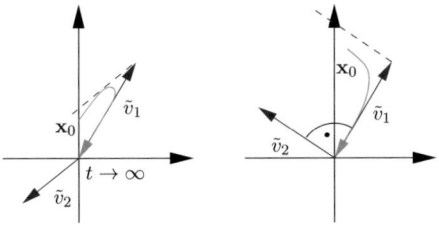

Bild 1: Illustration des Eigenverhaltens bei nicht-hermitescher Matrix, bei dem ein Anwachsen auch bei stabilem System möglich ist (links) und hermitescher Matrix $\mathbf{A}$, bei dem kein Anwachsen möglich ist (rechts)

Ein einfaches Beispiel (Bild 2) zeigt die Konsequenzen bzgl. TS-Systemen. Im dargestellten TS-Modell mit $c = 4$ Teilmodellen möge die Abbildung $\dot{\mathbf{x}}(t) = \mathbf{A} \cdot \mathbf{x}(t)$ in den schraffierten Bereichen anwachsen. Dieses Anwachsen ist dadurch bedingt, dass im Lö-

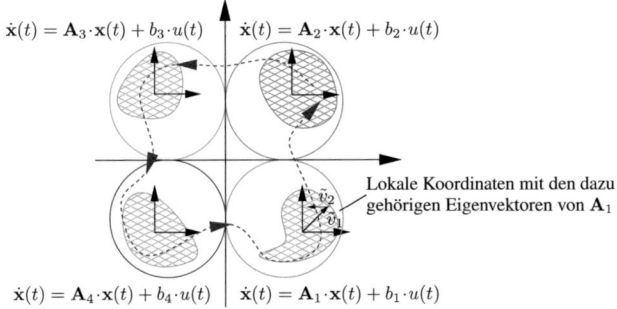

Bild 2: Zustandsraum eines TS-Systems

sungsansatz ($\tilde{\mathbf{v}}_1$, $\tilde{\mathbf{v}}_2$ Eigenvektoren zu Eigenwerten λ_1, λ_2 von $\mathbf{A}$) $\mathbf{x}(t) = e^{\lambda_1 \cdot t} \cdot k_1 \cdot \tilde{\mathbf{v}}_1 + e^{\lambda_2 \cdot t} \cdot k_2 \cdot \tilde{\mathbf{v}}_2$ wegen $\mathrm{Re}\lambda_1 \ll \mathrm{Re}\lambda_2$ der $e^{\lambda_1 \cdot t} \cdot k_1 \cdot \tilde{\mathbf{v}}_1$-Anteil wesentlich schneller abfällt als der $e^{\lambda_2 \cdot t} \cdot k_2 \cdot \tilde{\mathbf{v}}_2$-Anteil. Die Summe der Lösungsanteile bezüglich der Aufspaltung der

Lösung in die Eigenvektorkomponenten wächst damit in jedem schraffierten Bereich an. Sind die Zwischenräume zwischen den schraffierten Bereichen klein, so kann dies dazu führen, dass das TS-System, das aus den dargestellten linearen stabilen Systemen gebildet wird, instabil wird. Ein System mit derartigem Verhalten ist schwer zu regeln. Für hermitesche Matrizen $\mathbf{A}$ ist dieser Effekt ausgeschlossen. Da für sie

$$\mathbf{A} = \bar{\mathbf{A}}^\mathsf{T} \tag{18}$$

gilt, soll mit dieser Beziehung bewertet werden, wie nahe $\mathbf{A}$ der Hermitizität kommt. Eine Möglichkeit besteht darin, für jedes Teilsystem getrennt die Abweichung zu bewerten zu bewerten:

$$J_{\text{Hermit},i} = ||\mathbf{A}_i - \bar{\mathbf{A}}_i^\mathsf{T}||^2 \overset{!}{=} \min. \tag{19}$$

Dabei ist $||\ ||$ eine Matrixnorm. Im Folgenden wird die Euklidische Norm verwendet

$$||\mathbf{A}||_2 = \sqrt{\sum_{i,j} a_{ij}^2}. \tag{20}$$

Dieses Kriterium liefert nur eine qualitative Bewertung des Eigenverhaltens, ist aber sehr viel einfacher handhabbar als die etablierten Lyapunov-basierten Analysemethoden für TS-Systeme, z.B. [9].

3.1.4 Mehrzieloptimierung

Das Ziel besteht in der bestmöglichen Erfüllung von J_{Hermit}, J_{Steuer} und J_{Approx} für alle Teilsysteme, also in einer Minimierung von J J_{Hermit} und J_{Approx} sowie einer Maximierung von J_{Steuer}. Zur Vereinfachung werden die drei Teilziele mittels

$$J_i = \frac{\alpha}{J_{\text{Hermit},i} + 1} + \frac{\beta}{J_{\text{Approx},i} + 1} + \gamma \cdot J_{Steuer,i} \tag{21}$$

gewichtet zu einem Optimierungs- (Maximierungs-)problem zusammengezogen: Je nach Anforderungssituation im Einzelfall kann dann durch entsprechende Gewichtung der gewünschte Kompromiss eingestellt werden.

Zur Lösung des Optimierungsproblems wird ein einfacher Greedy-Algorithmus eingesetzt, der für die Demonstration der Methodik ausreicht: Für einen EP nach dem anderen wird die Position testweise um einen Schritt sukzessive in allen Koordinatenrichtungen verändert und die Änderung mit der größten Verbesserung vermerkt. Wenn alle EPs geprüft wurden, werden alle vermerkten Änderungen implementiert und eine neue Iteration durchgeführt. Die Iterationen enden wenn ein Abbruchkriterium erfüllt ist, d.h. es sich keine weitere Verbesserung von J_i mehr ergibt.

Um eine Mehrzieloptimierung zu vermeiden, werden die drei Einzelkriterien gewichtet so überlagert, das eine Einzeloptimierungsaufgabe entsteht. Da die Gewichtung einzelproblemorientiert erfolgen sollte, wird statt dessen im Rahmen der Fallstudie aufgezeigt, welchen Einfluss eine EP-Verschiebung im Sinne eines Kriteriums auf die Regelperformance gemäß der definierten Kriterien hat.

3.2 Reglerperformance

Die Bewertung der Performance eines Regelungssystems kann z.b. mittels dreier aus der modellprädiktiven Regelung bekannter integraler Kriterien erfolgen: Die Bewertung, wie gut die Führungsgröße verfolgt wird, mittels des quadratischen Regelfehlers

$$I_e = \int_{T_u}^{T_o} (w(t) - y(t))^2 \mathrm{d}t = \int_{T_u}^{T_o} e^2(t) \mathrm{d}t, \tag{22}$$

die Bewertung der Stellamplitude, die häufig ein Maß für den energetischen Aufwand ist

$$I_u = \int_{T_u}^{T_o} u^2(t) \mathrm{d}t, \tag{23}$$

sowie die Bewertung der Varianz der Stellaktivität, die ein Maß für die (mechanische) Belastung des Systems darstellt

$$I_{\dot{u}} = \int_{T_u}^{T_o} \dot{u}^2(t) \mathrm{d}t \tag{24}$$

Dabei ist $[T_u, T_o]$ der Bewertungszeitraum. Alle Kriterien sind dabei auf Mehrgrößensysteme erweiterbar:

$$I_e = \int_{T_u}^{T_o} \mathbf{e}^{\mathsf{T}}(t) \cdot \mathbf{e}(t) \mathrm{d}t, \quad I_u = \int_{T_u}^{T_o} \mathbf{u}^{\mathsf{T}}(t) \cdot \mathbf{u}(t) \mathrm{d}t, \quad I_{\dot{u}} = \int_{T_u}^{T_o} \dot{\mathbf{u}}^{\mathsf{T}}(t) \cdot \dot{\mathbf{u}}(t) \mathrm{d}t. \tag{25}$$

Des Weiteren interessiert, wie weit sich die Zustandstrajektorie beim Ausregelvorgang von der Zielruhelage temporär entfernt. Dieses kann z.B. durch den im Trajektorienverlauf maximal auftretenden Abstand vom Zielpunkt charakterisiert werden:

$$d_{\mathrm{max}} = \max_{t \in [T_u, T_o]} ||\mathbf{x}(t)||. \tag{26}$$

Im Folgenden wird hierzu die Euklidische Norm verwendet.

Zu den Standardkriterien für die Regelgüte gehört auch die Ausregelzeit T_{aus}, d.h. die Zeit bis die Regelgröße permanent in einem Toleranzbereich um den Zielwert verbleibt. Überschwingen soll hier nicht betrachtet werden, da in der folgenden Fallstudie Anfangswertausregelaufgaben betrachtet werden.

4 Fallstudie

Als Anwendungsbeispiel wird das vereinfachte inverse Pendel aus Bild 3 verwendet:

Aufgabe des Reglers ist es, das Pendel senkrecht ($\varphi = 0$) zu stabilisieren.

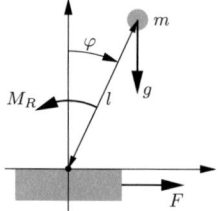

Var	Bedeutung	Wert	Einheit
l	Länge des Pendels	0,2	m
m	Masse des Pendels	0,15	kg
r	Reibungkoeffizient	0,02	Ns/m
g	Erdbeschleunigung	9,81	m/s^2
F	externe Kraft auf Pendel	–	N

Bild 3: Inverses Pendel

4.1 Physikalisches Modell

Für die Simulation des Systems werden die nichtlinearen Modellgleichungen des inversen Pendels verwendet, die sich aus dem Drallsatz um das Pendelgelenk ergeben:

$$J \cdot \ddot{\varphi} = \sum_i M_i = M_R + M_g + M_F. \tag{27}$$

Mit dem Reibmoment $M_R = c \cdot \dot{\varphi}$, dem Moment der Gewichtskraft $M_g = m \cdot g \cdot l \cdot \sin \varphi$ und dem Moment durch die externe Kraft F: $M_F = -F \cdot l \cdot \cos \varphi$ und $J = m \cdot l^2$ ergibt sich das nichtlineare Modell:

$$J \cdot \ddot{\varphi} = m \cdot g \cdot l \cdot \sin \varphi - r \cdot \dot{\varphi} - F \cdot l \cdot \cos \varphi. \tag{28}$$

Mit den beiden Zustandsgrößen $x_1 = \varphi$ und $x_2 = \dot{\varphi}$ folgt die Zustandsraumsdarstellung zu:

$$\dot{x}_1 = x_2$$
$$\dot{x}_2 = \frac{m \cdot g \cdot l}{J} \cdot \sin x_1 - \frac{r}{J} \cdot x_2 - \frac{F \cdot l}{J} \cdot \cos x_1. \tag{29}$$

4.2 Lokal linearisierte Modelle

Für den Entwurf des TS-Systems werden in verschiedenen EP linearisierte Modelle benötigt:

$$\begin{bmatrix} \dot{x}_1 \\ \dot{x}_2 \end{bmatrix} = \underbrace{\begin{bmatrix} 0 & 1 \\ \dfrac{m \cdot g \cdot l}{J} - \dfrac{F \cdot l \cdot \sin x_{10i}}{J} & -\dfrac{r}{J} \end{bmatrix}}_{=:\mathbf{A}_i} \cdot \begin{bmatrix} x_1 \\ x_2 \end{bmatrix} + \underbrace{\begin{bmatrix} 0 \\ -\dfrac{l \cdot \cos x_{10i}}{J} \end{bmatrix}}_{=:\mathbf{b}_i} \cdot u + \underbrace{\begin{bmatrix} f_{10i} \\ f_{20i} \end{bmatrix}}_{\mathbf{f}_{0i}}$$

$$\tag{30}$$

$$y = \underbrace{\begin{bmatrix} 1 & | & 0 \end{bmatrix}}_{=:C_i} \cdot \begin{bmatrix} x_1 \\ x_2 \end{bmatrix} + g_{0i} \tag{31}$$

und den Absolutgliedern

$$f_{10i} = x_{2i}, \qquad f_{20i} = \frac{m \cdot g \cdot l}{J} \cdot \sin x_{10i} - \frac{r}{J} \cdot x_{20i} - \frac{l \cdot F}{J} \cdot \cos x_{10i} \tag{32}$$

Die Linearisierung der TS-Teilmodelle erfolgt in den Linearisierungspunkten ($x_{10i} = \varphi_{0i}, x_{20i} = \dot{\varphi}_{0i}, u_{0i} = F = 0$).

4.3 Analytische Kriterienauswertung

Für das Anwendungsbeispiel 4.2 ergibt die analytische Auswertung für (21) folgende Ergebnisse:

- Hermite-Kriterium

$$J_{\text{Hermit},i} = ||\mathbf{A}_i - \bar{\mathbf{A}}_i^{\mathsf{T}}||_2^2 = 2 \cdot \left(\frac{g}{l} \cdot \cos x_{10i} - \frac{F}{m \cdot l} \cdot \sin x_{10i} - 1 \right)^2 \tag{33}$$

mit eingesetzten Modellparametern

$$J_{\text{Hermit},i} \approx 4811,81 \cdot \cos^2 x_{10i} - 196,2 \cdot \cos x_{10i} + 2. \tag{34}$$

$J_{\text{Hermit},i}$ ist somit nicht von x_{2i0} abhängig. Es nimmt sein Maximum für $0°$ und sein Minimum bei $\pm 88,2$ (und den periodischen Wiederholungen) an.

- Steuerbarkeitskriterium

$$J_{\text{Steuer},i} = \underline{\sigma}\left(\mathbf{C}_i\right) = \underline{\sigma}\left([\mathbf{b}_i, \mathbf{A}_i | \mathbf{b}_i]\right) = \underline{\sigma}\left(\left[\begin{array}{c|c} 0 & \dfrac{-1}{m \cdot l} \cdot \cos x_{10i} \\ \hline \dfrac{-1}{m \cdot l} \cdot \cos x_{10i} & \dfrac{r}{m^2 \cdot l^3} \cdot \cos x_{10i} \end{array} \right] \right)$$

$$= \frac{\sqrt{(2 \cdot l^4 \cdot m^2 + r^2) - \sqrt{4 \cdot r^2 \cdot l^4 \cdot m^2 + r^4}}}{\sqrt{2} \cdot l^3 \cdot m^2} \cdot |\cos x_{10i}| \tag{35}$$

Auch $J_{\text{Steuer},i}$ ist nicht von x_{20i} abhängig. Mit eingesetzten Modellparametern folgt:

$$J_{\text{Steuer},i} \approx 9,233 \cdot |\cos x_{1i}| \tag{36}$$

D.h. es gibt ein lokales Minimum für

$$x_{10i} = -90 \pm 180° \tag{37}$$

bzw. ein Maximum für

$$x_{10i} = 0 \pm 180°, \tag{38}$$

was intuitiv verständlich ist.

- Approximationskriterium

J_{Approx} nimmt für die Referenz-/Anfangslage der Prototypen sein Minimum an und steigt monoton mit wachsenden Abständen der EPs von ihren Referenzlagen.

Insgesamt bedeutet dies, dass für näherungsweise Hermitizität bevorzugt φ bei ca. $90°$ linearisiert werden sollte, dort aber die Steuerbarkeit am schlechtesten ist.

4.4 Simulationsergebnisse

Bei den folgenden Simulationen besteht das Ziel darin, eine Anfangsauslenkung des Pendels möglichst schnell wieder in die Ruhelage $x_1 = \varphi = 0°$ zu regeln. Dazu werden Zustandsregler mittels Polvorgabe ausgelegt.

Zur Illustration, was die Verwendung regelungs- statt prädiktionsfehlerorientierter Modelle für den Entwurf von Regelungssystemen bedeutet, werden 4 Regelungskonzepte miteinander verglichen: (a) das System wird in der Ruhelage ($\varphi = 0; \dot{\varphi} = 0$) linearisiert und ein linearer Zustandsregler entworfen (PVG), (b) ein Referenz-TS-Modell (TS reg) wird für das regelmäßige Linearisierungspunktraster $\mathbf{v}_{i0}$ erzeugt und lokale Zustandsregler entworfen, (c) das TS-System (TS steuer) wird bzgl. Steuerbarkeit (unter Beachtung von Approximationseigenschaften) mit $\alpha = 0, \beta = 0.1, \gamma = 1$ (Gleichung (21)) optimiert, und (d) das TS-System (TS hermit) wird bzgl. Hermitizität (unter Beachtung von Approximationseigenschaften) $\alpha = 1, \beta = 0.1, \gamma = 0$ (Gleichung (21)) optimiert.

Die Linearisierungspunkte liegen beim Referenz-TS-System in einem regelmäßigen Gitter mit $\varphi = [-80; -40; 0; 40; 80]$ Grad und $\dot{\varphi} = [-100; 0; 100]$ Grad/s. Die Pole werden für alle lokalen Systeme in $[-3; -4]$ vorgegeben. Die Simulation wird mit der nichtlinearen Strecke (29) ohne Stellgrößenbeschränkung durchgeführt.

Der Verlauf der Fuzzy-Basisfunktionen $\phi_i(x)$ der beiden TS-Systeme (Steuerbarkeit und Hermite) ist exemplarisch mit $\varphi = -80, -40, 0, 40, 80$ Grad und $\dot{\varphi} = 0$ Grad/s in Bild 4 dargestellt.

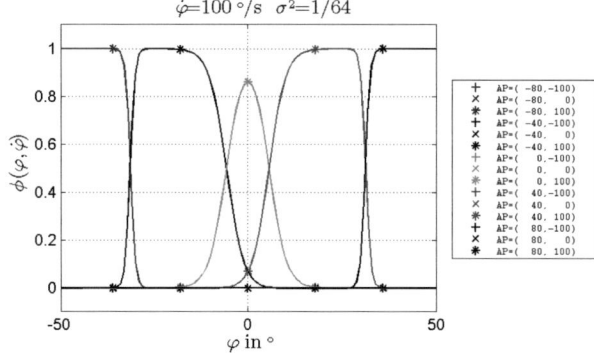

Bild 4: Fuzzy-Basisfunktionen $\phi(\varphi, \dot{\varphi})$ für EP = $\mathbf{v}_{i0}$ des regulären Gitters mit $\dot{\varphi} = 100$

Der Verlauf der Bewertungskriterien ist in Bild 5 dargestellt, die markierten Stellen zeigen die gesuchten Extrema des jeweiligen Kriteriums.

Bild 8 zeigt die Ausregelvorgänge und Bild 6 die zugehörigen Zustandstrajektorien für die 4 verschiedenen Regelungskonzepte. Bild 7 zeigt die zugehörigen Lagen der Entwicklungspunkte im Referenzgitter, sowie für Optimierung bzgl. Hermitizität oder Steuerbarkeit. Der lineare Regler wurde für ein im Ursprung linearisiertes Modell entworfen. Ein einfacher TS-Regler verbessert den Ausregelvorgang gegenüber einem linearen Regler in allen Kriterien, bis auf die zu verzeichnende erhöhte Stellaktivität. Eine Modellgenerierung für verbesserte Hermitizität führt zu der geringsten Wegbewegung der Trajektorie

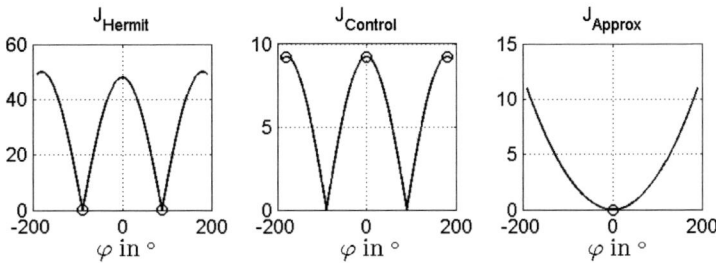

Bild 5: Verlauf der Bewertungskriterien für ein Teilsystem (30) bei Variation der Lage des EPs in Richtung von x_1 bzw. φ

von allen TS-Reglern. Auch die Stellaktivität liegt etwa 15% geringer. Andererseits verlangsamt sich der Ausregelvorgang gegenüber dem Standard-TS-Regler. Bei Optimierung auf Steuerbarkeit lassen sich quadratischer Regelfehler und Ausregelzeit deutlich gegenüber einem Standard-TS-Regler verbessern und zwar um 35 % bzw. 20%. Zudem lässt sich der Stellaufwand um ca. 15% reduzieren. Die Tabellen 1 und 2 zeigen die Kennwerte im Überblick. Hierbei ist $J_{\text{Approx}} = \sum_{i=1}^{c} J_{\text{Approx},i}$.

Reglertyp	J_{Approx}	$J_{\text{Hermit},i}$			$J_{\text{Steuer},i}$		
		min	max	mittel	min	max	mittel
Linear	—	48,0500	48,0500	48,0500	9,2300	9,2300	9,2300
TS regulär	0,000	1,60326	9,2328	5,3169	7,5174	48,05	27,2468
TS Steuer	3,000	5,76618	9,2328	7,7739	29,6333	48,05	40,2995
TS Hermit	2,135	0,22648	9,2328	3,1311	0,2032	48,05	15,6343

Tabelle 1: In der Fallstudie erreichte Modellgütewerte

Reglertyp	$d_{\max}$	T_{aus}	$\sum e^2$	$\sum u^2$	$\sum \dot{u}^2$
Linear	31,8	1,03	1953,96	5713,56	10825,43
TS regulär	35,8	0,90	1641,52	5050,27	15118,81
TS Steuer	43,2	0,73	1283,72	4370,54	30525,29
TS Hermit	33,9	0,96	1769,67	5312,83	13030,10

Tabelle 2: In der Fallstudie erreichte Reglerperformance

Unterschiede zeigen sich auch in dem stabilisierbaren Anfangswertebereich:Exemplarisch wird dabei für verschwindende Anfangswinkelgeschwindigkeit der maximal noch stabilisierbare Anfangswinkel betrachtet. Bei Anwendung des linearen Zustandsregler führen Anfangswinkel größer 42° zum Durchschwingen des Pendels. Der Referenz-TS-Regler kann bereits Anfangswinkel bis 66° stabilisieren. Der auf Steuerbarkeit optimierte Regler stabilisiert bis zu einem Anfangswinkel von 70° und der auf Hermitizität optimierte bis 60°.

Wie von der in diesem Fall einfach durchzuführenden analytische Untersuchung erwartet, bedeutet eine Optimierung auf Hermitizität eine Verschiebung der Entwicklungspunkte in Richtung ±88.8°. Die Weite der Verschiebung wird begrenzt, wenn wie in diesem Fall auch das Approximationskriterium berücksichtigt wird, das eine Änderung des regelmäßigen Gitters bestraft. Analoges folgt für das Steuerbarkeitskriterium, nur dass dies

Entwicklungspunkte nahe $0°$ empfiehlt, da dann (wegen direkter Krafteinwirkung) die Steuerbarkeit optimal ist.

4.5 Diskussion

Die vorgeschlagenen Kriterien erlauben die Ableitung von Auslegungshinweisen, wenn Ziel und Kriterien für einen Regelungsentwurf feststehen. Die erreichbare Reduzierung des Integralkriteriums bzgl. der Stellgröße bei dennoch verbesserter Verfolgung / besserem Erreichen des Sollwertes zeigt zudem, dass derartige Regelungsstrategien einen wichtigen Beitrag zur Energieeffizienzsteigerung von Systemen liefern können.

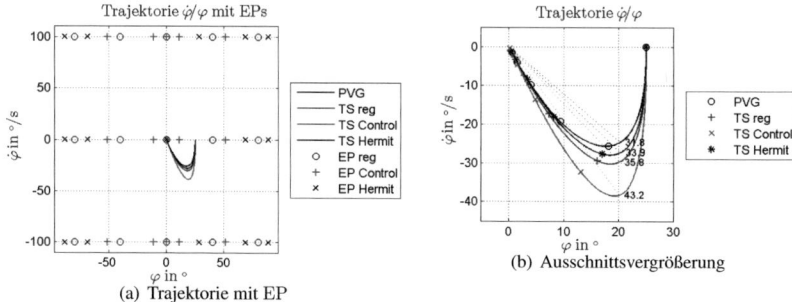

(a) Trajektorie mit EP

(b) Ausschnittsvergrößerung

Bild 6: Zustandstrajektorien der Regelungskonzepte

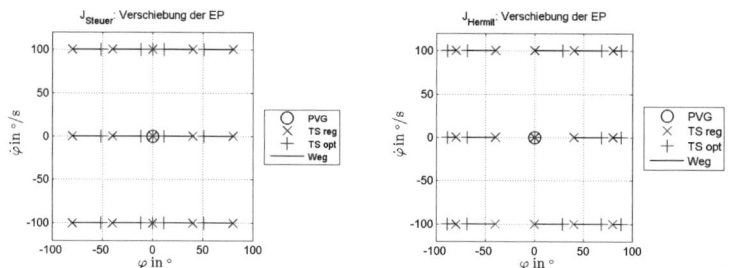

Bild 7: Verschiebung der Entwicklungspunkte für Optimierung bzgl. Steuerbarkeits- (l) oder Hermite-Kriterium (r)

5 Zusammenfassung und Ausblick

Im Beitrag wurden erste Ergebnisse zur Ableitung regelungsspezifischer TS-Modelle aus rigorosen bzw. physikalischen Systemmodellen in Form von Differentialgleichungen behandelt. Hierzu wurden strukturelle Kriterien zur Bewertung der Modellgüte eingeführt, die es gestatten die Linearisierungspunkte für die lokalen Modelle so zu platzieren, dass das resultierende Modell gut für den Regelungsentwurf geeignet ist. Anhand einer Fallstudie mit einem instabilen inversen Pendel konnte ein signifikantes Verbesserungspotential aufgezeigt werden.

Zukünftig wäre die Entwicklung eines Approximationskriterium interessant, dass eine bessere strukturelle Aussage zur Approximationsgüte im Hinblick auf die Abbildung der Systemnichtlinearitäten liefert. Der verwendete einfache Greedy-Algorithmus könnte durch effizientere und effektivere Optimierungsverfahren ersetzt werden. Zuerst ist aber die Durchführung weiterer Fallstudien geplant, um die Übertragbarkeit der viel versprechenden Zwischenergebnisse zu untersuchen.

Danksagung

Die Autoren danken Dr. H.-J. Sommer für wertvolle Diskussionen und Anregungen sowie Dipl.-Ing. V. Weingardt für die Durchführung von Simulationsstudien.

Literatur

[1] LUNZE, Jan: *Regelungstechnik 1: Systemtheoretische Grundlagen, Analyse und Entwurf einschleifiger Regelungen*. 8., neu bearb. Aufl. Springer, 2010

[2] SCHULTE, Horst: *Approximative Modellierung, Systemidentifikation und Reglerentwurf mittels gewichteter Kombinationen lokaler Zustandsraummodelle am Beispiel fluidischer Antriebe*. Universität Kassel, Fachgebiet Regelungstechnik und Systemdynamik (Maschinenbau), Diss., 2005

[3] LUNZE, Jan: *Regelungstechnik 2: Mehrgrößensysteme, Digitale Regelung*. 6., neu bearb. Aufl. Springer, 2010

[4] REINSCHKE, Kurt: *Lineare Regelungs- und Steuerungstheorie*. 1. Springer, 2005

[5] SCHWARZ, H.: *Nichtlineare Regelungssysteme*. Oldenbourg München, 1991

[6] ISIDORI, Alberto: *Nonlinear Control Systems (Communications and Control Engineering)*. Springer, 1995

[7] WANG, H. O. ; TANAKA, K. ; GRIFFIN, M. F.: Parallel Distributed Compensation of Nonlinear Systems by Tagaki-Sugeno Fuzzy Model. In: *Fuzz-IEEE/IFES'95*, 1995, S. 531–538

[8] SKOGESTAD, S. ; POSTLETHWAITE, I.: *Multivariable feedback control: Analysis and Design*. Wiley New York, 1996

[9] TANAKA, K. ; SUGENO, M.: Stability analysis and design of fuzzy control systems. In: *Fuzzy sets and systems* 45 (1992), Nr. 2, S. 135–156

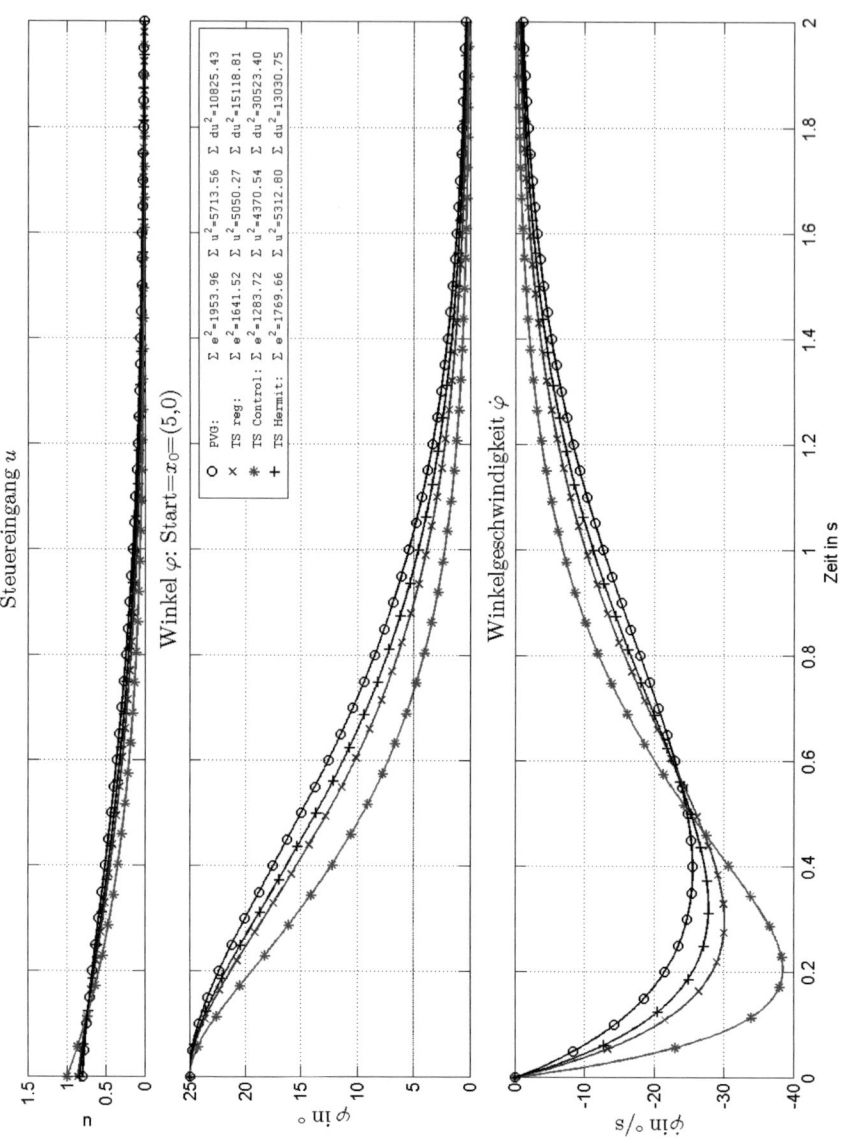

Bild 8: Ausregelvoränge der Regelungskonzepte für Startwinkel $x_{10} = 25°$

Erlernen kausaler Zusammenhänge aus Messdaten mittels gerichteter azyklischer Graphen

Christian Kühnert, Thomas Bernard, Christian Frey

Fraunhofer IOSB
Fraunhoferstraße 1, 76131 Karlsruhe
Tel.: 0721 6091-511
E-Mail: {christian.kuehnert, thomas.bernard, christian.frey}@iosb.fraunhofer.de

Zusammenfassung

Um unbekannte Zusammenhänge in komplexen Prozessen zu erkennen, werden in zunehmendem Maße maschinelle Lernverfahren eingesetzt. Die extrahierten Prozessmuster können allerdings nicht ohne weiteres dazu eingesetzt werden, Ursachen und Wirkungen zwischen einzelnen Prozessgrößen zu erkennen. Im vorliegenden Beitrag wird daher untersucht, inwiefern anhand von Messdaten und dem Einsatz gerichteter azyklischer Graphen die kausale Struktur eines Prozesses erlernt werden kann. Diese Graphen bieten dabei die Möglichkeit, mittels der Berechnung bedingter Wahrscheinlichkeiten die Struktur eines Systems zu lernen und Schlussfolgerungen bezüglich der Wirkzusammenhänge des Prozesses zu geben. Die Graphenstruktur wird zunächst durch ungerichtete Kanten initialisiert und daraufhin die Kanten bis zur Markov-Äquivalenz gerichtet. Anhand des resultierenden Graphen werden Randbedingungen für die Struktur definiert und in einer zweiten Phase werden die Kantengewichte in Form von Wahrscheinlichkeiten berechnet. Das Verfahren wird anhand simulierter Daten eines chemischen Prozesses sowie anhand von realen Messdaten eines Laborprozesses untersucht.

1 Einleitung

Moderne verfahrenstechnische Prozesse zeichnen sich durch einen hohen Komplexitätsgrad aus, was dazu führt, dass die Wirkzusammenhänge nicht immer im Detail bekannt sind (z.B. Teilreaktionen bei chemischen Prozessen). Zudem ist die Messdatenerfassung wichtiger Prozessgrößen nicht immer möglich (z.b. aufgrund zu hoher Temperaturen). Um wichtige und bisher unbekannte Zusammenhänge zwischen einzelnen Prozessparametern zu erkennen, werden daher in den letzten Jahren in zunehmendem Maße maschinelle Lernverfahren eingesetzt, um Muster aus archivierten Prozessdaten zu extrahieren und unbekannte Zusammenhänge zwischen einzelnen Prozessgrößen zu erkennen ([15] [9]).
Die extrahierten Prozessmuster erklären allerdings i.d.R. nicht Ursache und Wirkung zwischen den einzelnen Prozessgrößen. Ohne analytisches Prozesswissen oder gezielte Versuche ist es daher oft nicht möglich, eine Aussage darüber zu treffen, wie sich die Umsetzung des gewonnenen Wissens (z.B. durch Modifikation der Prozessführung) am Prozess auswirken wird.
Einen Ansatz, den Einfluss von Prozessgrößen abzuschätzen und somit kausale Zusammenhänge zu beschreiben, bieten gerichtete azyklische Graphen (Directed Acyclic Graphs, DAGs) [11]. DAGs bieten die Möglichkeit, mittels der Berechnung bedingter Wahrscheinlichkeiten die Struktur eines Systems zu lernen und Schlussfolgerungen bezüglich

der Kausalstruktur des Prozesses zu geben. Verwendung finden DAGs beispielsweise bereits in der Systembiologie [4] oder Psychologie [10]. Der Einsatz von DAGs in der Verfahrenstechnik wurde bisher nur unzureichend untersucht. Im vorliegenden Beitrag soll daher ein Ansatz vorgestellt werden, mit dem es möglich ist, in Messdaten kausale Abhängigkeiten ohne Verwendung physikalischer Modelle zu finden.

Die Arbeit gliedert sich wie folgt. In Abschnitt 2 wird das auf DAGs basierende Lösungskonzept vorgestellt. Zur Untersuchung der Leistungsfähigkeit des vorgeschlagenen Konzeptes wird in Abschnitt 3 untersucht, ob anhand von Simulationsdaten eines Rührkesselreaktors die Prozessstruktur maschinell erlernt werden kann. In Abschnitt 4 wird das Konzept zur Analyse eines Laborprozesses angewandt. Anhand von realen Messdaten soll die Sensor-Aktor-Struktur rekonstruiert werden.

2 Lösungsansatz

Es wird ein zweistufiges Konzept zum datengetriebenen Lernen von kausalen Wirkzusammenhängen vorgeschlagen. In der ersten Phase werden die Zusammenhänge des Systems mittels eines ungerichteten Graphen, welcher alle relevanten Messgrößen enthält, initialisiert. Es wird mittels eines strukturellen Lernverfahrens basierend auf bedingten Unabhängigkeitswahrscheinlichkeiten die Struktur des Graphen bis zu seiner Markov-Äquivalenz erlernt. Markov-Äquivalenz bedeutet in diesem Zusammenhang, dass ein Graph erlernt wird, bei dem alle möglichen gerichteten Graphen die gleichen bedingten Unabhängigkeitswahrscheinlichkeiten abbilden.

In der zweiten Phase wird mittels der Berechnung des marginalisierten Likelihoods eine Kantengewichtung durchgeführt [2], welche angibt, inwiefern die einzelnen Prozessgrößen voneinander abhängen.

Der sich zuvor ergebende Graph wird dazu verwendet, Randbedingungen bezüglich der Berechnung der Kantengewichte zu definieren.

2.1 Gerichtete azyklische Graphen

Formal beschrieben besteht ein Graph aus einer Anzahl von Variablen $X_i, X_j, X_k, ..$, welche durch gerichtete oder ungerichtete Kanten miteinander verbunden sind. Bei der Anwendung von Graphen zur Analyse von Prozessen werden die Variablen mit Prozessgrößen (z.B. Temperatursensor oder Pumpendrehzahl) beschrieben, so dass die Kanten kausale Abhängigkeiten zwischen den Prozessgrößen widerspiegeln.

Um diese kausalen Abhängigkeiten abbilden zu können, werden für die Berechnung der Wirkzusammenhänge strukturelle Lernverfahren eingesetzt, welche eine Graphenstruktur mittels bedingter Abhängigkeiten erlernen und nicht darauf basieren Informationskriterien zu maximieren [6].

Ein gerichteter azyklischer Graph (Directed Acyclic Graph, DAG) kann durch die in Tabelle 1 dargestellten Verbindungen und bedingten Unabhängigkeiten charakterisiert werden. Eine ausführliche Erklärung ist in [11] zu finden.

2.2 Phase 1: PC-Algorithmus zum Lernen der Wirkzusammenhänge

Zur Analyse der kausalen Wirkzusammenhänge wird angenommen, dass die vorhandenen Daten nicht durch gezielte Versuche erzeugt wurden, sondern normale Prozessverläufe re-

DAG	Darstellung	Bedingte Unabhängigkeiten
Kompletter Graph	$X_i \leftrightarrow X_j, X_i \leftrightarrow X_k, X_j \leftrightarrow X_k$	Keine
Unverbundener Graph	X_i, X_j, X_k	$X_i \perp X_j, X_i \perp X_k, X_k \perp X_j$
Kette mit Einzelpfeil	$X_i \leftrightarrow X_j, X_k$	$X_i \perp X_k, X_j \perp X_k$
Kette	$X_i \to X_k \to X_j$	$X_i \perp X_j \mid X_k$
Gabel	$X_i \leftarrow X_k \to X_j$	$X_i \perp X_j \mid X_k$
Kollision (V-Struktur)	$X_i \to X_k \leftarrow X_j$	$X_i \perp X_j$ aber $X_i \not\perp X_j \mid X_k$

Tabelle 1: Mögliche Darstellungsformen eines DAGs und die damit verbundenen bedingten Unabhängigkeiten.

präsentieren und eine gewisse statistische Schwankung der Eingangs- oder Störgrößen in den Daten enthalten sind. Weiter wird vorausgesetzt, dass die Anzahl der ausgewählten Prozessgrößen ausreichend ist, um alle kausalen Abhängigkeiten zu erkennen. Schließlich wird angenommen, dass die kausale Struktur des zu analysierenden Systems unverändert bleibt bezüglich Änderungen am Prozess (siehe [11]).

Die Vorgehensweise des so genannten PC-Algorithmus, welcher als Ergebnis einen teilweise gerichteten azyklischen Graphen (partial directed acyclic graph, PDAG) ausgibt, ist im Folgenden kurz zusammengefasst und in [12] ausführlich erklärt.

Initialisierung Erzeuge einen komplett verbundenen gerichteten Graphen mit allen vorhandenen Knoten.

Phase 1 Finde Kanten für die gilt, dass eine Variable X_i eine Kante mit Variable X_j bildet, wenn keine andere Variable existiert, welche diese beiden Variablen bedingt unabhängig machen kann. Dieser Test erfolgt mit dem in 2.2.1 beschriebenen Test auf Unabhängigkeit.

Phase 2 Orientiere die Kanten unter Verwendung von V-Strukturen. Existieren keine direkten Kanten zwischen X_i und X_j, aber zwischen X_i und X_k sowie zwischen X_k und X_j, dann muss es sich um eine V-Struktur in der Form $X_i \to X_k \leftarrow X_j$ handeln.

Phase 3 Weitere Orientierung der Kanten unter Berücksichtigung der folgenden Kriterien.

- Wenn $X_i \to X_k \leftrightarrow X_j$ erkannt wurde, dann wird dies erweitert zu $X_i \to X_k \to X_j$ (sonst würde es sich um eine V-Struktur handeln)

- Wenn $X_i \to X_k \to X_j$ vorhanden und $X_i \leftrightarrow X_j$ gilt, erweitern zu $X_i \to X_j$, da sonst ein Zyklus vorliegt.

2.2.1 Test auf bedingte Unabhängigkeit

Zum Testen der bedingten Unabhängigkeit von zwei Variablen unter Berücksichtigung einer dritten wird ein Hypothesentest durchgeführt (G^2-Test, [13]). Hierbei erfolgt für die Messdaten zunächst eine Kategorisierung [7]. Um zu testen, ob für eine Variable $X_i \perp X_j \mid X_k$ gilt, wird der folgende Wert berechnet [13]:

$$G^2 = 2 \sum_{a,b,c} S_{ijk}^{abc} \ln \frac{S_{ijk}^{abc} S_k^c}{S_{ik}^{ac} S_{jk}^{bc}} \tag{1}$$

Hierbei ist die Variable S_{ijk}^{abc} die Anzahl, in der die Variable i den Wert a hat, die Variable j den Wert b und die Variablen in k den Wert c. Die gleiche Definition gilt für die weiteren

Variablen S_k^c, S_{ik}^{ac}, S_{jk}^{bc}.

Um einen Hypothesentest durchzuführen, ob die bedingte Unabhängigkeit erfüllt oder nicht erfüllt ist, muss zudem die Anzahl der Freiheitsgrade df berechnet werden. Diese ergibt sich aus folgender Gleichung, wobei $D(X_i)$ die Anzahl der möglichen Zustände der Variablen X beschreibt.

$$df = (D(X_i) - 1)(D(X_j) - 1) \prod_{X_l \in X_k} D(X_l) \tag{2}$$

Mittels der Werte von G^2 und dem Freiheitsgrad df wird schließlich ein Hypothesentest mit einem definierten Signifikanzniveau α durchgeführt werden. Hierbei nimmt die Nullhypothese an, das eine bedingte Unabhängigkeit zwischen den beiden Variablen vorliegt. Ist der p-Wert aus der χ^2 Verteilung niedriger als das definierte Signifikanzniveau α, kann die Nullhypothese abgelehnt werden (die Knoten X_i und X_j sind abhängig). Wird die Nullhypothese nicht abgelehnt, wird angenommen, dass die Knoten X_i und X_j unabhängig sind.

2.3 Phase 2: Berechnung der Kantengewichte

Zur Berechnung der Kantengewichte wird der unter [5] beschriebene marginalisierte Likelihood berechnet. Unter der Annahme, dass alle Knoten X vorhanden und a priori global unabhängig voneinander sind, ergibt sich der marginalisierte Likelihood eines Graphen aus dem Produkt der jeweiligen marginalisierten Likelihoods einzelner Familien (also eines Knotens mit seinen Eltern). Dies lässt sich durch folgende Gleichung ausdrücken:

$$P(X^{1:N}|G) = \prod_{i=1}^{d} p(x_i^{1:N}|x_{G_i}^{1:N}) \tag{3}$$

x_i^n beschreibt hierbei den Wert des Knotens i. n beschreibt die jeweils möglichen Zustände der betrachteten Familie, bezeichnet durch den Graphen G_i.

Zur Berechnung des margnalisierten Likelihoods einer Familie müssen die a priori angenommenen Wahrscheinlichkeiten zudem lokal unabhängig voneinander sein. Dies ist erfüllt für die BDeu (Bayesian Dirichlet equivalence uniform) Gewichtungsmetrik und der Likelihood für eine Familie ergibt sich durch folgende Gleichung [1]:

$$p(x_i^{1:N}|x_{G_i}^{1:N}) = \prod_{j=1}^{q_i} \frac{\Gamma(\alpha_{ij})}{\Gamma(\alpha_{ij} + N_{ij})} \prod_{k=1}^{q_i} \frac{\Gamma(\alpha_{ij} + N_{ij})}{\Gamma(\alpha_{ij})} \tag{4}$$

Hierbei gilt

$$\alpha_{ij} = \frac{1}{q_i r_i} \tag{5}$$

r_i bezeichnet dabei die Anzahl der Zustände in X_i und q_i die Anzahl der möglichen Zustände des Graphen X_{G_i}. Γ steht für die Gamma-Funktion.

Die Berechnung der Kantengewichte erfolgt durch den in [5] beschriebenen Ansatz. Hierbei werden jeweils für eine gerichtete Kante die DAGs verwendet, welche sich aus dem PDAG ergeben und die Kante enthalten. Die Gewichtung lässt sich dann durch folgende Gleichung berechnen (G_j bezeichnet die Anzahl der Graphen, die das Merkmal für eine Kantengewichtung enthalten):

$$P(f_{x_k \to x_j}|G_j, X^{1:N}) = \frac{P(f_{x_k \to x_j}, X^{1:N}|G_j)}{P(X^{1:N}|G_j)} \tag{6}$$

Der Zähler ergibt sich durch folgende Gleichung und beschreibt die Summe der einzelnen marginalisierten Likelihoods der Graphen:

$$P(f_{x_k \to x_j}, X^{1:N}|G_j) = \sum_{G_k \in G_j} P(G_k|G_j)P(X^{1:N}|G_k) \tag{7}$$

Der Nenner ergibt sich durch folgende Gleichung:

$$P(X^{1:N}|G_j) = \prod_k^j \sum_{G_k \in G_j} P(G_k|G_j)p(x_k^{1:N}|x_{G_k}^{1:N}) \tag{8}$$

Der Nenner ergibt sich also durch die Summe der marginalisierten Likelihoods der möglichen Familien für jeden Knoten und anschließender Multiplikation über die Anzahl der Knoten.

2.4 Illustratives Beispiel

Das vorgeschlagene Verfahren wird anhand eines einfachen Beispiels illustriert. Es soll der Wirkzusammenanng des folgenden Strukturbildes ermittelt werden:

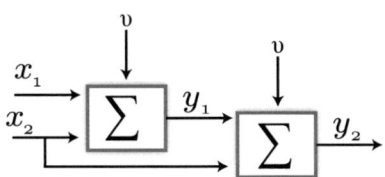 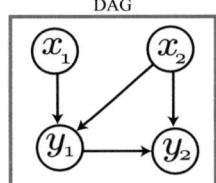

Bild 1: Strukturbild und gerichteter azyklischer Graph des illustrativen Beispiels.

Die Variablen x_1 und x_2 dienen als Eingangsvariablen, die Variable v ist eine Rauschvariable mit halber Amplitude des Eingangssignals. Eine Rauschvariable ist in diesem Fall notwendig, da ansonsten der PC-Algorithmus direkt die richtige Struktur erlernen kann und eine Gewichtung der Kanten unnötig wäre.
Das System wird durch weißes Rauschen für die Variablen x_1 und x_2 angeregt. Es werden insgesamt 1000 Datentupel verwendet, um eine genügend große Anzahl an Eingangsdaten zu garantieren.
Die Ergebnisse der einzelnen Berechnungsphasen sind in Abbildung 2 dargestellt.
Es zeigt sich, dass es möglich ist, nur anhand der Kenntniss der Messgrößen die Wirkzusammenhänge im System zu erkennen und dadurch die ursprüngliche Struktur zu reproduzieren.

3 Anwendung 1: Erlernen der Prozessstruktur eines Rührkesselreaktors

Die Untersuchung des Verfahrens erfolgt anhand der Simulationsdaten eines Rührkesselreaktors [8] mit Parallel- und Folgereaktion.

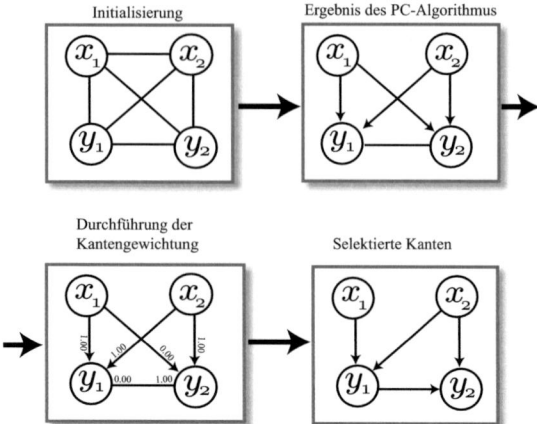

Bild 2: Darstellung der einzelnen Berechnungsphasen des illustrativen Beispiels.

Dem Reaktor liegt der Reaktionsmechanismus zugrunde, bei dem aus einem Edukt ein gewünschtes Produkt gebildet wird und in einer Folgereaktion sich das Produkt teilweise in zwei weiteren Produkte aufspaltet. Das Edukt liegt hierbei in einer verdünnten Lösung c_{in} vor und reagiert folgendermaßen zu den Produkten c_A, c_B und c_C.

$$c_{in} \longrightarrow c_A, \quad c_A \longrightarrow c_B, \quad c_A \longrightarrow c_C$$

Die gewünschte Reaktion ist endotherm, die Folgereaktionen dazu sind jeweils exotherm und der Rührkessel ist mit einer Mantelkühlung versehen (siehe Abbildung 3). Der Rührkessel wird kontinuierlich mit dem Edukt befüllt und das gewünschte Produkt wird kontinuierlich abgezogen.

Das Produkt soll in einer gewünschten Konzentration c_A vorliegen. Dies wird dadurch erreicht, dass der Kessel mittels der Heizleistung Q auf einer konstanten Arbeitstemperatur geregelt wird. Der zugeführte Volumenstrom $\dot{V}$ ist konstant mit einer leicht schwankenden Eintrittstemperatur T_{in} und beinhaltet die Lösung des Eduktes c_{in}, sowie schon geringe Konzentrationen der Produkte c_A, c_B und c_C.

Zusätzlich wird angenommen, dass der Einfluss der Temperatur, welche bei den einzelnen Reaktionen erzeugt wird, vernachlässigbar niedrig ist und somit lediglich ein Einfluss der Fluidtemperatur auf die Reaktionsgeschwindigkeit besteht (ohne Rückkopplungseffekt).

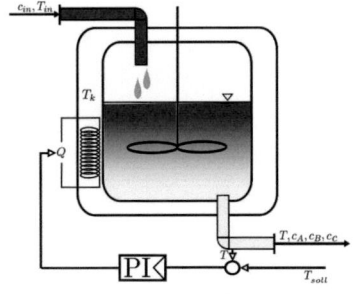 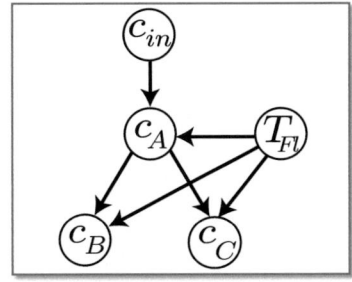

Bild 3: Verwendeter Chemiereaktor zur Analyse des Verfahrens.

Bild 4: Graph des Chemiereaktors basierend auf Systemgleichungen

3.1 Nichtlineares dynamisches Prozessmodell

Die nichtlinearen dynamischen Systemgleichungen der prozessrelevanten Größen c_A, c_B und c_C lauten [14]:

$$\dot{c}_A = -k_1(T)c_A - k_3(T)c_A^2 + [c_{in} - c_A]\dot{V}_{in} \tag{9}$$

$$\dot{c}_B = k_1(T)c_A - k_2(T)c_B - c_B\dot{V}_{in} \tag{10}$$

$$\dot{c}_C = k_3(T)c_A^2 - k_4(T)c_A - c_C\dot{V}_{in} \tag{11}$$

Die drei Geschwindigkeitskonstanten $k_1(T)$, $k_2(T)$, $k_3(T)$ und $k_4(T)$ werden dabei als unterschiedliche Arrhenius-Funktionen angesetzt und die Parameter werden wie in [14] dargestellt, gewählt.

$$k_i(T) = k_{i0}e^{\left(\frac{-E_i}{T_i+273.15}\right)} \tag{12}$$

Die Enthalpiebilanzen für Reaktor und Kühlmantel führen zu zwei Differentialgleichungen für die Temperatur des Reaktors T und die des Kühlmantels T_k.

$$\dot{T} = \beta[T_k - T] + [T_{in} - T]\dot{V}_{in} \tag{13}$$

$$\dot{T}_k = \beta[T - T_k] + \gamma Q \tag{14}$$

Der Parameter β ist ein zusammengesetzter Faktor und beschreibt den Koeffizienten der Reaktor- und Fluidtemperatur. γ beschreibt den Wärmeleitkoeffizient zwischen der Heizleistung und der sich einstellenden Reaktortemperatur.

Der Strukturgraph, welcher die einzelnen Prozessgrößen enthält, ist in Abbildung 4 dargestellt.

Dieser soll mit dem in Abschnitt 2 vorgestellten Konzept aus Simulationsdaten erlernt werden. Da mit dem vorgestellten Verfahren azyklische Graphen erlernt werden, wird der Regelkreis der Temperaturregelung nicht berücksichtigt und die Stellgröße Q, sowie die Reaktortemperatur T_k aus dem Datensatz der Prozessgrößen entfernt. Da die Temperatur T_{in} als konstant angenommen wird, wird diese ebenfalls nicht in dem Graphen berücksichtigt. Das strukturelle Lernverfahren wird daher mit dem in Abbildung 6 dargestellten ungerichteten Graphen initialisiert.

3.2 Testdatensatz

Durch den Einfluss der Regelung, welche bewirkt, dass die Konzentration c_A auf einem konstanten Wert gehalten wird, enthält die Stationärphase nicht genug Information für das Erkennen der Wirkzusammenhänge des Prozesses. Durch unterschiedliche Initialisierungswerte der einzelnen Konzentrationen c_A, c_B, c_C sowie der schwankenden Fluidtemperatur T_{Fl} wird eine Varianz in den Daten erzeugt. Zusätzlich wird der Mittelwert der Konzentration c_{in} variiert. Der Zufluss $\dot{V}$ wird hingegen konstant gehalten.

Es wurden die Daten von 1000 simulierten Anfahrvorgängen verwendet. Abbildung 5 zeigt exemplarisch einige der verwendeten Anfahrvorgänge.

3.2.1 Merkmalsextraktion

Da es sich bei den Anfahrvorgängen um eine instationäre Prozessphase handelt, können nicht die direkten Messdaten verwendet werden, sondern es muss zuvor eine Merkmalsextraktion erfolgen. Als beschreibendes Merkmal wird dazu der Mittelwert verwendet. Das heißt, aus den einzelnen Konzentrationen c_A, c_B, c_C sowie der Fluidtemperatur T_{Fl} werden jeweils für einen Anfahrvorgang Mittelwerte berechnet und als Datensatz verwendet.

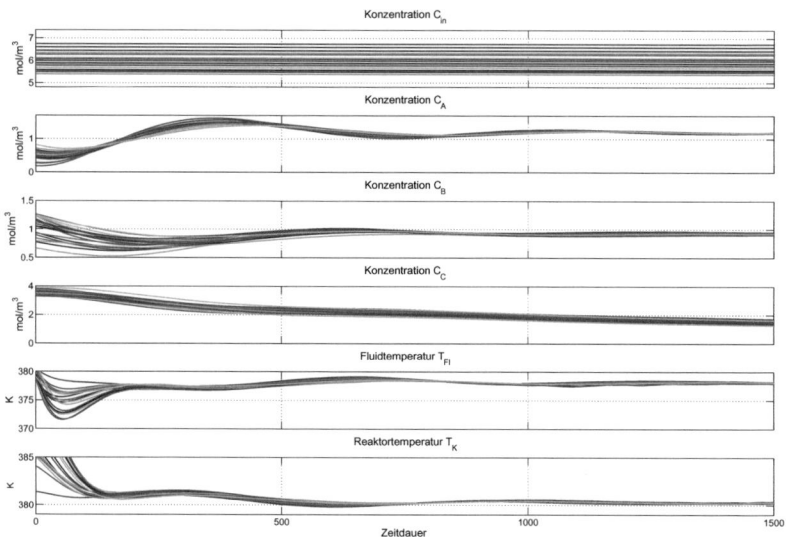

Bild 5: Beispielhafte Produktionen des verwendeten Testdatensatzes.

3.3 Ergebnisse

3.3.1 Phase 1: Anwendung des PC-Algorithmus

Zunächst wird die Struktur des Prozesses, wie in Abbildung 4 dargestellt, als komplett ungerichteter Graph vorgegeben. Das Ergebnis des PC-Algorithmus liefert den in Abbildung

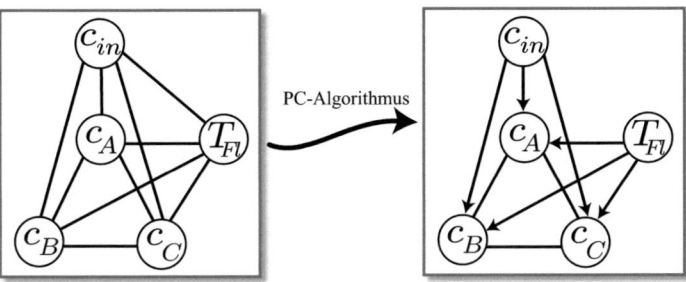

Bild 6: Initialisierungsgraph des Chemiereaktors und resultierender Graph nach Durchführung des PC-Algorithmus. Der tatsächliche azyklische Graph ist in der Markov-Äquivalenzklasse enthalten.

6 dargestellten Graphen. Es lässt sich erkennen, dass die Struktur des Chemiereaktors, wie sie sich aus den Strukturgleichungen ergibt, in dem resultierenden partiell gerichteten Graphen des PC-Algorithmus enthalten ist.

Es wurde erkannt, dass die Konzentrationen c_A, c_B und c_C keine Auswirkungen auf c_{in} haben. Zudem sind alle Kanten von der Fluidtemperatur T_{Fl} auf die drei resultierenden Konzentrationen gerichtet. Die Kante zwischen c_{in} und der Fluidtemperatur T_{Fl} wurde entfernt. Der PC-Algorithmus liefert durch dieses Ergebnis schon Hinweise auf die Abhängigkeiten zwischen den einzelnen Prozessgrößen. Ein Einfluss der Konzentrationen c_A, c_B, c_C auf c_{in} kann genauso ausgeschlossen werden wie ein Einfluss der resultierenden Konzentrationen auf die Fluidtemperatur T_{Fl}. In dem Graph nach Phase 1 ist nicht enthalten, dass c_{in} lediglich einen direkten Einfluss auf c_A hat, die bedingten Unabhängigkeiten wurden also nicht erkannt.

Außerdem ist in dem PDAG nicht wiedergegeben, dass es sich bei den Konzentrationen c_B und c_C um eine Folgereaktion von c_A handelt. Aus dem Graph lässt sich daher schließen, dass die bedingte Unabhängigkeit $A \perp B|C$ aus den Daten nicht erlernt wurde, da weder Kette oder Gabel erkannt wurden (vergl. Tabelle 1).

3.3.2 Phase 2: Berechnen der Kantengewichte

Im zweiten Schritt erfolgt die Berechnung der Kantengewichte aus dem resultierenden Graphen des PC-Algorithmus. Dazu werden die sich ergebenen gerichteten Kanten festgehalten und dadurch die Marginalisierung beeinflusst. Das heißt, hierbei ist nun von besonderem Interesse, ob es mittels der Kantengewichtung möglich ist, Rückschlüsse auf das Reaktionsverhalten der Konzentrationen c_A, c_B, c_C zu erhalten. Das Ergebnis der Gewichtung der Kanten ist in Abbildung 7 dargestellt. Zur besseren Veranschaulichung ist

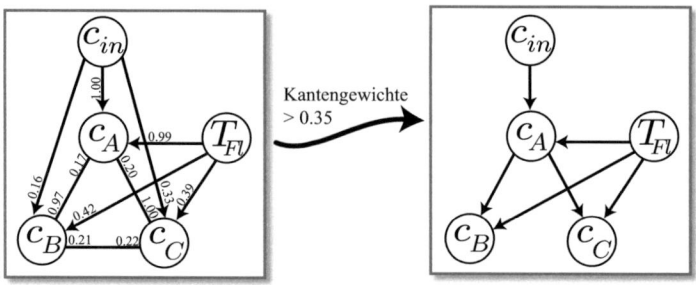

Bild 7: Resultierender Graph nach Durchführung der Kantenmarginalisierung.

in Abbildung 7 der resultierende Graph dargestellt, der sich ergibt, wenn alle Kanten die unter einer Gewichtung von 0.35 liegen, entfernt werden. Es ergibt sich der ursprüngliche Graph des chemischen Reaktors, der die Wirkzusammenhänge beschreibt.

Mittels der Kantengewichtung werden die Reaktionsrichtungen $c_A \rightarrow c_B$ und $c_A \rightarrow c_C$ sowie $c_B \not\rightarrow c_C$ richtig erkannt. Zudem wird die Abhängigkeit $c_{in} \rightarrow c_A$, sowie $c_{in} \not\rightarrow c_B$ richtig wiedergegeben. Leidglich die Kante $c_B \rightarrow c_C$ erhält eine etwas zu hohe Gewichtung.

Bezüglich der Fluidtemperatur T_{Fl} wird für alle drei Konzentrationen eine Abhängigkeit festgestellt. Allerdings fällt die Wahrscheinlichkeit für $T_{Fl} \rightarrow c_B$ (0.42) und $T_{Fl} \rightarrow c_C$ (0.39) niedrig aus.

Das Ergebnis hat gezeigt, dass es möglich ist, rein basierend auf Daten und ohne Kenntnis von Prozesswissen Wirkzusammenhänge zwischen einzelnen Prozessgrößen zu erkennen. Der PC-Algorithmus hat den Graphen bis zu seiner Markov-Äquivalenz erlernt, mittels der Kantengewichtung ist es danach möglich, weitere Kanten zu richten. Eine Kantengewichtung ist gerade dann sinnvoll, wenn dadurch die bei dem PC-Algorithmus nicht erkannten bedingten Unabhängigkeiten durch eine niedrige Kantengewichtung entfernt werden.

4 Anwendung 2: Erlernen der Sensor-Aktorstruktur eines Laborprozesses

Im Folgenden wird untersucht, ob es möglich ist, basierend auf Messdaten die Sensor-Aktorstruktur eines Laborprozesses zu rekonstruieren. Bei der Versuchsanlage handelt es sich um zwei Behälter, zwischen denen zyklisch Wasser bei variierender Pumpenleistung und Ventilstellung in einem Kreislauf umgepumpt wird [3]. Gleichzeitig wird in der Anlage der Duchfluss sowie der Druck gemessen. Der schematische Aufbau sowie der Graph der Anlage ist in Abbildung 8 dargestellt. Der Aufbau ist insofern interessant, da er über keinerlei V-Strukturen verfügt und daher mittels des PC-Algorithmus nur ein Teil der Kanten gerichtet werden kann. Die verwendeten Produktionsdaten sind in Abbildung 9 dargestellt. Die Anlage wird über das Einschalten der Pumpe aktiviert, so dass per Definition keine Kante auf die Pumpe gerichtet sein darf. Daher sind im Initialisierungsgraph alle Kanten von der Pumpe weggehend gerichtet (siehe Abbildung 10). Es wird angenommen, dass außer der Aktivierung durch die Pumpe keine weiteren Informationen verfügbar sind.

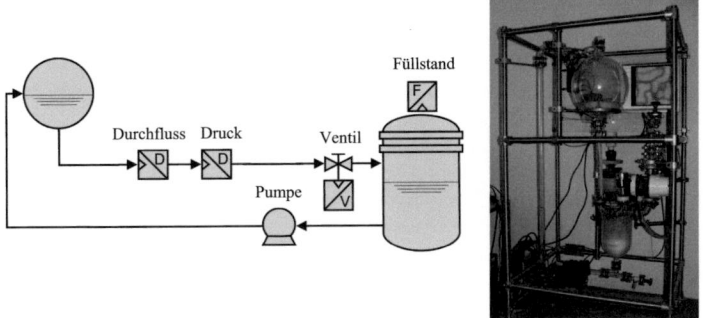

Bild 8: Dargestellt die installierte Versuchsanlage sowie das zu erlernende Sensor/Aktornetzwerk.

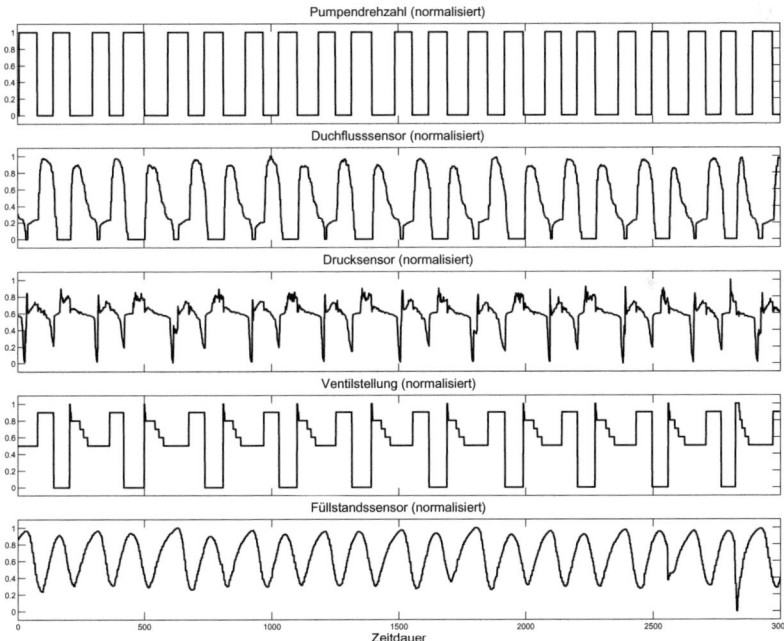

Bild 9: Verwendeter Datensatz der Versuchsanlage.

4.1 Ergebnisse

4.1.1 Phase 1: Anwendung des PC-Algorithmus

Die Durchführung des PC-Algorithmus liefert den in Abbildung 10 dargestellten Wirkzusammenhang. Grau schattiert ist zusätzlich der tatsächliche Verlauf der Sensoren/Aktoren eingezeichnet. Wie bei dem in Abschnitt 3 untersuchten Chemiereaktor ist der tatsächliche Pfad einer von mehreren möglichen Pfaden innerhalb der durch den Algorithmus gefundenen Markov-Äquivalenzklasse.
Es zeigt sich, dass mittels des PC-Algorithmus erkannt wurde, dass die Pumpe direkten Einfluss auf den Durchfluss hat und nicht auf die anderen Prozessgrößen. Allerdings konnte keine bedingte Unabhängigkeit erkannt werden zwischen dem Durchflusssensor und dem Ventil beziehungsweise dem Füllstandsensor. Da es sich hierbei aber um eine Kette handelt (vergl. Tabelle 1), kann lediglich die Richtung des Einflusses erkannt werden.
Des weiteren kann die bedingte Unabhängigkeit zwischen Füllstand und Druck nicht erkannt werden und es ergibt sich daher bezüglich Druck, Ventil und Füllstand ein ungerichteter Graph.

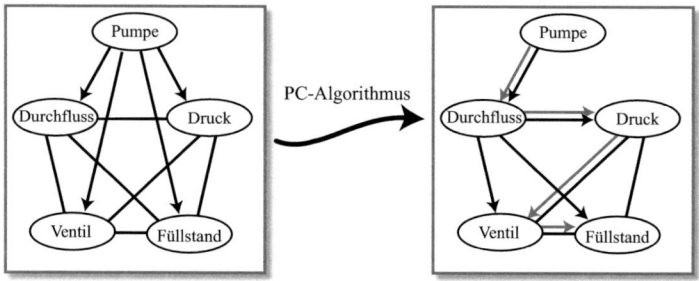

Bild 10: Resultierender Graph nach Durchführung der Kantengewichtung.

4.1.2 Phase 1: Berechnen der Kantengewichte

Entsprechend dem entwickelten Konzept wird der resultierende Graph des PC-Algorithmus dazu verwendet, eine Kantengewichtung durchzuführen. Durch die durchgeführte Marginalisierung der Kanten ergibt sich der in Abbildung 11 dargestellte Strukturgraph.
Es zeigt sich, dass die Graphenstruktur durch die Kantengewichtung weiter eingeschränkt werden kann. Nach der Marginalisierung kann ausgeschlossen werden, dass das Ventil nach dem Durchflusssensor folgt und es kann angenommen werden, dass der Füllstandssensor auf das Ventil folgt. Drucksensor und Füllstandssensor besitzen dabei eine niedrige Gewichtung.
Zur besseren Übersicht wird als Schwellwert 0.5 definiert. Der resultierende Graph ist in Abbildung 11 dargestellt. Es lässt sich auch nach der Marginalisierung nicht erkennen, ob nach dem Durchflusssensor der Füllstandsensor folgt oder der Drucksensor. Zudem kann

nicht erkannt werden, ob zwischen Druck und Füllstandssensor noch das Ventil sitzt. Es sind also weiterhin mehrere Kombinationen der Prozessstruktur möglich, die Auswahl konnte aber mittels der Marginalisierung weiter eingeschränkt werden.

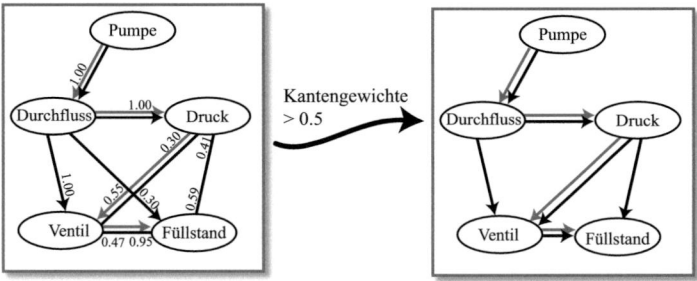

Bild 11: Initialisierungsgraph der Versuchsanlage und resultierender Graph nach Anwendung des PC-Algorithmus.

5 Zusammenfassung und Ausblick

Es wurde untersucht, inwieweit es möglich ist, anhand von Messdaten nicht nur Abhängigkeiten zwischen einzelnen Prozessgrößen zu erkennen, sondern die tatsächliche Wirkungskette darzustellen. Die Ergebnisse haben gezeigt, dass es möglich ist, anhand gerichteter azyklischer Graphen und einer darauffolgenden Kantengewichtung Grundzüge des deterministischen Verhaltens zu erkennen. Hierbei wurde vorausgesetzt, dass eine genügend große Anzahl an Daten vorhanden ist, welche nicht durch gezielte Versuche erhalten wurden, sondern aus dem normalen Betrieb entnommen wurden.

Das entwickelte Verfahren wurde zuerst anhand von simulierten Anfahrphasen eines Rührkesselreaktors untersucht. Hierbei konnte ohne genaue Kenntnis der Prozessgrößen erkannt werden, dass der Reaktionsmechanismus aus einer Folge- und einer Parallelreaktion besteht.

Anhand einer Versuchsanlage wurde das Verfahren daraufhin auf Praxistauglichkeit untersucht. Hierbei hat sich gezeigt, dass ein Großteil der Struktur erkannt werden konnte.

Die Ergebnisse haben aber auch gezeigt, dass nicht immer die bedingten Unabhängigkeiten in den Daten erkannt werden können. Sowohl bei dem Chemiereaktor als auch bei der Versuchsanlage wurden mittels des G^2 Tests nicht alle vorhandenen bedingten Unabhängigkeiten erkannt. Es sind daher weitere Verfahren zum Test auf bedingte Unabhängigkeiten zu untersuchen.

Ein logischer nächster Schritt ist das so genannte aktive Lernen. Das bedeutet, dass mittels der erlernten Wirkzusammenhänge die einzelnen Kanten als Hypothesen aufgefasst werden und durch aktive Stelleingriffe verändert und auf ihren Wahrheitsgehalt untersucht werden können.

Eine weitere interessante Fragestellung ist, inwiefern Eingriffe in die Prozessstruktur mittels dieser Graphen simuliert werden können, also beispielsweise wie sich der Einfluss eines defekten Aktors auf den Prozess auswirken würde.

[1] D. Chickering: *Learning Equivalence Classes of Bayesian-Network Structures.* Journal of Machine Learning Research 2 2002.

[2] D. Eaton, and K. Murphy: *Belief net structure learning from uncertain interventions.* Journal of Machine Learning Research 1 2000.

[3] C. Frey *Diagnosis and Monitoring of Complex Industrial Processes based on Self-Organizing Maps and Watershed Transformations.* IEEE International Conference on Computational Intelligence for Measurement Systems and Applications 2008.

[4] N. Friedman: *Inferring Cellular Networks Using Probabilistic Graphical Models.* Science(5659, 303:799-805 2004.

[5] N. Friedmann: *Being Bayesian about Network Structure.* Conference on Uncertainty in Artificial Intelligence 2000.

[6] I. Guyon, et al.: *Causal feature selection.* NIPS Workshop on Causality and Feature Selection 2006.

[7] T. Hastie et al.: *The Elements of Statistical Learning.* Spring Series in Statistics 2008.

[8] K. U Klatt, S. Engell: *Rührkesselreaktor mit Parallel- und Folgereaktion* VDI-Bericht Nr. 1026: Nichtlineare Regelung 1993

[9] C. Kühnert: *Extraction of optimal control patterns in industrial batch processes based on support vector machines.* IEEE Multi-conference on systems and control 2009.

[10] B. Meder: *Seeing versus Doing: Causal Bayes Nets as Psychological Models of Causal Reasoning.* Dissertation, http://webdoc.sub.gwdg.de/diss/2006/meder/meder.pdf 2006.

[11] J. Pearl: *Causality.* Cambridge University press 2000.

[12] P. Spirtes et al.: *Causation, Prediction, and Search.* The MIT Press, 2nd edition 2000.

[13] I. Tsamardinos et al.: *The max-min hill-climbing bayesian network structure learning algorithm.* Machine Learning 65 2006.

[14] T. Utz et al.: *Nonlinear Model Predictive and Flatness-Based Two-Degree-of Freedom Control Design: A Comparative Evaluation in View of Industrial Application.* IEEE Conference on Control Applications 2006.

[15] J. XU, Z. Hou.: *Notes on Data-driven System Approaches.* ACTA Automatica Sinica 2009.

Interactive Learning of Inverse Kinematics with Nullspace Constraints using Recurrent Neural Networks[1]

Sebastian Wrede, Michael Johannfunke, Andre Lemme, Arne Nordmann, Stefan Rüther, Alicia Weirich and Jochen Steil

Research Institute for Cognition and Robotics (CoR-Lab),
Bielefeld University
Universitätsstr. 25, 33615 Bielefeld
Tel.: (0521) 106-5214
Fax: (0521) 106-89042
E-Mail: {swrede,mjohannf,alemme,anordman,sruether,aweirich,jsteil}
@cor-lab.uni-bielefeld.de

Abstract

It is a major goal of current robotics research to enable robots to become co-workers that collaborate with humans efficiently, safely and that adapt to changing environments or workflows. In this contribution, we present an approach that integrates the interaction capabilities of state-of-the-art compliant robotics with data-driven and model-free learning in a coherent system (FlexIRob – Flexible Interactive Robot) in order to make fast reconfiguration of redundant robots feasible. FlexIRob allows to teach a multi-DOF robot several null-space constraints in different areas of the workspace. Users with no particular robotics knowledge can perform this task in physical interaction with the compliant robot, for example to reconfigure a work cell due to changes in the environment. For fast and efficient training the respective mapping, an associative reservoir neural network is employed. It is embedded in the motion controller of the system, hence allowing for execution of arbitrary motions in task space. We describe the systems' workflow, the training and the underlying software-architecture and present some evaluation on the KUKA Light-Weight Robot. Our results show that the learned model solves the inverse kinematics problem under the given constraints with sufficient accuracy and generalizes to generate valid joint-space trajectories even in untrained areas of the workspace.

1 Introduction

The EUROP strategic research agenda [1] promotes robotics and automation systems as increasingly important tools for small-and-medium enterprises (SME) to keep a competitive edge in a fully globalized economy. The targets are higher process efficiency and improved production quality as exemplified in [2]. However, the benefit of deploying state-of-the-art automation technology in SME's is limited as the gain in process efficiency is often reduced through high costs for the frequent adaptation of manufacturing processes. Reconfiguration, affects robotic systems in several ways: different tools mounted to a robot or different kinematic setups for modular robots yield different kinematics and dynamics, or changed work cell layouts may require path planning and obstacle avoidance strategies. Collectively, these *configuration* changes yield high costs for manual re-programming and testing of robotic systems and their accompanying software.

[1]This work has been partially supported by the AMARSi - Adaptive Modular Architectures for Rich Motor Skill project (EU FP7-ICT 248311, http://www.amarsi-project.eu/).

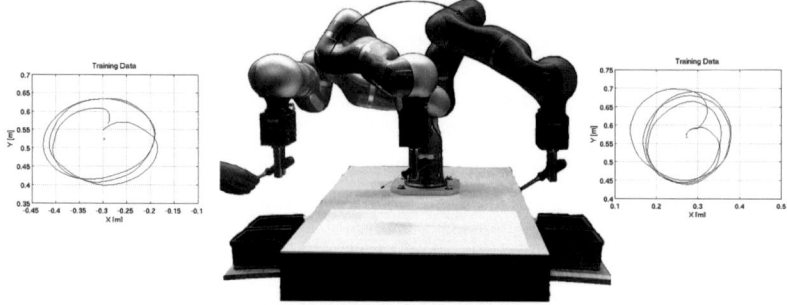

Figure 1: During execution of trajectories, the FlexIRob system respects null-space constraints taught in human-robot interaction (cf. areas left and right above the blue boxes).

Furthermore, future applications will likely involve robotic systems for complex tasks such as multi-part assembly and use several non-standard, e.g., redundant manipulators or other specific tools in close HRI scenarios [3, 4] resulting in even more complex adaptation processes.

Consequently, the configuration problem of advanced robotics systems is entitled as one of the major challenges of current robotics research [1]. Our approach to this challenge is based on *(i) human-robot interaction, (ii) model-free learning* techniques and an integrating *(iii) system architecture.* In this contribution, we focus on two important parts of the re-configuration problem, namely the change of kinematic setups and the introduction of constraints for redundancy resolution in the joint space of the robot.

While the presented approach is not bound to a specific robot platform, we developed our current system using a recent version of the KUKA Light-Weight Robot (LWR IV)[5]. Its control scheme yields active compliance of the manipulator which is beneficial for the desired human-robot interaction. The LWR IV is a redundant manipulator allowing a manifold of configurations in joint space for a single end-effector position and thereby provides high flexibility for complex movements in workspace. Section 2 discusses some requirements from the perspective of human-robot interaction and learning on robotic platforms and presents some details about the platform actually used in our experiments.

The prototype robotic system described in this contribution, termed *FlexIRob*, allows to teach a *redundant* robot several particular null-space constraints in different areas of the workspace as shown in Figure 1. Users with no particular robotics knowledge can perform this task in physical interaction with the compliant robot, for example to reconfigure a working cell according to changes in the environment. Section 3 summarizes the resulting challenges for the control architecture and the learning scheme. Subsequently, Section 4 presents a purely data-driven learning algorithm to encode the inverse kinematics mapping with null-space constraints in a single Recurrent-Neural Network (RNN). After training, the learned inverse kinematics controller is embedded in the control strategy of the overall system, allowing for execution of arbitrary motions in task space, respecting the learned null-space constraints. This interplay between a sophisticated industrial robot platform, human-robot interaction strategies and learning algorithms is an example for the tight integration we envision to be necessary to match the given challenge.

In order to demonstrate and evaluate the benefits the system, all components need to be orchestrated in a coherent system architecture. For the presented approach, we realized a generic control architecture exploiting the compliance features of the robot and connecting low-level control with learning components that shall similarly be applicable for other scenarios integrating compliant robots, interaction and learning. It provides a set of coherent tools for high-level simulation, programming of individual and re-use of complete learning or interaction components. In Section 5, this software architecture, its different control modes as well as the overall integration concept providing the technological basis for FlexIRob are explained briefly. Finally, Section 6 describes first results from quantitative evaluation experiments. They show that the approach solves the inverse kinematics problem under the given null-space constraints accurately and even generates valid joint-space trajectories in untrained areas of the workspace without explicit motion planning.

2   Taking the Human-in-the-Loop with Compliant Robots

In this contribution, we use the KUKA Lightweight Robot (LWR). The LWR is a proto-typical research platform developed in a collaboration between KUKA and the German Aerospace Center. We chose the LWR as robot platform since it is well suited to demonstrate the application of our proposed methods in an industrial context while providing advanced features for sophisticated robot control as needed by new research applications. Advantages are the movement flexibility introduced by the redundancy of the system. It provides rich sensory feedback providing an avenue for novel types of human-machine interaction and effectively taking the human in the loop between perception, learning and action of the robot system.

The LWR has seven axes and therefore one redundant degree of freedom. Torque sensors in all its seven joints and a dynamic model of the entire robot allow active compliance control, both on joint level and in task space. The control has a cycle rate of 3 kHz in each joint and 1 kHz over-all. This enables the robot to act as a spring-damper system in which the parameters (stiffness and damping) can be set within wide limits. The compliance feature allows manual guidance of the robot via interaction with a human operator [5]. Additionally the LWR system provides a gravitation compensation mode in which the robot holds its position but at the same time fully complies to external forces applied to the manipulator. This is done in active control based on the dynamic model and force sensory feedback, which allows to distinguish between gravitation force which needs to be compensated and the external interaction force which the robot complies to.

Nowadays, physical interaction is also possible with conventional 6 DOF industrial robots if force sensors are added at the end-effector. However, only the redundancy of the LWR in combination with the force sensors in each of the joints allows intuitive teaching of null-space constraints along the entire joint configuration via physical interaction.

3   Problem Statement

Redundant robots such as the KUKA LWR IV provide high flexibility for the realization of complex scenarios, e.g., in car-manufacturing. However, this flexibility induces challenges such as solving inverse kinematics with redundancy resolution in joint space for arbitrary movements.

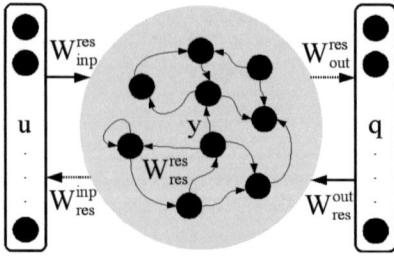

Figure 2: The associative reservoir network architecture connects task- and joint-space variables bidirectionally. Inverse and forward kinematics can be be queried continuously.

The analytic determination of this inverse kinematics requires expert knowledge and the availability of rigorous kinematic models of the robot. Typically, either a single solution in joint-space is selected as redundancy resolution or an energy function that is minimized [6]. Furthermore, alternative schemes for redundancy resolution exist based on devising additional criteria in null-space, i.e., "home" positions or joint angle limits.

While the resolution of the redundancy in case of the KUKA LWR IV can also be done with the built-in tool-set provided by KUKA Robot Control (KRC) framework, this just provides one generic solution, not allowing for adaptation of constraints in a flexible manner. An additional challenge is the handling of rich sensory feedback in combination with tight real-time constraints defined by the KRC architecture. This real-time constraint needs to be matched with larger timescales of sensory processing and movement generation as well as variable timescales of interaction with a human operator.

4 NDMP-based Learning of Redundancy Resolution

The framework we utilize in FlexIRob to address learning aspects in the aforementioned questions is the so-called Neural Dynamic Movement Primitives (NDMP) approach [7]. Training is conducted by recording postures along trajectories in the desired areas of the workspace where a posture is a pair of task and joint space sample vectors. Subsequently, a fast learning scheme based on backpropagation-decorrelation (BPDC) configures a recurrent neural network to approximate the inverse kinematics. In the following, this computational model is introduced.

NDMP is a dynamical fully data driven bidirectional mapping between end effector positions $\mathbf{u}$ and joint values $\mathbf{q}$ by means of a fixed recurrent neural network, a reservoir. It has no explicit model knowledge of the target platform, here the KUKA LWR IV robot. Figure 2 visualizes the architecture of the reservoir network. Here, the inverse kinematic (IK) mapping $\mathbf{q} = IK(\mathbf{u})$ is from left to right (input-to-output) and the forward kinematic (FK) mapping $\mathbf{u} = FK(\mathbf{q})$ from right to left (output-to-input).

We denote the network state at time step k by:

$$\mathbf{z}(k) = (\mathbf{u}(k)^T, \ \mathbf{y}(k)^T, \ \mathbf{q}(k)^T)^T$$

W^{net} captures all connection sub-matrices between neurons in the RNN and is defined by

$$
W^{net} = \begin{pmatrix} 0 & W^{inp}_{res} & 0 \\ W^{res}_{inp} & W^{res}_{res} & W^{res}_{out} \\ 0 & W^{out}_{res} & 0 \end{pmatrix},
$$

where we denote by $W^{\square}_{\star}$ all connections from $\star$ to $\square$ using inp for input, out for output, and res for inner reservoir neurons. Only connections W^{out}_{res} and W^{inp}_{res} projecting to the input and output neurons are trained by error correction (illustrated by dashed arrows in Fig. 2). All other weights are initialized randomly with small weights and remain fixed. We consider recurrent network dynamics

$$
\mathbf{x}(k{+}1) = (1{-}\Delta t)\,\mathbf{x}(k) + \Delta t\,\mathbf{W}^{net}\mathbf{z}(k) \tag{1}
$$
$$
\mathbf{z}(k) = \mathbf{f}(\mathbf{x}(k)), \tag{2}
$$

where for small Δt continuous time dynamics are approximated. $\mathbf{z}$ is obtained by applying activation functions component-wise to the neural activations $x_i, i = 1 \dots N$. We use parametrized logistic activation functions $y_i = f_i(x_i, a_i, b_i) = (1 + \exp{(-a_i x_i - b_i)})^{-1}$ for the reservoir neurons. Input and output neurons have a identity as activation function, i.e. are linear neurons.

We use the associative neural reservoir learning (ANRL) approach to learn from data samples. We start by training the dynamic network with trajectories, e.g. demonstrated by a teacher, to learn the kinematic mapping. Learning proceeds supervised, i.e. needs corresponding task/joint space data for training.

In ANRL, the read-out weights W^{out}_{res} and W^{inp}_{res} are trained by backpropagation-decorrelation (BPDC) learning, an efficient supervised online training scheme introduced in [8]. In this network configuration the BPDC learning rule is

$$
\Delta w_{ij}(k) = \frac{\eta}{\|\mathbf{y}(k{-}1)\|^2}\, y_j(k{-}1)\,(d_i^*(k) - d_i(k)), \tag{3}
$$

where $\mathbf{d}(k) = (\mathbf{u}(k)^T, \mathbf{q}(k)^T)^T$ collects all visible neurons and $d_i^*(k)$ is the desired target value of visible neuron i at time step k.

Additionally to the supervised learning of the weights, an unsupervised learning method called Intrinsic plasticity (IP) is used. IP was first introduced in [9] in the context of feed-forward networks. The biologically inspired learning rule changes the neurons' gains a_i and biases b_i of the logistic activation functions and is used here in order to optimize information transmission of the inner reservoir neurons [10].

That is, neurons should be active only sparsely according to an approximately exponential distribution. In the following the online gradient rule with learning rate η_{IP} and desired mean activity μ is shown:

$$
\Delta b_i(k) = \eta_{IP}\left(1 - \left(2 + \frac{1}{\mu}\right)y_i(k) + \frac{1}{\mu}y_i(k)^2\right), \tag{4}
$$
$$
\Delta a_i(k) = \eta_{IP}\frac{1}{a_i(k)} + x_i(k)\Delta b_i(k). \tag{5}
$$

This unsupervised self-adaptation rule is local in time and space and therefore efficient to compute. This learning scheme has been applied for high-dimension humanoids, however using analytically generated training data. Details on the parameters used in the FlexIRob context are explained in Section 6.

5   System Architecture

To facilitate the necessary teaching in physical human-robot interaction and the application of the learned NDMP controller in the control scheme of the overall robotics system, we developed an integrating system architecture taking into account the specifics of compliant robots.

While the application and robot control components of the architecture are currently rather specific for the the given scenario and the KUKA LWR IV, safety and learning components are re-usable across this single application. After an initial explanation of the fundamental modus operandi of the presented system, the resulting control flow and the integration of its components in a distributed control architecture capable of real-time control will be discussed.

As a first design decision, we introduce two distinct operational modes, namely an exploration and execution to clearly structure the desired human-robot interaction. In the *exploration phase* parts of the task space are explored in physical interaction with a human operator, providing the data for the training of the NDMP. Utilizing a trained NDMP, the *execution phase* allows to execute a movement task defined by a human user (or some other system component), using the trained RNN as inverse kinematics solver. Figure 3 shows a UML activity diagram highlighting the high-level activities of the relevant system parts and the human teacher in both of the two phases.

The exploration phase starts with an untrained NDMP. For recording training data the application control switches the robot to gravitation compensation mode in order to allow a human teacher to move the robot to the desired position, considering the constraints in the environment. Subsequently, the robot is switched to impedance control allowing the human operator to move the end-effector of the robot to record end-effector positions and the corresponding joint angles. After recording the training data and hence the redundancy resolution in this area of the workspace another constraint can be taught. Otherwise, the recorded data is sent to the NDMP component in order to allow the data-driven training, which takes around $3 - 4$ minutes depending on the number of training data.

Once the NDMP is trained, the system can be used in its execution mode. For actually moving the robot, the user has to generate end-effector trajectories, which can currently be done by providing a 2D trajectory in the workspace on a tablet PC. This end-effector trajectory is sent to the NDMP component that is now used as a trajectory controller. The NDMP performs the mapping from end-effector coordinated to joint angle configurations, respecting and generalizing the constraints given in the exploration phase when traversing to new positions in task space. For executing the resulting joint space trajectories, the robot is switched to position impedance mode and moved by a position controller.

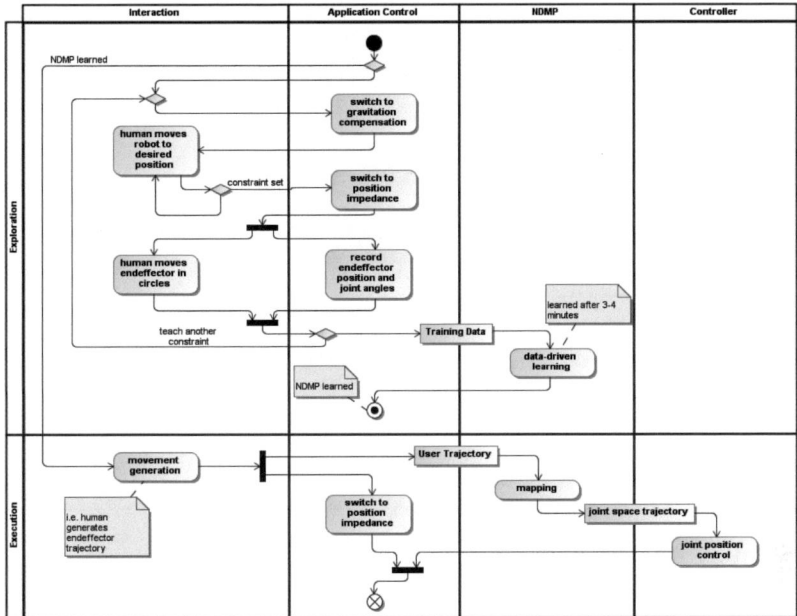

Figure 3: Exploration and execution activities in the FlexIRob system.

5.1 Control Architecture

In order to explain the overall control scheme of FlexIRob, including the use of compliance features of the robot for kinesthetic teaching and position impedance control with the learned NDMP controller, we provide a systems engineering perspective to the system. Hence, we understand the major system components as functional blocks of a control system and the communication between the components as flow of information between these functional blocks, as shown in Figure 4. In its two modes, exploration and execution, the system selectively activates different control flows.

5.1.1 Exploration

In a first phase of exploration the robot is in a so called *gravitation compensation* mode, where forces applied to the robot are not counteracted by the controller. This phase is used to let the operator position the robot via kinesthetic teaching to an initial joint angle configuration q_{init}. After the desired configuration is reached, the robot is switched to impedance control for recording training data. In this phase the *Controller* component and the *User Interface* is inactive. The only active control loop in this phase is the inner impedance control loop. While the operator applies an interaction force f_{int} to the robot in order to produce training data, f_{int} in combination with the initial joint angle configuration q_{init} is the reference for an impedance control loop executed on the robot.

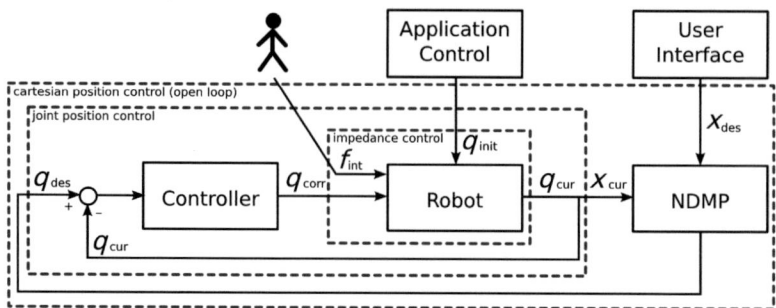

Figure 4: Block diagram showing the FlexIRob control scheme with its three control loops. Physical interaction between the human operator and the robot is modeled as interaction force f_{int}.

Parameters for the impedance controller are stiffness and damping in cartesian coordinates, which are carefully chosen by us to allow easy physical interaction with the robot. During the training the current joint angles q_{cur} and the corresponding cartesian end-effector positions x_{cur} are recorded and afterwards passed to the *NDMP* component. The *NDMP* component feeds the recurrent neural net with the recorded data to enable the net to learn the forward and inverse kinematics.

5.1.2   Execution

In the execution phase the *User Interface* component as well as the *Controller* are now active. As shown in Figure 4 a user provides a trajectory of desired end-effector positions x_{des} via the *User Interface*. x_{des} is passed to the *NDMP* component, where the trained recurrent neural net maps the end-effector positions x_{des} to desired joint values q_{des}, which provides the reference for a joint position control loop built with the *Controller* component. In order to to that q_{des} is constantly compared to the reported current joint angles q_{cur}, which leads to joint angle corrections q_{corr}. q_{des} together with the interaction force f_{int} applied by a user during execution, provides the reference for the inner impedance control loop. Stiffness and damping values can be chosen according to the executed task.

In our experiments, the outer position control loop is executed with a 12 ms control cycle, the inner impedance control loop on the KUKA LWR is executed with a 1 ms control cycle. Note that the outer control loop, the cartesian position control, is an open-loop control in our current setup.

5.2   Software Architecture

The actual software architecture realizing the presented operational modes and the three control loops features a rather coarse decomposition of the different functionalities into high-level services accessible through a service oriented middleware framework (XCF) [11] developed at Bielefeld University.

The FlexIRob system architecture thereby realizes a distributed control system. According to the information-driven design principles [12] the different services were designed to be re-usable as complete services across different applications. For instance, the learning service is neither from an algorithmic nor from a software perspective coupled to the KUKA LWR robot platform. The following subsections briefly describe informally the fundamental services in each layer needed for the realization of the described scenario.

5.2.1 Control Components

The responsibilities of the three software components implementing the control service in our FlexIRob system are to provide an external API accepting asynchronous Task requests which allow the robot to change its configuration accordingly, perform collision checking and allow joint-level position control. The latter is realized through the integration of a generic and hierarchical position controller component, based on ideas by Grupen and Huber[13]. Collision checking is realized by forwarding all requests to the service first through a collision-checking pipeline using a detailed simulation of the robot and its environment. Finally, the control service embeds a real-time communication interface connecting to the embedded industrial control PC on the robot. As the communication with this research-oriented industrial robot is non-standard, some extra explanation for this component is needed.

At the time of writing, KUKA provides two software interfaces for the Lightweight Robot IV, the *RSI-XML* interface [14] and the more up-to-date *Fast Research Interface* [15] (FRI). In the current system, we use the RSI-XML interface. Communication using RSI-XML follows a client-server pattern. The client is implemented by a KRL application running on the KUKA Robot Control (KRC) system providing the RSI-XML interface. In our software we provide an RSI-XML server using OpenKC (Open KUKA Control[16]), an RSI-XML wrapper developed in Bielefeld. We use OpenKC as a library in the main control component to the robot and realize thereby a real-time cycle, communicating via a a Gigabit Ethernet point-to-point network connection. Messages between our system and the KRC are sent as XML documents via TCP in a 12 ms cycle.

Documents sent to the robot are control mode switches and commands, which could be on joint level (joint position control, joint stiffness/damping, ...) or in cartesian coordinates. The OpenKC part of the *Controller* component translates the high-level commands from our application to the specified XML format. In case of position control absolute positions have to be transformed to a continuous set of corrections, since the RSI-XML interface just takes corrections instead of absolute values as commands. Documents received from the robot contain all status information of the robot on joint level and in task space (positions, forces, ...). These documents are parsed and instantiate the domain specific object information-driven object passed to the interface of the control service.

An additional responsibility of the control service is to publish relevant state variables on the event bus, representing all relevant information available, e.g, about joint angles, end-effector position, contact forces as well as information about possibly collisions or the currently accepted tasks. All components in this layer were developed in C/C++.

5.2.2 Interaction Components

Since physical human-robot interaction is a core requirement for our system, the management of interaction state is an essential pre-requisite for the integration of the learning functions in the architecture. To manage this state and control the user interaction, the service is comprised by three software components: an application controller implementing the scenario-specific behavior using a finite state machine for modeling the application work-flow and two separate graphical user interfaces, one for monitoring system operation as well as safety status and the other one for a graphical user interaction allowing end-users to draw 2D trajectories on a tablet PC simulating movement generation in the workspace.

The interaction service components communicate via asynchronous Task events with the robot control service while subscribing and processing the Eigenmodel events about the robot and control status. In our case this is setting impedance on joints, and commanding trajectories in task and joint space. The application controller component is written in C++ while the graphical user interfaces were developed in Java for the sake of simplicity.

5.2.3 Learning Components

The learning service features the NDMP component as described in Section 4 and exports its interface at a service level to other software components. Its primary responsibilities are to perform the actual learning task where it processes a set of recorded end-effector and corresponding joint angle trajectories and provide a query interface generating trajectories in order to control the robot system with the learned inverse kinematics. According to the scenario we use the learning approach to plan a user trajectory in joint space by generating a seven dimensional output vector for each three dimensional input vector, describing the task trajectory. According to our first experiments, a training set of about 250 samples is needed to cover a sufficient area for a 7-DOF robot arm in the learning phase. Further information about the use of the NDMP component is presented in Section 6. The NDMP component is written in C++ and is as a service component reusable on other robot platforms.

6 Prototype Evaluation

In its current setup FlexIRob is configured to execute arbitrary two dimensional end-effector trajectories. To reduce complexity for providing a proof of concept test, the z-coordinate and rotation of the trajectories are left constant. The experiment's setup uses a workspace configuration as shown in Figure 1, with a training space on the left and right side of the table. The training spaces are unconnected, so there is an untrained space in between. The length of the area where no training data is recorded can be chosen in preface. For this initial evaluation, we used values between 600mm and 800mm as distance between training data center points.

During the exploration phase each of the training space is explored by kinesthetic moving the end-effector in circles around training space's center point. Each training data set consists of 200 up to 300 points of end-effector positions with corresponding joint angles.

These two sets are used to teach the RNN, as described in Section 4 with parameters given in Table 1. These parameters are proposed in [7] and in [17] for controlling a humanoid robot respecting specific constraints. We adjusted the parameters for our setup in a way that we do not use a linear mapping in this framework, which is biologically more plausible.

During exploration we record training data in both sub workspaces and change axis configuration in each training space (e.g. 'elbow up on the left side, elbow down on the right'). After learning has finished, the system is ready to execute arbitrary trajectories.

The expectation is that joint space constraints, intrinsically defined through the training data, are at least satisfied in each of the trained areas. For exploring the system behavior we have done the process of i) *recording* two training data sets with different axis configurations and ii) *executing* several end-effector trajectories. While executing a trajectory we use the hierarchical position controller already introduced in Section 5 to evaluate the joint angles generated by the RNN. The controller calculates the joint angles corresponding to a given end-effector position but it has no null-space redundancy solving. Hence, we generate a posture consisting of the end-effector position (input to the RNN) and the corresponding joint angles with redundancy resolution (output of the RNN). The controller generates joint angles based on the posture, with priority to the end-effector position so that the given end-effector position is always executed, with the given joint angle configuration as secondary constraint. Note, that the hierarchical controller also uses blending for time-optimal execution and due to interface requirements for LWR. The blending results in an interpolated trajectory are visible in Figure 5(8) and 6(8). A comparison of the RNN-generated joint angles and the executed joint values generated by CBF controller is given in Figure 6(1-7) and 6(1..7). This demonstrates that the model-free RNN controller is able to realize the desired trajectory execution.

The experiments also show a generalization of null-space constraints while executing an arbitrary trajectory. As shown on-site during AUTOMATICA2010, the taught constraints for the additional DOF are satisfied while executing the end-effector trajectory, even in the untrained areas of the workspace where the RNN generates intermediate solutions generalizing the constraints. Even though no training data was recorded between both workspaces, the redundancy resolution works in this unexplored space as a function of distance: the more the end-effector moves towards one workspace, the more the redundancy resolution is adapted to the previously taught constraint for this workspace. Further work will investigate on and quantify the constraint generalization of given constraints in unexplored spaces.

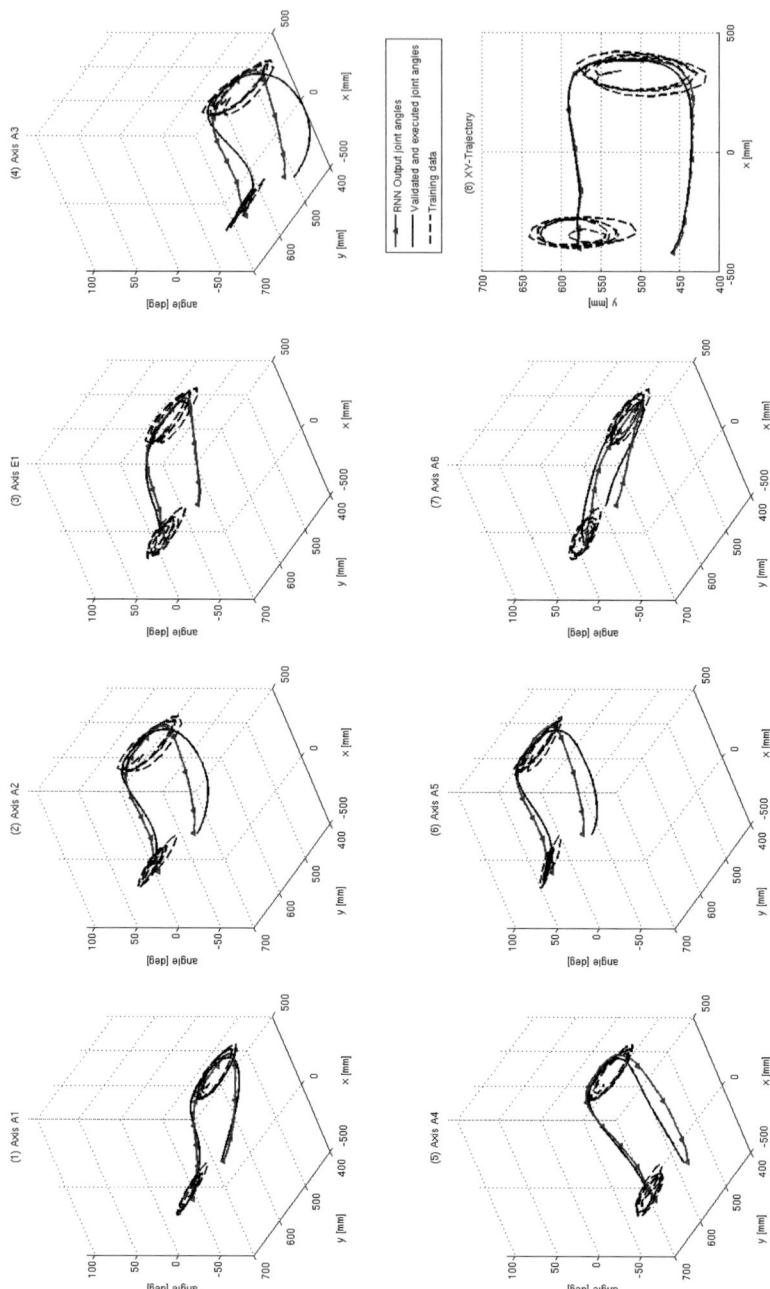

Figure 5: Joint angles with regard to x-y-end-effector position (1-7) and trained areas visualized as 2D-trajectories (8) for trial experiment A

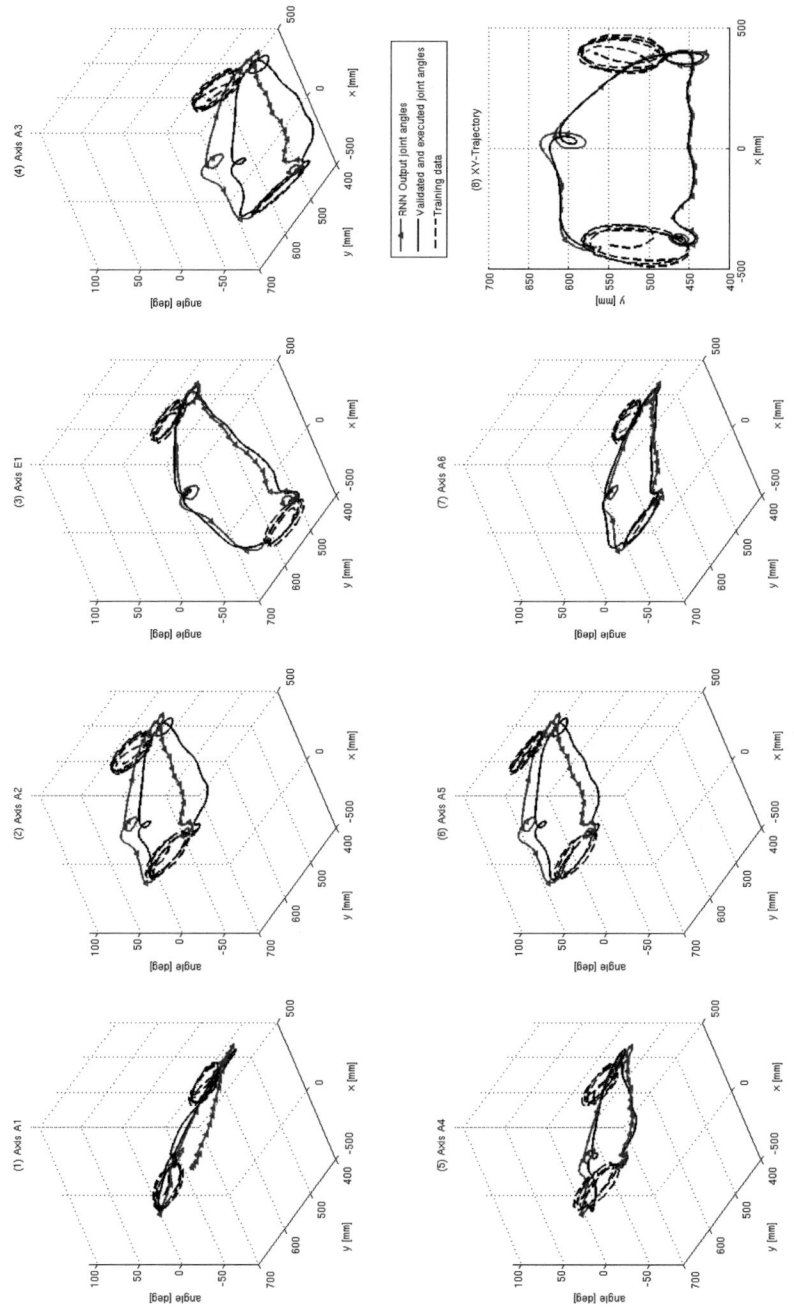

Figure 6: Joint angles with regard to x-y-end-effector position (1-7) and trained areas visualized as 2D-trajectories (8) for trial experiment B

	FlexIRob	
Reservoir Size	300	
Connection	ρ	a
Input-Reservoir	0.2	0.1
Reservoir-Reservoir	0.02	0.02
Reservoir-Output	0.2	0.1
Output-Reservoir	0.2	0.1
Learning	η	
IP	0.00015	
BPDC	0.015	
Cycles	100	

Table 1: Parameters for network construction and learning.

7 Conclusion

In this contribution, we presented an integrated interaction and machine learning approach for re-configuration of robotics systems with respect to constraints given by the workspace environment. We use a compliant and redundant robot arm and created a system architecture integrating a set of learning and interaction components. Configuration of the system can even be done by users without deep robotics knowledge, using kinesthetic teaching to provide training data intrinsically containing constraints given by the environment or set by the intended task. The learning component uses a data-driven and model-free approach for training the recurrent neural net. The applied learning rule allows to perform the training of the underyling NDMP controller in a few minutes, which makes the approach fast and flexible.

As an initial evaluation of our prototype system, we demonstrated its ability to execute user-generated trajectories. This showed that FlexIRob allows task execution not only in the trained areas of the workspace, but also provides reasonable intermediate solutions for untrained areas.

Further work will assess the applicability of the approach in industrial co-worker scenarios and extend the evaluation to analysis of stability aspects, influence of training data sample rates and execution sample rates. Functionally, we will extended our system to handle arbitrary 6D-trajectories and include perceptual processing for online trajectory adapation in task space.

Concluding, the features and the first promising results of this FlexIRob prototype system present a first step towards easier re-configurabition of robotic systems through integration of learning technology, human-robot interaction and advanced robotics technology.

References

[1] European Robotics Technology Platform (EUROP). Robotic visions to 2020 and beyond - the strategic research agenda for robotics in europe, 2009. http://www.robotics-platform.eu/sra.

[2] Daimler. Leichtbauroboter im Piloteinsatz im Mercedes-Benz Werk Untertürkheim, 2009.

[3] Sami Haddadin, Michael Suppa, Stefan Fuchs, T. Bodenmüller, A. Albu-Schäffer, and Gerd Hirzinger. Towards the Robotic Co-Worker. In *International Symposium on Robotics Research (ISRR2007), Lausanne, Switzerland*, volume 1, 2009.

[4] Ingo Lütkebohle, Julia Peltason, Lars Schillingmann, Christof Elbrechter, Britta Wrede, Sven Wachsmuth, and Robert Haschke. The curious robot - structuring interactive robot learning. In *International Conference on Robotics and Automation*, Kobe, Japan, 14/05/2009 2009. IEEE, IEEE.

[5] Rainer Bischoff, Johannes Kurth, Günter Schreiber, Ralf Koeppe, Alin Albuschäffer, Der Beyer, Oliver Eiberger, Sami Haddadin, Andreas Stemmer, Gerhard Grunwald, and Kuka Roboter Gmbh. The KUKA-DLR Lightweight Robot arm – a new reference platform for robotics research and manufacturing. *Automatica*, 2010.

[6] Bruno Siciliano. Kinematic control of redundant robot manipulators: A tutorial. *Journal of Intelligent and Robotic Systems*, 3(3):201–212, September 1990.

[7] M. Rolf, R. F. Reinhart, and J. J. Steil. Neural Dynamic Movement Primitives based on Associative Reservoir Learning. 2010.

[8] J. J. Steil. Backpropagation-decorrelation: recurrent learning with O(N) complexity. In *Proc. IJCNN*, volume 1, pages 843–848, 2004.

[9] J. Triesch. A gradient rule for the plasticity of a neuron's intrinsic excitability. In *Proc. ICANN*, pages 65–79, 2005.

[10] Jochen J Steil. Online reservoir adaptation by intrinsic plasticity for backpropagation-decorrelation and echo state learning. *Neural networks : the official journal of the International Neural Network Society*, 20(3):353–64, April 2007.

[11] J. Fritsch and S. Wrede. *Software Engineering for Experimental Robotics*, volume 30 of *Springer Tracts in Advanced Robotics*, chapter An Integration Framework for Developing Interactive Robots, pages 291–305. Springer, 2007.

[12] Sebastian Wrede. *An Information-Driven Architecture for Cognitive Systems Research*. PhD thesis, Technical Faculty, Bielefeld University, Germany, 2008.

[13] R.A. Grupen and Manfred Huber. A framework for the development of robot behavior. In *2005 AAAI Spring Symposium Series: Developmental Robotics*. Stanford University, 2005.

[14] KUKA. KUKA.Ethernet RSI XML 1.2. *System*, pages 1–85, 2008.

[15] G. Schreiber, A. Stemmer, and R. Bischoff. The Fast Research Interface for the KUKA Lightweight Robot. *IEEE ICRA 2010 Workshop on Innovative Robot Control Architectures*, 2010.

[16] Matthias Schoepfer, Florian Schmidt, Michael Pardowitz, and Helge Ritter. Open Source Real-Time Control Software for the Kuka Light Weight Robot. pages 444–449, 2010.

[17] Klaus Neumann, Matthias Rolf, Jochen J Steil, and Michael Gienger. Learning inverse kinematics for pose-constraint bi-manual movements. In *Simulation of Adaptive Behavior – SAB 2010*, Paris, Aug 2010.

A Real-time Object Detection Framework using Resource Optimized Cascaded Perceptron Classifiers and its Application to US Speed Limits

Armin Staudenmaier, Ulrich Klauck

Hochschule Aalen
E-Mail: armin.staudenmaier@gmx.de

Ulrich Kreßel, Frank Lindner

Daimler AG

Christian Wöhler

Technische Universität Dortmund

Abstract

In this study we present a machine learning framework for object detection which consists of a training stage and a detection stage. We use a *cascaded classifier* which is composed of different *perceptron classifiers* differing in dimensionality, geometrical peculiarity, and feature types.In contrast to many other systems we do not use the classical AdaBoost approach and the concept of weak classifiers, but instead employ perceptrons of variable dimensionality and features,which are chosen in a classifier selection process and are added in each stage to the cascade classifier. The basic idea of the selection is that we start with a set of classifiers in a *very low resolution subspace*, which is achieved by geometrical constraints of the classifiers themselves rather than by resizing the image. A further contribution of this study is the introduction of a *cost-performance function* for rating a binary classifier which consists of a weighted ratio of the operational cost required for a single classification operation and the classifiers recognition performance. We explain how this cost-performance function models the probability of false operations and therefore can produce very effective cascaded classifiers when used as a *selection criterion* and as a *stopping criterion* for classifiers. We also show how this function can be used with cascaded classifiers for cost-performance prediction. Our cascaded classifier is composed of resolution subcascades. As long as the cost-performance function decreases, we stay in the current resolution subspace and add the classifier which yields the minimum value until the function increases. We thus obtain a cascade that consists of subcascades of increasing resolution with a decreasing cost-performance ratio for each new stage minimizing the probability of false operations. The training algorithm which is a Fisher Linear Discriminant Analysis yields a high generalization performance also for nonseparable data due to the effective computation of weights and margins by statistical modelling in feature space. The combination of linear classifiers of variable dimension and the integration of different resolution levels, which can be seen as a coarse-to-fine-search, yields very short computation times both for the training and for the detection stage.

1 Introduction

Object detection systems are used in a wide variety of applications. This is due to the growth of computational performance and at the same time decreasing dimensions of controllers. Especially, the field of Advanced driver assistance systems (ADAS) for cars offers a wide area of different detection tasks such as traffic sign detection, pedestrian detection or curb detection just to mention a few. Such systems can be used on the one hand as information advising systems to show the driver relevant information or, integrated into an adaptive cruise control system (ACC) assist the driver. Detecting potentially dangerous situations can help to minimize accidents. Even the strict adherence to speed limits for example can reduce the risk of accidents while at the same time saving energy. Most systems evolving in recent years use different stages during the detection. Our aim is to design a general system that automatically builds a classifier system being resource optimized and therefore working efficiently for a wide variety of detection tasks.

2 Related Work

Machine learning algorithms are increasingly applied to object detection tasks. One of the most famous systems is the face detection system presented by Viola and Jones [7, 6]. In that work, cascaded classifiers consisting of strong classifiers are trained. Each strong classifier consists of weak classifiers that have fast computation times due to the use of integral images for their computation. The strong classifiers are created by the AdaBoost algorithm [8, 9], where each weak classifier is assigned a weight dependent on its classification performance and therefore the decision of the strong classifier can be seen as a weighted majority vote. Many other authors introduce new fast features for the weak classifiers based on integral images. Dalal and Triggs introduce HOG features [12] which are used for example in combination with a SVM classifier for pedestrian detection [13] and with a cascaded classifier [11]. The detection of U.S. speed limits is presented in [18, 19], both using in the first stage a shape based detector followed by a Viola Jones classifier [18] and a neural network digit recognition module [19].

Nearly all the mentioned methods contain a classifier selection process where quality functions are needed for the rating of the classifiers. Mostly the cost functions depend on the type of misclassifications. The model described by Zhang [14] assigns different losses to different kinds of mistakes depending on the type of faces in a face recognition system. Another algorithm called stacking, which is adapted to the task of classifier learning for misclassification cost performance, is presented in [15]. A detailed introduction and overview is given in [16]. A cost model for a cascaded AdaBoost classifier which is solved there as a constrained numerical nonlinear optimization problem is presented in [17]. This model also incorporates the operational cost of the AdaBoost classifier.

While AdaBoost provides an effective learning algorithm ensuring strong bounds on generalization performance [9], Freund and Schapire also use large margins to achieve generalization performance with the perceptron algorithm [10].

3   Base classifiers

The main algorithm described here is a greedy method. We have a pool of different binary classifiers $h_i \in \mathcal{H}$ which we call *base classifiers*. In a selection process we iteratively choose a classifier from the pool and add this classifier to a *cascaded classifier* [7] by means of a quality function.

A cascade classifier is in principle a series of ordered binary classifiers. The decision function of a cascade classifier h_C with T stages containing $h_1, \ldots h_T$ binary classifiers is as follows:

$$h_C^T = (h_1, \ldots, h_T) = \begin{cases} 1 & \text{if } T = 0 \\ 0 & \text{if } h_j = 0, 1 \leq j \leq T \\ 1 & \text{else} \end{cases} \tag{1}$$

The first case ensures that if no classifier is contained in the cascade, it will always answer with "yes" and therefore never produce a false negative. If a sample is presented to the cascade, it will ask the first classifier. If it answers with "no", no other classifier has to be considered. The cascade will only answer with "yes" if one classifier after the other answers "yes" including the last one. This is shown in figure 1. The famous detection system

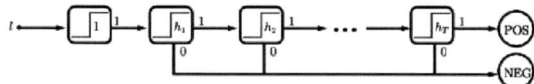

Figure 1: Cascade classifier composed of binary classifiers.

of Viola and Jones uses so-called strong classifiers in the cascade which consist of several weak classifiers. The weight of each weak classifier is chosen depending on its classification performance. A weak classifier is one-dimensional and uses simple but fast features. Here we present an algorithm that only uses one type of base classifiers and automatically rates the classifiers depending on the classification performance and operational costs. Arbitrary features can be used for the base classifiers which can be multidimensional and the weighting of the features is done with a flexible learning method, therefore the algorithm is not only restricted to detection tasks in image processing.

The base classifiers are linear perceptron classifiers with n-dimensional weight vectors that are trained by a linear discriminant analysis procedure. The classification function is a perceptron[4]:

$$h = \begin{cases} 1 & \text{if } \vec{w}^T \vec{x} - \theta > 0 \\ 0 & \text{otherwise} \end{cases} \tag{2}$$

$$\tag{3}$$

where $\vec{x}$ is the extracted feature vector, $\vec{w}$ is the trained weight vector and θ is a specific threshold. The perceptron classifier is the most simple feedforward neural network and consists of one output layer with one node. This classifier is linear, since the weight vector can be regarded as the normal of a multidimensional plane in feature space which separates the samples. The features x_i are the components of the feature vector $\vec{x}$. They are multiplied by the weights of the weight vector and summed up afterwards. The original perceptron learning rule iteratively updates the weights of a perceptron depending on the classification of a sample. Since we claim specific characteristics concerning the classification and time performance we use a different learning method for the determination of the weight vector $\vec{w}$ and the threshold θ.

3.1 Base classifier training

The weight vector $\vec{w}$ of the base classifiers can be interpreted as an axis with a specific direction in feature-space, which should have best discrimination properties. To compute this direction for each classifier we use Fisher's Linear Discriminant Analysis [5, 3]. We have a list of positive feature vectors $\vec{x}_{pos} \in \mathcal{P}$ generated with the feature extraction function from the positive samples containing objects and a list of negative feature vectors $\vec{x}_{neg}$ generated by negative samples without objects which have approximately the same size. The negative examples are randomly chosen from a huge set of negative examples that do not contain any positive objects. Out of these vectors we compute the mean vectors $\vec{m}_{pos}, \vec{m}_{neg}$ and the scatter matrices S_{pos}, S_{neg} and $S_w = S_{pos} + S_{neg}$. Then $\vec{w}$ is computed by

$$\vec{w} = \alpha S_w^{-1}(\vec{m}_{pos} - \vec{m}_{neg}) \tag{4}$$

and normalized such that $\|\vec{w}\| = 1$.

For the computation of the threshold θ there are three main aspects. First we should guarantee a high detection rate. Second we should be aware that not all positive samples must be *correct* positive samples. It could be the case that the human expert made some mistakes during the label process or that some very "difficult" labels are contained. For the classifier it could be better to leave out these perhaps wrong or difficult samples. And third we should incorporate a separability measure which tells us the difficulty of the separation. For easy problems we can set the threshold nearer to the positive samples.

We use the p-quantile to leave out positive samples which we expect to be unusual. The computation of the p-quantile $\mathcal{Q}_p$ of positive samples is done by projecting all positive features $\vec{x}_i^T \vec{w}$ and sorting according to the projected value. The lower the values, the smaller is the distance to the projected negative mean. The sample with the lowest projected value that is contained in $\mathcal{Q}_p$ is $\vec{x}_q$. We compute the threshold according to

$$\theta = \vec{x}_p^T \vec{w} - g \tag{5}$$

where $g \geq 0$ can be regarded as a generalization constant. The larger this value is, the more space is between the projected quantile $\vec{x}_p$ and the threshold θ.

We compute the constant g based on the weighted variance of the projected positive samples and on an additional constant value q_2.

$$g = q_1 \sigma_{\mathcal{Q}_P}^2 + q_2 \tag{6}$$

Figure 2 shows two scatter plots of the first two features from two perceptron classifiers. The green points are object points in feature space and the red points are non-object points.

4 Performance Measurement

As described above we use perceptron classifiers with variable dimensions and a large variety of features which have differing operational costs. Therefore we introduce a power

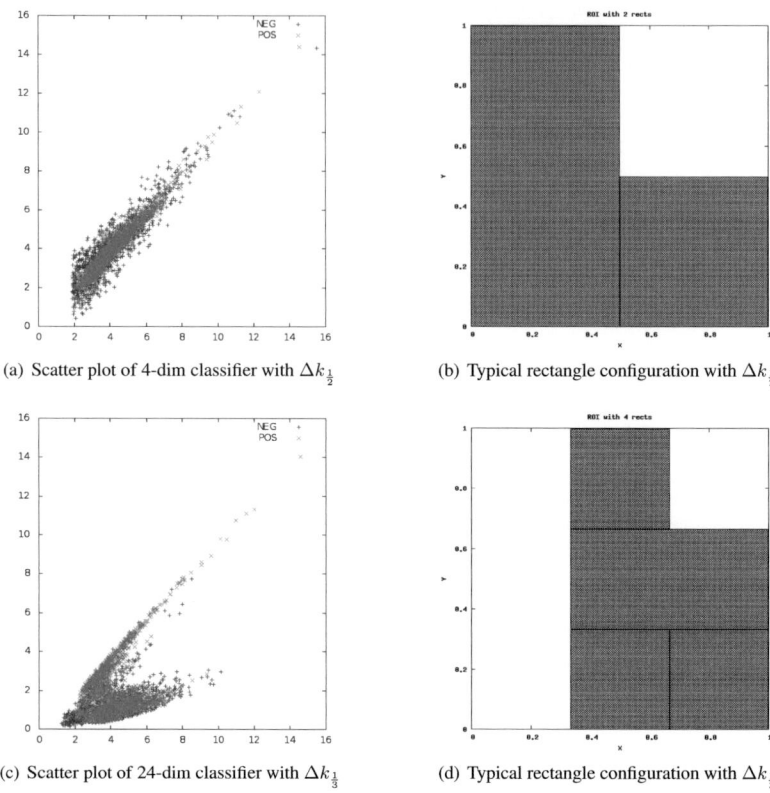

(a) Scatter plot of 4-dim classifier with $\Delta k_{\frac{1}{2}}$

(b) Typical rectangle configuration with $\Delta k_{\frac{1}{2}}$

(c) Scatter plot of 24-dim classifier with $\Delta k_{\frac{1}{3}}$

(d) Typical rectangle configuration with $\Delta k_{\frac{1}{3}}$

Figure 2: Scatter plots of two perceptron classifiers together with their corresponding rectangle configurations. Green points are object points, red points are non-object points. The features shown are average intensity and variance of pixel gray levels.

function that combines the operational cost for a classifier with its classification performance as a general performance measurement method for arbitrary classifiers. Since we always have the opportunity to add another classifier to the cascaded classifier the idea is that the classifiers should have a favorable ratio between classification performance and operational costs needed for a classification. We also show a way how the operational cost of a classifier can additionally be weighted by its classification performance. By doing this we can give good classifiers more computational resources. This cost-performance ratio should implicitly rate how strong or weak a classifier is, regarding its operational cost and classification performance. The cost-performance function measures "likely false operations per classification". This function can be used on the one hand for the base *classifier selection* and on the other hand as a *stopping criterion* for the cascade training. We also show a way how a cost-performance prediction on a small sample set can be achieved.

4.1 Cost-Performance Function

We use the probability of a wrong decision $P(h)$ of a classifier h as a *classification performance* measurement since we expect that a wrong decision will generate additional operational costs for the classifier for compensation or additional costs resulting from the misbehavior of the detection system itself. Therefore a low probability of a wrong decision yields a low probability of additional operational costs and vice versa. We use the operational cost $C(h)$ for one classification as a *operational cost performance* measurement. The unit of the operational cost can be chosen arbitrary, for example in mips or as absolute time. Therefore we are independent of a specific architecture and the training and recall can run on different platforms, since the cost for each operation of a classifier can be assigned according to the target platform of the recall. We define the cost-performance function as

$$\Psi(h) = C(h)^X P(h). \tag{7}$$

The exponent X is a cost weighting factor. For the case where $X = 1$ the costs have the unit [operations/classification], and multiplied with the probability of a wrong decision we can interpret the unit of Ψ as [likely false operations/classification] which we want to minimize since they will generate additional costs.

If we know in each stage of a cascade classifier h_C the probability of appearance of costs , "likely costs" of the cascade can be computed. We approximate the appearance probabilities of costs with the probability of a wrong decision of the previous stage since we claim that wrong classified costs will survive the actual stage.

The probability of costs in stage k in the cascade for example is $(\prod_{j=0}^{k-1} p_j) c_k$. The absolute expected costs of the cascade classifier per classification are[17]:

$$C(h_C) = \sum_{i=1}^{T} (\prod_{j=0}^{i-1} p_j) c_i \tag{8}$$

with $c_i = c(h_i)$ the cost of the base classifier h_i in stage i and $p_i = p(h_i), p_0 = 1$ the probability of a wrong decision.

Expected global costs of a classifier can then easily be computed with the total amount of classifications n:

$$C_G(h) = C_0 + nC(h) \tag{9}$$

where C_0 are initialization costs for the computation of integral images for example. We measure the performance of a cascade classifier based on the wrong decision probabilities of the base classifiers:

$$P(h_C) = \prod_{i=0}^{T} p_i \tag{10}$$

The cost-performance function of the cascaded classifier can then be computed with equation 7.

4.2 Classification Performance

As described above, we measure the classification performance of a classifier regarding the probability of a wrong decision which is in our case the probability of a false classified sample. This can be measured for a negative sample with the false positive rate

$p(\text{false}_h|neg) = FP_R(h)$ and for a positive sample with the false negative rate $p(\text{false}_h|pos) = FN_R(h)$. In other words, the higher the false positive rate of a classifier, the higher is the probability that a negative sample is misclassified. Therefore, our classification performance function corresponds to:

$$P(h) = \alpha\, FP_R(h) + \beta\, FN_R(h) \tag{11}$$

The rating between false positives and false negatives is specified by the parameters α and β. For typical detection tasks false negatives are often more disadvantageous than false positives. To assign higher costs for false negatives we could set $\alpha \ll \beta$.

4.3 Performance-dependent cost weighting

In the training phase of a cascade classifier, only misclassified samples are considered in the following stages. Therefore, the higher the stage, the more difficult are the samples presented to the base classifiers but the better is the performance of the cascade classifier. The idea is now to focus more on the classification performance the better the classifier is:

$$\Psi_W(h) = P(h)C(h)^{P(h)} \tag{12}$$

The higher the stage, the better the performance. This means a low probability of a wrong decision $P(h)$, and therefore the cost factor $C(h)^{P(h)}$ approaching to 1. As a result we reduce the total number of base classifiers in higher stages.

4.4 Cost-performance prediction

Since we optimize our cascade in a greedy process we can predict the cost-performance function for the cascade based on our trained perceptron classifiers. The prediction with the current Cascade $C_T = C(h_C^T)$, $P_T = P(h_C^T)$ for the next k stages and base classifiers h_i for $1 \leq i \leq k$ can be computed with:

$$\Psi_{Pred}(h_C, h_1, \ldots h_k) = (C_T + \sum_{i=1}^{k}(\prod_{j=1}^{i-1} P_T p_j(\mathcal{S}_j))c_i(\mathcal{S}_j))^X P_T \prod_{i=0}^{k} p_i(\mathcal{S}_i) \tag{13}$$

Where $p_0 = 1$ and $\mathcal{S}_i = \{\mathcal{P}, \mathcal{N}_i\} = \{\mathcal{P}, FP(\mathcal{N}, h_C(h_1, \ldots, h_i)\}$ are the misclassified samples in each stage. Again, X is the weight factor that can be set according to equation 12. We refer to the term prediction since the number of negative samples can be adjusted according to the available computational resources for the training by using an appropriately sized subset of randomly chosen samples from the original set of negatives. Also the amount of classifiers for the computation of Ψ can be set for the search. If we use one classifier, we have to evaluate $\Psi(C_T, h_i)$ for all $h_i \in \mathcal{H}$. For two classifiers we have to evaluate $\Psi(C_T, h_i, h_j)$ for all $(h_i, h_j) \in \mathcal{H}$ which are all pairs. Using all classifiers with all combinations would then result in a global search which would require to evaluate the function on all combinations of classifiers .

5 Cascade Training

The overall performance of a detection system is heavily dependent on the type and amount of features. The first consideration is that the extraction of features in a rectangular regions is nothing else than a local transformation of the underlying signal into a specific resolution subspace which depends on the structure of that region. For example, taking the sum of pixel grey values and dividing by the area is in principle a convolution with a constant kernel mask. The next consideration is that the oscillation of the classifier signal depends on that transformation. Put differently, the lower the resolution the lower the oscillation of the signal of each classifier. We use this behavior to improve both the training and the recall.

5.1 Resolution dependent training

Our perceptron classifiers have assigned a list of rectangles, from which features are extracted. Each classifier is assigned a k-elementary subset of rectangles from a n-elementary set of rectangles which do not overlap:

$$\mathcal{R}_i = \{r_k | \, w(r_k) \geq \Delta k \,, \, h(r_k) \geq \Delta k\} \tag{14}$$

where $w(r)$ is the width and $h(r)$ is the height of a rectangle r. A perceptron classifier b_i extracts features only within the regions of rectangles $\mathcal{R}_{b_i}$. Since we train with a discriminant analysis, the overlap of rectangles will partly override the information contained and we remove rectangles that overlap with other rectangles. Figure 3 shows the extraction of features with a specific extraction function for each rectangle r_i.

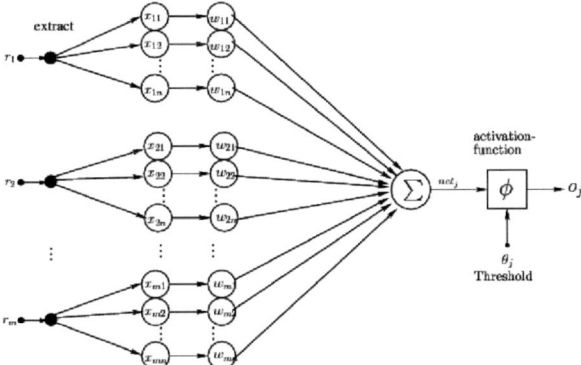

Figure 3: Perceptron classifier. Features are extracted from within the rectangles $r_1, \ldots, r_m$.

For the evaluation we hold a large set of samples $\mathcal{G} = \{\mathcal{P}, \mathcal{N}_{\Delta k}\}$ where the negative samples are generated by moving detection boxes R_i at different sizes over all images I and collecting all samples that do not intersect with a positive sample. The step size depends on the actual size of the box and on the actual resolution Δk. Then we generate a smaller set $\mathcal{S}$ by random sampling of $\mathcal{G}$ and filtering FPs and TPs by the actual cascade h_C^T:

$$\mathcal{N}^T = \{FP(h_C^T, \mathcal{N}_{\Delta k})\} \tag{15}$$

$$\mathcal{P}^T = \{\mathcal{P}\} = const \tag{16}$$

The size of $\mathcal{N}^T$ is restricted to $|\mathcal{N}^T| \simeq |\mathcal{P}^T|$. We train each classifier $h_i \in \mathcal{H}_{\Delta k}$ as described above on the set $\mathcal{S} = \{\mathcal{P}^T, \mathcal{N}^T\}$. The "best" base classifier h_{min} is the one with a minimum Ψ_{Pred}, which is the *selection criterion*:

$$h_{min} = \arg\min_i \{\Psi_{\text{Pred}}(h_C^T, h_i) \mid h_i \in \mathcal{H}_{\Delta k}\} \tag{17}$$

This classifier is added to the existing cascade $h_C^{T+1} = h_C^T \otimes h_{min}$. The selection process is repeated as long as the cost-performance function is decreasing on the global set $\mathcal{G} = \{\mathcal{P}, \mathcal{N}_{\Delta k}\}$:

$$\Psi(h_C^{T+1}, \mathcal{G}) < \Psi(h_C^T, \mathcal{G}) \tag{18}$$

which is our *stopping criterion* for the selection process. If this relation is violated, we increase the resolution by decreasing the minimum rectangle length $\Delta k' < \Delta k$. Then we generate a new set of perceptron classifiers with $\Delta k'$ and new samples and go on with the selection of perceptron classifiers as long as equation 18 holds. Then the selection process can be divided into *resolution stages*, where only classifiers $\mathcal{H}_{\Delta k}$ with constant resolution $\Delta k = const$ are used and each scale stage has its subcascade $h_{C,\Delta k}$. If we use different resolutions $\Delta k_1 > \Delta k_2 > \cdots > \Delta k_m$, each resolution is assigned a cascade. This is shown in Figure 4.

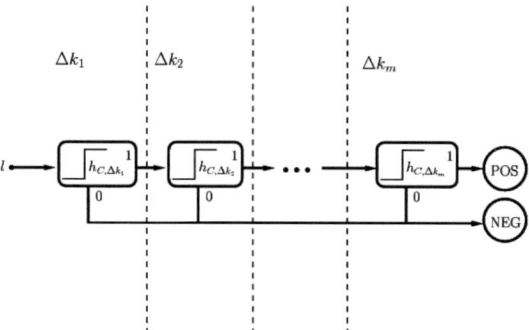

Figure 4: Resolution cascade containing resolution dependent subcascades.

6 Detection

The basic idea for the detection algorithm is that we use our resolution subcascades for a coarse-to-fine search in the image at increasing resolutions. A subcascade only triggers the transition to the next higher resolution inside the current box if it detects an object. This *recursive* coarse-to-fine search is very effective.

For the detection algorithm we start with the first resolution and generate all boxes $\mathcal{R}_{\Delta k_1}$ inside the image.For each box we request the subcascade $h_{C,\Delta k_i}$ for the current resolution level. If it rejects the box, we continue with the next box. Otherwise, if it detects an object, we pass this box to the next higher resolution subcascade $h_{C,\Delta k_{i+1}}$ and generate a new set of boxes depending on Δk_{i+1} where we again start to classify each box. If the subcascade in the last resolution stage affirms an object, we have achieved the terminating condition of the recursion, and the detection is deemed to be successful. An example is given in Figure 5 with three different resolution stages.

Figure 5: Detection with three different resolutions and subcascades. First stage is red, second stage is yellow and third stage is green.

7 Experiments

The different parameters and the cost-performance function as selection and stopping criterion make it difficult to determine an appropriate parameter combination. This is why we trained 144 cascades with starting resolution 0.5 and 144 cascades with starting resolution 0.25 using different parameter combinations and we picked out those cascades with a false positive rate below 0.0005. For training we used 2800 positive samples extracted from about 250 Sequences of US-Speed-Limit signs containing 13 different numbers ranging from 10 to 70. The average training time for a cascade was about 4 hours. After each resolution stage we evaluated the resolution cascades and the contained base classifiers on a validation set. The following tables show important attributes of the cascades concerning their structure and parameters. We used a consistent numbering of the different cascades as unique id. Since for all cascades the overall stopping criterion for the training and for each resolution subcascade was done with equation 18 we show the configuration of cascades with the total amount of base classifiers and the amount of classifiers in each resolution stage in Table 1. For Δk_1 only the rectangle over the whole detection area is assigned to the base classifiers. For $\Delta k_{\frac{1}{2}}$ the detection area is divided by two and therefore there are 9 possible sub-rectangles. The cascades 6, 9, 10 and 13 were trained by skipping resolution $\Delta k_{\frac{1}{2}}$ and $\Delta k_{\frac{1}{3}}$. The same basis features which are extracted from inside the rectangle regions are used for all experiments. To compare the performance we listed the detection rate and the false positive rate together with the operations per classification in table 3. The operations per classification are measured as average time needed for one classification in [microseconds/classification]. The values are averaged over 4000 classifications. Table

Id	Total	Δk_1	$\Delta k_{\frac{1}{2}}$	$\Delta k_{\frac{1}{3}}$	$\Delta k_{\frac{1}{4}}$
1	255	5	42	208	0
2	255	5	39	211	0
3	174	2	16	60	96
4	120	3	11	44	62
5	117	2	7	20	88
6	112	3	0	0	109
7	109	2	7	20	80
8	105	2	0	0	103
9	97	3	0	0	94
10	44	1	0	0	43
11	41	1	1	1	38
12	30	1	2	3	24
13	30	5	6	8	11
14	27	5	0	0	22

Table 1: Overview of the amount of base classifiers contained in the resolution stages of cascade with Id j where Δk_i is the current resolution.

Id	α	β	X	g	$\mathcal{Q}$
1	1	1	$0.1P(h)$	g_1	1
2	1	1	0.1	g_1	1
3	1	1000	$P(h)$	g_2	1
4	1	1000	$P(h)$	g_1	1
5	1	1	$P(h)$	g_4	0.999
6	1	1000	$P(h)$	g_3	1
7	1	1	$P(h)$	g_1	0.999
8	1	1	$P(h)$	g_3	1.
9	1	1000	$P(h)$	g_3	1.
10	1	1	2	g_3	0.999
11	1	1	2	g_2	0.999
12	1	1	2	g_4	0.99
13	1	1	0.1	g_5	0.99
14	1	1	$0.1P(h)$	g_4	0.99

Table 2: Parameters used for the different cascades with $g_1 = 0.001\sigma^2 + 0.001$, $g_2 = 0.001\sigma^2$, $g_3 = 0.01\sigma^2$, $g_4 = 0.01\sigma^2 + 0.001$ and $g_5 = 0.1\sigma^2 + 0.001$.

Id	TP_R	FP_R	Operations
1	0.931	2.7×10^{-4}	33.2
2	0.936	2.3×10^{-4}	34.6
3	0.921	2.5×10^{-5}	0.3
4	0.950	2.2×10^{-4}	0.7
5	0.897	1.4×10^{-5}	0.9
6	0.941	3.7×10^{-4}	1.9
7	0.897	1.6×10^{-5}	1.5
8	0.916	2.6×10^{-4}	2.0
9	0.936	2.6×10^{-4}	1.2
10	0.936	2.7×10^{-4}	0.7
11	0.936	2.8×10^{-4}	3.3
12	0.848	4.0×10^{-6}	1.7
13	0.789	3.0×10^{-6}	1.4
14	0.833	4.0×10^{-6}	1.0

Table 3: Performance of each cascade measured by its detection rate, false positive rate and average operational costs in [microseconds/classification].

2 shows the different parameters used for training. For the quantiles with $Q = 1$. we did not sort out any positive objects, for $Q = 0.999$ we sorted out the lower permille and for $Q = 0.99$ we sorted out the lower percent of positive objects along the discrimination axis. Since the weighting of α and β influences the selection function, we used $\alpha_1 = \alpha_2 = 1$ which means that we rate false positives the same as false negative samples and therefore the selection function chooses classifiers dependent on wrong classifications equally rating positives and negatives. The detection rate is then dependent on the threshold of each base classifiers computation of each base classifiers threshold for which we used five combinations: $g_1 = 0.001\sigma^2 + 0.001$, $g_2 = 0.001\sigma^2$, $g_3 = 0.01\sigma^2$, $g_4 = 0.01\sigma^2 + 0.001$ and $g_5 = 0.1\sigma^2 + 0.001$.

7.1 Performance discussion

Table 2 clearly shows that the cascades with a low cost weighting have much higher averaged operational cost than those with a higher weighting when claiming comparable detection rates. To illustrate the effect of different cost weighting we compare the values of the cost-performance function with the whole pool of classifiers during the training of cascade 2 and 7 since they have large differing average operational costs but the same performance weight parameters α and β. Figure 6 shows 2D plots of the cost-performance function Ψ_{Pred} of all trained base classifiers $\mathcal{H}_{\Delta k_{\frac{1}{2}}}$ on the training set in the first stage with resolution $\Delta k_{\frac{1}{2}}$ of cascade classifier 7 and 2. The false positive rate is assigned to the X axis and the averaged operations are assigned to the Y axis. Since we use the same feature types in each resolution step the amount of base classifiers was the same for both cascades, $|\mathcal{H}_{\Delta k_{\frac{1}{2}}}| = 1000$ and $|\mathcal{H}_{\Delta k_{\frac{1}{2}}}| = 30000$. Images 6(a) and 6(b) show a vertical color gradient while image 6(c) and 6(d) shows a more diagonal gradient since the costs have more influence.

Images 7(a) and 7(b) show 3D plots with an additional axis for the false negative rate. These plots show that the classifiers are clustered for $\alpha = \beta$ and $Q < 1$. The selected classifier of cascade 7 produces a false negative on the training set. All positive samples sorted out according to the quantile criterion were stored. Figure 8 shows the first 6 quantile objects from a total of 303 objects that were sorted out from the cascade classifier 7 during the training. In each stage approximately three images have been sorted out. These images show all distortions regarding the average luminance being very dark or very bright. The images 8(b) and 8(d) are partially shaded and images 8(e) and 8(f) show a strong blurring effect.

8 Results

The cascades already presented in the experiments section have been evaluated on 2981 single images extracted from 279 different real world tracks of US speed limit signs not contained in the training set. The signs also contain 13 different speed limits ranging from 10 to 70 mph, with large variations in illumination and contrast (see figure 8). A sign is considered as detected, if there is at least one detected rectangle that covers 30 percent area of the correct speed limit box. The detection algorithm was scanning the whole image which has the dimension 752x480 pixels while the processing time was measured in milliseconds on a fast 3.2 GHz processor including all steps needed for the complete detection.

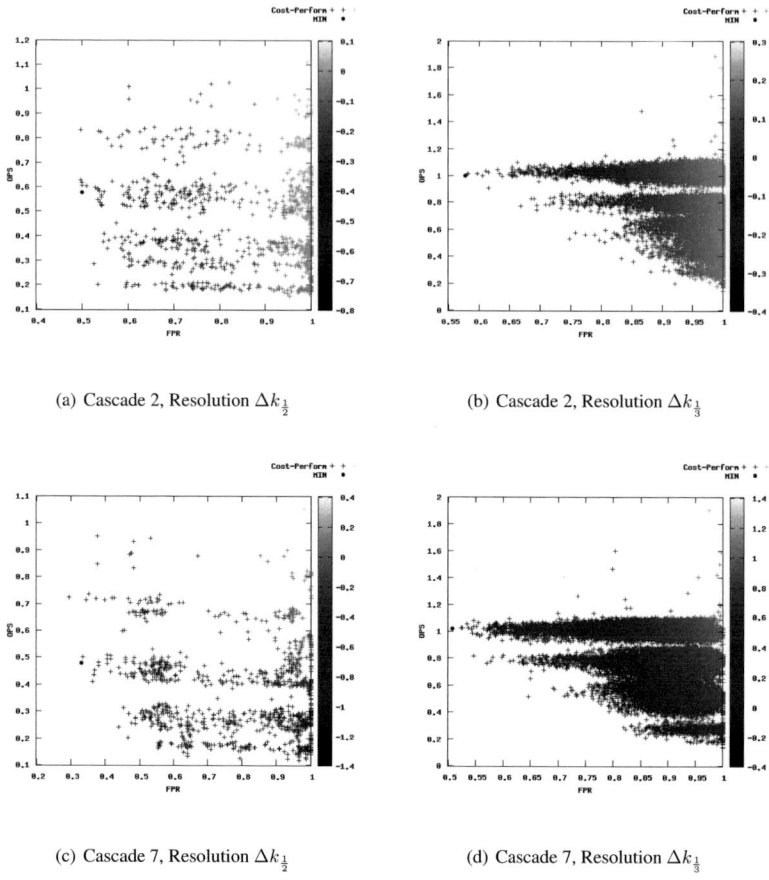

(a) Cascade 2, Resolution $\Delta k_{\frac{1}{2}}$ (b) Cascade 2, Resolution $\Delta k_{\frac{1}{3}}$

(c) Cascade 7, Resolution $\Delta k_{\frac{1}{2}}$ (d) Cascade 7, Resolution $\Delta k_{\frac{1}{3}}$

Figure 6: Cost-performance function of classifiers $\mathcal{H}$ using logarithmic color coding. Operational cost on Y axis and false positive rate on X axis. The black point is the selected base classifier in the first resolution stage.

The detection boxes used range from 20 pixel width to 80 pixel width. Table 4 compares the total averaged cost and performance of each cascade with the computed costs during the training. Cascades $6, 8, 9$ and 10 all have detection rates over 80% with comparable false positive rates. This indicates that the use of parameter $g_3 = 0.01\sigma^2$ which was the largest weight for σ^2, works good for the application case. For speed limit detection single images from one object appear in a track. Therefore a detector must not necessarily detect all single images. We evaluated the detection rates dependent on the minimum detected images per track in table 5. This shows on the one hand that there are only few completely missed signs and that we achieve very good track based detection rates. The results show that very effective classifiers can be generated using the presented methods.

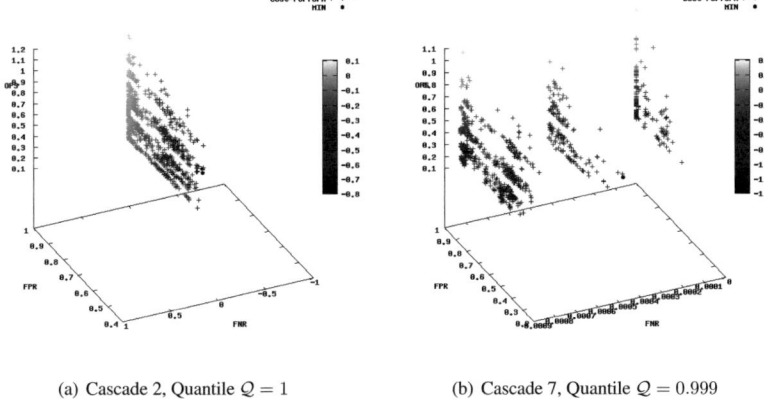

(a) Cascade 2, Quantile $Q = 1$ (b) Cascade 7, Quantile $Q = 0.999$

Figure 7: Cost-performance function of classifiers $\mathcal{H}_{\Delta k_{\frac{1}{2}}}$ using logarithmic color coding. Additional axis with false negative rate. Using $\alpha = \beta$, the classifiers are clustered for quantiles with $Q < 1$.

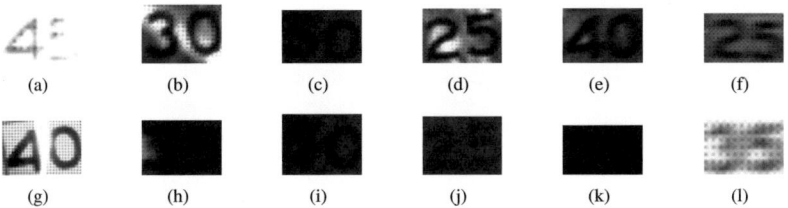

Figure 8: Samples sorted out according to the quantile criterion.

The correct adjustment of the base classifiers parameters is crucial for the performance of the cascade in the final detection application. Nevertheless, the differing costs and performances between the validation during training and the final application clearly indicate overtraining.

9 Conclusion

In this study we presented a framework for object detection that consists of cascaded perceptron classifiers and applied the Fisher LDA method as an fast and effective learning method, since weights are specified with a statistical analysis of the data. On the other hand we showed how statistical methods can be applied to sort out unusual samples but nevertheless achieve a good generalization performance of the perceptrons. We introduced a quality function for the measurement of classifiers which incorporates the operational costs per classification and the classification performance of the classifier. This function is used as a selection criterion and as a stopping criterion for the selection process. Due to

Id	TP_R	FP/I	COST(ms)
1	0.634	18.0	19.4
2	0.611	16.2	18.0
3	0.553	3.6	13.5
4	0.697	47.0	18.1
5	0.564	2.6	13.8
6	0.826	18.8	25.0
7	0.566	2.2	13.8
8	0.806	13.0	24.3
9	0.810	14.1	27.4
10	0.844	10.9	19.7
11	0.915	122.3	105.9
12	0.581	1.2	13.2
13	0.323	0.9	7.9
14	0.603	0.5	20.2

Id	50 %	40 %	30 %	20 %
1	0.61	0.70	0.77	0.80
2	0.61	0.69	0.78	0.82
3	0.55	0.63	0.72	0.78
4	0.71	0.79	0.84	0.88
5	0.55	0.64	0.72	0.78
6	0.85	0.89	0.91	0.91
7	0.56	0.66	0.71	0.78
8	0.83	0.89	0.91	0.93
9	0.83	0.86	0.88	0.90
10	0.87	0.92	0.93	0.95
11	0.91	0.94	0.95	0.96
12	0.60	0.67	0.75	0.81
13	0.23	0.33	0.43	0.55
14	0.62	0.70	0.79	0.83

Table 4: Performance of each cascade applied to whole images, average operational costs in [milliseconds], false positives per image.

Table 5: Detection rate of each cascade dependent on the average detection rate per track.

this quality function our method handles arbitrary features differing in their operational costs. We showed that very effective detectors can be generated when applied to a difficult real world task of US speed limit detection. The experiments showed that a crucial step in building the classifier is the adjustment of parameters due to its cascaded structure.

References

[1] Tony Lindeberg: *Scale-Space for Discrete Signals*. In: PAMI, pages 234-254 1990.

[2] Tony Lindeberg: *Feature Detection with Automatic Scale Selection*. In: International Journal of Computer Vision, pages 79-116. 1998.

[3] Seung-Jean Kim Alessandro and Alessandro Magnani and Stephen P. Boyd: *Robust Fisher Discriminant Analysis*. In: Advances in Neural Information Processing Systems, pages 659-666, MIT Presss. 2006.

[4] Frank Rosenblatt: *The Perceptron: A Probabilistic Model for Information Storage and Organization in the Brain*. In: Psychological Review, pages 386-408. 1958.

[5] Fisher, R.A.: *The Statistical Utilization of Multiple Measurements*. In: Annals of Eugenics, pages 376-386. 1938.

[6] Paul Viola and Michael Jones: *Rapid object detection using a boosted cascade of simple features*. 2001.

[7] Paul Viola and Michael Jones: *Robust Real-time Object Detection*. In: International Journal of Computer Vision. 2001.

[8] Yoav Freund and Robert E. Schapire: *A decision-theoretic generalization of on-line learning and an application to boosting.* In: *Computational Learning Theory: Eurocolt 95*, pages 23-37. Springer-Verlag 1995.

[9] R. E. Schapire, Y. Freund, P. Bartlett, and W. S. Lee. *Boosting the margin: a new explanation for the effectiveness of voting methods.* In: Ann. Stat., 26(5):1651-1686. 1998.

[10] Yoav Freund and Robert E. Schapire: *Large Margin Classification Using the Perceptron Algorithm.* In: Machine Learning, 37(3):277-296. 1999.

[11] Qiang Zhu , Shai Avidan , Mei-Chen Yeh , and Kwang-Ting Cheng: *Fast Human Detection Using a Cascade of Histograms of Oriented Gradients.*

[12] Navneet Dalal and Bill Triggs: *Histograms of Oriented Gradients for Human Detection.* In: CVPR, pages 886-893 2005.

[13] M. Bertozzi and A. Broggi and M. Del Rose and M. Felisa and A. Rakotomamonjy and F. Suard: *Pedestrian Detection using Infrared images and Histograms of Oriented Gradients.* In: Intelligent Vehicles Symposium 2006

[14] Yin Zhang and Zhi-Hua Zhou: *Cost-Sensitive Face Recognition.* In: IEEE Transactions on Pattern Analysis and Machine Intelligence, VOL. 32, NO. 10. 2010.

[15] Cameron-Jones, R. Mike and Charman-Williams, Andrew: *Stacking for Misclassification Cost Performance.* In: Proceedings of the 14th Biennial Conference of the Canadian Society on Computational Studies of Intelligence, pages 215-224, Springer-Verlag. 2001.

[16] Charles Elkan: *The Foundations of Cost-Sensitive Learning.* In: Proceedings of the Seventeenth International Joint Conference on Artificial Intelligence, pages 973-978 2001.

[17] Brendan Mccane, Kevin Novins, Michael Albert and Pack Kaelbling: *Optimizing Cascade Classifiers.*

[18] Christoph Gustav Keller and Christoph Sprunk and Claus Bahlmann and Jan Giebel and Gregory Baratoff: *Real-Time Recognition of U.S. Speed Signs.* In: IEEE Intelligent Vehicles Symposium (IV 2008) 2008.

[19] Fabien Moutarde, Alexandre Bargeton, Anne Herbin, and Lowik Chanussot: *Robust on-vehicle real-time visual detection of American and European speed limit signs, with a modular Traffic Signs Recognition system.* 2007.

Zur Robustheitssteigerung eines klassifikationsgestützten adaptiven Fehlerdiagnoseansatzes

Patrick Gerland

Universität Kassel, FB Maschinenbau, FG Mess- und Regelungstechnik
E-Mail: patrick.gerland@mrt.uni-kassel.de

In dieser Arbeit wird ein beobachterbasierter Fehlerdiagnoseansatz für eine Klasse nichtlinearer Systeme präsentiert, die sich durch Takagi-Sugeno-Fuzzy-Modelle (TS) beschreiben lassen. Es wird ein Sliding-Mode-Fuzzy-Beobachter vorgeschlagen, der zum Einen robust gegenüber begrenzten Unsicherheiten im System ist und zum Anderen eine Fehlerschätzung basierend auf dem *equivalent output error injection approach* [3] ermöglicht. Die Fehlersensitivität dieses Diagnoseansatzes lässt sich mithilfe einer klassifikationsgestützten Adaptionsstrategie on-line an die aktuelle Betriebsphase des zu überwachenden Systems anpassen. Zur Vermeidung von Fehlalarmen in unbekannten Fahrsituationen wird ein Fuzzy-Noise-Clustering-Algorithmus angewandt. Die Effektivität des vorgeschlagenen Fehlerdiagnoseansatzes wird anhand einer umfangreichen Simulation einer mobilen Arbeitsmaschine demonstriert.

1 Einleitung

Bau-, Land-, Forstmaschinen sowie Flurförder- und Kommunalfahrzeuge werden unter dem Begriff *Mobile Arbeitsmaschinen* zusammengefasst. Während stationäre Arbeitsmaschinen vorwiegend definierte, feste Arbeitsabläufe zyklisch durchlaufen, unterliegen mobile Arbeitsmaschinen vielfältigeren Anforderungen mit sich möglicherweise deutlich ändernden Umgebungsbedingungen. Zur Steigerung von Produktivität und Energieeffizienz werden zunehmend druck- und leistungsgeregelte hydrostatische Getriebe eingesetzt. Der zuverlässige und sichere Betrieb erfordert daher eine kontinuierliche Überwachung der integrierten Aktoren und Sensoren. Beispielsweise kann die Fehlfunktion eines Drucksensors zu Situationen führen, die ein enormes Sicherheitsrisiko für Mensch und Maschine darstellen. Der in dieser Arbeit vorgeschlagene neue Diagnoseansatz eignet sich zur Aktor- und Sensorfehlerüberwachung, wobei hier jedoch die Sensorfehlerdiagnose hydrostatischer Fahrantriebe im Fokus steht.

Derzeit kommen in mobilen Arbeitsmaschinen ausschließlich Schwellwertüberwachungen und Messdatenplausibilisierungen zur Sensorüberwachung zum Einsatz. Diese erlauben jedoch keine ausreichend zuverlässige Drucksensorüberwachung. Eine Alternative ist der Ansatz der beobachterbasierten Fehlerdiagnose (siehe z. B. [1]). Schwierigkeiten resultieren jedoch aus der stark nichtlinearen Dynamik hydrostatischer Fahrantriebe [2]. Daneben stellen Leckverluste im hydraulischen Kreis sowie der Einfluß externer Lasten durch die Umwelt große Unsicherheiten bei der Modellbildung dar, wobei diese noch dazu von der aktuellen Betriebsphase abhängen und sich daher stark ändern.

In [3] schlagen Edwards et al. einen auf Sliding-Mode-Beobachtern (SMO) basierenden Fehlerdetektions- und Identifikationsansatz (FDI) für unsichere Systeme vor. Deren Kernidee zur Fehlererkennung besteht in der Auswertung des sogenannten *equivalent output injection* Signals, welches den notwendigen Aufwand zur Aufrechterhaltung der Gleitbewegung (engl.: sliding-motion) darstellt. Allerdings basiert deren Beobachterentwurf im wesentlichen auf einem linearen Streckenmodell, wodurch bei der Anwendung auf nichtlineare Systeme eine verringerte Fehlersensitivität resultiert.

Daher schlagen Yan & Edwards in [4] einen Beobachter zur Aktorfehlererkennung ähnlich zu [3] für eine Klasse von nichtlinearen Systemen vor. Dieser Ansatz ist jedoch nicht für die Sensorfehlererkennung vorgesehen und damit nicht geeignet, eine funktionsfähige und zuverlässige Drucksensorüberwachung zu gewähren.

Einen weiteren wohlbekannten nichtlinearen Beobachtertyp stellt der TS-Fuzzy-Beobachter basierend auf dem *parallel distributed compensation* (PDC) Konzept dar [5]. Allerdings stellt dieser Beobachtertyp jedoch nur eine nichtlineare Erweiterung des klassischen linearen Luenberger-Beobachters dar und ist somit nur bedingt robust gegenüber Modellunsicherheiten. Außerdem wird FDI hierbei nicht betrachtet.

Einen alternativen Ansatz mit Ähnlichkeit zur Kernidee der FDI in [3] stellen Gao et al. in [6] vor. Hierbei verwenden die Autoren einen TS-Fuzzy-Beobachter basierend auf einem erweiterten Fuzzy-Deskriptor-System zur Sensorfehlerrekonstruktion. Allerdings ist auch dieser Beobachter nicht robust gegenüber Modellunsicherheiten. Um genau diese für praktische Anwendungen bedeutsame Robustheit für nichtlineare Anwendungen zu erreichen, werden in [7] und [8] Kombinationen von TS-Fuzzy-Beobachtern und Sliding-Mode-Beobachtern vorgestellt. Bergsten et al. [7] schlagen zwei verschiedene TS-SM-Beobachter vor, wobei aber auch hier nicht die Anwendung auf FDI betrachtet wird. Anders jedoch in [8], wo die Residuen einer Bank von TS-SM-Beobachtern zur FDI ausgewertet werden. Dieses Vorgehen erfordert jedoch einen komplizierten und aufwendigen Beobachterentwurf und Auswertungsprozess. Klassische Ansätze hierzu sind das *dedicated and generalized observer scheme* [1].

In dieser Arbeit wird eine Kombination des Sliding-Mode-FDI Ansatzes nach ([3],[4]) mit dem TS-Beobachter nach [5] präsentiert. Dies liefert einen robusten Beobachter, mittels dessen sich unter gewissen Voraussetzungen mehrere, zeitgleich auftretende Sensor- und/oder Aktorfehler in unsicheren nichtlinearen Systemen erkennen lassen. Gegenüber anderen Ansätzen erlaubt dies eine direkte Fehlerschätzung oder sogar eine Fehlerrekonstruktion. Weiterhin lassen sich hierüber gleichzeitig auch optimale Fehlerschwellen für eine robuste Fehlerdetektion aus dem pysikalischen Vorwissen berechnen [4].

Zweitens wird ein neuer Ansatz vorgeschlagen, um die Schwellenwerte des FDI-Ansatzes on-line an die aktuelle Betriebsphase anzupassen. Hierdurch ergibt sich in Betriebsphasen mit geringen Modellunsicherheiten eine stark erhöhte Fehlersensitivität. In Betriebsphasen mit großen Modellunsicherheiten werden Fehlalarme vermieden. Die Kernidee hierbei ist die, die aktuelle Betriebsphase mittels eines Bayes-Klassifikators zu ermitteln und darüber die Fehlerschwellen an die a-priori definierten Unsicherheiten dieser Betriebsphasen anzupassen. Bei vielen Anwendungen wie auch mobilen Arbeitsmaschinen ist es z. B. aufgrund fehlender Sensorinformationen nicht möglich, die aktuelle Betriebsphase des Systems direkt anhand eines oder auch mehrerer Signale zu bestimmen. In diesen Fällen bietet sich der Einsatz von Mustererkennungsalgorithmen an.

Drittens wird demonstriert, wie sich Fehlalarme aufgrund von bisher unbekannten Betriebssituationen, d. h. Situationen, die nicht zum Anlernen der Betriebsphasenerkennung herangezogen wurden, vermeiden bzw. reduzieren lassen. Hierfür wird eine Ausreißererkennung mittels eines Fuzzy-Noise-Clustering-Algorithmus zur Selbstüberwachung der Betriebsphasenerkennung vorgeschlagen.

Diese Arbeit ist folgendermaßen gegliedert: Zunächst wird im zweiten Abschnitt das TS-Modell eines hydrostatischen Getriebes vorgestellt. Basierend auf diesem Modell werden im dritten Abschnitt ein TS-SM-Beobachter (TS-SMO) und eine FDI-Methode vorgestellt, bei der das equivalent output injection Signal in Kombination mit einer Betriebsphasenerkennung ausgewertet wird. Im darauffolgenden Abschnitt wird die Effektivität des vorgeschlagenen FDI-Ansatzes für die Anwendung der Sensorfehlerdetektion auf hydrostatische Fahrantriebe im Rahmen einer Simulationsstudie demonstriert.

2 Modellbildung eines hydrostatischen Fahrantriebs

Hydrostatische Getriebe übertragen die Leistung eines Verbrennungsmotors ohne starre Kopplung. Dabei erzeugt eine Hydraulikpumpe einen Differenzdruck, der wiederum einen Hydraulikmotor antreibt. Die Abtriebsdrehzahl des hydrostatischen Getriebes wird mittels eines elektronischen Steuergeräts (ECU) eingestellt. In der ECU werden die Signale zur Ansteuerung der elektrohydraulischen Verstellelemente berechnet, so dass sich eine gewünschte Getriebeübersetzung einstellt. In Abhängigkeit dieser Verstellungen ändern sich Volumenstrom und Druck im geschlossenen Ölkreis und somit auch die Abtriebsdrehzahl des Hydromotors. Die Abtriebsleistung wird weiter über den mechanischen Antriebsstrang an die Triebachse des Fahrzeugs übertragen. In [9] wird ein TS-Fuzzy-Modell basierend auf dem Konzept der Sektornichtlinearitäten nach [5] hergeleitet, welches die nichtlineare Dynamik eines hydrostatischen Fahrantriebs exakt, d. h. ohne Approximationsfehler abbildet. Aufgrund des Ziels der FDI (vgl. Abschnitt 3) wird dieses Modell noch um die Unsicherheiten durch Leckverluste im hydraulischen Kreis sowie den Einfluß externer Lasten durch die Umwelt erweitert. Mit dem Zustandsvektor $\mathbf{x}(t) = [\tilde{\alpha}_P(t)\ \tilde{\alpha}_M(t)\ \Delta p(t)\ \omega_M(t)]^T$, dem Eingangsvektor $\mathbf{u}(t) = [u_P(t)\ u_M(t)]^T$ und dem sogenannten Premissenvektor $\boldsymbol{\alpha}(t) = [\tilde{\alpha}_M(t)\ \omega_p(t)]^T$ ergibt sich das TS-Fuzzy-Modell

$$
\dot{\mathbf{x}}(t) = \sum_{j=1}^{2}\sum_{k=1}^{2} w_{1,j}(\boldsymbol{\alpha}(t))\ w_{2,k}(\boldsymbol{\alpha}(t)) \cdot \left\{ \begin{bmatrix} -\frac{1}{T_{u_P}} & 0 & 0 & 0 \\ 0 & -\frac{1}{T_{u_M}} & 0 & 0 \\ \frac{10}{C_H}\tilde{V}_{\max_P}c_l & 0 & \frac{-10}{C_H}k_{leak} & \frac{-10}{C_H}\tilde{V}_{max_M}b_j \\ 0 & 0 & \gamma b_j & -\frac{1}{J_v}\tilde{d}_{vc}i_a^2 \end{bmatrix} \mathbf{x}(t) \right.
$$

$$
\left. + \begin{bmatrix} \frac{k_P}{T_{u_P}} & 0 \\ 0 & \frac{k_M}{T_{u_M}} \\ 0 & 0 \\ 0 & 0 \end{bmatrix} \mathbf{u}(t) \right\} + \begin{bmatrix} 0 & 0 \\ 0 & 0 \\ \frac{-10}{C_H} & 0 \\ 0 & \frac{-i_g i_a}{J_v} \end{bmatrix} \begin{bmatrix} \Delta k_{leak}x_3(t) \\ M_L(t) \end{bmatrix} \tag{1}
$$

mit $\gamma = \frac{1}{J_v}i_g^2 i_a^2 \eta_g \eta_{mh}\tilde{V}_{\max_P} \cdot 10^{-4}$ sowie den nichtlinearen Zugehörigkeitsfunktionen $w_{r,1}(\boldsymbol{\alpha}(t))$, $w_{r,2}(\boldsymbol{\alpha}(t))$ für $r = 1, \ldots, n_l$[1]

$$
w_{1,1}(\tilde{\alpha}_M(t)) = \frac{b_1 - \tilde{\alpha}_M(t)}{b_1 - b_2}\ , \qquad w_{2,1}(\omega_P(t)) = \frac{c_1 - \omega_P(t)}{c_1 - c_2} \tag{2}
$$

mit den Sektorgrenzen $b_1 = \max(\tilde{\alpha}_M(t))$, $b_2 = \min(\tilde{\alpha}_M(t))$, $c_1 = \max(\omega_P(t))$ und $c_2 = \min(\omega_P(t))$. Es ist zu beachten, dass $w_{r,2}(\boldsymbol{\alpha}(t)) = 1 - w_{r,1}(\boldsymbol{\alpha}(t))$ gilt. Sämtliche Modellparameter sind in Tabelle 1 aufgelistet. Letztlich lassen sich durch die Kombination aller n_l Sektorfunktionen $w_{r,g}(\boldsymbol{\alpha}(t))$ mit $g = 1, 2$ untereinander aggregierte Zugehörigkeitsfunktionen $h_i(\boldsymbol{\alpha}(t))$ berechnen, wobei diese die Bedingungen $\sum_{i=1}^{n_r} h_i(\boldsymbol{\alpha}(t)) = 1$ und $0 \leq h_i(\boldsymbol{\alpha}(t)) \leq 1$ erfüllen (vgl. [5]):

$$
h_1(\alpha_1(t), \alpha_2(t)) = w_{1,1}(\alpha_1(t)) \cdot w_{2,1}(\alpha_2(t))\ , \quad \ldots,
$$
$$
h_4(\alpha_1(t), \alpha_2(t)) = w_{1,2}(\alpha_1(t)) \cdot w_{2,2}(\alpha_2(t))\quad .
$$

---

[1] n_l ist die Anzahl der einzelnen nichtlinearen Terme des physikalischen Modells, von dem das TS-Fuzzy-Modell abgeleitet wurde. In (1) beträgt $n_l = 2$ (vgl. [9]).

Tabelle 1: Zustände und Parameter des hydrostatischen Fahrantriebs

Symbol	Beschreibung	Wert	Einheit
x_1	normierter Hydropumpenschwenkwinkel ($x_1 = \tilde{\alpha}_P$)	$[-1\,;\,1]$	-
x_2	normierter Hydromotorschwenkwinkel ($x_2 = \tilde{\alpha}_M$)	$[0\,;\,1]$	-
x_3	Differenzdruck ($x_3 = \Delta_p$)	$[-450\,;\,450]$	bar
x_4	Drehzahl Hydromotor ($x_4 = \omega_M$)	$[-340\,;\,340]$	rad/s
u_1	normiertes Stellsignal Hydropumpe ($u_1 = u_P$)	$[-1\,;\,1]$	-
u_2	normiertes Stellsignal Hydromotor ($u_2 = u_M$)	$[0\,;\,1]$	-
T_{u_P}	Zeitkonstante Hydropumpe	0.13	s
T_{u_M}	Zeitkonstante Hydromotor	0.22	s
k_P	Verstärkung Hydropumpenstellsignal	241.67	-
k_M	Verstärkung Hydromotorstellsignal	283.33	-
k_{leak}	Leckflusskoeffizient	0.14	mm^3/(s bar)
$\Delta_{k_{leak}}$	Unsicherheit des Leckflusskoeffizienten	$[-15\,;\,15]$	%
C_H	Hydraulische Kapazität	1840.8	mm^5/N
$\tilde{V}_{\max_P}$	max. Verdrängungsvolumen Hydropumpe	145	cm^3
$\tilde{V}_{\max_M}$	max. Verdrängungsvolumen Hydromotor	170	cm^3
ω_P	Drehzahl Hydropumpe	$[105\,;\,300]$	rad/s
J_v	Massenträgheitsmoment	16512	Nms^2
i_g	Getriebeübersetzung	-6.12	-
i_a	Achsübersetzung	-23.3	-
η_g	mechanischer Getriebewirkungsgrad	0.98	-
η_{mh}	hydromechanischer Wirkungsgrad	0.697	-
$\tilde{d}_{vc}$	viskoser Dämpfungskoeffizient	0.0126	Nms
M_L	externes Lastmoment an der Antriebsachse	$[3.5\,;\,1300]$	kNm

Mit den zugehörigen Matrizen $\mathbf{A}_i$, $\mathbf{B}$, $\mathbf{D}$, $\mathbf{C}$ und dem Vektor der Unsicherheiten $\boldsymbol{\xi}(t)$ kann (1) auch als eine Kombination aus $n_r = 2^{n_l} = 4$ linearen Teilmodellen dargestellt werden:

$$\dot{\mathbf{x}}(t) = \sum_{i=1}^{n_r} h_i(\boldsymbol{\alpha}(t)) \left[\mathbf{A}_i \mathbf{x}(t) + \mathbf{B}\mathbf{u}(t) + \mathbf{D}\boldsymbol{\xi}(t) \right], \quad \mathbf{y}(t) = \mathbf{C}\mathbf{x}(t) \qquad (3)$$

3 Fehlerdetektionsansatz

3.1 Betriebsphasenerkennung

In dem hier vorgeschlagenen Fehlerdetektionsansatz wird ein Bayes-Klassifikator [10] eingesetzt, um die aktuelle globale Betriebsphase des Systems zu ermitteln. Dies erfordert die Verfügbarkeit eines gekennzeichneten Trainingsdatensatzes, aus dem die freien Parameter des Klassifikators bestimmt werden müssen. Das Ziel einer Klassifikation besteht darin, eine Trennung eines gegebenen Datensatzes in Klassen zu erreichen. Wesentliche Charakteristika der Daten sollen in möglichst kompakter Form zusammengefasst werden.

Ein Klassifikator wird in zwei verschiedenen Phasen betrieben, dies sind die Lern- und die Betriebsphase. Das Ziel der Lernphase besteht in dem Auffinden geeigneter Merkmale, die Eingangsmuster wiederspiegeln und dem Anlernen des Klassifikators zur Trennung der Eingangsmuster. In der Betriebsphase weist der Klassifikator neue, frische Eingangsdaten einer der vorab definierten Klassen zu. Im ersten Schritt der Lernphase ist ein Merkmalsvektor $\boldsymbol{\phi}^T = (\phi_1, \ldots, \phi_s)$, bestehend aus s potentiell geeigneten und informationstragenden Merkmalen ϕ_i aus den verfügbaren Lerndaten zu extrahieren. Hierbei kommen typischerweise Filterungen zur Signalvorverarbeitung zum Einsatz. Für die weiteren Berechnungen lassen sich die Merkmale ϕ alle N Tupel in der Matrix $\Phi \in \mathbb{R}^{N \times s}$

$$\Phi = \begin{pmatrix} \phi_{1,1} & \phi_{1,2} & \cdots & \phi_{1,s} \\ \phi_{2,1} & \phi_{2,2} & \cdots & \phi_{2,s} \\ \vdots & \vdots & & \vdots \\ \phi_{N,1} & \phi_{N,2} & \cdots & \phi_{N,s} \end{pmatrix} = \begin{pmatrix} \phi_1^T \\ \phi_2^T \\ \vdots \\ \phi_N^T \end{pmatrix} \tag{4}$$

und dem Ausgangsvektor $\vartheta = [\vartheta_1, \vartheta_2, \ldots, \vartheta_N]^T$ mit den diskreten Werten $\Omega_c, c = 1, \ldots, C$, die die unterschiedlichen Klassen c repräsentieren, zusammenfassen. Oftmals hängt der Erfolg zur Lösung der gestellten Klassifikationsaufgabe wesentlich von der Merkmalsextraktion und dem Auffinden von wichtigen bzw. diskriminierenden Merkmalen ab. Daher besteht das Ziel darin, eine möglichst kleine und aussagekräftige Gruppe $\mathcal{I}$, zusammengesetzt aus s_m aller s Merkmalen aufzufinden. Hierfür kann die Multivariate Varianzanalyse (MANOVA) [11] angewandt werden. Dieses statistische Verfahren bewertet Kombinationen von s_m Merkmalen durch das Likelihood-Quotienten-Maß

$$M_{\mathcal{I}} = 1 - \prod_{i=1}^{s_m} \frac{1}{1 + \lambda_i}, \tag{5}$$

wobei $M_{\mathcal{I}}$ Werte zwischen 0 (ungeeignete) und 1 (sehr geeignete Merkmalskombination) annimmt. Dieses Maß bewertet die resultierenden Eigenwerte λ_i aus

$$(\mathbf{W}^{-1}\mathbf{K} - \lambda_i \mathbf{I})\mathbf{v}_i = 0 \quad \text{mit} \quad \mathbf{K} = \mathbf{T} - \mathbf{W}, \ \mathbf{W} = \sum_{c=1}^{C} N_c \cdot \mathbf{S}_c, \tag{6}$$

worin $\mathbf{T} = N \cdot \mathbf{S}$, $\mathbf{K}$, $\mathbf{W}$ die Schätzungen der Gesamt-, der Zwischen- und Innerklassenvariationsmatrizen sind. Weiterhin sind $\mathbf{S}$ und $\mathbf{S}_c$ in (6) Schätzungen der Kovarianz- und Klassenkovarianzmatrizen und $\mathbf{I}$ ist die Einheitsmatix. N_c ist der Umfang der Merkmale der jeweiligen Klassen $c = 1 \ldots C$. Der Bayes-Klassifikator schätzt a-posteriori-Wahrscheinlichkeiten für jede Klasse c

$$\gamma_c = \frac{\hat{p}(\vartheta = c) \cdot \hat{p}(\phi_m | \vartheta = c)}{\sum_{c=1}^{C} \hat{p}(\vartheta = c) \cdot \hat{p}(\phi_m | \vartheta = c)} \tag{7}$$

mit der jeweils geschätzten a-priori-Wahrscheinlichkeit $\hat{p}(\vartheta = c)$ und der mehrdimensionalen Wahrscheinlichkeitsdichte

$$\hat{p}(\phi_m | \vartheta = c) = \frac{1}{(2\pi)^{\frac{s_m}{2}} \sqrt{|\mathbf{S}_c|}} \cdot e^{\left(-\frac{1}{2}(\phi_m - \mu_c)^T \mathbf{S}_c^{-1}(\phi_m - \mu_c)\right)} \tag{8}$$

unter Annahme einer Normalverteilung der Merkmale ϕ_m. μ_c ist der Vektor der Erwartungswerte aller Merkmale der c-ten Ausgangsklasse. Typischerweise wird bezüglich der Klasse c mit der größten geschätzten Wahrscheinlichkeit γ_c entschieden.

3.2 Sliding-Mode-Fuzzy-Beobachter

Edwards & Spurgeon stellen in ([3],[12]) einen SMO und dessen Entwurfsverfahren vor. Bei diesem Ansatz sorgt ein diskontinuierlicher Schaltterm dafür, dass die Schaltfläche in endlicher Zeit erreicht wird und eine Gleitbewegung darauf einsetzt und erhalten bleibt. Während dieser Gleitbewegung klingt der Ausgangsfehler $\mathbf{e}_{\hat{y}}(t) = \hat{\mathbf{y}}(t) - \tilde{\mathbf{y}}(t)$ ab, d. h. die Differenz zwischen Beobachter- und Systemausgang verschwindet. Ein wesentlicher Nachteil dieses SMO ist der, dass der Entwurf auf einem linearen Streckenmodell beruht und sich daher beispielsweise zur FDI in nichtlinearen hydrostatischen Fahrantrieben nicht eignet [2]. Daher schlagen wir einen zu ([3],[12]) ähnlichen SMO basierend auf dem Konzept der TS-Fuzzy-Systeme [5] für eine Klasse von nichtlinearen Systemen vor.

Man nehme an, ein unsicheres nichtlineares System ist Lipschitz-stetig für alle $\mathbf{x}(t) \in \mathbb{R}^n$ und dieses System lässt sich durch das unsichere TS-Fuzzy-System aus Abschnitt 2 darstellen

$$\dot{\mathbf{x}}(t) = \sum_{i=1}^{n_r} h_i(\boldsymbol{\alpha}(t))[\mathbf{A}_i\mathbf{x}(t) + \mathbf{B}_i\mathbf{u}(t) + \mathbf{D}_i\boldsymbol{\xi}(t) + \mathbf{E}_i\mathbf{f}_a(t)], \quad \tilde{\mathbf{y}}(t) = \mathbf{C}\mathbf{x}(t) + \mathbf{f}_s(t), \quad (9)$$

worin die Matrizen $\mathbf{A}_i \in \mathbb{R}^{n \times n}$, $\mathbf{B}_i \in \mathbb{R}^{n \times m}$, $\mathbf{D}_i \in \mathbb{R}^{n \times q}$ und $\mathbf{E}_i \in \mathbb{R}^{n \times a}$ die System-, Steuer- und die Verteilungsmatrizen der unsicheren Eingänge beschreiben. Die unbekannte Funktion $\boldsymbol{\xi}(t) \in \mathbb{R}^q$ repräsentiert alle Modellunsicherheiten und die auf das System einwirkenden Störungen mit Ausnahme von Aktorfehlern $\mathbf{f}_a(t) \in \mathbb{R}^a$ und Sensorfehlern $\mathbf{f}_s(t) \in \mathbb{R}^p$. Die Ausgangssmatrix $\mathbf{C} \in \mathbb{R}^{p \times n}$ besitzt im Folgenden vollen Zeilenrang. Weitere notwendige Annahmen an das System (9) sind:

Annahme 1 *Die Eingangsunsicherheiten und Aktorfehler sind unbekannt, aber durch die Euklidische Norm $\|[\boldsymbol{\xi}^T(t) \ \mathbf{f}_a^T(t)]^T\| \leq \Xi$ begrenzt. Weiterhin wird angenommen, dass individuelle Grenzen $\|\boldsymbol{\xi}(t)\| \leq \Xi_\xi$ und $\|\mathbf{f}_a(t)\| \leq \Xi_{f_a}$ existieren und die Systemzustände $\mathbf{x}(t)$ sowie die Eingänge $\mathbf{u}(t)$ begrenzt sind.*

Annahme 2 $rg(\mathbf{C}[\mathbf{D}_i \ \mathbf{E}_i]) = rg([\mathbf{D}_i \ \mathbf{E}_i])$ *und* $rg([\mathbf{D}_i \ \mathbf{E}_i]) = \tilde{q}$. *Dies impliziert* $\tilde{q} \leq p$.

Annahme 3 *Alle invarianten Nullstellen von* $(\mathbf{A}_i, [\mathbf{D}_i \ \mathbf{E}_i], \mathbf{C})$ *liegen in* $\mathbb{C}_-$. *Andernfalls existiert kein stabiler Beobachter.*

Annahme 4 *Fehler auf den gemessenen Ausgängen sind unbekannt aber begrenzt, so dass $\|f_s(t)\| \leq \Psi$. Weiterhin sind deren Ableitungen begrenzt auf $\|\dot{f}_s(t)\| \leq \Psi_d$.*

Annahme 5 *Fehlerfreie Messungen der Premissenvariablen $\boldsymbol{\alpha}(t)$ sind verfügbar.*

Ein TS-SMO für das unsichere System (9) mit $\mathbf{e}_{\tilde{y}}(t) = \hat{\mathbf{y}}(t) - \tilde{\mathbf{y}}(t)$ ist gegeben durch

$$\dot{\hat{\mathbf{x}}}(t) = \sum_{i=1}^{n_r} h_i(\boldsymbol{\alpha}(t))[\mathbf{A}_i\hat{\mathbf{x}}(t) + \mathbf{B}_i\mathbf{u}(t) - \mathbf{G}_{l,i}\mathbf{e}_{\tilde{y}}(t) + \mathbf{G}_{n,i}\boldsymbol{\nu}(t)], \quad \hat{\mathbf{y}}(t) = \mathbf{C}\hat{\mathbf{x}}(t), \quad (10)$$

worin $\mathbf{G}_{l,i}, \mathbf{G}_{n,i} \in \mathbb{R}^{n \times p}$ geeignete Verstärkungsmatizen mit der Struktur [12]

$$\mathbf{G}_{l,i} = \mathbf{T}_i^{-1}\begin{bmatrix} \boldsymbol{\mathcal{A}}_{12,i} \\ \boldsymbol{\mathcal{A}}_{22,i} - \boldsymbol{\mathcal{A}}_{22}^s \end{bmatrix}, \quad \mathbf{G}_{n,i} = \mathbf{T}_i^{-1}\begin{bmatrix} \mathbf{0}_{(n-p) \times p} \\ \mathbf{I}_p \end{bmatrix} \quad (11)$$

und $\boldsymbol{\nu}(t) \in \mathbb{R}^p$ der diskontinuierliche Schaltvektor zum Einsetzen der Gleitbewegung auf der Beobachterschaltfläche $\mathcal{S} = \{\mathbf{e}(t) \in \mathbb{R}^n : \mathcal{C}\mathbf{e}(t) = \mathbf{e}_{\tilde{y}}(t) = 0\}$ sind. $\boldsymbol{\nu}(t)$ ist definiert als

$$\boldsymbol{\nu}(t) = \begin{cases} -\rho \dfrac{\mathbf{P}_2\mathbf{e}_{\tilde{y}}(t)}{\|\mathbf{P}_2\mathbf{e}_{\tilde{y}}(t)\|} & \text{, wenn } \mathbf{e}_{\tilde{y}}(t) \neq 0 \\ 0 & \text{, sonst} \end{cases} \quad (12)$$

Darin ist ρ ein positiver Skalar und $\mathbf{P}_2 \in \mathbb{R}^{p \times p}$ ist die symmetrisch positiv definite (s.p.d.) Lösung der Lyapunovgleichung mit der ebenfalls s.p.d. Entwurfsmatrix $\mathbf{Q}_2 \in \mathbb{R}^{p \times p}$:

$$\mathbf{P}_2\boldsymbol{\mathcal{A}}_{22}^s + \boldsymbol{\mathcal{A}}_{22}^{s\,T}\mathbf{P}_2 = -\mathbf{Q}_2 \quad (13)$$

Man beachte, dass die stabile Entwurfsmatrix $\boldsymbol{\mathcal{A}}_{22}^s$ nicht von den Premissenvariablen abhängt und daher für alle n_r Teilmodelle identisch ist. Die Matrizen $\boldsymbol{\mathcal{A}}_{12,i}$ und $\boldsymbol{\mathcal{A}}_{22,i}$ in (11) lassen sich durch individuelle Koordinatentransformationen auf jedes der n_r linearen Teilmodelle des TS-Fuzzy-Systems (9) berechnen.

$$\mathcal{A}_i = T_i A_i T_i^{-1} = \begin{bmatrix} \mathcal{A}_{11,i} & \mathcal{A}_{12,i} \\ \mathcal{A}_{21,i} & \mathcal{A}_{22,i} \end{bmatrix} \tag{14}$$

Die notwendigen Transformationen erhält man aus einer Serie von Transformationen $T_i = \bar{T}_{L,i}\,\tilde{T}_{DE,i}\,\tilde{T}_c$. Mit Ausnahme von $\bar{T}_{L,i}$ lassen sich diese Transformationen durch das Entwurfsschema aus [12] für jedes Teilmodell individuell berechnen. Ähnlich zu Edwards & Spurgeon [12] kann eine nichtsinguläre Transformation $\bar{T}_{L,i}$ definiert werden

$$\bar{T}_{L,i} = \begin{bmatrix} I_{(n-p)} & [L_i\ 0_{(n-p)\times\tilde{q}}] \\ 0_{p\times(n-p)} & \tilde{Y}_i^T \end{bmatrix}, \tag{15}$$

wobei $\tilde{Y}_i$ vorab (vergl. [12]) zu bestimmen ist. L_i kann aus der Lösung der n_r Lyapunov-Gleichungen [5]

$$P_1 \mathcal{A}_{11,i} + \mathcal{A}_{11,i}^T P_1 \le -2\beta P_1 \qquad i = 1, ..., n_r \tag{16}$$

mit Abklingrate β [13] und s.p.d. Matrix P_1 berechnet werden. Mit $\mathcal{A}_{11,i} = \bar{A}_{11,i} + L_i \bar{A}_{211,i}$ [12] sowie der Substitution $N_i = P_1 L_i$ folgen aus (16) die LMI's [13]

$$P_1 \bar{A}_{11,i} + N_i \bar{A}_{211,i} + \left(\bar{A}_{11,i}\right)^T P_1 + \left(\bar{A}_{211,i} N_i\right)^T \le -2\beta P_1, \tag{17}$$

woraus sich die Verstärkungen L_i mit $L_i = P_1^{-1} N_i$ berechnen lassen, falls (17) für ein vorgegebenes β lösbar ist. Bei Lösbarkeit von (17) ist gleichzeitig die Stabilität des Beobachters (10) garantiert. Der vollständige Stabilitätsnachweis ist wegen des begrenzten Platzes in [14] nachzulesen.

3.3 Schätzung von Sensorfehlern

Wie in [14] gezeigt, lässt sich unter Vernachlässigung von Störungen und Aktorfehlern

$$\hat{f}_s(t) = \mathcal{W}(\alpha(t))\nu_{eq}(t) \tag{18}$$

als Detektorsignal zur Schätzung von Sensorfehlern ableiten, worin $\mathcal{W}(\alpha(t))$ eine geeignete Gewichtungsmatrix darstellt. In (18) ist mit $\mathscr{A}(\alpha(t)) = -\sum_{i=1}^{n_r} h_i(\alpha(t))(\mathcal{A}_{22,i} - \mathcal{A}_{21,i}\mathcal{A}_{11,i}^{-1}\mathcal{A}_{12,i})$, $\mathscr{D}(\alpha(t)) = \sum_{i=1}^{n_r} h_i(\alpha(t))\mathcal{D}_{2,i}$ und $\mathscr{E}(\alpha(t)) = \sum_{i=1}^{n_r} h_i(\alpha(t))\mathcal{E}_{2,i}$

$$\nu_{eq}(t) \approx [\mathscr{A}(\alpha(t))\ \mathscr{D}(\alpha(t))\ \mathscr{E}(\alpha(t))] \begin{bmatrix} f_s(t) \\ \xi(t) \\ f_a(t) \end{bmatrix} \tag{19}$$

das sogenannte *equivalent output injection* Signal, welches das durchschnittliche Verhalten des diskontinuierlichen Vektors $\nu(t)$ repräsentiert und somit den Aufwand zur Aufrechterhaltung der Bewegung auf der Schaltfläche darstellt. Die Matrizen $\mathcal{D}_{2,i}$, $\mathcal{E}_{2,i}$ folgen aus den Transformationen

$$T_i [D_i\ E_i] = \begin{bmatrix} 0 & 0 \\ \mathcal{D}_{2,i} & \mathcal{E}_{2,i} \end{bmatrix} \tag{20}$$

Mögliche Fehlentscheidungen (Fehlalarme) aufgrund unbekannter Eingänge (Störungen) und Aktorfehler[2] bei der Sensordiagnose können durch geeignete Fehlerschwellen vermeiden werden. Dazu sind aus dem Wissen über das zu überwachende System maximale und minimale Unsicherheiten (Störungen) ξ_{max} und ξ_{min} sowie Aktorfehler $f_{a_{max}}$ und

---

[2]Diese wirken ebenso auf $\nu_{eq}(t)$ wie anhand von (19) zu erkennen ist.

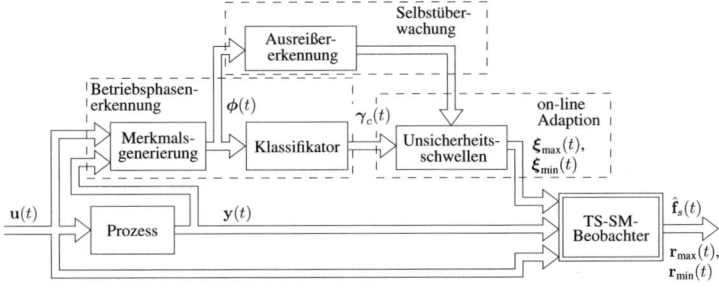

Bild 1: Adaptionsschema des TS-SM-Beobachters zur Fehlerdetektion.

$\mathbf{f}_{a_{\min}}$ zu definieren. Durch das Ersetzen von $\boldsymbol{\xi}(t)$ und $\mathbf{f}_a(t)$ mit diesen Werten, dem Streichen von $\mathbf{f}_s(t)$ und der Multiplikation mit der Gewichtungsmatrix $\mathscr{W}(\boldsymbol{\alpha}(t))$ kann aus (19) die Matrix

$$\mathbf{G}(t) = \left[\mathscr{W}(\boldsymbol{\alpha}(t))\,[\mathscr{D}(\boldsymbol{\alpha}(t))\ \mathscr{E}(\boldsymbol{\alpha}(t))] \begin{bmatrix} \boldsymbol{\xi}_{\max} & \boldsymbol{\xi}_{\min} \\ \mathbf{f}_{a_{\max}} & \mathbf{f}_{a_{\min}} \end{bmatrix} \right] \tag{21}$$

mit der Dimension $\mathbf{G}(t) \in \mathbb{R}^{n \times 2}$ berechnet werden. Aus dem jeweiligen Zeilenmaximum bzw. Zeilenminimum dieser Matrix lassen sich daraufhin die Fehlerschwellen $\mathbf{r}_{\max}(t)$ und $\mathbf{r}_{\min}(t)$ bestimmen. Falls nun der Einfluß von Unsicherheiten/Störungen und Aktorfehlern klein gegenüber den Sensorfehlern ist, dann wird das Detektorsignal (18) diese Fehlerschwellen überschreiten, so dass $\mathscr{W}(\boldsymbol{\alpha}(t))\boldsymbol{\nu}_{eq}(t) > \mathbf{r}_{\max}(t)$ oder $\mathscr{W}(\boldsymbol{\alpha}(t))\boldsymbol{\nu}_{eq}(t) < \mathbf{r}_{\min}(t)$.

3.4 On-line Adaption der Fehlersensitvität

An Gleichung (21) ist erkennbar, dass die Fehlersensitivität direkt mit der Größe der Unsicherheiten und den Aktorfehlern verknüpft ist. Bei einigen technischen Systemen können die Modellunsicherheiten von der aktuellen Betriebsphase abhängen. Ein Beispiel hierfür ist das externe Moment $M_L(t)$ an der Antriebsachse des Radladers in Abschnitt 2. $M_L(t)$ ist bei der Fahrt in der Ebene gering und steigt beim Einstechen in ein Haufwerk deutlich an. Bild 1 zeigt einen Ansatz, um die (üblicherweise konstanten) Fehlerschwellen so zu adaptieren, dass die Empfindlichkeit an die aktuelle Betriebssituation angepasst ist.

In diesem Ansatz wird die aktuelle Wahrscheinlichkeit $\gamma_c(t)$ jeder Betriebsphase mit einem Bayes-Klassifikator geschätzt. Diese Schätzung basiert auf den Merkmalen $\phi(t)$, die aus Eingangs-, Ausgangs- sowie daraus on-line berechneten Größen bestehen. Die aktuellen Unsicherheitsschwellen $\boldsymbol{\xi}_{\max/\min}(t)$ werden hier folgendermaßen bestimmt: Aus dem Wissen über das System werden a-priori Unsicherheiten $\boldsymbol{\xi}'_{\max}, \boldsymbol{\xi}'_{\min}$ für jede einzelne Betriebsphase definiert. Diese Werte werden on-line mit den aktuell zugehörigen Wahrscheinlichkeiten $\gamma_c(t)$ der Betriebsphasen multipliziert und aufsummiert. Dies liefert nun Schätzungen $\boldsymbol{\xi}_{\max/\min}(t)$ der maximalen und minimalen aktuellen Unsicherheiten, aus denen sich nach Abschnitt 3.3 die Fehlerschwellen $\mathbf{r}_{\max/\min}(t)$ berechnen lassen. Hieraus ergibt sich in Betriebsphasen mit kleinen Modellunsicherheiten eine stark erhöhte Fehlersensitivität, d. h. auch geringe Sensorfehler können erkannt werden. In Betriebsphasen mit großen Modellunsicherheiten werden jedoch Fehlalarme vermieden. Die Performance dieses Ansatzes hängt dabei stark von der Qualität der Betriebsphasenerkennung ab. Fehlklassikationen können durch die Adaption der Fehlerschwellen zum Übersehen von Fehlern oder auch zu Fehlalarmen führen.

3.5 Selbstüberwachung der Betriebsphasenerkennung

Der Bayes-Klassifikator ordnet einen Merkmalsvektor stets einer der zuvor angelernten Klassen $c = 1 \dots C$ zu. Diese Zuordnung erfolgt auch in Situationen, die nicht zum Anlernen des Klassifikators vorlagen und sich unter Umständen deutlich von allen anderen unterscheiden. In solchen Situationen ist das Klassifikationsergebnis höchst unsicher und sollte daher möglichst zurückgewiesen werden. Entsprechende Algorithmen für diese Aufgabe finden sich in einschlägiger Literatur unter dem Begriff der Ausreißererkennung. Ausreißer sind definiert als Beobachtungen, die zu weit entfernt von allen anderen Beobachtungen liegen und u. U. zu Fehlinterpretationen führen. Entsprechende Algorithmen werten in der Regel die minimalen Abstände zu anderen Merkmalsvektoren oder repräsentativen Kenngrößen von Klassen im Lerndatensatz aus [15]. In dieser Arbeit wird auf das bekannte Verfahren des Fuzzy-Noise-Clusterings (FNC) [16] zurückgegriffen. Das FNC ist eine robuste Erweiterung des klassischen Fuzzy c-Means-Algorithmus (FCM), bei dem Datensätze automatisch in eine Menge von C' Clustern[3] eingeteilt werden. Robustheit bedeutet in diesem Zusammenhang, dass die Performance des Algorithmus durch kleine Abweichungen des angenommenen Modells, z. B. durch Messrauschen und Ausreißer, nicht wesentlich beeinflusst wird. Bei dem klassischen FCM werden auch die Daten, die die gestörten Daten beinhalten, in die einzelnen Cluster aufgeteilt. Das FNC wurde entwickelt, um diesen Nachteil zu verringern. Die Kernidee des Algorithmus besteht in der Einführung eines separaten Rausch-Clusters. Dieses Rausch-Cluster wird durch einen Prototypvektor (Clusterzentrum) repräsentiert, der denselben Abstand δ (auch als Rausch-Abstand bezeichnet) von *allen* Merkmalsvektoren besitzt. Dies impliziert, dass all diese Merkmalsvektoren mit derselben a-priori Wahrscheinlichkeit zum Rausch-Cluster gehören. Der entscheidende Punkt ist die Wahl von δ.

Der FNC-Algorithmus lässt sich folgendermaßen in das Adaptionsschema aus Bild 1 integrieren: Wird eine Betriebsphase durch den FNC als Ausreißer (also als eine unbekannte Situation) erkannt, wird daraufhin zur Vermeidung von Fehlalarmen die maximale Unsicherheit angenommen, wodurch sich die maximalen Fehlerschwellen einstellen und somit Fehlalarmierungen unterdrückt werden. Allerdings können in diesen Situationen somit gleichzeitig auch keine Fehler erkannt werden.

Man nehme an, der zu partitionierende Datensatz enthält $C' - 1$ gute Cluster. Das C'-te Cluster wird als Rausch-Cluster definiert. Die Partitionierung aller N betrachteten Merkmalsvektoren in die C' Cluster (einschließlich des Rausch-Clusters) erfolgt beim FNC durch die Minimierung der Kostenfunktion

$$J_{FNC} = \sum_{n=1}^{N} \sum_{c'=1}^{C'} (\mu_{nc'})^q \cdot d_{nc'} \qquad (22)$$

mit dem Zugehörigkeitsgrad des Merkmalsvektors $\mathbf{x}_n$ zu dem Prototypvektor $\mathbf{v}_{c'}$, den gewichteten Distanzen $d_{nc'}$ sowie dem Unschärfeparameter (engl.: fuzzyfier) q. Die Distanzen $d_{nc'}$ in (22) sind für alle n definiert als

$$d_{nc'} = d^2(\mathbf{x}_n, \mathbf{v}_{c'}) = (\mathbf{x}_n - \mathbf{v}_{c'})^T \mathbf{A}_{c'} (\mathbf{x}_n - \mathbf{v}_{c'}) \quad \text{für} \quad c' = 1 \dots (C'-1) \qquad (23)$$

und

$$d_{nc'} = \delta^2 = \lambda \left(\sum_{n=1}^{N} \sum_{c'=1}^{C'} (d_{nc'})^2 \right) / N \cdot C' \quad \text{für} \quad c' = C' \qquad (24)$$

---

[3]Dabei ist zu beachten, dass die Klassen C und die Cluster C' in der Regel nicht identisch sind.

Gleichung (23) ist eine gewöhnliche Abstandsnorm (Vektornorm). Darin ist $\mathbf{A}_{c'}$ die Formenmatrix. Je kleiner δ in (24) gewählt wird, desto mehr Merkmalsvektoren werden dem Rausch-Cluster zugeordnet.

Unter Berücksichtigung der Nebenbedingungen $\sum_{c'=1}^{C'} \mu_{nc'} = 1$ und $0 < \sum_{n=1}^{N} \mu_{nc'} < N$ erfolgt die Minimierung der Zielfunktion (22) durch eine alternierende Optimierung der Parameter Zugehörigkeitsgrad $\mu_{nc'}$ und Prototypvektor $\mathbf{v}_{c'}$ solange, bis entweder eine maximale Anzahl von Schritten erreicht ist oder die Änderung der Clusterzentren zwischen zwei Schritten eine Terminierungsgrenze unterschreitet. Für weitere Details sei aufgrund des Platzes auf [16] verwiesen.

4 Simulationstudie

4.1 Sensorfehlerdiagnose

Zur Demonstration des adaptiven FDI-Ansatzes wurde ein umfangreiches Simulationsmodell eines Radladers entwickelt, welches neben dem nichtlinearen hydrostatischen Getriebe noch Modelle eines Verbrennungsmotors, des Antriebsstrangs und des Geländes umfasst. Ein einfaches Fahrermodell regelt die Referenzgeschwindigkeit $v_{ref}(t)$ des Fahrzeugs ein. Die Ausgangsmatrix $\mathbf{C} = [\mathbf{0}_{3\times1} \ \mathbf{I}]$ des Beobachters wurde in dieser Studie bewußt so gewählt, dass nicht alle Ausgänge zurückgeführt werden. Weiterhin wurden die Parameter $\rho = 10^{5.5}$, $\delta = 130$, $\mathbf{A}_{22}^s = \text{diag}([-8- \, 8- \, 8])$, $\beta = 4$ und eine Simulationsschrittweite von $\Delta T = 0.01$s verwendet, wobei deren Wahl z.T. auf Expertenwissen beruht. Da $\mathscr{A}(\boldsymbol{\alpha}(t))$ hier nichtsingulär ist, kann deren Inverse als Gewichtungsmatrix verwendet werden $(\mathscr{W}(\boldsymbol{\alpha}(t)) = \mathscr{A}(\boldsymbol{\alpha}(t))^{-1})$. Es lassen sich Betriebsphasen wie z. B. Vorwärtsfahrt in der Ebene, Hangfahrt oder auch das Einstechen in ein Haufwerk simulieren. Insgesamt liefert die Simulation 24 nicht direkt abhängige Signale, wovon jedoch 7 Signale nicht zur Fahrsituationserkennung verwendet werden können. Der Grund liegt darin, dass diese Signale direkt oder indirekt durch die zu überwachenden Sensorfehler beeinflusst werden oder in einem Serienfahrzeug nicht verfügbar sind. Die von den Sensorfehlern betroffenen Signale werden jedoch zur FDI verwendet. Neben diesen Signalen werden 19 weitere Signale mittels on-line Filterung (Tiefpassfilterung, Trend) berechnet. Der angelernte Bayes-Klassifikator trifft eine Entscheidung basierend auf 29 Signalen/Merkmalen, welche mittels MANOVA ausgewählt wurden. Bild 2 zeigt die wahren Betriebsphasen und die zugehörigen Klassifikatorentscheidungen des in dieser Studie betrachteten Arbeitszyklusses. Abgesehen von geringfügig verzögerten Entscheidungen in den Übergängen der Betriebsphasen arbeitet der Klassifikator schnell und zuverlässig. Bild 3 zeigt die Sensorfehler $\mathbf{f}_s(t)$, deren Schätzungen $\hat{\mathbf{f}}_s(t)$ und die zugehörigen on-line adaptierten Fehlerschwellen $\mathbf{r}_{\text{max/min}}(t)$. Beispielsweise sind die Fehlerschwellen während des Einstechens in das Haufwerk gegenüber denen während der Fahrt in der Ebene deutlich aufgeweitet. Wie in Bild 3 gezeigt, wird der kleine Fehler $f_{s_{\Delta_p}}(t)$ auf dem Drucksensorsignal (12bar) unmittelbar nach dem Wechsel der Betriebsphase mit geringerer Unsicherheit erkannt $(t = 13\text{s})$. Dasselbe gilt für die zwei Fehler $f_{s_{\omega_M}}(t)$ auf dem Winkelgeschwindigkeitssignal (erkannt bei $t = 14.2$s und $t = 38$s). Währe die Betriebsphase jedoch unbekannt, so müsste stets die maximale Unsicherheit (hier die der Situation Einstechen in ein Haufwerk) verwendet werden, um potentielle Fehlalarme zu vermeiden. Hierdurch ließen sich dann nur Fehler größer 430bar detektieren. Dies demonstriert, dass der vorgeschlagene adaptive FDI-Ansatz die Fehlersensitivität wesentlich erhöhen kann. Weiterhin interessant ist, dass trotz der Vernachlässigung von $\dot{\mathbf{f}}_s(t)$ (vgl. hierzu [14]) die Form der Fehler bei den Fehlerschätzungen erhalten bleibt (vgl. $\dot{f}_{s_{\omega_M}}(t)$ bei $t = 14\ldots24$s). Wie erwartet

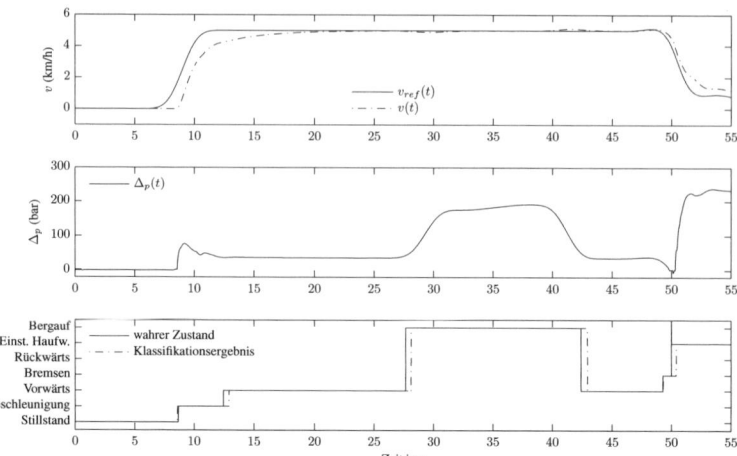

Bild 2: Zur Demonstration des adaptiven Fehlerdiagnoseansatzes verwendeter Arbeitszyklus bestehend aus den Betriebsphasen Stillstand, Beschleunigung, Konstantfahrt in der Ebene bei 5 km/h, Bergauffahrt und Einstechen in einen Sandhaufen.

lassen sich auch mehrere gleichzeitig auftretende Fehler gut schätzen. Bedauerlicherweise werden jedoch auch kurze Fehlalarme aufgrund der zuvor genannten verzögerten Entscheidungen des Klassifikators in den Übergängen einzelner Betriebsphasen ($t = 26.8$s und $t = 50.2$s) ausgelöst. Dies ist nochmals in den vergrößerten Ausschnitten in Bild 4 dargestellt. Die verzögerten Entscheidungen resultieren aus den Zeitkonstanten der verwendeten Filter. Daher bestehen mögliche Maßnahmen zur Vermeidung dieser Fehlalarme in der Anwendung von Filtern mit geringeren Zeitkonstanten sowie der weiteren Signalverarbeitung des Detektorsignals und der Fehlerschwellen.

4.2 Sensorfehlerdiagnose mit überlagerter Selbstüberwachung

Zur Demonstration der Funktionsweise der Selbstüberwachung mittels FNC wird wie im Abschnitt zuvor wieder ein simuliertes Fahrmanöver des Radladers herangezogen. Dieses Manöver setzt sich aus den Betriebsphasen Stillstand, Vorwärtsfahrt in der Ebene und Bergabfahrt zusammen. Die Betriebsphase Bergabfahrt stellt in dem hier behandelten Szenario eine unbekannte Betriebsphase dar, d. h. Daten dieser Betriebsphase wurden *nicht* zum Anlernen des Klassifikators sowie der Ausreißererkennung verwendet. Der Klassifikator wurde auf die Unterscheidung von 5 Klassen, der FNC-Algorithmus auf die Partitionierung der Anlerndaten in 6 Cluster (5 gute Cluster sowie 1 Rausch-Cluster) angelernt. In dieser Untersuchung entscheidet der Klassifikator basierend auf 2 aggregierten Merkmalen. Dieselben Merkmale verwendet auch der FNC zur Entscheidungsfindung. Das Bild 5 zeigt das entsprechende Fahrmanöver sowie die Ergebnisse der on-line Klassifikation und Ausreißererkennung. Während der für den Klassifikator unbekannten Betriebsphase Bergabfahrt entscheidet dieser fälschlicherweise zu den Betriebsphasen Einstechen in das Haufwerk sowie Bergauffahrt. Die Ausreißererkennung basierend auf dem FNC erkennt diese unbekannte Betriebsphase jedoch sicher. In dieser Simulation wurde der Parameter λ zur Berechnung des Rausch-Abstands in Gl. (24) zu

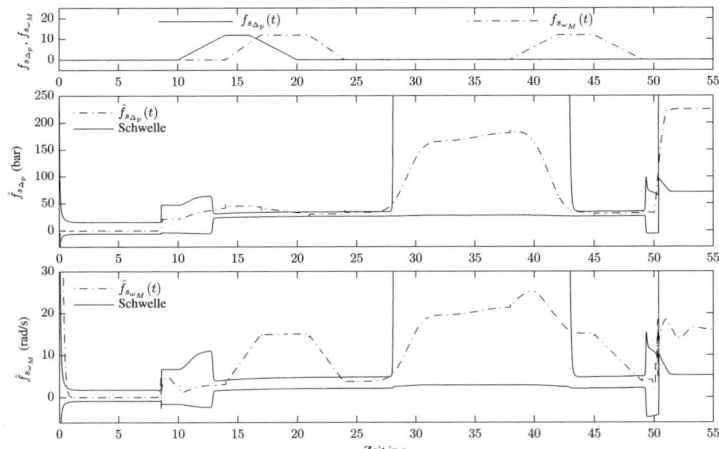

Bild 3: FDI-Ergebnis des in Bild 2 dargestellten Arbeitszyklusses. Das obere Teilbild zeigt die Sensorfehler $f_{s_{\Delta_p}}(t)$ und $f_{s_{\omega_M}}(t)$ auf dem Druck- sowie dem Winkelgeschwindigkeitssensor, die zwei unteren Teilbilder die zugehörigen Fehlerschätzungen und die adaptiven Fehlerschwellen. Alle drei Sensorfehler werden erkannt (durch das Verlassen des zwischen den Fehlerschwellen eingeschlossenen Bereichs), wobei $f_{s_{\Delta_p}}(t)$ und der ab dem Zeitpunkt $t = 38$s einsetzende Fehler $f_{s_{\omega_M}}(t)$ unmittelbar nach Adaption der Fehlerschwellen an die aktuellen Betriebsphasen mit geringerer Unsicherheit und somit kleineren Fehlerschwellen erkannt werden.

0,2 und die Mahalanobis-Norm zur Distanzberechnung gewählt. Den Einfluß der Variation des Parameters λ von 0,2 zu 0,9 bei der Ausreißererkennung ist in Bild 6 für das Manöver aus Bild 5 im Merkmalsraum dargestellt. Das linke Teilbild zeigt das Ergebnis für $\lambda = 0, 2$, das rechte Teilbild entsprechend das Ergebnis für $\lambda = 0, 9$. In diesen Bildern kennzeichnen die graue Kreise Daten bekannter Situationen, die grauen Dreiecke Daten der unbekannten Situation, die schwarzen Kreise erkannte Ausreißer. Die restlichen schwarzen Symbole kennzeichnen die 6 Clusterzentren des FNC nach dem Anlernen. Es ist deutlich zu erkennen, dass bei zunehmend kleinerem λ mehr Daten dem Rausch-Cluster zugeordnet werden. Das FDI-Ergebnis des in Bild 5 dargestellten Szenarios zeigt Bild 7. Das obere Teilbild zeigt den zwischen $t = 38 \ldots 49$s vorliegenden Sensorfehler $f_{s_{\omega_M}}(t)$ auf dem Winkelgeschwindigkeitssensor, die zwei unteren Teilbilder die zugehörigen Fehlerschätzungen und die adaptiven Fehlerschwellen für $f_{s_{\omega_M}}(t)$ ohne (Bild 7 Mitte)

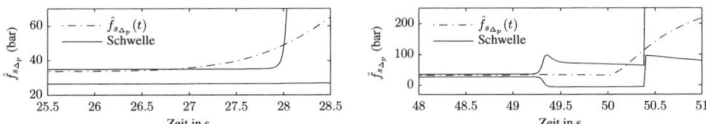

Bild 4: Vergrößerte Ausschnitte aus Bild 3. Diese zeigen die Fehlalarmierungen, die aus den zeitlich geringfügig verzögerten Entscheidungen des Klassifikators resultieren.

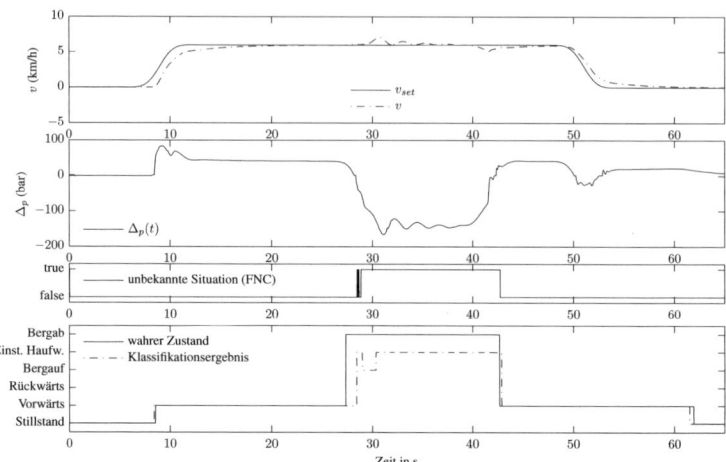

Bild 5: Zur Demonstration der Einbindung der Ausreißererkennung in den adaptiven FDI-Ansatz verwendeter Arbeitszyklus bestehend aus den für den Klassifikator bekannten Betriebsphasen Stillstand und Vorwärtsfahrt sowie der unbekannten Betriebsphase Bergabfahrt.

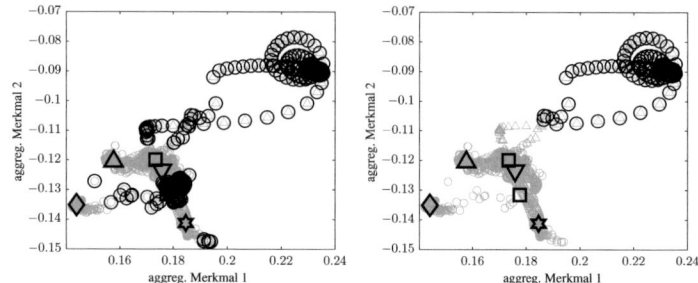

Bild 6: Einfluss des Parameters λ bei der Ausreißererkennung mittels FNC dargestellt im Merkmalsraum (links: $\lambda = 0, 2$, rechts: $\lambda = 0, 9$). Bedeutung der Symbole: Graue Kreise (Daten bekannter Situationen), graue Dreiecke (Daten unbekannter Situation), schwarze Kreise (erkannte Ausreißer), restliche schwarze Symbole (Clusterzentren des FNC). Bei zunehmend kleinerem λ werden mehr Daten dem Rausch-Cluster zugeordnet.

und mit (Bild 7 unten) Einbeziehung der Ausreißererkennung. Ohne Ausreißererkennung wird zum Zeitpunkt $t = 29$s ein Fehlalarm ausgelöst (Bild 7 Mitte), mit Ausreißererkennung werden die Fehlerschwellen soweit aufgespreizt, dass kein Fehlalarm ausgelöst wird (Bild 7 unten). Nachdem die Betriebsphase durch den FNC wieder als bekannt gekennzeichnet wird ($t = 42, 7$s), wird auch der Sensorfehler $f_{s_{\omega_M}}(t)$ unmittelbar darauf erkannt. Der Klassifikator sowie die Ausreißererkennung wurden in dieser Arbeit mit der freien Matlab Toolbox Gait-Cad [17] angelernt.

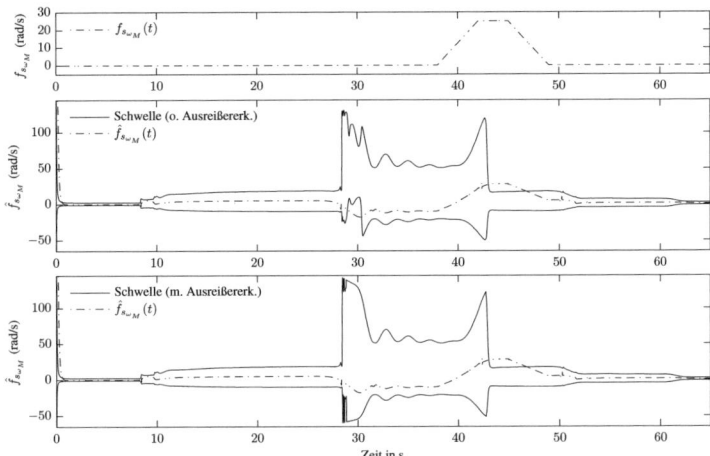

Bild 7: FDI-Ergebnis des in Bild 5 dargestellten Arbeitszyklusses mit dem Sensorfehler $f_{s_{\omega_M}}(t)$ im oberen Teilbild und den zugehörigen Fehlerschätzungen und den adaptiven Fehlerschwellen ohne (Mitte) und mit (unten) Einbeziehung der Ausreißererkennung in den zwei unteren Teilbildern. Ohne Ausreißererkennung wird zum Zeitpunkt $t = 29$s ein Fehlalarm ausgelöst (Bild Mitte). Mit Ausreißererkennung werden die Fehlerschwellen soweit aufgespreizt, dass kein Fehlalarm ausgelöst wird. Nachdem die Betriebsphase durch den FNC wieder als bekannt gekennzeichnet wird ($t = 42, 7$s), wird auch der Sensorfehler $f_{s_{\omega_M}}(t)$ unmittelbar darauf erkannt.

5 Zusammenfassung und Ausblick

In diesem Beitrag wurde ein Sliding-Mode-Fuzzy-Beobachter zur Aktor- und Sensor-fehlerschätzung in Gegenwart von Modellunsicherheiten präsentiert. Basierend auf dem Sliding-Mode-Ansatz von [12] wurden notwendige Bedingungen zur Existenz eines stabilen robusten Beobachters abgeleitet und dessen Entwurf dargestellt. Weiterhin wurde ein Ansatz präsentiert, um die Fehlerschwellen des Fehlerdetektionsalgorithmus on-line so zu adaptieren, dass die Empfindlichkeit bezüglich der aktuellen Betriebssituation wesentlich optimiert wird. Dieser Adaptionsalgorithmus basiert auf einem Bayes-Klassifikator zur Schätzung der aktuellen Betriebsphase. Die Leistungsfähigkeit des adaptiven Fehler-detektionsansatzes wurde in einer Simulationsstudie zur Sensorfehlerüberwachung eines hydrostatisch angetriebenen Radladers demonstriert. Zukünftige Forschungsarbeiten werden sich mit den Problemen bei dem Übergang zwischen den Betriebsphasen befassen.

Danksagung: Der Autor dankt Herr Dr. habil. R. Mikut herzlichst für die stets anregenden Diskussionen und Hilfestellungen im Umgang mit der Matlab-Toolbox Gait-Cad.

Literatur

[1] J. Chen, R.J. Patton: *Robust model-based fault diagnosis for dynamic systems*. Kluwer Academic Publishers, Norwell, MA; 1999.

[2] P. Gerland, H. Schulte, A. Kroll: Vergleichende Untersuchung nichtlinearer Beobachterkonzepte zur Fehlerdiagnose am Beispiel hydrostatischer Fahrantriebe. *In Proc., 19. Workshop Computational Intelligence*, Vol. 19, 2009, S. 61-74.

[3] C. Edwards, S.K. Spurgeon, R.J. Patton: Sliding mode observers for fault detection and isolation. *Automatica*, 36(4), 2000, S. 541-553.

[4] X.G. Yan, C. Edwards: Nonlinear robust fault reconstruction and estimation using a sliding mode observer. *Automatica*, 43(9), 2007, S. 1605-1614.

[5] K. Tanaka, H.O. Wang: *Fuzzy Control Systems Design and Analysis: A Linear Matrix Inequality Approach*. J. Wiley&Sons; 2001.

[6] Z. Gao, X. Shi, S.X. Ding: Fuzzy State/Disturbance Observer Design for TS Fuzzy Systems With Application to Sensor Fault Estimation. *IEEE Transactions on Systems, Man, and Cybernetics, Part B: Cybernetics*, 38(3), Juni 2008, S. 875-880.

[7] P. Bergsten, R. Palm, D. Driankov: Observers for Takagi-Sugeno fuzzy systems. *IEEE Transactions on Systems, Man, and Cybernetics, Part B: Cybernetics*, 32(1), August 2002, S. 114-121.

[8] A. Akhenak, M. Chadli, J. Ragot, D. Maquin: Fault detection and isolation using sliding mode observer for uncertain Takagi-Sugeno fuzzy model. *In Mediterranean Conference on Control and Automation*, Ajaccio, Frankreich, 2008.

[9] H. Schulte, P. Gerland: Observer Design using T-S Fuzzy Systems for pressure estimation in hydrostatic transmissions. *In International Conference on Intelligent Systems Design and Applications (ISDA)*, Pisa, Italy, 2009.

[10] A. K. Jain, P. W. Duin, J. Mao: Statistical pattern recognition: A review. *IEEE Transactions on pattern analysis and machine intelligence*, 22(1), 2000, S. 4-37.

[11] M. M. Tatsuoka: *Multivariate Analysis*. Macmillan, New York; 1988.

[12] C. Edwards, S.K. Spurgeon: *Sliding Mode Control: Theory and Applications*. Taylor and Francis, London; 1998.

[13] S.P. Boyd, L.E. Ghaoui, E. Feron, V. Balakrishnan. *Linear Matrix Inequalities in System & Control Theory*. SIAM, Philadelphia, 1994.

[14] P. Gerland, D. Gross, H. Schulte, A. Kroll: Robust Adaptive Fault Detection Using Global State Information and Application to Mobile Working Machines. *In Conference on Control and Fault-Tolerant Systems (SysTol)*, Nizza, Frankreich, 2010.

[15] R. Mikut: *Data Mining in der Medizin und Medizintechnik*. Habilitation, Universitätsverlag Karlsruhe, 2008.

[16] R. N. Dave: Characterization and detection of noise in clustering. *Pattern Recognition Letters*, 12, 1991, S. 657-664.

[17] R. Mikut, O. Burmeister, S. Braun, M. Reischl: The Open Source Matlab Toolbox Gait-CAD and its Application to Bioelectric Signal Processing. *In Proc., DGBMT-Workshop Biosignalverarbeitung*, Potsdam, Deutschland, 2008, pp. 109-111.

Koevolutionärer Algorithmus zur Analyse struktureller Steuerbarkeit - Eine Methode der „komplexen Netzwerke" zur Systemanalyse

Andreas Geiger, Hanns Sommer und Andreas Kroll

Universität Kassel, Fachbereich Maschinenbau, Fachgebiet Mess- und Regelungstechnik
Mönchebergstr. 7
34125 Kassel
Tel.: (0561) 804 - 2953
Fax: (0561) 804 - 2847
E-Mail: andreas.geiger@mrt.uni-kassel.de

Zusammenfassung

Die zunehmende Vernetzung und Integration innerhalb von technischen Systemen, wie z.b. Infrastruktureinrichtungen, Fertigungs- und Produktionsanlagen, sowie der Wunsch die jeweiligen Systemgrenzen zu erweitern, begründen eine Komplexitätszunahme technischer Systeme und führen zu neuen Herausforderungen und Fragestellungen an die Regelungstechnik. So stellt sich bei der Betrachtung von großen und komplexen Systemen die Frage, wie diese sinnvoll auf ihr Verhalten hin analysiert werden können und welche Anforderungen sie z.b. in Bezug auf ihre Beeinflussbarkeit erfüllen müssen.

Eine Möglichkeit zur Analyse solcher Systeme bietet die Methode der Systembeschreibung mittels komplexer Netzwerke. Sie erlaubt es, auf Basis von abstrahierten Graphen, Systeme bezüglich ihres Verhaltens zu klassifizieren und ihrer Struktur zugrunde liegende Eigenschaften aufzudecken. Solche Netzwerkverfahren wurden bereits in der klassischen Regelungstechnik zur Untersuchung struktureller Eigenschaften wie Steuerbarkeit und Beobachtbarkeit eingeführt.

Auf die bereits erwähnten komplexen Anlagensystemen sind die klassischen Methoden allerdings meist schwer anwendbar, da diese Systeme zu groß sind und dadurch auch Eigenschaften auftreten können, welche bisher nicht berücksichtigt wurden.

Der vorliegende Beitrag wendet sich dieser Problematik zu, in dem er die Verwendung von Methoden der komplexen Netze diskutiert und, zum Nachweis der strukturellen Steuerbarkeit mit Hilfe des Lin-Hahn'schen Kriteriums, einen koevolutionären Algorithmus vorstellt.

1 Einleitung

Um die Konkurrenzfähigkeit von Anlagen der Fertigungs- und Produktionsindustrie auf lange Sicht hin zu erhalten und zusätzlich zu steigern, werden immer neue Anforderungen an moderne Anlagen gestellt. Zu diesen Anforderungen zählen unter anderem die Dezentralisierung, sowie eine erhöhte Flexibilität und Wandlungsfähigkeit, um eine größere Variantenvielfalt, kleine Losgrößen (bis hin zur Einzelfertigung), kürzere Lebenszyklen und kurze Reaktionszeiten zu ermöglichen. Weitere Anforderungen sind die Selbstoptimierung und die Arbeit in Kreisläufen, zur Verringerung von Abfällen und der optimalen Werkstoffnutzung [1, 2]. Als Folge all dieser Anforderungen kommt es bei der Entwicklung passender Automatisierungssysteme zu einer Steigerung der integrierten Intelligenz und zu einer zunehmenden Vernetzung der Anlagen. Daneben ist zu beachten, dass eine Anlage ständigen Anpassungen und Änderungen unterworfen ist und sich somit in einem dynamischen Wandel befindet.

Bei der Entwicklung von Regelungssystemen für Anlagen ist es erforderlich, das vorliegende System zu analysieren und zu modellieren. Hierbei kommt es nun im Falle von modernen Produktions- und Fertigungsanlagen zu Problemen, da diese als Gesamtsystem eine Größe erreicht haben, die nicht mehr als ganzes handhabbar ist. Eine Möglichkeit, dieses Problem anzugehen ist es, das Gesamtsystem aufzuspalten und kleinere Teilsysteme zu bilden. Diese Teilsysteme können dann einzeln mit den konventionellen Methoden behandelt werden. Bei der Reduktion des Problems auf die einzelnen Teilprobleme werden die Kopplungen zwischen den Teilsystemen durch Einsparungen oder Linearisierung stark vereinfacht. Durch die vorgenommenen Vereinfachungen wird die Struktur des Gesamtsystems verändert und Eigenschaften, welche in der Systemstruktur zu finden sind können nicht mehr korrekt analysiert und eine übergreifende, optimale Lösung kann nicht gewährleistet werden. Ein weiteres Problem der Analyse der beschriebenen Anlagen liegt in deren kontinuierlichen Veränderungen, da im Laufe ihrer Lebenszeit eine Anlage an neue Anforderungen und Technologien Angepasst wird. Diese Veränderungen machen eine erneute Betrachtung und Anpassung des Regelungssystems erforderlich, wobei nicht jede Änderung zwingend eine komplett neue Regelung erfordert. Eine schnelle Untersuchung der strukturellen Eigenschaften des veränderten Systems sollte es vielmehr erlauben, die erforderlichen Änderungen gezielt vorzunehmen. Ein weiterer Lösungsansatz zur Analyse großer, komplexer Systeme, besteht darin, diese auf einem abstrakteren Niveau zu untersuchen, zum Beispiel durch die Modellierung als Graph. Diese Art der Modellierung wird unter anderem durch die vernetzte Struktur von modernen Anlagen begünstigt. Durch die Analyse der so erstellten Graphen können Aussagen über die strukturellen Eigenschaften getroffen werden und es kann eine Klassifizierung von Systemen bezüglich ihres Verhaltens erfolgen. In der Vergangenheit untersuchte bereits Lin [3] die strukturelle Steuerbarkeit von linearen Systemen, Reinschke [4] verwendete einen Graphenansatz zur Regelung von Mehrgrößensystemen und Svaricek [5] untersuchte die Berechnung der Nullstellen im Unendlichen bei nichtlinearen Systemen. Hahn und Sommer [6, 7] erweiterten die Analyse der strukturellen Steuerbarkeit mittels Graphen auf eine Klasse von nichtlinearen Systemen.

Im vorliegende Beitrag wird das Lin-Hahn'sche Kriterium für strukturelle Steuerbarkeit aufgegriffen und für die Analyse großer Systeme verwendet. Die strukturelle Steuerbarkeit ermöglicht es, eine Aussage über die Steuerbarkeit eines Systems zu treffen, wobei vorhandene Parameter berücksichtigt werden, ohne das ihr genauer Wert vorliegt. Dabei sollen große, komplexe Anlagen auf mögliche Phasenübergänge, das heißt sprunghafte Änderungen von Systemeigenschaften, in Abhängigkeit des strukturellen Aufbaus, untersucht werden. Hierfür wird das zu analysierende System mit Hilfe eines Netzgraphen abstrahiert und anschließend nach der sogenannte „Kaktusstruktur" durchsucht. Die Hauptaufgabe der Analyse liegt somit bei der Suche nach entsprechenden Strukturen, wobei der Aufwand für die Struktursuche mit der Größe des Systems anwächst. Um den Rechenaufwand bei der Suche klein zu halten, sind insbesondere Methoden der Computational Intelligence geeignet, z.B. evolutionäre Suchalgorithmen.

Der Beitrag geht zunächst in Abschnitt 2 auf die Untersuchung von Systemen ein, hierzu wird auf die Beschreibung von Systemen, sowie ihre Darstellung als Graph eingegangen. Es wird der Begriff der Steuerbarkeit sowie deren Ermittlung mit Hilfe von Graphen besprochen und die Idee von Phasenübergängen in Systemeneigenschaften erläutert. Hierbei wird auch das Lin-Hahn'sche Kaktuskriterium vorgestellt. Im Abschnitt 3 wird dann der Suchalgorithmus, sowie dessen Erweiterung zu einem koevolutionären Algorithmus behandelt. Den Abschluss bildet in Abschnitt 4 eine Zusammenfassung mit kurzem Ausblick.

2 Systembetrachtung

2.1 Der System-Begriff

Viele verschiedene Wissenschaften verwenden den Begriff des Systems, dazu zählen neben den Ingenieurswissenschaften die Physik, die Sozial- und Wirtschaftswissenschaften [8]. Allgemein verstehen wir unter einem System eine Einheit, die durch Eingangsfunktionen $u_1, ..., u_p$ beeinflusst werden kann und in Abhängigkeit von diesen reagiert. Die Reaktionen seien durch die Funktionen $y_1, ..., y_q$ beschrieben. Im Falle eines dynamischen Systems hängt die Reaktion zum Zeitpunkt t nicht nur von den Eingangswerten zu diesem Zeitpunkt, sondern auch von Werten früherer Zeitpunkte ab. Wird angenommen, dass zur Erinnerung die Speicher $S_1, ..., S_n$ zur Verfügungen stehen und, dass in jedem Speicher zum Zeitpunkt t genau ein Wert $x_i(t)(i = 1, ..., n)$ gespeichert ist, so ist ein deterministisches System durch zwei Systemgleichungen beschreibbar:

Die Ausgangsgleichung [8]

$$y = g(x, u) \; ; \; y \in \mathbb{R}^q, \; x \in \mathbb{R}^n, \; u \in \mathbb{R}^p \tag{1}$$

und die Zustandsgleichung für zeitdiskrete bzw. kontinuierliche Systeme [8]

$$x(t+1) = f(x(t), u(t)) \quad \text{bzw.} \quad \dot{x} = f(x(t), u(t)) \tag{2}$$

wobei $h : \mathbb{R}^n \times \mathbb{R}^p \to \mathbb{R}^q$ und $f : \mathbb{R}^n \times \mathbb{R}^p \to \mathbb{R}^n$ zunächst beliebige Funktionen sein können.

Eine noch allgemeinere Darstellung von Systemen wurde von J.C. Willems vorgeschlagen [9]. Er bezeichnet diese als Verhaltensbeschreibung eines Systems. Ein System besteht in dieser Sichtweise aus einem Universum $\mathfrak{U}$ von Funktionen: z.B. $\mathfrak{U} = \{w_1, w_2, ..., w_m\} = \{u_1, ..., u_p, y_1, ..., y_q, x_1, ..., x_n\}$, wobei nur ein Teil dieser Funktionsmenge im Systemverhalten $\mathfrak{B}$ tatsächlich zugelassen ist, $\mathfrak{B} \subseteq \mathfrak{U}$. Das Systemverhalten $\mathfrak{B}$ wird dann durch Konsistenzbedingungen an die Systemfunktion $\mathfrak{U}$ festgelegt. Die Gleichungen (1) und (2) stellen solche möglichen Konsistenzbedingungen dar, aber deren Form kann natürlich wesentlich allgemeiner sein. Jede allgemeine Relation, die zwischen den Elementen von $\mathfrak{U}$ gefordert wird, ist eine mögliche Konsistenzbedingung. Funktionen in $\mathfrak{U}$, die frei vorgegeben werden können und die wir mit $u_1, ..., u_p$ bezeichnet haben, werden Eingangsfunktionen genannt, wohingegen Funktionen $y_1, ..., y_q$, die rein algebraisch von den restlichen Funktionen $u_1, ..., u_p, x_1, ..., x_n$ abhängen als Ausgangsfunktionen bezeichnet werden. Die übrigen Funktionen sind die Zustandsbeschreibungsfunktionen des Systems.

Die Systembeschreibung nach J.C. Willems bietet die Möglichkeit, Systemeigenschaften direkt in die Systembeschreibung zu integrieren. So ist es z.B. möglich die Steuerbarkeit eines Systems dadurch zu implementieren, dass die hierfür notwendige Bedingung als Konsistenzbedingung des Systems definiert wird. Daraus ergibt sich dann für das Systemverhalten wiederum die Frage nach der Erfüllbarkeit und Eindeutigkeit der Konsistenzbedingung. Im Abschnitt 2.5 wird hierfür ein Beispiel angeführt.

Die einheitliche Form der Systembeschreibung hatte zunächst in den Sozialwissenschaften die Hoffnung gestärkt, dass es nun möglich sein werde, viele der Methoden der Physik und der Ingenieurwissenschaften auch nutzbringend übernehmen zu können. Aber diese Hoffnung hat sich nur zu geringen Teilen erfüllt. Es hat sich vielmehr herausgestellt, dass Systeme der Sozial- und Wirtschaftswissenschaften, zur Wettervorhersage und der Softwaretechnik Eigenschaften besitzen, welche sie von den üblichen technischen Systemen auch qualitativ unterscheiden. Während technische Systeme innerhalb ihres Nominalverhaltens mit einem Modell beschrieben werden können und ihre „Beeinflussbarkeit" gewährleistet werden kann, haben Systeme der Sozial- und Wirtschaftswissenschaften und auch der Klimaforschung diese Eigenschaft nicht [10]. Es werden daher andere Kriterien zur Charakterisierung von Systemen dieser Bereiche benötigt, als sie uns der reine Systembegriff liefert.

Wie einführend erläutert, weisen auch große technische Anlagen Eigenschaften auf, welche es nur schwer erlauben, diese in einem exakten Modell zu beschreiben. So können Fertigungs- und Produktionsanlagen wegen ihrer Größe und Komplexität ebenfalls in die Reihe der oben genannten Systeme mit aufgenommen werden. Eine wichtige Methode zur Klassifizierung und Beschreibung von Systemen auf einem abstrakteren Niveau, ist deren Beschreibung mit Hilfe eines Systemgraphen. Diese Methode wurde in den letzten Jahrzehnten insbesondere von Physikern zu einem effektiven Werkzeug entwickelt, jedoch auch die Beiträge der Regelungstechniker Lin, Reinschke, Hahn und Svaricek haben diese Methode wesentlich beeinflusst. Das Ziel des vorliegenden Beitrags ist es, aufzuzeigen wie sich diese Ergebnisse der Regelungstechnik in eine allgemeine „Graphenmethode" einfügen lässt und welche Ergebnisse von dieser Methode zu erwarten sind.

2.2 Strukturellen Steuerbarkeit von Systemen

In der Praxis haben Begriffe der Erreichbarkeit [11], Steuerbarkeit [12] und Sensitivität [13] große Bedeutung. Unter der Steuerbarkeit eines Systems versteht man dabei die Möglichkeit, das System von einem Zustand $(x_1(t_0), ..., x_n(t_0))$ zum Zeitpunkt t_0 durch Wahl geeigneter Steuerfunktionen $(u_1(t), ..., u_p(t))$ $t \in [t_0, t_e]$ in einen vorgegebenen Zustand $(x_1(t_e), ..., x_n(t_e))$ zu überführen. Umgekehrt wird für die Erreichbarkeit die Frage gestellt welche Zustände $(x_1(T), ..., x_n(T))$ von einem gegebenen Startzustand $(x_1(t_0), ..., x_n(t_0))$ mittels einer Steuerung $(u_1(t), ..., u_p(t))$ in der Zeit $T \geq t \geq t_0$ erreicht werden können. Die Sensitivität des Systems beschreibt wiederum, wie stark die Zustandswerte $(x_1(t_e), ..., x_n(t_e))$ von den Steuerfunktionen abhängen.

Formal definiert man Steuerbarkeit durch den Ausdruck:

$$\forall \, \boldsymbol{x}, \, \tilde{\boldsymbol{x}} \in M, \, \exists \, \boldsymbol{u}(t) \text{ mit } t \in [t_0, t_e] \,, \text{ so dass } \boldsymbol{u}(t) \text{ den Zustand } \boldsymbol{x}(t_0) \text{ in den Zustand}$$
$$\boldsymbol{x}(t_e) = \tilde{\boldsymbol{x}} \text{ überführt, wobei } \boldsymbol{x}(t) \in M \text{ erfüllt ist.} \tag{3}$$

Der Ausdruck (3) erlaubt folgende Unterscheidungen:

- **globale Steuerbarkeit:** $M = \mathbb{R}^n$

- **lokale Steuerbarkeit:** M = eine kleine Umgebung von $\boldsymbol{x}(t_0) \in \mathbb{R}^n$

- **Halbraumsteuerbarkeit:** M = nichtleere offene Schnittmenge aus n dimensionalen Halbräumen

- **lokale Halbraumsteuerbarkeit:** M = nichtleere offene Schnittmenge aus n dimensionalen Halbräumen in einer Umgebung von $\boldsymbol{x}(t_0)$

Ein System heißt strukturell steuerbar, wenn es durch eine beliebig kleine Änderung seiner Parameter in ein steuerbares System überführt werden kann.

Es ist wichtig zu beachten, dass die angegebenen Steuerbarkeitsbegriffe nur für lineare Systeme gleichwertig sind. D.h. für lineare Systeme gilt, dass die Erfülltheit von einem der Steuerbarkeitsbegriffe die anderen impliziert. Für nichtlineare Systeme sind die beschriebenen Steuerbarkeitseigenschaften dagegen nicht gleichwertig. Selbst die globale Steuerbarkeit würde die lokale Steuerbarkeit nicht notwendigerweise implizieren.

2.3 Die Graphenmethode zur Untersuchung von Systemen

Eine wesentliche Erfahrung der Softwaretechnik, welche in die Systemtheorie eingeflossen ist, ist die, dass die Beherrschbarkeit von Systemen wesentlich von der Art und Weise abhängt, wie die Teile des Systems miteinander verknüpft sind. Beherrschbare Softwaresysteme sollten modular aufgebaut sein, was eine Aufteilung des komplexe Systems in Teilsysteme bedeutet [14]. Die Funktionalität innerhalb der Teilsysteme wird dabei verborgen und lediglich deren Eingangs- und Ausgangsschnittstellen möglichst einfach dem Gesamtsystem zugänglich gemacht. Werden nun Fertigungs- und Produktionsanlagen betrachtet, so lassen sich diese auch in einzelne Module zerlegen, welche wiederum über festgelegte Ein- und Ausgänge miteinander verbunden sind. Es interessiert dann weniger das Verhalten innerhalb der Teile, als vielmehr ihr Gesamtverhalten, als vernetztes System. Da die Softwaretechnik zur Beschreibung ihrer komplexen Systeme unter anderem auf abstrakte Graphen zurückgreift, um die Verknüpfungen zwischen den Teilsystemen zu beschreiben, liegt der Schritt nahe, dies auch auf Anlagen anzuwenden.

Da der Systemgraph auch zur Untersuchung der strukturellen Steuerbarkeit herangezogen werden soll, wird er im Folgenden eingeführt.

Systemknoten: Jeder Funktion w_i, mit $i = 1, ..., m$, des Systems wird ein Knoten n_i zugewiesen. $\mathcal{V} = \{n_1, n_2, ..., n_m\}$ sei die Menge aller Knoten des Systemgraphen $\mathcal{G}$ bzw. $\widetilde{\mathcal{G}}$.

Verallgemeinerte Systemkante: Knoten $n_{i_1}, n_{i_2}, ..., n_{i_k}$, deren zugeordnete Funktionen $w_{i_1}, w_{i_2}, ..., w_{i_k}$, in einer Konsistenzbedingung gemeinsam vorkommen, werden zu einer Kante $e = (n_{i_1}, n_{i_2}, ..., n_{i_k}) \in \mathcal{V}^k$ zusammengefasst.

Die Menge $\widetilde{\mathcal{E}} \subseteq \mathcal{V}^2 \cup \mathcal{V}^3 \cup ...$, beschreibt die Menge der so entstehenden Kanten. Das Paar $\widetilde{\mathcal{G}} = \left(\mathcal{V}, \widetilde{\mathcal{E}} \right)$ wird als verallgemeinerter Systemgraph bezeichnet. Aus diesem erhält man den Systemgraphen $\mathcal{G} = (\mathcal{V}, \mathcal{E})$, durch bilden von Paaren aus den Elementen der verallgemeinerten Systemkanten:

$$\mathcal{E} := \left\{ e = (n_i, n_j) \in \mathcal{V} \times \mathcal{V} \mid \exists \, \widetilde{e} \in \widetilde{\mathcal{E}} : n_i \in \widetilde{e} \text{ und } n_j \in \widetilde{e} \right\}$$

Für Systeme, die durch die Gleichungen (1) und (2) darstellbar sind kann auch ein gerichteter Systemgraph definiert werden:

Gerichteter Systemgraph: Die Knotenmenge $\mathcal{V} = \{n_1, ..., n_m\}$ besteht aus je einem Knoten, der einer der Funktionen $u_1, ..., u_p, x_1, ..., x_n$ zugeordnet ist ($m = p + n$). Die Knotenmenge $\mathcal{E}_g \subseteq \mathcal{V} \times \mathcal{V}$ wird wie folgt definiert:

$$\mathcal{E}_g := \{(n_i, n_j) \in \mathcal{V} \times \mathcal{V} \mid x_i \text{ kommt in der Knotenmenge } f_j \text{ zur Berechnung von}$$
$$x_j(t+1) \text{ bzw. } \dot{x}_j(t) \text{ in Gleichung (2) vor }\}$$

Das Paar $\mathcal{G}_g = (\mathcal{V}, \mathcal{E}_g)$ wird als gerichteter Systemgraph bezeichnet.

Der zu einem System gebildete Systemgraph beschreibt ein System nicht vollständig, sondern er erfasst nur dessen Verkopplungsbedingungen. Es ergibt sich so eine grobere Sichtweise auf ein System, von der wir uns erhoffen, dass sie das „Wesentliche" dieses Systems in vereinfachter WForm zum Ausdruck bringt. Das Ziel einer gröberen Systembetrachtung ist es, strukturelle Eigenschaften sowie deren Verhalten bei Änderungen des Systems, so genannten Phasenübergängen, zu untersuchen und zu bewerten. Abbildung 1 zeigt den gerichteten Systemgraphen des Systems 4, welches als Beispiel verwendet wird.

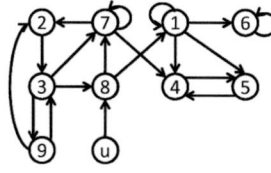

$$\dot{x}_1 = f(x_1, x_8) \,;\; \dot{x}_2 = f(x_7, x_9) \,;$$
$$\dot{x}_3 = f(x_2, x_9) \,;\; \dot{x}_4 = f(x_1, x_5, x_7) \,;$$
$$\dot{x}_5 = f(x_1, x_4) \,;\; \dot{x}_6 = f(x_1, x_6) \,;$$
$$\dot{x}_7 = f(x_3, x_7, x_8) \,;\; \dot{x}_8 = f(x_3, u) \,;$$
$$\dot{x}_9 = f(x_3)$$

Bild 1: Gerichteter Systemgraph des Systems 4. Die Knoten repräsentieren die Funktionen $x_1, ..., x_9, u$.

$$(4)$$

2.4 Strukturelle Steuerbarkeit von Systemen mit der Graphenmethode

Eine wichtige Frage ist, inwieweit die Betrachtungsweise mittels der Graphenmethode in der Lage ist den Steuerbarkeitsbegriff zu erfassen. Die folgenden Sätze beantworten diese Frage für spezielle Systemklassen.

Definition (Kaktus): Ein gerichteter Graph $(\mathcal{V}, \mathcal{E})$ wird als Kaktus bezeichnet, falls er zusammengesetzt ist aus:

i. einem Stamm, d.h. einer Menge von Knoten $\{n_1, n_2, ..., n_n\} \in \mathcal{V}$ und den Kanten $\{e_1 = (n_1, n_2), e_2 = (n_2, n_3), ..., e_{k-1} = (n_{k-1}, n_k)\} \in \mathcal{E}$ und

ii. keiner Knospe oder mehreren Knospen, d.h. Zyklen aus Knoten $n_{i_1}, n_{i_2}, ..., n_{i_j}$ mit den Kanten $(n_{i_1}, n_{i_2}), ..., (n_{i_j}, n_{i_1})$ die über eine zusätzliche Kante $(n, n_{i_{j+\rho}})$ mit dem Stamm ($0 \leq \rho \leq j$) oder mit anderen Knospen des Graphen verbunden sind. Dabei ist n ein Knoten des Stamms oder einer bereits am Kaktus befindlichen Knospe. Hingegen dürfen die Knoten $n_{i_1}, n_{i_2}, ..., n_{i_j}$ nicht bereits dem Stamm oder anderen Knospen angehören.

Eine Kaktushecke besteht aus einer Menge von disjunkten Kakteen, zwischen denen keine Kanten verlaufen. □

Ein System hat die Kakteeneigenschaft, wenn es folgende Eigenschaften erfüllt:

Der zugeordnete gerichtete Systemgraph zu den Eingangsfunktionen $u_1, ..., u_p$ und den Zustandsfunktionen $x_1, ..., x_n$, der bezüglich Gleichung (2) entsteht, kann durch Weglassen von Kanten in eine Kaktushecke so umgeformt werden, dass die Anfangsknoten jedes Stammes jeweils den Eingangsfunktionen u_i entsprechen.

Mit dem Begriff des Kaktus sind die folgenden Sätze zur Steuerbarkeit von Systemen formulierbar.

Satz von Lin: Ein lineares System ist genau dann strukturell steuerbar, falls sein gerichteter Systemgraph die Kaktuseigenschaft erfüllt [3]. □

Satz von Hahn: Ein polynomiales System (bei dem die Funktion f mit Polynomen definiert werden kann) ist genau dann strukturell lokal halbraumsteuerbar, falls sein gerichteter Systemgraph die Kaktuseigenschaft erfüllt [6]. □

In Abbildung 2 ist der Kaktus für das Beispiel aus Abschnitt 2.3 farbig eingezeichnet und die überflüssigen Kanten wurden entfernt. Die Sätze von Lin und Hahn zeigen, dass

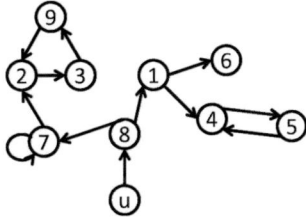

Bild 2: Kaktus zum Beispielsystem 4, die Knoten (8,1,6) bilden den Stamm, (7), (2,3,9) und (4,5) jeweils Knospen.

wichtige Eigenschaften von Systemen, wie z.B. deren Steuerbarkeit, aus der vereinfachten Betrachtungsweise, welche der Systemgraph bietet, erkannt werden können. Da alle stetigen Funktionen mit Polynomen beliebig genau approximiert werden können, kommt damit dem Satz von Hahn eine besondere Bedeutung zu. Dieser Satz zeigt aber auch, dass es nicht immer einfach ist, die strukturell und generell erkennbaren Eigenschaften als Aussagen für ein individuelles System zu formulieren.

Wie wir gesehen haben ist es zur Verwendung der Graphenmethode notwendig, die Aussagen über den Systemgraphen in effektiver und robuster Weise erkennen zu können. Effektiv bedeutet dabei, dass der Suchalgorithmus auch für große Systeme nach kurzer Rechenzeit ein Ergebnis liefert. Unter robustem Erkennen wird verstanden, dass dieses Ergebnis nicht von kleinen Details und singulären Erscheinungen des Systems abhängt, sondern das System im Kontext „ähnlicher" Systeme bewertet. Diese Forderung entspricht derjenigen nach dem Erkennen „der Phase", zu der das System gehört.

Beispielhaft wird im nächsten Abschnitt ein Algorithmus, der dieses für das Kaktuskriterium leistet, hergeleitet.

2.5 Phasenübergänge bei Systemen

Einführend wurde auf die Anforderungen von Infrastruktureinrichtungen, Fertigungs- und Produktionsanlagen eingegangen und diese als große, komplexe Systeme eingeführt. Bedingt durch ihre Größe ist es bei diesen Systemen aufwändig, eine klassische Systemanalyse durchzuführen. Ein erster Analyseschritt mit Hilfe von abstrahierten Modellen ermöglicht eine rasche Untersuchung der strukturellen Eigenschaften von Systemen, ohne auf das Detailverhalten einzugehen. Bedingt durch die Abstrahierung müssen jedoch auch Einschnitte im Untersuchungsergebnis hingenommen werden und zur anschließenden Auslegung einzelner Regler kann nicht in jedem Fall auf eine klassische Analyse verzichtet werden. Neben der Analyse des Systems auf strukturelle Eigenschaften, ist es auch von Interesse, das Verhalten der Systemeigenschaften genauer zu betrachten. Es stellt sich die Frage nach dem Verhalten der strukturellen Systemeigenschaften bei Änderungen des Systems. Was passiert also, wenn Komponenten hinzukommen oder Kopplungen wegfallen? Ein bekanntes Beispiel für ein solches Ereignis hat sich am 4. November 2006 zugetragen. Während der Fahrt eines Kreuzfahrtschiffs von der Werft an die Küste, wurde eine Hochspannungsleitung über der Ems abgeschaltet, was dann zu Stromausfällen in mehreren Ländern Europas führte. Das abschalten einer einzelnen Leitung hatte ein scharfes Umschlagen des Systemverhaltens zur Folge. Neben der Untersuchung, welche Eigenschaften ein System aufweist, ist es zudem wichtig, zu analysieren, unter welchen Bedingungen ein System diese Eigenschaften erfüllt, bzw. plötzlich andere aufweist. Die Suche nach den Umschlagpunkten der Systemeigenschaften sollte also ebenfalls Bestandteil der Systemanalyse sein und es ermöglichen, die Schwachstellen der Struktur zu identifizieren um sie durch entsprechende Anpassungen zu kompensieren. Der Grund für eine erweiterte Betrachtung der Eigenschaften ist in der Art der Systemeigenschaften zu finden. In unserem Fall werden strukturelle Eigenschaften untersucht, welche sich nicht nur auf ein einzelnes konkreten Systems beziehen, sondern auf eine Menge von Systemen mit gleicher Struktur. Daneben sollen robuste Aussagen getroffen werden, wofür es wichtig ist zu wissen, wie sich das System bei Änderungen, wie dem Hinzunehmen oder Entfernen einer einzelnen Kante, verhält. Die Umschlagpunkte grenzen die veränderten Systemeigenschaften und die dazugehörige Menge von Systemen, welche diese erfüllen, voneinander ab. Sie zeigen die Stelle im strukturellen Aufbau des Systems auf, an denen auch eine kleine Änderung eine generelle Veränderung der Systemeigenschaften zur Folge hat. Die Bereiche zwischen den Umschlagpunkten werden als Systemphasen bezeichnet.

Das folgende Beispiel soll die Charakterisierung mittels Systemphasen verdeutlichen, durch welche sich große Systeme der Fertigungs- und Produktionstechnik oder auch der Sozialwissenschaften, gegenüber kleinen, aus technischen Geräten gebildeten, Systemen unterscheiden. Da auch technische Anlagen steigende Komplexität aufweisen, wird es zunehmend wichtiger, diese Unterscheidung zu verstehen. Weiter oben wurde die Systembeschreibung von J.C. Willems vorgestellt, in welcher die Systemeigenschaften mittels Konsistenzbedingungen in die Modellierung integriert werden können. So kann beispielsweise die Eigenschaft der Steuerbarkeit über die Bedingung, welche ein System zum Nachweisen der Steuerbarkeit erfüllen muss, in das Systemmodell integriert werden. Die so gebildeten Konsistenzbedingungen sind Gleichungen der Systemfunktionen, welche wiederum im Allgemeinen durch (viele) binäre Funktionen approximiert werden können, wie sie im folgenden Beispiel verwendet werden.

Beispiel: (Binäre Funktionsmengen mit Konsistenzbedingungen) [15, 16, 17]

Wir betrachten m Funktionen $w_1, w_2, ..., w_m$, welche nur die Werte 0 oder 1 annehmen können und beschreiben das Systemverhalten dieser Funktionen durch K Konsistenzbedingungen von der Form:

$$c_k := (w_{i_1} = t_{k_1} \lor w_{i_2} = t_{k_2} \lor ... \lor w_{i_n} = t_{k_n}) \quad k = 1, ..., K \tag{5}$$

wobei t_{k_i} jeweils einen vorgegebenen Wert 0 oder 1 bezeichnet.

Bezüglich der Erfüllbarkeitseigenschaft d.h. der Existenz von m Funktionen, welche alle K Konsistenzbedingungen erfüllen gilt:

Satz : Zu einer festen Länge n der Konsistenzbedingungen gibt es einen Umschlagpunkt α_c mit $0 < \alpha_c < 1$, so dass für das Verhältnis $\alpha = \frac{K}{m}$, von Konsistenzbedingungen zur Anzahl der Funktionen gilt:

   i. $\alpha < \alpha_c$: dann existiert mit einer Wahrscheinlichkeit, die für $m \to \infty$ gegen 1 strebt ein Funktionentupel $w_1, ..., w_m$, das alle Konsistenzbedingungen (5) erfüllt.

   ii. $\alpha > \alpha_c$: dann sind alle Konsistenzbedingungen (5) mit einer Wahrscheinlichkeit, die für $m \to \infty$ gegen 1 strebt, nicht erfüllbar. □

Der angegebene Satz zeigt, dass für große Systeme, die den Bedingungen des Beispiels entsprechen (d.h. für große m), das Erfüllbarkeitsverhalten von Mengen von Konsistenzbedingungen bezüglich dem Parameter α in Phasen aufgeteilt wird. Werden die Konsistenzbedingungen als Systemeigenschaften interpretiert, kann das Phasenverhalten auch auf diese übertragen werden. Es lassen sich also zwei Gruppen von Systemen bilden, wobei bei der einen die Systemeigenschaft mit hoher Wahrscheinlichkeit erfüllt ist und bei der anderen mit hoher Wahrscheinlichkeit nicht. Dabei hat die Größe des Systems Einfluss auf das Übergangsverhalten bei a_c, da mit steigender Größe der Übergang von einer Phase zur andern schärfer wird.

Folgerung: Charakteristische Systemeigenschaften ändern sich in sehr großen Systemen nicht stetig und langsam, sondern sprunghaft beim Überschreiten von Phasengrenzen.

Die gefundene Folgerung zeigt einen wesentlichen Unterschied der Systemeigenschaften von großen Systemen im Vergleich zu kleinen. Bei großen Systemen und der Betrachtung ihrer strukturellen Eigenschaften ist neben den individuellen Eigenschaften eines Systems auch interessant, zu untersuchen unter welchen Bedingungen eine kleine Strukturänderung zu einem komplett neuen Verhalten führt. Es stellt sich die Frage nach den Umschlagpunkten, da diese die Robustheit der analysierten Systemeigenschaften beschreiben. Es müssen Unterscheidungsmerkmale zwischen Systemen gefunden werden, welche nicht von den Details des Systems sondern von dessen genereller Struktur abhängen. Hierzu bietet sich die Systembeschreibung durch Systemgraphen an, wobei dessen Eigenschaften dann mittels CI-Methoden ermittelt werden können.

3 Algorithmus

Zur Untersuchung der strukturellen Steuerbarkeit von Systemen wurde oben das Lin-Hahn'sche Kriterium vorgestellt. Dabei wird das zu analysierende System mittels eines Graphen abstrahiert und anschließend in diesem Graphen nach der Kaktusstruktur gesucht. Für die erforderliche Suche wurde zunächst ein Suchalgorithmus implementiert, der jedoch nicht die gewünschte Performance in Bezug auf die Lösungsqualität liefert. Daher soll der bereits vorhandene Algorithmus, unter Verwendung von Methoden der Computational Intelligence, erweitert werden. In diesem Abschnitt wird kurz der aktuell implementierte Suchalgorithmus beschrieben, wobei seine Schwächen aufgezeigt werden. Anschließend wird die Erweiterung zu einem koevolutionären Algorithmus diskutiert und in groben Zügen dargestellt.

3.1 Suchalgorithmus

Für die Anwendung des Lin-Hahn'schen Kriteriums wurde ein Suchalgorithmus implementiert, welcher einen Graphen auf einen Kaktus hin untersucht. Hierzu muss ein Startpunkt gewählt werden, von dem aus die Kaktussuche im Graphen erfolgen soll. Ausgehend von diesem Punkt wird daraufhin nach Stamm- oder Knospenelementen gesucht, welche den bereits gebildeten Kaktus erweitern. Abbildung 3 zeigt das Flussdiagramm des Algorithmus.

Wird der Algorithmus auf das Beispiel aus Abbildung 1 angewandt, so findet er die gewünschte Kaktusstruktur, wie in Abbildung 2. Spaltet sich ein System jedoch in verschiedene Teilsysteme, welche untereinander gar nicht oder nicht ausstreichend miteinander verbunden sind, wie in Abbildung 4 dargestellt, so führt eine Suche, ausgehend von nur einem Startpunkt, zu keinem Ergebnis. Für eine allgemeine Suche ist es also erforderlich, von mehreren Startpunkten aus die Suche zu starten und somit die Suche nach einer Kaktushecke zu ermöglichen. Ein weiterer kritischer Punkt ist die Entscheidung über das Element, welches als nächstes hinzugefügt werden soll, sowie seine Größe. In Abbildung 5 hat der Suchalgorithmus verschieden Möglichkeiten, ein weiteres Element auszusuchen, wobei die Entscheidung für ein Element das weitere Vorgehen des Algorithmus beeinflusst und zu unterschiedlichen Lösungen führen kann.

Um die Bildung von Kaktushecken zu ermöglichen, ist es erforderlich, mehr als einen Startpunkt für eine Lösung vorzusehen. Bei einer weiteren Verwendung des Suchalgorithmus besteht daher die Möglichkeit, mehrere Suchagenten für die Lösungssuche einzusetzen. Hierfür müssen die Einzelnen Lösungen der Suchalgorithmen, die nun jeweils einen Suchagenten darstellen, zusammengefügt werden. Es muss also eine Plattform geschaffen werden, auf der die Teillösungen zusammengesetzt werden. Hierzu werden die Suchagenten, welche gemeinsam nach einer Lösung suchen, zu einer Population zusammengefasst. Das zweite Problem des Suchalgorithmus war die starre Entscheidungsfindung und die damit verbundenen Einschränkungen bei der Gestaltung der Lösung. In diesem Fall bietet die Gruppierung der Suchagenten in Populationen, die Möglichkeit, Methoden der evolutionären Algorithmen einzusetzen. Somit wird die Anpassung und Optimierung der Suchagenten, bzw. ihrer Parameter, zur Laufzeit erreicht. Den identifizierten Problemen kann also durch den Aufbau von Populationen von Suchagenten und der Verwendung von evolutionären Methoden entgegengewirkt werden, wobei das Suchergebnis durch Zusammenfügen der Teilergebnisse erstellt wird. Im Falle der Kaktus-

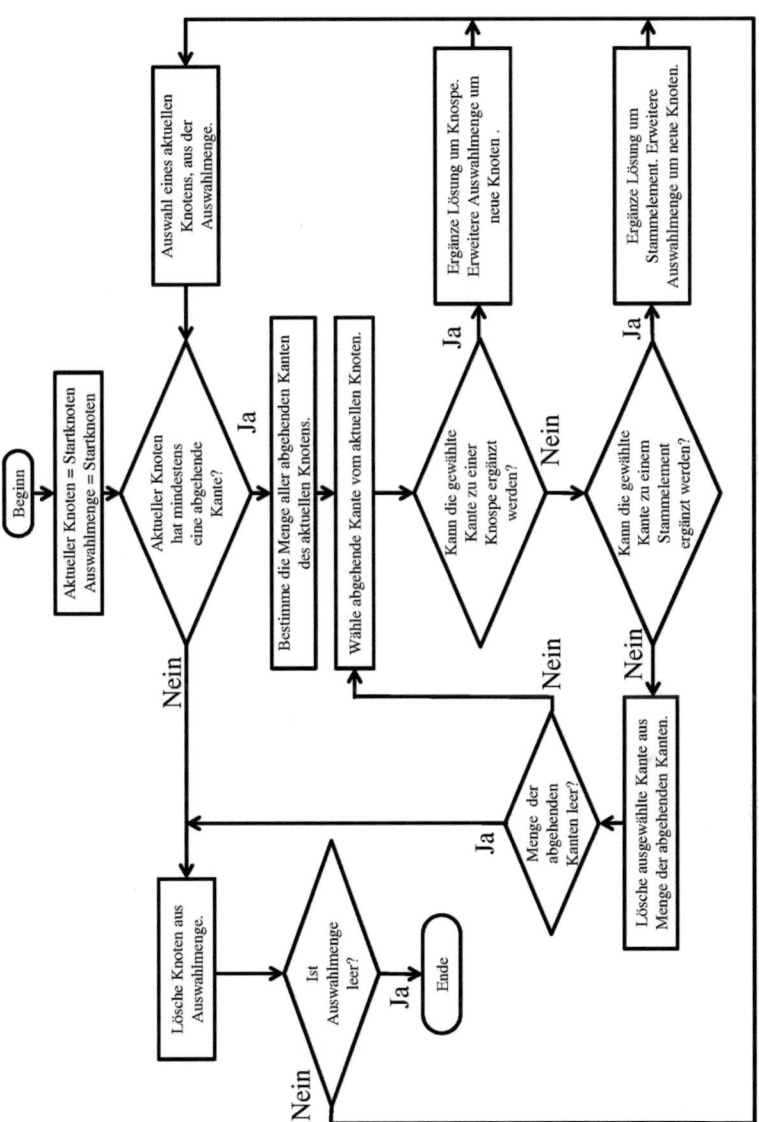

Bild 3: Flussdiagramm des Suchalgorithmus.

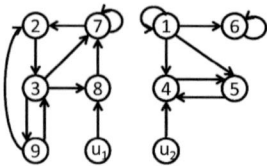

Bild 4: Geteiltes System, kann nicht mit einem Suchagenten gelöst werden.

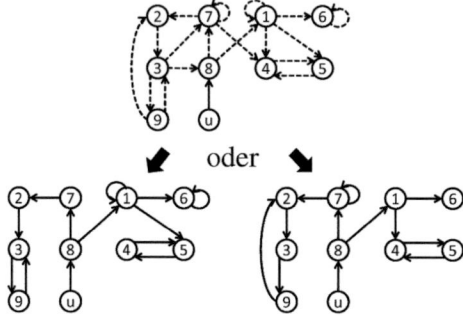

oder

Bild 5: Die Entscheidung, die Verbindung von 8 nach 1 bzw. von 8 nach 7, als Stammelement hinzuzunehmen, führt zu unterschiedlichen Ergebnissen.

suche ist es erforderlich, alle vorhandenen Knoten des Graphen in die Lösung zu integrieren. Da es bei der Lösungssuche einer einzelnen Population zu Situationen kommen kann, in denen eine vollständige Abdeckung des Graphen nicht mehr durch Hinzufügen von Elementen ermöglicht wird, muss die Möglichkeit zum Rückbauen von Lösungsteilen bestehen. Ein weiterer Weg ist jedoch auch die Verwendung mehrerer Populationen und somit das Erstellen unterschiedlich gearteter Lösungen. Wenn dann ein Austausch von Lösungsansätzen und Teillösungen zwischen den Populationen stattfindet, trägt dies wesentlich zum Auffinden einer Lösung bei, die alle Knoten des Graphen beinhaltet. Die nun aufgezählten Punkte für eine Verbesserung des Algorithmus lassen sich im Konzept der Koevolutionären Algorithmen vereinigen. Diese soll daher kurz vorgestellt werden.

3.2 Koevolutionäre Algorithmen

Evolutionäre Algorithmen verwenden, wie der Name schon sagt, Konzepte und Methoden der, aus der Biologie bekannten, Evolutionstheorie. Entsprechend dem biologischen Vorbild, bei dem eine Optimierung mittels Evolution stattfindet, wurde dieser Gedanke auf Algorithmen zur Lösung von Optimierungsaufgaben eingeführt. Die dabei verwendeten Konzepte sind die Mutation, Rekombination und Selektion, welche auf die Parameter des Optimierungsproblems angewandt werden. Die Parameter entwickeln sich somit evolutionär, wobei die Entstehung und Wahl neuer Parameter durch den Wert der zu optimierenden Zielfunktion beeinflusst werden. Die Koevolution ist nun eine Ergänzung der klassischen Evolution, bei der nur die Entwicklung einer Art betrachtet wird, hin zur Berücksichtigung der Einflüsse anderer Arten auf die evolutionäre Entwicklung.

Weite Verbreitung fand der Gedanke der Koevolution durch Ehrlich und Raven [18]. In ihrer Arbeit beschrieben sie mit Hilfe der Koevolution die gegenseitigen, wechselwirkenden Einflüsse zweier von einander abhängigen Arten auf ihre jeweilige evolutionäre Entwicklung. Als Beispiel führten sie die Wechselwirkung zwischen Schmetterlingen und Futterpflanzen an. In den folgenden Jahren wurde das Konzept der Koevolution in der Biologie weiter aufgegriffen, so zum Beispiel von Janzen [19], welcher die Koevolution als die evolutionären Änderungen von Merkmalen einer Art, durch die Merkmale einer anderen Art und umgekehrt definierte. Des weiteren hielt die Koevolution auch Einzug in andere Wissenschaftsbereiche, wie zum Beispiel die Sozial- und Wirtschaftswissenschaften. Dabei beschreibt die Koevolution die gegenseitige Beeinflussung der Entwicklung des Individuums bzw. der Gesellschaft oder, im Falle der Wirtschaftswissenschaften, die wechselseitigen Einflüsse von Unternehmen und Märkten aufeinander. Es liegt also nahe den Gedanken der Koevolution auch in die Technik zu übertragen. Anwendungen, welche die Koevolution als Ergänzung der klassischen evolutionären Algorithmen einführen, gibt es bereits. Dabei wird zwischen konkurrierender und kooperierender Koevolution unterschieden [20]. Bei den konkurrierenden Verfahren wird die Evolution einer Population durch den Vergleich der Fitness mit der einer anderen Population beeinflusst. Der klassische, evolutionäre Ansatz wird also dadurch ergänzt, dass die Selektions- und Mutationsoperationen nicht nur auf die Fitness der eigenen Population, sondern auch auf die der konkurrierenden Population zurückgreifen. Das Endergebnis des Algorithmus ist also dennoch nur die Lösung eines Individuums, die des fittesten. Dem hingegen bieten die Verfahren mit kooperierender Koevolution eine größere Bandbreite an Einflussmöglichkeiten. Bei diesem Verfahren sind die Populationen nicht zu anderen Populationen hin komplett abgegrenzt, wie bei den konkurrierenden, koevolutionären Algorithmen. Die Grenze kann eher als durchlässig angesehen werden, so dass es Agenten aus anderen Populationen erlaubt ist auf die Lösungen anderer Populationen zurückzugreifen. Potter und Jong [21] stellten zum Beispiel einen kooperierenden, koevolutionären Algorithmus vor, welcher das Endergebnis aus verschiedenen Teillösungen der einzelnen Individuen selektiert und somit am Ende eine weitere Verbesserung der Fitness erreicht.

Die vorgeschlagene Erweiterung des Suchalgorithmus kann in die Klasse der kooperierenden, koevolutionären Algorithmen eingeordnet werden, da die Populationen nicht miteinander um die optimale Lösung konkurrieren, sondern sich gegenseitig unterstützen, indem der Austausch von Lösungen ermöglicht wird. Die verwendeten Populationen stellen Parallelgesellschaften dar, welche sich zunächst unabhängig voneinander entwickeln und unabhängig voneinander nach einer Lösung suchen. Der Idee der Koevolution folgend, ist es den Agenten möglich, über die Populationsgrenze hinweg miteinander zu interagieren und Lösungen bzw. Lösungsansätze aus anderen Populationen zu übernehmen.

4 Zusammenfassung und Ausblick

Einführend wurde dargestellt, dass moderne Produktions- und Fertigungssysteme, sowie Infrastruktureinrichtungen, basierend auf ihrer Größe und den an sie gestellten Anforderungen als „komplexe Systeme" bezeichnet werden können. Dabei spielt das Zusammenwirken von Mensch und Maschine, sowie die lange Lebensdauer der Anlagen, eine wichtige Rolle. Ausgehend von dieser Feststellung ist die, für die Entwicklung von Automatisierungssystemen notwendige, Anlagenanalyse mit den herkömmlichen, in der Regelungstechnik verbreiteten Methoden, zunehmend aufwändiger. Dazu trägt wesentlich die Komplexität der Systeme bei, da diese sich nur schwierig mit Hilfe der bekannten Modellierungsmethoden darstellen lassen und die Systemeigenschaften ein neuartiges Verhalten aufweisen, wie z.b. Phasenübergänge. Ein Blick in andere Wissenschaftsbereiche wie z.b. in die Soziologie, Biologie oder Wirtschaftswissenschaften zeigen schnell, dass dort bereits seit längerem komplexe Systeme betrachtet werden. So beschäftigt sich zum Beispiel seit Mitte der 80er Jahre das Santa Fe Institut mit komplexen, adaptiven Systemen und ihren Anwendungen in verschiedensten Gebieten [22].

Eine Möglichkeit, welche in den genannten Bereichen bereits zur Analyse komplexer Systeme verwendet wird, sind die Methoden der Netzwerkanalyse auf Basis von Graphen. Auch in der Regelungstechnik gab es bereits Ansätze zur Analyse mit Hilfe von Graphen. So z.B. das Lin-Hahn'sche Kriterium zum Nachweis struktureller Steuerbarkeit einer Klasse nichtlinearer Systeme. Dies wurde im vorliegenden Beitrag zur Analyse großer komplexer Systeme aufgegriffen und verwendet. Zur Untersuchung auf strukturelle Steuerbarkeit, muss der Graph auf eine Kaktusstruktur hin durchsucht werden. Da ein einzelner Suchagent nicht die gewünschte Performance, sowie Lösungsqualität aufweist, wurde die Idee der Verwendung von CI Methoden vorgestellt. Genauer gesagt soll die Suche mit Hilfe eines koevolutionären Algorithmus erfolgen, bei dem die Suchagenten auch über Populationsgrenzen hinweg kooperieren und Teillösungen austauschen. Nach der Implementierung des koevolutionären Algorithmus sollen Graphennetze technischer Systeme auf ihre Eigenschaften untersucht werden, wobei die Untersuchung der Phasenübergänge im Vordergrund stehen soll.

Literatur

[1] Neugebauer, R.: Intelligente Produktion - innovative Zukunftssicherung. *Frauenhofer-Jahresbericht 2003* (2003).

[2] BMWi: Nernetzte Produktionsanlagen. In: *Innovationspolitik, Informationsgesellschaft, Telekommunikation* (Bundesministerium für Wirtschaft und Technologie, Hg.), Bd. 4. 2008.

[3] Lin, C.-T.: Structural controllability. *Automatic Control, IEEE Transactions on* 19 (1974) 3, S. 201 – 208.

[4] Reinschke, K.: *Multivariable control.* Lecture notes in control and information sciences. Springer Berlin [u.a.]. 1988.

[5] Svaricek, F.: A graph-theoretic approach for the determination of the structure at infinity of nonlinear systems. In: *Nonlinear Control System Design Symposium NOLCOS, Bordeaux, France.* 1992.

[6] Sommer, H.; Hahn, H.: Global structural approximate controllability of polynomial nonlinear systems. In: *Computer Aided Systems Theory - EUROCAST'97* (Pichler, F.; Moreno-Diaz, R., Hg.), Bd. 1333 von *Lecture Notes in Computer Science*, S. 170–176. Springer Berlin / Heidelberg. 1997.

[7] Sommer, H. J.; Hahn, H.: A New Approach to the Global Controllability of Nonlinear Sampled Data Systems. *RTS-Internal Report* (1998) 27.

[8] Deutsche Kommission Elektrotechnik Elektronik Informationstechnik im DIN und VDE: Internationales Elektrisches Wörterbuch - Teil 351: Leittechnik (DIN IEC 60050-351). 2006.

[9] Willems, J.: Paradigms and puzzles in the theory of dynamical systems. *Automatic Control, IEEE Transactions on* 36 (1991) 3, S. 259 –294.

[10] Parker, W. S.: Predicting weather and climate: Uncertainty, ensembles and probability. *Studies In History and Philosophy of Science Part B: Studies In History and Philosophy of Modern Physics* In Press, Corrected Proof (2010).

[11] Schwarz, H.: *Nichtlineare Regelungssysteme*. Oldenbourg München [u.a.]. 1991.

[12] Nijmeijer, H.; van der Schaft, A.: *Nonlinear dynamical control systems*. Springer New York [u.a.]. 1990.

[13] Khalil, H. K.: *Nonlinear systems*. Prentice Hall Upper Saddle River, NJ. 2002.

[14] Klemm, P.: Grundlagen der Prozessrechentechnik und Softwaretechnik. 2007.

[15] Biroli, G.; Monasson, R.; Weigt, M.: A variational description of the ground state structure in random satisfiability problems. *The European Physical Journal B - Condensed Matter and Complex Systems* 14 (2000), S. 551–568.

[16] Achlioptas, D.; Coja-Oghlan, A.: Algorithmic Barriers from Phase Transitions. *Foundations of Computer Science, Annual IEEE Symposium on* 0 (2008), S. 793–802.

[17] Zweig, K. A.; Palla, G.; Vicsek, T.: What makes a phase transition? Analysis of the random satisfiability problem. *Physica A: Statistical Mechanics and its Applications* 389 (2010) 8, S. 1501 – 1511.

[18] Ehrlich, P. R.; Raven, P. H.: Butterflies and Plants: A Study in Coevolution. *Evolution* 18 (1964) 4, S. 586–608.

[19] Janzen, D. H.: When is it coevolution. *Evolution* 34 (1980) 3, S. 611–612.

[20] Wiegand, R. P.; Liles, W. C.; Jong, K. A. D.: An empirical analysis of collaboration methods in cooperative coevolutionary algorithms. In: *Proceedings of theGenetic and Evolutionary Computation Conference (GECCO)* (Spector, L.; e. a., Hg.), S. 1–8. 2001.

[21] Potter, M.; De Jong, K.: A cooperative coevolutionary approach to function optimization. In: *Parallel Problem Solving from Nature - PPSN III* (Davidor, Y.; Schwefel, H.-P.; Männer, R., Hg.), Bd. 866 von *Lecture Notes in Computer Science*, S. 249–257. Springer Berlin / Heidelberg. 1994.

[22] Gell-Mann, M.: Complex adaptive systems (1999), S. 17–45.

LERNEN DURCH DEMONSTRATION UND KOLLISIONSVERMEIDUNG MIT DYNAMISCHEN BEWEGUNGSPRIMITIVEN

Anh Son Phung, Jörn Malzahn, Frank Hoffmann, Torsten Bertram

Lehrstuhl für Regelungssystemtechnik, Technische Universität Dortmund
Otto-Hahn-Str. 4, 44221 Dortmund
Tel.: (0231) 755-3592
Fax: (0231) 755-2752
E-Mail: anhson.phung@tu-dortmund.de

1 Einführung

Überall dort, wo häufig wiederkehrende und monotone Aufgaben bei gleichbleibender Präzision zu erledigen sind, haben heute Industrieroboter in die industrielle Fertigung Einzug gefunden. Die eingesetzten Roboter werden durch Roboterspezialisten mithilfe einer herstellerspezifischen Beschreibungssprache für ihre jeweilige Aufgabe programmiert. Dabei werden prozessspezifische Bahnparameter, wie Bahngeschwindigkeit und Orientierungen für jeden Punkt zwischen Start- und Zielpunkten jeder Bewegung im Programm abgestimmt. Geringe Variationen der Fertigungsaufgabe erfordern aufwändige Anpassungen des Roboterprogramms, wodurch der Einsatz von konventionell programmierten Industrierobotern erst in der Serienfertigung mit großen Losgrößen wirtschaftlich wird. Für Serviceroboter, die einem ungeschulten Benutzer in der sich ständig verändernden Umgebung des Menschen behilflich sein sollen, ist diese Programmierweise ungeeignet. Ein Beispiel aus der Servicerobotik stellt das Servieren einer gefüllten Kaffeetasse dar. Der Serviceroboter soll den heißen Kaffee schnell servieren, dabei aber keinen Kaffee verschütten. Während ein Mensch diese Aufgabe nach einer Lernphase mühelos unter verschiedenen Randbedingungen bewältigt, stellt die explizite Planung erforderlicher Beschleunigungsprofile für unterschiedliche Randbedingungen eine mühsame Aufgabe dar.

Eine Alternative zur expliziten textuellen Programmierung stellt die Programmierung des Roboters durch Demonstration dar. Drei Phasen sind diesbezüglich zu unterscheiden: Demonstrationsphase, die Lernphase und die Reproduktionsphase. In der Demonstrationsphase beobachtet der Roboter Aktionen und Bewegungen eines Instruktors. In der Lernphase werden Beobachtungen durch eine verallgemeinerte Darstellungsform approximiert. Diese Darstellungsform erlaubt allgemein neben der Adaption der demonstrierten Bewegung eine Reproduktion der gleichen oder einer im Kontext ähnlichen Bewegung in der Reproduktionsphase.

In [1] wird ein Konzept vorgestellt, welches das Erlernen und die Reproduktion einer demonstrierten Bewegung mithilfe nichtlinearer Differentialgleichungen ermöglicht. Durch die Generalisierungsfähigkeit des Ansatzes wird die abgefahrene Bahn bei Veränderung von Start- und Zielpunkt automatisch adaptiert. Der Eingriff eines Programmierers ist nicht erforderlich.

Für die Praxistauglichkeit eines Serviceroboters muss er in der Lage sein, über die rein erlernte Bewegung hinaus auf unvorhergesehene Ereignisse spontan zu reagieren. Beispielsweise muss der Roboter in der Lage sein Kollisionen mit plötzlich im Arbeitsraum auftauchenden Hindernissen zu vermeiden und dennoch die von ihm geforderte Aufgabe zu erfüllen.

Ein verbreitetes Werkzeug zur Kollisionsvermeidung in der Robotik sind Potenzialfelder. Das Grundprinzip wird in [2] vorgestellt. Darin stellt ein Hindernis die Quelle eines virtuellen räumlich beschränkten repulsiven Potenzialfelds dar. Der Roboterendeffektor wird durch einen Punkt innerhalb des Potenzialfeldes repräsentiert. Um sprunghafte Roboterbewegungen zu vermeiden wird das Grundprinzip in [3] durch die Berücksichtigung der Relativgeschwindigkeit zwischen Roboter und Hindernis zu dynamischen Potenzialfeldern erweitert.

Potenzielle Kollisionsgefahr besteht nicht allein zwischen dem Roboter-Endeffektor und seiner Umgebung, sondern auch zwischen den übrigen Roboterstrukturen und Hindernissen. In [4] wird für einen kinematisch redundanten Roboter anstelle des Endeffektors zu jedem Zeitschritt der Punkt der Armstruktur betrachtet, der dem Hindernis am nächsten ist. Die kinematische Redundanz erlaubt es, die Endeffektor-Bewegung fortzuführen, während für den zur Kollisionsvermeidung betrachteten Armpunkt eine Ausweichgeschwindigkeit und -richtung vorgegeben wird. Die Geschwindigkeitsvorgabe in [4] ähnelt dem Prinzip statischer Potenzialfelder. In diesem Beitrag wird der Ansatz über den hindernisnächsten Punkt in das Konzept der dynamischen Potenzialfelder in Kombination mit Dynamischen Bewegungsprimitiven integriert. Dabei werden Limitationen des klassischen Konzepts Dynamischer Bewegungsprimitve durch das Lernen einer zusätzlichen nichtlinearen Funktion überwunden. Die diesbezüglichen in diesem Beitrag vorgestellten Erweiterungen verbessern die Generalisierungsfähigkeit des Ansatzes für Bewegungen in niederdimensionalen Unterräumen und großen Variation des Bahnendpunkts.

Im Folgenden werden in Abschnitt 2 dynamische Bewegungsprimitive inklusive der in diesem Beitrag entwickelten Erweiterungen dargestellt. In Abschnitt 3 wird das dynamische Potenzialfeld zur Kollisionsvermeidung entwickelt. Die Hindernisdetektion unter Verwendung einer externen Kamera mit Photonen-Misch-Detektor (PMD-Kamera) wird in Abschnitt 4 vorgestellt. Ergebnisse sowohl aus Simulationen, als auch aus Experimenten werden in Abschnitt 5 gezeigt. Der Beitrag schließt mit einer Zusammenfassung und einem Ausblick auf Erweiterungen und mögliche Anwendungsfelder des vorgestellten neuen integrierten Konzepts.

2 Dynamische Bewegungsprimitive

2.1 Prinzip des dynamischen Bewegungsprimitivs

Das Prinzip des Dynamischen Bewegungsprimitivs (DP) wird in [1] eingeführt. Es erlaubt die Generierung diskreter oder rhytmischer Bewegungen über ein dynamisches System. Die folgende Differenzialgleichung stellt ein lineares System dar, dessen Zustandsgrößen x, v und $\dot{v}$ beispielsweise die Position, Geschwindigkeit und Beschleunigung für eine Bewegung von einem Startpunkt x_0 zu einem Endpunkt g sind:

$$\tau\dot{v} = K(g - x) - Dv, \tag{1}$$

$$\tau\dot{x} = v. \tag{2}$$

In diesem System beschreibt D den Dämpfungsfaktor, K die Federkonstante und τ eine Zeitskalierung des Systems. Die Parameter K und D sind so gewählt, dass das System aperiodisch gedämpft ist. Das System wird um eine nichtlineare Funktion $f_2(\theta)$ wie folgt erweitert:

$$\tau \dot{v} = K(g - x) - Dv + (g - x_0)f_2(\theta). \tag{3}$$

Die nichtlineare Erweiterung wirkt wie eine externe Kraft auf das System und dient zur Erzeugung komplexerer Trajektorien. Sie hat die Gestalt:

$$f(\theta) = \frac{\sum_{i=1}^{N} \omega_i \psi_i(\theta)\, \theta}{\sum_{i=1}^{N} \psi_i(\theta)}, \tag{4}$$

und ist keine Funktion der Zeit, sondern eine Funktion der Phasenvariablen θ. Als Kernfunktionen werden phasenabhängige Gaußfunktionen $\psi_i(\theta) = e^{-h_i(\theta - c_i)^2}$ mit Zentren c_i und der Breite h_i verwendet. Alle N Kernfunktionen werden mit den Faktoren w_i gewichtet überlagert. Die Phasevariable θ und damit auch $f_2(\theta)$ stehen über den Zusammenhang:

$$\tau_k \dot{\theta} = -\alpha\theta \tag{5}$$

mit der Zeitskalierung τ_k in Beziehung. Das System (5) wird kanonisches System genannt. Über eine Anpassung von τ_k wird die zeitliche Einwirkung von $f_2(\theta)$ beeinflusst.

Die Gleichungen (1) bis (5) bilden zusammen ein dynamisches Bewegungsprimitiv. Ein solches Dynamisches Bewegungsprimitiv hat folgende Eigenschaften:

- Konvergenz von x zum Zielpunkt g ist garantiert, da das System (1) asymptotisch stabil ist und die Funktion f_2 mit begrenzten Gewichtungsfaktoren w_i mit dem Zeitverhalten in Abhängigkeit von τ_k zu Null konvergiert.

- Die Adaption der Gewichtungsfaktoren w_i ermöglicht, beliebige Trajektorien von x zu generieren.

- Die Gestalt der Trajektorie kann im Phasenraum unabhängig vom Zeitverhalten und den Arbeitsraumabmessungen trainiert werden. Die Anpassung der Trajektorie an das geforderte Zeitverhalten und den Arbeitsraum erfolgt über die Zeitkonstanten t und τ_k, sowie die Lage des Zielpunktes g.

Um eine demonstrierte Bewegung zu erlernen werden die Positionen, die Geschwindigkeiten und die Beschleunigungen (x_{demo}, v_{demo} und a_{demo}) der Demonstration aufgezeichnet. Aus diesen Daten wird die Zielfunktion:

$$f_{demo} = \frac{\tau a_{demo} - K(g - x_{demo}) + Dv_{demo}}{g - x_0} \tag{6}$$

gebildet. Diese Funktion wird durch Minimierung des quadratischen Fehlers:

$$\varepsilon = (f_2 - f_{demo})^2 \tag{7}$$

in Abhängigkeit der Parameter c_i, h_i und w_i aus Gleichung (4) gelernt.

Zur Vereinfachung des Minimierungsproblems, werden die Zentren der Kernfunktionen des Dynamischen Bewegungsprimitivs äquidistant im ganzen Zeitbereich von 0 bis τ verteilt. Die Breite der Kernfunktionen beträgt zwei drittel des Abstands zwischen den Zentren benachbarter Kernfunktionen. Unter diesen Voraussetzungen geht die Aufgabenstellung in ein lineares Minimierungsproblem über. Es wird durch einen Gradientenabstieg gelöst.

Anzahl der Kernfunktionen	20	25	30	35
Fehler (%) in X Richtung	0,18	0,11	0,05	0,02
Fehler (%) in Y Richtung	1,33	0,85	0,46	0,21
Fehler (%) in Z Richtung	1,99	1,31	0,35	0,23

Tabelle 1: Zusammenhang zwischen quadratischem Fehler und der Anzahl der Kernfunktionen

Die Anzahl der Kernfunktionen beeinflusst die Größe des Residuums zwischen demonstrierter und gelernter Zielfunktion f_{demo}. Tabelle 2 zeigt den prozentualen quadratischen Fehler. Es wird deutlich, dass der residuale Fehler mit der Anzahl der verwendeten Kernfunktionen sinkt, während der Rechenaufwand zur Laufzeit steigt. In diesem Beitrag wird als Kompromiss jedes dynamische Bewegungsprimitiv mit dreißig Kernfunktionen trainiert wird. Der Fehler liegt somit unter 0,5% und der Rechenaufwand ist mit dem verwendeten Rechnersystem noch vertretbar.

2.2 Erweiterung des Dynamischen Bewegungsprimitivs

Eine Einschränkung für das Erlernen eines durch die Gleichungen (1) bis (5) dargestellten Dynamischen Bewegungsprimitivs stellt das Verschwinden des nichtlinearen Anteils f_2 dar, wenn Startpunkt x_0 und Zielpunkt g nahe beieinander liegen. Dies hat im Wesentlichen zwei Effekte:

- Wenn die Bewegung der Reproduktionsphase nahezu oder vollständig in einem niederdimensionalen Unterraum des ursprünglichen Arbeitsraums stattfindet, kann die erlernte Trajektorie nicht realisiert werden.

- Wenn in der Demonstrationsphase zwischen Start- und Zielpunkt nur eine kurze Strecke liegt, dann treten große Beschleunigungen auf, wenn der Zielpunkt in der Reproduktionsphase stark verändert wird. Wie Gleichung (3) zu entnehmen ist, verschwindet für große Differenzen $g - x_0$ der Einfluss des Dämpfungsterms Dv. Der Effekt ist im Bild 1 (links) veranschaulicht. Eine kleine Variation des Zielpunktes führt zu einem hinsichtlich Krümmung und Weglänge stark unterschiedlichen Bahnverlauf zwischen demonstrierter und reproduzierter Bahn.

In diesem Beitrag wird ein neuartiger Ansatz vorgestellt, der die genannten Limitationen überwindet. Die Grundlage bildet die Erweiterung von Gleichung (3) um einen weiteren nichtlinearen Term f_1 Das Dynamische Bewegungsprimitiv verfügt damit über zwei überlagerte und unabhängig voneinander lernbare nichtlineare Anteile:

$$\tau\dot{v} = K(g - x) - Dv + Kf_1(\theta) + (g - x_0)f_2(\theta), \qquad (8)$$

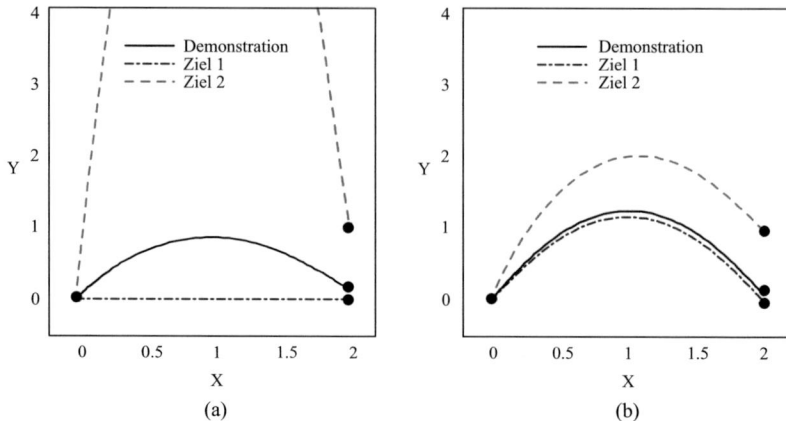

Bild 1: Vergleich der Zielanpassung zwischen originalen (links) und modifizierten (rechts) System

$$\tau \dot{x} = v. \tag{9}$$

Aus der Struktur von Gleichung (8) wird ersichtlich, dass im Fall $g \approx x_0$ lediglich der Anteil f_1 wirksam ist. Wird die Differenz $g - x_0$ groß, so überwiegt der Anteil mit f_2. Beide nichtlinearen Anteile werden unabhängig voneinander gelernt, indem die Demonstrations- und Lernphase entsprechend der beiden Fälle in zwei Schritten durchgeführt werden. Im ersten Schritt wird für die Demonstration $g_1 \approx x_0$ gefordert. Anhand der so erhaltenen Lerndaten wird die Funktion f_1 bestimmt:

$$f_{1demo} = \frac{\tau a_{1demo} + D v_{1demo}}{K} - (g_1 - x_{1demo}). \tag{10}$$

Im zweiten Schritt wird der Fall $g_2 \neq x_0$ demonstriert um f_2:

$$f_{2demo} = \frac{\tau a_{2demo} + D v_{2demo} - K (g_2 - x_{2demo}) - K f_1}{g_2 - x_0}. \tag{11}$$

Im zweiten Schritt sind die Parameter der Funktion f_1 konstant und über f_2 erfolgt die Anpassung an variable Zielpunkte. Wie Bild 1 (rechts) veranschaulicht, erlaubt die Überlagerung der beiden Funktionen die Generalisierung der demonstrierten Bewegung auf zuvor nicht demonstrierte Zielpunkte, ohne die Gestalt der Trajektorie hinsichtlich Krümmung zu verletzen.

3 Potenzialfeldbasierte Kollisionsvermeidung.

3.1 Dynamisches Potentialfeld zur Kollisionsvermeidung am Endeffektor.

Das Grundprinzip der Kollisionsvermeidung für Roboter über Potenzialfelder wird in [2] vorgestellt. Darin stellt ein Hindernis die Quelle eines virtuellen räumlich beschränkten repulsiven Potenzialfelds $U(\mathbf{x})$ dar. Der Roboter wird durch einen Punkt innerhalb des

Potenzialfeldes repräsentiert. Zunächst entspreche dieser Punkt dem Zentrum des Endeffektors. Um sprunghafte Roboterbewegungen zu vermeiden wird das Grundprinzip in [3] durch die Berücksichtigung der Relativgeschwindigkeit zwischen Roboter und Hindernis zu dynamischen Potenzialfeldern erweitert. In dieser Arbeit wird darauf aufbauend das dynamische Potenzialfeld:

$$\mathbf{U}_{dyn}\left(\mathbf{x}, \mathbf{v}\right) = \begin{cases} \lambda\left(-\cos\alpha\right)^{\beta} \frac{\|\mathbf{v}\|}{d(\mathbf{x})} & wenn \quad 0 < |\alpha| < \pi/2 \\ 0 & wenn \quad \pi/2 \leq |\alpha| \leq \pi \end{cases} \tag{12}$$

verwendet. Das Potenzial eines Punktes im Raum ist durch den positiven Verstärkungsfaktor λ, dem positiven exponentiellen Gewicht β, der Relativgeschwindigkeit $\mathbf{v}$ und dem Ortsvektor $\mathbf{x}$ vom Roboter zum Hindernis definiert. Der Winkel α zwischen Relativgeschwindigkeit und Ortsvektor ergibt sich gemäß:

$$\alpha = \arccos\left(\frac{\mathbf{v}^T\mathbf{x}}{\|\mathbf{v}\| d(\mathbf{x})}\right). \tag{13}$$

Taucht der Roboter in das Potenzialfeld ein, so wirkt auf ihn die virtuelle externe Kraft F($\mathbf{x}$), deren Betrag und Richtung für $0 < |\alpha| < \pi/2$ durch den Gradienten $\varphi(\mathbf{x}, \mathbf{v})$ bestimmt ist:

$$\varphi\left(\mathbf{x}, \mathbf{v}\right) = \lambda\left(-\cos\alpha\right)^{\beta-1}\left(\frac{\beta}{d} grad\left(\cos\alpha\right) - \frac{\cos\alpha}{d^2} grad\left(d\left(\mathbf{x}\right)\right)\right). \tag{14}$$

Bild 2 zeigt ein Beispiel vom dynamischen Potentialfeld. Im Vergleich zum statischen

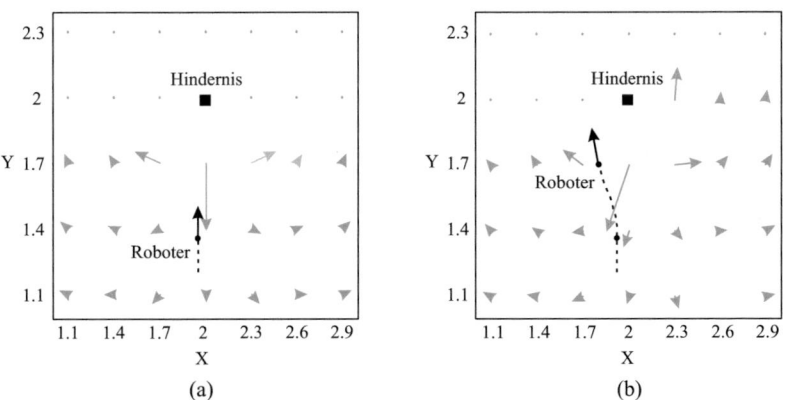

Bild 2: Dynamisches Potentialfeld

Potentialfeld, indem die Gradienten des Potentialfeldes in Umgebung unverändert sind, ändern sich die Gradienten des dynamischen Potentialfeld stets in Abhängigkeit von der relativen Bewegung zwischen dem Roboter und dem Hindernis. Bild (b) zeigt ein anderes Potentialfeld im Vergleich zum Bild (a).

Zusammenfassend charakterisieren folgende Eigenschaften das dynamische Potentialfeld:

- Das Potenzial eines Punktes im Feld verhält sich antiproportional zum Abstand vom erzeugenden Hindernis.

- Das Potenzial in einem Punkt ist am größten, wenn Ortsvektor $\mathbf{x}$ und Geschwindigkeitsvektor $\mathbf{v}$ in diesem Punkt parallel sind und verschwindet, wenn sich Roboter und Hindernis voneinander entfernen.

- Das Potential in allen Punkten verschwindet, wenn die Relativgeschwindigkeit zwischen Roboter und Hindernis zu null wird.

3.2 Erweiterte Kollisionsvermeidung in Gegenwart redundanter Kinematik.

Potenzielle Kollisionsgefahr besteht nicht allein zwischen dem Roboter-Endeffektor und seiner Umgebung, sondern auch zwischen den übrigen Roboterstrukturen und Hindernissen. In [4] wird für einen kinematisch redundanten Roboter anstelle des Endeffektors zu jedem Zeitschritt der Punkt der Armstruktur betrachtet, der dem Hindernis am nächsten ist. Die kinematische Redundanz erlaubt es, die Endeffektor-Bewegung fortzuführen, während für den zur Kollisionsvermeidung betrachteten Armpunkt eine Ausweichgeschwindigkeit und -richtung vorgegeben wird.

Bild 3 veranschaulicht dies für zwei unterschiedliche Konfigurationen des Roboterarms mit gleicher kartesischer Endeffektorposition. Ohne Betrachtung der Endeffektororientierung sind beide Konfigurationen äquivalent. Der minimale Abstand zwischen dem Hindernis und dem Arm in der hell dargestellten Konfiguration (1) ist kleiner als der minimale Abstand zwischen dem Hindernis und der dunkel dargestellten Konfiguration (2).

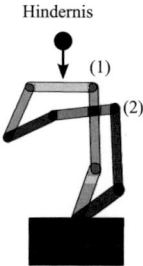

Bild 3: Verschiedenen Konfiguration eines redundanten Manipulators für gleiche End-Position

Dieses Vorgehen ähnelt dem Prinzip statischer Potenzialfelder. In diesem Beitrag wird der Ansatz über den hindernisnächsten Punkt in das Konzept der dynamischen Potenzialfelder in Kombination mit Dynamischen Bewegungsprimitiven integriert.

Die Trajektorienplanung findet im kartesischen Raum statt. Die im Bild 4 dargestellte Folgeregelung wird im Achsraum gemäß [5] über die Endeffektorjakobimatrix $\mathbf{J}$ für den Fall kinematischer Redundanz realisiert. Das Reglergesetz lautet:

$$\dot{\mathbf{q}} = \mathbf{J}^{\dagger}\left(\dot{\mathbf{x}} + K\mathbf{e}\right) + \left(\mathbf{I} - \mathbf{J}^{\dagger}\mathbf{J}\right)\dot{\mathbf{q}}_0, \tag{15}$$

wobei $\mathbf{e}$ den kartesischen Bahnfehler des Endeffektors, $\mathbf{I}$ die Einheitsmatrix und $\mathbf{J}^{\dagger}$ die rechte Pseudoinverse von $\mathbf{J}$ bezeichnet. Der Anteil $\left(\mathbf{I} - \mathbf{J}^{\dagger}\mathbf{J}\right)\dot{\mathbf{q}}_0$ dient der Ausnutzung

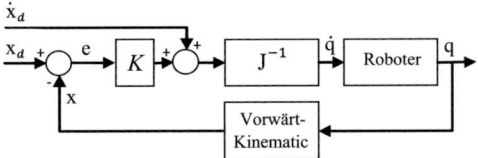

Bild 4: Blockschaltbild einer Rückwärtstransformationen mittels inverser Jakobi-Matrix

der kinematischen Redundanz durch Vorgabe der sogenannten Nullraumbewegung über zusätzliche Achsgeschwindigkeiten $\dot{q}_0$. Über die Auswertung des dynamischen Potenzialfelds U_{dyn} wird für den hindernisnächsten Punkt an der Stelle x_0 eine kartesische Geschwindigkeit $\dot{x}_0$:

$$\dot{x}_0 = -grad\left(U_{dyn}\left(x_0, v_0\right)\right) \tag{16}$$

vorgegeben. Über die Jakobimatrix J_0 für diesen Punkt lässt sich diese kartesische Geschwindigkeit in den Achsraum abbilden:

$$\dot{q} = J^\dagger\left(\dot{x} + Ke\right). \tag{17}$$

Diese Beziehung in Gleichung (15) eingesetzt ergibt:

$$\dot{x}_0 = J_0 J^\dagger\left(\dot{x} + Ke\right) + J_0\left(I - J^\dagger J\right)\dot{q}_0. \tag{18}$$

Daraus folgt:

$$\dot{q}_0 = \left(J_0\left(I - J^\dagger J\right)\right)^\dagger\left(\dot{x}_0 - J_0 J^\dagger\left(\dot{x} + Ke\right)\right), \tag{19}$$

und nach erneuter Betrachtung von Gleichung (15):

$$\dot{q} = J^\dagger\left(\dot{x} + Ke\right) + \left(I - J^\dagger J\right)\left(J_0\left(I - J^\dagger J\right)\right)^\dagger\left(\dot{x}_0 - J_0 J^\dagger\left(\dot{x} + Ke\right)\right). \tag{20}$$

4 PMD-basierte Hindernisdetektion

In dieser Arbeit wird eine extern aufgestellte Kamera mit einem sogenannten Photonen-Misch-Detektor (PMD) zur Hindernisdetektion verwendet. Die PMD-Kamera liefert zusätzlich zum konventionellen 2D-Bild für jedes Pixel die Abstandsinformation auf Basis von Laufzeitmessungen ausgesendeten Lichts. Diese Tiefeninformation wird zur Rauschunterdrückung tiefpassgefiltert und mit der 2D-Information zu einem 3D-Bild der Szene fusioniert. Es folgt eine Segmentierung der Datenpunkte in Roboter- und Hindernisregionen. Hierzu wird der "Region Growing"-Algorithmus verwendet. Der Algorithmus segmentiert indem er ausgehend von zuvor definierten Startpunkten Bildregionen auf Basis eines Ähnlichkeitsmaßes zusammenfasst. Das Ähnlichkeitsmaß beruht in diesem Fall auf der Änderung der Szenentiefe benachbarter Pixel. Zwei benachbarte Pixel sind ähnlich und werden zusammengefasst, wenn sich Änderung der zugehörigen Tiefenwerte unterhalb eines Schwellwerts befindet. Als Startpunkte zur Segmentierung des Arms vom übrigen Bildinhalt dienen die über die Vorwärtskinematik bestimmbaren Gelenkpositionen. Alle verbliebenen Datenpunkte, die nicht zum Roboterarm zugeordnet werden können, werden von diesem als Hindernis segmentiert. Durch Berücksichtigung aller Gelenkpunkte wird auch ein Hindernis detektiert, dass sich vor dem Roboter befindet und diesen aus der Perspektive der Kamera in zwei Bildsegmente unterteilt.

Bild 5 zeigt schrittweise das Ergebnis einer Segmentierung. In (a) wird ein von der PMD-Kamera aufgenommenes rohes Tiefenprofil der Szene dargestellt, während in (b) das 3D-Bild aus der Fusion der 2D- mit Tiefeninformationen anstelle der Intensität eines dargestellt ist. Bild (c) zeigt die drei Hauptsegmente: Hintergrund (Weiß), Roboterarm (Hellgrau) und Hindernisse (Dunkelgrau). Über die mittlere Entfernung aller Punkte eines Segments lässt sich das Hintergrundsegment identifizieren. Nach Verwerfen des Hintergrundsegments und des Robotersegments verbleiben in (d) nur noch Datenpunkte, die Hindernisse darstellen. Die Datenpunkte bestehen aus den Sensorkoordinaten x_n und y_n,

(a)   (b)   (c)   (d)

Bild 5: Hinderniserkennung aus einem 3D-Tiefenbild.

sowie der Abstandsinformation r. Die Sensorkoordinaten ergeben sich aus den Koordinaten $[X, Y, Z]^T$ des zugehörigen Weltpunkts im Kamerakoordinatensystem durch die perspektivische Abbildung:

$$x_n = \alpha_x \frac{X}{Z} + o_x, \tag{21}$$

$$y_n = \alpha_y \frac{Y}{Z} + o_y. \tag{22}$$

Darin sind α_x, α_y, o_x, o_y die intrinsischen Kameraparameter. Sie werden ebenso, wie die Koeffizienten zur Beseitigung der radialen Verzerrung durch eine klassische Kamerakalibrierung [6] bestimmt.

Die Abstandsinformation entsteht aus den Koordinaten des Weltpunkts gemäß:

$$r = \sqrt{X^2 + Y^2 + Z^2}. \tag{23}$$

Für die im vorangegangenen Abschnitt dargestellte Kollisionsvermeidung werden die Weltkoordinaten der Hindernispunkte aus den Datenpunkten bestimmt, indem Gleichung (21) und (22) nach X beziehungsweise Y umgeformt und in Gleichung (23) eingesetzt werden:

$$Z = \frac{r}{\sqrt{\left(\frac{x_n - o_x}{\alpha_x}\right)^2 + \left(\frac{y_n - o_y}{\alpha_y}\right)^2 + 1}}, \tag{24}$$

$$X = \frac{x_n - o_x}{\alpha_x} Z, \tag{25}$$

$$Y = \frac{y_n - o_y}{\alpha_y} Z. \tag{26}$$

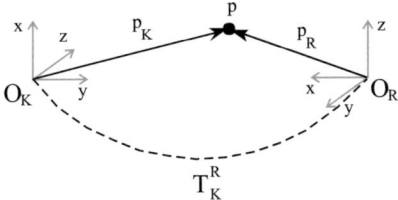

Bild 6: Transformation zwischen zwei Koordinatensystemen

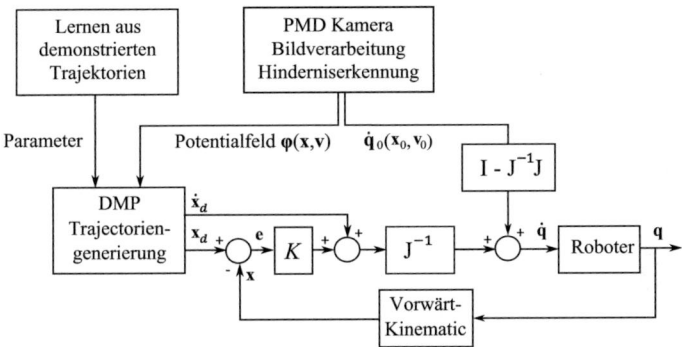

Bild 7: Reglerarchitektur

Die so erhaltene Beschreibung der Hindernisposition im Kamerakoordinatensystem wird über eine homogene Transformation in eine Beschreibung der Hindernisposition im Basiskoordinatensystem des Roboters überführt. Bild 6 verdeutlicht die Geometrie der Anordnung für einen beispielhaften Weltpunkt $\mathbf{p}$ der im Kamerakoordinatensystem $\mathbf{O}_K$ durch den Vektor $\mathbf{p}_K$ und im Basiskoordinatensystem $\mathbf{O}_R$ des Roboters durch den Vektor $\mathbf{p}_R$ dargestellt wird. Die Translation und die Rotation zwischen beiden Koordinatensystemen beschreibt die Transformation $\mathbf{T}_K^R$, sodass beide Vektoren durch:

$$\mathbf{p}_R = \mathbf{T}_K^R \, \mathbf{p}_K \tag{27}$$

ineinander überführt werden. Die Transformation wird zuvor aus Kalibrierbewegungen bestimmt.

5 Ergebnisse

5.1 Simulationsergebnisse

Bild 7 beinhaltet die Reglerarchitektur bestehend aus erweitertem Dynamischem Bewegungsprimitiv zur Bahngenerierung, Bildverarbeitung zur Hindernisdetektion und der Bahnregelung. Die Simulation erfolgt in Matlab/Simulink. Es wird die in Bild 8 in hellgrau dargestellte Trajektorie vorgegeben. Entlang der Vorgabe wird ein Hindernis platziert, das durch einen schwarzen Kasten repräsentiert wird. Die gestrichelte Linie verdeutlicht, wie die gefahrene Bahn ohne Kollisionsvermeidung durch das Hindernis hindurch verläuft. Das durch die Pfeile angedeutete dynamische Potenzialfeld führt den Endeffektor, wie in schwarz dargestellt, um das Hindernis herum, sodass die Kollision erfolgreich vermieden wird.

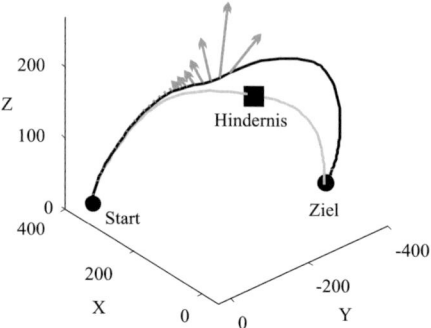

Bild 8: Kollisionsvermeidung mithilfe des Potentialfeldes.

Bild 9 zeigt das Ergebnis einer Simulation für die erweiterte Kollisionsvermeidung am gesamten Roboterarm. Im dargestellten Szenario passiert der Roboterarm dicht ein Hindernis. In der Praxis würde dies eine hohe Kollisionsgefahr im Fall einer unvorhergesehenen Bewegung des Hindernisses bedeuten. Im Bild (a) stellt die hellgraue Linie die Bewegung des hindernisnächsten Armpunkts dar. Die schwarze Linie zeigt die Trajektorie des hindernisnächsten Punkts bei aktivierter Kollisionsvermeidung über das dynamische Potenzialfeld. Die gestrichelten Linien stellen die Endeffektor-Trajektorie für die beiden Fälle dar. Es wird in Bild (b) deutlich, dass der Abstand des hindernisnächsten Punkts erhöht wird, wobei zugleich die Endeffektor-Trajektorie unverändert bleibt. In der Praxis bedeutet dies eine verminderte Kollisionsgefahr bei sonst unveränderter Ausführung der Aufgabe.

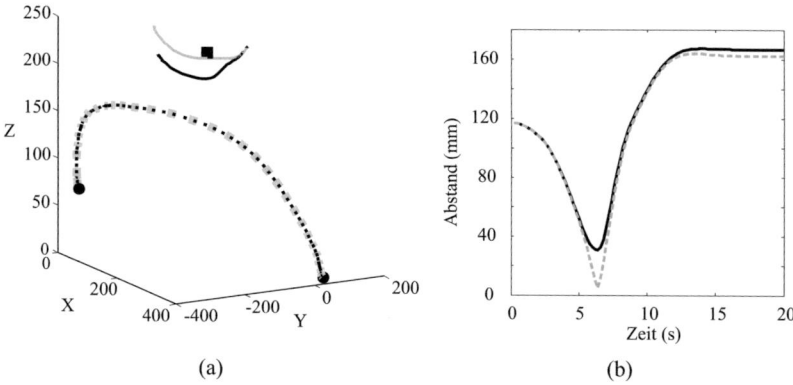

(a)   (b)

Bild 9: Kollisionsfrei für Manipulator.

5.2 Experimentelle Ergebnisse

Als Experimentalsystem dient ein fünfachsiger Roboterarm mit den nominellen DH-Parametern aus Tabelle 2. Es werden ausschließlich die Translationsfreiheitsgrade des Endeffektors berücksichtigt. Das letzte Gelenk des Experimentalsystems beeinflusst lediglich die Orientierung des Endeffektors. Bezüglich der Endeffektorposition besitzt das Experimentalsystem also einen redundanten Freiheitsgrad. In der Demonstrationsphase

i	θ(rad)	d(mm)	a(mm)	α(rad)
1	0	0	0	$\pi/2$
2	0	0	190	0
3	0	0	138	0
4	$\pi/2$	0	0	$\pi/2$
5	0	287,9	0	0

Tabelle 2: DH Parameter des Experimentalsystems

wird der Roboter von einem Instruktor per Hand geführt, wobei sich die Motoren in stromlosen Zustand befinden. Die Winkelverläufe aller Achsen werden aufgenommen und daraus die Trajektorie des Endeffektors aus der Vorwärtskinematik bestimmt. Für die drei Freiheitsgrade dieser Trajektorie wird jeweils ein Dynamisches Bewegungsprimitiv trainiert.

Bild 10 zeigt das Ergebnis der Experimente am realen Roboterarm. Der Roboterarm reproduziert die hellgrau dargestellte Demonstrierte Bahn. Das von der PMD-Kamera detektierte Hindernis wird, wie in schwarz eingezeichnet, zuverlässig umfahren. Anschließend wird der Zielpunkt entsprechend dem Fall ohne Hindernis erreicht. Ein Vergleich der tatsächlich gefahrenen Trajektorie (hellgrau gestrichelt) zur Beispieltrajektorie (hellgrau) zeigt Abweichungen auf. Diese Abweichungen werden auf eingeschränkte Präzision der Aktuatoren, sowie die hohe Abtastzeit bei der Übertragung der Bewegungsbefehle zurückgeführt. Bild 11 zeigt Einzelbilder aus dem Video eines Experiments, bei dem der Roboterarm über ein Hindernis hinwegfährt. Die oberen Bilder zeigen eine Bewegung des Roboterarms ohne Kollisionsvermeidung. Es kommt zur Kollision des Roboters mit dem Hindernis in Form eines Tischtennisballs (mittleres Bild). Die untere Bildreihe zeigt das gleiche Experiment mit aktivierter Kollisionsvermeidung, wobei deutlich sichtbar ein Abstand zum Hindernis eingehalten wird.

6 Zusammenfassung und Ausblick

Dieser Beitrag präsentiert ein neues Verfahren zur Roboterprogrammierung durch Demonstration, das in der Lage ist, die gelernte Bewegung auf neue Zielpunkte zu übertragen. Der Ansatz erlaubt überdies durch Ausweichen Kollisionen mit unvorhergesehenen Hindernissen zu vermeiden. Kern des Beitrages ist die Erweiterung des Prinzips dynamischer Bewegungsprimitive um eine zusätzliche nichtlineare lernbare Funktion zur Verbesserung der Generalisierungsfähigkeit des ursprünglichen Ansatzes. Die verbesserte Generalisierungsfähigkeit betrifft besonders jene Szenarien, in denen die Wegstrecke entlang unterschiedlicher Dimensionen stark variiert. Das erweiterte Konzept wird mit einem

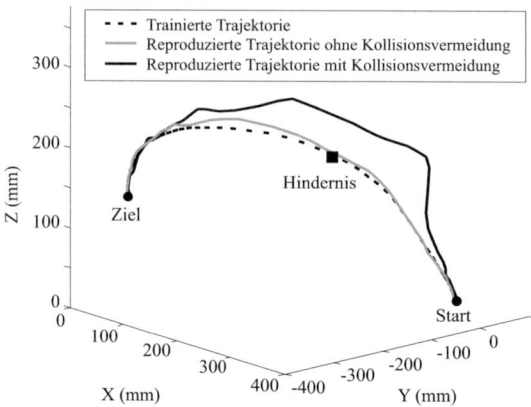

Bild 10: Kollisionsvermeidung für Endeffektor eines fünfachsigen Roboterarms

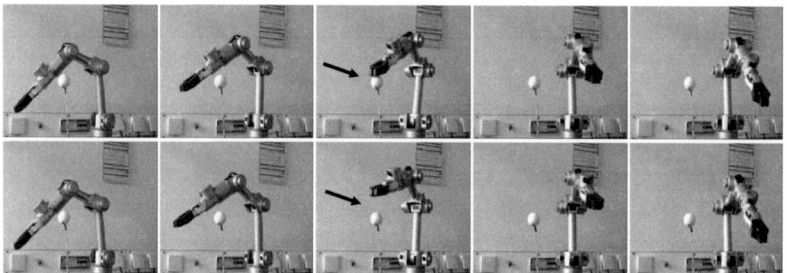

Bild 11: Kollisionsvermeidung mit einem fünfachsigen Roboterarm

dynamischen Potenzialfeld zur Vermeidung von Kollisionen des Roboterendeffektors mit unvorhergesehenen Hindernissen kombiniert. Diese Strategie wird darüber hinaus über die Bestimmung des Hindernisnächsten Armpunktes auf den ganzen Roboterarm ausgeweitet. Das in diesem Beitrag entwickelte Verfahren erlaubt für redundante Roboterkinematiken Kollisionen zu vermeiden, ohne von der zuvor demonstrierten Positionieraufgabe für den Endeffektor abzuweichen. Simulationen mit unterschiedlichen Konfigurationen, Start- und Zielpunkten sowie Hindernissen zeigen die Zuverlässigkeit des Systems. Abschließend erfolgt eine experimentelle Evaluierung des Konzepts an einem fünfachsigen Roboterarm. Die Bewegung wird händisch durch einen Instruktor demonstriert. Die Detektion des Hindernisses erfolgt über eine externe PMD-Kamera. Die Konzentration auf die translatorischen Freiheitsgrade des Endeffektors ermöglicht die experimentelle Erprobung auch für den kinematisch redundanten Fall. Die Experimente mit unterschiedlichen Positionen und Armkonfigurationen zeigen Abweichungen zwischen demonstrierten und reproduzierten Bewegungen auf. Diese werden durch technische Eigenschaften des Experimentalsystems erklärt und liegen nicht im vorgestellten Verfahren begründet. Die Experimente belegen die Anwendbarkeit des Verfahrens zur kollisionsfreien Reproduktion und Adaption zuvor durch Demonstration programmierter Bewegungen. Es handelt sich um ein viel versprechendes Verfahren für den Einsatz in der Servicerobotik in dem sich ständig verändernden Umfeld des Menschen.

Bislang werden Hindernisse beliebiger Form und Ausdehnung nur durch einen zentralen Punkt repräsentiert. Der Abstand zwischen Roboterarm und Hindernis wird durch Koordinatentransformationen berechnet. Prinzipiell erlaubt die eingesetzte PMD-Kamera die direkte Messung des Abstands, sodass der Punkt größter Kollisionsgefahr unmittelbar aus der Messung identifiziert werden kann. Auf diese Weise wird zur Kollisionsvermeidung kein explizites Objektmodell benötigt und das Verfahren wird universeller einsetzbar. Zukünftige Arbeiten befassen sich vor diesem Hintergrund mit der Generalisierung des Potenzialfeldansatzes auf Punktewolken.

Literatur

[1] Schaal, S.; Mohajerian, P.; Ijspeert, A.: Dynamics systems vs. optimal control a unifying view. *Progress in Brain Research* 165 (2007), S. 425–445.

[2] Krogh, B.: A generalized potential field approach to obstacle avoidance control. *International Journal of Robotic Research* (1984), S. 155–186.

[3] Park, D. H.; Hoffmann, H.; Pastor, P.; Schaal, S.: Movement reproduction and obstacle avoidance with dynamic movement primitives and potential fields. In: *IEEE international conference on humanoid robots, 2008.*. 2008.

[4] Maciejewski, A. A.; Klein, C. A.: Obstacle Avoidance for Kinematically Redundant Manipulators in Dynamically Varying Environments. *International Journal of Robotic Research* 4 (1985), S. 109–117.

[5] Sciavicco, L.; Siciliano, B.: *Modelling and Control of Robot Manipulators (Advanced Textbooks in Control and Signal Processing)*. Advanced textbooks in control and signal processing. Springer, 2nd Aufl. ISBN 1852332212. 2005.

[6] Zhang, Z.: Flexible Camera Calibration by Viewing a Plane from Unknown Orientations. *Computer Vision, IEEE International Conference on* 1 (1999), S. 666.

SPOT: A Toolbox for Interactive and Automatic Tuning in the R Environment

Thomas Bartz-Beielstein, Oliver Flasch, Patrick Koch, and Wolfgang Konen

Fakultät für Informatik und Ingenieurwissenschaften, Fachhochschule Köln
E-Mail: {thomas.bartz-beielstein | oliver.flasch |
patrick.koch | wolfgang.konen}@fh-koeln.de

Abstract

Sequential parameter optimization is a heuristic that combines classical and modern statistical techniques to improve the performance of search algorithms. It includes methods for tuning based on classical regression and analysis of variance techniques; tree-based models such as CART and random forest; Gaussian process models (Kriging), and combinations of different meta-modeling approaches. The suitability of these different meta models for parameter tuning is analyzed in this article. Automated and interactive approaches are compared..

1 Introduction

Sequential parameter optimization (SPO) is a heuristic that combines classical and modern statistical techniques to improve the performance of search algorithms. Bartz-Beielstein [1] present an introduction to the state-of-the-art R implementation of SPO, the so-called *sequential parameter optimization toolbox* (SPOT). This article describes important aspects of parameter tuning related to algorithm design and meta models. A short case study illustrates our considerations. This paper is organized as follows: the sequential parameter optimization is introduced in Section 2. Exogenous parameters of algorithms such as population size define an algorithm design. Algorithm design used in our experiments are described in Section 3. SPOT uses several prediction models (meta models) in order to predict the performance of an algorithm. Meta models are introduced in Section 4. In order to compare different meta models, a case study is presented in Section 5. Tuning procedures considered so far use SPOT in an automated manner. Section 6 presents an interactive approach, which is related to classical *response surface methodology* (rsm). Section 7 presents a summary and an outlook.

2 Sequential Parameter Optimization

Sequential parameter optimization uses the available budget (e.g., simulator runs, number of function evaluations) sequentially, i.e., it uses information from the exploration of the search space to guide the search by building one or several meta models. Predictions from the meta models are used to select new design points. The meta model is refined to improve knowledge about the search space. SPOT provides tools to cope with noise, which typically occurs when randomized search

Algorithm 1: Sequential parameter optimization toolbox (SPOT)

```
// phase 1, building the model:
```
let A be the tuned algorithm;
```
// design considerations necessary:
```
generate an initial population $X = \{\bar{x}^1, \ldots, \bar{x}^m\}$ of m parameter vectors;
let $k = k_0$ be the initial number of tests for determining estimated utilities;
foreach $\bar{x} \in X$ **do**
$\quad$ run A with $\bar{x}$ k times to determine the estimated utility y of $\bar{x}$;
end
```
// phase 2, using and improving the model:
```
while *termination criterion not true* **do**
$\quad$ let $\bar{a}$ denote the parameter vector from X with best estimated utility;
$\quad$ let k the number of repeats already computed for $\bar{a}$;
$\quad$ `// model considerations necessary:`
$\quad$ build meta model f based on X and $\{y^1, \ldots, y^{|X|}\}$;
$\quad$ `// design considerations necessary:`
$\quad$ generate a set X' of l new parameter vectors by random sampling;
$\quad$ **foreach** $\bar{x} \in X'$ **do**
$\quad\quad$ calculate $f(\bar{x})$ to determine the predicted utility $f(\bar{x})$ of $\bar{x}$;
$\quad$ **end**
$\quad$ select set X'' of d parameter vectors from X' with best predicted utility $(d \ll l)$;
$\quad$ run A with $\bar{a}$ once and recalculate its estimated utility using all $k + 1$ test
$\quad\quad$ results; `// (improve confidence)`
$\quad$ let $k = k + 1$;
$\quad$ run A k times with each $\bar{x} \in X''$ to determine the estimated utility $\bar{x}$;
$\quad$ extend the population by $X = X \cup X''$;
end

heuristics are run. It guarantees comparable confidence for search points. Users can collect information to learn from this tuning process, e.g., by applying exploratory data analysis. Last, but not least, SPOT provides mechanisms both for interactive and automated tuning. SPOT is described in [2, 3]. An R version of this toolbox for interactive and automatic optimization of algorithms can be downloaded from CRAN[1]. Programs and files from this study can be downloaded from the author's WWW page[2]. As can be seen from Algorithm 1, meta models are used to determine new algorithm designs. This article compares several standard and non-standard meta-modeling approaches.

3 Algorithm Designs

There is a strong interaction between meta models and algorithm designs, because the optimality of an algorithm design depends on the meta model [4, 5].

SPOT generates new design points during the init and during the sequential step. Many algorithm designs generators are available in R, see, e.g., the *CRAN Task*

---

[1] http://cran.r-project.org/web/packages/SPOT/index.html
[2] http://www.gm.fh-koeln.de/campus/personen/lehrende/thomas.bartz-beielstein/00489/

Table 1: SPOT initial design plugins

Type	Name of the SPOT plugin
Fractional factorial design (Resolution III)	spotCreateDesignDoe3
Factorial design	spotCreateDesignBasicDoe
Latin hypercube	spotCreateDesignLhd
Latin hypercube	spotCreateDesignLhs

Table 2: SPOT meta models

Type	Name of the SPOT plugin	R package
Linear model	spotPredictLm	base
Response surface methodology	spotPredictLmOptim	rsm
Regression trees	spotPredictTree	rpart
Random forest	spotPredictRandomForest	randomForest
Gaussian processes (Kriging)	spotPredictMlegg	mlegp
Tree based Gaussian processes	spotPredictTgp	tgp

View: Design of Experiments (DoE) & Analysis of Experimental Data.[3] This is one of the main reasons why SPOT is implemented in R. The user can use state of the art design generators for tuning his algorithm. Or, he can write his own design generator and use it as a *plugin* for SPOT. The default SPOT installation contains several design plugins (and further design plugins will be added in forthcoming versions). Table 1 summarizes design plugins from the current SPOT version (0.1.888).[4]

A *Latin hypercube design* (LHD) was chosen as the default initial design in Section 5, because it is easy to implement and understand. Section 6 uses fractional-factorial designs, because classical RSM techniques are used. This paper modifies SPOT's meta models, while design generators remain unchanged. The impact of the variation of the design generators on the algorithm's performance will be subject of a forthcoming paper.

4 Meta Models

SPOT processes data sequentially, i.e., starting from a small initial design, further design points (parameter settings for the algorithm) are generated using a meta model. Many meta models are available in R. The user can use state of the art meta models for tuning his algorithm. Or, he can write his own meta model and use it as a plugin for SPOT. The default SPOT installation contains several meta models (and further meta models will be added in forthcoming versions). Table 2 summarizes meta models from the current SPOT version (0.1.888).

The R implementation of randomForest was chosen as SPOT's default meta model, because it is quite robust and can handle categorical and numerical values.

---

[3]http://cran.r-project.org/web/views/ExperimentalDesign.html
[4]The command spotVersion() displays the actual version of your local SPOT package.

Note, these meta models and design plugins should be considered as templates. They were implemented in order to demonstrate how the interfaces should look like. We strongly recommend an adaptation of these plugins to your specific needs, if real-world tuning tasks are performed. However, we will use these simple and generic plugins for the following case study.

5 Case Study: Tuning Simulated Annealing

5.1 Goals of this Study

The following case study is devoted to the question: "Which meta models can be recommended for tuning algorithms?" The experimental setup is generic, i.e., we have chosen a set of meta models from statistics (linear models, tree based models, Gaussian processes or Kriging) which were used for tuning an algorithm (stochastic search heuristic), i.e., simulated annealing.

5.2 Simulated Annealing

Simulated annealing (SANN) belongs to the class of stochastic global optimization methods. The R implementation, which was investigated in our study, uses the Metropolis function for the acceptance probability. It is a variant of the simulated annealing algorithm given in [6]. SANN uses only function values but is relatively slow. It will also work for non-differentiable functions. By default the next candidate point is generated from a Gaussian Markov kernel with scale proportional to the actual temperature. Temperatures are decreased according to the logarithmic cooling schedule as given in [6]; specifically, the temperature is set to `temp`$/\log(((t-1)/$`tmax`$) \times$ `tmax` $+ \exp(1))$, where t is the current iteration step and `temp` and `tmax` are specifiable via control. SANN is not a general-purpose method but can be very useful in getting to a good value on a very rough surface.

SANN uses two design variables, which were tuned during our study:

`temp` is the starting temperature for the cooling schedule. Defaults to 10.

`tmax` is the number of function evaluations at each temperature. Defaults to 10.

The interval from 1 to 50 was chosen as the *region of interest* (ROI) for both design variables in our experiments. The total number of function evaluations (of the Branin function, see Section 5.3) was set to `maxit` $= 250$ for all experiments. The starting point, i.e., the initial value for the parameters to be optimized over, was $\vec{x}_0 = (10, 10)$.

5.3 Description of the Objective Function

The Branin function

$$f(x_1, x_2) = \left(x_2 - \frac{5.1}{4\pi^2} x_1^2 + \frac{5}{\pi} x_1 - 6 \right)^2 + 10 \times \left(1 - \frac{1}{8\pi} \right) \cos(x_1) + 10,$$

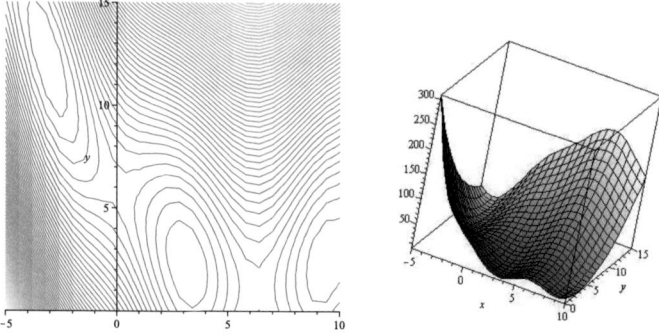

Figure 1: Plots of the Branin function. The contour plot (*left*) shows the location of the three global minima

with

$$x_1 \in [-5, 10] \text{ and } x_2 \in [0, 15]. \tag{1}$$

was chosen as a test function, because it is well-known in the global optimization community, so results are comparable. It has three global minima, $\vec{x}_1^* = [3.1416, 2.2750]$, $\vec{x}_2^* = [9.4248, 2.4750]$ and $\vec{x}_3^* = [-3.1416, 12.2750]$ with $y^* = f(\vec{x}_i^*) = 0.3979$, $(i = 1, 2, 3)$, see Fig. 1.

5.4 Results from Default and Random Settings

As a baseline for our experiments, we run SANN one hundred times—first, with default parameters (tmax = temp = 10), and second, with randomly chosen parameter values from the interval $[1, 50]$.[5] These experiments were performed to quantify the benefit of tuning for our experiments. Results from theses two experiments are shown in the first and second result row from Tab. 3. SANN was not able to determine the optimal function value with these settings. Now that the baseline results are available, we can examine SANN's tunability.

5.5 SPOT Setup

The SPOT based tuning procedure uses the following parameter settings: SPOT uses a budget of one hundred algorithm runs (auto.loop.nevals = 100) and an initial design size of ten (init.design.size = 10). Each initial design point was evaluated twice (init.design.repeats = 2). A Latin hypercube design was chosen as the initial design. The interval from 1 to 50 was chosen as the ROI for both design variables, i.e., temp and tmax, respectively, in our experiments.

---

[5]SPOT can generate one hundred randomly chosen design points of the SANN by using the following setting in the CONF file: init.design.size = 100 and init.design.repeats = 1.

Table 3: SANN results. Results from $n = 100$ repeats. Smaller values are better. The optimal function value is $y^* = 0.3979$

Model	Min.	1st Qu.	Median	Mean	3rd Qu.	Max.
Default	0.3982	0.4037	0.4130	0.8281	0.5032	6.1120
Random	0.3988	0.5326	1.2160	2.0720	2.9820	8.8800
Tree (rpart)	**0.3979**	0.4001	0.4044	0.4184	0.4106	0.8576
RF	**0.3979**	**0.3987**	0.4000	**0.4010**	**0.4022**	**0.4184**
lm	0.3981	0.4034	0.4077	0.5325	0.4789	4.1570
mlegp	0.3980	0.4022	0.4089	0.4691	0.4349	2.7180
tgp	**0.3979**	0.3991	0.4002	0.4030	0.4034	0.4530
rsm + rpart	**0.3979**	**0.3987**	**0.3997**	0.4014	0.4027	0.4203

5.6 Tree-based Parameter Tuning

The first tuning procedure uses a (simple) regression tree, which is implemented in SPOT as a plugin (seq.predictionModel.func = "spotPredictTree"). This meta model plugin uses R's rpart package. The function rpart follows [7] very closely. The final best solution from the SPOT tuning run reads temp = 3 and tmax = 31.

Finally, one hundred SANN runs were performed with this design point. Results are shown in the third result row in Tab. 3. The tree-tuned SANN algorithm was able to detect the global minimum.

5.7 Random Forest-based Parameter Tuning

Next, a Random Forest based meta model was used, originating from the R package randomForest implements Breiman's algorithm, which is based on Breiman and Cutler's original Fortran code, for classification and regression. It is implemented as a SPOT plugin which can be selected via the command seq.predictionModel.func = "spotPredictRandomForest" in SPOT's configuration file. The best algorithm design point determined by Random Forest is temp = 1.116 and tmax = 38. Finally, one hundred SANN runs were performed with this design point. Results are shown in the fourth result row in Tab. 3. The SANN algorithm with SPOT tuned parameters was able to detect the global minimum.

5.8 Linear Model-based Parameter Tuning

A standard linear regression model was used as a meta model in the SPOT. It is implemented as a SPOT plugin, which can be selected via the command seq.predictionModel.func = "spotPredictLm" in SPOT's configuration file. The best algorithm design point determined by this linear model is temp = 5.0664 and tmax = 49. Finally, one hundred SANN runs were performed with this design point. Results are shown in the fifth result row in Tab. 3. The SANN algorithm with tuned parameters, which were generated with a linear regression model was not able to detect the global minimum. However, SANN with these tuned algorithm design obtained better function value than the SANN algorithm with standard or the randomized algorithm design points.

5.9 Maximum Likelihood Estimates of Gaussian Processes

SPOT provides a plugin for the *maximum likelihood estimation of Gaussian process* (`mlegp`) package which is available in R. The package `mlegp` finds maximum likelihood estimates of Gaussian processes for univariate and multi-dimensional responses, for Gaussian processes with product exponential correlation structures; constant or linear regression mean functions; no nugget term, constant nugget terms, or a nugget matrix that can be specified up to a multiplicative constant [8].

`mlegp` is implemented as a SPOT plugin, which can be selected via the command `seq.predictionModel.func = "spotPredictMlegp"` in SPOT's configuration file. The best algorithm design point determined by `mlegp` is `temp` = 5.3510 and `tmax` = 37. Finally, one hundred SANN runs were performed with this design point. Results are shown in the sixth result row in Tab. 3. The SANN algorithm with `mlegp`-tuned parameters was not able to detect the global minimum. However, SANN with these tuned algorithm design obtained better function value than the SANN algorithm with standard or the randomized algorithm design points.

5.10 Treed Gaussian Process Models

`tgp` is an R package for fully Bayesian nonstationary, semiparametric nonlinear regression and design by treed Gaussian processes with jumps to the limiting linear model [9]. The SPOT plugin to `tgp` can be invoked via `seq.predictionModel.func = "spotPredictTgp"` in SPOT's configuration file. The best algorithm design point determined by `tgp` is `temp` = 1.4692 and `tmax` = 34. The SANN algorithm with SPOT tuned parameters was able to detect the global minimum.

5.11 Comparison of the Meta Model Results

Random Forest was able to determine an algorithms design point which reduced the variance between different SANN runs and enables SANN to determine the optimal function value, y^*, or a value close to y^*. The `tgp` tuned SANN shows a similar performance. Random Forest is preferred, because `tgp` runs require significantly more CPU time than Random Forest runs, or, as stated by Gramacy [10]: "Fully Bayesian analyses with MCMC are not the super-speediest of all statistical models."

We used Random Forest to generate a sensitivity plot[6]. Figure 2 shows sensitivity plots based on results from different meta models used in the tuning process.

All plots show that `temp` affects SANN's performance significantly, whereas `tmax` has nearly no effect at all. Smaller `temp` values improve the algorithms performance.

---

[6]SPOT provides a report plugin to generate theses plots. The report plugin was written by Wolfgang Konen and can be invoked via `report.func = "spotReportSens"` in SPOT's CONF file.

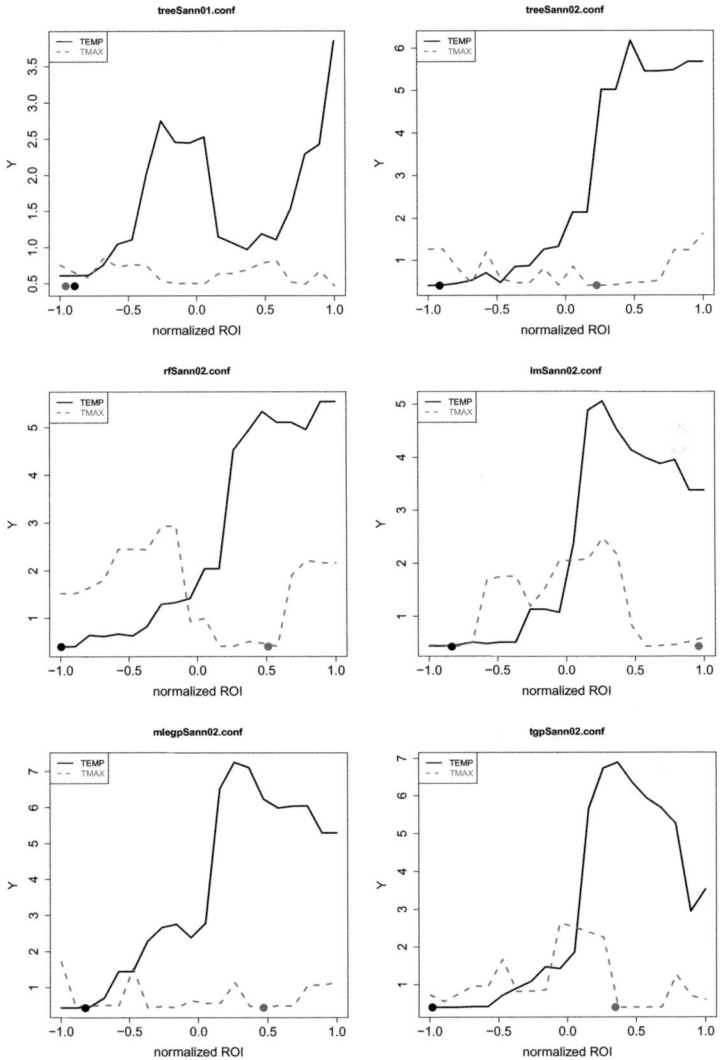

Figure 2: Sensitivity plots (generated by random forest). *Top left:* One hundred random samples, *Top right:* Regression tree, *Middle left:* Random forest. *Middle right:* Linear model, *Bottom left:* Mlegp, and *Bottom right:* Tree Gaussian process models

Dots denote the best design points with respect to the normalized ROI. These sensitivity plots reveal that Random Forest and `rpart` were able to explore the search space better than their competitors. The results from these sensitivity plots are in accordance with results from the response surface analysis which will be discussed later on, see Fig. 4.

6 Interactive Tuning

In Section 5, SPOT was run as an automatic tuner. Steps from the automatic mode can be used in an interactive manner: The user can perform one of the tasks `init`, `seq`, `run`, or `rep` sequentially, see [1]. She can also add and delete design points or modify the region of interest.

In the following, different meta models, namely tree based regression (`rpart`) and response surface modeling (`rsm`), are combined and the region of interest is adapted.

6.1 Designs

A *central composite design* (CCD) was chosen as the starting point of the tuning process. SPOT's `spotCreateDesignFrF2` plugin can be used to generate CCD points. After the first run is finished, we can use SPOT's report facility to analyze results. In the following, we will use RSM. [11] describes an implementation of RSM in R. This R package `rsm` has many useful tools for an analysis of the results from the SPOT runs. After evaluating the algorithm in these design points, a second order regression model with interactions is fitted to the data. Functions from the `rsm` package were used by the SPOT plugin `spotPredictLmOptim`. Before meta models are build, data are standardized. Data in the original units are mapped to coded data, i.e., data with values in the interval $[-1, 1]$.

6.2 Response Surface Models and Gradient Information

Based on the number of design points, SPOT automatically determines whether a first-order, two-way interaction, pure quadratic, or second order model can be fitted to the data. The CCD generated by `spotCreateDesignFrF2` allows the fit of an second-order model which can be summarized as shown in Fig. 3.

The response surface analysis (cf. Fig. 3) determines the following stationary point on the response surface: $(0.4886822 0.2712242)$, or, in the original units `temp` $= 37.47271$ and `tmax` $= 32.14499$. The eigenanalysis shows that the eigenvalues ($\lambda_1 = 1.848425$; $\lambda_2 = -2.010494$) have different signs, so this is a saddle point, as can also be seen in Fig. 4. SPOT determines the most steeply rising ridge in both directions, see also [11] for details. In addition to the points from the steepest descent, the best point from the first design, i.e., $(1,50)$ is evaluated again, see Fig. 5.

Now, these points are evaluated and a new `rsm` model is build. Summarizing, the SPOT tasks `init`, `run`, `seq`, `run`, `seq`, `run`, `seq`, `run`, `seq` were performed. Each `seq` step generates information as shown in Fig. 3 and a plot of the response surface as shown in Fig. 4. The resulting surface plots from four steps of these procedure are shown in Fig. 4.

```
Coefficients:
            Estimate Std. Error t value Pr(>|t|)
(Intercept)   2.7383     0.5075   5.396   0.0125 *
x1            2.0779     0.3995   5.201   0.0138 *
x2           -0.7664     0.3987  -1.922   0.1503
x1:x2        -0.4677     0.4467  -1.047   0.3720
x1^2         -1.9963     0.9581  -2.084   0.1286
x2^2          1.8342     0.9591   1.912   0.1518
---
Signif. codes:  0 '***' 0.001 '**' 0.01 '*' 0.05 '.' 0.1 ' ' 1
Residual standard error: 0.8934 on 3 degrees of freedom
Multiple R-squared: 0.9242,       Adjusted R-squared: 0.798
F-statistic: 7.319 on 5 and 3 DF,  p-value: 0.06605

Stationary point of response surface:
       x1        x2
0.4886822 0.2712242

Stationary point in original units:
    TEMP     TMAX
37.47271 32.14499

Eigenanalysis:
$values
[1]  1.848425 -2.010494
```

Figure 3: Output from the first regression model in the interactive approach

6.3 Automatic Adaptation of the Region of Interest

SPOT modifies the region of interest, if seq.useAdaptiveRoi = TRUE. This procedure consists of two phases, which are repeated in an alternating manner.

During the *orientation* phase, the direction of the largest improvement is determined as described in Section 6.2. Based on an existing design and related function values, the path of the steepest descent is determined. A small number of points is chosen from this path. Optimization runs are performed on these design points. In some situations, where no gradient information is available, the best point from a large number of design points, which were evaluated on the regression model, is chosen as the set of improvement points.

The *recalibration* phase determines the best point $\vec{x}_b$. It can be selected from the complete set of evaluated design points or from the points along the steepest descent only. The best point $\vec{x}_b$ defines the new center point of a central composite design. The minimal distance of $\vec{x}_b$ to the borders of the actual region of interest defines the radius of this design. If $\vec{x}_b$ is located at (or very close to) the borders of the region of interest, a Latin hypercube design which covers the whole region of interest is determined. This can be interpreted as a restart. To prevent premature convergence of this procedure, one additional new design point is generated by a tree based model. Next, the orientation phase is repeated.

This tuning process, which is based on regression models (rsm) and tree based regression (rpart), results in a tuned algorithm design point with temp =1 and tmax = 50. As in Section 5, one hundred repeats of the best solution from this tuning

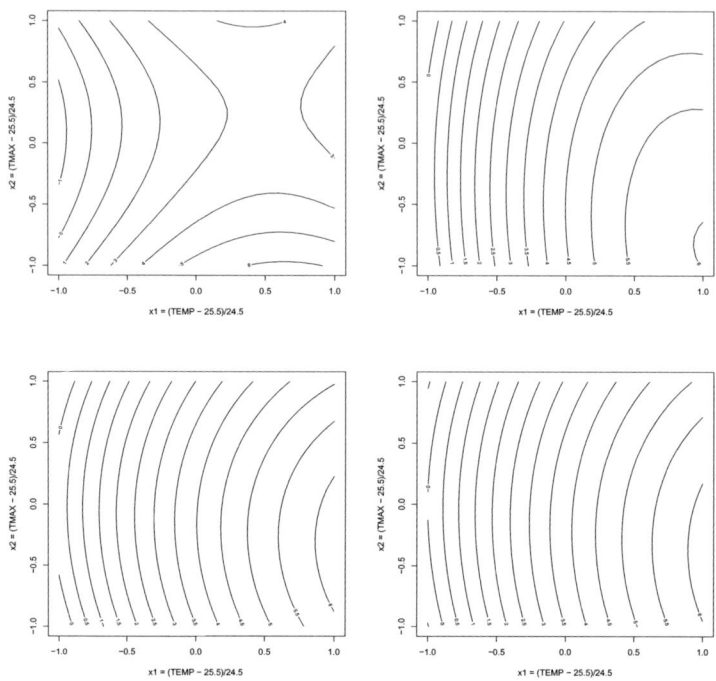

Figure 4: Response surface model based on the initial design. rsm was used to generate this plot

TEMP	TMAX
1.0000	50.0000
42.3560	32.4335
39.9060	32.2865
37.4805	32.1395
35.0305	31.9925
32.5805	31.8455

Figure 5: Second algorithm design. The best design point is evaluated again and five new design points are determined. Gradient information was used to generate this design

process are generated. Results are shown in the last result row from Tab. 3.

7 Summary

All meta models improved SANN's performance. Random Forest performs very
well compared to other meta models. The interactive approach provides additional
information, e.g., gradient, eigenvalues, plots of the response surface, which might
accelerate the tuning process. Users can add or delete design points manually, e.g.,
after studying the response surface or using additional tools from exploratory data
analysis. However, this feature was not used in the current study. In comparison to
the automated approaches, the interactive approach performed competitively. This
short study recommends random forest meta models for "lazy" tuning of algorithms.
As an additional interesting feature, Random Forests can handle categorical and
numerical design variables in one model.

Note, results from this study shed some light on the behavior of meta models in the
tuning process. However, we do not claim that these results are correct in every
situation. Further studies, which include different algorithm design generators as
well, are necessary.

8 Acknowledgments

This work has been supported by the Bundesministerium für Bildung und Forschung
(BMBF) under the grants FIWA and SOMA (AIF FKZ 17N1009, "Ingenieurnachwuchs") and by the Cologne University of Applied Sciences under the research focus
grant COSA.

References

[1] Bartz-Beielstein, T.: SPOT: An R Package For Automatic and Interactive Tun-
    ing of Optimization Algorithms by Sequential Parameter Optimization. Techn. Ber.
    arXiv:1006.4645. CIOP Technical Report 05-10, Cologne University of Applied Sci-
    ences. URL http://arxiv.org/abs/1006.4645. Comments: Related software can be
    downloaded from http://cran.r-project.org/web/packages/SPOT/index.html. 2010.

[2] Bartz-Beielstein, T.; Preuss, M.: The Future of Experimental Research. In: *Exper-
    imental Methods for the Analysis of Optimization Algorithms* (Bartz-Beielstein, T.;
    Chiarandini, M.; Paquete, L.; Preuss, M., Hg.), S. 17–46. Berlin, Heidelberg, New
    York: Springer. 2010.

[3] Bartz-Beielstein, T.; Lasarczyk, C.; Preuss, M.: The Sequential Parameter Optimiza-
    tion Toolbox. In: *Experimental Methods for the Analysis of Optimization Algorithms*
    (Bartz-Beielstein, T.; Chiarandini, M.; Paquete, L.; Preuss, M., Hg.), S. 337–360.
    Berlin, Heidelberg, New York: Springer. 2010.

[4] Pukelsheim, F.: *Optimal Design of Experiments*. New York NY: Wiley. 1993.

[5] Santner, T. J.; Williams, B. J.; Notz, W. I.: *The Design and Analysis of Computer
    Experiments*. Berlin, Heidelberg, New York: Springer. 2003.

[6] Belisle, C. J. P.: Convergence theorems for a class of simulated annealing algorithms. *Journal Applied Probability* 29 (1992), S. 885–895.

[7] Breiman, L.; Friedman, J. H.; Olshen, R. A.; Stone, C. J.: *Classification and Regression Trees.* Monterey CA: Wadsworth. 1984.

[8] Dancik, G. M.; Dorman, K. S.: mlegp. *Bioinformatics* 24 (2008) 17, S. 1966–1967.

[9] Gramacy, R. B.; Taddy, M.: Categorical Inputs, Sensitivity Analysis, Optimization and Importance Tempering with tgp Version 2, an R Package for Treed Gaussian Process Models (2010). URL http://www.jstatsoft.org/v33/i06/paper.

[10] Gramacy, R. B.: tgp: An R Package for Bayesian Nonstationary, Semiparametric Nonlinear Regression and Design by Treed Gaussian Process Models. *Journal of Statistical Software* 19 (2007) 9, S. 1–46. URL http://www.jstatsoft.org/v19/i09.

[11] Lenth, R. V.: Response-Surface Methods in R, Using rsm. *Journal of Statistical Software* 32 (2009) 7, S. 1–17.

Robuste Fehlerdiagnose bei aktuator- und sensorähnlichen Fehlern am Beispiel eines Dreitanksystems

Horst Schulte[1], Patrick Gerland[2], Dominic Groß[3]

[1]Hochschule für Technik und Wirtschaft Berlin, Studiengang Elektrotechnik und Angewandte Automation
[2]Universität Kassel, FB Maschinenbau, FG Mess- und Regelungstechnik
[3]Universität Kassel, FB Elektrotechnik, Institut für Regelungs- und Systemtheorie
E-Mail: horst.schulte@htw-berlin.de

Dieser Beitrag beschreibt die systematische Vorgehensweise bei der Anwendung eines robusten Beobachterkonzeptes zur Fehlerdiagnose nichtlinearer dynamischer Systeme mit konzentrierten Parametern und begrenzten Modellunsicherheiten. Am Beispiel des Benchmarkproblems Dreitanksystem, vgl. Abb. 1, wird anhand von Simulationen und experimentellen Untersuchungen gezeigt, wie mittels der quantitativen Berücksichtigung von Modellunsicherheiten und definierten a-priori Fehlerschranken aktuator- und sensorähnliche Fehler detektier- und isolierbar sind. Das Konzept basiert auf der Erweiterung des Sliding-Mode (SM) Beobachters von Edwards und Spurgeon [1] durch die Klasse der Takagi-Sugeno Fuzzy Systeme, im folgenden TS-SM Beobachter genannt, der erstmals in den Arbeiten [2] und [3] vorgestellt wurde. Die Erweiterung bezieht sich dabei auf die vorgegebene Modellstruktur des nominalen Streckenmodells, welche in [1] auf LTI Systeme beschränkt und durch die Integration von Takagi-Sugeno Fuzzy Systemen allgemeingültiger ist.

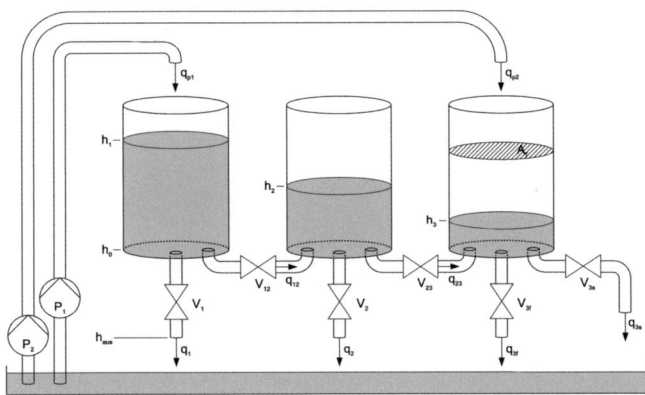

Abbildung 1: Konfiguration des untersuchten Dreitanksystems

Im ersten Abschnitt dieser Arbeit wird eine Takagi-Sugeno Modellbeschreibung eines in Abb. 1 dargestellten Dreitanksystems basierend auf dem Ansatz der Sektornichtlinearitäten vorgestellt. Beim fehlerfreien Dreitanksystem sind die Ventile V_{12}, V_{23}, V_{3s} geöffnet und die restlichen Ventile geschlossen. Die Pumpen können kontinuierlich zwischen 0 und 100 Prozent der Fördernennleistung eingestellt werden.

Anschließend werden die nominalen Modellunsicherheiten experimentell mittels Parameterschätzung bestimmt sowie die Fehlerschranken der zu erwartenden Aktuator- und Sensorfehler festgelegt. Zusätzliche Fehler in Form von Leckflüssen können durch das Öffnen der Ventile V_1, V_2, V_{3f} eingeleitet werden. Anschließend werden alle notwendigen Schritte des Entwurfsverfahrens systematisch vorgestellt und anhand von simulierten und experimentellen Untersuchungen diskutiert. In Abb. 2 sind erste Ergebnisse zur Detektion eines sprungförmigen Fehlers e_{Sen2} am Pegelsensor vom zweiten Tank durch den Beobachterfehler e_{x1} bei Variation der Dynamik des TS-Beobachters dargestellt. Die vorgestellten Ergebnisse werden mit Simulations- und Messdaten aus [4] und [5] verglichen.

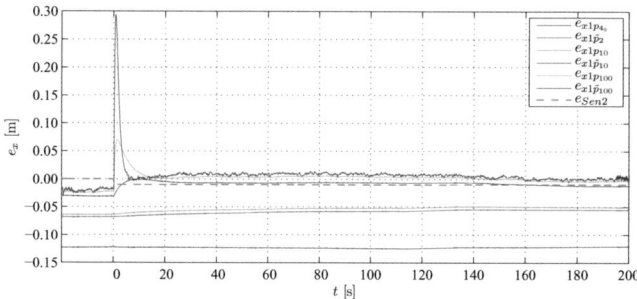

Abbildung 2: TS Beobachterfehler bei einem Pegelsensorfehler vom zweiten Tank

Literatur

[1] C. Edwards, S. K. Spurgeon: *Sliding mode control: Theory and applications*. London: Taylor & Francis, 1998.

[2] P. Gerland, D. Groß, H. Schulte, A. Kroll: Robust Adaptive Fault Detection Using Global State Information and Application to Mobile Working Machines, *In Proc., Conference on Control and Fault-Tolerant Systems*, Nancy, Frankreich, submitted, 2010.

[3] P. Gerland, D. Groß, H. Schulte, A. Kroll: Design of Sliding Mode Observers for TS Fuzzy Systems with Application to Disturbance and Actuator Fault Estimation *In Proc., 49th IEEE Conference on Decision and Control*, Atlanta, USA, submitted, 2010.

[4] P. Mai, C. Hillermeier: Fehlertolerante Regelung bei aktuatorähnlichen Fehlern mittels Ableitungsschätzung, *Automatisierungstechnik (at)*, 2, 2010.

[5] H. Noura, D. Theilliol, J.-C. Ponsart, A. Chamseddine: *Fault-tolerant Control Systems*, Springer Verlag, 2009.

[6] H. Schulte, LMI-based observer design on a power-split continuously variable transmission for off-road vehicles, *In Proc., IEEE Multi-conference on Systems and Control*, Yokohama, Japan, 2010.

3D Off-Line Path Planning for Autonomous Airships in Known Environments by using Genetic Algorithms.

Naef Al-Rashedi and Michael Gerke

Fakultät für Mathematik und Informatik
Lehrgebiet Prozesssteuerung und Regelungstechnik
Fernuniversität in Hagen
Universitätstrasse 27, D-58097 Hagen.
Tel: +49 23 31 / 9 87 – 17 02
Fax: +49 23 31 /9 87 – 3 54
Naef.Al-Rashedi@FernUni-Hagen.de

Abstract

The paper presents a Genetic Algorithm (G.A.) off-line path planning of Autonomous Small Airships (ASAs) in known 3D environments. The algorithm assumes that the airship is used in Fire Fighting and Mine Detection projects, so the aircraft will fly only a few meters above the ground, which means there is a high possibility of collision with obstacles. The task of the Off-Line Path Planner algorithm is to find an optimal route to visit all the predefined locations for airborne measurement exactly once per mission and without any collisions with environmental obstacles. The planner task posed here is an NP problem. This paper proposes a 3D Off-Line Path Planner using G.A. including chromosome representation, G.A. crossover and collision avoidance with known obstacles. The proposed algorithm is implemented using MATLAB with Genetic Algorithms and Mapping Toolboxes. The proposed algorithm is tested using real maps of our research airfield and the result shows that the algorithm finds a near-optimal collision free path for the airship.

1. Introduction

Autonomous Small Airships (ASAs) have many applications in civil and military areas[3], e.g. for different missions including fire fighting, mine detection, traffic monitoring, monitoring and maintenance of high power electric lines and advertising. The main advantages of using the ASA are: it has low energy consumption, there is no vital risk for operators during performance of hazardous missions, and its long endurance in the air.

The ASAs need a control system that can make both low-level control decisions in realtime, medium-level decisions such as path planning, and high-level decisions, such as cooperative task assignment, for long time missions without human interference. Task assignment is crucial for designing successful missions in difficult environments while the path planners which generate collision-free and optimized paths are needed to give autonomous operation capability to the ASAs. The combined solution of both aspects for the mission planning problem of the ASAs lead to a near optimal flight trajectory [6].

Figure (1): Fernuniversität ASA.

The paper is organized as follows. The next section 2 formulates the path planning problem. The description of the proposed path planner follows in section 3. In section 4 experiments and results are given. The conclusion of this paper in is drawn in section 5.

2. Problem Definition

The mobile robot path planning problem is typically formulated as follows: given a mobile robot and a description of an environment and set of user-defined way-points (wp), in order to calculate a route that visits all user-defined way-points exactly once. The resulting path should be free of collision and satisfies certain optimization criteria (i.e., shortest path)[3]. This problem corresponds to finding the shortest Hamiltonian cycle in a complete graph $G = (V, E)$ of an n nodes. Thus the path planner consists of finding a permutation of the set $\{wp_1, wp_2, wp_3, \ldots, wp_N\}$ that minimize the quantity:

$$\text{Minimize} \quad \left[\sum_{i=1}^{N-1} d\left(wp_i, wp_{i+1}\right) + d\left(wp_N, wp_1\right) \right]$$

Where $d(wp_i, wp_j)$ denotes the distance between waypoint wp_i and waypoint wp_j.

Researchers distinguish between various methods used to solve the path planning problem according to two factors, (1) the environment type (i.e., static or dynamic), (2) the path planning algorithms (i.e., Off-Line or On-Line). A static environment is defined as the environment which doesn't contain any moving objects other than a navigating robot; while any dynamic environment includes moving objects (i.e., human beings, moving machines and moving robots).

The Off-Line path planning algorithms requires a complete knowledge about the search environment and is based on the fact that all terrain should be static. On the other hand, On-Line path planning means that the path planning algorithm is calculated in realtime while the robot is moving around. In other words, the algorithm is capable of producing a new path in response to environmental changes [2].

3. The Proposed Path Planner

The proposed path planner accomplishes its task into two phases: the preparation phase and the G.A.

3.1. The Preparation Phase

In this phase all inputs data such as digital 3D maps and user-defined way-points are represented and prepared to be use by the genetic algorithm.

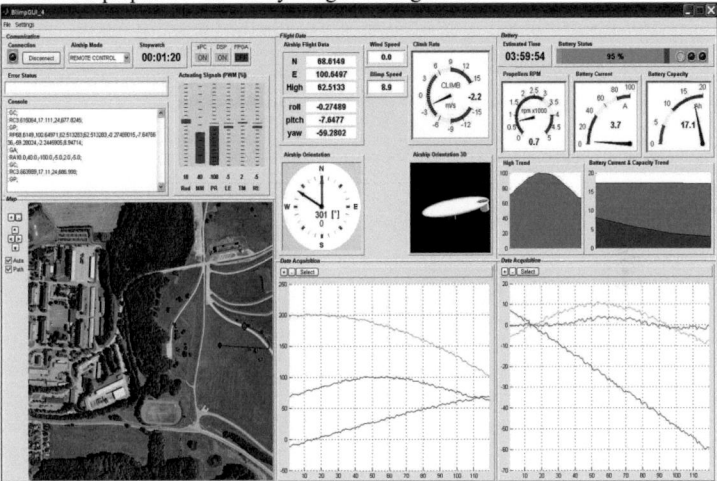

Figure (2): Control System User Interface of the Fernuniversität ASA.

3.1.1 Environment Representation

This paper considers that the ASA will fly in static and well known environments, while these environments are represented as digital maps (e.g. for processing in MATLAB Mapping Tool Box).

3.1.2. Verifying Feasibility and Adding New Sub-way Points

The Feasibility of all direct paths between each set of user-defined way-point are verified and if there is a feasible direct path between any pair of these points, its path length is calculated and stored in a cost table, otherwise (i.e. there is an obstacles between two waypoints), a process is being started to find an indirect feasible path between these two user-defined way-points by adding a new sub-way-point to avoid this disturbing obstacle. The strategy of adding new sub-way-points is based on making a displacement around the obstacle in all directions in order to find an intermediate way-point that is feasible from both user-defined way-points under consideration. The main advantage of this step is to reduce the calculation and the execution time of G.A.

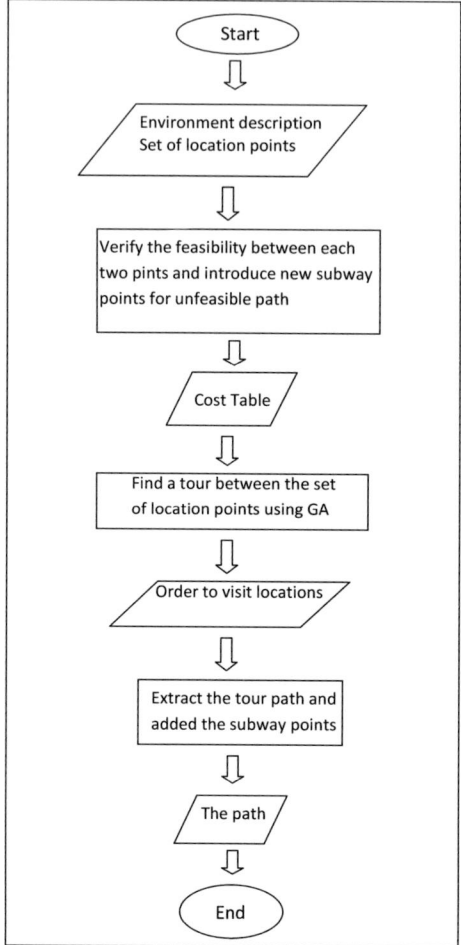

Figure (3): Path Planner Process Flowchart

3.2. The G.A. Algorithm:

This new pre-processing strategy enhances the G.A. search that is used to solve the travel salesman problem in [8] to be used as an optimization tool for the ASA path planner. A description of the G.A. search for 3D-problems is as follows:

3.2.1 Path Representation:

The proposed algorithm represents a robot mission as an Upper Triangle Binary Matrix (UTBM) as in **Figure (4)** which represents the tour (0, 2, 4, 1, 3, 5). Every gene /chromosome is represented in binary form, which means: if the element (i,j) of the matrix is equal (1) there is a feasible path between user-defined way-points (i) and (j) in the tour.

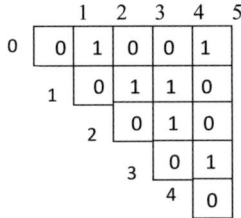

Figure (4): The Proposed Representation of a Chromosome

The matrix representation must satisfy the following conditions in order to represent a feasible tour:

1- The number of elements in the matrix that have the value (1) must be equal to the number of the user-defined way-points.
2- The number of matrix elements that have the value of (1) in each row and each

$$\sum_{i=0}^{N-2} \sum_{j=1}^{N-1} wp_{ij} = N$$

column of the same way-point must be equal to two.

$$Col_j = \sum_{i=0}^{N-2} c_{ij}$$

$$Row_i = \sum_{j=1}^{N-1} c_{ij}$$

$$\forall\, (i = j): Row_i + Col_j = 2$$

3.2.2. The Crossover

The crossover operation generates an offspring from two parents as follows:

1- Unify the two parents matrices in one matrix by executing (Or) operation.
2- The result matrix from step 1 may be an invalid tour (do not satisfy the two conditions from above). So it must be repaired by counting the number of elements that have the value of (1) in each row and column for the same way-point. If this number is greater than 2 edges then delete the longest edges and

remain just 2. If the number is less than 2, then add this way-point to a path list called List_of_Way-point_that_Must_Add_Edge_To_It (LWMAETI).

3- Adding the missing edges to the way-points in the LWMAETI list by using the greedy algorithm.

3.2.3. The Evaluation Function:

The evaluation function is an important part of any evolutionary process using G.A. Only an appropriate selection of the evaluation function will lead the search towards the desired optimal solution. For the airship that is used in Fire fighting and mine detection, the optimal path has two type of constrains:

- Hard constrains: the path should be free of collision and every user-defined way- point of the flight mission should be visited exactly once. (The algorithm proposed here guarantees that all the solutions that are produced meet these conditions).
- Soft constrains which can be defined by user requirements: in specific scenarios such as fire fighting and mine detection some additional constrains can be formulated, e.g. enforcement of a shortest path and of path types keeping the ASA in low altitude above the ground. The following equation is used as evaluation function for the algorithm proposed here:

$$F = \text{minimize} \; [\; |T| + H \;]$$

Where:

Parameter $|T|$ is the length of the flight mission [e.g. in meters] and is computed as the sum of the paths lengths between every two way-points of the tour.

Parameter H is a value computed as following:

$$H = h * Hf$$

Where:

h is the sum of the difference between the maximum height of the airship during the tour and the height of the user-defined way-points.

Hf is a user defined value; for a large value the GA will select the solution that ASA will not assume to go up even if the tour will be longer.

4. Experiments and Results

The proposed algorithm is implemented using MATLAB and tested both in a virtual terrain generated by Gaussian functions and with a real three-dimensional map of our experimental area in Hemer (Northrhine-Westfalia), the following figures showing the results of the experiments.

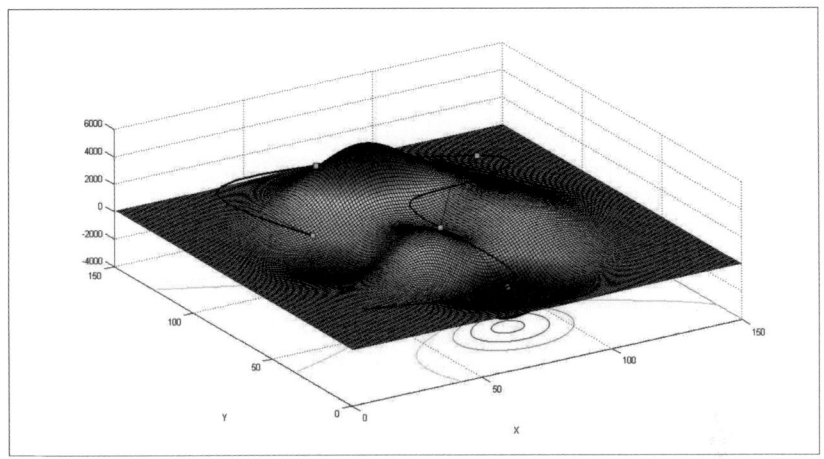

Figure (5): Sample tour for 6 user defined way-points in a terrain generated by Gaussian function.

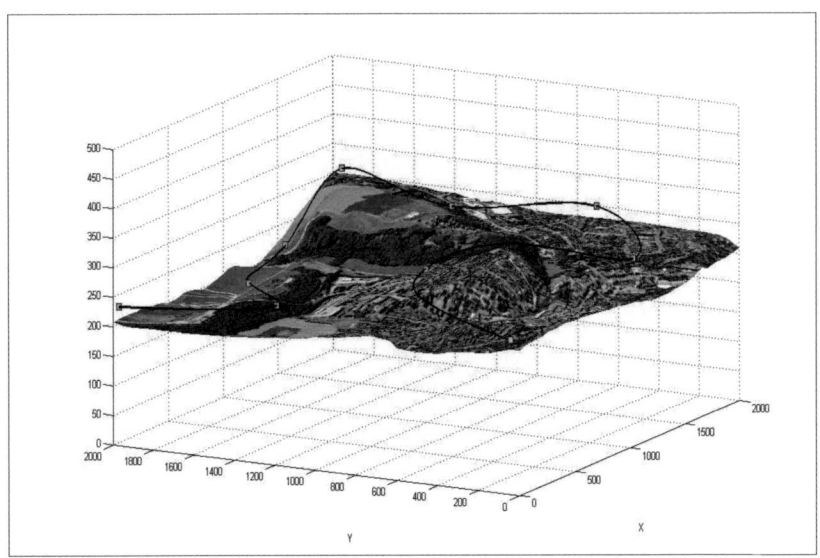

Figure (6): a sample tour of 10 user defined way-points in map of Hemmer.

5. Conclusion:

This paper represents an Off-Line path planner for small autonomously operating airships in well known static 3D environments. Using G.A. search, the separation between Preparation phase and the G.A. process reduces the execution time of G.A. and makes the path planner more flexible. For example, it is relatively simple to modify the proposed G.A., or to integrate optimization criteria considering further factors of influence (like the direction of wind force, the energy consumed by airship devices ...etc.).

6. References

[1]. Anargyros N. Kostaras, Ioannis K. Nikolos, Nikos C. Tsourveloudis, and Kimon P.Valavanis: *Evolutionary Algorithm Based Off-Line/On-Line Path Planner for UAV Navigation*. Proceedings of the 10th Mediterranean Conference on Control and Automation – MED 2002 Lisbon, Portugal, July 9-12. 2002.

[2]. Bruno Siciliano, Oussama Khatib, Frans Groen: *Robot Navigation from Nature Simultaneous Localisation, Mapping, and Path Planning Based on Hippocampal Models*. Springer Tracts in Advanced Robotics Volume 41 ISSN 1610-7438. Springer-Verlag Berlin Heidelberg.2008

[3]. Christopher Bolkcom, *Potential Military Use of Airships and Aerostats*, CRS Report for Congress, USA, 2004

[4]. Florian Adolf, Franz Andert, Sven Lorenz, Lukas Goormann, and Jörg Dittrich: *An Unmanned Helicopter for Autonomous Flights in Urban Terrain*. German Workshop on Robotics GWR2009, Braunschwrig-Germany, 2009.

[5]. Francois C.J. Allaire, Mohamed Tarbouchi, Gilles Labonte and Giovanni Fusina: *FPGA Implementation of Genetic Algorithm for UAV Real-Time Path Planning*. Springer Science. 2008

[6]. Isil Hasirciolgu Haluk Rahmi Murat Ermis: *3-D Path Planning for the Navigation of Unmanned Aerial Vehicles by Using Evolutionary Algorithms*, GECCO'08, Atlanta-Georgia USA, 2008

[7]. Ismail Al-Taharwa, Alaa Sheta and Mohammed Al-Weshah: *A Mobile Robot Path Planning Using Genetic Algorithm in Static Environment*, Journal of Computer Science 4 (4): 341-344, ISSN 1549-3636, Science Publication, 2008.

[8]. Naef Taher Al-Rashedi and Jalal Atoum: *Solving Travel salesman Problem Using New Operator in Genetic Algorithms*, American Journals of Applied Sciences 6 (8): 1586-1590, 2009.

[9]. Zixing, CAI., Lingli, YU., Chang, XIAO., Lijue, LIU.: *Path Planning for Mobile Robots in Irregular Environment Using Immune Evolutionary Algorithm.* Proceedings of the 17th World Congress The International Federation of Automatic Control Seoul, Korea, July 6-11, 2008.

Robuste Boden-Hindernis Segmentierung durch ein Ensemble von Experten für die Navigation mobiler Roboter

Luis Felipe Posada, Krishna Kumar Narayanan, Frank Hoffmann, Torsten Bertram

Lehrstuhl für Regelungssystemtechnik
Fakultät für Elektrotechnik und Informationtechnik
Technische Universität Dortmund
44221 Dortmund
E-Mail: {felipe.posada}{krishna.narayanan}{frank.hoffmann}{torsten.bertram}@tu-dortmund.de

Zusammenfassung

Dieser Beitrag stellt eine neue Methode zur Segmentierung von Boden und Hindernissen in omnidirektionalen Ansichten vor. Die Segmentierung beruht auf der Fusion mehrerer Klassifikationen die auf heterogenen Segmentierungsverfahren mit unterschiedlichen visuellen Merkmalen basieren. Die Daten zum Antrainieren und Testen der Klassifikatoren werden mit Hilfe einer Photonic Mixer Device (PMD) Kamera aus 3D Scans der lokalen Umgebung generiert. Die Klassifikation wird zusätzlich durch eine Kantenerkennung und Ultraschallabstandsmessungen unterstützt. Die unabhängigen, sich ergänzenden Expertenentscheidungen werden durch drei unterschiedliche Verfahren zusammengefasst: Stacked Generalisation, Behavior Knowledge Space und Kombination durch Abstimmung. Der kombinierte Klassifikator erreicht eine Klassifikationsgüte von bis zu 0.96 korrekt Positiven bei nur 0.03 falsch Positiven. Ein robustes Navigationsverhalten erwächst aus der situationsabhängigen Auswahl zwischen einem Hindernisvermeidungs- und einem Flurfolgeverhalten, welche beide auf der Wahrnehmung der lokalen, freien Umgebung des Roboters beruhen.

1 Einführung

In der zurückliegenden Dekade hat das Interesse an bildbasierter Navigation in der mobilen Robotik beständig zugenommen [1]. Im Gegensatz zu herkömmlichen Abstandssensoren ermöglicht die Bildverarbeitung die erscheinungsbasierte Unterscheidung von Objekten, wie Boden, Hindernissen, Personen, Türen, Wänden und Möbeln. Dafür jedoch steht die Bildverarbeitung vor der Herausforderung, die für die jeweilige Aufgabe relevanten Signale und Merkmale zu definieren und aus der hochdimensionalen Rohbildinformation effektiv in Echtzeit zu extrahieren. Die Bildanalyse einer Szene wird durch das Fehlen von Tiefeninformationen erschwert. Zudem variieren visuelle Signale wie Intensität, Farbe, Textur und optischer Fluß stark mit dem Erscheinungsbild der Umgebung, der Blickrichtung und den vorherrschenden Beleuchtungsverhältnissen. Eine robuste Klassifikation des freien lokalen Raumes ist ein wichtiger Baustein für die bildbasierte Navigation, Lokalisation und Kartenbildung mobiler Roboter. Im Zusammenhang kartenunabhängiger lokaler Hindernisvermeidung ersetzt oder ergänzt die bildbasierte Klassifikation der unmittelbaren Umgebung konventionelle Abstandssensoren und ermöglicht reaktive Ausweichmanöver des Roboters auch in schwierigen Situationen.

In der Literatur finden sich zahlreiche Ansätze zur Segmentierung des freien Bodens, unter anderem Verfahren welche die Erscheinung von Objekten durch Farbhistogramme repräsentieren [2, 3, 4]. Der in [3] vorgestellte Ansatz extrahiert den freien Raum durch die fortlaufende Anpassung eines erscheinungsbasierten Modells des Bodens. Dieses Model wird fortlaufend anhand der als hindernisfrei angenommenen Pixel in unmittelbarer Nähe des Roboters aktualisiert. Der Ansatz von [4] schätzt die Ausdehnung des freien Raumes und ersetzt damit auf der Laufzeit basierende Abstandssensoren. In [5] entwirft und optimiert ein evolutionärer Algorithmus einen visuellen Abstandssensor durch die Identifikation domänenspezifischen Merkmale und Einschränkungen.

Die in [6] präsentierte Methode beruht auf der Erkennung von Bodenregionen mit Hilfe planarer Homographien, welche über die Verfolgung von Ecken über mehrere Ansichten bestimmt werden. Das Verfahren von [7] segmentiert die Bodenebene durch die Abschätzung der Oberflächennormalen mittels optischem Fluß. In [8] beruht die Segmentierung auf einem zweistufigen K-means Clustering unter Verwending lokaler Farbinformation und Texturbeschreibungen. Die Schätzung des freien Bodens in [9] basiert auf einem Gaußschen Prozessmodell entweder von Kantenmerkmalen oder den Hauptkomponenten des Bildes.

Der selbstüberwachten Erkennung passierbaren Terrains kommt beim autonomen Fahren auf unbefestigten Wegen zunehmende Bedeutung zu. Die sogenannten nah-zu-fern Onlinelernverfahren [10, 11, 12] ermitteln zunächst die tatsächliche Begrenzung der unmittelbar vor dem Fahrzeug befindlichen Fahrbahn mit Hilfe von Laserabstandssensoren. Aus diesen Daten wird ein erscheinungsbasiertes Model der Fahrbahn erzeugt, welches dann über die Bildverarbeitung die korrekte Klassifikation weiter entfernt liegender befahrbarer Abschnitte ermöglicht.

Die Grundidee aus einer Menge heterogener Segmentierungsverfahren und Merkmale, den für die jeweilige Situation am besten geeigneten Experten auszuwählen wurde in [13] präsentiert. Eine PMD-Kamera stellt die Keime und Valdierungsdaten für die Überwachung und Auswahl mehrerer erscheinungsbasierter Segmentierungen in der omnidirektionalen Ansicht zur Verfügung. In dem hier vorgestellten Ansatz, dient die mit Hilfe der PMD-Kamera um die Tiefe ergänzte Bildinformation lediglich dazu Trainingsbeispiele für das Offline-Training der bildbasierten Klassifikatoren zu generieren. Während der Laufzeit, dienen Pixel die bereits in der vorherigen Segmentierung mit hoher Konfidenz klassifiziert wurden als Keime für eine markerbasierte Segmentierung mit Region Growing und Watershed.

Obwohl die Literatur über eine Reihe robusten Boden-Hindernis Segmentierungsmethoden berichtet, liegt die Neuartigkeit des hier vorgestellten Ansatz in der Kombination der Entscheidungen mehrerer heterogener Experten [14]. Die Grundidee besteht darin mehrere Segmentierungen in einer Weise zu kombinieren, bei welcher die Gesamtentscheidung von den kontextabhängigen, gegenseitigen Stärken der Einzelmethoden profitiert. Die Analyse bestätigt, dass sich durch die Kombination verschiedenartiger Klassifikatoren eine Klassifikationgüte erzielen lässt, welche die über das gesamte Spektrum an Situationen betrachtete Genauigkeit jedes einzelnen Klassifikators deutlich übertrifft.

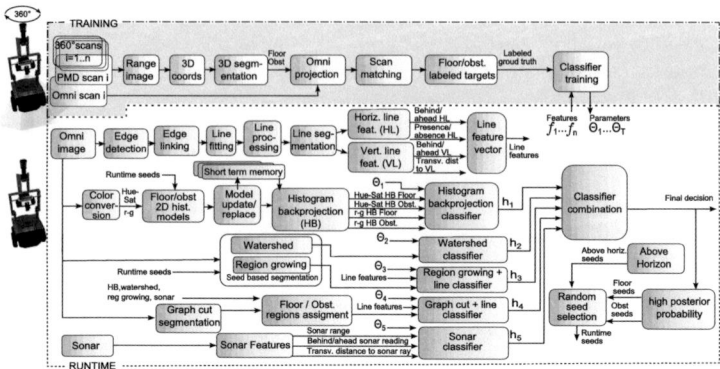

Bild 1: Systemarchitektur

2 Systemarchitektur

Die Gesamtarchitektur des Systems ist in Abbildung Fig. 1 dargestellt. Der obere Teil illustriert die Erzeugung der gelabelten Beispieldaten für das Training der Klassifikatoren. Der untere Teil zeigt die Merkmalsgenerierung, Segmentierungsverfahren und die Kombination der Expertenentscheidungen. Die Trainingsdaten werden mit Hilfe einer PMD Kamera generiert, welche zusätzlich zur Intensität des 204 x 204 Pixel großen Bildes auch dessen Tiefeninformation über einen Blickwinkel von $40° \times 40°$ zur Verfügung stellt. Zur Laufzeit verzichtet das Verfahren auf die PMD Kamera. Zur Aufnahme eines Panoramatiefenbild verschiedenartiger Szenen, wie Flur, Räume und mit Objekten verstellten Umgebungen werden Roboter und PMD Kamera um 360° gedreht. Das Panaromabild ensteht aus der Überlagerung und Registrierung der Einzelaufnahmen mit Hilfe von Scanmatching. Aus den in Form einer Punktwolke vorliegenden 3D Daten werden mit Hilfe des RANSAC-Algorithmus die wesentlichen in der Szene enthaltenen planaren Oberflächen bestimmt. Die zuverlässige Klassifikation eines 3D Punktes in Boden oder Hindernis erfolgt dann anhand der Orientierung der Oberflächennormale, des Abstands zur Kamera und von Nachbarschaftsbeziehungen. Die Klassifikation der 3D-Punkte wird durch Projektion in das Bild der omnidirektionalen Ansicht übertragen. Abbildung 2 illustriert die Projektion der beiden Klassen Boden und Hindernis vom 3D-Scan auf die omnidirektionale Ansicht. Im linken Tiefenbild (a) entsprechen helleren Regionen niedrigen Abstände zur Kamera. Die aus dem Tiefenbild der Szene mit Hilfe von RANSAC extrahierten und anschließend klassifizierten Ebenen, in diesem Falle die Bodenebene und zwei Wände, sind in Abbildung (b) zu sehen. Die Übertragung der Klassifikation auf den zugehörigen Sektor der omnidirektionalen Anicht ist in Abbildung (c) dargestellt. Abbildung (d) zeigt die vollständige Klassifikation, die sich aus der Überlagerung der Einzelscans ergibt. Der äußere Ring entspricht Bildpunkten die oberhalb des Horizonts liegen und daher unter der Annahme eines ebenen Bodens als Hindernispixel gelten.

Zur Laufzeit beruht die lokale Navigation des Pioneer 3DX Roboters ausschließlich auf der erscheinungsbasierten Segmentierung der omnidirektionalen Ansicht ohne die Unterstützung der PMD Kamera. Die omnidirektionale Bildverarbeitung für die Bodensegmentierung besteht aus einer konventionellen CCD Kamera auf der ein hyperbolischer

Spiegel mit einem vertikalen Blickfeld von 75° montiert ist. Der überwiegende Anteil des Blickfeldes dient der Wahrnehmung des Bodens, lediglich ein Blickfeld von 15° erfasst die Szene oberhalb des Horizontes.

3 Boden Hindernis Klassifikation

Das Expertengremium konstituiert sich, wie in Abbildung dargestellt 1 aus fünf Naiven Bayes Klassifikatoren. Vier unterschiedliche Segmentierungsverfahren generieren heterogene Segmentierungen: 2D Histogram Backprojection; markerbasiertes Watershed und Region Growing und Graph Cut. Ein zusätzlicher Klassifikator verwendet die von den Ultraschallsensoren bereitgestellte Abstandsinformation. Aufgrund der Ausbreitungs- und Reflektionseigenschaften von Ultraschall sind diese Daten fehlerbehaftet und besitzen eine niedrige Winkelauflösung. Region Growing und Graph Cut werden zudem durch die Erkennung vertikaler und horizontaler Linienmerkmale unterstützt indem sich beide Segmentierungsverfahren an den Kanten orientieren. Die beiden übrigen Segmentierungsalgorithmen verzichten auf Linienmerkmale um die Heterogenität der Segmentierungen zu gewährleisten. Diese bewusst erzeugte Diversität gewährleistet die Unabhängigkeit der Fehler der zugeordneten Klassifikatoren. Diese Unabhängigkeit der Fehlerverteilungen ist eine wesentliche Voraussetzung dafür, dass Ensemble von Klassifikatoren die Klassifikationsgüte gegenüber den Einzelentscheidern tatsächlich verbessern.

Eine Segmentierung an sich ist zunächst einmal nicht gleichbedeutend mit einer Klassifikation. Vielmehr stellt die Segmentierung lediglich die Merkmale für die nachgeschaltete Klassifikation durch einen Naive Bayes Klassifikator zur Verfügung. Einzelne Segmentierungsverfahren erzeugen dabei gleichzeitig mehrere Merkmale, so berechnet Histogram Backprojection beispielsweise die Ähnlichkeit der lokalen Umgebung des Pixels mit den Histogrammen des Boden- und Hindernismodells in verschiedenen Farbräumen. Der Naive Bayes Klassifikator schätzt die Zugehörigkeit eines einzelnen Pixels zu den beiden Klassen Boden und Hindernis anhand der mit Hilfe der Segmentierung generierten Merkmale. Die bedingte Wahrscheinlichkeit $p(f_i|C_j)$ des Auftretens eines Merkmals f_i bei bekannter Klassenzugehörigkeit C_j wird im Fall kontinuierlicher Merkmale durch eine Normalverteilung und im Falle diskreter Merkmale durch eine Multnomialverteilung charakterisiert. Die Wahrscheinlichkeiten der Merkmale und die a priori Wahrscheinlichkeiten der Klassen werden anhand ihrer beobachteten Häufigkeit in den Trainingsdaten geschätzt. Der Naive Bayes Klassifikator berechnet für einen Merkmalsvektor f die a posteriori Wahrscheinlichkeiten der Klassen $C = \{Floor, Obstacle\}$ anhand der Wahrscheinlichkeiten der als voneinander unabhängig angenommenen Einzelmerkmale f_i.

$$p(C_j|f_i) = \frac{1}{Z}p(C_j)\prod_{i=1}^{n}p(f_i|C_j) \tag{1}$$

Dabei beschreibt die im nachhinein bestimmte Normalisierung Z die Wahrscheinlichkeit des Merkmalsvektor f. Die letztendliche Entscheidungsgrenze ist problemspezifisch und bestimmt sich aus den relativen Kosten für falsch negative und falsche positive Klassifikationsfehler. Obwohl die Unabhängigkeitsannahme der Merkmale nur teilweise erfüllt ist, erzielt der Naive Bayes Klassifikator eine gute Klassifikationsgüte bei gegenüber Bayes Netzwerken vergleichsweise geringem Rechenaufwand. Die geringe Rechenkomplexität erlaubt die Klassifikation aller Bildpunkte mit einer für die Navigation des mobilen Roboters ausreichend hohen Abtastrate von 3Hz.

Für die Kombination der Einzelentscheidungen der Klassifikatoren zu einem Gesamtvotum untersuchen wir vier unterschiedliche Methoden [14]: Bei der Stacked Generalization fungieren die Klassifikationen der Einzelentscheider als Merkmale eines nachgeschalteten Metaklassifikators. Die Behavior Knowledge Space (BKS) Methode erzeugt eine Look-Up Tabelle, welche den möglichen Kombinationen der Einzelentscheidungen die in den Trainingsdaten beobachtete Klassenhäufigkeit dieser Kombination zuordnet. Ausserdem betrachten wir eine Entscheidungsfindung über die Mehrheitsklasse und den Median der Einzelentscheidungen. An dieser Stelle sei angemerkt, dass die markerbasierten Segmentierungsalgorithmen ihre Keime aus den im vorherigen Bild mit hoher Eindeutigkeit klassifizierten Pixeln beziehen. Diese Vorgehensweise rechtfertigt sich durch den durch das weite Blickfeld der omnidirektionalen Kamera und die hohe Bildrate vergleichsweise geringen optischen Fluß. Daher ändert sich die Klassifikation zweier aufeinanderfolgender Bilder hauptsächlich in den Grenzregionen zwischen Boden und Hindernis, die sich durch mehrdeutige Klassenwahrscheinlichkeiten auszeichnen.

(a) (b) (c) (d)

Bild 2: Generierung der Trainingsdaten mit Hilfe der PMD Kamera: (a) Tiefenbild, (b) aus den 3D Daten mit RANSAC extrahierte Ebenen, (c) Projektion der Klassen in die omnidirektionale Ansicht, (d) Klassifikation der vollständigen Ansicht nach Registrierung und Überlagerung der Einzelbilder und Maskierung der sich oberhalb des Horizontes befindlichen Szene

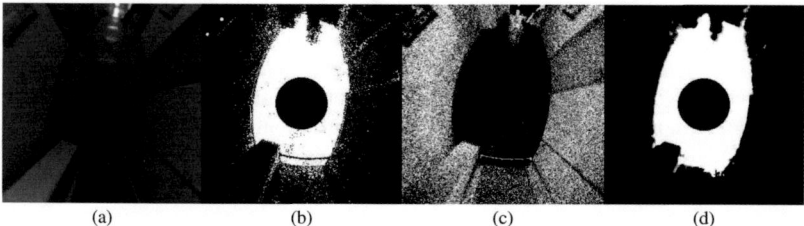

(a) (b) (c) (d)

Bild 3: Histogram Backprojection Segmentierung: (a) Eingangsbild, (b) Rückprojektion mit dem H-S Bodenmodel, (c) Rückprojektion mit dem H-S Hindernismodel, (d) Ausgabe des Histogram Backprojection Klassifikators unter Berücksichtigung der H-S und r-g Boden- und Hindernismodelle.

3.1 Histogram Backprojection

Histogram backprojection [15] erkennt Bildregionen, die in ihrer Erscheinung einem Referenzmodell ähneln. Das normalisierte Histogrammreferenzmodell M im normierten, zweidimensionalen Farbraum wird mit dem normalisierten Histogramm H des aktuellen

Bildes I verglichen. Das rückprojezierte Bild B beschreibt den Ähnlichkeitsgrad einer Region mit dem Referenzmodell und berechnet sich zu

$$B(u, v) = min \left(\frac{M(c(u, v))}{H(c(u, v))}, 1 \right) \in [0, 1] \tag{2}$$

wobei $c(u, v)$ die zweikomponentige Farbinformation des Pixel (u, v) darstellt.

Anstatt lediglich ein Farbmodell des Flures zu generieren, verwendet unser Ansatz zusätzlich ein explizites Modell der Wände und Hindernisse. Dadurch lässt sich die Entscheidungsgrenze zwischen beiden Klassen präziser festlegen, als dies bei einer Abgrenzung des Flures gegenüber einem unspezifischem Hintergrund der Fall wäre. Das Hindernismodell wird anhand der über der Horizontlinie befindlichen Pixel fortlaufend aktualisiert. Um eine ausreichende Generalisierungsfähigkeit zu gewährleisten werden die 2D Histogramme in 32-32 Bins quantisiert und über mehrere Bilder gemittelt und normalisiert.

Der auf rückprojezierten Histogrammen basierende Naive Bayes Klassifikator fusioniert Merkmale der vier folgenden visuellen Kanäle: Das Boden- und Hindernismodell verwenden einerseits den Buntton (hue) und den Sättigungskanal (saturation) Kanal des HSV Farbraumes und in analoger Weise die Rot-Grün-Kanäle des normalisierten RGB Farbraumes. Die Ähnlichkeit der Szene (a) mit den beiden Modelle Flur (b) und Hindernis (c) ist in in Abbildung 3 dargestellt. Aus diesen Merkmalen berechnet der Naive Bayes Klassifikators die durch die Helligkeit in Abbildung (d) repräsentierte Wahrscheinlichkeit der Klasse Boden.

Um den durch die Bewegung verursachten allmählichen Änderungen in der Erscheinung des Bodens und der Umgebung Rechnung zu tragen werden die Referenzhistogramme mit Hilfe eines gleitenden Mittelwertes fortlaufend aktualisiert.

$$\bar{M}(x, y)_t = \alpha M(x, y)_t + (1 - \alpha)\bar{M}(x, y)_{t-1} \tag{3}$$

wobei M_t das Histogramm des aktuellen Bildes und $\bar{M}_{t-1}$ den vorherigen gleitenden Mittelwert beschreibt. Die Abklingrate von $\alpha = 0.6$ gewichtet Beobachtungen der jüngeren Vergangenheit stärker. Im Falle abrupter Änderungen der Szene, beispielsweise bei Übergängen zwischen unterschiedlichen Bodenbelägen, werden jeweils neue Modelle aufgesetzt, anstatt die bisherigen Modelle anzupassen. Ein neues Model wird instanziert sobald das Histogramm einer signifikant ausgedehnten Bildregion sich mit keinem der bis dato im Kurzzeitgedächtnis gespeicherten Referenzhistogramme deckt. Aufgrund der begrenzten Rechenzeit speichert das Kurzzeitgedächtnis gleichzeitig maximal fünf unterschiedliche Hindernis- und zwei unterschiedliche Bodenmodelle. Die Histogrammähnlichkeit ergibt sich aus der Schnittmenge:

$$d(M_1, M_2) = \sum_{x,y} min(M_1(x, y), M_2(x, y)) \in [0, 1] \tag{4}$$

In der Praxis, wird ein neues Model instanziert sobald die Histogrammähnlichkeit zwischen dem aktuellen Bild und dem ähnlichsten gespeicherten Modell unter einen Schwellwert von 0.4 fällt. Das neue Histogrammmodell ersetzt dabei im Kurzzeitgedächtnis dasjenige Modell, dessen letzter erfolgreicher Vergleich am weitesten in der Vergangenheit zurückliegt. Modelle die über die letzten dreissig Bilder keinen einzigen Vergleich gewinnen konnten werden automatisch verworfen.

3.2 Markerbasiertes Watershed

Markerbasierte Watershed Segmentierung [15] lässt sich am besten verstehen, indem man das Gradientbild als ein topologisches Höhenprofil interpretiert. Die Wasserscheiden stimmen mit den Maxima des Gradientenbildes überein. Ausgehend von den Markierungen werden Pixel, analog zu Wasser das sich den Weg bahnt, dem nächstgelegenen lokalen Minimum zugeordnet und formen durch Fluten des Profils Becken. Dieser Prozess kommt zum Stillstand, sobald der Pegel die höchstgelegenen Wasserscheiden erreicht hat. Becken die ursprünglich mit der gleichen Markierung verbunden sind vereinigen sich zu einer Region. Ein Beispiel für markerbasiertes Watershed Segmentierung bei der eine zufällige Auswahl von Pixeln mit hoher Klassenkonfidenz als Marker dienen ist in Abbildung 4 zu sehen.

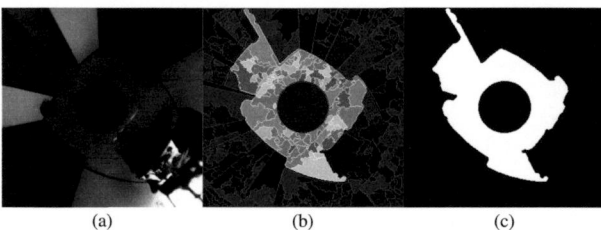

(a)   (b)   (c)

Bild 4: Watershed Segmentierung: (a) Eingangsbild (b) markerbasiertes Watershed mit zufälligen Keimen (c) auf Watershed Segmentierung basierende Klassifikation anhand der Zuordnung verlässlicher Boden-Hindernis Marker

3.3 Linienmerkmale

Kanten stimmen oftmals mit Bildregionen überein in welcher die Szene diskontinuierliche Änderungen in der Form, Tiefe oder Materialeigenschaften aufweist. Kanten entstehen allerdings ebenso bei Variation der Beleuchtung wie beispielsweise Reflektionen oder Schattenwurf. Nichtdestotrotz, bieten insbesondere geradlinige Kanten Anhaltspunkte für die Anwesenheit von Hindernissen und damit einen wertvollen Fingerzeig um die Klassifikation der Region Growing und Graph Cut Segmentierungen zu verbessern.

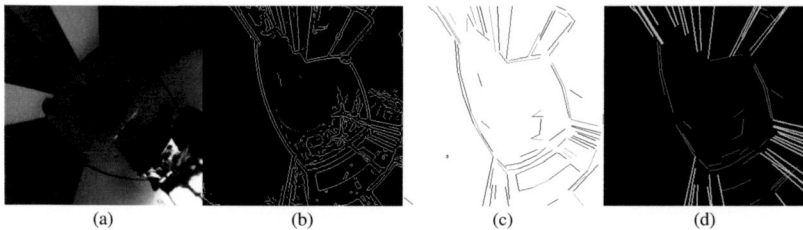

(a)   (b)   (c)   (d)

Bild 5: Linienmerkmale: (a) Eingangsbild (b) Canny Kantenerkennung (c) Kantenverfolgung und Liniensuche (d) vertikale und horizontale Linien

Anstatt lediglich die Kantenzugehörigkeit einzelner Pixel zu betrachten berücksichtigt unser Ansatz deren Konnektivität. Kanten werden zunächst durch Konturverfolgung vervollständigt und anschliessend sukzessive in Linienzüge unterteilt. Dazu wird eine Kontur zunächst global durch eine Gerade zwischen ihren beiden Endpunkten grob approximiert. Diese gerade Linie wird rekursiv in mehreren Linien zerlegt, indem an den Punkten maximaler lateraler Abweichung der Kontur von der bisherigen Linie ein neuer Anfangs- und Endpunkt eingefügt wird. Die sich ergebenden Linien werden anhand ihrer Orientierung im omnidirektionalen Bild hinsichtlich ihrer tatsächliche räumlichen Orientierung in vertikale und horizontale Linien klassifiziert. Radiale Linien im omnidirektionalen Bild entsprechen dabei räumlich vertikalen Strukturen wie Regalen, Schränken oder Tischbeinen. Tangentiale Linien in der omnidirektionalen Ansicht verweisen auf horizontale Strukturen und deuten auf Boden-Objekt-Kanten von Hindernissen oder Wänden hin.

Entsprechend dieser Einteilung lassen sich für die Lage eines Pixels bezüglich der ihm nächstgelegenen Linie vier Anordnungen unterscheiden: a) oberhalb oder unterhalb einer horizontalen Linie; b) Anwesenheit oder Abwesenheit einer horizontalen Linie in der Nachbarschaft; für diese Eigenschaft überprüft man ob sich die nächstgelegene horizontale Linie und die Verbindungsgeraden zwischen dem Bildmittelpunkt und dem Pixel u, v schneiden; c) oberhalb oder unterhalb einer vertikalen Linie; d) senkrechter Abstand zur nächstgelegenen vertikalen Linie.

3.4 Region Growing

Dieser Klassifikator fusioniert die Segmentierung durch Region Growing [16] mit den horizontalen und vertikalen Linienmerkmalen. Region growing fügt ausgehend von einer Menge von isolierten Pixeln die als Keime fungieren einer Region sukzessive benachbarte Bildpunkte anhand ihrer Ähnlichkeit hinzu. Der Klassifikator beruht auf zwei unterschiedlichen Segmentierungen, einer welche als zuverlässig geltende Flurpixel als anfängliche Keime verwendet und einer zweiten Segmentierung die aus Keimen die zu Hindernissen zählen wächst. Das Segmentierungsergebnis hängt stark von der Wahl der initialen Keime ab. Daher wird die Segmentierung für beide Typen mehrmals mit zufällig gewählten Keimen wiederholt. Als Merkmale der Zugehörigkeit eines Pixels dient die Differenz der Anzahl der Segmentierungen in denen er der jeweiligen Region Flur oder Hindernis zugehört. Die Gesamtausgabe des Klassifikators unter zusätzlicher Unterstützung der Linienmerkmale ist in den Abbildungen 6(b) und (c) zu sehen.

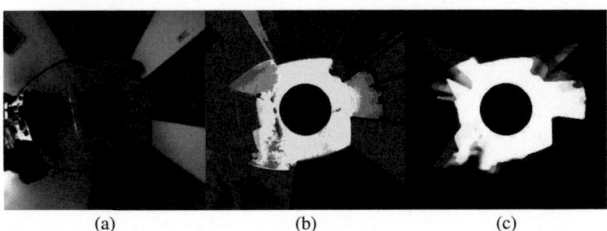

(a) (b) (c)

Bild 6: Region Growing Segmentierung: (a) Eingangsbild (b) Region Growing (c) Ausgabe des Klassifikators unter Einbeziehung der Linienmerkmale

3.5 Ultraschall Abstandsmessungen

Der auf den Ultraschallabstandsmessungen basierende Klassifikator berechnet die Wahrscheinlichkeiten der beiden Klassen Boden und Hindernis auf der Basis der beobachteten Häufigkeit $p(C_i|r, d, a)$ einer Messung (r, d, a). Das Merkmal r entspricht dem vom Sensor entlang seiner Achse gemessenen Reichweite zum nächstgelegenen Objekt und ist auf zehn Intervalle diskretisiert. d bezeichnet den lateralen Abstand des Pixels zu der in das omnidirektionale Bild projizierten Hauptachse des nächstgelegenen Ultraschallsensors. Das binäre Merkmal a definiert, ob der entsprechende Pixel in radialer Richtung vor oder hinter der vom Sensor gemessenen Reichweite liegt. Die Ausgabe des Ultraschallklassifikators für eine Abstandsmessung der sechzehn Sensoren ist in Abbildung 7 dargestellt. Die Unzuverlässigkeit von Ultraschallabstandsmessungen wird aus den beiden nordwestlichen Messungen deutlich, welche die Ausdehnung des freien Raumes in diese Richtung deutlich überschätzen. Diese Fehleranfälligkeit motiviert die Verwendung bildgebender Sensoren um eine höhere Zuverlässigkeit und gegenüber Sonarsensoren deutlich verbesserte Winkelauflösung zu erzielen.

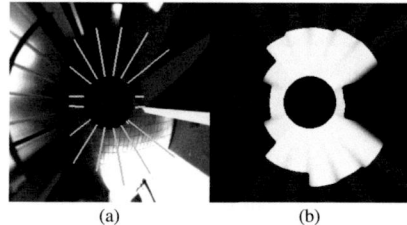

(a)   (b)

Bild 7: Auf Ultraschallabstandsmessungen basierender Klassifikator: (a) Eingangsbild mit projezierten Abstandsmessungen (b) Ausgabe des Klassifikators

3.6 Graph Cut

Das Verfahren der Graph Cut Segmentierung ist in [16] beschrieben. Es handelt sich um eine sehr effiziente Methode, bei welcher die resultierenden Segmentierungen auf dem Vergleich der entstehenden Teilregionen basiert. Dabei entsprechen Regionen den Knoten eines Graphen und die Unterschiedlichkeit zweier benachbarter Regionen wird durch eine Kante repräsentiert. Der Graph wird konstruiert indem Bildpunkte in einen Merkmalsraum transformiert werden welche die Bildkoordinaten (x, y) des Pixels mit seinem RGB Farbwert vereint. Kanten im Graphen verbinden im Merkmalsraum benachbarte Punkte. Ziel ist es, das Bild so in Regionen zu unterteilen, dass deren Ähnlichkeit minimal wird. Ob eine durch Graph Cut segmentierte Region letztendlich dem Boden oder den Hindernissen zugeordnet wird, ergibt sich aus der Zuordnung der vorhergehenden Klassifikation.

Der Algorithmus arbeitet von Natur aus unüberwacht, so dass sich in bestimmten Situationen eine Region ungrenzt ausdehnt. Daher erscheint es sinnvoll bei der Klassifikation die Graph Cut Segmentierung gemeinsam mit den Linienmerkmalen zu betrachten. Fig. 8 verdeutlicht die Graph Cut Segmentierung, die Zuweisung von Teilregionen zu Boden und Hindernis und die Vorteile der Einbeziehung der Linienmerkmale zur Begrenzung der Ausbreitung von Regionen.

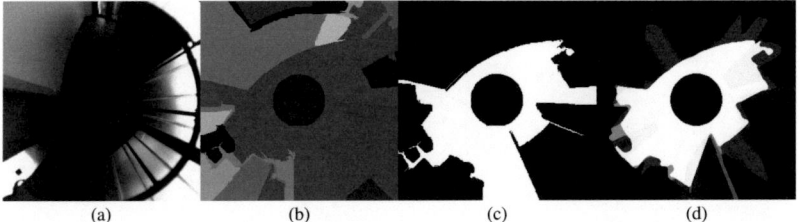

(a)   (b)   (c)   (d)

Bild 8: Graph Cut Segmentierung: (a) Eingangsbild (b) Graph Cut Segmentierung (c) Boden-Hindernis-Zuweisung der Graph Cut Regionen auf der Basis vorheriger Segmentierungen d) Ausgabe des Klassifikators unter Einbeziehung der Linienmerkmale

4 Experimentelle Ergebnisse

Die Trainingsdaten umfassen annähernd zwei Millionen Pixel aus 500 Bildern, für welche die Klassenzugehörigkeit aus der Tiefeninformation und der räumlichen Ebenensegmentierung bestimmt wurde. Die Klassifikationsgüte wird auf der Basis 500 weiterer klassifizierter, jedoch beim Training nicht präsentierter Bilder bestimmt. Das Anlernen bei der Stacked Generalization basiert auf einer k-fachen Kreuzvalidierung, bei der die Trainingsdaten in T disjunkte Blöcke unterteilt werden, wobei T der Anzahl der am Ensemble partizipierenden Klassifikatoren entspricht. Jeder einzelne Klassifikator wird auf $T - 1$ Datensätzen trainiert, so dass jeweils ein ungesehener Block von Daten zum Antrainieren des Ensemble-Klassifikators verbleibt. Die Ausgaben der Klassifikatoren auf ihren jeweilen Validierungsdaten in Verbindung mit deren bekannter Klasse dienen dem Antrainieren des übergeordneten Ensembleklassifikators. Nach dem Training des Metaklassifikators, werden die T Basisklassifikatoren noch einmal mit dem gesamten Trainingsdatensatz angelernt.

Die Klassifikationsgüte bestimmt sich aus der Rate der falsch Positiven FPR, derem Verhältnis zu den gesamten Negativen, der Rate der korrekt Positiven TPR und deren Verhältnis zu den gesamten Positiven. Eine falsch negative Klassifikation entspricht einem Bodenpixel, welches fälschlicherweise als Hindernis klassifiziert wird, eine falsch positive Klassifikation einem Hindernispixel das fälschlicherweise als Boden markiert wird.

Die Tabelle 1 vergleicht die Raten der falsch Positiven und falsch Negativen der einzelnen Basisklassifikatoren, als da wären Histogram Backprojection, Watershed, Region Growing, Graph Cut und Sonar. Die Einbeziehung vertikaler und horizontaler Linien beim Region Growing und Graph Cut führt zu einer deutlichen Verbesserung beider Klassifikatoren. Linienmerkmalein Verbindung mit Watershed führt zu keiner Verbesserung, da Watershed bereits selber auf der Segmentierung des Gradientenbildes entlang von Kanten beruht.

Stacked Generalization weist unter allen Metaklassifikatoren die höchste korrekt positive Rate auf. Die unterlegene Klassifikationsgüte des Behavior Knowledge Space Klassifikators ist auf die Binarisierung der a posteriori Wahrscheinlichkeiten im Rahmen der Generierung der Look-Up Tabellen und dem damit einhergehenden Informationsverlust zurückzuführen. Die konzeptionell einfachen, da keiner zweiten Trainingsstufe bedürfenden Median- und Mehrheitsklassifikator zeigen die geringste falsch positiv Rate, die jedoch zu

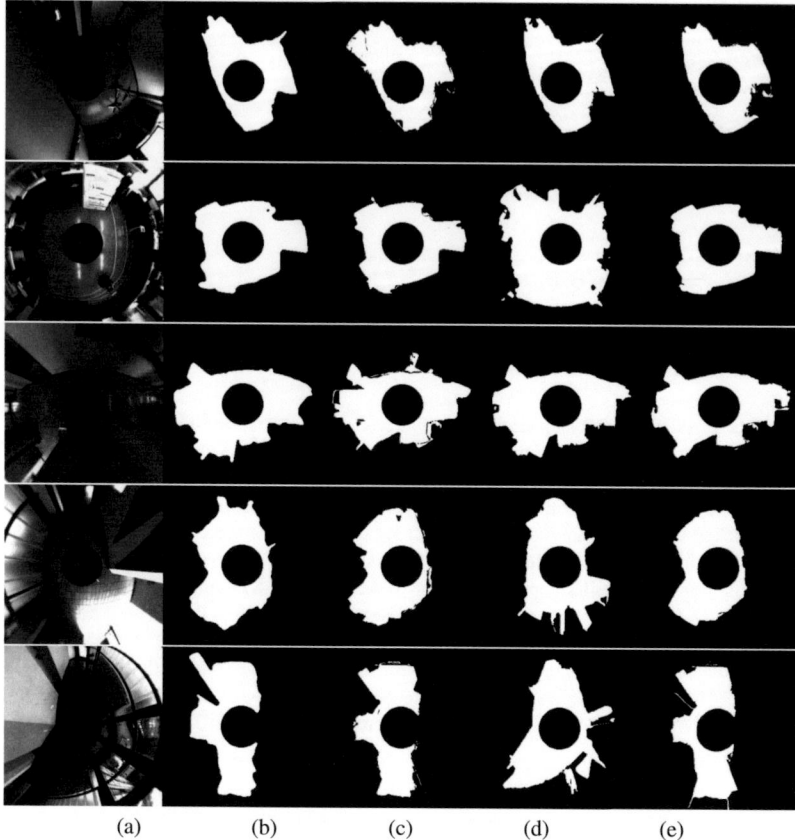

| (a) | (b) | (c) | (d) | (e) |

Bild 9: Klassifikationsergebnisse: (a) Eingangsbild, (b) Stacked Generalization, (c) Behavior Knowledge Space, (d) medianbasierte Kombination, (e) mehrheitsbasierte Kombination.

Lasten der korrekt positiv erkannten Instanzen geht. Im Kontext der Hindernisvermeidung besitzt die falsch positiv Rate die höchste Relevanz´, da das Übersehen eines Hindernis wesentlich kritischer als die Unterschätzung der Ausdehnung des freien Raumes ist. Eine der Haupteigenschaft der Median-Kombination ist die Filterung von Ausreißern einzelner Segmentierungsverfahren.

Abbildung 9 zeigt die Ergebnisse vierer prototypischer Szenarien mit den jeweiligen Segmentierungen der vier Metaklassifikatoren. Das erste Szenario zeichnet sich durch störende Reflektionen und Schatten aus, welche alleine auf Basis der Farbinformation fälschlicherweise als Hindernisse erkannt werden. Die Hinzunahme der vertikalen Linienmerkmale verbessert die Segmentierung deutlich, da die drei vertikalen Stative im unteren rechten Bildteil korrekt vom Boden segmentiert werden, obwohl sie einige der Basisklassifikatoren nicht als Hindernisse erkennen. Die zweite Szene entspricht einer typischen Büroumgebungen mit hohem Kontrast zwischen Boden und Hindernissen. Die

Tabelle 1: Klassifikationsgüte

Methode	FPR	TPR
Histogram Backprojection	0.085	0.889
Watershed	0.042	0.945
Watershed + Linienmerkmale	0.036	0.938
Region Growing	0.120	0.718
Region Growing + Linienmerkmale	0.044	0.907
Graph Cut	0.064	0.869
Graph Cut + Linienmerkmale	0.023	0.917
Sonar	0.045	0.890
Kombination mit Stacked Generalization	0.032	0.958
Kombination mit BKS	0.030	0.912
Kombination durch Median	0.024	0.945
Kombination durch Mehrheit	0.024	0.927

durch Lichtreflektionen überstrahlten Bereiche werden korrekt dem Boden zugeordnet. Das dritte bis fünfte Szenario beinhalten Segmentierungsaufgaben, die sich durch eine erhebliche Variation der Beleuchtung, Reflektionen und Schatten auszeichnen.

Die Bildverarbeitung des Pioneer 3DX Roboter läuft auf einem 1.8 GHz Dual-Core Standardlaptop. Trotz des nicht laufzeitoptimierten Programmcodes beansprucht die vollständige Klassifikation eines omnidirektionalen 310x310 Pixel Bildes lediglich ungefähr 300ms. Eine vollständige 2D Histogram Backprojection Segmentierung bedarf 15ms, Watershed Segmentierung benötigt 10mn und Region Growing im Mittel 50ms, die Extraktion der Linien benötigt 30ms und Graph Cut weitere 180 ms.

Der als freier Raum klassifizierte Ausschnitt bildet die Wahrnehmung eines reaktiven bildbasierten Navigationsverhaltens. Die Roboterbewegung erwächst aus der situationsabhängigen Verhaltensauswahl zwischen einem Hindernisvermeidungs- und einem Flurfolgeverhalten. Die Wahrnehmung wird auf charakteristische Merkmale wie die Richtung des nächstgelegenen Hindernis und die Orientierung der kleinen und großen Hauptachse der lokalen Verteilung des freien Raumes reduziert. Die Merkmale selber und der Entwurf der beiden reaktiven Navigationsverhalten sind im Detail in [13] beschrieben. Basierend auf der hier vorgestellten Boden-Hindernis Segmentierung gelingt es dem Roboter sich über längere Zeiträume autonom ohne Kollisionen in seiner Umgebung fortzubewegen. Die Zuverlässigkeit der Methodik wurde in zahlreichen Tests in unterschiedlichen Umgebungen, von denen einzelne mehr als 15 Minuten dauerten und die sich insgesamt zu mehreren Betriebsstunden akkumulieren, nachgewiesen.

5 Zusammenfassung

Dieser Beitrag präsentiert einen neuartigen Ansatz zu einer vorwiegend bildbasierten Klassifikation von Boden und Hindernissen zur Unterstützung der Navigation mobiler Roboter. Als Trainingsdaten dienen durch räumliche Segmentierung von Ebenen aus 3D Scans einer PMD-Kamera gewonnene korrekt gelabelte omnidirektionale Bilder. Die Klassifikation basiert auf der kombinierten Entscheidung heterogener Basisklassifikatoren, deren Entscheidung ihrerseits auf unterschiedlichen Segmentierungen und visuellen Kanälen beruht.

Das Ensemble setzt sich zusammen aus Histogram Backprojection, markerbasiertem Watershed, Region Growing und Graph Cut Segmentierung. Die Region Growing und Graph Cut Segmentierung wird durch die Einbeziehung zusätzlicher Linienmerkmale verbessert. Weiterhin bilden Ultraschallabstandsmessungen eine zusätzliche Informationsquelle. Die Entscheidungen der Basisklassifikatoren werden durch Stacked Generalisation, Behavior Knowledge Space oder Median- oder Mehrheitsvotum aggregiert. Der Ensembleklassifikator erreicht dabei eine Klassifikationsgüte von 0.96 korrekt Positiven bei lediglich 0.03 falsch Positiven. Die statistische Analyse belegt, dass die Klassifikationsgüte des Ensemble von Experten die der einzelnen Basisklassifikatoren deutlich übertrifft. Die sehr genaue Segmentierung des lokalen freien Raumes bestätigt sich in mehreren Szenarien unter diverser Ausleuchtung, Textur und Farbe. Die aus dem klassifizierten, omnidirektionalen Bild gewonnene Abstandsinformation ist bezüglich Robustheit, Genauigkeit und räumlicher Auflösung mit der von Laserabstandssensoren vergleichbar. Sie bietet die Basis für ein auch in räumlich eng begrenzten Situationen zuverlässiges reaktives Hindernisvermeidungs- und Flurfolgeverhalten. Die Robustheit des Ansatzes ist durch die mehrstündige, autonome, kollisionsfreie Navigation des Roboters in unstrukturierten Umgebungen belegt. Zukünftige Untersuchungen fokussieren sich auf die Verwendung der omnidirektionalen Segmentierung im Kontext der Lokalisation und Kartenbildung mobiler Roboter.

Literatur

[1] Bonin-Font, F.; Ortiz, A.; Oliver, G.: Visual Navigation for Mobile Robots: A Survey. *Journal of Intelligent Robotics System* 53 (2008) 3, S. 263–296.

[2] Lorigo, L.; Brooks, R.; Grimsou, W.: Visually-guided obstacle avoidance in unstructured environments. In: *Proc. IEEE/RSJ IROS'97*, Bd. 1, S. 373–379. 1997.

[3] Ulrich, I.; Nourbakhsh, I.: Appearance-Based Obstacle Detection with Monocular Color Vision. In: *Proc. AAAI 2000*. Austin, TX. 2000.

[4] Lenser, S.; Veloso, M.: Visual sonar: fast obstacle avoidance using monocular vision. In: *Proc. IEEE/RSJ Int. Conf. on Intelligent Robots and Systems (IROS 2003).*, Bd. 1, S. 886–891. 2003.

[5] Martin, C. M.: Evolving visual sonar: Depth from monocular images. *Pattern Recognition Letters* 27 (2006) 11, S. 1174–1180.

[6] Pears, N.; Liang, B.: Ground plane segmentation for mobile robot visual navigation. In: *Proc. IEEE/RSJ Int. Conf. on Intelligent Robots and Systems*, Bd. 3, S. 1513–1518. 2001.

[7] Kim, Y.; Kim, H.: Layered ground floor detection for vision-based mobile robot navigation. In: *Proc. IEEE Int. Conf. on Robotics and Automation*, Bd. 1, S. 13–18. 2004.

[8] Blas, M. R.; Agrawal, M.; Sundaresan, A.; Konolige, K.: Fast color/texture segmentation for outdoor robots. In: *Proc. of IEEE/RSJ Int. Conf. on Intelligent Robots and Systems*, S. 4078–4085. 2008.

[9] Plagemann, C.; Endres, F.; Hess, J.; Stachniss, C.; Burgard, W.: Monocular range sensing: A non-parametric learning approach. In: *IEEE Int. Conf. on Robotics and Automation*. 2008.

[10] Dahlkamp, H.; Kaehler, A.; Stavens, D.; Thrun, S.; G., B.: Self-supervised monocular road detection in desert terrain. In: *Proc. of the Robotics Science and Systems Conference*. 2006.

[11] Grudic, G.; Mulligan, J.; Otte, M.; Bates, A.: Online Learning of Multiple Perceptual Models for Navigation in Unknown Terrain. In: *6th International Conference on Field and Service Robotics*. 2007.

[12] Kim, D.; Sun, J.; Min, S.; James, O.; Rehg, M.; Bobick, A. F.: Traversability Classification Using Unsupervised On-Line Visual Learning for Outdoor Robot Navigation. In: *In Proc. of Int. Conf. on Robotics and Automation (ICRA)*. 2006.

[13] Posada, L.; Narayanan, K.; Hoffmann, F.; Bertram, T.: Floor Segmentation of Omnidirectional Images for Mobile Robot Visual Navigation. In: *Proc. of IEEE/RSJ Int. Conf. on Intelligent Robots and Systems*. 2010, to be published.

[14] Polikar, R.: Ensemble Based Systems in Decision Making. *IEEE Circuits and Systems Magazine* 6 (2006) 3, S. 21–45.

[15] Swain, M. J.; Ballard, D. H.: Color indexing. *International Journal of Computer Vision* 7 (1991), S. 11–32.

[16] Felzenszwalb, P.; Huttenlocher, D.: Efficient Graph-Based Image Segmentation. *International Journal of Computer Vision* 59 (2004) 2, S. 167–181.

Self-learning with confidence bands

Matthias Hillebrand[1], Christian Wöhler[2], Lars Krüger[1],
Ulrich Kreßel[1], Franz Kummert[3]

[1]Daimler AG, Group Research and Advanced Engineering, 89081 Ulm, Germany
[2]Image Analysis Group, Technische Universität Dortmund, 44221 Dortmund, Germany
[3]Applied Informatics Group, Universität Bielefeld, 33615 Bielefeld, Germany
matthias.hillebrand@daimler.com, christian.woehler@tu-dortmund.de,
lars.krueger@daimler.com, ulrich.kressel@daimler.com, franz@techfak.uni-bielefeld.de

Abstract

Since manual labelling of huge data sets is costly and time-consuming, we propose a framework for iterative confidence-based self-learning of classifiers which autonomously extends its knowledge gained based on a small amount of initial, manually labelled training samples towards increasingly different representatives of the regarded pattern classes. During each iteration, the labels of newly selected samples are determined and the samples are added to the training set, subsequently. The crucial step is the selection of the samples which are used for re-training the classifier during each iteration. For this purpose, we rely as a new approach on the concept of confidence bands known from the field of statistics.

1 Introduction

In general, classifiers require a large number of labelled training samples preferably covering a wide range of variation to yield a comprehensive and generalising recognition behaviour. However, acquiring unlabelled data often can be done with justifiable expenditure while labelling of the data by experienced human annotators is time consuming and binds resources.

For instance, large amounts of traffic sign images can easily be recorded by driving around with camera-equipped cars and preprocessed by automatic detection algorithms, while human annotators need considerable amount of experience especially if the original data was recorded under difficult lighting or weather conditions. Furthermore, once the training of a classification system with the whole available training set of labelled samples has been completed, continuing the system training with newly recorded samples necessiate to restart the operational labelling procedures.

Once a classification system is trained that is to be designed to operate in a continuously but permanently changing environment (e.g. the real world) a difficult problem arises: The system will be confronted with the task to keep pace with changes of the environment.

A car equipped with a traffic sign recognition system that was trained with images of german traffic signs will still recognise speed limit signs on motorways in France or Belgium since traffic signs of all western European countries bear marked similarities, but the recognition will not be as accurate as in Germany. The car requires the ability to adapt its classifier(s) to the similar-looking traffic signs of other countries – supervised by a human teacher or, better yet, unsupervised and on its own.

We rise to this challenge by the use of self-learning classification systems that get along with training sets containing only small numbers of labelled samples.

Our research focus is the field of image recognition and classification. During our experiments, we concentrated on two data sets which are available to us fully labelled. The first set is the well-known MNIST database of handwritten digits [1] which contains 60.000 training and 10.000 test samples. The second set is a database with a huge amount of traffic sign images mainly consisting of speed limit and no-overtake signs recorded on German motorways.

We want to touch on the data preprocessing algorithms only shortly here because they merely involve well-known image processing and statistical methods. This includes a resizing of all images to a standard size, the adjustment of lightning conditions and a Principal Component Analysis in combination with a whitening of the data.

2 State of the Art

2.1 Self-learning

An innumerable amount of algorithmic approaches dealing with learning from data have been published so far. When dealing with data samples representing a predetermined number of defined classes a system can learn from the data with classification algorithms. In contrast, data samples without predefined classes can be handled by clustering algorithms.

A second distinction must be made between learning from labelled and unlabelled data. In general, supervised learning refers to the use of labelled data only and unsupervised learning in contrast refers to the use of unlabelled data only.

Since the examined data sets are partly labelled, it is appropriate to utilise semi-supervised techniques which are located between supervised and unsupervised learning techniques. The survey by Grira et al. [2] provides a brief introduction to semi-supervised clustering techniques. However, due to the fact that both of our data sets have predefined class structures, we will concentrate on semi-supervised classification approaches.

A considerable number of semi-supervised learning approaches with different classifier architectures have been examined in recent years. The surveys by Zhu [3] and Seeger [4] and the book by Chapelle et al. [5] give a comprehensive overview to the field of semi-supervised learning.

According to Zhu, a frequently used semi-supervised learning technique is commonly referred to as *self-training*: In an iterative process, new samples are selected from the large set of available unlabelled samples. The selected samples are then classified or rejected by the classifier, and, if not rejected, are finally added to the training set along with their classifier-predicted labels. In the end of each iteration, the classifier is re-trained with the extended training set and the training procedure is repeated.

2.2 Sample selection

The crucial step in the training procedure is the selection of informative samples to re-train the classifier during each iteration. The most unpretending selection method is random selection of samples. Here the problem arises that the classifier must be capable of classifying the selected, unseen samples. This proves difficult especially if the initial training set consists only of a small amount of manually labelled samples and therefore the classifier is only basically trained. As a consequence, a more specific method for the selection of samples is to be called for.

Two common approaches are the use of the classifier posterior probabilities of the sample as described by Jeon and Liu [6] or some kind of confidence measure e.g. described by Juszczak and Duin [7]. Here, we take up on the idea of using a confidence measure and rely as a new approach on the concept of confidence bands known from the field of statistics.

2.3 Confidence and prediction bands

Confidence bands and the closely related prediction bands (see e.g. Kardaun [8]) may be described as statistical tools in the context of regression. Of course one may find a huge amount of references where these tools are used for the purpose of evaluating measurements or other data sets, but references describing the use of confidence bands going beyond these applications are rather limited, especially in the field of machine learning. For example, Martos et al. [9] make use of prediction surfaces (prediction bands calculated for a two-dimensional domain) for active selection of image correspondences in camera calibration systems.

3 Confidence bands

3.1 Definition

Confidence bands are curves enclosing a model (function) being estimated by a regression analysis. They represent the areas where the true model is expected to reside with a probability of $1 - \alpha$. In the majority of cases a value of 0.05 is used for α so that the bands are expected to enclose the true model with a probability of 95%. The extent of the bands in different areas of the data space gives an idea of how well the estimated function fits the data.

There exist many approaches to compute confidence bands, e.g. by Monte Carlo [10] or bootstrapping methods [11]. Martos et al. [9] present an analytical approach for computing prediction bands by linear error propagation. While they make use of predicton bands in camera calibration, we will adapt their algorithm to compute the closely related confidence bands for application in the context of polynomial classification or regression.

3.2 Classification

Since the samples in the initial training set are labelled, a class structure ist already given and does not have to be determined automatically from unlabelled data by a kind of unsupervised clustering algorithm.

Not all classifiers are equally well suited for our classification task. The self-learning process nearly always associates a certain amount of samples to the wrong classes, which is hard to detect. Different classifiers show considerable differences in their sensitivity towards these mislabelled samples. For instance, standard Support Vector Machines (SVM) are sensitive against outliers and mislabeled training samples [12] while classifiers with a neural network like architecture relying on continuous input, output, and weight values can be trained with partially mislabelled data and is nontheless capable of producing good classification results [13]. In this study, we use polynomial classifier. The decision in favor of this classifier was due to more than one reason: The training is fast, the classifier is well-researched and easy to understand, it behaves robustly with respect to partially mislabelled data, and re-training can be performed easily by mixing old and new moment matrices.

The functional principle of a N-dimensional polynomial classifier respectively regressor obeys the equation

$$d(\mathbf{v}) = \mathbf{A}^T x(\mathbf{v}) \tag{1}$$

which estimates the class membership of the sample. Here $\mathbf{A} = (\mathbf{a}_1, \ldots, \mathbf{a}_N)$ denotes the coefficient matrix which is adjusted during the training process. The function $x(\mathbf{v})$ denotes the polynomial structure of the feature vector $\mathbf{v}$ which is taken to be completely quadratic in our case. For a more detailed description of polynomial classifier one should refer to the introduction by Schürmann [14].

In order to minimise the complexity of the classification problem we reduce the number of classes N to two by harmonising the labels of the other $(N-1)$ classes, respectively. In case of the ten-class digit classification problem this leads us to the necessity of training ten classifiers, each of them handling a two-class problem. The evaluation benefits from this strategy to the extend that classificaion results of two-class classifiers depend on classification thresholds between both classes. By changing these thresholds we are able to present Receiver Operating Characteristic (ROC) curves in the evaluation section. In contrast, a N-class classifier would lead us to diagrams only with N ROC points (one for each class).

3.3 Confidence bands in polynomial classification

As stated before, we will adapt the algorithm of Martos et al. [9] for our application. A more detailed description can be found in the introduction by Kardaun [8].

The computation of confidence bands requires the covariance matrix of the parameters. In our implementation we use the Jacobian $\mathbf{J}$ with

$$\mathbf{J}_{ij} = \frac{\partial r_i}{\partial a_j} = -x(\mathbf{v}_i)_j \tag{2}$$

$$\mathbf{K}_{ij} = \frac{J_{ij}}{\sigma_i}, \tag{3}$$

where $r_i = y(\mathbf{v}_i) - d(\mathbf{v}_i)$ denotes the regression error of the sample $\mathbf{v}_i$ and a_j denotes the elements of the coefficient matrix which are to be estimated. $\mathbf{K}$ is the Jacobian weighted by the uncertainty σ_i of the label $y(\mathbf{v_i})$ of the sample. The uncertainty may refer to samples that have been mislabelled by human experts or whose class membership cannot be determined unequivocally because of bad image quality. Another source for uncertainty of labels is the self-learning process itself since classifier-generated labels may be wrong. $\mathbf{K}$ is now utilised to compute the covariance matrix $\mathbf{C}$ according to

$$\mathbf{C} = (\mathbf{K}^T\mathbf{K})^{-1}. \tag{4}$$

As confidence band value computations for each sample are independent of each other, we illustrate the computation for an arbitrary sample $\mathbf{w} = x(\mathbf{v_i})$. To compute confidence band values, we use the Jacobian vector $\mathbf{g}$ of the model function f with $g_j(\mathbf{w}) = \partial f(\mathbf{w})/\partial a_j$ and the covariance matrix $\mathbf{C}$ to achieve the dimensionless value c according to

$$c(\mathbf{w}) = \mathbf{g}\mathbf{C}\mathbf{g}^{\mathbf{T}}. \tag{5}$$

The half width σ_C of the confidence interval then corresponds to

$$\sigma_C(\mathbf{w}) = \frac{\beta}{2}\sqrt{c(\mathbf{w})\frac{\mathrm{R}}{\nu}}, \tag{6}$$

where $R = \sum_i r_i^2$ is the residual sum of squares with r_i being the regression resuidal of sample i, $\nu = N - N_P$ are the degrees of freedom with N_P corresponding to the number of free model parameters, and β is a constant derived from the inverse cumulative t-student distribution t_{cdf}^{-1} according to $\beta = t_{\mathrm{cdf}}^{-1}(1 - \alpha/2, \nu)$ with α as the probability of the desired confidence level for the bands. At a confidence level of 95% we use $\alpha = 0.05$ throughout this paper.

We assume identical uncertainties for all labels, i.e. $\sigma_i = \sigma$. A problem occuring under normal preconditions is that in Eq. (3) the uncertainty σ of the label is unknown. Therefore we propose the definition of the normalised confidence band

$$\sigma_C/\sigma, \tag{7}$$

with the effect that we are no longer dependent on an estimate of σ.

A further simplification results from the fact that we utilise only the confidence band's relative differences of all samples in one learning iteration for our purposes. We do not use absolute sample's confidence values from more than one learning iteration at a time. Therefore Eq. (6) can be simplified by setting to 1 the constant factors β, R and ν which do not change within one learning iteration. The confidence band value for the sample $\mathbf{w}$ may now be calculated according to

$$\sigma_{C,norm}(\mathbf{w}) = \sqrt{c(\mathbf{w})}. \tag{8}$$

3.4   Usage and interpretation

The confidence bands during each learning iteration are computed from all samples the training set contains so far. Accordingly, a confidence band value can be computed for each unlabelled sample that was not yet included into the training set.

We use these confidence values to select samples that are to be classified and added to the training set along with their classifier-generated labels (see Sec. 2.1). The main idea is that it would improve the classifier most of all to add samples from areas in the data space with low confidence values. Here the problem arises that the classifier is incapable of determining trustful classification results, i.e. labels, for these samples. In contrast, it would be capable of determining trustful labels for samples with high confidence values, but our experiences show that we should not let the training set being inundated by high-confidence samples from data space areas that are already well-represented by the model function.

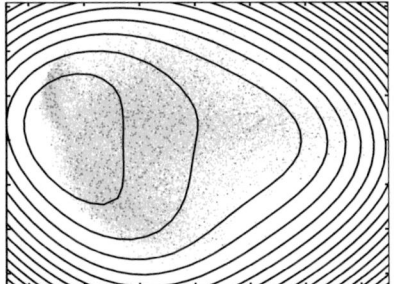 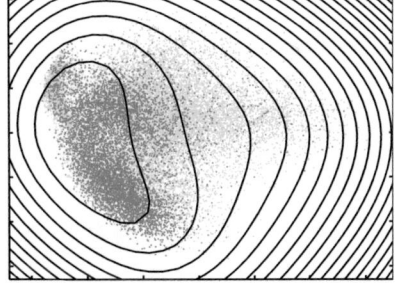

Figure 1: Digit training sample feature vector's first two dimensions overlaid by confidence band iso lines. The light grey points denote unlabelled samples, the dark grey points samples that have been added to the training set. Left: first iteration of a self-learning process (learning class "4" vs. all other classes; compare to Fig. 4) with the training set containing approximately 5% of all samples. Right: later iteration where the amount of labelled samples has increased to approximately 35%.

We obtained a good balance between both extrema by computing the mean of all training sample's confidence values and defining a maximum relative deviation of e.g. 5% around it. If no unlabelled sample's confidence value complies with this requirement, the maximum deviation allowed will be extended. In general, all unclassified samples with confidence values within this range are located in areas of the data space with medium classifier performance. As a next step, they are being classified and added to the training set which is then used to re-train the classifier. Also, the confidence bands will be computed again and change their topology after each addition to the training set as exemplary depicted in Fig. 1.

4 Evaluation

4.1 Experimental setup

We evaluate our self-learning approach by applying it to two data sets, an excerpt from the MNIST database of handwritten digits [1] (see Fig. 2) and an excerpt from a huge traffic sign image database (see Fig. 3).

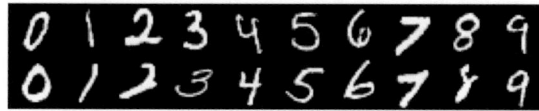

Figure 2: MNIST handwritten digits samples. Two samples of each class.

The MNIST data set contains 10 classes of normalised grey-value images with a size of 28×28 pixels. For the purpose of feature reduction we transform the data by a Principal Component Analysis (PCA) [15] with 33 dimensions, for which the reconstruction error amounts to 25.0%. The fully quadratic polynomial feature vector of each sample computed for polynomial classification comprises 528 values. The initial training set size is 960 samples (randomly chosen and uniformly distributed across all 10 classes) while another 19.040 samples have to be self-learned. The independent test set contains 10.000 samples.

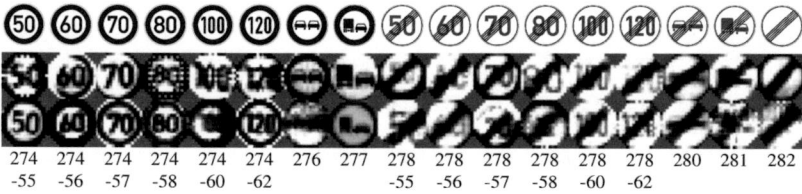

| 274 | 274 | 274 | 274 | 274 | 274 | 276 | 277 | 278 | 278 | 278 | 278 | 278 | 278 | 280 | 281 | 282 |
| -55 | -56 | -57 | -58 | -60 | -62 | | | -55 | -56 | -57 | -58 | -60 | -62 | | | |

Figure 3: German traffic sign samples and categorisation. Upper row: ideal pictogram of each class. Middle rows: two samples of each class. Lower row: official categorisation.

The traffic sign data set contains 17 classes of normalised grey-value images with a size of 17×17 pixels. The data is transformed using a PCA here, too, in this case with 30 dimensions, for which the reconstruction error amounts to 17.5%. The polynomial feature vector of each sample comprises 496 values. The initial training set size is 800 samples (randomly chosen and uniformly distributed across all 17 classes) while another 16.016 samples have to be self-learned. The independent test set contains 16.802 samples. Fig. 4 shows the first two data dimensions of both sets after being transformed by the PCA with one class highlighted, respectively.

Comparing the exemplarily depicted samples of both data sets (see Figs. 2 and 3) the fact that the quality of the samples is much better for the digits set than for the signs set is immediately apparent. This is due to the fact that the samples of the digits data set were scanned from paper in contrast to the samples of the signs data set which were recorded by camera-equipped cars under variable conditions. Furthermore, the signs data set contains

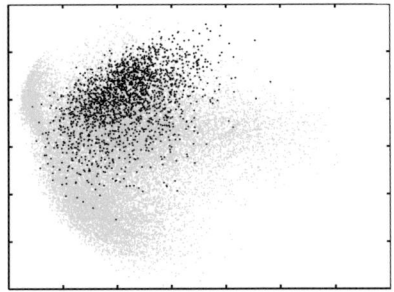 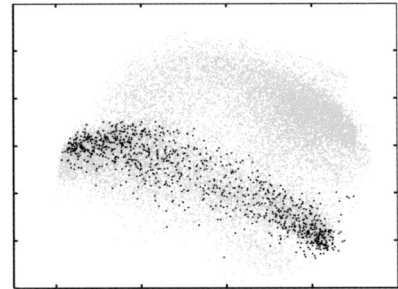

Figure 4: Point clouds composed of the first two components of each feature vector (after PCA transformation), the digits with class "4" emphasised as dark points on the left and the signs with class "274-58" (speed limit 80 km/h) emphasised on the right.

a considerable amount of *bad samples* e.g. with inaccurate cutouts. A classifier trained on this data will never gain a recognition performance of 100%.

On independent test sets, we compare the classifiers (as stated before in Sec. 3.2 we train one classifier for each class) by computing the true positive rate at a fixed false positive rate of 5% and the false positive rate at a fixed true positive rate of 95%. These rates give an idea of the classifier performance, they do not dispend with further performance analyses like ROC curves.

4.2 Self-learning from data

class	initial		self-learning			reference	
names	TP	FP	TP	FP	FL	TP	FP
"1"	96.8	3.07	99.6	0.16	0.13	1.00	0.07
"2"	75.2	29.5	96.7	3.23	1.58	98.9	0.98
"3"	83.0	20.9	98.6	1.42	0.00	99.6	0.44
"4"	87.3	18.0	97.6	2.12	0.36	99.1	0.61
"5"	94.8	5.49	99.1	0.28	0.19	99.8	0.12
"6"	82.7	26.9	96.8	3.92	1.87	99.7	0.34
"7"	87.4	11.9	98.5	1.10	0.37	1.00	0.44
"8"	86.8	16.1	98.0	1.99	0.73	99.2	0.50
"9"	85.1	15.4	97.6	1.01	0.34	99.3	0.43
"0"	99.0	0.38	99.6	0.02	0.15	99.8	0.01

Table 1: Performance of three different classifiers (self-learning classifier with initial training, self-learning classifier at the end of training process, reference classifier) for each of the 10 digits data set classes: true positive rates at fixed false positive rates of 5% (TP) and false positive rates at fixed true positive rates of 95% (FP), additionally the amount of false labels (FL) produced by the self-learning classifier during the training process. All information given in percent.

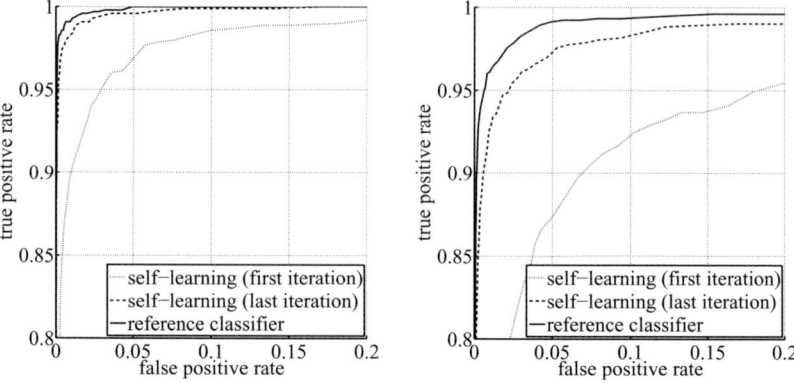

Figure 5: ROC curves of three different classifiers (self-learning classifier with initial training, self-learning classifier at the end of training process, reference classifier) for digits data set classes "1" (left) and "4" (right).

A comparison of the recognition rates between self-learning and reference classifiers on the digits data set indicates that although the self-learning classifiers do not fully achieve the performance of the reference classifiers due to classifier-generated erroneous labels they come close to them. The examined "1 vs. all" self-learning scenarios are capable of separating each class very well. For instance, Table 1 shows that class "4" obtains a true positive rate of 97.6% at a fixed false positive rate of 5% for self-learning (initial value 87.3%) vs. 99.1% for the reference classifier, the false positive rate amounts to 2.1% at a fixed true positive rate of 95% for self-learning (initial value 18.0%) and 0.6% for the reference classifier. The true positive rates rise above 96% in each experiment and above 98% in 6 of 10 experiments. Furthermore, the recognition performance of each classifier improves massively during the iterative training process as exemplarily depicted by the ROC curves in Fig. 5.

Comparing the recognition rates of the signs data set the results are not as clear as before. The self-learning process appears to fail or give unsatisfactory results in some cases like the classes "274-62" (speed limit 120 km/h), "276" (no-overtake for cars), "278-56" (end of speed limit 60 km/h) and "258-62" (end of speed limit 120 km/h). On the other hand there are also some classes with excellent self-learning performance and nearly no mislabelled training samples like "274-58" (speed limit 80 km/h) and "281" (end of no-overtake for trucks). For instance, Table 2 shows that class "274-58" obtains a true positive rate of 97.7% for self-learning (initial value 88.1%) vs. 98.5% for the reference classifier, the false positive rate amounts to 1.4% for self-learning (initial value 22.8%) and 0.7% for the reference classifier. As previously observed for the digits, all classifiers except the ones for which self-learning has failed show a substantial increase in performance during the self-learning process. For clarity, we exemplify the learning results by confining ourselves to ROC curves of the classifications of "speed limit 80 km/h" respectively "end of no-overtake for cars" signs vs. all other signs in Fig. 6.

class names	initial		self-learning			reference	
	TP	FP	TP	FP	FL	TP	FP
"274-55"	84.0	44.6	85.3	9.62	3.40	96.5	3.31
"274-56"	68.2	50.7	89.3	9.76	2.63	95.0	4.70
"274-57"	79.6	37.4	95.0	4.79	0.48	97.6	2.54
"274-58"	88.1	22.8	97.7	1.39	0.30	98.5	0.68
"274-60"	60.9	61.2	74.3	30.3	3.75	88.1	13.5
"274-62"	26.1	78.5	48.3	63.5	6.55	86.2	13.0
"276"	27.9	79.1	24.2	64.1	8.71	76.4	17.9
"277"	79.1	58.2	88.8	19.0	0.65	95.3	4.36
"278-55"	50.1	60.2	82.1	19.9	2.68	91.1	9.43
"278-56"	47.9	54.8	59.5	41.1	3.63	88.5	14.2
"278-57"	97.8	2.02	99.2	0.41	0.60	99.5	0.12
"278-58"	97.6	1.26	98.5	0.16	0.30	99.7	0.06
"258-60"	83.5	27.5	97.1	3.61	1.97	98.6	0.16
"258-62"	71.4	84.0	59.9	12.9	5,74	94.2	5.85
"280"	75.4	59.0	67.5	20.5	5.63	96.0	3.99
"281"	89.6	21.3	97.9	1.24	0.23	98.9	0.32
"282"	85.1	44.0	93.7	7.70	0.81	97.5	1.59

Table 2: Performance of three different classifiers (self-learning classifier with initial training, self-learning classifier at the end of training process, reference classifier) for each of the 17 signs data set classes: true positive rates at fixed false positive rates of 5% (TP) and false positive rates at fixed true positive rates of 95% (FP), additionally the amount of false labels (FL) produced by the self-learning classifier during the training process. All information given in percent.

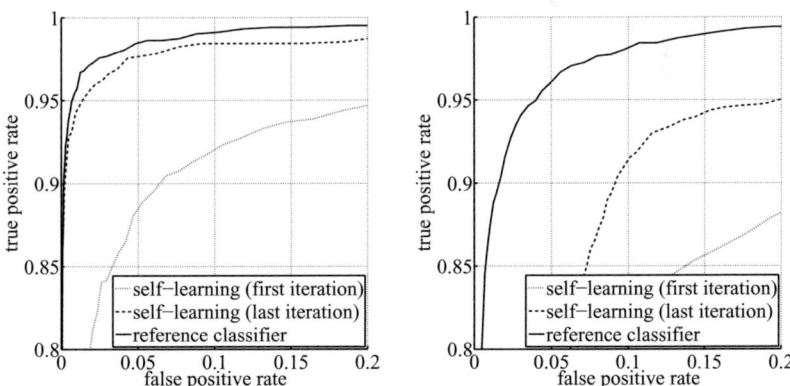

Figure 6: ROC curves of three different classifiers (self-learning classifier with initial training, self-learning classifier at the end of training process, reference classifier) for signs data set classes "274-58" (speed limit 80 km/h; left) and "280" (end of no-overtake for cars; right).

5 Summary, Conclusions, and Future Work

The self-learning method proposed in this paper can be used to perform training of a classifier with nearly ground-truth performance without labelling the whole set of training samples beforehand. But with the data set becoming less and less ideal, the more difficult the self-learning task will be for a classifier, as we have experienced with the signs data set. One possible reason is that the initial training set was too small to cover the feature space up to a sufficient amount. As we stated before, the signs data set contains a considerable amount of bad samples which may have "contaminated" the initial training set and lead to an unsuccessful self-learning process.

As we have seen in Section 4 our self-learning strategy cannot guarantee that automatically generated labels are free of errors. This problem grows with increasing amount of unclassified samples because once a sample is associated to the wrong class it will remain there. The sooner wrong associations occur in the training process the more harmful may be their influence on the self-learning process. We are currently working on strategies to detect false classifications to be able to re-classify them.

It was our objective to use preferably small training sets for the initial training step. Here one should keep in mind that the smaller the amount of samples in the initial training set are without forfeiting a good initial training, the lesser the labelling efforts by human experts have to be in the forefront. Although our classifiers achieve the aim of self-learning on our data sets with a particularly small amount of manually labelled samples (less than 5%) this is no revolution in machine learning since other semi-supervised learning algorithms would presumably be able to to achieve this, too. However, with the normalised confidence bands approach we have presented a new, easy-to-implement confidence-based method for sample selection during the self-learning process.

With good reason Zhu [3] instances that a self-learning system reduces the labelling effort, but instead someone needs to spend reasonable amount of effort to design this self-learning system. However, if we think a bit further, the argument of less labelling efforts gets stronger again. What if we do not have all possible training data collected yet at the time of the classifier training? Think of a system which is designed to operate in a continuously changing environment. New possible training samples that bear resemblances to already seen samples will occur continuously, and the system has to be adapted to the changing environment from time to time by re-training its classifier(s). There may not always be a human expert at hand for labelling new training samples. Some systems are even supposed to operate fully autonomously, such that the system has to adapt itself to the changing environment on his own by a self-learning architecture. These cases are addressed in our ongoing work.

References

[1] Lecun, Y.; Cortes, C.: The MNIST database of handwritten digits URL `http://yann.lecun.com/exdb/mnist/`.

[2] Grira, N.; Crucianu, M.; Boujemaa, N.: Unsupervised and Semi-supervised Clustering: a Brief Survey. In: *A Review of Machine Learning Techniques for Processing Multimedia Content, Report of the MUSCLE European Network of Excellence (FP6)*. 2004.

[3] Zhu, X.: Semi-Supervised Learning Literature Survey. Techn. Ber. 1530, Computer Sciences, University of Wisconsin-Madison. 2005.

[4] Seeger, M.: Learning with Labeled and Unlabeled Data. Techn. Ber., Institute for Adaptive and Neural Computation, University of Edinburgh. 2001.

[5] Chapelle, O.; Schölkopf, B.; Zien, A. (Hg.): *Semi-Supervised Learning (Adaptive Computation and Machine Learning)*. The MIT Press. 2006.

[6] Jeon, J. H.; Liu, Y.: Semi-supervised learning for automatic prosodic event detection using co-training algorithm. In: *ACL-IJCNLP '09: Proceedings of the Joint Conference of the 47th Annual Meeting of the ACL and the 4th International Joint Conference on Natural Language Processing of the AFNLP: Volume 2*, S. 540–548. Morristown, NJ, USA: Association for Computational Linguistics. 2009.

[7] Juszczak, P.; Duin, R. P. W.: Selective Sampling Methods in One-Class Classification Problems. In: *Artificial Neural Networks and Neural Information Processing - ICANN/ICONIP 2003, Joint International Conference ICANN/ICONIP 2003, Istanbul, Turkey, June 26-29, 2003, Proceedings* (Kaynak, O.; Alpaydin, E.; Oja, E.; Xu, L., Hg.), Bd. 2714 von *Lecture Notes in Computer Science*, S. 140–148. Springer. 2003.

[8] Kardaun, O. J. W. F.: *Classical Methods of Statistics*. Springer. 2005.

[9] Martos, A.; Krüger, L.; Wöhler, C.: Towards Real Time Camera Self Calibration: Significance and Active Selection. In: *3DPVT '10: Proceedings of the 4th International Symposium on 3D Data Processing, Visualization and Transmission, Paris, France, 2010*. 2010.

[10] Kendall, W. S.; Marin, J.-M.; Robert, C. P.: Confidence bands for Brownian motion and applications to Monte Carlo simulation. *Statistics and Computing* 17 (2007) 1, S. 1–10.

[11] Härdle, W. K.; Ritov, Y.; Song, S.: Partial Linear Quantile Regression and Bootstrap Confidence Bands. SFB 649 Discussion Papers SFB649DP2010-002, Sonderforschungsbereich 649, Humboldt University, Berlin, Germany. 2010.

[12] Xu, L.; Crammer, K.; Schuurmans, D.: Robust support vector machine training via convex outlier ablation. In: *AAAI'06: Proceedings of the 21st national conference on Artificial intelligence*, S. 536–542. AAAI Press. 2006.

[13] Wöhler, C.: Autonomous in situ training of classification modules in real-time vision systems and its application to pedestrian recognition. *Pattern Recognition Letters* 23 (2002) 11, S. 1263–1270.

[14] Schürmann, J.: *Pattern classification: a unified view of statistical and neural approaches*. John Wiley & Sons, Inc. 1996.

[15] Fodor, I.: A Survey of Dimension Reduction Techniques. Techn. Ber., US DOE Office of Scientific and Technical Information. 2002.

Bereits veröffentlicht wurden in der Schriftenreihe des Instituts für Angewandte Informatik / Automatisierungstechnik bei KIT Scientific Publishing:

Nr. 1: BECK, S.: Ein Konzept zur automatischen Lösung von Entscheidungsproblemen bei Unsicherheit mittels der Theorie der unscharfen Mengen und der Evidenztheorie, 2005

Nr. 2: MARTIN, J.: Ein Beitrag zur Integration von Sensoren in eine anthropomorphe künstliche Hand mit flexiblen Fluidaktoren, 2004

Nr. 3: TRAICHEL, A.: Neue Verfahren zur Modellierung nichtlinearer thermodynamischer Prozesse in einem Druckbehälter mit siedendem Wasser-Dampf Gemisch bei negativen Drucktransienten, 2005

Nr. 4: LOOSE, T.: Konzept für eine modellgestützte Diagnostik mittels Data Mining am Beispiel der Bewegungsanalyse, 2004

Nr. 5: MATTHES, J.: Eine neue Methode zur Quellenlokalisierung auf der Basis räumlich verteilter, punktweiser Konzentrationsmessungen, 2004

Nr. 6: MIKUT, R.; REISCHL, M.: Proceedings – 14. Workshop Fuzzy-Systeme und Computational Intelligence: Dortmund, 10. - 12. November 2004, 2004

Nr. 7: ZIPSER, S.: Beitrag zur modellbasierten Regelung von Verbrennungsprozessen, 2004

Nr. 8: STADLER, A.: Ein Beitrag zur Ableitung regelbasierter Modelle aus Zeitreihen, 2005

Nr. 9: MIKUT, R.; REISCHL, M.: Proceedings – 15. Workshop Computational Intelligence: Dortmund, 16. - 18. November 2005, 2005

Nr. 10: BÄR, M.: µFEMOS – Mikro-Fertigungstechniken für hybride mikrooptische Sensoren, 2005

Nr. 11: SCHAUDEL, F.: Entropie- und Störungssensitivität als neues Kriterium zum Vergleich verschiedener Entscheidungskalküle, 2006

Nr. 12: SCHABLOWSKI-TRAUTMANN, M.: Konzept zur Analyse der Lokomotion auf dem Laufband bei inkompletter Querschnittlähmung mit Verfahren der nichtlinearen Dynamik, 2006

Nr. 13: REISCHL, M.: Ein Verfahren zum automatischen Entwurf von Mensch-Maschine-Schnittstellen am Beispiel myoelektrischer Handprothesen, 2006

Nr. 14: KOKER, T.: Konzeption und Realisierung einer neuen Prozesskette zur Integration von Kohlenstoff-Nanoröhren über Handhabung in technische Anwendungen, 2007

Nr. 15: MIKUT, R.; REISCHL, M.: Proceedings – 16. Workshop Computational Intelligence: Dortmund, 29. November - 1. Dezember 2006

Nr. 16: LI, S.: Entwicklung eines Verfahrens zur Automatisierung der CAD/CAM-Kette in der Einzelfertigung am Beispiel von Mauerwerksteinen, 2007

Nr. 17: BERGEMANN, M.: Neues mechatronisches System für die Wiederherstellung der Akkommodationsfähigkeit des menschlichen Auges, 2007

Nr. 18: HEINTZ, R.: Neues Verfahren zur invarianten Objekterkennung und -lokalisierung auf der Basis lokaler Merkmale, 2007

Nr. 19: RUCHTER, M.: A New Concept for Mobile Environmental Education, 2007

Nr. 20: MIKUT, R.; REISCHL, M.: Proceedings – 17. Workshop Computational Intelligence: Dortmund, 5. - 7. Dezember 2007

Nr. 21: LEHMANN, A.: Neues Konzept zur Planung, Ausführung und Überwachung von Roboteraufgaben mit hierarchischen Petri-Netzen, 2008

Nr. 22: MIKUT, R.: Data Mining in der Medizin und Medizintechnik, 2008

Nr. 23: KLINK, S.: Neues System zur Erfassung des Akkommodationsbedarfs im menschlichen Auge, 2008

Nr. 24: MIKUT, R.; REISCHL, M.: Proceedings – 18. Workshop Computational Intelligence: Dortmund, 3. - 5. Dezember 2008

Nr. 25: WANG, L.: Virtual environments for grid computing, 2009

Nr. 26: BURMEISTER, O.: Entwicklung von Klassifikatoren zur Analyse und Interpretation zeitvarianter Signale und deren Anwendung auf Biosignale, 2009

Nr. 27: DICKERHOF, M.: Ein neues Konzept für das bedarfsgerechte Informations- und Wissensmanagement in Unternehmenskooperationen der Multimaterial-Mikrosystemtechnik, 2009

Nr. 28: MACK, G.: Eine neue Methodik zur modellbasierten Bestimmung dynamischer Betriebslasten im mechatronischen Fahrwerkentwicklungsprozess, 2009

Nr. 29: HOFFMANN, F.; HÜLLERMEIER, E.: Proceedings – 19. Workshop Computational Intelligence: Dortmund, 2. - 4. Dezember 2009

Nr. 30: GRAUER, M.: Neue Methodik zur Planung globaler Produktionsverbünde unter Berücksichtigung der Einflussgrößen Produktdesign, Prozessgestaltung und Standortentscheidung, 2009

Nr. 31: SCHINDLER, A.: Neue Konzeption und erstmalige Realisierung eines aktiven Fahrwerks mit Preview-Strategie, 2009

Nr. 32: BLUME, C.; JAKOB, W.: GLEAN. General Learning Evolutionary Algorithm and Method: Ein Evolutionärer Algorithmus und seine Anwendungen, 2009

Nr. 33: HOFFMANN, F.; HÜLLERMEIER, E.: Proceedings – 20. Workshop Computational Intelligence: Dortmund, 1. - 3. Dezember 2010

Die Schriften sind als PDF frei verfügbar, eine Nachbestellung der Printversion ist möglich. Nähere Informationen unter www.ksp.kit.edu.